A PLURALISTIC NATION

THE LANGUAGE ISSUE IN THE UNITED STATES

EDITORS

Margaret A. Lourie
Nancy Faires Conklin

University of Michigan

NEWBURY HOUSE PUBLISHERS, INC.
ROWLEY, MASSACHUSETTS 01969

Library of Congress Cataloging in Publication Data

Main entry under title:

A Pluralistic Nation.

   (Series in sociolinguistics)
   Bibliography: p.
   1. United States--Languages--Addresses, essays,
lectures. 2. Language and languages--Variation--
Addresses, essays, lectures. 3. Language and
education--United States--Addresses, essays, lec-
tures. I. Lourie, Margaret A. II. Conklin,
Nancy Faires.
P377.P55   301.2'1   78-7792
ISBN 0-88377-116-0

Series cover design by Lois Jefferson Kordaszewski. Cover art by Kathe Harvey.

NEWBURY HOUSE PUBLISHERS, INC.

Language Science
Language Teaching
Language Learning

ROWLEY, MASSACHUSETTS 01969

First printing: November 1978
                                   5   4   3   2
Printed in the U.S.A.

FOREWORD

by Roger W. Shuy

Within the past decade, a great deal of attention in linguistic studies has turned toward variability in language and what this variability means or can mean to education. Perhaps because linguistics has traditionally and necessarily focussed for decades on the unity of language, the real meaning of language diversity has been slow to develop. Lourie and Conklin have put together a collection of individual articles and chapters written in the past decade which point out some important patterns concerning the meaning and usefulness of language diversity in the United States. Three basic questions dealt with in the book are: Where does language diversity exist? How does it work? How can education best take advantage of it?

New areas of thought have been introduced in America as an outgrowth of recent sociolinguistic research and theory. Language variability had to be accounted for, of course, in linguistic theory. It also had to be addressed by the courts as they faced bilingual issues, by the schools as they developed procedures to deal with people whose language evidences this diversity and by society as a whole as it redefined its policies toward the human and social differences which are brought together in the United States. These issues are not merely applications of old information; they force the creation of new ways of thinking. They are directed at the greater issue of what it means to be a pluralistic society. No better case study of pluralism can be found than language. Lourie and Conklin have melded some outlines of the three basic questions here with helpful classroom guides as well. Pluralism through language is a pivotal aspect of sociolinguistic studies and this book is an important effort toward making the concept available for examination.

SERIES IN
SOCIOLINGUISTICS

Roger W. Shuy, *Series Editor*
Georgetown University and
Center for Applied Linguistics

The term *sociolinguistics* has been used since approximately the mid-1960s to designate the complex intersection of the fields of language and society. Sociologists have used linguistic data, often referring to the expression, *the sociology of language,* to describe and explain social behavior. Linguists, on the other hand, have tended to make use of social behavior to interpret linguistic variation. Still others have conceived of sociolinguistics in a more practical or applied sense, usually related to social dialects in an educational setting or language teaching. These three perspectives, sociological, linguistic and educational, are all legitimate, for it would be difficult to claim that any one group has an exclusive right to the term. It has become apparent increasingly that those who are interested in the ethnography of speaking, language planning, linguistic variation, the dynamics of language change, language attitudes, pragmatics, multi-lingualism and applied sociolinguistics are all concerned with sociolinguistics in one sense or another. As might be expected in any field, some scholars prefer the more linguistically dominating aspects, some the social or ethnographic, and some the applied or relational. Thus sociolinguistics may be studied in a number of different contexts.

This new series of books will cover a broad spectrum of topics which bear on important and changing issues in language and in society. The significance of social, linguistic, and psychological factors as they relate to the understanding of human speech and writing will be emphasized. In the past most language analyses have not taken these factors into account. The most exciting development of recent linguistic theory and research has been the recognition of the roles of context, variability, the continuum, and cross-disciplinary understanding.

PREFACE

As a result of the racial turbulence of the 1960s, which exploded the myth of a monolithic American way of life, cultural pluralism finally came of age in the mid-1970s. Americans now acknowledge their many ethnic differences with increasing pride. Ethnic studies programs are springing up on the heels of Black studies and women's studies. Even the AAA now encourages cultural and linguistic diversity with "Bring 'em Back Alive" bumper stickers in fourteen different languages.

In our schools this cultural pluralism has created a controversy centered in the language arts. The nurturant attitude toward ethnic differences is reflected in new bilingual education laws and tolerance for a child's native language or dialect in the classroom. But one result of liberalized attitudes toward language variation is that a growing number of parents, teachers, and Black community leaders share *Newsweek*'s view (Dec. 8, 1975) that "Johnny can't write." Pointing to declining College Board verbal scores, they fear that tolerance for language differences has made many children functional illiterates and substantially damaged their chances for success. Clearly, the language issue is a crucial test of our commitment to cultural diversity in this country. Whether we choose to enforce a standard language or to encourage language diversity in the schools will to a large extent determine how we function as a multicultural society. And informed, effective policy in the language area must be based on what sociolinguists have lately discovered about the complexity of the language situation in the United States and its implications for education. It is to these concerns that the present anthology is chiefly addressed.

In the decade since the publication of William Labov's monumental study of *The Social Stratification of English in New York City*, sociolinguistic research has burgeoned, and its impact on public policy has been profound. Following the early burst of studies demonstrating the systematic nature of language varieties and the reliability of language use as a predictor of social attitude, there was a rush to integrate the newly legitimized nonstandard varieties into the educational environment. The mixed results of these experiments stem from an oversimplified view of both the systematic variation in language and the motives influencing choice of language variety. We are now in a better position to evaluate sociolinguistic insights into public policy and the effects of language intervention because the body of sociolinguistic research has become more substantial. The study of social dialects now no longer focuses primarily on Black English Vernacular. Appalachian, Puerto Rican, and Chicano communities have been studied in some detail. Analysis of variation in discourse structure and nonverbal communication has begun. Research into male/female language differences has shown the inadequacy of a purely socioeconomic approach. This broadening of the dimensions of sociolinguistics is represented in the readings below.

In order to orient the reader to key concepts in the study of linguistic pluralism, the selections are grouped topically. Part I, "Some Speech Communities in the United States," introduces major American language varieties. Representative studies show the central role of language in the maintenance of community identity. Part II, "Variation within Speech Communities," focuses on the complex inner dynamics of sociolinguistic groups and illustrates the range of stylistic variation, the impact of language attitudes on group members, and the conflicting pressures for and against assimilation to Standard English. The symbiotic relationship between attitudes and individual behavior demonstrates the impossibility of separating language from its social and political context. With this background, Part III turns to "Educational Implications." These selections present a range of opinion on how best to approach instruction of nonstandard and non-English-speaking students. Again, examples are drawn from a variety of American speech communities. The information in these readings should facilitate informed and intelligent decision making on the level of policy formulation as well as on the level of daily interaction in the classroom.

The readings in this collection have been augmented in several ways to reach the entire audience concerned with these issues: teachers and prospective teachers in English, English as a second language, bilingual education, language arts, as well as any educator in a multicultural community; teachers and students of linguistics; community leaders and organizers; educational and public policy makers. The General Introduction, written for nonlinguists, briefly summarizes the basic concepts and terminology in linguistics, sociolinguistics, and the study of interaction. Many readers will want to refer back to it as they proceed through the collection. The discussion of Standard English in this introduction will be a useful guide to the issues in Part III. The General Introduction concludes with an annotated list of further readings, both introductory and technical. In addition, an introductory essay to each section contextualizes the articles, discusses common themes, and suggests further readings.

Headnotes to individual articles offer necessary background to independent readers and guidelines for discussion to course instructors. Terms or concepts peculiar to one essay are explicated in footnotes. A set of appendixes offers further aid to teachers. Each questionnaire, test, and sample text may serve as the basis for an assignment or class project, enabling students to research linguistic variation and language attitudes for themselves.

Margaret A. Lourie
Nancy Faires Conklin

University of Michigan
June 1978

ACKNOWLEDGMENTS

The editors wish to thank the individuals and publishers mentioned below for permission to reprint their copyrighted materials:

Roger W. Shuy, "The Reasons for Dialect Differences" and "American Dialects Today" from *Discovering American Dialects.* Copyright © 1967 by the National Council of Teachers of English. Reprinted by permission of the publisher and the author.

Nathan Glazer, "The Process and Problems of Language Maintenance: An Integrative Review." Reprinted with permission of the publisher from *Language Loyalty in the United States: The Maintenance and Perpetuation of Non-English Mother Tongues by American Ethnic and Religious Groups* by Joshua A. Fishman. Copyright 1966 by Mouton & Co., Publishers.

Muriel R. Saville, "Language and the Disadvantaged: Spanish, Acadian French, Navajo." From "Language and the Disadvantaged" by Muriel R. Saville in *Reading for the Disadvantaged*, edited by Thomas D. Horn, copyright © 1970 by Harcourt Brace Jovanovich, Inc., and reprinted with their permission.

C. Allen Tucker, "The Chinese Immigrant's Language Handicap: Its Extent and Its Effects." Reprinted by permission of the author and the *Florida FL Reporter* (Alfred C. Aarons, editor), vol. 7, no. 1, spring/summer 1969, pp. 44-45, 170. (The theme of copyrighted vol. 7, no. 1 is "Linguistic-Cultural Differences and American Education.")

Gail Raimi Dreyfuss, "Pidgin and Creole Languages in the United States." © 1977 by Gail Raimi Dreyfuss. Published here for the first time.

Margaret A. Lourie, "Black English Vernacular: A Comparative Description." © 1977 by Margaret A. Lourie. Published here for the first time.

Thomas Kochman, "Toward an Ethnography of Black American Speech Behavior." Reprinted with permission of Macmillan Publishing Co., Inc., from *Afro-American Anthropology: Contemporary Perspectives*, edited by Norman E. Whitten, Jr., and John F. Szwed. Copyright © 1970 by The Free Press, a Division of The Macmillan Company.

Benjamin G. Cooke, "Nonverbal Communication among Afro-Americans: An Initial Classification." From *Rappin' and Stylin' Out: Communication in Urban Black America*, edited by Thomas Kochman, University of Illinois Press. Copyright © 1972 by The Board of Trustees of the University of Illinois and reprinted with their permission.

Walt Wolfram, "Objective and Subjective Parameters of Language Assimilation among Second-Generation Puerto Ricans in East Harlem." Reprinted with permission of the publisher from *Language Attitudes: Current Trends and Prospects*, edited by Roger W. Shuy and Ralph W. Fasold (Washington, D.C.: Georgetown University Press), 1973. 148-173.

Robert W. Young, "English as a Second Language for Navajos." By permission from *Teaching the Bilingual*, Frank Pialorsi, editor, Tucson: University of Arizona Press, copyright 1974.

Raven I. McDavid, Jr., "Postvocalic /-r/ in South Carolina: A Social Analysis." Reprinted by permission of the author from *American Speech*, 1948, 23: 194-203.

William Labov, "General Attitudes towards the Speech of New York City." Reprinted by permission of the author from *The Social Stratification of English in New York City* (Washington, D.C.: Center for Applied Linguistics), 1966.

William Labov, "The Linguistic Consequences of Being a Lame." Reprinted in abridged form from *Language in the Inner City: Studies in the Black English Vernacular*. Copyright © 1972 by University of Pennsylvania Press.

Nancy Faires Conklin, "The Language of the Majority: Women and American English." © 1977 by Nancy Faires Conklin. Published here for the first time.

Nancy M. Henley, "Power, Sex, and Nonverbal Communication." Reprinted with permission of the author from *Berkeley Journal of Sociology*, 1973-74, 18: 1-26. Copyright © 1973 by Nancy M. Henley.

Don H. Zimmerman and Candace West, "Sex Roles, Interruptions and Silences in Conversation." Reprinted from *Language and Sex: Difference and Dominance*, edited by Barrie Thorne and Nancy M. Henley. Copyright © 1975 by Newbury House Publishers.

John J. Gumperz and Eduardo Hernández-Chavez, "Bilingualism, Bidialectalism, and Classroom Interaction." Reprinted by permission of the publisher from John J. Gumperz and Eduardo Hernández-Chavez, "Bilingualism, Bidialectalism, and Classroom Interaction," in Courtney B. Cazden, Vera P. John, and Dell Hymes, editors, *Functions of Language in the Classroom*. (New York: Teachers College Press, © 1972 by Teachers College, Columbia University), pp. 84-108.

Robbins Burling, "What Should We Do about It?" From *English in Black and White* by Robbins Burling. Copyright © 1973 by Holt, Rinehart and Winston, Inc. Reprinted by permission of Holt, Rinehart and Winston.

Committee on CCCC Language Statement, "Students' Right to Their Own Language." Excerpted from *College Composition and Communication* 25 (Special Issue, separately paginated). Copyright © 1974 by the National Council of Teachers of English. Reprinted by permission of the publisher.

Milton Baxter, "Educating Teachers about Educating the Oppressed." From *College English* 37: 677-681. Copyright © 1976 by the National Council of Teachers of English. Reprinted by permission of the publisher and the author.

William A. Stewart, "The Laissez-Faire Movement in English Teaching: Advance to the Rear?" Reprinted by permission of the author and the *Florida FL Reporter* (Alfred C. Aarons, editor), vol. 12, nos. 1 and 2, spring/fall 1974, pp. 81-90, 98-99. (The theme of copyrighted vol. 12 is "Issues in the Teaching of Standard English.")

Walt Wolfram and Donna Christian, "Educational Implications of Dialect Diversity." Extracted with permission of the publisher from *Appalachian Speech.* Copyright © 1976 by the Center for Applied Linguistics.

William Labov, "Modes of Mitigation and Politeness" and "Asking Questions." Reprinted from *The Study of Nonstandard English* (Urbana, Ill.: National Council of Teachers of English), 1970.

Susan U. Philips, "Participant Structures and Communicative Competence: Warm Springs Children in Community and Classroom." Originally titled "Acquisition of Rules for Appropriate Speech Usage." Reprinted with permission from Georgetown University Round Table on Languages and Linguistics 1970, *Bilingualism and Language Contact: Anthropological, Linguistic, Psychological, and Sociological Aspects.* Edited by James E. Alatis. Washington, D.C.: Georgetown University Press. 77-96. The article as it appears here was reprinted from Susan U. Philips, "Participant Structures and Communicative Competence: Warm Springs Children in Community and Classroom," in Courtney B. Cazden, Vera P. John, and Dell Hymes, editors, *Functions of Language in the Classroom.* (New York: Teachers College Press, © 1972 by Teachers College, Columbia University), pp. 370-394.

Joshua A. Fishman, "Bilingual Education: What and Why?" Reprinted from *Bilingual Education: An International Sociological Perspective.* Copyright © 1976 by Newbury House Publishers.

"Word Lists for Regional Pronunciation," "Rating Scales for Attitudes toward Sex-Marked Language," "Worksheets for Analyzing Interaction." Copyright © 1977 by Margaret A. Lourie and Nancy Faires Conklin. Published here for the first time.

"Linguistic Attitudes Questionnaire," "A Test of Linguistic Insecurity." Adapted from *The Social Stratification of English in New York City* by William Labov (Washington, D.C.: Center for Applied Linguistics). Copyright © 1966 by William Labov and used with his permission.

Black English Vernacular Text. Reprinted by permission of William Labov.

Appalachian English Text. Reprinted by permission of the publisher from *Appalachian Speech* by Walt Wolfram and Donna Christian. Copyright © 1976 by the Center for Applied Linguistics.

We also wish to express our personal gratitude to Richard W. Bailey and Gail Raimi Dreyfuss, who generously read and commented on our introductory materials, and to James W. Conklin, Linda Garnets, Julie Jensen, Lydia Kleiner, Betty A. Lourie, and Vivian M. Patraka, who provided invaluable technical assistance and moral support.

CONTENTS

GENERAL INTRODUCTION

The truth of the matter is that language is an essentially perfect means
of expression and communication among every known people.

—Edward Sapir

The Structure of Language

With the above pronouncement the eminent linguist Edward Sapir dismisses one
of the most persistent and pernicious of popular misconceptions about language:
that some languages and dialects are inherently inferior to others. In the last two
hundred years travelers and explorers have fueled this misconception with a
number of inaccurate observations, claiming that certain "primitive" peoples
communicate only by gesture, pronounce their words indistinctly, or command
vocabularies of fewer than a hundred words. Hollywood, for example, used to
perpetuate the myth that Plains Indians could communicate only in a crude sign
language, while the truth was that, because they spoke many different mother
tongues, these Native Americans had developed a sophisticated nonverbal lingua
franca for intergroup communication. Reasons ranging from cultural laziness or
stupidity to racial traits like thick lips or short stature have been advanced to
explain such presumed linguistic inadequacies. This blatant ethnocentrism may
seem benighted in an age of cultural pluralism. Yet as recently as the 1960s
educators believed that the language of Black preschoolers was illogical,
underdeveloped, and incoherent, and that the only way for Black children to
overcome this language "deficit" was to participate in government-sponsored
Head Start programs.

American schools have done much to foster the kind of thinking about
language that Sapir and other linguists have been struggling to controvert. Many of
us learn in school that some constructions constitute "good grammar" and others
"bad grammar." We learn that *He don't know nothing* is "bad grammar" because
it contains a double negative and lacks subject-verb agreement. And we learn not
to use *It's me*—even though the alternative may be the stilted construction *It is I*.
What we learn, in short, is a list of rules which are supposed to produce "good
grammar" (and, just as importantly, social acceptability) in the same way that
rules like *Never begin eating before the hostess raises her fork* produce "good

1

manners." They are not rules which govern the way Americans actually do speak—many speakers regularly utter constructions like *He don't know nothing* and *It's me* and are understood by their listeners. Rather, these rules codify the way certain grammarians have decided Americans should speak. Because these school grammars prescribe rules for proper language use, linguists call them *prescriptive* grammars.

Modern linguistics, however, differs considerably from prescriptive grammar. One of its chief tenets is that all languages and all varieties of a single language are equally logical and expressive, rich and complex. Without evaluating "correctness," modern linguists try to describe objectively and nonjudgmentally how language actually operates. Hence they develop what are called *descriptive* grammars. Most of the articles in Part I of this book are partial descriptive grammars of language varieties spoken in the United States.

What descriptive linguists have discovered is that language does indeed operate according to rules, though the rules they formulate describe actual language use rather than some socially sanctioned norm. There is, for instance, a rule in English that adverbs of place must precede adverbs of time when both occur after the verb. Thus *Josephine had to go home Friday* and *She wants me to be there soon* are perfectly regular sentences, but any native speaker of English would find something odd in **Josephine had to go Friday home* and **She wants me to be soon there.* (Constructions which violate descriptive rules are conventionally marked by asterisks.) In fact, any language is governed by such a complicated set of descriptive rules that linguists are still far from being able to specify all of them, even for English. It is surely one of the greatest marvels of the human brain that every normal six-year-old has a good intuitive grasp of this intricate system of rules. That is what allows even young children to produce utterances which are at once original and totally comprehensible; in other words, to combine a finite set of language resources into an infinite number of well-formed constructions. The child who conjectures that the plural of *sheep* must be *sheeps* is simply applying the pluralization rule a bit too enthusiastically, attributing to English more systematic elegance than it actually possesses.

All languages, then, are systematic. One characteristic of this system is that it is arbitrary; that is, there is no causal or natural connection between the form of language and its meaning, as there is between the sun and daylight. All languages are simply artificial constructs or sets of conventions which speakers have agreed to associate with certain meanings. It is thus absurd to attribute to one language more correspondence with nature or "reality" than another language. Another characteristic of language system is that it is hierarchical, at the lowest level consisting of sound units, and at the highest levels of whole conversations or texts. Since most linguistic discussions assume a basic grasp of concepts and terminology within this hierarchy, it will be useful to know something about each level.

Form   Because the fundamental medium of language is speech, not writing, *phonology*, or the study of sound systems, is the first step in the study of language system. Within phonology, *phonetics* is the study of that continuous stream of sounds and pauses which comprise any speech event. Technically, this stream of sounds (conventionally transcribed in a modified alphabet and between square brackets) is infinitely various. Any two utterances of the same sentence never sound exactly alike even when the speaker is the same. To impose order on this infinite variety, speakers of a language unconsciously agree to consider certain sound differences nonsignificant and have a hard time distinguishing the differences among these sounds even when they are demonstrated. For example, most speakers of English do not notice that the [t] sound in *top* (accompanied by a slight puff of air, or *aspiration*) is not the same as the [t] sound in *stop* (unaspirated). In English this difference between the two [t]s is nonsignificant. Similarly, differences between the [r] and [l] sounds in Japanese or [v] and [w] sounds in German are nonsignificant and difficult for speakers of those languages to distinguish in English. There are, of course, other sound differences which speakers of a language agree to consider significant. These are sounds which, like the initial sounds in English *park* and *bark*, differentiate units of meaning. Linguists call these significant units of sound *phonemes*. A phoneme is not an actual sound but an abstraction which stands for a range of sounds perceived as "the same" by speakers of a given language. The actual utterances of a phoneme, which vary nonsignificantly from each other, are called *allophones*. Hence the [t] sounds in *top* and *stop*, as well as those in *bottom* and *pot*, are all separate allophones of the phoneme /t/. (Phonemes are conventionally represented between slant lines.)

Happily for the would-be systematizer, the number of phonemes in any language is never overwhelming. English has thirty-five by most counts. What differentiates these sounds from one another is the place and manner of articulation along the human vocal tract. A knowledge of where and how the sounds of English are articulated can explain why certain sounds merge with or replace other similar sounds in some varieties of English. (See the sketch of the human vocal apparatus on p. 4.) Consonants are formed by stopping or obstructing the airflow along the vocal tract as it is exhaled from the lungs. The obstruction may be caused by the lips, the walls of the glottis, or most frequently, the tongue. Consonants can be classified according to their point of articulation, according to whether they are *voiced* (vocal cords vibrating) or *voiceless* (vocal cords relaxed), and according to their manner of articulation; i.e., whether they are *stops*, which shut off the airflow completely; *fricatives*, which narrow the vocal passage at some point; *affricates*, which are stops followed by fricatives; *nasals*, which shut off the airflow in the mouth but allow it to be released through the nose; *liquids*, which divert the air around the sides (/l/) or over the top (/r/) of the tongue; or *semivowels*, which glide to or from the articulation point of related vowels. The table on p. 5 uses these classifications to group English consonants. Vowels, which are transitional sounds intervening between consonants or consonant clusters to make words pronounceable, shape rather than obstruct the airflow along the vocal passage. Since the tongue, the most movable part of the vocal apparatus, is crucial in shaping the air for vowels, they can be classified according to tongue position, as shown in the table on p. 6. Pronouncing aloud

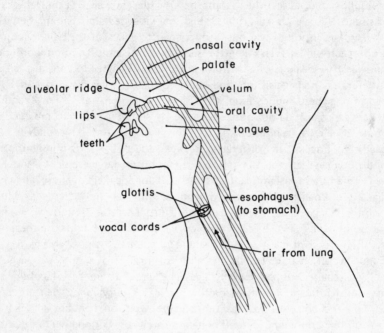

each of these consonant and vowel sounds should clarify their classifications and the relationships among the various sounds of English.

Stress and pitch, which are superimposed on the sequence of phonemes, play a significant role in sound systems as well. Stress may differentiate one word from another (the noun *pérmit* from the verb *permít*). Sequences of pitches form *intonation contours*, which have important implications for the meaning of sentences (e.g., *Jerry's here*, with falling pitch at the end of the sentence and *Jerry's here?* with the rising question intonation, indicating doubt and request for confirmation).

At the next level in the hierarchy of language system, phonemes build into sequences which speakers recognize as minimal units of meaning, or *morphemes*. The study of these meaning units and the way they combine into words is *morphology*. The highlights of English morphology can be briefly summarized. Morphemes are classed as *free* when they can stand independently as words (for example, *swim*, *girl*) and as *bound* when they must be accompanied by other morphemes to stand as words (*dis-*, *-ment*, *kniv-*, *-ed*). Two free morphemes can combine in a new word: *break-water*. Bound morphemes, in turn, fall into two main categories: *derivational* and *inflectional*. Derivational morphemes are affixes, which can be attached to either the beginning (e.g., <u>un</u>do, <u>re</u>pay) or the end (e.g., *slow<u>ly</u>, hand<u>ful</u>*) of another morpheme. More than one derivational morpheme can, of course, occur in one word: <u>un</u>-read-<u>able</u>-<u>ness</u>. The other major class of bound morphemes is the inflectional morpheme, which indicates grammatical

CONSONANT TABLE

Point of articulation

Manner of articulation	Bilabial (both lips)	Labiodental (lower lip, upper teeth)	Interdental (tongue between teeth)	Alveolar (tongue on alveolar ridge)	Palatal (tongue on palate)	Velar (tongue on velum)	Glottal (glottis constricted)
Stops:							
Voiceless	p			t		k	
Voiced	b			d		g	
Fricatives:							
Voiceless		f	Θ (thin)	s	š (ash)		h
Voiced		v	ð (then)	z	ž (rouge)		
Affricates:							
Voiceless					č /t + š/ (cheap)		
Voiced					ǰ /d + ž/ (jeep)		
Nasals, voiced	m			n		ŋ (sing)	
Liquids, voiced				l, r			
Semivowels, voiced	w				y		

VOWEL TABLE

	Tongue front	Tongue center	Tongue back
Monophthongs (one sound)			
Tongue high	i (beat)*		u (boot)
	I (bit)		U (put)
Tongue mid	e (bait)	ə (but)	o (boat)
	ɛ (bet)		
Tongue low	æ (bat)	a (pot)	ɔ (bought)
Diphthongs (two sounds combined)		ai (bite)	ɔi (Boyd)
		au (bout)	

*Pronunciation guide words are not valid for all varieties of American English. Some varieties collapse contrasts shown here.

relationship and in English is usually a suffix, including the plural, the past tense, the possessive. Morphemes, like phonemes, are idealizations and can receive different pronunciations in different phonological environments. For instance, the plural morpheme becomes /s/ when attached to the word *fork*, /z/ when attached to *spoon*, and /əz/ when attached to *glass*. These various manifestations of a morpheme are called *allomorphs*.

Above the level of morphology in the language hierarchy is *syntax*, or the combination of words into sentences—a considerably more complicated level than either phonology or morphology and one that linguists are only beginning to understand. One reason for the complexity of the syntactic level is that syntax actually consists of several hierarchical levels: words combine into phrases (e.g., *in the morning, the first green bed quilt, carried away*), phrases into clauses (e.g., *to come back in the morning, after she had laboriously stitched the first green bed quilt, carried away by their own enthusiasm*), and clauses into sentences. To cite just one syntactic rule at the level of phrase formation, English requires that modifiers in noun phrases occur in a certain order: determiners (*the, some, this,* etc.), then ordinators, which place items in the context of other related items (*three, first, best,* etc.), then adjectives (*interesting, old, yellow,* etc.), then nouns acting as modifiers (as in *bus* station). *The best local woman announcer* is thus a well-formed English noun phrase, while any other word order would not be. There are scores of other rules for assembling clauses out of phrases and sentences out of clauses. Linguists have recently begun to discover that even units above the sentence, like question-and-answer or discourse, operate systematically. But at these upper levels in the hierarchy there is so much freedom of choice that the principles of structure are increasingly difficult to discern.

Meaning   The structural hierarchy outlined so far pertains only to the form of language. The systematic analysis of meaning—called *semantics*—is much more elusive, partly because meaning changes so quickly, partly because it is so intimately bound up with private associations, and partly because it encodes cultural assumptions which are so fundamental that they are almost impossible to decode consciously. Nevertheless, it is the demanding job of the semanticist to analyze both the grammar and the vocabulary (*lexicon*) of a language to discover how it conveys what its speakers perceive as "reality."

Some semanticists concentrate on explaining the logical relationships among words and/or assertions in a single language. They study linguistic phenomena like these: the distinction between sense (*The mare trotted obediently into her stall*) and nonsense (*The daisy trotted obediently into her stall*); ambiguity, in which one construction has more than one possible interpretation (*Ask the butcher if he has any brains*); paraphrase, in which two different constructions convey the same meaning (*She was too short* and *She was not tall enough*); implication, in which the truth of one statement implies the truth of another (*Terry is a nun* implies that Terry is a woman).

Other semanticists study meaning cross-culturally and can suggest ways that language parallels world view. For instance, the noun-verb orientation of English and related languages implies a view of the world in which every action or process must be performed by something or someone. English speakers cannot simply say *blowing, flashing,* or *snowing,* as speakers of the Native American language Hopi could, but must find a subject, however weak, for each of these verbs: *The wind blows, The light flashes, It's snowing.*

Cross-culturally-oriented semanticists also examine items in the lexicon to discover how various languages classify reality. English pronouns, for instance, classify objects in the world according to whether they are nonhuman (*it*) or human (*she, he*) and further subclassify human objects by gender. Some non-European languages have much more elaborate classification systems which reveal something of how their speakers view reality. In Thai and Laotian, for example, there are special noun classes reserved for elephants, which are sacred in those cultures. Especially in a cross-cultural context, then, semantics, like other aspects of language system, reaffirms the initial proposition of this introduction: that every language is uniquely and perfectly suited to express all the richness and variety of its culture.

The Nature of Communication

The systematic analysis of language structure has led scholars from many disciplines to begin the systematic analysis of the entire communication process. Linguists have clearly established that our languages offer us complex, sophisticated, and largely unconscious systems of rules which enable us to process the constantly new and infinitely varied sound sequences we hear into meaningful messages. Each language's phonological system allows the listener to screen out extraneous noise and personal variations in pronunciation and concentrate on meaningful articulatory distinctions. (We even compensate for foreigners' errors and children's unpracticed articulations.) The language's morphological system cues the listener to the meaningful units in the continuous speech stream, and the syntactic rules that all speakers have internalized hold the key for organizing those units into meaningful relationships.

When linguists turned to studying semantics, to questioning, among other things, how listeners interpret messages with many possible meanings, they discovered they had opened a Pandora's box. How, for instance, do we know that *I bought a real white elephant yesterday* between zookeepers refers to an albino pachyderm but between antique dealers to a snuff box, a gilded clock, or a potbellied stove? Our ability to guess the correct interpretation lies not in our understanding of English alone but in our knowledge of American culture. Effective communication does not begin and end with a shared language; it begins and ends with shared cultural knowledge and values, for which language serves as the principal medium of exchange. This method of analyzing language within its cultural matrix is often called *ethnography of communication.*

Correct interpretation of individual vocabulary items or even whole sentences is only a minor test of our verbal skills and cultural knowledge. We face infinitely more difficult communicational barriers every day. In face-to-face encounters we make a great many other observations at the same time as we interpret the speech stream itself. Facial expression, body postures and gestures, dress, and other factors of physical appearance such as height and subtleties in tone of voice all contribute to our assessment of a speaker's remarks.

Consider, for example, a job interview—an encounter especially designed to permit employer and applicant to evaluate each other subjectively, as well as objectively. The applicant is seeking a job which fulfills her interests, which pays adequately, and which provides room for advancement in a pleasant and companionable work environment. The employer is concerned about the applicant's professional skills, her longevity once trained for the job, and her potential for "fitting in" to what the boss considers the proper office structure and atmosphere.

The interviewer makes the following observations among countless others during the interview: The applicant is casually but neatly dressed. She graciously accepts the proffered first-name basis as well as the obligatory cup of coffee. As the interviewee takes the chair beside, not that opposite, the desk, the boss thinks that she might be a little "pushy." The applicant demonstrates adequate familiarity with the professional field by easily handling the highly specialized jargon. She also expresses herself articulately, though an overlay of regional accent is somewhat distracting to the employer. The applicant follows the employer's remarks with respect and interest, watching closely and nodding affirmatively when appropriate. Yet the somewhat "pushy" impression is recreated when the interviewee raises the question of wages before the boss has a chance to. However, she admires the confidence and self-assertion so expressed.

On the applicant's part similarly subtle observations are taking place, likewise unconscious, but important to her impression of the encounter: First-name basis seems to indicate an egalitarianism which is, however, belied when the boss fails to rise to greet her. The interviewer has remained seated behind the large desk facing the door, observing the applicant from a secure (and physically undisclosing) position as she crosses the room. The employer apparently maintains a position of distance and authority toward the staff. To avoid the teacher-pupil relationship which she associates with sitting on the opposite side of the desk, the applicant takes the chair beside it and accepts a cup of coffee, hoping thereby to appear friendly and relaxed. The interviewee pays close attention to the description of the job, smiling appreciatively but with dignity and follows the employer's gestures and facial expression as closely as her words. However, salary and benefits have not been addressed, and after waiting until she feels that an adequate impression of professional commitment has been established, the applicant raises the "bread and butter" issues herself. The employer's apparent avoidance of these issues makes the applicant somewhat uneasy about the boss's concern for her employees' welfare. At the close of the interview, signaled by the employer's indirect remark about an upcoming meeting, the boss does walk out into the lobby with the applicant, publicly thanking her for her time.

The above example pinpoints just a few of the thousands of bits of verbal and nonverbal information which go into an individual's understanding of a speech event. Many are both informative and possible sources of breakdown in communication, for they are liable to multiple interpretation. For instance, the applicant must realize that *Actually, there is an important staff meeting coming up* really means *I've spent as much time as I wish on the interview.* The interviewer's offer of first-name address implies informality, but this gesture must be weighed against the nonverbal one in which the boss chose to remain seated and physically hidden behind her desk. How much use of professional jargon does the employer want to hear? The applicant must use enough to satisfy the inquiry about professional competence implied in the boss's conversation but not so much that she appears a show-off without substantial experience. After all, words can be cheap.

To realize the potential for misunderstanding inherent in all our encounters, imagine the same interview taking place between persons who are not of the same ethnic and social group. Is the offer of a cup of coffee really a question? In many American homes, for example, those of families with southeastern European heritage, refusal to accept food or drink can be construed as an intentional insult. In many offices coffee drinking is the basis for most of the social interaction among the staff. (This kind of failure in communication due to different definitions of the same event is aptly termed *cultural slippage* by Roger Abrahams.) The boss in the above example was impressed by the attentiveness with which the applicant followed her description of the job. She formed this impression because the applicant followed her eyes and gestures and murmured affirmatives. Suppose the applicant had come from a Chicano background in which deference, attention, and respect are indicated by lowered eyes or an Afro-American community in which intermittent *yes . . . yes . . . I see* is not necessary to ensure that the speaker has an attentive audience. First-name address between superiors and inferiors is largely unknown outside the United States and would be disconcerting to immigrants from many cultures. Indeed, its use varies widely within the United States according to region and to specific industry. Detecting regional speech differences always leads to judgments about the speaker. A Bostonian interviewing in Atlanta might approach an employer with a local accent with some condescension, while the interviewer is simultaneously trying to ascertain whether the applicant is as "cold" and "stuffy" as his Down East pronunciation would imply.

Even within a single ethnic and social class differing interpretations of communicational behavior may result from age or sex differences. A comment on dress or personal appearance may have different implications between two women than between a man and a woman. Suppose in the interview example a male applicant had taken the chair beside, not that opposite, the interviewer's desk. This would constitute a more powerful intrusion upon the employer's personal space, for men and women in a nonsexual relationship are expected to maintain considerable physical distance. Her failure to rise, however, when he entered would not have been so unfriendly but rather acceptable female gender behavior.

When speakers come from entirely different linguistic and cultural backgrounds, the barriers to effective communication multiply. An American may have offended a Burmese business acquaintance even before the conversation begins by offering the Southeast Asian a low chair, thereby implying that the visitor is socially inferior. Each culture selects some aspects of language and behavior to which it assigns special salience. In some societies strict rules govern who may open a conversation, and one waits in silence for a sign that talk is to begin. In our own culture time is a very important consideration. In another society time may not be encoded into the language as a commodity which can be "spent," "wasted," or "lost," but rather each day or season is conceptualized as a rotation to another opportunity to start one's work anew.

The study of communication has only recently proceeded beyond the structure of language to the communicational process as a systemic event. Short discourses and brief conversations are now being subjected to systematic analysis. Video recording is augmenting the traditional sound-tape recordings so that nonverbal cues can be taken into account. Most work so far is on English only. The analysis of intercultural, cross-linguistic communication has barely begun.

Variation in Language

The structure of language provides its speakers with a framework in which they can operate to assess information and to communicate with others. But a language does not exist apart from its speakers. Each generation of new speakers makes changes in the language; they are constantly evolving new forms, supplanting and supplementing old ones. What we call "English" is not an abstract system to which all English speakers subject themselves. Rather, "English" is a consensus, the vehicle that its speakers have agreed upon and which they amend and alter as necessary to fulfill their communicational needs. There are general norms for language behavior—both verbal and nonverbal—but constantly new communicational situations require innovation as well as new assessments of appropriate behavior. Speakers also may choose to alter their behavior from the norm for purposes of impact and individuation (e.g., continually new "slang" among pop musicians).

Thus speakers are not mere captives of the norms for language behavior but rather make continual choices during the course of the communicational process. Through the choices each makes, all speakers contribute to the direction in which language is changing. It has long been recognized that speakers have not just one but a range of styles and that they make judgments as to which is most appropriate at any given time. However, systematic study of linguistic decision making was not begun until the 1960s. *Sociolinguistics* attempts not only to describe variation but also to explain the factors governing people's use of particular linguistic alternatives, or *variants*. The investigation of language variation began with the study of regional *dialects*. This approach emphasizes description of subsystems of a language but fails to take into account stylistic variation, age-graded language differences, multilingual situations, or the impact of socioeconomic factors on language use. Regional dialectologists had shown that different parts of the country have some differences in vocabulary, accent, and standards for "correctness." But it had become increasingly impossible to ignore the fact that within geographic regions, particularly in the supposed "melting pots" of our large cities, different speech patterns prevail among the various ethnic communities. Large-scale linguistic surveys of New York, Detroit, and other cities revealed some shared speech norms, but also standards which are unique to particular groups. Subjects of these studies demonstrated remarkable ability to manipulate their language subtly in order to express their personal identification with their peers or with some other group which they held in esteem.

Furthermore, people use the speech of those outside their own group as a basis for value judgments which are often totally unrelated to the language use itself. Studies show that, based only on a tape recording of a set passage, speakers of the more prestigious language in a bilingual community or the more prestigious dialect in a monolingual community are consistently perceived as more intelligent, ambitious, and personable than the speakers of the less prestigious variety. Like other members of their communities, teachers are susceptible to this stereotyping by language and have been shown to evaluate a student's academic potential merely on the basis of language behavior. Such stereotypical judgments are particularly insidious because largely unconscious.

Most negative judgments about speakers are based on detected deviations from what the listener defines as "standard" speech. All speakers of English have some model in their minds against which they measure their own speech and that of others. Many would say that they never speak anything but "standard," but their actual linguistic performance varies from formal to casual according to the situation and to the degree of familiarity and relative status of other participants in the conversation. In reality there is no one speech which can be labeled "American Standard." Regional differences, for instance, can play a part. Any native Georgian would feel that the speech of a well-educated Atlanta banker is near the ideal "standard," but a non-Southerner might disagree. It has been asserted that a "General American" standard is found in the educated speech of the Midwest, but to many Eastern ears Midwest regionalisms such as /rʊf/ for *roof* or *pop* for "carbonated beverage" are rustic at best and at worst "wrong." Even the supposedly monolithic "Broadcast English" permits an ever larger range of regional and some ethnic variation, as evidenced by the increasing variety of pronunciation among network newscasters.

Still, there are many speech forms which are generally agreed to be "standard" among all English-speaking Americans. The particular linguistic features which are deemed "standard" are arbitrary, no more "right" or "logical" than those which are considered "nonstandard." There is no more "logic," for example, in the rule of single negation in standard English (*I don't need any help*) than in the multiple negation employed in many nonstandard varieties of English (*I don't need no help*), and indeed no one is ever mistaken as to the intended meaning of the latter. However, the sources for the linguistic features which come to constitute "correct" speech are *not* arbitrary. The notion of standard language is restricted to literate cultures. That speech used by major literary and journalistic figures often becomes the basis for codification of the language by lexicographers and grammarians, for it constitutes the most significant body of printed material available for analysis. The personal prestige of the individuals employing the literary dialect lends credence to the notion that this variety is "better." Thus speech forms which are most highly valued devolve largely from the most powerful social and political group in the society. In the case of the United States this has traditionally been the professional and upper classes in the industrial Northeast states. As the South becomes economically and politically more powerful, it is not surprising that Southern regionalisms are coming to be accepted on national television. And as various racial and ethnic groups assert their rights, it follows that their terms and their speech habits are finding their way into general usage.

Like all communication, "standard" speech does not exist in isolation. The notion of "correct" language cannot be understood separate from the context of the situation in which it is used. For years vain attempts to teach children "correct" grammar have gone unheeded once the pupils leave the classroom. Children know that those schoolbook forms are simply inappropriate on the playground. Similarly, most would agree that *I ain't* is not as "correct" as *I am not.* But whereas some persons avoid the use of *I ain't* at all times, for others it is entirely appropriate to use the nonstandard form in situations where informality in speech and behavior is called for.

Sociolinguistic studies demonstrate clearly that not only the communicational context but also the larger social context bears directly on language use.

Socioeconomic status and ethnicity largely determine the "standardness" of the speaker. "Standard English" is, by definition, the speech of mainstream society, and those outside the mainstream have less opportunity to be exposed to it at home, at work, or in social groups. The casual speech of these people is usually not Standard English but some less prestigious variety of English or perhaps an entirely different language. And that variety or language is less prestigious by the very fact of being spoken by them.

Knowing what is the "best" language does not always lead to a desire to emulate it. Just as a child using overly proper speech in the schoolyard might get punched by the class bully for behaving like a "smart aleck," so a household worker and urban-ghetto dweller who uses standard speech is setting herself off from her peer group and would be just as justifiably ostracized. Use of in-group speech, including nonstandard forms, is one of the most important indicators of belonging to a group, as the linguistic behavior of adolescents makes clear. A factory worker may well agree that the company president speaks the "best" English he hears, but his own aspirations would be better fulfilled if he could learn to speak like the foreman and not the boss, for there lies his real possibility for advancement.

"Standard English" is not the language most of the privileged speak all the time. It is nobody's real language. Instead, it is a norm toward which speakers gravitate when they wish to communicate formally, particularly with persons outside their peer group. And, undefinable as it is, it is the measure against which, however unjustly, our personal value is assessed each time we open our mouths. The selections which follow offer some insights into language variation, language attitudes, and language teaching in the United States. And, to paraphrase, as language goes, so goes the country.

Further Readings

The Structure of Language

Dwight Bolinger, *Aspects of Language,* 2d ed. (Harcourt Brace Jovanovich, 1975). The best broad introduction to the study of language.

Ronald Wardhaugh, *Introduction to Linguistics* (McGraw-Hill, 1972). A good introduction, particularly strong on the structure of language; excellent glossary; use of International Phonetic Alphabet and generative-transformational terminology may present obstacles.

Edward Sapir, "Language," *Encyclopedia of the Social Sciences,* vol. IX (1933). Reprinted in Harold Hungerford, Jay Robinson, and James Sledd, eds., *English Linguistics: An Introduction* (Scott, Foresman, 1970). A brief essay which captures the major theoretical issues in the structure of language and linguistic variation.

John Lyons, *Introduction to Theoretical Linguistics* (Cambridge University Press, 1969). Comprehensive analysis of major questions in the study of syntax; requires considerable background.

The Nature of Communication

Dell Hymes, "Toward Ethnographies of Communication: The Analysis of Communicative Events," Pier Paolo Giglioli, ed., *Language and Social Context* (Penguin, 1972). Good introductory essay on the ethnographic approach to the study of language by a primary figure in the field.

Robbins Burling, *Man's Many Voices: Language in Its Cultural Context* (Holt, Rinehart and Winston, 1970). An accessible introduction to language and culture; each chapter is a separate essay on one problem in the ethnography of communication; some American examples.

John J. Gumperz and Dell Hymes, *Directions in Sociolinguistics: The Ethnography of Communication* (Holt, Rinehart and Winston, 1972). An anthology with essays of varying difficulty; consideration of discourse; good bibliography; guidelines for projects in ethnography of communication.

Erving Goffman, *Frame Analysis* (Harper & Row, 1974). Sociological framework for the observation of interpersonal interaction, particularly nonverbal behavior.

Variation in Language

Peter Trudgill, *Sociolinguistics: An Introduction* (Penguin, 1974). The most readable introduction to sociolinguistics; avoids technical terminology; primarily on British English with some examples from American English and other European languages.

Joshua A. Fishman, *Sociolinguistics: A Brief Introduction* (Newbury House, 1971). Lays out basic concepts in sociolinguistics, bilingualism, and language planning; ethnographic approach; examples primarily on languages other than English, including European languages in America.

William Labov, "The Place of Linguistic Research in American Society," *Linguistics in the 1970's* (Center for Applied Linguistics, 1971). Leading sociolinguist summarizes advances in the field and major issues raised by sociolinguistics for researchers and educators.

Walt Wolfram and Ralph W. Fasold, *The Study of Social Dialects in American English* (Prentice-Hall, 1974). Analyzes data from urban sociolinguistic studies with remarks on their pedagogical implications.

PART I

SOME SPEECH COMMUNITIES
IN THE UNITED STATES

The mere fact of a common speech serves as a peculiarly potent symbol of the social solidarity of the people who speak the language.
—Edward Sapir

Americans have recently begun to recognize the nation's linguistic and cultural diversity and appreciate the contributions of many and varied groups to this society. This pluralistic view that each subculture is unique and equally valuable allows us to capitalize on the country's wealth of human resources. In our eagerness to consider ourselves a unified culture, we have for too long overlooked the cohesiveness and resilience of individual communities, which have always provided a primary forum for social interaction. Indeed, any society as huge and complex as the United States breaks down into smaller units to live, work, worship, socialize, and relax. People naturally affiliate with those who share their interests, values, or background. These smaller groups within a large society provide their members with a sense of self-worth, a comfortable interpersonal environment, and protection from alien ways of life.

For the linguist these natural social groups are also important because they are *speech communities.* In general, a speech community can be any network of frequent social interaction and shared speech norms. Depending on how broadly the term is construed, speech communities may share a variety of speech norms: use of one language (e.g., monolingual Chicanos) or language variety (e.g., Tidewater Virginians); use of several languages or varieties in different contexts (e.g., Jewish immigrants who might use Yiddish, English, an East European language, or a combination depending on the situation); or use of a small lexical subset of one language (e.g., the jargon of ballet dancers).

Another characteristic of speech communities is that language functions as a symbol for other shared values and provides an instant and accurate means of distinguishing between insiders and outsiders. Thus the United States can be seen as a single speech community since we recognize one national language and agree on certain grammatical norms for use in public situations like television newscasts or political speeches. Or a speech community can be as small as three or four children who develop a secret language to confuse or exclude anyone outside their play group.

Speech communities can coalesce around a number of other variables besides nationality and play group, and one individual typically belongs to several. Locality is certainly the most obvious of these variables. Especially in the years before rapid transportation and electronic media, one inescapable determinant of social networks was simple physical proximity. Hence Northerners are known to speak differently from Southerners and Bostonians from New Yorkers. Other variables are vocation and avocation. Part of what insulates the medical community, for instance, is its highly specialized and Latinate vocabulary, which both allows group members to recognize colleagues and effectively shuts out intruders. Similarly, hobbyists like photographers or numismatists (whose very name separates initiates from those unfamiliar with the word) create their own specific vocabularies. Any woman who has ever felt cheated by a garage mechanic or ignored in a sports discussion is suffering partly from being outside those particular speech communities. Still another determinant of speech communities can be age. Teenagers, who value peer-group status highly, develop complicated and quickly changing slangs to identify group members and are seldom taken in when a nongroup member (like their middle-aged teacher) tries to manipulate their style and vocabulary.

Yet probably the most salient variables that distinguish among speech communities in an urban America are the overlapping factors of race, class, and ethnicity, for it is these factors that constitute the greatest determinants of reference group in today's cities. Employment, neighborhood, religious, and socializing patterns all provide ample sociological evidence for group cohesion by race, class, and ethnicity. But there is also linguistic evidence: most middle-class Americans do not speak like most working-class Americans, nor do most Blacks or Puerto Ricans speak like most Whites. It is to these crucial differences in contemporary American speech communities that most of the articles in this section are addressed.

Not surprisingly, the study of speech communities in the United States has more or less paralleled our national sense of what lines most deeply divide our population. Beginning with the foundation of the American Dialect Society in 1889 and persisting until quite recently, the chief division among speakers of American English was considered to be regional. American regional dialectology owes its greatest debt to Hans Kurath, who in the 1930s established the Linguistic Atlas Project. Kurath's goal was to map the influence of settlement history and migration patterns on language variation. He therefore focused primarily on the varieties of American English derived from British settlers and sought out older informants and usages. His method was to dispatch field workers to communities throughout the country to elicit regional differences in pronunciation, grammar, and syntax by means of a questionnaire. Kurath himself published the *Linguistic Atlas of New England*, and atlases for other sections of the United States have since been published or soon will be. The excerpt from Shuy's *Discovering American Dialects* summarizes the major concepts and findings of the linguistic geographers, who pointed the way for all subsequent studies of language variation in the United States.

In the early 1960s, American dialectology came to a crossroads when William Labov set off to execute a regional study on Martha's Vineyard, a resort island off the coast of Massachusetts. What he discovered there began to turn American dialectologists toward sociological explanations for differences among speech communities. He found that language variation among residents of Martha's Vineyard had less to do with geography than with reference group: speakers who identified with the island culture pronounced certain vowels as early settlers of the island had, while those who identified with the mainland pronounced them like mainland speakers. According to this analysis, even brothers in the same family could and did belong to different reference groups and therefore different speech communities. In 1966, Labov's *Social Stratification of English in New York City* introduced modern sampling and interview techniques into linguistic studies and established the primacy of class and ethnic differences among speakers of American English. The New York survey ushered in modern sociolinguistics.

It is no coincidence that class and race differences in American speech began to receive serious attention during the Civil Rights era. In fact, it is largely because of the Civil Rights movement that our most detailed sociolinguistic studies—many of them sponsored by the federal government and aimed at improving education—focus on Black English Vernacular (BEV). The consequent richness of resources in this area is reflected here by articles on the origin and on the structural features of BEV as well as by taxonomies of Black speech events and nonverbal modes of communication.

The 1970s, perhaps partly as an outgrowth of the racial and economic issues raised in the 1960s, have witnessed a burgeoning concern for and pride in the cultural pluralism of American society. Most major cities now have annual ethnic festivals, students come to college eager to study the language and heritage of their immigrant or minority families, and bumper stickers proclaim, "Proud to Be American. Proud to Be Polish." In keeping with the emphasis on these social issues, linguists are also turning increased attention to the variety of speech habits inherent in a multicultural and multilingual society. In this collection the articles by Saville, Glazer, Wolfram, Young, and Tucker describe some linguistic dimensions of diversity in such a society.

There is, of course, much more diversity among American speech communities than can possibly be suggested by a few selections. For one thing, there are many more speech communities than those represented here: there are several hundred Native American speech communities, of which Navajo is the largest; there are urban and rural poor white speech communities, which in themselves vary regionally (See "Educational Implications of Dialect Diversity" in Part III for some data on Appalachian speech); there are rural immigrant communities including Scandinavians in Minnesota and Germans in Pennsylvania. A list of American speech communities could be expanded to considerable length. In addition, language and language study vary in more ways than linguists have yet described. We need ethnographies of communication on all these speech communities and need to know more about the cultures that stand behind the languages. We also need to know more about the variety of nonverbal communication in different speech communities. And we should ask how speech communities are affected by their immediate neighbors and by the total American verbal environment. The communities studied and linguistic approaches taken in this section are clearly only a foundation. Much exciting work remains to be done.

Further Readings

Raven I. McDavid, Jr., "The Dialects of American English," W. Nelson Francis, *The Structure of American English* (The Ronald Press, 1958). Outlines the history of regional dialects and regional dialectology in the United States; details pronunciation, vocabulary, and grammatical features for major U.S. dialect regions.

Harold B. Allen and Gary N. Underwood, eds., *Readings in American Dialectology* (Appleton-Century-Crofts, 1971). Best anthology of regional dialect studies, drawn largely from the Linguistic Atlas surveys.

Einar Haugen, *The Norwegian Language in America: A Study in Bilingual Behavior* (Indiana University Press, 1969). Best detailed study of an immigrant community's language maintenance and assimilation in the English-speaking environment.

Robbins Burling, *English in Black and White* (Holt, Rinehart and Winston, 1973). An accessible but not oversimplified account of the origin, features, stigmatization, and educational implications of Black English Vernacular; most reliable of the many books on the subject.

Walter A. Wolfram, *A Sociolinguistic Description of Detroit Negro Speech* (Center for Applied Linguistics, 1969). Most readable of the reports on major urban sociolinguistic studies; differences in socioeconomic status, age, and sex analyzed for each feature.

Walt Wolfram and Donna Christian, *Appalachian Speech* (Center for Applied Linguistics, 1976). Nontechnical description of Appalachian speech with sociological background on the Appalachian speech community.

THE REASONS FOR DIALECT DIFFERENCES

Roger W. Shuy

Regional variation was the subject of the first serious and systematic study of differences among American speech communities. Hans Kurath, founder of the American Linguistic Atlas Project and author of the *Linguistic Atlas of New England*, discerned three major American dialect areas along the East Coast: Northern (New England, New York, northern Pennsylvania), Midland (southern New Jersey, southern Pennsylvania, northern Maryland, northern Delaware, western Virginia, the western Carolinas), and Southern (southern Delaware, southern Maryland, eastern Virginia, the eastern Carolinas). As Map 7 indicates, Kurath and other linguistic geographers have also discovered subdivisions within these major areas, but they agree that Northern, Midland, and Southern dialects remained more or less intact as settlers from these Eastern regions moved west to the Mississippi. West of the Mississippi, however, settlement patterns became more complicated, and as a result, the Eastern dialect boundaries grew increasingly less distinct. In the selection below from the pamphlet *Discovering American Dialects*, written for students and teachers of high school English, Roger W. Shuy explains how regional dialect differences arose and spread and how linguistic geographers go about mapping them.

Field workers in regional dialectology typically interview at least two natives of each of the selected communities in their region—one older and less educated, the other younger and better educated. Interviewers strive for the tone of a casual conversation with their informants in order to encourage the use of colloquial features. They work through questionnaires designed to elicit specific items of pronunciation (e.g., *greasy* with an /s/ for Northern speakers, with a /z/ for Midland and Southern speakers) and vocabulary (e.g., *pail* for Northern speakers, *bucket* in Midland and Southern speakers) which have been found to discriminate among dialect areas. Readers can replicate or update this field work by administering the pronunciation and vocabulary tests in Appendixes A and B of this volume.

The Patterns of Settlement History   Recently I was driving through the rural Midwest with some friends from California, who noticed things which I had always taken for granted. One Californian, for example, was struck by what he called "little red lollipops" in the front yards of the farmhouses. Later, when he saw another one and called my attention to it, I saw only a red reflector on a stick, used by Indianans as a guide to their driveways at night. My guests were also impressed with poppies growing along the roadside and the quaint country grocery stores with cases of empty soft drink bottles stacked near the front steps. If one grows up in an area in which people usually say "quarter to four," a different but equally common expression, "quarter till four," may seem as strange as the little red lollipops seemed to my friend.

Whether we realize it or not, our language is influenced by the people who settled and established our area. The influence of the early settlers may remain strong for many years; for example, German pronunciations and vocabulary are still found in Grundy County, Illinois; the linguistic effects of the Irish are present on Beaver Island in Lake Michigan; the Dutch influences, in Holland and Grand Rapids, Michigan; and Briticisms, in many American communities which were settled directly from England (such as Albion, Illinois, and New Harmony, Indiana). The first large migration of English people to our country came chiefly from the southeastern counties of England, but there were also some families from Yorkshire, Lancashire, and even the counties farther north. Each of these counties in England has its own local dialects, and the settlers brought these dialects to the New World with them. Later, Ulster Scots, Palatinate Germans,

Dutchmen, and others brought features of their own languages or dialects to America, and remnants of these may be clearly seen over one hundred years later.

Sometimes we find a relatively small dialect area surrounded by another, larger one; the former is called a dialect "island." A good example roughly includes parts of northwestern Illinois and southeastern Wisconsin. This lead mining region was settled in the 1850s primarily by people from the Ohio River area, especially Kentucky. Traveling to the region on the Ohio and Mississippi Rivers, these Midland people and some immigrant Cornishmen formed the nucleus of the Lead Region population. To this day, Midland speech predominates here, even though people in all the surrounding areas of both states use Northern speech. Note, too, that this "island" has no regard for political boundaries; it spreads over parts of Illinois, Wisconsin, and Iowa.

Local settlement history, a study often neglected, is vital to the dialectologist as he begins his research. Sometimes he can even supply "missing links" to settlement histories by observing and analyzing speech; for example, a Midwestern area with dialect features usually found in New England is quite likely to have been settled by New Englanders.

The current dialect, although useful, is not a foolproof guide to settlement history, for later layers of settlement may tend to cancel out earlier speech characteristics.

The first American settlers, of course, came from England. At the time of the earliest settlements in Massachusetts, Virginia, Maryland, and Rhode Island, dialect differences in England were even greater than they are today—and today they are still more striking than ours. Speakers of these various dialects crossed the Atlantic Ocean and settled, dialect and all, on the eastern coast of America. The various colonies of the New World found communication very difficult, and the mixed dialects of English settlers who inhabited each colony gradually became distinctive in themselves. The infrequent visits from "outsiders," the lack of safe and efficient transportation methods, and the tendency of each colony to act as a social unit did much to make their dialects distinctive. To this day the eastern coast of our country has smaller and more clearly defined dialect areas than does almost any region to the west.

Patterns of Population Shift   Ask almost anyone what the dialects of America are, and you probably will be told that they are Southern, Eastern, and General American (meaning Midwestern and Western). Even though some textbooks encourage this notion, Americans simply are not divided that neatly. Nor are regional dialects organized along state lines, as we have already seen. There is simply no such thing as a single New York, Ohio, or Florida dialect; the dialects of these and other states are formed along the lines of population shift. Nor do national borders necessarily mark dialect (or, for that matter, language) differences. The U.S.-Canadian border has been crossed many times by immigrants from both nations. One interesting example of this movement occurred during the Civil War when groups of New Englanders, hoping to avoid conscription, felt the urge to move to New Brunswick. Such immigrants were referred to as

Skedaddlers, and to this day one of their settlements is known locally as Skedaddlers Ridge.

Since the American population shift generally has been from east to west, dialect boundaries are more apt to run horizontally than vertically. People from, say, western New York who moved to Michigan, Wisconsin, northern Illinois, and northern Ohio took their western New York dialect with them.

Population shift is affected by the opening of new travel routes, by the invention of new means of transportation, by the development of industry, and by other aspects of American history. And speech patterns are thus moved and changed. For instance, the steamboat ushered in a whole new concept of American migration, allowing New Englanders and the more recent immigrants to move west across the Great Lakes.

The effects of population shift caused by industrialization can be seen in cities like Akron, Ohio. This area was settled later than most urban areas of Ohio because it is located on a high spot (Summit County) just south of the general migration route through Cleveland and just north of the route through Columbus. When the rubber industry began to develop, Akron drew thousands of laborers from the handiest source of labor: southern Ohio, West Virginia, and Kentucky. The tremendous in-pouring of Midlanders has had such a noticeable effect on the speech of Akronites that, despite its Northern location, Akron might well be considered part of the Midland speech area. The migration of Midlanders, especially West Virginians, in the past twenty years is also clearly evident in the Cleveland area, where it is estimated that Cuyahoga County has received 150,000 migrants from other states since World War II. Professor Raven I. McDavid, Jr., of the University of Chicago has observed that Kentucky and West Virginia, like western New England in our country's earlier days, have the two qualities necessary for emigration: a high fertility in the population and a low fertility in the soil.

Along with mention of the shift of population, we must also note the development of urban prestige. Cities like New York, Philadelphia, New Orleans, and San Francisco have acquired a certain prestige and have become culturally influential. Of course, no one city dominates American culture or American speech; a combination of factors causes Americans to use regional forms rather than a "national" pattern of speech.

One such factor is found in the very size of our country. It is simply too large for one city to develop a network of influence over every other city. If such an influence had ever existed, today we would most likely be imitating the speech of New York City, Boston, Philadelphia, Washington, D.C., or some other city significant in our nation's history.

Democracy also affects the thinking of Americans. If we should be told suddenly that we should pattern our speech, dress, buying habits, religion, and political views after those of Cedar Rapids, Iowa, most of us would react violently. Why Cedar Rapids? The spirit of American regionalism may be seen in people from almost any area of the country. The most traditional example might be a Texan, whose loyalty is notorious. But it can also be seen in the regional loyalty of the natives of Washington state, the Great Lakes area, and New England. This feeling is encouraged by local businessmen whose constant plea is "Buy local products," and by the pressures of family life which cause people to take local jobs rather than to move to some other part of the country.

As a result of this loyalty, various urban areas become focal points in the culture, including the dialect, of a given area. Pronunciations, words, and even grammatical choices of a city are often copied, consciously or subconsciously, by people around it. The influence of Chicago speech patterns can be clearly seen as far west as Wheaton, Illinois (twenty-five miles from Chicago), for example, where such characteristic Chicago words as *prairie* (for vacant lot) and *clout* (political influence) are known. The spread of the Minneapolis influence into Wisconsin was recently noted by Frederic G. Cassidy, who observed that the Minneapolis term *rubber-binder* (for rubber band) was gaining across the state line. On the other hand, the exact influence of an urban area is difficult to judge. The mere presence of a word or pronunciation in the city and its surrounding area does not guarantee that the primary influence came from the city. The flat farmland west of Chicago was actually settled before that city began its phenomenal growth, and it is difficult to sort out the influences of both areas. William Labov has recently observed that lower-income New York City residents often ridicule their own speech. The pronunciations *dis* and *dese* (for *this* and *these*) are thought of as characteristic of lower social levels and are not highly valued.

More recent immigration patterns also have had their influence on American English. There can be little doubt about the impact of foreign languages in the past century. The influence of German settlers on the vocabulary and syntax of certain parts of Pennsylvania has long been recognized; likewise, one can easily find Polish terms in Detroit, Hungarian in Cleveland, and Spanish in Los Angeles. New people bring new customs and, quite frequently, new ways of expressing them. Other aspects of American history have also contributed to the dialect mixtures of the present day. Many of our earlier settlements in the Rocky Mountains, for example, dissolved along with the mines which attracted the settlers in the first place. Similarly, those early eastern Coloradans who tried the wrong farming techniques soon moved to other parts, taking their dialect heritage with them and leaving the dust bowl behind.

Patterns of Physical Geography   Today we are seldom hindered in our travels by physical barriers such as rivers, deserts, or mountains. Bridge building, improved water travel, earthmoving techniques, and air transportation have removed most of the barriers which hampered communications and population shift in the last century. Consequently, dialect differences which are found on opposite sides of a river, a mountain range, or a desert were probably established many years ago. In more recently settled areas we find the influences of physical geography less important; however, there are some recent examples of cultural and linguistic isolation. Until about forty years ago river transportation was almost the only way for residents of Calhoun County, Illinois, to travel outside the county to Alton, Illinois, for a distance of about one hundred miles. Likewise

Leslie County, Kentucky, had only one paved road as recently as ten years ago. This type of isolation can be seen today in parts of eastern Kentucky and southern Virginia, and more examples might be found in many other states.

In the East, rivers, mostly because they were early physical barriers, are rather clear markers of dialect areas. The Connecticut River still separates *pahk the cah* from *park the car.* As far west as Illinois, the prairie south of the Rock River and north of the Illinois River provided easy access for the settlement of Yankees who came to Illinois across the Great Lakes and Midlanders who came north by way of the Mississippi and Illinois Rivers. Today this prairie area contains a mixture of Northern and Midland dialects. West of the Mississippi, however, geographical barriers are seldom important, since settlement often developed along with the railroad or even followed it, instead of being determined by water routes and boundaries.

Field Work in Historical Background and Social Structure

One of the first things a dialectologist does in his investigation of a given area is to find out as much as he can about its settlement history. Sometimes he can discover a little from published histories of the city or state. In some parts of the country, county histories are available through local libraries or county historical societies. State historical societies may provide useful information, often through an official publication or journal. A good beginning point for a class studying dialects, therefore, is the available historical material. Teacher and students alike might want to go beyond the school library's collection to that of the local, county, or state historical society.

The dialectologist is interested in the basic patterns of settlement history, population shift, physical geography, and social structure. Of these patterns, the social structure may be the most difficult to determine. An investigation of the speech of your area, along with the education, the occupation, and the age of your informants, may tell you as much about social structure as any kind of information can. Try to answer these questions:

Where did the people who settled this area come from?   This information is sometimes stated directly in state or county histories, but more often we must guess, using maps which show population density at different times. For example, some of the earliest settlers in Illinois came to the southern part of the state. This suggests that they came from neighboring southern areas. See such standard references as Charles O. Paullin and John K. Wright, *Atlas of the Historical Geography of the United States* (Washington and New York: Carnegie Institution of Washington and the American Geographical Society of New York, 1932), or the U.S. Census publications.

How did they come?   If your area is on or near a river, a canal, the Great Lakes, an early national highway, a valley pass through a mountain range, or a seacoast, you can expect to find traces of the speech of people who traveled these routes. Early southern settlements in Illinois, for example, point to migrations from Kentucky and Tennessee via the Ohio and Mississippi Rivers. The end of the Black Hawk War, the invention of the steamboat, and the financial depression of 1831-1840 all facilitated a second period of Illinois settlement, this time by Yankees. Most of these western New England settlers came by way of the Great Lakes and settled in the northeast corner of the state—largely north of the Illinois River. Some New Englanders went on south and west into easily reached prairie farming areas such as Bureau, Henry, Knox, and Stark Counties. Midlanders settled near rivers and avoided the prairie because they were more interested in hunting and trapping than in farming.

What changes in population have taken place since original settlement? Frequently this question may be answered by tracing the economic history of the area. Have recent industrial developments attracted migrant laborers? The construction of the Chrysler Motors plant at Hudson, Ohio, for example, has had a profound effect on the former New England character of that community.

Sometimes a simple examination of U.S. Census statistics will vividly illustrate such things as an increase in the Negro population of a Northern urban center, a decrease in upper- and middle-income professional people in a particular area, an increase or decrease of county population (from 1950 to 1960, DuPage County, Illinois, increased its population by 102.8 percent as compared to the total state of Illinois increase of 15.7 percent), or the increase of Negroes of professional status—as in Washington, D.C., in recent years.

Map 1 will give a rough idea of what can be discovered about population mobility within an American city. In the city of Detroit, we can observe definite patterns of group mobility. The movement of a Negro from Inner City to Middle City may show his climb in socioeconomic status; research now indicates that this climb is also reflected in his pronunciation, vocabulary, and grammar. Recent white migrants from Southern states, particularly from Appalachia, tend to settle in three parts of the city, as the map indicates, or in the less affluent suburban areas where they have small farms. The Detroit Polish population likewise moves in a fairly well-established pattern, although it is certainly less restricted than that of the Negro or, more interestingly perhaps, the Mexican. Mexican immigrants, as the map indicates, have a much shorter mobility pattern—at least so far.

These factors, usually seen as the special property of history or social studies courses, are also significant in the study of American English. Our language, after all, reflects our history, geography, and social contacts. American education is finally showing awareness of the fact that we must study the speech of people who are prevented by any reason—economics, race, religion, or national background—from reaching the success they are capable of. And studying the speech of a particular group will help us understand and appreciate the group itself. Many Northerners need to learn that Southern or Midland speech is not necessarily substandard; many Southerners and Midlanders need to learn that a Northern speaker is not just "conceited." Many need to learn that climate, thickness of lips, or skin color have absolutely nothing to do with speech.

MAP 1

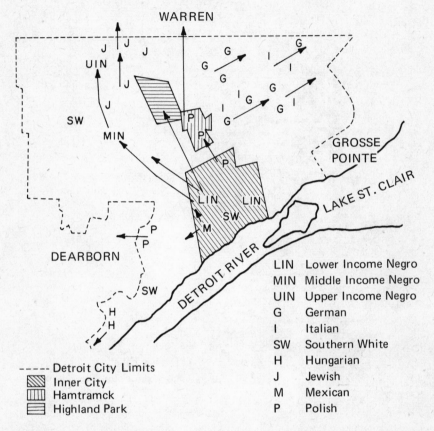

LIN	Lower Income Negro
MIN	Middle Income Negro
UIN	Upper Income Negro
G	German
I	Italian
SW	Southern White
H	Hungarian
J	Jewish
M	Mexican
P	Polish

- - - - - Detroit City Limits
Inner City
Hamtramck
Highland Park

Specific problems that arise accidentally can sometimes be traced to language. White citizens in Las Vegas, Nevada, only recently learned that Negroes in that city prefer to be called "Negroes," not "colored people." This sort of situation can cause one group to feel uncomfortable or even insulted, though the other group had no idea their choice of words was offensive.

The study of speech, therefore, has two potential benefits:

1. to the person whose speech keeps him from the success he wants—so that he can learn acceptable forms;

2. to the person who has already learned at least some acceptable forms—so that he will not scorn acceptable speech from other parts of the country, from other social levels, or from other races.

Finding the Dialect Areas of American English

Dialectologists record on maps the pronunciations, words, and grammatical forms which they find in an area. These items are represented by various symbols. Map 2, a map of several Eastern states, illustrates this procedure.[1] The circles indicate

MAP 2

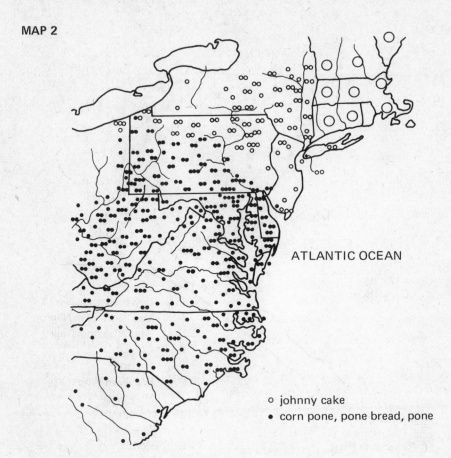

ATLANTIC OCEAN

o johnny cake
• corn pone, pone bread, pone

the communities investigated. As the legend explains, informants represented by solid circles say either *corn pone, pone bread*, or *pone*. Informants from the other communites (open circles) say *johnnycake*. Map 3 shows the distribution of the two ways the verb *dive* is used in the past tense in northern Illinois.[2]

Once a number of such maps has been made, the dialectologist looks for similar patterns. Where he finds that one pronunciation or word is used almost entirely in one area, he draws a line which encloses the use of that item. This line, called an isogloss, marks the boundary of the pronunciation, word, or grammatical form. Such isoglosses can be seen in Map 4,[3] where the solid line indicates how far south the term *tow sack* (burlap bag) extends. The dotted line shows how far north the term *croker sack* (burlap bag) can be found. The arrows at the end of each line point toward the areas enclosed by them. Isoglosses marking the distribution of *frijoles* (pinto beans) and *pilón* (something extra) in Texas are found in Map 5.[4] Examining these isoglosses, the dialectologist finds patterns of their direction. He determines whether or not several isoglosses are found in the same place. One way to do this is to draw several isoglosses on the same map and see where they

MAP 3

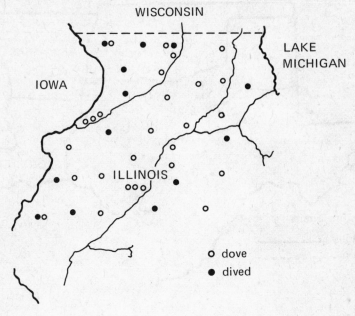

○ dove
● dived

MAP 4

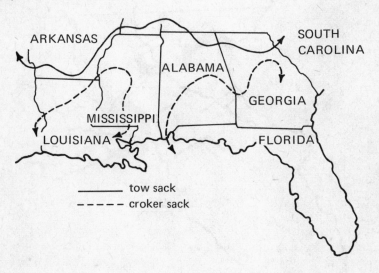

——— tow sack
- - - - croker sack

coincide. Map 6 shows how this technique was carried out in Northern Illinois. The dark line symbolizes areas where twelve to seventeen isoglosses pattern identically. The double line describes areas where ten or eleven isoglosses converge. The single line stands for nine isoglosses in the same area.[5]

MAP 5

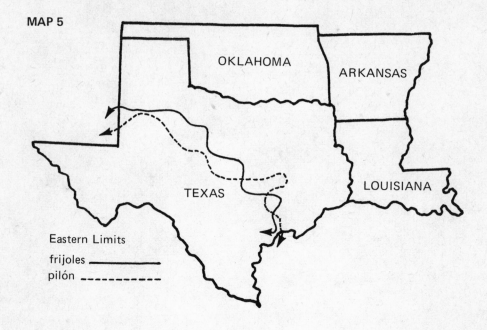

Eastern Limits

frijoles ——————

pilón - - - - - - -

MAP 6

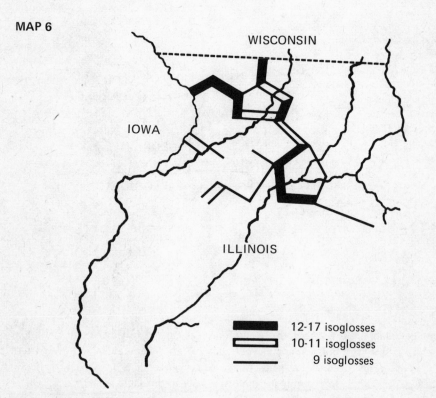

12-17 isoglosses
10-11 isoglosses
9 isoglosses

MAP 7

Using such techniques, then, American dialect geographers have tried to find the major and minor dialect areas of our country. Map 7 shows some of the major boundaries that have been established so far, although a great deal of work remains to be done.

NOTES

1. Adapted from Hans Kurath, *A Word Geography of the Eastern United States* (Ann Arbor: University of Michigan Press, 1949), Fig. 116; used by permission of University of Michigan Press.

2. Adapted from Roger W. Shuy, "The Northern-Midland Dialect Boundary in Illinois," *Publication of the American Dialect Society*, No. 38 (November 1962), p. 50; used by permission of the American Dialect Society.

3. Adapted from Gordon R. Wood, "Dialect Contours in the Southern States," *American Speech* (December 1963), p. 244; used by permission of Columbia University Press, 2960 Broadway, New York, N.Y. 10027.

4. Adapted from E. Bagby Atwood, *The Regional Vocabulary of Texas* (Austin: University of Texas Press, 1962), p. 246; used by permission of University of Texas Press.

5. It is clear from Map 2, which represents a fairly sharp geographical division between *johnny cake* and *corn pone*, where to draw the isogloss boundary. But an isogloss would be much more difficult to identify on Map 3, where the distribution of *dived* and *dove* is scattered. Given the data on Map 3, the regional dialectologist would need to map the distribution of a number of other features before it would be possible to draw the lines on Map 6, which represent bundles of isoglosses, confidently. [Eds.]

THE PROCESS AND PROBLEMS OF
LANGUAGE-MAINTENANCE: AN INTEGRATIVE REVIEW

Nathan Glazer

In the preceding selection, Roger W. Shuy discussed the geographical dimension of diversity among speakers of American English and mentioned that regional dialects have their roots mainly in the dialects brought to the United States by various English-speaking settlers. But many Americans, past and present, have not been native English speakers. We too often forget the scores of separate Native American languages and dialects still extant, the three major colonial languages other than English—Spanish, French, and German—and the numerous other languages spoken by later U.S. immigrants. In fact, a July 1975 survey by the National Center for Educational Statistics found that 13 percent of the U.S. population lives in households in which languages other than English are spoken. And the 1970 U.S. Census reports that 16.3 percent of our population claims a mother tongue—whether or not still spoken—other than English, a 5 percent rise from the corresponding 1960 figure. Here are the 1970 census statistics on U.S. mother tongues:

English: 160,717,113; Spanish: 7,823,583; German: 6,093,054; Italian: 4,144,315; French: 2,598,408; Polish: 2,437,938; Yiddish: 1,593,993; Swedish: 626,102; Norwegian: 612,862; Slovak: 510,366; Greek: 458,699; Czech: 452,812; Hungarian: 447,497; Japanese: 408,504; Portuguese: 365,300; Dutch: 350,748; Chinese: 345,431; Russian: 334,615; Lithuanian: 292,820; American Indian languages: 268,205 (see headnote to Robert W. Young's article for breakdown); Ukrainian: 249,351; Serbo-Croatian: 239,455; Finnish: 214,168; Danish: 194,462; Arabic: 193,520; Slovenian: 82,321; other: 1,780,053; not reported: 9,317,873.

Non-English speech communities present unique challenges to students and teachers of language—challenges that are only recently being met by multicultural and bilingual education programs. Such speech communities also present certain challenges to their members, who must respond to conflicting pressures to retain their primary allegiance to their mother tongue and culture, or to become bilingual and bicultural, or to abandon all vestiges of their original ethnicity. Nathan Glazer in this article summarizes the several factors that bear on the maintenance of non-English mother tongues in the United States. As an overview of the data on foreign-language communities and institutions presented in Joshua Fishman's *Language Loyalty in the United States*, this selection synthesizes the insights of other contributors (Fishman, Kloss, Chester and Jane Christian, Nahirny) to Fishman's book.

More than forty years ago, Robert E. Park published *The Immigrant Press and Its Control.*[1] No other study has described as well the incredible variety of immigrant experience in America and the way in which it found expression in print. The title clearly indicated that Park had a practical as well as a scholarly objective in undertaking this study. He was answering the question: is the immigrant press a menace? Were subversive and un-American sentiments lurking behind the strange alphabets and ideographs? Was not the immigrant press—not only the German newspapers, but also those of other Central and East European groups—influenced by German money in World War I? Had not immigrant newspapers supported the countries that became our enemies? And were they not maintaining distinct and separate loyalties, and preventing the immigrants from becoming good citizens?

It was part of Park's uniqueness as a sociologist of American ethnic groups—perhaps it came from his journalistic background—that he was able to consider soberly the idea that there was some truth in these accusations and that control of the foreign press was an issue that at least deserved discussion. He was no Pollyanna; he knew perfectly well what subsidies and judiciously placed advertisements could do to influence impoverished editors and publishers struggling to keep a newspaper alive. His conclusions therefore came with all the more force and effectiveness. He opposed any formal controls and favored the natural control that was exercised by a real interest in and knowledge of the foreign communities and their newspapers. "If immigrant editors and readers know that their newspaper is read outside its own language group, that America is interested in what it says and takes account of its opinions—that very fact establishes a measure of control."

But his larger conclusion was that the very nature of immigrant hopes and objectives in this country made this issue a temporary one, and one which would find a solution without the need for any formal governmental intervention: "In America, the immigrant wants to preserve, as far as possible, his heritage from the old country. These are represented preeminently by his language and his religion. At the same time, he wants to participate in the common life and find a place in the American community. In these two motives, we have at once the problem of the foreign-language press and its solution."

Forty years later, and after the appearance of many other books dealing with American ethnic groups, we again have witnessed a heightening of interest in the peculiar cultural treasures which the vast numbers of immigrants brought to this country. Once again, there is both official and scholarly interest in the topic. But immigrant tenacity in holding on to specific cultural characteristics is no longer seen as the problem; rather, the new problem is, as Park's conclusions suggested they would be, the rapidity with which values and resources are abandoned. In particular, our new international position leads us to consider with concern the rapid attenuation of facility in languages, a facility which almost all human beings seem to acquire almost effortlessly early in life, and to which most can add only with great difficulty when they are grown. This country, which can find within its borders native speakers of the most outlandish and exotic languages—and very often sizable numbers of them—seems to be one of the most linguistically limited of the great nations in its international contacts. Tens of millions of people in this country were raised speaking languages other than English, yet these Americans are, it seems, tongue-tied abroad and unable to make use of the huge literature published in other languages—including, commonly, the ones they or their parents used in their childhood.

The nature of official interest has consequently changed. We are no longer interested in the control of a rich, unrestrained, and possibly menacing natural growth; we are now more interested in the factors that have led to the rapid decline of language facility and of all the institutions that expressed and to some degree supported it. We have also become interested in the question of whether these institutions might be strengthened for the benefit of the country. And once again, as in Park's book forty years ago, we are confronted with the incredible variety and complexity of immigrant experience in this country.

The major intellectual problem with which we are faced is perfectly clear: how can we explain why, in the country which was most open to immigration, and most undisturbed when it came to the maintenance of immigrant cultures, there was also the most rapid flight from and abandonment of most key aspects of immigrant cultures on the part of the children and grandchildren of immigrants as well as on the part of immigrants themselves?

On the one hand, in contrast to some other countries with sizable minorities or heavy immigration, immigrants to the United States were allowed a remarkable degree of cultural freedom. There were no established religions, there was rarely any great restraint on private schooling, there was usually no control of publications, and cultural and social organizations of the greatest variety could do what they wished. Indeed, even the public institutions could sometimes be used for language maintenance, as in the case of the many public schools that were conducted wholly or partly in German, and as in the case of the successful effort to introduce the languages of major ethnic groups into public high schools in New York and elsewhere.

It is, of course, only by contrast with *some* other countries that the United States may be considered liberal in its attitudes toward the cultures of incoming ethnic groups. If we apply a more absolute standard of freedom our record is not nearly as good. In many parts of the country native Americans of Anglo-American background resisted public support for other languages. It took a good deal of political muscle by Italians and Jews to introduce their languages into the New York City high schools. And during the First World War and after, there was a hysterical attack on German by public bodies and public opinion, and to a lesser degree on other foreign languages. But apart from any public actions, there is the character of American culture itself, and in particular the strong pressures— remarked upon by Toqueville and other European travelers—toward conformity. Even without any formal legal requirements, these could be devastatingly effective in hastening the abandonment of foreign dress, habits, language, and accent. Just why America produced *without* laws that which other countries, desiring a culturally unified population, were not able to produce *with* laws—is not an easy question.

Elsewhere in this volume, Joshua A. Fishman suggests one important point which explains the enormous assimilative power of American civilization: assimilation in America was not to another folk, another ethnic group, but to a rather abstract concept involving freedom for all and loyalty to democratic ideals. In America one assimilated not to another *people*—which inevitably means abandoning or betraying one's "own" people—but to an ideology marked by an easily attained formal citizenship. Thus, Fishman suggests, even the very first Puritan settlers emphasized ideology rather than ethnicity. The ideology, in time, underwent many changes, and today's "Americanism" is a very different affair from the Enlightenment philosophy of the founding fathers. But all the ideologies held in common a refusal to accept the typical European nationalism which ascribed special virtues, many unanalyzed, to a natural phenomenon, the ethnically based nation, which had as one of its natural features a special language. Thus even the recurrent waves of exclusivism in this country, which were vicious and bigoted in their attitudes toward those they wished to *exclude* (Catholics, Jews, Orientals, Communists), were remarkably *inclusive* in their interpretations of those they considered true Americans. At worst, the true Americans were white Protestant Christians. But this includes Englishmen, Scots, Welshmen, Netherlanders, Germans, Danes, Norwegians, Swedes, and members of other ethnic-nationality groups as well.

The significance of this is that American nationalism rarely attacked foreign cultures directly, except in the special case of Germans during and after the First World War. It attacked "ideas" and "conditions": authoritarianism, poverty, ignorance, and inefficiency. Since most immigrants were without a sharply developed opposing ideology, it was easy to accept Americanism. And since their specific cultural and linguistic attributes were not under attack directly, they developed little loyalty in defending them. Culture and language became an *embarrassment* and an *obstacle* in the way of becoming true Americans, rather than something of value to be cherished.

Thus when compared with many other countries, the United States has put relatively few restrictions on the public and private use of foreign languages. And yet, as so many language loyalists sadly noted, their languages shriveled in the air of freedom, while they had apparently flourished under adversity in Europe. Obviously, there was more than freedom in the United States. There were other aspects to American society and culture which reduced all languages to the same sad state. Whether it was one of the great international tongues with a vast literature, such as German, Spanish, or French; or a language of peasants with a scanty literature or press, such as Ukrainian; or an exotic and proud language not widely known, such as Hungarian;[2] or a language, such as Yiddish,[3] that incorporated in itself a major national and cultural movement—all, it seems, regardless of their position, their history, their strength, the character of the groups that brought them to this country and maintained them through one or two or three generations have come to a similar condition. The newspapers die out; the schools, full-time and part-time, close; the organizations, religious or secular, shift to English; and the maintenance of the ethnic mother tongue becomes the desperate struggle of a small group committed to it, who will have to find their most effective future support less among the descendants of the immigrants who brought the language to this country than in governmental and educational institutions that might find some practical or scholarly value in training and maintaining a corps of experts who know and can use it.

And yet the diversity among the groups that carried foreign languages to this country, and the circumstances they encountered, was so great that it is hard to see what common factors could have affected them all. We can document—from the studies reported by Fishman and his colleagues—a number of major types of diversity which logically should have played some role in affecting the use and history of immigrant-group languages in this country. Without attempting to order them in degree of significance, we can distinguish at least five factors of major importance.

There was, first of all, the time of arrival in this country of the bulk of the immigrant group. In the first half of the nineteenth century, when many German immigrants arrived, the United States was, in fact, culturally underdeveloped. Colleges and universities were few and inferior to those in Europe; the public school system was just beginning; sectionalism was strong and the federal government weak. Under these circumstances, it was no special sign of cultural nationalism for German immigrants to feel a strong obligation to maintain what they conceived of as a higher culture. Indeed, the German language gave access to as much or more of science and literature than did English.

The situation after the second half of the nineteenth century was quite different. With the passage of time, American institutions became stronger, their assimilating power much greater. Since the early 1930s, immigrants to this country have been distinguished from their same-homeland predecessors by more education, more frequent professional backgrounds, and more experienced intellectual and cultural leadership. Nevertheless, they have come to an America of enormous cultural strength and significance, with powerful educational and political institutions and with tremendous economic opportunities, and this has inevitably inhibited the development of separate social and cultural organizations and of direct language-maintenance institutions (settlements, schools, newspapers, theaters) among these new immigrants, even though they are far more competent to build such institutions than were their predecessors.

In his essay on German in the United States, Heinz Kloss points to an important factor related to the time of arrival of the first large bodies of non-English language users: some of their languages had official status *before* the establishment of the political authority of England or the United States. In particular, one must note the position of Spanish in New Mexico, and of French in Louisiana. One can hardly overestimate the importance of some official status in maintaining a language. It gives it social status among its native users, and serves in part as a barrier against self-deprecation and embarrassment. A little of state support, in the form of official printing presses, court proceedings, and school use, can, at times, do much more to establish a language than can a vast amount of energetic activity by language loyalists. However, we may add to the significance of *official* status in maintaining these early established languages the *social* status derivable from the fact that the first settlers, the makers of history in the area, the givers of names to natural features and towns, spoke these languages. Thus the colonial tongues, French, Spanish, and German, have been stronger than the more recently introduced languages of the period of mass immigration.

But this factor, of course, is closely linked to a second factor which Heinz Kloss also emphasizes: the area and pattern of settlement. Thus the mother tongue was maintained longer in the German language islands of Texas or the Great Plains than in mixed areas of settlement, urban or rural. Language maintenance was more successful in smaller industrial and mining towns with large relative concentrations of a particular immigrant group cut off from cosmopolitan influences than in the mixed areas of the great cities where larger numbers of immigrants of diversified backgrounds resided side by side. Ethnic mother tongues were maintained longer where immigrant groups were, in effect, almost geographic extensions of homelands near at hand than where immigrants were cut off from their homelands by oceans. Thus the French-Canadians in New England, the Puerto Ricans in New York, the Cubans in Florida, the Mexicans in the Southwest are all better able to maintain their languages owing to the relative ease of contact with Canada, Puerto Rico, Cuba, and Mexico, as well as the relative concentration of their settlements.

But in comparison with these factors of time and pattern of settlement, the social and cultural factors—more elusive and complex—are at least of equal significance. Hasidic Jews created—at least for a time—a community in the heart of Brooklyn as completely cut off from the influence of the city as the German sectarian groups in their colonies in the sparsely populated Dakotas. Immigrant groups arrived in this country with quite different social structures. The Germans represented almost a whole nation—intellectuals, professionals, priests, artisans, farmers, workers. Other groups, such as the Ukrainians, represented a much less extended social range, limited primarily to peasants and workers and a handful of priests. What was the significance of the presence of a substantial intellectual or professional class, or of a large middle class, among immigrants? It would seem that they strengthened the institutions that supported language use directly, such as schools and cultural societies and publications. And yet, a peasant group without intellectuals, such as the Ukrainians, freed from the presence of a Russified or Polonized upper and middle class, could find within itself cultural resources that would not have flourished in the homeland and that offered strong support for language maintenance. Perhaps more important than the simple *presence* of intellectual and middle-class groups among the immigrants was their *relationship* to the less educated masses. In the case of Ukrainians, Russians, Hungarians, Croatians, political history led to a pattern in which one had an earlier working-class migration, followed by later migrations of better-educated professional and middle-class groups. In all these cases, the later middle-class immigrants felt superior to the earlier immigrants of the peasant class. They did little or nothing to strengthen the institutions these had created. But if the entire group, those of middle-class and of peasant origin, had been bound together by a national struggle, if a sense of common nationality had been strengthened in them, then undoubtedly the educated middle-class elements were a resource for language maintenance. The Germans in the middle of the nineteenth century, and the Eastern European Jews in the early twentieth century, are examples of such groups.

Of all the groups reported on in this volume, it is the Spanish-speaking of the Southwest who seem to have been most completely without middle-class, intellectual, and professional groups. Paradoxically, while less "high cultural" activity is reported for them than for any other group, at the same time they reveal less attrition in the use of their mother tongue than does any other group! Of course, one cannot take the position that the development of any serious cultural interest in a minority language is a sign that it is losing its hold as a medium of daily life. The explanation of the paradox of continued mass use without high cultural development is obviously to be found in the special circumstances of both the early Spanish-speaking population and later immigrants. The early Spanish-speaking groups, largely Indian in origin, developed a folk culture in which there was almost no written communication. Later Mexican immigrants also came from an illiterate environment. In this country, as Chester and Jane Christian have pointed out, both groups adopted patterns of communication and entertainment by means that either preceded or succeeded the age of print—fiestas, markets, and family life from the period *before*; radio and television from the period *after*. Certain political services for this group were more often carried out by Mexican consular representatives than by their own leaders. Thus they may be seen as a lower-class extension of a society which, however small its middle, intellectual, and professional classes, does have them—back in Mexico.

But this link with Mexico is being broken as the immigrants become city dwellers and American citizens. Mexican-Americans seem to be at a point which French-Canadians in New England reached one hundred years ago. If the folk use of the language is still strong, this is primarily the effect of social isolation which is bound to break down as the commitment to American citizenship increases. And yet it would be hazardous to predict that Spanish in the Southwest will go through the same evolution as French in New England. On the one hand, its present complement of high cultural institutions is nowhere near what French had and has. On the other hand, its evolution will take place in an America that may be far more supportive of facility in a language as important to this nation as Spanish. One suspects that just as Spanish in New York is developing an official position that no other immigrant language ever attained, so Spanish in the Southwest has a history marked out for it that will be rather different from the histories of languages spoken by other peasant immigrant groups. Once again— Spanish *is* the official language of one part of the American polity (and Puerto Rico may yet become a state), and this too will certainly make a difference.

As Heinz Kloss has pointed out, these elements of social structure of immigrant groups have ambiguous effects on language-maintenance. We must analyze complex interrelationships of time, place, and social structure for each group. Religion has an equally complex relationship to language-maintenance. One of the most interesting generalizations one can draw from this series of studies on the experiences of many different ethnic groups in the United States is that the Catholic Church became indifferent or opposed to the language-maintenance efforts of immigrant groups within its fold. Thus among the Germans, it was the Lutheran churches rather than the Catholic that were most concerned with maintaining German schools. The French had to fight consistently against the Irish-American hierarchy in order to maintain their French-language schools and French-language parishes. The Ukrainians encountered the same difficulties. Nor was the Roman Catholic hierarchy much friendlier to Italian, Hungarian, Polish, or any other language-maintenance efforts. But if the Roman Catholic hierarchy in America generally played a grudging and unwilling role in helping foreign languages, the situation was, of course, quite different where the groups were able to maintain their own distinct parishes, with priests stemming from the language groups themselves. The French-Canadians were most successful in doing so, and some of their parishes became strong supporters of language-maintenance efforts.

Among the Spanish-speaking of the Southwest, the church is deeply concerned with the social and economic problems of Mexican-Americans and accepts the fact that they are Spanish-speaking. However, once again, there is no evidence that it places any great value on this fact. It defends the rights of the Spanish-speaking, and in the present situation this means acknowledgment of the fact that teachers and social workers and policemen and government employees who do not know Spanish cannot do as good a job as those who can. Thus we find a purely instrumental accommodation to Spanish, rather than—as in the truly nationally oriented churches—a fight for the language itself.

In many ethnic groups there were also non-Catholic, nationally oriented churches, and these were among the most powerful forces in strengthening language loyalty. This was the case among the German Lutherans, the Hungarian Calvinists, and the various Eastern Churches separated in varying degrees from Roman Catholicism. Was the indifference or antagonism of American Catholicism to foreign languages affected by the overwhelming domination of the American hierarchy by the Irish, who spoke English and had become ardent 100 percent American patriots by the time mass Eastern and Central European immigration had begun? Was "Americanism" in the church related to the strong American nationalism that the Irish developed in the United States?

Religion, we may conclude, played a role in maintaining language skill when it was a *national* religion, closely linked to and identified with the historical trials of a single nation. If it was truly "catholic," religion could not long serve as a vehicle by which particular national languages, cultures, or customs were maintained. And indeed, with the passage of time, as the religious denominations which stemmed from European national churches came ever closer together on the basis of theological ties—as the lines between German, Swedish, Norwegian, Danish, and other Lutherans blurred (and as the same thing happened to Calvinists)—even these national religions no longer played major roles in maintaining language competence. They became American religions, with the same assimilating effects as other American institutions.

We have spoken of the time of immigration, the spatial pattern of settlement, the social structure of the immigrant group (and in particular of the role of professional, intellectual, and middle-class elements within it) and of the role of religion. To these four factors we will add one more: the degree of ideological mobilization in the group. We may ask, is the emigration to be explained solely by economic factors, or are religious and political factors also important? It seems reasonable that if people emigrate because of oppression, because they are not allowed national freedom, cultural freedom, religious freedom, they will cling more strongly to the national language than if they emigrate only to improve their economic situation. If the language has become an instrument in the national struggle—as in the case of Polish—there is even stronger reason to set up communities, schools, newspapers, organizations. We are all familiar with political refugees—whether from Bourbon Italy or Castro Cuba—who expected to return to their homelands and who maintained a vigorous associational life and a lively press in their native languages. And yet, it is also true that, on a lower social level, those who emigrate to make money, and who expect to return to their homes, will also—with less sophisticated instruments perhaps—maintain language facility and move over to English slowly. Their within-group ties and everyday ethnicity may be strong enough to make up for the absence of conscious nationalism.

And yet, having listed all these factors, can one honestly say that they made a great difference in the outcome? Regardless of this wide range of differences in the circumstances of ethnic groups in America, language is always so intimate and valued a part of life that the immigrants clung to it—whether they were religious or freethinkers, in an international or a national church, concentrated in town or countryside or spread thinly over many states, and regardless of whether they had an appropriate complement of intellectuals and journalists and teachers. Indeed, as Fishman points out in several chapters, one of the most striking facts about immigrant languages in America was the way in which groups without intellectuals and ignorant of the approved form of their language were able to develop newspapers, organizations, and schools to maintain this valued part of their heritage.

The basic counter-maintenance factor, therefore, may very well have been American civilization. Probably mass, free education played the largest role—it taught almost all the children English, and it insidiously undermined the native language by implying (if not advocating) the superiority of English to any language their parents spoke. But an important role in undermining the foreign languages was also taken by American mass culture. This was gradually shaped under democracy so as to appeal, for the greater profit of its producers, to the largest numbers. American mass culture learned to create products which have, it appears, as great an appeal to the most diverse peoples of the world as to Americans. It has made English—along with its political and commercial importance—the language that the world's youth feels it must acquire first in order to become stylish and modern. If it has this effect in Japan, how much more effective is it in America? American mass culture was created to appeal to people of the most diverse backgrounds. Tested successfully among immigrants here, it now goes abroad to create new emigrants-in-spirit from their own country and from their own cultures.

Along then with the school, we must place mass culture. Consider the impact of television in teaching English—and much more than English—to the immigrants who have come to the United States since World War II. And before television, there were movies, comic strips, popular newspapers, gadgets, and innovations doing the same.

The openness of American politics must also be considered. It has made it relatively easy for immigrants to participate in political processes. By offering the rewards of office to a few, it makes the natural leaders of the immigrants the most effective propagandists for Americanization. Thus instead of defending the group culture and language—as minority leaders do in other countries—the leaders of immigrants join other Americans in urging the immigrant to put away his foreign ways, learn English, and become a citizen. Only then can he vote his leaders into office, and benefit most from the American social and economic system. Aspiring political leaders also appealed to ethnic groups as groups—they sought Polish, German, or Jewish votes by stressing some group demand, or by emphasizing their own identification with these groups. But they could not get the support they sought while the members of these groups remained unchanged. They encouraged a symbolic Polishness, Germanness, Jewishness—loyalty to a vague and contentless symbol, rather than a concrete cultural reality. The latter would threaten them, by preventing their people from entering into general political and communal life; the former mobilized a voting bloc for them. Once this mobilization had taken place, once the specific cultural content of the group had been reduced to almost nothing, the candidate could propose various symbolic balms to the group ego, such as teaching the ethnic language in public schools.

Finally, the economy also played a major role in undercutting immigrant languages and cultures. Workers were very often concentrated in industries dominated by a single or only a very few ethnic groups. Garment workers in New York, farmers in Minnesota, and coal miners in Pennsylvania could manage well enough with Yiddish or Swedish or Lithuanian. But few immigrants and their children wanted to remain workers in a land of expanding opportunities. Many opened small businesses; those who succeeded in educating themselves entered white-collar work and became professionals. These could not be effective economically or accepted socially without English.

And so, through education, mass culture, politics, the economy, the immigrant was assimilated. So powerful were these forces that, as Fishman and Nahirny both point out, we find not only the loss of language competence from one generation to another, we find the loss of competence within a single generation. The children of immigrants, fluent in childhood, lose their knowledge as they grow up. This happens even to the immigrants themselves. It is a result of the fact that the most effective and important institutions to which they have access as Americans are conducted in English.

What we must conclude is that many *natural* supports for language use are cut off in America. The family still exists. Insofar as language facility is communicated, it tends to be as a result of language use within the family in the earliest years of childhood. As soon as school begins, another language, of greater status and value, begins to compete. Even before school, television is in the home and with it, the language of television. Associations may support the old language—but the driving force of associations is self-perpetuation, and many an organization which began in a foreign language and as a supporter of foreign-language use continues its life in English.

But if the natural supports of language are cut down by the homogenizing aspects of American civilization, at the same time it must be pointed out there is no direct hostility to language use and language maintenance. Indeed, the mass media, which we have spoken of as one of the chief creators of a homogeneous culture, are not averse to adapting themselves to a foreign language if its use is widespread and if its bearers show little tendency to switch to English—as happens among the Spanish-speaking of the Southwest and New York. It is the peculiar nature of American culture and civilization—discussed by many of the chapters in this volume—that seems to undermine differences, in its creation of a common modern, changing, mobile, urbanized society. Just as the "socialist culture" of Soviet Russia can be spread in many languages, so can the "mass culture" that is one of the distinctive products of American civilization.

If the natural supports of language use remain strong, American institutions accommodate themselves to the situation. But this seems to be the situation—and it may remain so only temporarily—only in the case of Spanish. For the rest, we can no longer depend on the natural supports, in a distinctive culture, of language use. The people of this country are for the most part too mobile, geographically and socially, to maintain distinctive cultures, whether immigrant or regional. Thus just as hitherto many other "natural" functions (for example, the maintenance of the aged and of dependent children by their families) became state functions, or at any rate, formally organized functions, so too the natural process of language transmission, if it is to be strengthened and maintained, will very likely need formal and state support. More and more of the things that were done unthinkingly by groups and nations in the past will have to be done in a formally organized way, on the basis of common group decisions—in effect, political decisions—if they are to be done in the future.

Under these new circumstances, the chief supports of foreign-language facility—if there are to be any—will have to be found in those relatively efficient organized segments of American life. The schools, first of all; in a more limited way, the mass media and specialized voluntary organizations; and above all, public funds, which become more and more necessary for any large social objective. This is a country in which every natural—or traditional—social form is rapidly undermined by new forms of rational organization. The only hope for the maintenance of the valuable resource of foreign-language facility still available to us is for language loyalists and others interested in language-maintenance to learn the techniques of using rational organization and public commitment in support of their goals.

NOTES

1. New York and London, Harper & Brothers, 1922.

2. Joshua A. Fishman, *Hungarian Language Maintenance in the United States*, vol. 62 of *Uralic and Altaic Series*, ed. Thomas Sebeok (Bloomington, Ind.: Indiana University Press, 1966).

3. Joshua A. Fishman, "Yiddish in America: A Socio-Linguistic Analysis," in J.A. Fishman et al., *op cit.*, chap. 18. *International Journal of American Linguistics*, 31 (1965), no. 2, part II.

LANGUAGE AND THE DISADVANTAGED: SPANISH, ACADIAN FRENCH, NAVAJO

Muriel R. Saville

Muriel R. Saville's brief descriptions of three American languages will serve as references for those who come in contact with these minority languages and as models of how to formulate language contrasts for all concerned with transcending miscommunication in bilingual situations. Spanish is the second largest language community in the United States. In this book it is treated primarily in articles by Gumperz and Hernández-Chavez, who analyze Spanish-English bilinguals in the Southwest, and by Wolfram, who studies assimilation of Puerto Ricans to an English-speaking environment in New York. Saville also describes Louisiana Acadian French, which should be compared with the Louisiana French Creole discussed in the Dreyfuss article. Educators in northwestern New England will find a somewhat different linguistic background among French speakers influenced by neighboring Quebec Province. Navajo is described here as the largest representative of the language families which constitute the mother tongues of 268,205 Native Americans. Robert Young, in his report of Navajo culture, and Susan Philips, in her study of the Warm Springs, Oregon, Native American community, point out ways in which the educational establishment is particularly unprepared to understand the needs of children from non-European backgrounds, either linguistically or culturally.

Spanish

Disadvantaged children with Spanish-language backgrounds present a major educational challenge to many schools, particularly in New York and the Southwest. The degree of language handicap exhibited by these children in an English-language classroom setting is sufficiently great to explain much of their academic underachievement and their high dropout rate. Contrasts between English and Spanish have been well described by linguists, and Spanish-speaking children have so far received most of the attention in elementary-school programs for teaching English as a second language. More reading and oral language materials for them will be published soon.

Not all Spanish-speaking children have the same language system any more than all English-speaking children do. Some of their families have come to the United States from Puerto Rico, Cuba, and various parts of Mexico. Others have lived for generations in parts of the United States where various dialects of Spanish have developed. When one considers that there are social dialects within the regional ones, the language problem seems very complex. There has been sufficient research to show that these dialectal differences in Spanish influence the children's use of English, but no comprehensive analysis is yet available.

In general the Spanish sound system does not contrast /š/ and /č/, and substitution or interchange of these English phonemes is the most obvious error Spanish-speaking children make in pronouncing English words. They may often say /ču/ for *shoe* or /šer/ for *chair*. Spanish has one phoneme that covers the range of both English /b/ and /v/, and it often sounds as if the children say /beri/ for *very* and /kəvərd/ for *cupboard*. Other common substitutions are /s/, /f/, or /t/ for /θ/; and /z/, /v/, or /d/ for /ð/. Consonant clusters cause many problems, particularly when they contain a sibilant, such as /s/.

Spanish uses only five vowel phonemes; children learning English must distinguish several more. The range of Spanish /i/ includes the vowel sounds of *mit* and *meat*; /e/, those of *met* and *mate*; /u/, those of *pull* and *pool*; /o/, those of *coat* and *caught*; and /a/ covers a range that includes the vowel sounds of *cut* and *cot*.

There are several basic differences in the grammatical structures of Spanish and English that cause interference for a pupil learning English as a second language (Brengelman, 1964). The verb-noun pattern of *es un hombre* must be equated with the noun-verb-noun pattern of *this is a man*. Similarly, the interrogative-verb pattern of *¿qué es?* is patterned in English as interrogative-verb-noun, *what is that?* A difference in word order is seen in the following examples: *la mano derecha* (D-N-Adj): *the right hand* (D-Adj-N); *le da el sombrero* (IO-V-DO): *he gives him the hat* (S-V-IO-DO); *¿está abierta una ventana?* (V-Adj-N): *is a window* *open?* (V-N-Adj). A relationship that has been indicated by word order in *la cabeza de un perro* must be indicated by inflection in *a dog's head*; the situation is reversed in the case of *dará*, which is expressed in English as *he will give.* Many Spanish-speaking children transfer the use of double negatives from Spanish to English. It is good Spanish to say *no hay nada en la mesa,* but the sentence literally translated is *there's not nothing on the table.*

The semantic structure of English also presents a number of problems for speakers of Spanish. There are many cognates in the two languages. The most difficult new words to learn are the "false friends," words that sound the same but have different meanings. An example is the Spanish verb *asistir,* which means in English *to attend* and not *to assist.*

Teachers often comment that their Spanish-speaking pupils read without expression. To understand and correct the real problem, they should first know that the Spanish intonational system has one less degree of stress than the English system, different rhythm and stress patterns, and different intonational contours. A Spanish-speaker will pronounce every syllable for about the same length of time, shorten English stressed syllables, put the stress on the wrong syllable, and not reduce vowels in unstressed syllables. He will use a rising pitch for a confirmation response and a low-mid-low pitch pattern for statements instead of the mid-high-low contour usual in English.

Improper intonation in reading English questions and exclamations may be partly a problem with symbols. If the pupil has learned to read in Spanish, he is used to the signals *¿* and *¡* at the beginning of questions and exclamations, respectively. Because the initial signals are missing in English, he may get close to the end of these constructions before he realizes that they are questions or exclamations.

Most of the problems Spanish-speaking children have in learning to read and spell English words are due to the different correspondences between sounds and symbols. Vowels cause the greatest difficulty; pupils could conceivably write *cat* for *cot, mit* for *meat,* and *met* for *mate.* They might read *fine* as /fine/ instead of /fain/ and *but* as /but/ instead of /bət/. These reading and spelling errors cannot be corrected unless the pupils can first consistently hear and use the vowel phonemes of English. The symbols can then be related to these sounds.

A similar problem may be noted in arithmetic if pupils have learned to write numerals in Mexico or one of several other countries. They will write 1 as *1* and 7 as *7* . Consequently, teachers and pupils may confuse 1's and 7's in problems and answers.

Acadian French

Many families in the United States speak some variety of French as a native language. The largest concentration of French-speakers is found in Louisiana; they are primarily the descendents of Acadians who were forced to leave Nova Scotia in 1755. These groups of Louisiana French, or Cajuns as they are frequently called, have been very persistent in preserving their linguistic identity. Other French-speakers came directly to Louisiana from Europe, and a sizable black population in the region developed still another variety of French. The complex of French dialects in Louisiana transcends race, social status, and geographical boundaries.

In 1960, according to the U.S. Bureau of the Census, Louisiana had the highest rate of illiteracy in the United States, and the illiteracy rate within this state was highest in its twenty-six predominantly French-speaking parishes. A variety of factors contributes to this educational problem, and one of the most serious is the inability of pupils to cope with standard English in the classroom. A correlation between linguistic and economic factors was found by Bertrand and Beale (1965). They report that of the families they interviewed in the region who use predominantly French at home, 69 percent of the whites and 88 percent of the blacks had annual incomes under $1500, and 19 percent of the whites and 12 percent of the blacks had annual incomes between $1500 and $2999.

Cajuns typically have difficulties with standard English phonology, syntax, and vocabulary.[1] The phoneme /d/ is substituted for /ð/, resulting in /di/ for *the*, /diz/ for *these*, /doz/ for *those*, and /dæt/ for *that*. English phonemes /š/ and /č/, and /ž/ and /ǰ/ are not contrastive pairs in Cajun speech. The /č/ and /ǰ/ variants may be substituted for /š/ and /ž/ under emphatic stress. Final /-s/ is omitted in some words.

English consonant clusters are often simplified by Cajuns. The phonemes /l/ and /r/ are often dropped before a consonant, and *like to* may be pronounced without the /k/. Final /-nd/ may be reduced to /n/ in *mind*, /-bl/ to /b/ in *noble* or *terrible*, /-br/ to /b/ in *September*, /-kl/ to /k/ in *miracle*, and /-pl/ to /p/ in *simple* (Conwell and Juilland, 1963). Variant pronunciations are not uncommon; in one interview a single informant pronounced *ask* as /æks/, /æst/, and /æs/. Initial clusters may also be simplified: /pl/ to /p/, /pr/ to /pl/, and /str/ to /st/. Whenever /r/ or /l/ forms part of a cluster, that phoneme is the first element deleted.

Vowels present additional problems, for variant pronunciation is allowed within Louisiana French phonemes that cross phoneme boundaries in English, making an unwanted difference in meaning in English words. The phoneme /ə/ may alternate with /e/ in emphatic speech or be deleted after a single consonant or at the ends of words. An /o/ may alternate with /u/ in unstressed syllables or with /ɔ/ in some environments. An /e/ may alternate with either /a/ or /æ/ before /r/, /l/, or /m/.

The syntactical errors made by Cajun informants include the plural inflection of mass nouns (*hairs*), the deletion of *to* in infinitive constructions (*I'm going get it*), and the omission of modals and auxiliaries in questions (*What I do?*). Other common expressions are *talking at you, listening at you*, and *I have you an idea*.

Some French words are used by these speakers in otherwise English sentences. The most frequent seem to be the interjections /me/ *well* and /æ/ *what?* In many sentences the words are all English, but the sequence is nonstandard. At mealtime you may hear, *Put me some potatoes, please*, or *Save the sugar*, meaning "store" it. Instead of being "delivered," the mail *passes,* and a Cajun may ask, *Is the mail passed?* The same verb is used for *visit*: *You make a pass on town.*

In some parts of Louisiana a child may go through elementary school without hearing standard English spoken because his teachers come from the same region and speak the same dialect. The language system of the textbooks is therefore kept separate from the language system he speaks and hears. This barrier to learning is hurdled by some, but it is part of the educational and economic barricade surrounding thousands of French-speaking citizens.

Navajo

A number of unrelated languages are spoken by the more than half a million Indians who live on reservations in the United States. Many groups have adopted some form of English as a primary language, and some continue to use the languages of their ancestors. On the Navajo reservation, forty thousand pupils are now attending schools, and the number increases each year. The teaching of English is recognized there as one of the most serious problems in education and one that must be solved as part of the assault on generally low wages, high unemployment rates, and poor living conditions.

The specific problems Navajo children have with English are considered here because the Navajos are the largest tribe in the United States. Their problems, as well as those of speakers of Spanish and French, depend on the points of contrast between their language and English, and thus cannot be generalized to include all Indian languages. These points should serve to indicate, however, the types of problems that may be encountered by speakers of languages completely unrelated to English.

There are many differences between English and Navajo both in the articulation of sounds that have similar positions in the phonemic systems of the two languages and in the articulation of sounds that occur in one language but have no correspondents in the other.

Navajo-speakers do not distinguish between English /p/ and /b/ and usually substitute their own slightly different /b/ for both. This sound never occurs in syllable final position in Navajo, however; so they often substitute /ʔ/ (a glottal stop) for final /-p/ or /-b/ or reduce all final stops to the Navajo /-d/.[2] This /d/, which sounds like the /t/ in /stap/, is also typically substituted for English /t/ or /d/ in initial position. The /ʔ/ is frequently substituted for stopped consonants and added before initial vowels, making Navajo speech sound choppy to speakers of English. In Navajo there are no correspondents to /f/, /v/, /θ/, /ð/, and /ŋ/.

The primary differences between the vowel systems are the use of vowel length and nasalization to distinguish meaning in Navajo and the greater variety of vowel sounds in English. The vowels /æ/ and /ə/ do not occur in Navajo and are the hardest for pupils to learn. Navajo-speakers must also learn to distinguish among English /o/, /ʊ/, and /u/.

English consonant clusters present a major problem for Navajo-speakers, who often substitute similar affricates for them. Much of the Navajos' difficulty with noun and verb inflections may be traced to their failure to hear or produce final consonant clusters (Cook and Sharp, 1966).

Tonal pitch in Navajo serves as the only distinctive feature to differentiate meaning in such words as /níĺį/ *you are,* /nilį/ *he is,* /át?į/ *he does,* /at?į/ *he is rich,* /azéé?/ *mouth,* and /azee?/ *medicine.* Whereas Navajo uses fixed tones with relation to vowels and syllabic nasals to distinguish meaning, English uses a variety of sentence pitch patterns, or intonational contours. Navajo-speakers must learn to disregard the pitch of individual phonemes. On the other hand, English makes use of stress to distinguish meaning in some words, whereas stress is never distinctive in Navajo.

The use of a rising sentence inflection to indicate interrogation or the use of other types of pitch to convey, for example, the connotation of surprise is not possible in a tone language, is not used as a mechanism for this purpose, or is used in a different way. Particles in Navajo convey meanings expressed by intonation in English. For instance, /da?-íš/ and /-ša/ added to Navajo words signal questions, /-ga?/ gives emphasis, and /-?as/ indicates disbelief. Navajos may speak and read English without the appropriate modulations and inflections because they are unaccustomed to the use of intonation to express meaning in these situations (Young, 1961).

Other very general phonological problems that teachers of Navajo children should concentrate on are the voicing of stops, the production of most consonants in final position, and the production of glides.

Many features of English syntax are difficult for Navajo-speakers. Articles and adjectives are very troublesome because, with a few exceptions, they do not exist in Navajo. The idea of prettiness would be expressed by a verb and conjugated "I am pretty, you are pretty," and so forth. English adjectives present problems in both their word order and comparative patterns. Few Navajo nouns are inflected for plural; thus a common type of error in English is *four dog.* Possessive *-s* is also a problem, since the Navajo pattern for *the boy's book* would be *the boy his book.* English third-person pronouns are commonly confused. Navajo /bí/ translates as any of the following: *he, she, it, they, him, her, them, his, her, its, their.* This means that gender, number, and case distinctions must all be learned. Navajo makes other distinctions among third-person pronouns not found in English, however, such as distance from the subject. There are also numerous and complicated differences in the verb structure.

Even if a Navajo child has mastered the phonological and syntactic components of the English language, he is faced with a semantic system that categorizes experience in a very different way. English often uses several unrelated words to describe something that is seen as different aspects of the same action in Navajo, or one word to describe an action seen as unrelated events. For example, if the object of each action is the same, the English verbs *give, take, put,* and several others are translated by one Navajo verb stem that means roughly "to handle." Different Navajo verb stems will be used for *to handle* depending on the shape of the object.

There has been no interference from written Navajo because the language has been recorded only by linguists and missionaries. Programs are now under way to teach reading and writing to Navajos in their native language. A standardized orthography has been developed. Questions concerning its possible interference with learning the English writing system have been raised, but some leading educators agree that basing the orthography on the Navajo language itself is a far more important consideration than any interference with English that may result (Ohannessian, 1969).

NOTES

1. The description of Acadian French presented here draws on data collected by the author from speakers of the Lafayette region and on data collected by Marilyn Conwell in the same parish.

2. Saville uses the symbol /ʔ/ to represent the glottal stop, a full consonant phoneme in Navajo. It is used by English speakers in such expressions as *uh-uh* /ʔəˀə/. [Eds.]

References

Bertrand, Alvin L., and Calvin L. Beale, 1965   *The French and Non-French in Rural Louisiana: Study of the Relevance of Ethnic Factors to Rural Development.* Louisiana Agricultural Experiment Station 606.

Brengelman, Fred, 1964   "Contrasted Grammatical Structures in English and Spanish," unpublished.

Conwell, Marilyn J., and Alphonse Juilland, 1963   *Louisiana French Grammar I.* Mouton & Co.

Cook, Mary Jane, and Margaret Sharp, 1966   "Problems of Navajo Speakers in Learning English," *Language Learning* 16: 1-2, 21-30.

Ohannessian, Sirarpi, 1969   *Conference on Navajo Orthography.* Center for Applied Linguistics.

Young, Robert W., 1961   "A Sketch of the Navajo Language," *The Navajo Yearbook.* Navajo Agency, Window Rock.

THE CHINESE IMMIGRANT'S LANGUAGE HANDICAP: ITS EXTENT AND ITS EFFECTS

C. Allen Tucker

A large number of Asian languages are represented in the U.S. population. Cantonese speakers, whose social and linguistic situation C. Allen Tucker discusses here, are the second largest group, after Japanese. Asian-speaking people are concentrated on the West Coast, predominantly in urban areas (over half a million Japanese live in Los Angeles alone), although most large American cities have significant Asian populations. Asian immigration began in the latter half of the nineteenth century, when Chinese men were brought in as a cheap labor force. For many years the Chinese were denied rights of citizenship and forbidden to establish families here. Kept in low-paying, unskilled jobs, they lived in barracks-like conditions and later established their communities in tightly knit neighborhoods, some of which have become virtual ghettos because of overcrowding and lack of city services. In recent years Asian people have become outspoken leaders in the struggles to maintain inner-city neighborhoods and to assert community control of schools, city planning, and city services. The Chinese, and later Japanese, communities have been replenished by a stream of immigration from Asia, first of wives, later of relatives and friends.

In more recent years, other Asians have entered the United States. In addition to Japanese and Chinese (some Mandarin speakers as well as Cantonese), Koreans, Philippinos, Vietnamese, and Thais are among the larger populations. Many Asians live in ethnic communities in which knowledge of English is not necessary to survival but is a key to high-paying employment and mobility. Others, often professionals, may be found in any community. Asian women who marry American servicemen are often quite isolated from others of their nationality.

Tucker's study of the problems facing Chinese immigrants can be applied to any immigrant group in this country, but the seriousness of the situation is exacerbated for Asians, whose language and culture are so radically different from the European majority and who face barriers of race as well. Although Tucker focuses exclusively on recent immigrants, longer-term residents and second-generation Asian-Americans who have remained largely isolated from English-speaking society may not differ greatly from new arrivals. His arguments raise important issues for English as a second language and bilingual education programs. Readers may wish to consult Fishman's article in Part III for further information on the educational and legal status of programs for non-English-speaking communities.

Tucker contends that some knowledge of the structure of the native language is important for teachers of non-English-speaking students. A note on Japanese, Korean, Vietnamese, and Philippine languages is attached to this article for readers who come into contact with speakers of those languages.

The major urban centers in the United States, as well as outlying communities, are receiving rapidly increasing numbers of Chinese immigrants. Prior to Oct. 3, 1965, the U.S. immigration quotas permitted a very small number of Chinese to enter this country annually. Public Law 89.236, an amendment to the Immigration and Nationalities Act, which was passed in 1965 and fully implemented on July 1, 1968, provided an interim quota phase during which Chinese immigration began to burgeon. Now, through the implementation of our new immigration policies, at least 10,000 Chinese are expected to immigrate to the United States each year.

San Francisco, with a Chinese community of approximately 70,000, receives a substantial share, probably not less than 15 percent, of the total annual Chinese immigration to the United States. In one San Francisco elementary school in the heart of Chinatown more than 55 percent of the 1200 students are immigrants. Eight years ago non-native-born Chinese children made up no more than 10 percent of the same school's enrollment. As new families enter the community week after week, their children appear at this or other Chinatown schools. On the day following Christmas vacation this particular school received 31 new immigrant pupils; on Monday following Easter week they received 9.

Most of these children, along with a vast majority of their parents, must attempt to function here under the pressures of an extensive language handicap. In order to assess the extent of this handicap, it may be helpful to consider briefly some aspects of the psychological, socioeconomic, and linguistic factors contributing to the handicap.

In addition to the usual psychological problems that accompany second-language learning the Chinese immigrant manifests some special problems. This may stem from a tendency to confuse the problems of learning to speak a second language with the problems of becoming literate in the language. If in their earlier education they learned to read and write their first language, they tend to expect the study of English to involve the memorizing of thousands of strange new words and the characters which represent them. If, on the other hand, they are not literate in their first language, they are painfully conscious of the baffling complexities of its written form. They may approach the study of English assuming comparable complexities to be encountered in its written form. The contemporary written form of Chinese is a highly refined and conventionalized adaptation of an older, more directly pictorial representation of concepts and constructs. To become literate in such a language requires the memorization of thousands of different characters. From his experience with such a writing system the Chinese immigrant frequently finds it very difficult to think in terms of a writing system of 26 letters which, used repeatedly in various combinations, must represent an entire language. The prior education of many of the immigrants was a "copy book" sort of education with a great deal of emphasis on books in general. If they had any pre-immigration exposure to English, it was often a book-oriented exposure, resulting in little more than a degree of sight-translation ability. As a consequence, most adults and older children feel a strong need for the comfort and security of a textbook in their American English classes. They often appear to be psychologically unprepared to accept the audio-lingual approach to language learning.

Another psychological problem is that many of the immigrants have forgotten or have never learned how to learn in an academic environment. Many of the adults, after a few years in school, learned a skill or trade and have pursued it daily for many years. Unfortunately, some adults and some children too, have had no formal education before coming to the United States. For all these people any successful attempt at learning English must include careful and specific help in learning how to learn.

There are some important socioeconomic facts of life for the Chinese immigrant in the United States which contribute to the extent of his language handicap. All too often, he settles in a Chinese-speaking urban enclave. Here, he finds housing, some sort of subsistence employment, essential services, and schooling for the children. He continues to think, hear, and speak Chinese throughout his working day. The necessity to use the English he may be learning is slight. In fact, the occasions to do so may be few. The rate at which English can be learned in such an environment is very slow, with a great deal of daily "forgetting."

Because available employment for the non-English-speaking adult is apt to be low-paying and the cost of urban living high, many immigrant families suffer chronically from malnutrition. They tire easily at work or at school.

The immigrant child is often rejected at school by other children, even by American-born Chinese children. Part of this rejection is caused by the language barrier, but differences in dress and behavior are factors, too. In defense against this rejection, the immigrant children form tight subgroups on the school grounds and have little occasion to speak or hear any language other than their own. In the classroom, they are often unable to understand anything that is said by the teacher or by another student. They appear to be unduly passive and unwilling to interact or participate. It is not so much a matter of unwillingness as of inability because of their failure to understand instructions, directions, or the purpose of a classroom activity. Isolated behind their language barriers they become discouraged and withdrawn, and begin to accept failure as unavoidable. Fortunately, this problem is not nearly so severe for the very young pupil. His chances of learning English are reasonably good. For the older students, however, unless the teacher provides special opportunities for using the English he knows or is learning, his retention and rate of learning English will be regrettably low.

Clearly, the most significant factor contributing to the Chinese immigrant's language handicap is the linguistic factor. Most of the current immigrants are native speakers of one or more of the several dialects of the Cantonese language. Vast structural differences between English and Cantonese make it particularly difficult for the Cantonese speaker to learn English. Cantonese is a tone language. Every word that the Chinese child learns must be remembered in terms of a specific tone or pitch upon which that word depends largely for meaning. In listening to English words, he cannot help attending to their tone or pitch. Since pitch is a feature of stress which may vary on a particular word at different times, the Chinese student is predisposed to hear that word as several different words because of the several different stresses we have given it. For example the stressed, rising *mine* in "Is it mine?" sounds like a very different word from the low, even, weaker-stressed *mine* in "No, mine's at home."

Because of the importance of syllabic tone in Cantonese, the student attends to the tone and stress of each word in a sentence and finds it difficult to learn to attend to the sentence intonation patterns. Consequently, our tendency to alter stress on words because of the requirements of a sentence intonation pattern is very confusing to him.

Cantonese vowels occur in very strictly controlled consonant environments. Many vowels can occur only after certain consonants, never after others. When a Cantonese student listens to English vowels, his hearing of the vowel sound is often influenced more by the consonant sound which precedes or follows it than by the actual sound of the vowel itself. Even with English vowels that are similar to Cantonese vowels, he is apt to hear a sound which is possible in that consonant environment in Cantonese rather than the vowel which was really pronounced. He needs extensive practice on English vowels in all consonant environments, beginning with those environments in which he has always heard the similar Cantonese vowels.

Cantonese has very few consonants in word or syllable final position. Exceptions are chiefly nasals and some unreleased unaspirated stops. As a result, Cantonese speakers hear and pronounce words like *George* as *Georgie*.

There are no consonant clusters in Cantonese. As a result, the Cantonese student hears and usually pronounces only one of the sounds in an English cluster. The frequency of such clusters in English causes this to be a considerable problem. This is particularly true since many clusters are formed or augmented by important morphological or syntactic items. For example, in the sentence "What's this?" the addition of 's to *what* forms a cluster in which the presence of 's is very important, but the Cantonese student will neither hear nor say it.

The Cantonese speaker makes no singular/plural distinction for nouns in his language. In English, not only is he faced with the fact that many nouns are made plural through the formation of a final consonant cluster like *books*, but he must remember to make other choices in a sentence which depend upon the singular or plural state of a noun. That is, he must remember to say *these* rather than *this* and *are* instead of *is* if he is talking about *my books*.

Cantonese word order cannot be manipulated for meaning change as English word order can. A Cantonese speaker can reposition some words for purposes of emphasis, but he does not make the kind of change we make in English when we relocate *is* to convert the statement "He is a teacher" to a question. The habit of listening for words or phrases in different positions in a sentence develops slowly, and only with considerable practice, for the Cantonese student.

There is nothing in Cantonese that parallels the masculine/feminine distinction essential to a correct use of English pronouns. Even after extensive practice and memorization of our pronoun forms, the Cantonese-speaking student has difficulty in remembering which English form to use.

One of the most difficult problems for the Cantonese speaker learning English stems from the fact that a Cantonese verb has only one form. When he is required to learn different forms for third person singular, he is encountering a singular/plural concept as well as person concept, neither of which has an effect on a Cantonese verb. When, at the same time, he must learn and remember to choose correctly among various forms with respect to past, present, or future time, the problem is compounded. The eventual addition of further forms and choices required for perfect tenses, combinations of continuous and perfect along with the many passive forms creates a formidable array of forms to learn and choices to make for a student who has never thought of a verb as having more than a single form.

The combined weight of the many psychological, socioeconomic, and linguistic factors puts a very heavy language handicap upon the Chinese immigrant. The effects of this handicap are far-reaching and extend to most members of the immigrant family. Despite his training and experience, the adult is usually unable to find work which makes use of his existing skills, even though those skills may be viable ones. His inability to speak English forces him to compete for long-hour, low-paying, menial jobs in the Chinese enclave. For all too many such adults there is little opportunity to learn English because of the long working hours. However, until or unless they learn English, these working conditions must continue.

Because the father earns so little and costs of living are so high, the mother frequently is forced to find work at very low wages and for long hours. The usual close-knit family structure suffers because both parents are away from home during most of the children's waking day. Problems of child care are adequately met only at considerable expense to the underpaid parents, or they are inadequately met at the ultimate expense of the children.

Many of the most important concepts which lie at the heart of the primary school curriculum cannot be learned by the immigrant child. Such concepts would be available to him if they were offered through a bilingual curriculum. Lacking the opportunity provided by a bilingual curriculum, the child must wait to learn these concepts until he has learned English. By that time, he may be beyond his optimal learning stage for such concepts, or the opportunities to learn them may be few.

For the older elementary or junior high school child, the problems are somewhat greater. In the first place, it is more difficult for him to learn English than it is for the younger child. Also, there is a considerable body of curriculum content in all subjects which a child at that grade level is expected to know. Although the immigrant child has never been exposed to the greater part of this content, he must compete with other children who have had such exposure. Despite his native abilities, he is frequently relegated to low streams or tracks in the system because of his inability to compete effectively. Unless the older immigrant child knows English at the time of arrival, or is a highly gifted child, he needs extensive English training and special instruction to compensate for his background deficiencies if his success in school is to be, even to a degree, commensurate with his native ability.

Time and his language handicap combine to weigh heavily against chances of success for the high school student. The complexities of today's sophisticated high school curriculum and the degree of success necessary for college entrance are such that the immigrant student is often defeated at the outset. The dropout rate among such students is high and is a cause of great concern to the immigrant parents and to the community at large.

Education is highly valued by the Chinese. Many immigrant parents have transplanted their families in order to provide improved educational and career opportunities for their children. Such parents are bitterly disappointed when their children fail in school and often overlook the role of the language handicap in such failure. Unfortunately, the menial job held by the father is seen by some children as an equal sign of failure on his part. The alienation and bitterness resulting from such failures are coming to the surface in some communities. In San Francisco's Chinatown, street gangs of immigrant teenagers have formed and their numbers are growing. The plight of these young people epitomizes a pitiful waste of human potential. That they and their families may yet have a chance for something better and that others may be helped to avoid their present plight constitute a considerable challenge to our society and especially to those of us concerned with the teaching of English as a second language.

EDITORS' NOTE ON OTHER ASIAN LANGUAGES SPOKEN IN THE UNITED STATES

The Structure of Language section of the General Introduction defines terms and concepts used in the descriptions below.

Japanese

Phonology   The differences between the English and Japanese sound systems will cause difficulties for the English learner in two ways. First, English makes some phonemic contrasts that Japanese does not. Second, the range of allophonic variation is greater in some cases, so that sounds are more affected by their neighbors. The following are probable trouble spots:

/r/: [r] and [l] are not differentiated (*row=low*).

/s/: [s] and [š] are not differentiated (*see=she*).

/z/: [z] and [ž] are not differentiated (*bays=beige*).

/t/: [t] and [č] are not differentiated (*to=chew*); /t/ also becomes [ts] in certain contexts.

/h/: becomes [f] and [ts] in certain contexts.

Nasals: /ɲ/ (as in Spanish *señor*) becomes [m], [n], and [ŋ] in certain contexts; /g/ also becomes [ŋ] in certain contexts.

/θ/ and /ð/ do not occur.

Japanese has a five-vowel system—/i/, /e/, /a/, /o/, and /u/—compared with the nine- to eleven-vowel systems of American English. Each Japanese vowel has a correspondingly larger range of possible pronunciations, so that a Japanese speaker may fail to distinguish /i/ from /ɪ/; /e/ from /ɛ/, /æ/, or /ə/; /a/ from /æ/, /ə/, or /ɔ/; /o/ from /ɔ/; and /u/ from /ʊ/.

English consonant clusters present a formidable obstacle to Japanese speakers, for their language consists entirely of consonant-vowel sequences. In rendering English words, vowels are inserted to break up the unpronounceable consonant clusters (e.g., *Boston* becomes /bosotany/; *club* becomes /kurabu/).

In English, stress is used extensively to differentiate and to emphasize words. For instance, we change word class by shifts of stress (*lábor/labórious*). Japanese stress is distributed evenly across the syllables, and each syllable is the same length. It does not use pitch to make distinctions, as does Chinese. Cues of emphasis and distinctions dependent on stress and length will be lost on the learner. Similarly, questions are formed with special particles, not by a shift in intonation.

Grammar   Japanese grammar is organized very differently from English. The student must cope with an entirely new way of thinking about what constitutes a word, as well as how they can be arranged. Many categories that play important roles in English do not occur in Japanese, and vice versa. Some specific areas of difficulty are:

Gender: not marked at all in Japanese.

Number: not marked at all in Japanese.

Word order: English sentences are basically arranged subject-verb-object; Japanese are subject-object-verb.

Subject-verb agreement: concord of person or number does not occur in Japanese.

Word classes: Japanese has basically only two word classes—inflected forms (verbs, adjectives, copula) and uninflected forms (nouns, pronouns, adverbs, particles); pronouns do not really exist as a word class—certain nouns serve that purpose instead.

Tense: Japanese does not make the same distinctions as English (e.g., future time is expressed as an unreal or unrealized action).

Writing System   Japanese writing is derived from Chinese characters, which were not too well suited to the multisyllable word structure of Japanese. Over time, the characters evolved into a syllabary of approximately fifty signs, each representing a consonant-vowel combination. In addition, the Chinese characters remain in their original use, sometimes standing for whole words or concepts, sometimes for a sound associated with the basic meaning of the character. Thus the Japanese perceive writing as a complicated and multileveled problem and may have a great deal of difficulty with the English alphabetic system in which each sign represents only a single sound. The incongruity between spelling and pronunciation only adds to the confusion.

Interaction Japanese society tends to be more formal and hierarchical than American, and the language is correspondingly full of forms and rules for maintaining proper respect and social distance. For example, there are three different sets of terms of address: a familiar, a polite, and an honorific series. Deference is exhibited by use of honorific-level linguistic features, discourse rules that forbid an inferior to initiate an interaction, and aversion of the eyes. Interpersonal distance and posture norms are also different from English speakers'. Teachers of Japanese should be sensitive to their students' natural disinclination to participate aggressively in classroom exhibition and debate and to challenge the teacher with probing questions.

Korean

Phonology Korean consonants differ quite radically from those of English. The following are some of the most likely areas of difficulty for Korean speakers who are learning English:

Voiced stops are allophones of voiceless stops, so that /p/ is pronounced [b] in some contexts, /t/ can be pronounced [d], and /k/ can be pronounced [g].

/s/ becomes [š] in certain contexts.

/č/ becomes [ǰ] in certain contexts.

/l/ becomes [r] between vowels.

There are three series of voiceless stops and affricate: unaspirated /p, t, k, č/; aspirated /pʰ, tʰ, kʰ, čʰ/; and "tense" /p', t', k', č'/ where English has only one set (with allophonic aspiration in initial position).

The English phonemes /z/, /ž/, /θ/, and /ð/ do not occur. It is extremely difficult for Korean speakers to understand which distinctions among English stops are significant. The much more elaborated English fricatives present a challenge as well.

English and Korean vowel systems contrast in two ways. Korean has fewer vowels than English, so that our /i/ and /ɪ/, /e/ and /ɛ/, /o/ and /ɔ/, and /u/ and /ʊ/ will not be distinguished by the student. Further, Korean has a limited form of vowel harmony, in which a vowel affects the quality of the one in the following syllable. Thus the same word may have more than one vowel pronunciation depending on the vowel of the word preceding it in the sentence.

Syllable structure is confined to consonant-vowel, with a few consonants also appearing finally in consonant-vowel-consonant sequences. Students will have difficulty with English clusters and aid themselves by intrusive vowels. They may also not hear second and third consonants of clusters.

Korean is not a tone language, and stress is not used as a major contrasting element. Our various intonation contours will be confusing and often overlooked.

Grammar Korean grammar resembles that of Japanese, with which it is thought to be related. Syntactic categories are indicated by particles after the verb or at the end of sentences. For instance, where we use devices such as intonation to differentiate indicative, interrogative, and imperative moods, Korean has only a particle at the end of each sentence to indicate this.

Like other Asian languages, Korean does not demand concord of person and number among nouns and verbs, nor does it require gender distinctions. No "articles" are present either. The verbal system is highly complex, but based on different parameters from those in the English tense system. Students learning English will have to learn to divide time in new ways and to consider events from a different perspective.

Writing Korean has what has been called the most ideal writing system in the world. There are 28 symbols, each corresponding to a phoneme, which not only define the sound but show how the sound is produced by lips, tongue, and throat. Korean is not written linearly but in clusters of letters which form words. Korean speakers will find the totally abstract English alphabet signs and their lack of congruence with pronounced forms quite difficult.

Interaction Korean, too, has a series of language levels based on social class, age, and kinship. Each has its own pronouns, particles, and discourse rules, as well as nonverbal behaviors.

Vietnamese

Phonology and Grammar In Vietnamese, phonology and grammar are tightly bound up with one another. The most obvious difference between Vietnamese and English is the complex tone and stress system in Vietnamese, which is used to differentiate among otherwise homophonous words. Vietnamese vowels have six tones and, superimposed on these, four vowel intonations which function largely as gliding tones. Further, there are three distinct degrees of stress which may be attached to any word to designate whether the word is new information (strong stress), old information (weak stress), or the rest of the phrase (medium stress). For a Vietnamese student of English, our much less formally structured and atonal phonological system is extremely foreign.

In addition to the tone, intonation, and stress contrasts, the phonemic system of Vietnamese also presents some problematic contrasts to English. The syllable structure is basically consonant-vowel, with some consonants also occurring finally (consonant-vowel-consonant), and a large number of vowel clusters in midsyllable. Thus our consonant clusters are difficult and may result in intrusive vowels. In Vietnamese many consonants can occur only at the beginnings or at the endings of syllables. Thus:

/p/ becomes [b] in final position.
/t/ becomes [d] in final position.

It will be difficult for Vietnamese to hear and to pronounce these as separate phonemes. On the other hand, aspirated and unaspirated stops are all separate phonemes in Vietnamese. A Vietnamese will thus perceive the /p/ of *peer* ([pʰir]) as a distinct sound from that in *spear* ([spir]), the /t/ of *tool* ([tʰul]) as distinct from that in *stool* ([stul]), and the /k/ of *cool* ([kʰul]) as distinct from that in *school* ([skul]). The phonemes /š/, /r/, /Ө/, and /ð/ do not occur. Thus English /r/ and /l/ may be hard for the student to distinguish, as well as /s/ and /z/. /Ө/ and /ð/ will be difficult to pronounce. The vowel system in Vietnamese, even without considering tone, is more complex than English.

Vietnamese syntax is an extreme example of "isolating" languages. Words, in this case single syllables, occur as simple roots with no affixes indicating word class (as "-ly" indicates adverbs in English), number, person, or role in the sentence (as English does with case). A word might be functioning as a noun, a verb, an adjective; a topic, an object, an instrument. No connectors (copula, conjunctions, prepositions) are required. The syntactic roles of the individual words are defined by word order, by context, and by the rhythm with which they are spoken. Again, a fine phonological distinction serves a grammatical function: words which are in close syntactic relation are spoken in rhythmic groups. The difficulties that English suffixation, word-order shifts, and intonational contours present to the student are obvious. Also unlike English, no time indication is necessary in the verb. Tense, if it is not clear from context, is indicated by temporal or manner adverbials like *already* for past events and *slow* for future.

Writing System   Vietnamese employs a Latin alphabet with complex markings for tone and intonation. The primary difficulty for readers will be the discrepancy between our spelling and pronunciation, for Vietnamese is much truer to the written word.

Interaction   Although Vietnamese society is not as stratified as the Chinese, its language does exhibit a multitude of levels and different honorific markers.

Philippine Languages

Most of the native languages of the Philippines are members of the Malayo-Polynesian language family. Probably the most widely represented in the United States are Tagalog (the national language), Ilocano, and Cebuano. The impact of Spanish and American colonization has made itself felt in all these native languages as well as in education and government. And Philippinos who come to the United States—many as well-educated professionals—may speak fluent English upon arrival. In her article on pidgins and creoles, Gail Dreyfuss points to Cebuano and Ilocano as important languages in the Hawaiian linguistic situation. A few general features of the Malayo-Polynesian language group in the Philippines are explained below, using Tagalog as the central example.

Phonology Tagalog has fewer phonemes than English, both among the consonants and among the vowels. /s/ is the only fricative in native words; so students of English will have a large number of contrasts to learn. The voiceless stops are unaspirated in Tagalog, so that the puff of air following English initial sounds (e.g., *top*=[tʰap]) will sound like a stop + /h/ sequence. /l/ and /r/ are both present, and /d/ is pronounced as [r] between vowels. Consonant clusters are rare, and words are mostly two-syllable consonant-vowel-consonant-vowel sequences. Intrusive vowels will be necessary to make some English words pronounceable. There are only five vowels in Tagalog; so the difference between English /i/ and /ɪ/, /e/ and /ɛ/, /a/ and /ə/, /o/ and /ɔ/, and /u/ and /ʊ/ will be difficult for the learner to hear. However, the temporal length of vowels is used to make distinctions among words in Tagalog, so that the lengthening of vowels which English speakers use for emphasis may be interpreted as a new word.

Tagalog uses intonation contours to make meaning distinctions, much as English does. What each contour means differs, of course.

Writing Philippine languages are written with the Latin alphabet. Tagalog uses twenty letters, of which seven are exclusively for foreign words. Words are pronounced just as they are spelled; so English spelling will be quite an obstacle.

Grammar Malayo-Polynesian languages do not mark the same categories as European languages do. Number and gender are not ordinarily indicated. There are no articles like English *a* or *the* and no copula. In fact, the notions "subject" and "object" are not useful in describing their grammatical systems. Verbs and their particles go first in the sentence, followed by nouns, which are unmarked for case or concord with the verb. Sentential word order or a "focus" particle affixed to the verb indicates which is the topic ("focus") of the sentence. Tagalog verb forms are based on the status of the action as "completed," "not-yet-completed," and "contemplated" rather than on the location of the action in time, which is the basis of English tense. English students with Malayo-Polynesian backgrounds will have to acquire a whole new set of syntactic and semantic distinctions in order to become fluent in English.

PIDGIN AND CREOLE LANGUAGES
IN THE UNITED STATES

Gail Raimi Dreyfuss

In a nation such as the United States, where many speech communities have existed side by side since the colonial era, there are bound to be interesting linguistic developments when two divergent communities come into contact. Gail Raimi Dreyfuss describes one linguistic phenomenon which can result from these contacts: the emergence of pidgin and creole languages, which combine characteristics from two or more languages. Dreyfuss discusses the three major U.S. creoles—Gullah, Louisiana Creole, and Hawaiian Creole—as well as the creole origins of Black English Vernacular and Spanish-English language mixing among Chicanos.

For more detailed information on Black English Vernacular, see Lourie's article in this volume, as well as the Kochman selection on Black speech events and the Cooke essay on nonverbal communication in the Black community. In addition, Dreyfuss' section on Louisiana Creole can be usefully supplemented by Saville's brief description of Cajun French. And the section on Spanish-English language mixing should be compared with the discussion of code switching in the Gumperz and Hernández-Chavez paper. Appendix H contains passages of Gullah and Pennsylvania German. Readers may wish to examine the Pennsylvania German text with an eye to discov   g why Dreyfuss calls it a "doubtful" creole.

Most people think that a pidgin is a misspelled bird and a creole is either a kind of French spoken in Louisiana or else a style of cooking characterized by the liberal use of onions and tomatoes. In linguistics, however, these terms apply to special kinds of languages which differ from other languages in both their histories and their structures. This paper will first describe pidgins and creoles in general and then discuss those that are found in the United States.

According to Hancock's survey (1971) there are eighty pidgin and creole languages, both extant and extinct, whose existence has been reported. The vast majority of these are spoken in Africa and on islands in the Pacific and the Caribbean. Some of the best known of these languages are Louisiana French Creole, Jamaican Creole, and pidginized Swahili. Rather few pidgins or creoles are spoken in the United States or Europe.

The distinguishing characteristic of a pidgin is that no one speaks it as a first, or native, language. A pidgin arises when two or more groups of people who do not share a common language are in contact with each other. This contact must be extensive enough that the groups need to communicate with each other but not so extensive that one group abandons its own language and learns that of the other. Often pidgins have arisen with colonization, where the colonizers all spoke the same language and the colonized were linguistically heterogeneous. In these circumstances, a language evolves for purposes of basic communication by drawing its vocabulary and grammar from the languages that are in contact. In the case of colonization, the vocabulary is usually from the language of the colonizers while the grammar reflects mainly features of the languages of the colonized. In such cases, the pidgin will have a number of "grammars," with each speaker using the rules of his or her native language in arranging the words in a sentence.

Pidgins in general lack inflections, phonological and morphological variation, and obligatory categories such as number, case, and gender. Their vocabularies are also considerably smaller than those of "natural" languages, and their phonologies tend to be made up of sounds that are common in the languages of the world and to lack "rare" sounds like front rounded vowels and aspirated voiced stops.

This description of pidgins is a generalization and is probably not accurate for any particular pidgin. Where some of the languages involved in its formation are similar, a pidgin may well contain structures derived from these languages. For example, Saramaccan, an English-African creole spoken in Surinam, retains the phonological tone characteristic of West African languages. In Neo-Melanesian, a pidgin English spoken in New Guinea, there is a distinction between two kinds of we: *yumi* means "we including the person addressed" and *mipela* means "we not including the person addressed," a distinction characteristic of the Austronesian languages spoken in the area. The distinction is very important: Laycock (1970, p. xviii) reminds missionaries not to say *jisas i-dai long mipela*, "Jesus died for us," since that would mean he did not also die for non-Europeans.

Conditions that favor the development of a pidgin are those in which several groups of people are in frequent but rather limited contact with one another. This is often the case in Africa, where a number of pidgins, sometimes called *lingua francas,* are in use. These are languages which are used in nonpidginized form by one group as a mother tongue and as a pidgin by various other groups for trading purposes. The pidginized form is spoken as a second language by all who use it. Some examples of this are Twi, Arabic, and Wolof (Heine, 1970). In these cases, the people who use the lingua franca as a second language remain in contact with the social and linguistic group into which they were born, and have no motivation for abandoning their tribal languages in favor of a pidgin, just as an American who learns French does not cease to speak English.

A creole is distinguished from a pidgin by being spoken natively by a sizable group of people. This sometimes happens in an area where a pidgin is spoken when people from different language backgrounds marry and have children. Since the parents speak to each other in the pidgin, the children learn it as their first language and speak it to each other. A situation like this frequently arises when people of highly diverse language backgrounds migrate in considerable numbers from rural areas to urban centers. Some examples of creoles that have developed in this way are Tok Pisin, which was the creole derived from Neo-Melanesian Pidgin in New Guinea, and Sango in the Central African Republic, which is a creolized lingua franca.

In other cases, creoles have developed where there is no evidence that a pidgin ever existed. This occurred in the West Indies during the epoch of slavery, when the slave dealers had a policy of separating members of the same language group to discourage rebellions. Under these circumstances, a new language had to develop and become native almost simultaneously. The resultant creoles have mainly European (English, French, Spanish, Dutch, and Portuguese) vocabularies and reflect strong African influence in their grammars. There is considerable controversy as to the exact origins of these languages. One point of view holds that they are all derived from a common ancestral pidgin and changed their vocabularies ("relexified") according to the language of the colonizers in each island. Those who hold this opinion are impressed by the degree to which these creoles resemble each other despite the great differences in their vocabularies (Whinnom, 1965). Another controversy concerns whether or not these languages ever passed through a clear pidgin stage. In either case, the Caribbean creoles differ from noncreole (so-called "natural") languages on the one hand and from pidgin languages on the other. Unlike languages like English, Eskimo, and Chinese, they cannot trace their ancestry back to prehistory through an unbroken process of gradual language change. Instead, they came into existence rather recently and abruptly, usually under circumstances of great social upheaval, and they cannot be unambiguously assigned to any one language family. Unlike pidgins, on the other hand, creoles are mother tongues to large numbers of people. In this sense they are like the "natural languages" and fulfill Sapir's description as "essentially perfect means of expression and communication."

There is some question as to whether creoles are different in any way other than historically from other languages. The best answer seems to be that creoles share certain characteristics among themselves that make them like some other languages but unlike others. Creoles in general are relatively "isolating" languages: their morphological systems are fairly simple and their syntactic systems (that is, the rules for arranging words in various orders) are fairly complex. This makes them similar to languages like English and Chinese, and unlike Turkish and Latin, which make heavy use of inflections. In addition, the morphology of creole languages is likely to be regular in comparison with other languages. English, for example, has many irregularities in the way plurals are formed: the regular ending in /-s/, /-z/ and /-əz/, the ablaut, or vowel alternation as in *goose/geese,* the zero plural as in *sheep/sheep,* the /-ən/ endings as in *ox/oxen* or *child/children,* the Latinate endings as in *alumna/alumnae,* and so on. This irregularity occurs primarily because the rules for forming plurals have changed in the course of the history of the language, and some words have remained from each epoch. Creoles, lacking this long history, usually apply their rules more regularly. Characteristics such as these are not sufficient to mark creoles as essentially different from other languages. They should be considered to be as fully adequate as any other language in the world today.

The problem for linguists and other people who have been concerned with creole languages has often been that creoles are compared to the languages from which they derive the bulk of their vocabularies. Haitian Creole, for example, one of the Caribbean creoles discussed above, is often compared to French. The following is a Haitian sentence and its equivalent in French:

/bodye te-fèk fin fe mun ak bèt./

Dieu venait de faire les hommes et les bêtes.

God had just made men and beasts. (Comhaire-Sylvain, 1938, p. 221)

People were inclined to notice what Haitian "lacks" by comparison with French. For example, there is no verb agreement: the verb would be the same whether the noun was *I* or *you* or *s/he*. There also are no articles, and gender (masculine and feminine) is not distinguished. However, the Haitian version also has features which the French lacks. The pre-verbs *fèk fin* indicate that an action has just been completed. To render this in English would require an extra verb and adverb: "had just finished making." The point is that it is inappropriate to compare a creole's grammar with the grammar of the language from which its vocabulary is derived. The two systems are different, and are complex in different ways.

Children who come to school speaking a creole have problems of both a linguistic and a social nature. Linguistically, the situation for pidgin or creole speakers is identical to that for native speakers of any language other than English, whether it be Spanish, Chinese, or Navajo. They need to learn Standard English as a second language. Socially, however, the problems for these children may be more severe than they are for speakers of other languages, since pidgins and creoles have always been heavily stigmatized, both by the general community and, until recently, by linguists. They have been described by such terms as "baby talk," "broken English," and "reduced English." Speakers of these languages often have a negative image of themselves and their speech, and efforts to teach Standard English may only reinforce this feeling. It is important for the teacher to communicate to the students that they should be proud of their language, since it is linguistically as "good" as any other, including English, and that Standard English is taught because it is the national language, not because it is "clearer" or "more logical."

With these things in mind, we can begin an examination of the pidgin and creole languages in use today in the United States. This discussion will include only those languages which are indigenous to the United States and will exclude, for lack of space, languages spoken by relatively recent groups of immigrants. Some of these, however, are quite important in certain areas (e.g., Haitian Creole in New York City), and the interested reader can find references to them by consulting *A Bibliography of Pidgin and Creole Languages* by Reinecke et al.

The linguistic situation with regard to creoles in the United States is complicated by the fact that the pressure to learn and speak Standard English is very strong in all areas. This means that pidgin and creole languages exist in a variety of dialects that show more or less influence from Standard English. This process, by means of which creoles come more and more to resemble a standard language, is called *decreolization*. If a creole is undergoing decreolization, an individual speaker may control several varieties of the language, ranging from something very close to Standard English to something that is clearly a creole.

This means that it is impossible to describe, for example, Hawaiian Pidgin English; the term covers many dialects which may have quite different vocabularies and grammars. Variation is a feature of all languages, of course, but it is particularly marked in languages that are decreolizing. In turn, decreolization is particularly strong in the United States because of such factors as universal education, good transportation, and television. In this chapter, the form of the languages described is, unless otherwise noted, that variety which is furthest from English. However, teachers or visitors are likely to encounter more decreolized varieties.

The languages which are considered here are: Gullah, or Sea Islands Creole, spoken on the Sea Islands off the coast of South Carolina; Louisiana French Creole; Hawaiian Pidgin and Creole English; Black English from the point of view of its creole ancestry; and the Spanish-English mixing that characterizes the speech of some Chicanos.

Gullah

Gullah, or Geechee, is an English-African creole which is very closely related to the English creoles of the Caribbean such as Jamaican and Guyanese and the English-based languages of the west coast of Africa such as Krio and West African Pidgin. It is spoken primarily on the Sea Islands off the coast of South Carolina, of which Hilton Head is probably the best known. It is also spoken in the coastal areas of Georgia and Florida. Gullah has of course been heavily influenced by Standard English, but there are still many people who speak a variety which is quite far from English.

In his book *Africanisms in the Gullah Dialect*, Turner (1949, p. 1) explains the persistence of African customs and vocabulary in this region by the fact that slaves were transported there in great numbers directly from Africa, even as late as 1858. In other parts of the United States, slaves were more often brought from the West Indies. Also, the area was relatively isolated, and the white population was extremely small: Turner cites a ratio of 20 black to 1 white families. These same factors probably account for the persistence of creole in the face of a sea of English. Decreolization can occur only where the influence of the standard language is strong. In the Sea Islands region, however, the influence of Africa was strong and the presence of English was minimal, certainly until the 1860s and to some extent still today.

Prior to Turner's work, Gullah had been considered to be merely an extremely deviant dialect of English. Turner, however, discovered many African influences on the vocabulary and syntax, including more than 4000 given names and 250 other vocabulary items derived from about twenty West African languages, including Yoruba, Ibo, Wolof, Mandinka, and Twi. Some of the words occur in other dialects of American English, including:

/bakra/ "white man" from Ibo and Efik, both spoken in Nigeria
/guba/ "peanut" (goober) from Kimbundu *ngguba*. Also cognates in Umbanda and Kongo, all spoken in Angola
/jiga/ "insect, jigger" from Wolof and several other languages

/tot/ "to carry" from Kikongo *tota* and several other languages

/yam/ "yam" from Mende *yam, yambi* and several other languages

Most of the rest of the vocabulary of Gullah is derived from English. The phonology, however, is quite different. The vowels /i/, /e/, /o/, and /u/ are "pure" rather than diphthongized as they are in most varieties of English, and thus they more closely resemble the vowels of French and Spanish. The voiceless stops /p/, /t/, and /k/ are either unaspirated or only slightly aspirated. English /j/ is replaced by /ɟ/, a voiced palatal stop. (This is the actual sound in the Gullah word "jigger.") The /f/ of English is replaced by a bilabial voiceless fricative /Φ/, and /v/ and /w/ are replaced by /β/, a voiced bilabial fricative (as in Spanish *haber*). There are other phonological differences that make Gullah sound very unlike English at first.

The grammar of Gullah also reveals several striking similarities to African languages and differences from Standard English. One African characteristic, common to most of the African and Caribbean creoles, is the use of serial verbs, where verbs fulfill the function sometimes performed by prepositions in English. For example:

/den de tek am go Čalzten/. Then they take them to Charleston.

/yu beta go hom go si baut yo čɪlen/. You'd better go home to (in order to) see about your children.

/i tɛk stik kɪl əm/. He killed them with a stick. (Turner, 1949, pp. 210-211)

In all these cases, an English verb (*take* and *go*) has been reinterpreted to fulfill the functions required of serial verb constructions in African languages.

Another example is the use of /sɛ/, which occurs in many African languages such as Twi to mark the embedding of one sentence in another. It also has this function in Gullah, as in:

/dɛn di čɪlən dɛ in nyu yak sɛn wəd sɛ de ẽ gain gɪt natn/ (Turner, 1949, p. 211).[1] Then the children in New York sent word *that* they weren't going to get anything.

Note that /sɛ/ sounds similar to English *say*. This coincidence probably made it easier for /sɛ/ to occur in English-based creoles. In fact, it is quite common to find coincidences like this where a creole word has a dual etymology from at least two languages.

The following fragment of a story was recorded by Patricia Jackson in 1976 on Wadmalaw Island off the coast of Charleston. The speaker is a 95-year-old man. The transcription here is rather broad; it does not represent the sounds of Gullah with full accuracy but is used to make the text more intelligible. Some differences between this representation and the actual pronunciation are that /w/ here represents /β/ and /f/ represents /Φ/: the voiced and voiceless bilabial fricatives, respectively.

1 /da was wašǎ kɔl šaiklɔn. fɛs kɔl em a adem stɔm. . . . ai din imba gud. ai bin

2 arung elɛm yez ol. ðə naindi Ɵri stom də stat ɔn ə sɔndi mɔnin. . . ðə weðɛ

3 luk hezi. . . ɛn so mai məðə hi bin klɛč. ai wɔz de bigis bɔi. di čilin sɛva a wi

4 bin dɛ, ɛn dɛn wɔn ə mi ungəls fɔm ovə hat: wi bin livin ovə ya. . . we mai
5 ma lef mi fə kuk dina. wɛlɛs ai tɛl di pipl. . . se ẽ nutin hia fə kuk. . . so ai
6 kuk dina fid mi ankl n mai nɛfu n misɛf. ɛn də leda de gitin, gyal, luk de
7 wɛdə də klozin in. dɛn de sta lil drizlin rein. jis aftə yɛti git hom—ai kɔl mi
8 ma yɛti, i nem laiza but dɛn yu no ai rez up wit di ol pipl, wel i git hom lil fo
9 di ol man kɔm in. i sprenkl ren i wə. din lil bi lɔng. . . wɛn de ivnin endə sɔn
10 gitn loɛ n loɛ də hevia de wəz gitin./

Translation

That was what you call a cyclone. First (they) call them autumn storms. . . . I don't remember good. I was around 11 years old. The '93 storm started on a Sunday morning. . . . The weather looked hazy . . . and so my mother he was at church. I was the biggest boy. The children, several of us were there, and then one of my uncles from over Hart, we been living over there. . . . Well, my Ma left me to cook dinner. Well, as I told people . . . that ain't nothing here to cook . . . so I cooked dinner, fed my uncle and my nephew, and myself. And the later it's getting, gal, look the weather's closing in. Then it start a little drizzling rain. Just after Yatta get home—I call my mother Yatta, his name's Liza, but then you know I raised up with the old folks, well, he gets home a little before the old man come in, he sprinkle rain he was. Then a little longer . . . when it's evening and the sun getting lower and lower the heavier it was getting.

There are several points of interest in this passage. Notice the use of *de* or *də* for *it* or *it's*, as in lines 2, 6, 7, and 10. Also, there is no gender or case marked on pronouns: *he* is used for *mother* in lines 3 and 8 and *we* is used for *us* in line 3, *me* for *my* in lines 4, 6, and 7, and *he* for *his* in line 8. Notice also the use of *for* instead of *to* in line 5, the absence of tense markers, and the use of the *se* complementizer in line 5.

The most likely prediction for Gullah would be that it will continue to decreolize and will eventually merge with other dialects of English. However, it has already existed for a long time, maintaining its identity in an overwhelmingly English world; so we should not be too eager to lament its passing. A change in official policy or a desire for self-determination on the part of its speakers may give it the impetus it needs to continue to live.

Louisiana French Creole

Louisiana Creole is probably the best-known variety of creole in the United States. The number of speakers has been estimated at 80,000 (Voegelin, as cited in Reinecke et al.), but there has never been an accurate count. It became established among the slaves transported from Africa in the early eighteenth century by the French, who occupied Louisiana until 1763, when it was taken over by Spain, and again from 1800 to 1803. In addition to French Creole, there are two other varieties of French spoken in the area: Acadien, or Cajun, and Standard Louisiana French. Cajun is spoken by descendants of the Acadiens, Catholics who were expelled from Nova Scotia in 1755, and Standard Louisiana French by descendants of some of the original French settlers.

As is to be expected, the three varieties have influenced each other and all have also been influenced by English, both Black and Standard. Morgan (1970) reports that Cajun, Creole, and Standard have exactly the same vocabularies but that there still are some differences, primarily in word order, that mark Creole as different from the other two varieties. Compare, for example:

Creole: /ti - zwazo - y/
                     little bird plural
Standard Louisiana: /l - ti - z   wazo/
                     the little plural bird
Standard European: "les petits oiseaux"
                     "the little birds"   (Morgan, 1970, p. 60)

Goodman, who made a comparative study of all the French creoles in the world, described Louisiana as the most decreolized. However, it is still mutually intelligible with the other French creoles of the Caribbean.

The vocabulary of Louisiana Creole is largely derived from French with several African words and numerous English borrowings. The phonology is similar to French, but the front rounded vowels of French, /ü/ as in *fumer* /füme/, /ɔ̈/ as in *seul* /sɔ̈l/, and /ö/ as in *peu* /pö/ are unrounded.[2] Thus the words cited above are pronounced /fime/, /sɛl/, and /pe/, respectively. Many words in Louisiana Creole occur with a prefix that is derived from a French definite or indefinite article or the "partitive" *de,* "some." These prefixes are /n/ from French *un* or *une,* "a," /l/ or /la/ from French *le* or *la,* "the," and /d/ from French *de.* In Creole, however, these do not have the meanings they had in French; rather, they are simply part of the word. Some examples (from Morgan, 1960, p. 24a):

/nɔm/ "man" (French *homme* /ɔm/)
/lide/ "idea" (French *idée* /ide/)
/lavi/ "life" (French *vie* /vi/)
/diri/ "rice" (French *riz* /ri/)

These prefixes do not always occur with the word. For example:

/ɛ̃ lide/ "an idea"

but

/dɛz ide/ "two ideas"

Louisiana Creole grammar is very different from French, and many of the differences can be traced to the grammar of African languages. For example, the definite article /la/ occurs not before the noun as in French but after it. Thus "the woman" is /fɔm-la/. This word order is characteristic of African languages as well as the other French creoles. In contrast to French, there is usually no gender in Louisiana Creole, and verbs are not usually marked for tense. As in all French creoles, there is a set of aspect markers that distinguish continuing action from completed action. For example (from Lane, 1935, p. 14):

/m-ape-fini/ "I am finishing" (progressive)
/mo te-fini/ "I have finished" (completive)
/mo fini/ "I finish, I finished, I will finish"

Creole also uses serial verbs as in (Morgan, 1960, p. 24d):

Creole: /li prɔn yɛ li mɛt yɛ a lekɔl/.
European French vocabulary: il prendeux il met eux à l'école.
Standard English vocabulary: he take they he put they to school.
European French: Il les a envoyé à l'école.
Standard English: He sent them to (or he put them in) school.

As was noted in the section on Gullah, serial verbs occur in African languages and in the West Indian creoles.

The following is an excerpt from a text recorded by Morgan in Saint Martin Parish, Louisiana. The plot, that of an animal pretending to be dead in order to steal something, is a common one all over the world, but in this particular form it is found in Africa and the West Indies: Bouki is riding along in his cart full of couscous (itself an African food), and Rabbit runs ahead of him three times, playing dead each time. Finally, Bouki decides to go back and collect the three rabbits to cook, and while he is gone, Rabbit steals the cart. The first version below is in Morgan's phonemic orthography, the second is in standard French orthography for the benefit of those readers who know French, and the third is an English translation. Underlined words in the second version are those that have no obvious French equivalent.

1 /lapẽ fɛ l'tur dɛva buki, li kuše o bɔr šɛmɛ. buki di: ga ẽ lapẽ mɛ li muri.
2 buki pasɛ. aprɛ li pasɛ, lapẽ lɛvɛ. li fɛ ẽ gra tur e li kuše o bɔr šɛmɛ ãkɔr.
3 buki tɛ krwa sɛ ẽ nɔt lapẽ. buki di: sa fɛ dyɛ lapẽ ki mɔr e la li di: si mo
4 srɛ ramase dyɛ lapẽ-yɛ mo srɛ fɛ kwi yɛ pu mãžɛ avɛk mo kuškuš. mɛ li
5 kõtine. aprɛ li pasɛ, lapẽ lɛvɛ e li fɛ ẽ grã tur dɛva buki e li kuše pu la
6 trway ɛm fwa. e buki arɛtɛ so wagõ e li di: sa fɛ trwa lapẽ-ye ki muri. m alɛ
7 šarše ye. l,arɛtɛ so wagõ e li dẽsɔn pu kuri šarše prɛmye lapẽ li wa me lɛ
8 trwa lapẽ s ɛtɛ l mɛm kõpɛr lapẽ. kã buki parti, lapẽ ratrɛ da wagõ
9 kuškuš-la. buki pa truvɛ lapẽ-yɛ. li rɛvini, li pa truvɛ so wagõ kuškuš. kõpɛr
10 lap prõn wagõ kuškuš e li parti še li./

French Orthography

Lapin fait le tour devant Bouki, lui coucher au bord chemin. Bouki dit: ga un lapin, mais lui mouri. Bouki passer, après lui passer, Lapin lever. Lui fait un grand tour et lui coucher au bord chemin encore. Bouki te croire se un autre lapin. Bouki dit: "ça fait deux lapin qui mort" et la lui dit: "si moi serait

ramaser deux lapin-ye, moi serait fait cuit ye pour manger avec moi couscous.
Mais lui continuer. Après lui passer, Lapin lever et lui fait un grand tour devant
Bouki et lui coucher pour la troisième fois, et Bouki arrêter son wagon et lui
dit: "ça fait trois lapin-ye qui mouri. Moi aller chercher ye." Lui arrêter son
wagon et lui descend pour courrir chercher premier lapin lui voir mais le trois
lapin c'étais le même Compère Lapin. Quand Bouki parti, Lapin rentrer dans
wagon couscous-la. Bouki pas trouver lapin-ye. Lui revenir, lui pas trouver son
wagon couscous. Compère Lapin prend wagon couscous et lui parti chez lui.

Translation

Rabbit ran around in front of Bouki: he lay down by the side of the road.
Bouki said: there's a rabbit, but he's dead. Bouki went by. After he went by,
Rabbit got up, he ran around again, and he lay down by the side of the road
again. Bouki believed that it was another rabbit. Bouki said: that makes two
rabbits who are dead. And then he said: if I had picked up two rabbits, I would
have cooked them to eat with my couscous. But he went on. After he had
passed, Rabbit got up and went around in front of Bouki and lay down for the
third time, and Bouki stopped his wagon and said: that makes three rabbits
who are dead. I'll go look for them. He stopped his wagon and he went down
to run and look for the first rabbit he saw, but the three rabbits were the same
Friend Rabbit. When Bouki left, Rabbit went into the couscous wagon. Bouki
didn't find the rabbits. He returned, he didn't find his couscous wagon. Friend
Rabbit took the couscous wagon and went back to his house.

In this passage, note that the verbs are usually not conjugated in any way, but
/tɛ/ is used to express completed action in line 3, and /srɛ/ to express the
conditional in line 4. Also, in line 1, the adverb /muri/, "dead," occurs with no
verb "to be": this is typical of French creoles. The pronouns are not marked for
case: /mo/ or /m/ is always used for the first person singular, and /li/ for the third
person singular. /sɛ/, a relative of the embedded sentence-marker se referred to in
the section on Gullah, occurs in line 3. /yɛ/ occurs as a plural definite article after
/lapẽ/ in lines 4 and 9, and /la/ as a singular definite article marker after /wagɔ̃
kuškuš/ in line 9. Notice also that, except for this use of /la/ and /yɛ/, the
singular and plural are not distinguished.

The future of Louisiana Creole, like that of Gullah, probably holds increased
loss of prestige and speakers to some variety of Standard English. However, also
like Gullah, this is by no means certain and depends primarily on the attitude of
its speakers toward this language.

Hawaiian Pidgin and Creole English

The language situation in Hawaii is immensely complicated because of the extent
and diversity of immigration. At present, according to Reinecke et al. (1975, pp.
593-594) nearly the entire population speaks English as a first or second language,
but Ilocano, Cebuano (Philippine languages), Cantonese, Hakku (Chinese lan-

guages), Japanese, Spanish, Korean, Samoan, and Hawaiian are also spoken. Also according to Reinecke et al., about half the population speaks some variety of pidgin English.

Pidgin in Hawaii exists in many forms. Much of the variation can be ascribed to the differing ethnic backgrounds of immigrant speakers: native speakers of Japanese speak Pidgin quite differently from native speakers of Ilocano, for example. Thus "Japanese Pidgin English" is Pidgin as spoken by a native speaker of Japanese, and so on. Hawaiian Pidgin English, however, generally refers to any form of Pidgin English spoken in Hawaii. There also exists a considerable community which speaks a creolized form of Hawaiian Pidgin. This group is composed primarily of the children of couples from different ethnic groups who intermarried, but it also contains a large number of young people who never learned their parents' language or who learned it imperfectly. The Creole has rules of its own: some of them derived from the various pidgins, and others, perhaps the majority, created by the creole-forming generation. In addition, strong influence from Standard English has caused rapid decreolization, with the result that a whole range of dialects exists between Creole and each of the dialects of Pidgin on the one hand and Standard English on the other. The entire situation may be roughly represented as shown in the figure below, where the lines between circles represent pidgin and creole continua. It is likely that a speaker would be able to control several steps on the continuum that connects his or her variety of pidgin or creole with Standard English. However, according to Bickerton and Odo (1976, p. 21), many or most do not speak the variety farthest from Standard English; nearly everyone's speech is decreolized to some extent.

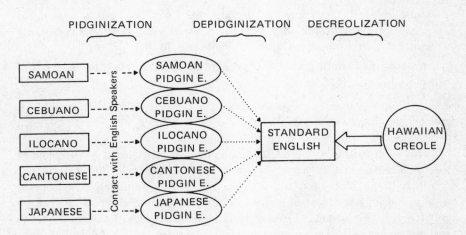

Because of this diversity, it is particularly difficult to make any definitive statements about the structure of Hawaiian Pidgin and Creole English. However, there are some general tendencies in the pidgin varieties described by Bickerton and Odo (pp. 222-244). First, the plural is usually not marked in any way.

Second, the definite article *the* is usually lacking, and the indefinite article *a* is sometimes replaced by *wan*. Third, the negative is invariably expressed by *no* placed before the verb. All these generalizations are illustrated in a few short passages from Bickerton and Odo in phonemic notation:

/kawpe preis tu mač hai, ei? æn wan paun, dæs fo paun seven sents, si./ The price of coffee was very high, eh? And then a pound, that was 7 cents for a pound, see. (Japanese-derived, p. 227)

/yu no go hom pilipin ailen?/ Didn't you go home to the Philippine Islands? (Philippine-derived, p. 236)

/no mœa wan olseim yu./ There is no one like you. (Philippine-derived, p. 236)

The following passage from Reinecke, cited in English orthography by Labov (1971, p. 20b), illustrates some other characteristics of Hawaiian Pidgin:

I no can read, so I take da letta to my friend and my friend he read it to me. One time, da letta, he speak for me come Honolulu. I come Honolulu wid wan friend. Dis fust time I see boat and I li-li [little] scared da water. But I no sick was day. Maybe because I too happy.

Note the absence of tense marking and the use of *for* to express intention.

Hawaiian Creole is spoken principally by young people, and it too exists in a variety of dialects. All the samples of Creole available at present show evidence of a considerable degree of decreolization. A few passages from Labov (1971) illustrate some of its characteristics:

Because, da kine. You know the coconut tree? I wen go climb up when I was one baby. I wen go climb all a way up, an' I wen go *chop* [chopping motion] the coconut, an' I missed, an' I wen go right down in the mud. (p. 48)

Then—soon pau [finish] school. I jus' wen' down to the park, for fight . . . So he never like. . . . (p. 55)

Note the use of *wen* and *wen go* to express the past tense in the affirmative and *never* in the negative, the continuing use of *one* for *a*, the word *pau* from Hawaiian, and the presence of *for* to indicate intent.

Teachers in Hawaii will probably encounter different levels of decreolized Hawaiian Creole, with the varieties farthest from English most likely on islands other than Oahu (Bickerton and Odo, p. 23). They are unlikely to encounter Hawaiian Pidgin, since most of its speakers are older people whose children either never learned their parents' language or at least encountered English very early. (The average age of Bickerton and Odo's informants for Hawaiian Pidgin was 62.)

The present language situation in Hawaii would seem to predict a continuation of the decreolization process, with the result that some variety of Standard English would predominate. This is due partly to the strength of Standard English in the area because of Hawaii's status as a state and partly to the slowing of immigration by speakers of other languages. A number of possible changes could reverse this trend. These would include a change in the immigration policy, a cessation of efforts to "Americanize" Hawaii, or a development of nationalistic consciousness which would encourage rather than stigmatize the use of creole.

Black English

Rather than outlining the complete structure of Black English, this section will document some of the evidence for the hypothesis that Black English originated as a creole, closely related to the Caribbean English creoles, and that this accounts for some of the features that differ from other dialects of English.

Prior to the 1960s, most researchers concerned with Black English believed that it derived its special characteristics from a wide variety of nonstandard British dialects. This conclusion was possible because in most respects Black English is similar to other dialects, particularly Southern. Investigators were motivated to emphasize these similarities in reaction against earlier popular notions that advanced racist explanations for the development of Black English. However, in the 1960s a combination of factors made it possible to reexamine theories of the origin of Black English. One factor was increased familiarity with Lorenzo Turner's book *Africanisms in the Gullah Dialect* (discussed in the section on Gullah). Another was a new political/cultural climate which permitted investigation into the unique characteristics of the Black community in America.

According to the creole theory of the origin of Black English, a form of African English Creole similar to Jamaican Creole or Gullah was spoken in this country by the slaves brought from Africa and their descendants. The process of decreolization was quite rapid because of the relatively small size of the Black population in most parts of the United States; so Black English came to resemble other forms of English in most respects. However, enough traces of its ancestry remain in the structure of Black English to enable the investigator to establish its creole (and therefore African) ancestry. Some of the evidence is summarized by Bailey (1965, reprinted 1971), Dillard (1972), and Bickerton (1975), and includes:

a. Absence of copula in sentences like:
Chester my best friend.
She real skinny. (Dillard, p. 41)
The Caribbean creoles and most West African languages have no copula between subjects and adjectives. Compare, for example:
Jamaican: /mi taiad/ "I am tired"; / di tiicha sari/ "the teacher is sorry"
Haitian: /mwẽ malad/ "I am sick"
Yoruba: /ʔyẹ́n burú/ "that is bad" (literally "that bad") (Bamgboṣe, 1966, p. 127)

b. The aspect markers *be* (habitual or iterative) and *done* (completive or perfective). *Be* indicates that an activity is performed regularly, over and over, and *done* that an action has been completed. These have no exact counterparts in Standard English. West Indian creoles and West African languages, however, do have comparable forms. Some examples of habitual *be* in Black English are:

He be waitin for me every night.

in contrast to:

He waitin for me right now.

Be could not be used in the above sentence, as the following ungrammatical example shows:

*He be waitin for me right now. (Dillard, p. 45)

Completive *done* is used in such sentences as:

I done go. (Dillard, p. 47)

Many Caribbean creoles have *done* as a marker of perfective aspect. Habitual aspect is usually indicated by *a* or *e* or *de* in the Caribbean. In Guyanese, for example, the habitual and continuous aspects are marked with *a*, and the completive with *done* (pronounced /don/). Also, in some dialects, the form *does be* exists, indicating a possible source for Black English *be*. Some examples:

/evri de mi a ron raisfiil/ Every day I run to the ricefield. (Bickerton, 1975, p. 34)

/we yu a go wid bondl?/ Where are you going with that bundle? (Bickerton, 1975, p. 34)

The sun does be hot some days, you know. (Bickerton, 1975, p. 119)

/wen mi kuk don, mi a hosl fiid op mi pikni/ When I've finished cooking, I hurry and feed my child. (Bickerton, 1975, p. 40)

/we dem don plau, dem čip/ When they finish ploughing, they harrow. (Bickerton, 1975, p. 40)

In most West African languages as well, the aspect categories of habitual and perfective are always marked on the verb. Consider these examples from Yoruba, where the habitual is usually with *a* or *a máa* and the perfective with *ti:*

/wɔn a máalọ/ They usually go

/èmí ti rá. lùfáá/ I have seen a priest (Bamgbose, 1966, pp. 69-71)

c. Negative concord. In Black English, a negative sentence has a negative marker in every possible position. For example:

I ain't paying that kind of bread for no iron.

I ain't afraid of nothing. (Bailey, 1965, p. 48)

Sentences like this are similar to Caribbean sentences, such as the following:

Jamaican: /non a di pikini-dem neba si notn/ None of the children never saw nothing. (Bailey, 1966, p. 92)

Guyanese: No, no potato never sell in British Guiana for cent a pound, never yet at no time. (Bickerton, 1975, p. 71)

There is still considerable controversy about the creole hypothesis for Black English. Labov (1969) claims that the absence of copula is a special consequence of a phonological rule in Black English that deletes the /s/ of contracted *is* in many circumstances. McDavid and McDavid (1971) argue that some features said to be creole in origin can be explained by reference to other southern dialects. However, the weight of the evidence seems to be clearly on the side of a creole origin for at least some features of Black English.

Spanish-English Mixing

Another language situation that ought to be considered here is the mutual influence of Spanish and English in Chicano communities. In the Southwest states, primarily California, Arizona, New Mexico, Colorado, and Texas, where both languages have been in use for a long time, they have become mixed by borrowing to a considerable degree. The borrowing has been primarily from English into Spanish in recent times because of the political dominance of Anglo culture in the area.

Speech in many Chicano areas is characterized by a high incidence of bilingualism, and as a result it is common for people to switch between English and Spanish, even in the middle of a sentence. Lance (1975) gives many examples from Texas bilinguals. The following sentences were spoken by Rachel, a twelve-year-old girl:

> they (the lions) were very nice to him and all and then ... he ... él vino [he came] ... a nice man and todo ese [all that], and ... y pues los quitaron, él ... él ... he ... él [and then he left them ... he] became on good con [with] Jesus y todo eso [and all that]. (Lance, p. 151. The ellipses represent pauses, not deleted material.)

The explanation for the extremely high frequency of switching and false starts in this passage is that Rachel was instructed to speak in Spanish to an Anglo interviewer who spoke little Spanish and she probably felt uncomfortable with the task.

Language of this kind has a great deal in common with a creole, in the sense that Rachel's speech in the example cited above cannot be clearly assigned to either English or Spanish. Nevertheless, it is not actually a creole, since Rachel and the other bilinguals are able to speak entirely in English or entirely in Spanish under appropriate circumstances with only minimal interference from the other language. Their Spanish is characterized by a large number of loan words from English, but it is clearly Spanish, since it maintains the verb conjugations, personal pronouns, genders, and other grammatical categories that characterize Spanish. Similarly, English is classified as a Germanic language and not as a creole despite the large number of French loans that entered the language after the Norman Conquest in 1066.

A type of Spanish-English creole could develop out of this language-mixing situation, but that would probably occur only if these bilinguals and their descendants lost contact with both the Spanish and English communities. Such a development seems sociologically unlikely at the present time.

Conclusion

In addition to the languages discussed here, a number of other pidgin and creole languages are in use in the United States. Some of these are spoken by immigrant groups, most notably from the West Indies. Others are doubtful as cases of creolization like Pennsylvania German. There may also be some Amerindian pidgins still in existence; at one time, many were used. All the pidgins and creoles, however, seem to be on their way to extinction at the present time. Hopefully, this trend will reverse itself: language diversity is an important part of the cultural wealth of a nation, and we should try to preserve it.

NOTES

1. Dreyfuss uses the symbol / ~/ over vowels to indicate nasalization. [Eds.]
2. The phonemes /ü/, /ȫ/, and /ö/ represent high, mid, and low front rounded vowels, respectively. [Eds.]

References

Bailey, Beryl, 1966   *Jamaican Creole Syntax*, The University Press, Cambridge. A technical grammar.

———, 1971   "Toward a New Perspective in Negro English Dialectology," in Wolfram and Clarke, 1971. Compares aspects of Creole and Black English grammars. Not too technical.

Bamgboṣe, Ayọ, 1966   *A Grammar of Yoruba*, The University Press, Cambridge. A technical grammar.

Bickerton, Derek, 1975   *Dynamics of a Creole System*, The University Press, Cambridge. Presentation and discussion of data from Guyanese Creole. Fairly technical.

——— and Carol Odo, 1976   *Change and Variation in Hawaiian English*, vol. I, Social Sciences and Linguistics Institute, University of Hawaii, Honolulu. The first of three volumes on language in Hawaii. Fairly technical.

Comhaire-Sylvain, Suzanne, 1938   "Creole Folk-Tales from Haiti," *Journal of the American Folk-Lore Society*, vol. 51, pp. 219-356. Stories in Haitian with English translations.

Dillard, J.L., 1972   *Black English*, Random House, New York. A good general summary of the history and structure of Black English. Not too technical.

Hancock, Ian, 1971   "A Map and List of Pidgin and Creole Languages," in Hymes, 1971, pp. 509-524. Just what the title says.

Heine, Bernd, 1970   *Status and Use of African Lingua Francas*, Weltforum Verlag, Munich. A census and brief discussion of many African languages.

Hernández-Chavez, Eduardo, Andrew Cohen, and Anthony Beltrano, 1975   *El Lengua de los Chicanos*, Center for Applied Linguistics, Washington, D.C. A collection of articles on Chicano speech, of varying technicality, in Spanish and English.

Hymes, Dell, ed., 1971   *Pidginization and Creolization of Languages*, The University Press, Cambridge. Mostly specialized articles, but many, particularly the introductions to each section, are not technical.

Jackson, Patricia, forthcoming University of Michigan dissertation, possible title: *The Status of Gullah: Creole or English Dialect.*

Labov, William, 1969 "Contraction, Deletion, and Inherent Variability of the English Copula," *Language*, vol. 45, pp. 715-762. Fairly technical sociolinguistic article.

———, 1971 "On the Adequacy of Natural Languages I: Tense." Unpublished but much circulated manuscript.

Lance, Donald M., 1975 "Spanish-English Code-Mixing," in Hernández-Chavez et al., 1975, pp. 138-153.

Lane, George S., 1935 "Notes on Louisiana French," *Language*, vol. 11, pp. 5-16. A brief discussion of some of the characteristics of Louisiana French.

Laycock, Don, 1970 *Materials in New Guinea Pidgin*, The Australian National University, Canberra. A good general grammar including several texts.

McDavid, Raven, and Virginia McDavid, 1971 "The Relationship of the Speech of American Negroes to the Speech of Whites," in Wolfram and Clarke, 1971, pp. 16-40.

Morgan, Raleigh, Jr., 1960 "Structural Sketch of Saint Martin Creole," *Anthropological Linguistics*, vol. 2, no. 1, pp. 7-29. A good short description, not too highly technical.

———, 1970 "Dialect Leveling in the Non-English Speech of Southwest Louisiana," in Glenn Gilbert, ed., *Texas Studies in Bilingualism*, 1970, pp. 50-62, de Gruyter, Berlin. A discussion of how the different varieties of French in Louisiana have become mixed.

———, 1975 "Playing Dead Thrice: Louisiana Creole Animal Tale," *Revue de Louisiane*, vol. 4, pp. 23-32. A good discussion of various aspects of the story, part of which appears in this chapter.

Reinecke, John E., Stanley M. Tsuzaki, David DeCamp, Ian Hancock, and Richard Wood, 1975 *A Bibliography of Pidgin and Creole Languages*, The University Press of Hawaii, Honolulu. The best general bibliography. Also provides a brief history and sociological description of the languages considered.

Turner, Lorenzo, 1949 *Africanisms in the Gullah Dialect*, University of Michigan Press, Ann Arbor. An excellent description of Gullah plus a careful documentation of its African heritage. Not too technical.

Vintilă-Rădulescu, Ioana, 1976 *Le Creole Français*, Mouton, The Hague. Not too technical description of French creoles in French.

Whinnom, Keith, 1965 "The Origin and Spread of the European-Based Pidgins and Creoles," *Orbis*, vol. 14, pp. 509-527.

Wolfram, Walt, and Nona Clarke, eds., 1971 *Black-White Speech Relationships*, Center for Applied Linguistics, Washington, D.C. Many interesting articles, some not technical.

BLACK ENGLISH VERNACULAR:
A COMPARATIVE DESCRIPTION

Margaret A. Lourie

Black Americans, who make up 11 percent of the U.S. population, comprise this country's largest minority group by far. Yet it has only been within the last decade that Black language and culture, along with their African roots, have received serious scholarly attention. One result of this belated attention is that we now have quite sophisticated sociolinguistic descriptions of Black English Vernacular (BEV). Yet we still do not fully understand the connections between this variety and other related varieties of American English. In the article below, Margaret A. Lourie summarizes the phonological and grammatical features that recent sociolinguistic studies attribute to BEV and also suggests its possible connections with other dialects. Her discussion of BEV features assumes familiarity with the concepts and sound tables in "The Structure of Language" section of the General Introduction. See Appendix H for a BEV text which exhibits many of the features mentioned here.

Readers should consult the Dreyfuss article for more information on the creole origins of BEV. And the selections by Kochman and Cooke extend the description of BEV into the areas of speech acts and nonverbal communication. A thorough comprehension of this series of articles should help readers evaluate the range of educational alternatives proposed for BEV speakers by Burling, the CCCC, Baxter, and Stewart in Part III of this collection.

The recent "back-to-basics" movement in American education urges that teachers must take immediate and serious action to reverse the marked decline in their students' reading and writing skills. In concomitant developments, educators are renewing their insistence that all students acquire the language of mainstream American society, called Standard English (SE), and are relying more extensively on standardized tests, which are often biased against nonmainstream language and culture, to measure reading and writing ability. Since 1974, for instance, the Scholastic Aptitude Test has included a Written Test of Standard English. Similarly, in June 1977, school systems in Chicago; Denver; Jacksonville, Florida; and elsewhere used standardized test results to determine which students to promote. In such an educational climate it is crucial that educators understand as much as possible about the nonmainstream language varieties their students bring to the classroom so that they can intelligently reevaluate how or whether to teach reading, writing, or speaking Standard English.

Sociolinguistic research, which in the last decade has largely focused on the nonmainstream language of Black Americans, leads to two conclusions that illuminate the issue of teaching Standard English to Blacks but that, unfortunately, fail to resolve it. The first conclusion has to do with the nature of the English spoken by many Black Americans, a variety which is at its purest and most consistent in the casual speech of Black youths who participate fully in their vernacular culture and which is therefore called Black English Vernacular (BEV). What linguists have concluded about BEV is that it has a great wealth of verbal rituals and resources, that it is entirely logical and systematic in its structure, that it is wholly adequate to express the most complicated abstractions. The stigma that attaches to BEV continues to be a sensitive indicator of American racism, but there is no sense in which this or any other nonmainstream variety is inherently inferior to SE.

Virtually every sociolinguist, then, agrees that Black students do not need to learn SE in order to express themselves fully or think clearly. Nor do speakers of BEV have any trouble understanding SE speakers or being understood by them. In addition, many linguists would argue that reading and writing problems among Black students owe far more to cultural conflicts between the values of the school and the values of the street than they do to language conflicts between BEV and SE. Based on findings like these, educators might readily conclude that they can best prepare their students to function as useful and literate members of American society by letting them retain their own language unless they explicitly ask to learn SE. In fact, the National Council of Teachers of English encourages just such an approach in its recent publication *Students' Right to Their Own Language* (NCTE, 1974).

But another conclusion drawn by sociolinguists militates against any such simple resolution to the problem of teaching SE in the schools. Linguists and psychologists who examine language attitudes agree that most Americans, whether Black or White, teacher or layman, respond more positively to SE speakers than to BEV speakers. One study, for example, found that, based only on short taped speech samples, both Black and White college students attributed more success and friendliness to SE speakers than to Black or White speakers of other varieties of American English (Tucker and Lambert, 1969). In short, speakers of BEV are at an automatic social disadvantage in mainstream American society. Educators must weigh this evidence of a deeply ingrained American prejudice against nonmainstream dialects in any decision they make about the teaching of SE.

If linguists cannot settle all the educational questions concerning the teaching of SE to speakers of BEV, they can nevertheless render valuable service to educators by describing in detail what this important minority dialect is like and how it differs from related varieties of English. Teachers can use such a description for at least four purposes: (1) to judge for themselves how different BEV is from SE and, hence, how necessary or difficult it might be to teach SE to BEV speakers; (2) to pinpoint which specific phonological and grammatical features of BEV are likely to pose the greatest obstacles to learning SE; (3) to distinguish whether a student's reading and/or writing problems should be ascribed to simple dialect interference or to more fundamental conceptual difficulties; and (4) to gain insight into and respect for the linguistic heritage of their Black students.

The Relationship of BEV to Other Varieties   Because the connections among BEV and other related varieties of American English are complicated and not entirely understood, they require a summary discussion before they can be itemized under the individual features of BEV. Basically, there are three varieties of American English that bear importantly on the structure of BEV: Standard English, Southern White English (SWE), and Gullah or Sea-Island Creole. Among the three, all the major features of BEV can be accounted for. But, as will be seen in the description below, these varieties sometimes seem to provide competing sources and explanations for the same feature of BEV. At this point in linguistic research, it is impossible to eliminate any of the possible sources confidently. One can only propose that the convergence of two or more sources on a single BEV feature may simply have reinforced its occurrence.

Standard English resembles far more than it differs from BEV and functions as a target language for many Black Americans. This means that in formal speaking styles almost all Blacks approximate SE forms even if their casual speaking styles exhibit predominantly BEV features, and Blacks who have assimilated to the dominant culture may speak SE exclusively. It also means, in general, that the more Black Americans are integrated into mainstream society, the more their language resembles SE. On this analysis, BEV seems to be gradually growing more like SE. On another analysis, however, SE may be growing more like BEV, since BEV often seems to extend or generalize changes that occur more slowly in SE. For example, all speakers of American English tend in casual conversation to convert /ɪŋ/ to /ɪn/ in words like *running* (often called "dropping the *g*"). But speakers of BEV make this conversion more frequently than SE speakers even though they usually join SE speakers in shifting to /ɪŋ/ in formal contexts. The description that follows calls attention to the many other features of BEV that can likewise be analyzed as extensions of SE rules.

Southern White English also bears a close but vexed relationship to BEV, as any Northerner who has mistaken a Southern White for a Black on the telephone can testify. Almost every feature of BEV except parts of the verb system has also been attested—though often at different frequency levels—in SWE. But linguists advance opposing explanations for this similarity. Some maintain that the various West African languages brought by slaves were all but obliterated in this country and were simply replaced by the largely Scottish and Irish English of plantation overseers, perhaps with a few surviving African words (McDavid and McDavid, 1951). According to this theory, slaves acquired the language of their masters, and any subsequent divergences are a product of the social distance between Black and White speech communities.

Yet, other linguists argue that Blacks have always had their own distinctive brand of English (see next paragraph) which, furthermore, influenced the language of their Southern white masters (Stewart, 1969; Dillard, 1972). There is, at least, lexical evidence that the language of Black Americans has influenced the speech of White Americans more than Whites have often wished to admit. Besides a number of indisputable vocabulary borrowings from African languages (*cola, okra, yam, banana*), the speech of White Americans contains such basic items as *okay, uh-uh,* and *uh-huh,* which may also have West African origins. Moreover, slang seems to travel quickly from the Black to the White community, as witness many jazz terms early in this century as well as more recent usages like *foxy* and *laid back.* It is not unreasonable, then, to theorize that Blacks may also have influenced the phonology and grammar of SWE. A middle position between these two theories of influence posits mutual influence between BEV and SWE. Whatever their explanation, the similarities between these two varieties are itemized in the description below.

Gullah, the third related variety of American English, is spoken by Blacks on the Sea Islands off the coast of Georgia and South Carolina. Like Jamaican Creole, it combines features of English and West African languages and is considered by some linguists to be an isolated survival of what was once the general language of Black Americans. According to the creole hypothesis, BEV began as a creole language, a variety that diverged in fundamental ways from SE, and its history is a process of *decreolization,* or gradual assimilation to the Standard. Thus creolists maintain that superficial similarities between current BEV and SE actually conceal significant underlying differences between the two language systems. Evidence for this theory (cited in the description below) consists of the numerous correspondences between BEV and creoles like Gullah.

Data on BEV have been gathered in urban centers such as New York, Detroit, Washington, D.C., and Los Angeles as well as in several Southern rural settings. Although BEV varies somewhat by region, it displays enough common features to validate the following compendium of the major phonological and grammatical contrasts between BEV and SE.

Phonological Contrasts

Forwarding of Stress   One of the greatest determinants of change in the history of the English language has been the tendency of English speakers for well over 1500 years to shift their pronunciation emphasis toward the first syllable of a word. This tendency especially affects the many vocabulary items English borrows from French. Hence, for example, the French *oránge* becomes the English *órange.* Furthermore, American and British pronunciations of French borrowings often forward stress at different rates and so provide instances of this phenomenon in progress: British stress has already been forwarded in *gárage* (vs. American *garáge*) while Americans have taken the lead in *láboratory* (vs. British *labóratory*). Nor is the forwarding of stress limited to French borrowings. The word *pecan,* borrowed from the Native American language Cree, seems to be currently shifting from *pecán* to *pécan* in the southeastern United States.

With respect to the general tendency to forward stress, BEV, along with many SWE varieties, seems to be in the vanguard. Where SE retains second-syllable stress in words such as *políce, motél, Detróit,* many BEV speakers would say *pólice, mótel, Détroit* instead. Or where a first syllable is unstressed in SE because it functions as a prefix, BEV and some SWE dialects manage to front their stress by omitting the prefix: *'ríthmetic, 'mémber, 'ccépt, 'féssor.*

Weakening of Final Consonants   A further result of the forwarding of stress in English words is a general reduction of articulation after the first stressed vowel. Historically, this reduction has caused the loss of some word-final sounds in SE. For instance, the "silent *e*" in words such as *love, fine, come* was once pronounced like the vowel in *but*, yet is now only preserved in spelling. As an intermediate stage in this process, sounds that are not entirely lost can be reduced by *devoicing*; that is, the voiced stop /d/, pronounced with the vocal cords vibrating, can turn into its voiceless counterpart /t/, pronounced with vocal cords still, as in the frequent SE pronunciation *hundret.*

BEV generalizes this tendency to reduce articulation at the ends of words. All word-final voiced stops—/b/, /d/, and /g/—can become their voiceless counterparts—/p/, /t/, and /k/, respectively—and voiceless stops can sometimes disappear entirely. Consequently, such words as *seed* and *seat* may sound almost identical (except for a slight difference in vowel quality), or both words may sound like *see.* This weakening of final consonants in BEV seems to affect /d/ and /t/ the most often but can sometimes apply to /g/ and /k/ or to /b/ and /p/, producing such potential homophones as *dig=Dick* or *robe=rope=row.* Interestingly, West African Pidgin English, a language related to Gullah, devoices all final stops so that *bad* becomes *bat*, *big* becomes *bik*, etc.—a characteristic that might further explain devoicing in BEV.

To a lesser extent, the nasals /m/, /n/, and /ŋ/ are also subject to weakening in final positions but, as in French, they leave a nasal coloring on the preceding vowel. Thus *rum, run,* and *rung* (but not *rug*) are possible homophones in BEV. A few speakers of BEV have so extended this weakening rule that almost all of their syllables consist only of a consonant-vowel sequence, which, incidentally, is a prevalent syllable pattern in Gullah.

Consonant-Cluster Simplification   The tendency in English to weaken final consonants is particularly strong when a word ends in a *consonant cluster*, a group of two or more consonants. The spelling of *gang, hung,* and *sing* (which for most Americans end in /ŋ/, not /g/; compare *sink*, which ends in /ŋk/) and of *dumb, lamb,* and *comb* make it clear that earlier speakers of English pronounced these words with final consonant clusters that SE speakers have since simplified. A number of additional consonant clusters can be simplified in SE provided that the style of speech is informal and the next word begins with a consonant. In other words, a teacher might say *Leave the res' for your brother!* in informal conversation with her child or in rapid speech but would probably shift to a more formal style to tell her large lecture class *The best four papers received "A"s.* Similarly, in a casual context she would be likely to say *Hilda lef' Friday* where the next word begins with a consonant but *Hilda left on Friday* where the next word begins with a vowel.

Furthermore, consonant clusters in any variety of English can only be simplified if they share voicing—that is, if they are totally voiceless or totally voiced—and if they end in a stop—that is, in /p/, /t/, /d/, or /k/. (Clusters ending in the two other stops /b/ and /g/ were simplified earlier in the history of English, as pointed out above.) According to these rules, then, candidates for simplification include /st/, /sp/, /sk/, /ft/, /pt/, and /kt/ among the voiceless clusters and /nd/ and /ld/ among the voiced clusters but not, for example, /mp/, /lt/, or /lp/, which combine voiced and voiceless consonants.

In BEV the SE rules for consonant-cluster simplification can be extended to environments with a following vowel or pause in addition to environments with a following consonant. Hence a BEV speaker might say *The ris' is great* or *We can take the ris'*. By this rule, some BEV speakers may always simplify consonant clusters and thus exhibit homophones not found in SE: *lass=last, coal=cold, mass=mask,* etc.

By further extension of the consonant-cluster simplification rules of SE, BEV can also simplify clusters ending in /s/ or /z/. In this way, *six* (pronounced "sicks" in SE) may be pronounced like *sick* and *Max* like *Mack*. But in the case of consonant clusters ending in /s/ or /z/, the first member may sometimes be omitted instead of the second, especially when the final /s/ or /z/ sound results from a contraction; hence, *tha's* or *le's*.

Another extension of consonant-cluster simplification allows BEV speakers to change or reduce some word-initial clusters. For example, *street* can become *skreet, threw* can become *th'ew,* or *specific* can be realized as *'pecific*. This kind of reduction is also part of the general history of English; *knight* and *gnat,* as their spellings indicate, were once pronounced with initial consonant clusters.

Strong evidence suggests that this phonological feature can be traced not only to rules generalized from SE but to West African creoles, which rarely display consonant clusters with shared voicing, especially in final positions. Gullah, for instance, has *groun'* for *ground, ol'* for *old, twis'* for *twist* but exhibits consonant clusters with mixed voicing in words like *jump*. Likewise, West African Pidgin English, a precursor of Gullah, has *'trong* for *strong* and *'peech* for *speech*. Siding with the creolists, then, it might be wiser to theorize that, as it decreolizes, BEV has been gradually *adding* consonants where SE requires them rather than generalizing SE rules for deleting them.

"th" Sounds   The voiceless "th" sound of *thin* /θ/ and the voiced "th" of *then* /ð/ do not occur in most of the world's languages, including creoles, and are usually the last sounds learned by new speakers of English. It is not, therefore, surprising that BEV speakers often substitute other sounds for /θ/ and /ð/; nor should it be surprising that the substituted sounds are related to /θ/ and /ð/ in systematic ways. Phonologically, /θ/ and /ð/ are interdental fricatives, differing only slightly in manner and place of articulation from the alveolar stops /t/ and /d/. Hence, especially in word-initial positions, the voiceless fricative /θ/ often becomes the voiceless stop /t/, while the voiced fricative /ð/ often becomes the voiced stop /d/. By this substitution, *thin* can become *tin,* and *then* can become *den* in BEV. The same thing can happen with medial and final "th" so that *aritmetic* and *mont* are possible variants of *arithmetic* and *month*, and *moder* and *wid* sometimes replace *mother* and *with*. As we might expect, /Ө/ also turns to /t/ and /ð/ to /d/ in West African creoles, as well as in white nonstandard varieties which have been influenced by non-native English speech (e.g., Brooklyn dialect).

Alternatively, medial or final /Ө/ in BEV and in some creoles can move its point of articulation slightly forward to become the voiceless labiodental fricative /f/. Resultant pronunciations are *aufor* for *author* and *bof* for *both*. Less frequently, medial or final /ð/ can turn into its voiced labiodental counterpart /v/, as in *brover* for *brother* or *bave* for *bathe*. The systematic nature of these substitutions can be handily summarized on a partial consonant chart:

	Point of articulation		
Manner of articulation	*Labiodental*	*Interdental*	*Alveolar*
Stops			
Voiceless			t
Voiced			d
Fricatives			
Voiceless	f ←	Ө →	
Voiced	v ←	ð →	

/r/ and /l/ Sounds The liquids /r/ and /l/ resemble vowels in that they allow a freer flow of air along the vocal tract than most other consonants do. That is why they can turn into vowel sounds or even merge entirely with a preceding vowel, as they have for many Americans who live in New England, New York, or the coastal South. This process affects the /r/ that occurs after vowels (*postvocalic /r/*) in words like *for, car, guard,* or *fort,* in which the /r/ is absorbed completely by the preceding vowel, and in words like *fear, sore,* or *care,* in which the /r/ is pronounced something like "uh." Even the vestigial "uh" can disappear in BEV and some SWE varieties so that *shore=show* and *stare=stay*.

In BEV and occasionally in SWE this /r/lessness can be further extended to environments where /r/ occurs between two vowel sounds (*intervocalic /r/*). Thus, *Carol=Cal, Paris=pass,* and *Irish=ash*. The same is true for the final /r/ that becomes intervocalic because the following word begins with a vowel. For most white /r/less speakers the final /r/ reappears in this environment, yielding *sister Edna* and *sore arm* even for speakers who would have *sistuh Barbara* and *souh leg*. But in BEV *sistuh Edna* and *souh arm* (or *so arm*) are also possible. (A parallel occurrence in BEV involves the absence of /n/ in the indefinite article *an*. Just as SE *four o'clock* becomes BEV *fo' o'clock*, so SE *an apple* becomes BEV *a apple*. The rules of SE do not allow two such vowel sounds to be pronounced in succession, but the rules of BEV do.)

West African creoles, too, lack postvocalic /r/. Creole /r/lessness could stem either from the /r/lessness of the British dialects with which West Africans first came in contact or from the /r/lessness of some West African languages—or from both. In any case, the /r/lessness of BEV is certain to owe something to this creole feature.

Like /r/, /l/ can be lost preconsonantally, as it has been for all American English speakers in words like *talk, could,* and *half* and for many SWE and BEV speakers in *help* and *wolf.* In addition, BEV can assimilate /l/ to the preceding vowel at the end of a word so that *toll* and *toe, soul* and *sow, all* and *awe* become nearly identical. And in BEV /l/ is never heard before /w/, /r/, or /y/ sounds in words like *always, already, million.* In combination with consonant cluster simplification, /l/lessness can produce such further BEV homophones as *told= toll=toe.*

Vowels Speakers of BEV, along with many SWE speakers, can collapse certain SE vowel contrasts, depending on what consonant follows them:

1. /I/=/ɛ/ before nasals; that is, the vowel sound in words like *pin* is the same as the vowel sound in words like *pen* when the vowel occurs before a nasal: /m/, /n/, or /ŋ/.

2. /i/=/e/ and /u/=/o/ before /r/; that is, the vowel sound in words like *beer* is the same as the vowel sound in words like *bear,* and the vowel sound in words like *lure* is the same as the vowel sound in words like *lore* when the vowel occurs before /r/.

3. /ai/=/au/=/a/; that is, the diphthongs in words like *find* and *found* become the monophthong of words like *fond* so that *find=found=fond,* especially before voiced consonants.

4. /ɔi/=/ɔ/; that is, the diphthong of words like *oil* becomes the monophthong of words like *all,* especially before /l/.

The Problem of Homophones It should be clear from the preceding discussion of BEV phonology that many speakers of this variety have certain homophones where SE speakers make phonological distinctions. Such homophones, however, need not be cause for educational alarm. Speakers of SE also have many homophones: *wright, right,* and *write; too, to,* and *two;* for Midwesterners *merry, marry,* and *Mary;* for Mid-Atlantic and Pacific coast residents *caught* and *cot.* And just as Midwesterners tend to be neither persuaded nor illuminated by the phonological contrasts that their New York friends perceive in *merry, marry,* and *Mary,* Black children are likely only to become needlessly frustrated if their teachers insist on pronunciation distinctions between *bowl* and *bold* or *since* and *sense.* Homophones are almost never confusing in the context of a sentence so need not be phonologically distinguished in order to keep their meanings distinct. In short, children are in no danger of thinking *sow* and *sore* mean the same thing even if they sound the same.

At worst, the greater number of homophones may cause spelling problems for BEV speakers, just as *their* and *there* do for SE speakers. And, as for SE speakers, spelling problems may arise from two other sources as well: (1) spelling words as they are pronounced, which can produce *lass* for *last* or *po* for *poor* in BEV; *lim* for *limb* or *wak* for *walk* in SE; (2) *hypercorrecting,* which means generalizing an

SE rule to cases where it does not apply; e.g., *speciment* for *specimen* or *lorn* for *lawn* in BEV; *owne* for *own* or *humb* for *hum* in SE. But spelling in English so little resembles anyone's pronunciation that the phonological system of BEV is hardly an extra handicap. Most linguists agree that BEV speakers need not change their phonology in order to read and write.

Grammatical Contrasts

Nouns and Pronouns   In SE nouns are inflected only for plural and possessive. Most BEV speakers follow SE rules for pluralization with a few exceptions:

1. Like many SWE speakers, BEV speakers often omit plural suffixes from nouns of measure, producing phrases like *thirty bushel of wheat* or *forty year ago*.

2. Where SE has irregular plurals, BEV and other nonmainstream dialects sometimes regularize them (e.g., *foots*) and sometimes mark them redundantly (e.g., *mens*).

3. In cases where consonant-cluster simplification produces nouns ending with /s/ or /z/ sounds, BEV can apply the SE rule for pluralizing nouns that end in /s/ or /z/. Hence, on the model of SE *dresses*, the BEV plurals could be *desses* for *desks*, *wasses* for *wasps*, and *tesses* for *tests*.

Very young speakers of BEV occasionally exhibit no plural noun inflections, just as there are none in most creoles, but the concept of plurality is clearly marked by contextual cues such as numeral modifiers.

Because creoles indicate possession by noun position rather than by inflection (e.g., *William mother*), BEV varies between inflected and uninflected possessives (*Jan dress* alternates with *Jan's dress*). Uninflected possessives are most common in second person and third person plural pronouns (e.g., *you house, they house*). Since the SE possessives for *you* and *they* both end in /r/, it seems likely that absence of postvocalic /r/ in BEV phonology has reinforced this grammatical feature.

In addition to the frequently uninflected possessive pronouns *you* for *your* and *they* for *their*, a few BEV speakers—mainly young children in the South—distinguish person and number but use one case, either subjective or objective, throughout the personal pronoun system and one gender in the third person singular. Such undifferentiated pronouns, inherited from creoles, result in constructions like these: *Me got juice* or *He a nice girl*. But for most BEV speakers all personal pronouns except possessive *you* and *they* are inflected according to SE rules.

The Verb System

Some of the most important and subtlest differences between BEV and SE involve the verb system, which thus requires detailed consideration.

Auxiliaries and Copulas In SE auxiliary verbs precede the main verb of a sentence, and a number of them can be contracted, giving *'ve* for *have*, *'s* for *has* or *is*, *'ll* for *will*, *'d* for *would* or *had*, *'m* for *am*, and *'re* for *are*. Sentences like these result: *You've barely begun your planting. Mary'll sell you some seeds. We're already weeding our vegetables.* The SE contraction rule cannot, however, operate when these auxiliaries occur at the end of a clause. Thus *Jennifer'd go if you would* cannot be further contracted to **Jennifer'd go if you'd.*

By an extension of the SE rule, auxiliaries that can be optionally contracted in SE can be optionally deleted in BEV, with the exception of *am*, which can be contracted but not deleted. By BEV rules, then, the example sentences in the preceding paragraph could become: *You barely begun you(r) planting. Mary sell you some seeds. We already weeding our vegetables.* But **Jennifer go if you would* would not occur in BEV. The phonological rules for absence of /r/ and /l/ favor the grammatical rule for deleting *'re* and *'ll* particularly. In fact, *are* is deleted more frequently than any of the other contracted auxiliaries both in BEV and in SWE.

Deletion of *'ll* might seem to endanger the existence of the future tense in BEV. Yet this dialect makes frequent use of the full form *will* and sometimes has the contracted form too. After all, auxiliary deletion is only a stylistic option in BEV, just as contraction is in SE. Furthermore, a very common alternative for expressing the future in BEV, as in other varieties, is some reduced form of *going to*, almost always with initial *are* or *is* deleted. In both BEV and SWE *going to* with *I* can be reduced to *I'ngna, I'mana, I'maw* or *I'ma* and elsewhere to *gonna, 'on,* or *gwin.*

The copula *to be* occurs in such sentences as *You are a nurse, She is real smart,* and *I am out of those.* As with auxiliaries, the copulas *is* and *are* (but not *am*) can be optionally deleted in BEV wherever they can be contracted in SE, yielding *You a nurse, She real smart,* but *I'm out of those.* And, as with auxiliaries, the phonological rule for /r/lessness favors deletion of *are* (also common in SWE) over the deletion of *is* (mainly confined to BEV). In the past tense the copula is not deleted but is regularized to *was* throughout the paradigm; hence, *they was, we wasn't.*

Optional absence of the present tense copula in BEV quite probably goes back to its variable absence in West African languages (as in numerous other world languages like Russian and Arabic) and in West African creoles. Consequently, it might be more historically accurate to describe this feature of BEV not as "copula deletion" but as optional "copula insertion" resulting from the decreolization process.

Tense The only inflected tenses in SE are the present, which typically carries an *-s* in third person singular, and the past, which typically shows an *-ed* suffix. BEV contrasts with SE in its use of inflections for both these tenses.

In the present tense, BEV almost obligatorily omits *-s* from the third person singular. Although English teachers have traditionally attributed this omission to negligence, linguists perceive this feature as eminently logical. They point out that

English verbs used to be inflected throughout the present tense (as archaisms like *thou hast* and *she cometh* remind us), but only the third person singular *-s* remains in SE. Speakers of BEV have simply taken the next logical step in the present tense paradigm by eliminating the last remaining inflection. For the same reason, they also use *have* and *do* throughout the present tense paradigm, which results in the famous stigmatized form *he don't*. SWE has this regularized present tense pattern to some extent, especially in *he don't*, but it seems much more prevalent in BEV. It may also be relevant that creoles often lack present tense inflections, probably because in creoles unmarked tense is assumed to be present.

The almost obligatory absence in BEV of this *-s* suffix makes it particularly difficult for BEV speakers to learn. One result of their attempts to learn this SE feature can be hypercorrection or adding the *-s* suffix to present tense verbs where it does not belong: *we walks, you thinks*. These constructions should not, however, be construed as evidence of yet another dialect or lack of any consistent rule in BEV. The inconsistency merely results from attempts to learn the SE rule.

Just as creoles tend to acquire past tense markers before they acquire present tense markers, so the past tense in BEV, unlike the present, seems to be definitely inflected. Yet its inflections are somewhat complicated by phonological rules. The simplification of consonant clusters with shared voicing can in BEV even more than in SE eliminate the past tense markers in verbs like *roped* (/ropt/ becomes /rop/) and *rolled* (/rold/ becomes /rol/). And the rules for weakening of final consonants can sometimes remove the inflection from such verbs as *rowed* (/rod/ becomes /ro/). (See the discussion of consonant-cluster simplification and weakening of final consonants in the section on Phonological Contrasts above.) In spite of these serious phonological assaults on the past tense marker, it still seems that such an inflection is well established in BEV. For one thing, verb stems that end in /t/ or /d/ acquire a whole extra syllable in the past tense (*coated, eroded*), and these past tense syllables are rarely absent in BEV. Second, in BEV the irregular past tense verbs *left, kept*, etc., almost always appear as *lef', kep'*, etc., in past tense contexts, not as *leave, keep*, etc. Apparently, then, BEV speakers understand the significance of the past inflection and therefore need not be taught to pronounce it in every phonological environment.

Aspect   Aspect is that part of the verb system which specifies the duration or completion of the action. Although SE has a relatively weak aspect system, it does distinguish completed action in the perfective (*Molly has/had arrived*) and continuing action in the progressive (*Molly is/was arriving*). By contrast, West African languages and the creoles that descend from them have highly elaborated aspect systems instead of highly developed tense systems. It is in its sophisticated aspect system (and, some linguists argue, in its weak tense system) that BEV shows its strongest ties to Gullah and other creoles. And it may also be here that BEV differs most profoundly from SE.

Linguists still do not fully comprehend the aspect system of BEV—partly because of its complexity and partly because it has been fragmented by contact with SE. Most agree, however, that BEV has the progressive and perfect aspects of

SE, even though the related auxiliaries can be deleted. In addition, BEV speakers, like Gullah speakers, use a habitual aspect, which is often called "invariant *be*" because it is never conjugated. Invariant *be* refers to intermittent or habitual action as opposed to continuous or momentary action. Thus it often occurs in constructions with adverbs like *sometimes* or *every day: Sometimes she be happy, Lenore be working every day,* or the negative *You don't be here much.* But it cannot occur in contexts where the action is either continuous or momentary, so that **She be my mother* and **Kathy be going right now* are not possible usages. Invariant *be* should not, incidentally, be confused with such constructions as *She be here tomorrow* or *She be here if she could,* which result from simply deleting the auxiliaries *will* and *would* and are therefore much closer to SE.

To the *have/had* perfective of SE, BEV adds two other markers for perfective: the completive *done* and the remote time *been. Done* can apparently apply to actions just completed (thus overlapping somewhat with perfective *have*) but sometimes seems just to serve as an emphatic marker, as in *I done forgot my hat!* Completive *done,* which has been assimilated to SE grammar and occurs regularly in SWE, usually takes a past form of the verb, perhaps on analogy with *have* and *had: I done told you already.* But *done* with unmarked verb forms, common in creoles, is occasionally possible in BEV: *She done go. Been,* on the other hand, seems to imply action begun long ago and continuing in the present, as in *I been had it a long time.* The remote time *been* seems to occur most often with unmarked verb forms, as in *I been know that,* probably because it is closer to its creole origins than is *done.*

An inventory of the BEV aspect system, then, would include these forms, with optional items in parentheses:

Progressive:	she (is) working
Habitual:	she be working
Perfective:	she (have/had) worked
Completive:	she done worked
Remote time:	she been work(ed)

Negation

Ain't   Probably the greatest shibboleth of English grammar, *ain't* has been a staple of all nonstandard English dialects since at least the eighteenth century. In BEV, as in other nonmainstream varieties, *ain't* can substitute for *am not, isn't, aren't, hasn't, haven't.* In addition, BEV speakers sometimes use *ain't* for *didn't.* Resultant constructions include *Janie ain't talking, Janie ain't talked,* and occasionally *Janie ain't talk. Ain't* is common in creoles, probably taken over from the nonstandard English of slave traders, and also appears regularly in SWE.

Negative Concord   Perhaps second only to the taboo against *ain't* in American schools is the proscription against the "double negative." Actually, negative concord was commonly used for emphasis in British English through Shakespeare's time, and it was clear to English speakers then, just as it is now, that two or more negatives simply increase the negative force of a sentence. But in the eighteenth century prescriptive grammarians decreed (contrary to every native speaker's intuition) that two negatives cancel each other and make a positive in grammar just as they do in multiplication. Since then, negative concord has disappeared from SE but still flourishes in all nonstandard varieties including BEV and creoles.

Basically, there are four possible places to negate an English sentence: an indefinite (if any) before the verb, the verbal auxiliary, an indefinite (if any) after the verb, and a negative adverb (if any). The rules of SE allow only one of these elements to carry the negative. Thus SE speakers have *Nobody will bring anything*, *They will not/won't bring anything* or in formal contexts *They will bring nothing*, and *They will never/scarcely bring anything*. Speakers of nonmainstream varieties simply reinterpret this SE rule so that the negative can be attached to any of the elements that permit it. Among nonstandard varieties, the most frequent type of negative concord involves the auxiliary and a postverbal indefinite, thus: *They won't bring nothing*. But *Nobody won't never bring nothing* (i.e., *Nobody will ever bring anything*) with its four negatives is quite acceptable for many BEV speakers. By a further rule, BEV speakers and an occasional SWE speaker can emphasize their negation by inverting the auxiliary and the first indefinite, yielding *Won't nobody never bring nothing*.

Clause Structure

Double Subject   Double subjects frequently occur in the speech of SE speakers, especially when a subject noun is widely separated from its verb, e.g., *That plant over there in the corner behind the chair with the embroidered cushions, it's almost as old as I am.* In BEV and SWE double subjects are more common and can occur closer together: *Jacob, he sick.* Although BEV double subjects may be derived from other nonstandard varieties, it should be mentioned that they are also nearly obligatory in West African Pidgin English, an ancestor of Gullah, where they might better be described as verbal affixes and transcribed something like this: *king i-aks* for *king he asks.*

Existential "It"   In BEV *it* substitutes for SE *there* in sentences like *It wasn't nothing to do* or *It's a boy in my room name Robert.* This is a relatively minor feature except that it can occasionally cause confusion in such ambiguous constructions as *It's something I want to say*, which for SE speakers would not exactly mean *There's something I want to say.* Existential *it* has been attested in a few SWE speakers but is a predominantly BEV form that also occurs in Gullah. For very young BEV speakers existential *it* can alternate with *here go* or *there go* (*Here go my house*).

Relative Clauses   In SE it is possible to delete the relative pronouns *who(m)*, *which*, and *that* when they serve as objects of relative clauses, thus: *Here is the new suit (that) I bought, Linda liked the women (whom) she met.* In BEV and SWE this rule is generalized so that relative pronouns serving as subjects of relative clauses can sometimes be deleted, thus: *There's a horse (that) goes by here* *sometimes*, *He's got a brother (who) was here yesterday.* Deletion of subject relatives also occurs in West African creoles.

Conjunctive "Which"   The relative pronoun *which* can often appear for BEV speakers in a context where SE speakers expect a conjunction or a period: *I went to Detroit, which my father lives there* or *She put nuts in the cake, which some of us can't eat it because we are allergic to nuts.* Similar constructions have been witnessed in creoles and in SWE.

Questions   Where SE indicates direct questions by inverted word order (e.g., *Where can she go?* or *Can she go?*) BEV and some SWE dialects have generalized this inversion to include indirect questions as well. Hence, BEV indirect questions would be *I wonder where can she go* and *I wonder can she go* where SE has *I wonder where she can go* and *I wonder if/whether she can go.* (Notice that because BEV signals indirect questions by inverted word order, the SE complementizers *if* and *whether* are unnecessary.) In a slightly different simplification of SE rules, a few BEV speakers can form direct questions without the inversion that SE requires, so that *Why she took it?* and *What that is?* are signaled as questions by rising intonation alone.

References

The foregoing description of Black English Vernacular has been synthesized from the following sources:

Burling, Robbins, 1973   *English in Black and White.* Holt, Rinehart and Winston. A readable description which concludes with two chapters on educating speakers of Black English Vernacular.

Closs-Traugott, Elizabeth, 1976   "Pidgins, Creoles, and the Origins of Vernacular Black English" in Deborah Sears Harrison and Tom Trabasso, eds., *Black English: A Seminar.* Lawrence Erlbaum Associates. A general discussion of pidgins and creoles, sample texts with short analyses of similarities among West African Pidgin English, Tok Pisin, Jamaican Creole, Gullah, and Vernacular Black English.

Dalby, David, 1972   "The African Element in American English" in Thomas Kochman, ed., *Rappin' and Stylin' Out.* University of Illinois Press. Lists English words with possible West African origins.

Dillard, J.L., 1972   *Black English: Its History and Usage in the United States.* Random House. Sustained argument for the creole origins of Black English Vernacular.

Labov, William, 1972   *Language in the Inner City: Studies in the Black English Vernacular.* University of Pennsylvania Press. Technical essays on the structure, social matrix, and discourse styles of Black English Vernacular.

McDavid, Raven I., and Virginia G. McDavid, 1951   "The Relationship of the Speech of American Negroes to the Speech of Whites," *American Speech* 26: 3-16. Reprinted with addendum in Walt Wolfram and Nona H. Clarke, eds., *Black-White Speech Relationships.* Center for Applied Linguistics, 1971. Argues that Black English Vernacular derives from the speech of Southern whites.

Stewart, William A., 1969   "Historical and Structural Bases for the Recognition of Negro Dialect" in James E. Alatis, ed., *Monograph Series on Language and Linguistics*, no. 22. Georgetown University Press. Argues here and in two articles reprinted in *Black-White Speech Relationships* for the creole origins of Black English Vernacular.

Tucker, G. Richard, and Wallace E. Lambert, 1969   "White and Negro Listeners' Reactions to Various American-English Dialects," *Social Forces* 47: 463-468. Reprinted in Richard

W. Bailey and Jay L. Robinson, eds., *Varieties of Present-Day English.* Macmillan, 1973. Uses subjective reaction tests to demonstrate that both Black and White subjects prefer Standard English to other varieties.

Wolfram, Walt, and Nona H. Clarke, eds., 1971 *Black-White Speech Relationships.* Center for Applied Linguistics. Essays by various linguists, some urging the creole hypothesis, some supporting the hypothesis that BEV originated in Southern white speech.

Wolfram, Walt, and Ralph W. Fasold, 1974 *The Study of Social Dialects in American English.* Prentice-Hall. Describes phonological and grammatical features common to nonstandard varieties of American English, including BEV. Chapter on educational implications.

Summary

Black English Vernacular feature	Example
	Phonological Contrasts
Forwarding of stress	pólice, féssor
Weakening of final consonants	seed=seat=see, rowed=row, run=rum=rung
Consonant-cluster simplification	lass=last, roped=rope, its=is, specific=pacific
/ɵ/ becomes / t / or / f /	thin=tin, Ruth=roof
/ð/ becomes / d / or / v /	then=den, clothe=clove
Absence of postvocalic / r /, / l /	guard=god, par=pa, four=foe, Paris=pass, help=hep, toll=toe
Collapse of certain vowel contrasts	tin=ten, fear=fair, sure=shore, pride=proud=prod, boil=ball
	Grammatical Contrasts
Nouns and pronouns:	
Nonstandard noun plurals	two *pound*, foots, mens, desses
Absence of possessive marker	*William* mother, *they* mother
Verbs:	
Variable absence of auxiliary and copula	she thinking, you happy
Uninflected present tense	she *go*
Phonological rules weaken past tense marker	She *talk* in class yesterday
Habitual *be*	she *be* working
Completive *done*	she *done* forgot
Remote time *been*	I *been* know it
Negation:	
Ain't	Jan *ain't* working/worked/work
Negative concord	Ca*n't* *no*body write *no* poetry
Clause structure:	
Double subject	*Lynn she* sick
Existential *it*	*It* wasn't nothing to do
Absence of relative pronoun in subject position	There's a horse goes by here
Conjunctive *which*	I went to Utah, which Sue lives there
Inverted word order in questions	I asked her *could I* go; Why *she took* it?

Summary (continued)

Relation to other varieties

Extended from SE
Extended from SE; devoicing and consonant-
vowel syllables in creoles
Extended from SE; few creole consonant
clusters
No "th" sounds in creoles
No "th" sounds in creoles
Extended from SE and SWE; absence of
postvocalic / r / in creoles
Also in SWE

Also in SWE; SE phonological rules
Absent in creoles

Extended from SE contractions; copula can be
absent in creoles
Extended from SE; uninflected in creoles
Extended from SE

From creoles
From creoles; also in SWE
From creoles

In other nonstandard dialects, creoles
In other nonstandard dialects, creoles

Extended from SE; verbal affixes in West African
Pidgin English
Also in Gullah, SWE

Also in SWE, creoles
Also in SWE, creoles
Also in SWE, creoles

TOWARD AN ETHNOGRAPHY OF
BLACK AMERICAN SPEECH BEHAVIOR

Thomas Kochman

As "The Nature of Communication" in the General Introduction to this volume points out, it takes more than a knowledge of phonological and grammatical features to understand the communication process in any culture. We must also understand the rules and forms of appropriate speech behavior within their cultural context: who is supposed to say what to whom in what order and under what circumstances. Thomas Kochman has discovered that in the vernacular culture of Black males such rules are highly formalized in speech events like "rapping," "shucking," "jiving," "signifying," and "sounding." The complex and creative nature of the verbal elaboration in these rituals should forever put to rest the mistaken notion held by many educators in the 1960s that Black youths are verbally deprived.

Thanks to researchers like Kochman and William Labov, we know a fair amount about the ethnography of communication among Black males in the street culture. But we still need comparable information about the communication process among Black women. Two articles have made a start in this direction. Claudia Mitchell-Kernan's "Signifying and Marking: Two Afro-American Speech Acts" in *Directions in Sociolinguistics*, edited by John J. Gumperz and Dell Hymes (Holt, Rinehart and Winston, 1972) uses largely female informants and notes that women do participate in speech events like sounding but less competitively than men do. Roger Abrahams' "Negotiating Respect: Patterns of Presentation among Black Women" in *Journal of American Folklore* (88: 58-80) suggests that Black women must constantly negotiate respect by a delicate combination of "sweet" and "tough" talk.

Many other cultures also have impressive verbal rituals. The Irish "blarney" in some ways resembles Afro-American "jiving" in the peer group. And Turkish males engage in ritualized verbal dueling which is something like sounding but focuses on accusations of homosexuality. See Wolfram's article for an analysis of how New York Puerto Ricans adapt the sounding rituals of their Black neighbors to suit their own culture. And see Appendix G for guidelines on analyzing discourse styles and structures in general.

In the black idiom of Chicago and elsewhere, there are several words that refer to talking: "rapping," "shucking," "jiving," "running it down," "gripping," "copping a plea," "signifying," and "sounding." Led by the assumption that these terms, as used by the speakers, referred to different kinds of verbal behavior, this writer has attempted to discover which features of form, style, and function distinguish one type of talk from the other. In this pursuit, I would hope to be able to identify the variable threads of the communication situation—speaker, setting, and audience—and how they influence the use of language within the social context of the black community. I also expect that some light would be shed on the black perspective behind a speech event, on those orientating values and attitudes of the speaker that cause him to behave or perform in one way as opposed to another.

The guidelines and descriptive framework for the type of approach used here have been articulated most ably by Hymes in his introduction to *The Ethnography of Communication*, from which I quote:

> In short, "ethnography of communication" implies two characteristics that an adequate approach to the problems of language which engage anthropologists must have. Firstly, such an approach cannot simply take results from linguistics, psychology, sociology, ethnology, as given, and seek to correlate them, however partially useful such work is. It must call attention to the need for fresh kinds of data, to the need to investigate directly the use of language in contexts of situation so as to discern patterns proper to speech activity, patterns which escape separate studies of grammar, of personality, of religion, of kinship and the like, each abstracting from the patterning of speech activity as such into some other frame of reference. Secondly, such an approach cannot take linguistic form, a given code, or speech itself, as frame of reference. It must take as context a community, investigating its communicative habits as a whole, so that any given use of channel and code takes its place as but part of the resources upon which the members of the community draw.
>
> It is not that linguistics does not have a vital role. Well analyzed linguistic materials are indispensable, and the logic of linguistic methodology is a principal influence in the ethnographic perspective of the approach. It is rather that it is not linguistics, but ethnography—not language, but communication—which must provide the frame of reference within which the place of language in culture and society is to be described.[1]

The following description and analysis is developed from information supplied mainly by blacks living within the inner city of Chicago. Their knowledge of the above terms, their ability to recognize and categorize the language behavior of others (e.g., "Man, stop shucking!"), and on occasion to give examples themselves, established them as reliable informants. Although a general attempt has been made here to illustrate the different types of language behavior from field sources, I have had, on occasion, to rely on published material to provide better examples, such as the writings of Malcolm X, Robert Conot, Iceberg Slim, and others. Each example cited from these authors, however, is regarded as authentic by my informants. In my own attempts at classification and analysis I have sought confirmation from the same group.

"Rapping," while used synonymously to mean ordinary conversation, is distinctively a fluent and lively way of talking which is always characterized by a high degree of personal style. To one's peer group, rapping may be descriptive of narration, a colorful rundown of some past event. A recorded example of this type of rap follows, an answer from a Chicago gang member to a youth worker who asked how his group became organized.

> Now I'm goin tell you how the jive really started. I'm goin tell you how the club got this big. 'Bout 1956 there used to be a time when the Jackson Park show was open and the Stony show was open. Sixty-six street, Jeff, Gene, all of 'em, little bitty dudes, little bitty. . . . Gene wasn't with 'em then. Gene was cribbin [living] over here. Jeff, all of 'em, real little bitty dudes, you dig? All of us were little.
>
> Sixty-six [the gang on Sixty-sixth Street], they wouldn't allow us in the Jackson Park show. That was when the parky [?] was headin it. Everybody say, If we want to go to the show, we go! One day, who was it? Carl Robinson. He went up to the show . . . and Jeff fired on him. He came back and all this was swelled up 'bout yay big, you know. He come back over to the hood [neighborhood]. He told [name unclear] and them dudes went up there. That was when mostly all the main Sixty-six boys was over here like Bett Riley. All of 'em was over here. People that quit gang-bangin [fighting, especially as a group], Marvell Gates, people like that.
>
> They went on up there, John, Roy and Skeeter went in there. And they start humbuggin [fighting] in there. That's how it all started. Sixty-six found out they couldn't beat us, at *that* time. They couldn't *whup* seven-0 [70]. Am I right Leroy? You was cribbin over here then. Am I right? We were dynamite! Used to be a time, you ain't have a passport, Man, you couldn't walk through here. And if didn't nobody know you it was worse than that. . . .

Rapping to a woman is a colorful way of "asking for some pussy." "One needs to throw a lively rap when he is 'putting the make' on a broad."[2]

According to one informant the woman is usually someone he had seen or just met, who looks good, and who might be willing to have sexual intercourse with him. My informant remarked that the term would not be descriptive of talk between a couple "who have had a relationship over any length of time." Rapping, then, is used by the speaker at the beginning of a relationship to create a favorable impression and be persuasive at the same time. The man who has the reputation for excelling at this is the "pimp," or "mack man." Both terms describe a person of considerable status in the street hierarchy, who, by his lively and persuasive rapping ("macking" is also used in this context), has acquired a stable of girls to hustle for him and give him money. For most street men and many teenagers he is the model whom they try to emulate. Thus, within the community you have a pimp walk, pimp-style boots and clothes, and perhaps most of all "pimp talk." A colorful literary example of a telephone rap (which one of my informants regards as extreme, but agrees that it illustrates the language, style, and technique of rapping) is set forth in Iceberg Slim's *Pimp: The Story of My Life.* Blood is rapping to an ex-whore named Christine in an effort to trap her into his stable.

Now try to control yourself baby. I'm the tall stud with the dreamy bedroom eyes across the hall in four-twenty. I'm the guy with the pretty towel wrapped around his sexy hips. I got the same hips on now that you x-rayed. Remember that hump of sugar your peepers feasted on?

She said, "Maybe, but you shouldn't call me. I don't want an incident. What do you want? A lady doesn't accept phone calls from strangers."

I said, "A million dollars and a trip to the moon with a bored, trapped, beautiful bitch, you dig? I'm no stranger. I've been popping the elastic in your panties since you saw me in the hall. . . ."[3]

Field examples of this kind of rapping were difficult to obtain, primarily because talk of this nature generally occurs in private, and when occurring in public places such as parties and taverns, it is carried on in an undertone. However, the first line of a rap, which might be regarded as introductory, is often overheard. What follows are several such lines collected by two of my students in and around the South Side and West Side of Chicago:

"Say pretty, I kin tell you need lovin' by the way you wiggle your ass when you walk—and I'm jus' the guy what' kin put out yo' fire."

"Let me rock you mamma, I kin satisfy your soul."

"Say, baby, give me the key to your pad. I want to play with your cat."

"Baby, you're fine enough to make me spend my rent money."

"Baby, I sho' dig your mellow action."

Rapping between men and women often is competitive and leads to a lively repartee, with the woman becoming as adept as the man. An example follows:

A man coming from the bathroom forgot to zip his pants. An unescorted party of women kept watching him and laughing among themselves. The man's friends hip [inform] him to what's going on. He approaches one woman—"Hey baby, did you see that big black Cadillac with the full tires ready to roll in action just for you?" She answers—"No mother-fucker, but I saw a little gray Volkswagen with two flat tires."

Everybody laughs. His rap was *capped* [excelled, topped].

When "whupping the game" on a "trick" or "lame" (trying to get goods or services from someone who looks like he can be swindled), rapping is often descriptive of the highly stylized verbal part of the maneuver. In well-established con games the verbal component is carefully prepared and used with great skill in directing the course of the transaction. An excellent illustration of this kind of rap came from an adept hustler who was playing the "murphy" game on a white trick. The maneuvers in the murphy game are designed to get the trick to give his money to the hustler, who in this instance poses as a "steerer" (one who directs or steers customers to a brothel), to keep the whore from stealing it. The hustler then skips with the money.

Look Buddy, I know a fabulous house not more than two blocks away. Brother you ain't never seen more beautiful, freakier broads than are in that house. One of them, the prettiest one, can do more with a swipe than a monkey can with a banana. She's like a rubber doll; she can take a hundred positions.

At this point the sucker is wild to get to this place of pure joy. He entreats the con player to take him there, not just direct him to it.

The "murphy" player will prat him [pretend rejection] to enhance his desire. He will say, "Man, don't be offended, but Aunt Kate that runs the house don't have nothing but high-class white men coming to her place. . . . you know, doctors, lawyers, big-shot politicians. You look like a clean-cut white man, but you ain't in that league are you?"[4]

After a few more exchanges of the murphy dialogue, "the mark is separated from his scratch."

An analysis of rapping indicates a number of things. For instance, it is revealing that one raps *to* rather than *with* a person, supporting the impression that rapping is to be regarded more as a performance than a verbal exchange. As with other performances, rapping projects the personality, physical appearance, and style of the performer. In each of the examples given above, in greater or lesser degree, the intrusive "I" of the speaker was instrumental in contributing to the total impression of the rap.

The relative degree of the personality-style component of rapping is generally highest when asking for some pussy (Rapping 2) and lower when whupping the game on someone (Rapping 3) or running something down (Rapping 1). In each instance, however, the personality-style component is higher than any other in producing the total effect on the listener.

In asking for some pussy, for example, where personality and style might be projected through nonverbal means (stance, clothing, walking, looking), one can speak of a "silent rap" where the woman is won without the use of words, or rather, with the words being implied that would generally accompany the nonverbal components.

As a lively way of running it down, the verbal element consists of two parts: the personality-style component and the information component. Someone *reading* my example of the gang member's narration might get the impression that the information component would be more influential in directing the audience response—that the youth worker would say, "So that's how the gang got so big," in which case he would be responding to the information component, instead of saying, "Man, that gang member is *bad* [strong, brave]," in which instance he would be responding to the personality-style component of the rap. However, if the reader could *listen* to the gang member on tape or could have been present (*watching-listening*) when the gang member spoke, he likely would have reacted more to the personality-style component, as my informants did.

Supporting this hypothesis is the fact that in attendance with the youth worker were members of the gang who *already knew* how the gang got started (e.g., "Am I right Leroy? You was cribbin over here then"), and for whom the information component by itself would have little interest. Their attention was held by the *way* the information was presented—i.e., directed toward the personality-style component.

The verbal element in whupping the game on someone, in the above illustration, was an integral part of an overall deception in which the information component and the personality-style component were skillfully manipulated to control the trick's response. But again, greater weight must be given to the personality-style component. In the murphy game, for example, it was this element which got the trick to *trust* the hustler and to leave his money with him for "safekeeping."

The function of rapping in each of the forms discussed above is *expressive.* By this I mean that the speaker raps to project his personality onto the scene or to evoke a generally favorable response from another person or group. In addition, when rapping is used to ask for some pussy (Rapping 2) or to whup the game on someone (Rapping 3), its function is *directive.* By this I mean that rapping here becomes the instrument used to manipulate and control people to get them to give up or do something. The difference between rapping to a "fox" (pretty girl) for the purpose of getting inside her pants and rapping to a "lame" to get something from him is operational rather than functional. The latter rap contains a concealed motivation, whereas the former does not. A statement made by one of my high school informants illustrates this distinction: "If I wanted something from a guy I would try to *trick* him out of it. If I wanted something from a girl I would try to *talk* her out of it [emphasis mine]."

"Shucking," "shucking it," "shucking and jiving," "S-ing and J-ing," or just "jiving," are terms that refer to one form of language behavior practiced by the black when interacting with The Man (the white man, the Establishment, or *any* authority figure), and to another form of language behavior practiced by blacks when interacting with each other on the peer-group level.

When referring to the black's dealings with the white man and the power structure, the above terms are descriptive of the talk and accompanying physical movements of the black that are appropriate to some momentary guise, posture, or facade.

Originally in the South, and later in the North, the black learned that American society had assigned him a restrictive role and status. Among whites his behavior had to conform to this imposed station, and he was constantly reminded to "keep his place." He learned that before white people it was not acceptable to show feelings of indignation, frustration, discontent, pride, ambition, or desire; that real feelings had to be concealed behind a mask of innocence, ignorance, childishness, obedience, humility, and deference. The terms used by the black to describe the role he played before white folks in the South was "tomming" or "jeffing." Failure to accommodate the white Southerner in this respect was almost certain to invite psychological and often physical brutality. The following description by black psychiatrist Alvin F. Poussaint is typical and revealing:

Once last year as I was leaving my office in Jackson, Miss., with my Negro secretary, a white policeman yelled, "Hey, boy! Come here!" Somewhat bothered, I retorted: "I'm no boy!" He then rushed at me, inflamed and stood towering over me, snorting "What d'ja say, boy?" Quickly he frisked me and demanded "What's your name, boy?" Frightened, I replied, "Dr. Poussaint, I'm a physician." He angrily chuckled and hissed, "What's your first name, boy?" When I hesitated he assumed a threatening stance and clenched his fists. As my heart palpitated, I muttered in profound humiliation, "Alvin."

He continued his psychological brutality, bellowing, "Alvin, the next time I call you, you come right away, you hear? You hear?" I hesitated. "You hear me, boy?" My voice trembling with helplessness, but *following my instincts of self-preservation*, I murmured, "Yes, sir." *Now fully satisfied that I had performed and acquiesced to my "boy" status*, he dismissed me with, "Now boy, go on and get out of here or next time we'll take you for a little ride down to the station house!"[5]

In Northern cities the black encountered authority figures equivalent to the Southern "crackers": policemen, judges, probation officers, truant officers, teachers, and "Mr. Charlies" (bosses), and he soon learned that the way to get by and avoid difficulty was to shuck. Thus he learned to accommodate The Man, to use the total orchestration of speech, intonation, gesture, and facial expression to produce whatever appearance would be acceptable. It was a technique and ability that was developed from fear, a respect for power, and a will to survive. This type of accommodation is exemplified by the "Yes sir, Mr. Charlie," or "Anything you say, Mr. Charlie," "Uncle Tom"-type Negro of the North. The language and behavior of accommodation were the prototype out of which other slightly modified forms of shucking evolved.

Through accommodation, many blacks became adept at concealing and controlling their emotions and at assuming a variety of postures. They became competent actors in the process. Many developed a keen perception of what affected, motivated, appeased, or satisfied the authority figures with whom they came into contact. What became an accomplished and effective coping mechanism for many blacks to "stay out of trouble" became for others a useful artifice for avoiding arrest or "getting out of trouble" when apprehended. Shucking it with a judge, for example, would be to feign repentance in the hope of receiving a lighter or suspended sentence; with a probation officer, to give the impression of being serious and responsible so that if you violate probation, you would not be sent back to jail. Robert Conot reports an example of the latter in his book: "Joe was found guilty of possession of narcotics. But he did an excellent job of shucking it with the probation officer." The probation officer interceded for Joe with the judge as follows: "His own attitude toward the present offense appears to be serious and responsible and it is believed that the defendant is an excellent subject for probation."[6]

The cartoon by Cal Barker illustrates this point nicely. (It appeared originally in the *Chicago Defender*.)

"Alright, alright! So what if I did sing a couple stanzas of Dixie and cut a few buck and wing steps back there. It saved the both of us from going to jail for vagrancy. The trouble with you is that you don't know how to differentiate between tomming and progressive maneuvering!"

Some field illustrations of shucking to get out of trouble after having been caught come from some seventh-grade children from an inner-city school in Chicago. The children were asked to "talk their way out of" a troublesome situation. Examples of the situation and their impromptu responses follow:

Situation: You're cursing at this old man and your mother comes walking down the stairs. She hears you. Response to "talk your way out of this": "I'd tell her that I was studying a scene in school for a play."

Situation: What if you were in a store and were stealing something and the manager caught you? Responses: "I would tell him that I was used to putting things in my pocket and then going to pay for them and show the cashier."

"I'd tell him that some of my friends was outside and they wanted some candy so I was goin to put it in my pocket to see if it would fit before I bought it."

"I would start stuttering. Then I would say, 'Oh, Oh, I forgot. Here the money is.' "

Situation: What do you do when you ditch school and you go to the beach and a truant officer walks up and says, "Are you having fun?" and you say, "Yeah," and you don't know he is a truant officer and then he says, "I'm a truant officer, what are you doing out of school?" Responses: "I'd tell him that I had been expelled from school, that I wasn't supposed to go back to school for seven days."

"I'd tell him that I had to go to the doctor to get a checkup and that my mother said I might as well stay out of school the whole day and so I came over here."

Situation: You're at the beach and they've got posted signs all over the beach and floating on the water and you go past the swimming mark and the sign says "Don't go past the mark!" How do you talk your way out of this to the lifeguard? Responses: "I'd tell him that I was having so much fun in the water that I didn't pay attention to the sign."

"I'd say that I was swimming under water and when I came back up I was behind the sign."

One literary and one field example of shucking to avoid arrest follow. The literary example of shucking comes from Iceberg Slim's autobiography. Iceberg, a pimp, shucks before "two red-faced Swede rollers [detectives]" who catch him in a motel room with his whore. My italics identify which elements of the passage constitute the shuck.

I put my shaking hands into the pajama pockets. . . . *I hoped I was keeping the fear out of my face. I gave them a wide toothy smile.* They came in and stood in the middle of the room. Their eyes were racing about the room. Stacy was open mouthed in the bed.

I said *"Yes gentlemen what can I do for you?"* Lanky said, "We wanta see your I.D."

I went to the closet and got the phony John Cato Frederickson I.D. I put it in his palm. I felt cold sweat running down my back. They looked at it, then looked at each other.

Lanky said, "You are in violation of the law. You signed the motel register improperly. Why didn't you sign your full name? What are you trying to hide? What are you doing here in town? It says here you're a dancer. We don't have a club in town that books entertainers."

I said, *"Officers, my professional name is Johnny Cato. I've got nothing to hide. My full name had always been too long for the marquees. I've fallen into the habit of using the shorter version. My legs went out last year. I don't dance anymore. My wife and I decided to go into business. We are making a tour of this part of the country. We think that in your town we've found the ideal site for a southern fried chicken shack. My wife has a secret recipe that should make us rich here."*[7]

The following example from the field was related to me by one of my colleagues. One black gang member was coming down the stairway from the club room with seven guns on him and encountered some policemen coming up the same stairs. If they stopped and frisked him, he and others would have been arrested. A paraphrase of his shuck follows: "Man, I gotta get away from up there. There's gonna be some trouble and I don't want no part of it." This shuck worked on the minds of the policemen. It anticipated their questions as to why he was leaving the club room, and why he would be in a hurry. He also gave *them* a reason for wanting to get up to the room fast.

It ought to be mentioned at this point that there was not uniform agreement among my informants in characterizing the above examples as shucking. One informant used shucking only in the sense in which it is used among the black peer group—viz., bull-shitting—and characterized the above examples as "jiving" or "whupping game." Others, however, identified the above examples as shucking and reserved "jiving" and "whupping game" for more offensive maneuvers. In fact, one of the apparent criterial features of shucking is that the posture of the black when interacting with members of the establishment be a *defensive* one. Some of my informants, for example, regarded the example of a domestic who changed into older clothing than she could afford before going to work in a white household as shucking, provided that she was doing it to keep her job. On the other hand, if she did the same thing to get a raise in pay, they regarded the example as whupping the game. Since the same guise and set of maneuvers are brought into play in working on the mind and feeling of the domestic's boss, the difference would seem to be whether the reason behind the pose were to protect oneself or to gain some advantage. Since this distinction is not always so clearly drawn, opinions are often divided. The following example is clearly ambiguous in this respect. Frederick Douglass, in telling of how he taught himself to read, would challenge a white boy with whom he was playing by saying that he could write as well as the white boy, whereupon he would write down all the letters he knew. The white boy would then write down more letters than Douglass did. In this way, Douglass eventually learned all the letters of the alphabet.[8] Some of my informants regarded the example as whupping game. Others regarded it as shucking. The former were perhaps focusing on the maneuver rather than the language used. The latter may have felt that any maneuvers designed to learn to read were justifiably defensive. One of my informants said Douglass was "shucking *in order to* whup the game." This latter response seems to be the most revealing. Just as one can rap to whup the game on someone, so one can shuck or jive for the same purpose—i.e., assume a guise or posture or perform some action in a certain way that is designed to work on someone's mind to get him to give up something. The following examples from Malcolm X illustrate the use of *shucking* and *jiving* in this context, though *jive* is the term used. Today, *whupping game* might also be the term used to describe the operation. "Whites who came at night got a better reception; the several Harlem nightclubs they patronized were geared to entertain and *jive* [flatter, cajole] the night white crowd to get their money."[9]

The maneuvers involved here are clearly designed to obtain some benefit or advantage.

> Freddy got on the stand and went to work on his own shoes. Brush, liquid polish, brush, paste wax, shine rag, lacquer sole dressing . . . step by step, Freddie showed me what to do.
>
> "But you got to get a whole lot faster. You can't waste time!" Freddie showed me how fast on my own shoes. Then because business was tapering off, he had time to give me a demonstration of how to make the shine rag pop like a firecracker. "Dig the action?" he asked. He did it in slow motion. I got down and tried it on his shoes. I had the principle of it. "Just got to do it faster," Freddie said. *"It's a jive noise, that's all. Cats tip better, they figure you're knocking yourself out!"*[10]

I was involved in a field example in which an eight-year-old boy whupped the game on me as follows:

> My colleague and I were sitting in a room listening to a tape. The door to the room was open and outside was a soda machine. Two boys came up in the elevator, stopped at the soda machine, and then came into the room and asked: "Do you have a dime for two nickels?" Presumably, the soda machine would not accept nickels. I took out the change in my pocket, found a dime and gave it to the boy for two nickels. After accepting the dime, he looked at the change in my hand and asked, "Can I have two cents? I need carfare to get home." I gave him the two cents.

At first I assumed the verbal component of the maneuver was the rather weak, transparently false reason for wanting the two cents. Actually, as was pointed out to me later, the maneuver began with the first question, which was designed to get me to show my money. He could then ask me for something that he knew I had, making my refusal more difficult. He apparently felt that the reason need not be more than plausible because the amount he wanted was small. Were the amount larger, he would no doubt have elaborated on the verbal element of the game. The form of the verbal element could be directed toward rapping or shucking and jiving. If he were to rap, the eight-year-old might say, "Man, you know a cat needs to have a little bread to keep the girls in line." Were he to shuck and jive he might make the reason for needing the money more compelling: look hungry, or something similar.

The function of shucking and jiving as it refers to transactions involving confrontation between blacks and The Man is both expressive and directive. It is language behavior designed to work on the mind and emotions of the authority figure to get him to feel a certain way or give up something that will be to the other's advantage. When viewed in its entirety, shucking must be regarded as a performance. Words and gestures become the instruments for promoting a certain image or posture. In the absence of words, shucking would be descriptive of the *actions* which constitute the deception, as in the above example from Malcolm X, where the movement of the shine rag in creating the "jive noise" was the deceptive element. Similarly, in another example, a seventh-grade boy recognized the value of stuttering before saying, "Oh, I forgot. Here the money is," knowing that stuttering would be an invaluable aid in presenting a picture of innocent intent. Iceberg showed a "toothy smile" which said to the detective, "I'm glad to see you," and "Would I be glad to see you if I had something to hide?" When the maneuvers seem to be defensive, most of my informants regarded the language behavior as shucking. When the maneuvers were offensive, my informants tended to regard the behavior as whupping the game. The difference in perception is culturally significant.

Also significant is the fact that the first form of shucking which I have described above, which developed out of accommodation, is becoming less frequently used today by many blacks as a result of a newfound self-assertiveness and pride, challenging the system "that is so brutally and unstintingly suppressive of self-assertion."[11] The willingness on the part of many blacks to accept the psychological and physical brutality and general social consequences of not "keeping one's place" is indicative of the changing self-concept of the black man. Ironically, the shocked reaction of the white power structure to the present militancy of the black is partly due to the fact that the black has been so successful at "putting whitey on" via shucking in the past—i.e., compelling a belief in whatever posture the black chose to assume. The extent to which this attitude has penetrated the black community can be seen from a conversation I recently had with a shoe-shine attendant at O'Hare airport in Chicago.

I was having my shoes shined and the black attendant was using a polishing machine instead of the rag that was generally used in the past. I asked whether the machine made his work any easier. He did not answer me until about ten seconds had passed and then responded in a loud voice that he "never had a job that was easy, that he would give me one hundred dollars for any *easy* job I could offer him, that the machine made his job 'faster' but not 'easier.' " I was startled at the response because it was so unexpected, and I realized that here was a new "breed of cat" who was not going to shuck for a big tip or ingratiate himself with "whitey" anymore. A few years ago his response would have been different.

The contrast between this shoe-shine scene and the one illustrated earlier from Malcolm X's autobiography, when "shucking whitey" was the common practice, is striking.

"Shucking," "jiving," "shucking and jiving," or "S-ing and J-ing," when referring to language behavior practiced by blacks when interacting with one another on the peer-group level, is descriptive of the talk and gestures that are appropriate to "putting someone on" by creating a false impression, conveying false information, and the like. The terms seem to cover a range from simply telling a lie, to bull-shitting, to subtly playing with someone's mind. An important difference between this form of shucking and that described earlier is that the same talk and gestures that are deceptive to The Man are often transparent to those members of one's own group who are able practitioners at shucking themselves. As Robert Conot has pointed out, "The Negro who often fools the white officer by 'shucking it' is much less likely to be successful with another Negro. . . ."[12] Also, S-ing and J-ing within the group often has play overtones in which the person being put on is aware of the attempts being made and goes along with it for the enjoyment of it or in appreciation of the style involved. An example from Iceberg Slim illustrates this latter point:

> He said, "Ain't you the little shit ball I chased outta the Roost?"
> I said, "Yeah, I'm one and the same. I want to beg your pardon for making you salty [angry] that night. Maybe I coulda gotten a pass if I had told you I'm your pal's nephew.
> "I ain't got no sense, Mr. Jones. I took after my idiot father."

Mr. Jones, perceiving Iceberg's shuck, says,

> "Top, this punk ain't hopeless. He's silly as a bitch grinning all the time, but dig how he butters the con to keep his balls outta the fire."[13]

Other citations showing the use of "shucking" and "jiving" to mean simply "lying" follow:

> It was a *jive* [false] tip but there were a lot of cats up there on humbles [framed up charges].[14]

> How would you like to have half a "G" [$500] in your slide [pocket]?
> I said, "All right, give me the poison and take me to the baby."
> He said, "I ain't *shucking* [lying]. It's creampuff work."[15]

"Running it down" is the term used by ghetto-dwellers when they intend to communicate information in the form of an explanation, narrative, giving advice, and the like. The information component in the field example cited under Rapping 1 would constitute the run down. In the following literary example, Sweet Mac is "running this Edith broad down" to his friends:

> Edith is the "saved" broad who can't marry out of her religion . . . or do anything else out of her religion for that matter, especially what I wanted her to do. A bogue religion, man! So dig, for the last couple weeks I been quoting the Good Book and all that stuff to her; telling her I am now saved myself, you dig.[16]

The following citation from Claude Brown uses the term with the additional sense of giving advice: "If I saw him [Claude's brother] hanging out with cats I knew were weak, who might be using drugs sooner or later, I'd *run it down* to him."[17]

Iceberg Slim asks a bartender regarding a prospective whore: "Sugar, *run her down* to me. Is the bitch qualified? Is she a whore? Does she have a man?"[18]

It seems clear that running it down has basically an informative function, telling somebody something that he doesn't already know.

"Gripping" is of fairly recent vintage, used by black high school students in Chicago to refer to the talk and facial expression that accompanies a *partial* loss of face or self-possession, or displaying of fear. Its appearance alongside "copping a plea," which refers to a total loss of face in which one begs one's adversary for mercy, is a significant new perception. Linking it with the street code which acclaims the ability to "look tough and inviolate, fearless, secure, 'cool,' "[19] suggests that even the slightest weakening of this posture will be held up to ridicule and contempt. There are always contemptuous overtones attached to the use of the term when applied to others' behavior. One is tempted to link it further with the degree of violence and level of toughness that is required to survive on the street. The intensity of both seems to be increasing. As one of my informants noted, "Today, you're *lucky* if you end up in the hospital [i.e., are not killed]."

Both "gripping" and "copping a plea" refer to behavior that stems from fear and a respect for superior power. An example of gripping comes from the record *Street and Gangland Rhythms.*[20] Lennie meets Calvin and asks him what happened to his lip. Calvin tells Lennie that a boy named Pierre hit him for copying off him in school. Lennie, pretending to be Calvin's brother, goes to confront Pierre. Their dialogue follows:

> *Lennie*: Hey you! What you hit my little brother for?
> *Pierre*: Did he tell you what happen man?
> *Lennie*: Yeah, he told me what happen.
> *Pierre*: But you ... but you ... but you should tell your people to teach him to go to school, man. (*pause*) I ... I know ... I know I didn't have a right to hit him.

Pierre, anticipating a fight with Lennie if he continued to justify his hitting of Calvin, tried to avoid it by gripping with the last line.

"Copping a plea" originally meant "to plead guilty to a lesser charge to save the state the cost of a trial"[21] (with the hope of receiving a lesser or suspended sentence), but is now generally used to mean "to beg, plead for mercy," as in, "Please cop, don't hit me. I give."[22] This change of meaning can be seen from its use by Piri Thomas in *Down These Mean Streets*: "The night before my hearing, I decided to make a prayer. It had to be on my knees, cause if I was gonna *cop a plea* to God, I couldn't play it cheap."[23] For the original meaning, Thomas uses "deal for a lower plea": "I was three or four months in the Tombs, waiting for a trial, going to court, waiting for adjournments, trying to *deal for a lower plea,* and what not."[24]

The function of gripping and copping a plea is obviously expressive. One evinces noticeable feelings of fear and insecurity which result in a loss of status among one's peers. At the same time one may arouse feelings of contempt in one's adversary.

An interesting point to consider with respect to copping a plea is whether the superficial features of the form may be borrowed to mitigate one's punishment, in which case it would have the same directive function as shucking, and would be used to arouse feelings of pity, mercy, and the like. The question whether one can arouse such feelings among one's street peers by copping a plea is unclear. In the example cited above from the record *Street and Gangland Rhythms*, which records the improvisations of eleven- and twelve-year-old boys, one of the boys convincingly *acts out* the form of language behavior, which was identified by all my informants as copping a plea with the police officer: "Please cop, don't hit me. I give." In this example it was clearly an artifice with a directive function; here we have the familiar dynamic opposition of black vs. authority figure discussed under shucking.

"Signifying" is the term used to describe the language behavior that, as Abrahams has defined it, attempts to "imply, goad, beg, boast by indirect verbal or gestural means."[25] In Chicago it is also used as a synonym to describe a form of language behavior which is more generally known as "sounding" elsewhere and will be discussed under the latter heading below.

Some excellent examples of signifying as well as of other forms of language behavior discussed above come from the well-known "toast" (narrative form), "The Signifying Monkey and the Lion," which was collected by Abrahams from black street-corner bards in Philadelphia. In the above toast the monkey is trying to get the lion involved in a fight with the elephant:

> Now the lion came through the jungle one peaceful day,
> When the signifying monkey stopped him, and that is what he started to say:
> He said, "Mr. Lion," he said, "A bad-assed motherfucker down your way,"
> He said, "Yeah! The way he talks about your folks is a certain shame.
> I've even heard him curse when he mentioned your grandmother's name."
> The lion's tail shot back like a forty-four
> When he went down that jungle in all uproar.

Thus the monkey has goaded the lion into a fight with the elephant by signifying, indicating that the elephant has been "sounding on" (insulting) the lion. When the lion comes back, thoroughly beaten up, the monkey again signifies by making fun of the lion:

> . . . a lion came back through the jungle more dead than alive,
> When the monkey started some more of that signifying jive.
> He said, "Damn, Mr. Lion, you went through here yesterday, the jungle rung.
> Now you come back today, damn near hung."

The monkey, of course, is delivering this taunt from a safe distance away on the limb of a tree when his foot slips and he falls to the ground, at which point

> Like a bolt of lightning, a stripe of white heat,
> The lion was on the monkey with all four feet.

In desperation the monkey quickly resorts to copping a plea:

> The monkey looked up with a tear in his eyes.
> He said, "Please, Mr. Lion, I apologize."

His plea, however, fails to move the lion to any show of pity or mercy; so the monkey tries another verbal ruse—shucking:

> He said, "You lemme get my head out of the sand
> Ass out of the grass, I'll fight you like a natural man."

In this he is more successful as

> The lion jumped back and squared for a fight.
> The motherfucking monkey jumped clear out of sight.

A safe distance away again, the monkey returns to signifying:

> He said, "Yeah, you had me down, you had me at last.
> But you left me free, now you can still kiss my ass."[26]

The above example illustrates the methods of provocation, goading, and taunting as artfully practiced by the signifier. Interestingly, when the *function* of signifying is *directive*, the *tactic* which is employed is one of *indirection*—i.e., the signifier reports or repeats what someone else has said about the listener; the "report" is couched in plausible language designed to compel belief and arouse feelings of anger and hostility. There is also the implication that if the listener fails to do anything about it—what has to be "done" is usually quite clear—his status will be seriously compromised. Thus the lion is compelled to vindicate the honor of his family by fighting or else leave the impression that he is afraid, and that he is not "king of the jungle." When used to direct action, signifying is like shucking in also being deceptive and subtle in approach and depending for success on the naïveté or gullibility of the person being put on.

When the function of signifying is only expressive (i.e., to arouse feelings of embarrassment, shame, frustration, or futility, for the purpose of diminishing someone's status, but without directive implication), the tactic employed is direct in the form of a taunt, as in the above example where the monkey is making fun of the lion. Signifying frequently occurs when things are dull and someone wishes to generate some excitement and interest within the group. This is shown in another version of the above toast:

> There hadn't been no disturbin in the jungle for quite a bit,
> For up jumped the monkey in the tree one day and laughed, "I guess I'll start some shit."

"Sounding" is the term which is today most widely known for the game of verbal insult known in the past as "playing the dozens," "the dirty dozens," or just "the dozens." Other current names for the game have regional distribution: "signifying" or "sigging" (Chicago), "joning" (Washington, D.C.), "screaming" (Harrisburg), and so on. In Chicago, the term "sounding" would describe the initial remarks which are designed to sound out the other person to see whether he will play the game. The verbal insult is also subdivided, the term "signifying" applying to insults which are hurled directly at the person and the "dozens" applying to insults hurled at your opponent's family, especially the mother.

Sounding is often catalyzed by signifying remarks referred to earlier, such as "Are you going to let him say that about your mama?" in order to spur on an exchange between two (or more) other members of the group. It is begun on a relatively low key and built up by means of verbal exchanges.

Abrahams describes the game:

One insults a member of another's family; others in the group make disapproving sounds to spur on the coming exchange. The one who has been insulted feels at this point that he must reply with a slur on the protagonist's family which is clever enough to defend his honor (and therefore that of his family). This, of course, leads the other (once again, more due to pressure from the crowd than actual insult) to make further jabs. This can proceed until everyone is bored with the whole affair, until one hits the other (fairly rare), or until some other subject comes up that interrupts the proceedings (the usual state of affairs).[27]

McCormick describes the dozens as a verbal contest

in which the players strive to bury one another with vituperation. In the play, the opponent's mother is especially slandered ... then, in turn fathers are identified as queer and syphilitic. Sisters are whores, brothers are defective, cousins are "funny," and the opponent is himself diseased.[28]

An example of the game collected by one of my students goes as follows:

Frank looked up and saw Leroy enter the Outpost. Leroy walked past the room where Quinton, Nap, Pretty Black, Cunny, Richard, Haywood, Bull, and Reese sat playing cards. As Leroy neared the T.V. room, Frank shouted to him.

Frank: Hey, Leroy, your mama—calling you man.

Leroy turned and walked toward the room where the sound came from. He stood in the door and looked at Frank.

Leroy: Look motherfuckers, I don't play that shit.

Frank (signifying): Man, I told you cats 'bout that mama jive (as if he were concerned about how Leroy felt).

Leroy: That's all right Frank; you don't have to tell those funky motherfuckers nothing; I'll fuck me up somebody yet.

Frank's face lit up as if he were ready to burst his side laughing. Cunny became pissed at Leroy.

Cunny: Leroy, you stupid bastard, you let Frank make a fool of you. He said that 'bout your mama.

Pretty Black: Aw, fat ass head, Cunny shut up.

Cunny: Ain't that some shit. This black slick head motor flicker got nerve 'nough to call somebody fathead. Boy, you so black, you sweat super Permalube Oil.

This eased the tension of the group as they burst into loud laughter.

Pretty Black: What'chu laughing 'bout Nap, with your funky mouth smelling like dog shit.

Even Leroy laughed at this.

Nap: Your mama motherfucker.

Pretty Black: Your funky mama too.

Nap, strongly: It takes twelve barrels of water to make a steamboat run; it takes an elephant's dick to make your Grandmammy come; she been elephant fucked, camel fucked and hit side the head with your Grandpappy's nuts.

Reese: Goddor damn; go on and rap motherfucker.

Reese began slapping each boy in his hand, giving his approval of Nap's comment. Pretty Black, in an effort not to be outdone but directing his verbal play elsewhere, stated:

Pretty Black: Reese, what you laughing 'bout? You so square you shit bricked shit.

Frank: Whoooowee!

Reese (sounded back): Square huh, what about your nappy ass hair before it was stewed; that shit was so bad till, when you went to bed at night, it would leave your head and go on the corner and meddle.

The boys slapped each other in the hand and cracked up.

Pretty Black: On the streets meddling, bet Dinky didn't offer me no pussy and I turned it down.

Frank: Reese scared of pussy.

Pretty Black: Hell yeah; the greasy mother rather fuck old, ugly, funky cock Sue Willie than get a piece of ass from a decent broad.

Frank: Goddor damn! Not Sue Willie.

Pretty Black: Yeah ol' meat beating Reese rather screw that cross-eyed, clapsy bitch, who when she cry, tears drip down her ass.

Haywood: Don't be so mean, Black.

Reese: Aw shut up, you half-white bastard.

Frank: Wait man, Haywood ain't gonna hear much more of that half-white shit; he's a brother too.

Reese: Brother, my black ass; that white ass landlord gotta be this motherfucker's paw.

Cunny: Man, you better stop foolin with Haywood; he's turning red.

Haywood: Fuck yall (*as he withdrew from the "sig" game*).

Frank: Yeah, fuck yall; let's go to the stick hall.

The above example of sounding is an excellent illustration of the game as played by fifteen-, sixteen-, and seventeen-year-old Negro boys, some of whom have already acquired the verbal skill which for them is often the basis for having a high "rep." Abrahams observed that "the ability with words is as highly valued as physical strength."[29] In the sense that the status of one of the participants in the game is diminished if he has to resort to fighting to answer a verbal attack, verbal ability may be even more highly regarded than physical ability. However, age within the peer group may be a factor in determining the relative value placed on verbal vis-à-vis physical ability.

Nevertheless, the relatively high value placed on verbal ability must be clear to most black boys at an early age in their cognitive development. Abrahams is probably correct in linking sounding to the taunt which is learned and practiced as a child and is part of signifying, which has its origins in childlike behavior.[30] The taunts of the Signifying Monkey, illustrated above, are good examples of this.

Most boys begin their activity in sounding by compiling a repertoire of one-liners. When the game is played among this age group, the one who has the greatest number of such remarks wins. Here are some examples of one-liners collected from fifth- and sixth-grade black boys in Chicago:

Yo mama is so bowlegged, she looks like the bite out of a donut.

You mama sent her picture to the lonely hearts club, and they sent it back and said, "We ain't that lonely!"

Your family is so poor the rats and roaches eat lunch out.

Your house is so small the roaches walk single file.

I walked in your house and your family was running around the table. I said, "Why you doin that?" Your mama say, "First one drops, we eat."

Real proficiency in the game comes to only a small percentage of those who play it, as might be expected. These players have the special skill in being able to turn what their opponents have said and attack them with it. Thus when someone indifferently said "Fuck you" to Concho, his retort was immediate and devastating: "Man, you haven't even kissed me yet."

The best talkers from this group often become the successful street-corner, barber shop, and pool hall storytellers who deliver the long, rhymed, witty narrative stories called "toasts." A portion of the toast "The Signifying Monkey and the Lion" was given above. However, it has also produced entertainers, such as Dick Gregory and Redd Foxx, who are virtuosos at repartee, and preachers whose verbal power has been traditionally esteemed.

The function of the dozens or sounding is invariably self-assertive. The speaker borrows status from his opponent through an exercise of verbal power. The opponent feels compelled to regain his status by sounding back on the speaker or some other member of the group whom he regards as more vulnerable. The social interaction of the group at the Outpost, for example, demonstrated less an extended verbal barrage between two people than a "pecking order." Frank sounds on Leroy; Cunny signifies on Leroy; Pretty Black sounds on Cunny;

Cunny sounds back on Pretty Black who (losing) turns on Nap; Nap sounds (winning) back on Pretty Black; Pretty Black finally borrows back his status by sounding on Reese. Reese sounds back on Pretty Black but gets the worst of the exchange and so borrows back his status from Haywood. Cunny also sounds on Haywood. Haywood defaults. Perhaps by being half-white, Haywood feels himself to be the most vulnerable.

The presence of a group seems to be especially important in controlling the game. First of all, one does not play with just anyone, since the subject matter is concerned with things that in reality one is quite sensitive about. It is precisely *because* Pretty Black has a "black slick head" that he is vulnerable to Cunny's barb, especially now when the Afro-American natural hairstyle is in vogue. It is precisely *because* Reese's girlfriend *is* ugly that he is vulnerable to Pretty Black's jibe that Reese can't get a "piece of ass from a decent broad." It is *because* the living conditions are so poor and intolerable that they can be used as subject matter for sounding. Without the control of the group, sounding will frequently lead to a fight. This was illustrated by a tragic epilogue concerning Haywood; when Haywood was being sounded on by his best friend in the presence of two girls (other members of the group were absent), he refused to tolerate it. He went home, got a rifle, came back, and shot and killed his friend. In the classroom from about the fourth grade on, fights among black boys invariably are caused by someone sounding on the other person's mother.

Significantly, the subject matter of sounding is changing with the changing self-concept of the black regarding those physical traits that are characteristically Negro, and which in the past were vulnerable points in the black psyche: blackness and "nappy" hair.

They still occur, as in the above example from the Outpost, and the change in the above illustration is notable more by what has been added than by what is subtracted—viz., the attack on black *slick* hair and half-white color. With regard to the latter, however, it ought to be said that, for many blacks, blackness was always highly esteemed; it might be more accurate to regard the present sentiment of the black community toward skin color as reflecting a shifted attitude for only a *portion* of the black community. This suggests that sounding on someone's light skin color is not new. Nevertheless, one can regard the previously favorable attitude toward light skin color and "good hair" as the prevailing one. "Other things being equal, the more closely a woman approached her white counterpart, the more attractive she was considered to be, by both men and women alike. 'Good hair' (hair that is long and soft) and light skin were the chief criteria."[31] Also, children's rhymes which before Black Power were

If you like black
Keep your black ass back

and

If you like white
You're all right

have respectively changed to

If you like black
You have a Cadillac

and

If you like white
You're looking for a fight.

Both Abrahams and McCormick link the dozens to the overall psychosocial growth of the black male. McCormick has stated that a "single round of a dozen or so exchanges frees more pent-up aggressions than will a dose of sodium pentothal." The fact that one permits a kind of abuse within the rules of the game and within the confines of the group which would otherwise not be tolerated is filled with psychological importance, and this aspect is fully discussed by Abrahams. It also seems important, however, to view its function from the perspective of the nonparticipating members of the group. Its function for them may be directive: i.e., they incite and prod individual members of the group to combat for the purpose of energizing the elements, of simply relieving the boredom of just "hanging around" and the malaise of living in a static and restrictive environment. One of my informants remarked that he and other members of the group used to feed insults to one member to hurl back at another if they felt that the contest was too uneven, "to keep the game going." In my above illustration from the Outpost, for example, Frank seemed to be the precipitating agent as well as chorus for what was going on and Bull did not directly participate at all. For them the dozens may have had the social function of "having a little fun," or, as Loubee said to Josh, of just "passing the time."[32]

A summary analysis of the different forms of language behavior which have been discussed permits the following generalizations.

The prestige norms which influence black speech behavior are those which have been successful in manipulating and controlling people and situations. The function of all forms of language behavior discussed above, with the exception of "running it down," was either expressive or expressive-directive. Specifically, this means that language was used to project personality, assert oneself, or arouse emotion, frequently with the additional purpose of getting the person to give up or do something which will be of some benefit to the speaker. Only "running it down" has as its primary function to communicate information—and often here, too, the personality and style of the speaker in the form of rapping are projected along with the information.

The purpose for which language is used suggests that the speaker views the social situations into which he moves as essentially agonistic, by which I mean that he sees his environment as consisting of a series of transactions which require that he be continually ready to take advantage of a person or situation or defend himself against being victimized. He has absorbed what Horton has called "street rationality."[33] As one of Horton's respondents put it: "The good hustler . . .

conditions his mind and must never put his guard down too far, to relax, or he'll be taken."

I have carefully avoided, throughout this paper, delimiting the group within the black community of whom the language behavior and perspective of their environment is characteristic. While I have no doubt that it is true of those who are generally called "street people," I am not certain of the extent to which it is also true of a much larger portion of the black community, especially the male segment. My informants consisted of street people, high school students, and blacks who by their occupation as community and youth workers possess what has been described as a "sharp sense of the streets." Yet it is difficult to find a black male in the community who has *not* witnessed or participated in the dozens or heard of signifying, or rapping, or shucking and jiving, at some time while he was growing up. It would be equally difficult to imagine a high school student in a Chicago inner-city school not being touched by what is generally regarded as street culture in some way.

In conclusion, by blending style and verbal power. through "rapping," "sounding," and "running it down," the black in the ghetto establishes his personality; through "shucking," "gripping," and "copping a plea" he shows his respect for power; through "jiving" and "signifying" he stirs up excitement. With all of the above, he hopes to manipulate and control people and situations to give himself a winning edge.

NOTES

1. John J. Gumperz and Dell Hymes, eds., *The Ethnography of Communication*, special publication of *American Anthropologist* 66, no. 6, pt. 2, pp. 2ff.

2. John Horton, "Time and Cool People," *Trans-action*, April 1967.

3. Iceberg Slim, *Pimp: The Story of My Life* (Los Angeles: Holloway House, 1969), p. 179.

4. Ibid., p. 38.

5. Alvin F. Poussaint, "A Negro Psychiatrist Explains the Negro Psyche," *New York Times*, Aug. 20, 1967, sec. 6, pp. 52ff.

6. Robert Conot, *Rivers of Blood, Years of Darkness* (New York: Bantam, 1967), p. 333.

7. Slim, *Pimp*, p. 294.

8. Frederick Douglass, *Narrative of the Life of an American Slave* (New York: New American Library, 1968), p. 57.

9. Malcolm X, *Autobiography* (New York: Grove Press, 1965), p. 87.

10. Ibid., p. 48. Italics mine.

11. Poussaint, "Negro Psychiatrist," p. 52.

12. Conot, *Rivers of Blood*, p. 161.

13. Slim, *Pimp*, p. 162.

14. Claude Brown, *Manchild in the Promised Land* (New York: Macmillan, 1965), p. 142.

15. Slim, *Pimp*, p. 68. Italics mine.

16. Woodie King, Jr., "The Game," *Liberator*, August 1965.

17. Brown, *Manchild*, p. 390. Italics mine.

18. Slim, *Pimp*, p. 79. Italics mine.

19. Horton, "Time and Cool People," p. 11.

20. *Street and Gangland Rhythms*, Band 4, "Dumb Boy."

21. Harold Wentworth and Stuart Berg Flexner, *Dictionary of American Slang* (New York: Crowell, 1960), p. 123.

22. *Street and Gangland Rhythms*, Band 1, "Gang Fight."

23. Piri Thomas, *Down These Mean Streets* (New York: Knopf, 1967), p. 316. Italics mine.

24. Ibid., p. 245. Italics mine.

25. Roger D. Abrahams, *Deep Down in the Jungle* (Hatboro, Pa.: Folklore Associates, 1964), p. 267.

26. Ibid., pp. 150ff.

27. Roger D. Abrahams, "Playing the Dozens," *Journal of American Folklore* 75 (1962): 209-210.

28. Mack McCormick, *The Dirty Dozens: The Unexpurgated Folksongs of Men*, Arhoolie record album, 1960.

29. Abrahams, *Deep Down*, p. 62.

30. Ibid., p. 53.

31. Elliot Liebow, *Tally's Corner* (Boston: Little, Brown, 1966), p. 138.

32. Earl Shorris, *Ofay* (New York: Dell, 1966).

33. Horton, "Time and Cool People," p. 8.

NONVERBAL COMMUNICATION AMONG AFRO-AMERICANS: AN INITIAL CLASSIFICATION

Benjamin G. Cooke

In face-to-face interaction, which modern linguists consider the most basic situation of language use, messages are communicated partly through speech sounds but also through such nonverbal visual cues as the use of the body—gestures, head and body movements, posture and stance, touching, facial expressions, eye movement and contact—and through situational factors such as seating arrangements and distance between speakers. The importance of this nonverbal information is easy to realize by contrasting a face-to-face interaction with a telephone conversation, the nemesis of second-language learners.

Sometimes nonverbal language has a clear, almost lexical meaning; e.g., a nod of the head in American society indicates agreement or assent. However, the nonverbal channel is primarily *affective* in its meaning, whereas the verbal channel is mainly *informational*. Listeners can indicate how they feel about a message without interrupting the speech stream by frowning, turning away, pretending not to hear, or by smiling or nodding. The verbal and nonverbal channels may reinforce each other, but speakers often use the nonverbal to mitigate or negate the information they are conveying in the verbal message. For instance, a child who has been reprimanded for disobedience and offers the required "I'm sorry" while shoving his hands into his pockets, pushing his foot around on the floor, and looking down with a pout of his face is likely to be told, "Say it again like you mean it."

A complete analysis of the communicative process requires the segmentation and classification of both verbal and nonverbal channels. "The Structure of Language" in the General Introduction explains how verbal elements can be arranged in a hierarchy of phonemes (with their allophonic variants), morphemes, and sentences. Ray L. Birdwhistell in *Kinesics and Context* (University of Pennsylvania Press, 1970) proposes a parallel hierarchy for nonverbal elements, or *kinesics.* In his system, *kinemes* are the smallest units of body motion with communicative significance (cf. phonemes), and their nonsignificant variants are *allokines* (cf. allophones). At the next level in the nonverbal hierarchy are *kinemorphs,* combinations of kinemes into the smallest nonverbal units to carry meaning (cf. morphemes). In the following article Benjamin G. Cooke uses Birdwhistell's system in his classification of several nonverbal features among Afro-Americans. He also distinguishes whether the nonverbal feature focuses on the sender (*expressive*) or the receiver (*directive*) of the message.

Cooke's article opens an important new field in the study of communication. Henley's "Power, Sex, and Nonverbal Communication" brings a somewhat different perspective to bear on nonverbal communication between the sexes. Yet we still need similar information on other cultures, as well as updates and other regional studies of Black kinesics. Appendix G offers guidelines for observing nonverbal behavior to the reader who wishes to pursue such research.

Introduction

Recent research has increasingly stressed the need to investigate nonverbal communication, the importance of which can no longer be ignored or overlooked in any comprehensive theory involving language and its relation to culture, learning, and psychology.

This article initiates such a study with respect to Afro-Americans by (1) describing the basic components of certain gestures and showing how these are altered to achieve variation in different social contexts, and (2) explaining the functions of these gestures along with other bodily movements.

Such a descriptive analysis illustrates the systemic nature of such communication, as well as illuminating something of the black cultural context in which nonverbal communication operates, especially that which might shape or reflect the world view of black people. Additionally, it might increase the reader's awareness of the significance of this channel and mode of communication and his appreciation of the integral part it plays in the Afro-American communication system.

Field-Study Technique

Field study consisted of informal interviews with several members of the black community in Chicago. Interviews were held in the summers of 1968 and 1969. Several of the informants were friends of the researcher and were chosen because of their diverse backgrounds and experiences. The occupational backgrounds included musicians, youth workers, ex-hustlers, artists, semiskilled workers, educational persons, and teenagers. The teenagers consisted of two different groups: one group from the West Side (middle-lower socioeconomic status) and the other group from the Southeast Side (upper-lower socioeconomic status). The various informants helped to describe and define the gestures considered here. The major factors considered in the interpretation and differentiation of the forms of nonverbal communication were:

1. The motives, attitudes, responses, conflicts, and personalities of the people involved in the communicative event
2. The context of the message
3. The entire social setting
4. The communicative event itself

Because of the importance of visual cues in nonverbal communication, illustrations assist in the discussion and help clarify certain points considered; motion pictures would, of course, be the most effective way to analyze the total expression. While some of the illustrations were posed, it was also possible to capture some spontaneous movements; these are always preferred because of their communicative value for conveying overall body movement and configuration. Whatever their imperfections, the illustrations give the reader a general idea of the features involved in nonverbal communication, since the study of kinesics—the area incorporating the present study—basically explores how man *sees* rather than how he *hears*.

Skin—Giving and Getting

The gestural expressions of "giving skin" and "getting skin" are very common in the black community. Harry Edwards, leader of the Olympic boycott, was recently quoted as saying: "Black people are communal by culture. They prepare communally. They dance, they play games communally. That slap on the hand you see Lew Alcindor give Mike Warren, or vice versa, that means something to those brothers. It means something to the brothers in the stands. It means something to the brothers who are watching the TV sets."[1]

In this paper the gestures of giving and getting skin will be considered as *kinemes* according to Birdwhistell's classification. They derive their meaning from the analysis of the entire range of components involved in a communicative act—sender, receiver, channel, code, setting, etc. The kinemes of giving and getting skin can be combined with facial expressions to produce *kinemorphs*. The variations within each of the kinemes represent subtle, individual *allokines* of giving skin.[2]

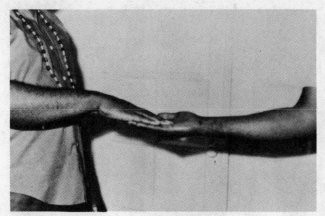

Fig. 1   Giving skin:
Palm-to-palm contact

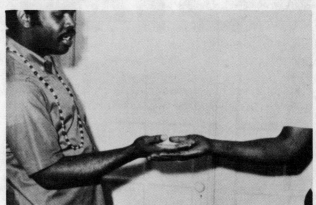

Fig. 2   Giving skin: Back of hand to upward-facing palm

Figures 1, 2, and 3 illustrate three regular kinemes of giving and getting skin. These gestures are tools used by individuals for their own specific needs, and there are as many varieties and styles of doing these simple acts as there are individual personalities. Figure 1 illustrates the palm-to-palm kineme of giving skin; it involves palm contact between two people with no significance attached to left-handedness or right-handedness. In other words, "skinning" can be accomplished with a right hand/right hand contact, a right hand/left hand contact, a left hand/right hand contact, or a left hand/left hand contact. Figure 2 illustrates the back-of-hand-to-upward-facing-palm kineme; it involves a back-of-hand contact with an upturned palm. The person receiving the skin can either cup his hand slightly or hold it straight out. One informant regularly uses these two kinemes together in a one-two sequence. As an example of how it is possible to achieve variation, the informant related the following: When especially tired or "beat" he may just use the first kineme in a lazy palm-to-palm contact, omitting kineme two completely. In this instance his walking and shoulder movements would reinforce the skinning comprising an entire kinemorph, and he would have effectively

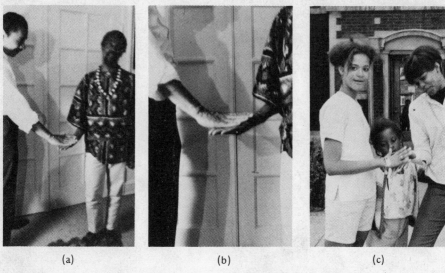

(a)   (b)   (c)

Fig. 3   Agreement skin

communicated that he was tired and in a weary mood without saying a word. Its function here would be *expressive*—that is, the focus is on the sender of the message.

Figure 3 illustrates the use of the first regular kineme (i.e., palm-to-palm contact) in a context of agreement between two people; but it should be remembered that the second kineme (i.e., back-of-hand-to-palm) could also have been used to indicate the same amount of agreement. Giving skin is often used as a gesture of agreement and approval; it can also be used to pay a compliment, as in Figure 4. In these situations its functions are both expressive and directive. What determines the minimal distinctions between complimentary skin and agreement skin is a function of the social interaction taking place between the two individuals and is *not* determined by any particular skin kineme.[3]

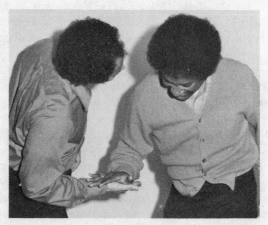

Fig. 4   Complimentary skin

Giving and getting skin are also used as gestures of greeting or parting; here again there are innumerable individual variations. Figures 5a and 5b are two informants' examples of greeting skin from a distance, perhaps to a friend across the street. This is not a part of any traditional waving motion associated with saying hello or good-by. It is a direct outward-and-upward thrust of the arm, exposing the skin of his palm to his comrade. Figures 5c and 5d illustrate greeting skin at close range. These same illustrations could be used to show parting skin, which is consistent with earlier statements that the kinemes of skin assume their total meaning from the consideration of the entire social context in which they occur.[4]

(a)

(b)

(c)

(d)

Fig. 5   Greeting skin

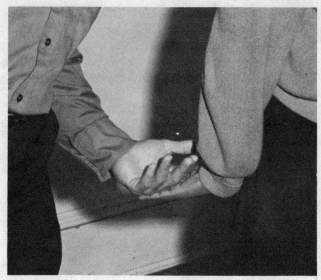

Fig. 6   "Five on the sly"

Figure 6 illustrates "five on the sly." This sort of contact would serve to heighten intimacy and rapport between two individuals. In this situation it would be a gesture of agreement or compliment concerning some facts or factors in the external environment, whether it be the comments they are hearing from someone (perhaps a speaker), or another event they are viewing together. For example, two "cats" are "digging" some speaker who is "tellin' it like it is."[5] Being in an unfamiliar environment, they are concerned with "keeping their cool."[6] However, they may also want to express inconspicuously their mutual agreement with some statement the speaker is making. They would then utilize this method of giving skin on the sly so that they could express the agreement between themselves and what the speaker has said and thus reestablish their solidarity. Its function in this case would be mainly expressive.

This manner of giving skin on the sly could also be utilized in a situation where complete secrecy or privacy would not be of prime necessity; in such a case it would be used for the element of style gained by using it. As an example, when Cat A is "cappin' on"[7] Cat B, Cat A has been so extra witty that a third Cat C is compelled to give him some skin on the sly to show his approval. Its function now would be directive. Another instance of this manner of giving skin can be seen in the following episode:

Several cats are standing together, digging a pretty girl walk by.

Cat A: Hey, baby; what's happenin'?

Pretty Girl (stops, turns around, and smiles approvingly to his "rap"[8]): Everything!

Cat A quickly turns his hand inward toward his friend so that the girl can't see, and Cat B encouragingly lays some "sly skin" on him. Whereupon Cat A takes off in hot pursuit of his would-be prey.

Skin can also be used as an exclamation mark for the purpose of emphasis. For example, if you really agree with someone and you want to accentuate this agreement more than usual, you might use some emphatic skin (Figures 7a and 7b). In this case the arm might be raised quite high and brought down with a great deal of exaggerated force; the contact is usually palm-to-palm in this situation. Although the contact seems to be hard, it is actually a quick, crisp movement. Emphatic skin derives its meaning from the total communicative event and must be analyzed with the social context in which it is being used. Its function is both expressive and directive.

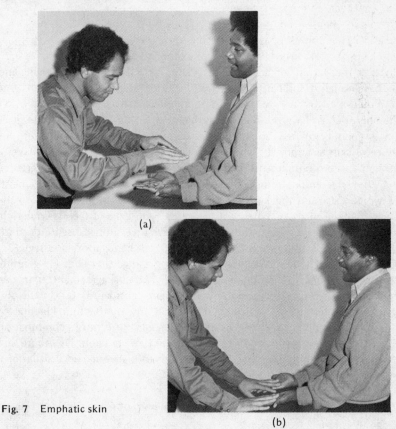

(a)

Fig. 7 Emphatic skin

(b)

One other variation observed in field study was the use of both hands cupped together to receive two hands full of skin in a superlative manner. This gesture expresses an added amount of happy agreement with a proposed suggestion by another. The other person might use one or two hands, depending on his mood. Although this is not the only way to express it, this kind of skin can be termed superlative skin. The complimentary skin and the agreement skin kinemes can be combined with the emphatic, superlative, or sly kinemes; that is, you can compliment or agree in an emphatic, superlative, or sly manner.

Another variation of skinning designed by drummers is as follows: (1) back-of-hand-to-palm, (2) palm-to-palm, (3) elbow-to-palm, and (4) palm-to-palm. This 1-2-3-4 sequence must be executed with lightning speed—something impossible to achieve without practice and something well-suited to drummers, who are concerned with hand and arm speed in relation to their playing. One variation includes elbow-to-elbow contact, reminiscent of the actions that accompany certain kinds of rhyming slang which are said for fun:

"You my frien'? Then gi' me some skin."

"How's it feel? Then gi' me some heel."

"If you a swinger, gi' me some finger."

"If all tha's so, then gi' me some elbow."

"Since all this has come to pass, now gi' me some ass."

The functions of these kinds of variations are expressive.

One look at this variety of meanings associated with the kinemes of giving and getting skin is enough to indicate that the only way to interpret the act in any one situation would be to analyze the entire communicative event. When a cat approaches his friends, he gives skin to say hello; when he "cuts out,"[9] he gives skin to say good-by. When an athlete makes a touchdown or a basket, his teammates give skin as approval; when a cat plays a "groovy"[10] solo or makes a fine speech, he gets complimentary skin; when two or more people agree to something, they give emphatic or superlative skin to accentuate their agreement. Girls and women also use the kinemes of giving and getting skin, but not to the same extent that the men do. When you give skin, you have to feel it; your style and body motion become a part of the way you give the skin because you cannot separate how your body moves and feels from how your hands move and feel.

We have considered four major kinemes of giving and getting skin: (1) greeting skin, (2) parting skin, (3) complimentary skin, and (4) agreement skin. In addition, four major means of execution have been considered: (a) on the sly, (b) emphatic, (c) superlative, and (d) regular. When any of the four kinemes of greeting, parting, compliment, or agreement is "regular," it is not in combination with any of the others. In addition to these four possibilities, there are twenty-eight other combinations that could conceivably arise in social situations. These possible combinations are shown in Table 1.

Table 1 Possible Combinations of Seven Basic Kinemes of Giving and Getting Skin

Interaction	Greeting G	Parting P	Compli-mentary C	Agreement A
Emphatic É	G+E	P+E	C+E	A+E
Superlative S	G+S	P+S	C+S	A+S
Sly Sl	G+Sl	P+Sl	C+Sl	A+Sl
Emphatic + Superlative	G+E+S	P+E+S	C+E+S	A+E+S
Emphatic + Sly	G+E+Sl	P+E+Sl	C+E+Sl	A+E+Sl
Superlative + Sly	G+S+Sl	P+S+Sl	C+S+Sl	A+S+Sl
Emphatic + Superlative + Sly	G+E+S+Sl	P+E+S+Sl	C+E+S+Sl	A+E+S+Sl

Standing Stances: Male

Standing stances are also communicative in the black community. Figures 8a and 8b represent, in a general way, the stance of a player. According to one informant, players are distinguishable from pimps in that the pimps have many lady friends for financial reasons, whereas the players have many lady friends for pleasurable reasons. Figure 8a also illustrates the use of the lowered-shoulder kineme which is common in the stances and walks of most males. One informant noted that usually a cat stands with one or both hands behind him. However, the hands-in-pocket is also a currently popular gesture associated with players and pimps (see Figure 9). Either one or both hands can be in the pocket or tucked underneath the belt; usually the back of the hands show so that actually only the fingers are inside. According to another informant, pimps usually stand with their legs spread apart—especially in bars, which are the centers for a great number of activities. They are the marketplaces for exchanging ideas and wares, socializing, finding out the happenings, checking out new styles, and making business deals of various sorts. Figure 9c illustrates a typical pimp stance; notice the hands are placed behind. The informant commented, "You seldom see a pimp with his legs close together." Figure 9d illustrates a regional variation of the pimp stance found in Virginia and the Carolinas.

(a)

(b)

Fig. 8 Player stance

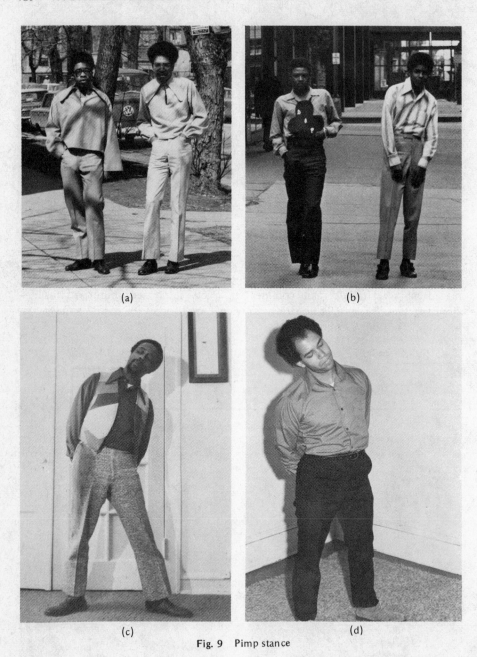

(a)

(b)

(c)

(d)

Fig. 9 Pimp stance

Figure 10 illustrates bodily motion associated with watching a girl walk by. The hands-in-pockets gesture can be seen here. This illustration is especially good for demonstrating the use of shoulder and spine motion, which is felt by this researcher to be the backbone of most bodily gestures. Also noticeable is the lowered-shoulder kineme, and the use of the eyes in the total facial expression to indicate pleasurable attention and interest in an approaching person (in this case, a pretty girl). The look on his face was readily identifiable among various informants as peeping, which is often associated with digging a girl's "action" (watching how she moves her derriere).

Figure 11 illustrates the use of the lowered-shoulder kineme in dancing. The lowered-shoulder kineme is often associated with "rapping"[11] stances, and although it has no unique or special meaning in this particular illustration, the young man interpreted his dance as being his way of showing the girl he digs her.

Fig. 10 Peeping   Fig. 11 Lowered-shoulder kineme

Compare Figure 11 with Figure 12 for a variation of the forward-lowered-shoulder kineme. Contrast Figure 11 with Figure 10 for the difference in the lowered-shoulder kineme. Figure 12 illustrates a rapping stance in a sequence which usually involves moving in toward the girl, closing the space between the two people. Contrast Figure 12 to Figure 13, which is obviously *not* rapping! First of all, the distance between the two is too great, and second, the stance of the cat lacks any characteristics thus far described for rapping (lowered-shoulder, facial expression, etc.).

Figures 14a and 14b are illustrations of rapping in a woofing fashion. "Woofing" is a style of bragging and boasting about how "bad" one is and is sometimes used by males and females when rapping to each other. This would be a sincere self-image, and the attitude is very emphatic, as, "I'm bad and I know I'm bad!"[12] This illustration is included to demonstrate the importance of interpreting an expression within the context of the whole event. Some may not see woofing and notice only the hair style which is expressive of black pride (see discussion of hair styles below). The informants in Figures 14a and 14b may look as though they are angry, possibly because of the extension of the lower lip, but this gesture of lowering the lip is a result of the emphatic manner in which they are "running it down."[13]

(a)

(b)

(c)

Fig. 12   Rapping stance

Fig. 13   Conversation

(a)

(b)

Fig. 14   Rapping styles:
"Woofing" and silent rap

Although rapping is most frequently associated with verbal adroitness, there exists a "silent rap" in which a cat may indicate what his desires are with his facial expression and intensity of eyes, etc. Figure 14c illustrates a cat digging a chick in such a way as to express his feelings without verbalizing. The silent rap can be used effectively across the distance of a room; this is actually one of its best features. In addition, it can be utilized when there are a great deal of noise and a

Fig. 14 (c)

great many people in the environment that would interrupt the flow of a verbal rap. The girl can respond to a silent rap with her own silent rap; or she can communicate lack of interest, also nonverbally.

Figure 15 illustrates the use of eyes in a directive function to focus on a particular person. Notice the lowered shoulder of the person in the background. Figures 16a and 16b show a girl's use of eyes in talking to her boyfriend. Figure 16b shows the use of the hands to achieve intimacy and privacy between two individuals, although in this case he is not necessarily rapping. The use of the eyes to communicate with cats is frequently employed by females as in the following examples: A girl may be in a crowd and see a cat she digs (i.e., one she finds attractive). To draw his attention, she will give him a persistent stare. When he finally looks her way, he will notice her persistent look, read her silent rap, and she will then smile and indicate with her facial expression a "ready"[14] look. When two girls are together and they want to attract some cat's attention, they will look him up and down intensely and when he turns their way they will whisper to each other about how fine he is. The cat may not hear what they are saying, but he will know they are talking about him and are interested in him. On the other hand, if a girl in a lounge does not want to be bothered when a cat comes up to rap, she might lift up one shoulder and sneer slightly, rolling her eyes upward in her head as though saying, "What a drag!" Her use of nonverbal communication is highly effective in all such cases.

Fig. 15   Use of eyes: Male

(a)   (b)

Fig. 16   Use of eyes: Female

Styles of Walking: Male

Each of the various walks described here has its own message when used in a particular social context; most blacks can alternate their walks depending on what the situation calls for. Perhaps the walks most noticeable to people outside the ethnic group are those commonly termed "catting" walks; they come under various individual names in different sections of the country and are constantly changing in style and method of execution. However, the function of the walk remains basically the same: to attract attention and admiration, especially from females. One informant compared it to the strutting of the peacock and his subsequent broad display of fine feathers. This seems to corroborate Hall's recent remarks on the adumbration features of a communicative event which indicates to others some notion of what is to follow.[15] Strutting and display among various fowls and fish have been reported by animal behaviorists for some time; it is also known that disruptions or alterations in the patterns or sequences of these displays can lead to abortive interactions between members of the species. When dealing with man, however, care must be taken not to oversimplify any seeming correlation.

The walks in general are more a matter of individual preference than of socioeconomic background, although those who aspire to be middle-class and white will abandon the ethnic walks and walk like the white folks—less rhythmical, or, as one informant said, "Like a robot." It is certainly erroneous to ascribe a certain combination of walking style, clothes, and vocabulary to just one role or type of personality. This results in a gross stereotyping of the blacks (similar to the Sambo myth) which ignores the true diversity and richness of communicative patterns which exist in the Afro-American culture. Herein possibly lies one of the pitfalls of "ethnic studies."

The chicken walk which Sammy Davis sometimes uses in his version of "Heah come de Judge" has an interesting history and possibly may connect to the catting walks. Similar to the peacock strut, the chicken walk derived its overall strutting appearance and name from its similarity to the strutting of the rooster at mating time. The rooster's mating strut consists of spreading one wing straight down, leaning toward that side, and then circling round the chicken just prior to copulation. The chicken walk consists of a lowered-shoulder kineme (either right or left side) and a simultaneous stiffening of that arm which is held close to the body and leg. When moving, the leg on the lowered-shoulder side bends abruptly and springs back into position abruptly; this results in a bobbing motion. It was suggested that this walk was first used as a catting walk; when black entertainers began to incorporate this strut into their performances, the white people were so amused by it that it gradually became associated with "Uncle Tomism."[16] Today it is not a current walking style, although some entertainers (such as Sammy Davis) still use it for a laugh. The chicken walk is similar to the more animated gowster walk of the bebop era of the early 1950s.

The Slu Foot is another walk which dates back some time. One informant who used the walk regularly referred to it as a "down-home"[17] walk. The feet are turned outward; if the heels were placed together to form the vertex of an angle, it would measure about 150 degrees. The foot lands on the side of the heel, and the weight of the body is actually carried on the sides of the feet. It is possible that this type of walk was first employed by people who had bad feet (perhaps from standing on their feet a lot, such as waiters, soldiers, etc.). However, others not suffering from foot ailments adopted it as a manner of style. This walk can also be seen among classical dancers. It is not currently popular among the teenage set.

The basic soul walk consists of placing one foot directly in front of the other, the heel hits first and the leg drops loosely, which results in a bended leg effect.

The shoulders sway very slightly and naturally, with a slight dropping of the shoulder which moves forward (the lowered-shoulder kineme). The overall motion is a gentle swing; the stride is rhythmic and graceful.

The cool walk (one informant uses this walk on Sundays only) involves the same leg movements as the soul walk. The difference lies in the movements of the arms and hands. With some, the hands are tucked under the belt or inside the pants in front (the hands-in-pockets kineme discussed under Standing Stances). The shoulders sway in a subtle forward-down and backward-up motion. With others, as is customary, individual variations of the cool walk develop. Compare Figure 17a with Figures 17b and 17c.

(a)

(b)　　　　　　　　　　　　　　　　(c)

Fig. 17　Styles of walking: Cool walk and pimp walk

Fig. 17   (d)

The pimp walk presently consists of the basic soul walk with some additional gestures. A cat using such a walk is described as pimping off. One arm swings completely free, crossing over in front of the trunk of the body. The other hand is tucked in the side of the pants, either under the belt or in the pocket; some variations keep both hands in the pockets. A regional variation of this type of walk can be seen in Figure 17d.

The hands in the pocket can be used to facilitate pulling up the trousers. According to one informant, this action results in revealing the outline of the genitals, which is again a recurrence of the display associated with the peacock strut. Whatever individual style a pimp adopts, usually when he walks into a bar everyone "hip"[18] to the culture can tell. Before rapping to a chick, a cat's walk would indicate to the chick what his "game" was so that any chick going for his game and interested in hearing his rap could then make her presence known to him. In this sense the walk could be considered adumbrative in nature and function.

Styles of Walking and Standing: Female

There are several ways a female may indicate to a man that she is interested in him by the way she walks. One basic kind of jaunt consisting of a back-and-forth hip-swinging movement is also found in other cultures. What is unique in the black culture is the overall rhythm of the walk, as well as the forward-and-backward motion of the shoulders which creates movement in the breast area. This kind of walk, which involves movement of many parts of the body (hips, shoulders, breasts), is referred to as "shaking it up." Figure 18 indicates such a walk; notice

Fig. 18   Style of walking: Female

in this the swinging backward of the shoulder. To indicate her availability and interest to a cat in a lounge, a chick may jaunt up to the juke box to play a record. Her walk is sufficient to draw attention. While at the juke box, there are various stances she may employ to further indicate her mood. Standing with her hands resting on the juke box and her derriere thrust outward ("ass tooched out"), she bends one leg forward and somewhat in front of the other leg, which is held straight in back. Figure 19a illustrates such a stance. A variation of this stance is achieved at a bar by resting one arm on the bar, tooching out the hip and

Fig. 19   Female stances   (a)

(b)

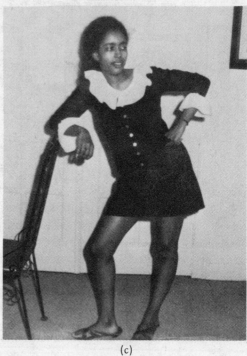

Fig. 19   (c)

placing the other hand on the hip. Again, one leg may be bent in order to accentuate the tooching of the hip (as in Figures 19b and 19c), although other variations of this stance can be seen in places other than bars.

Figure 20 is illustrative of another use of gestures in the black community. This particular interaction occurred spontaneously in a social situation involving the introduction of two people. The man in the middle, during his introduction of his musician friend to his buddy, makes the motions of playing a bass fiddle. This communicated to his buddy that the cat was not only a musician but that he was a bassist, yet nothing was said about music. This particular illustration does not capture the spontaneity of the original movements, but it is possible to see in it the use of such types of gestures to assist communication. Other motions used to indicate musicians and their "axes"[19] would be (1) a quick movement of the first two fingers up near the mouth area to indicate a trumpet player, (2) a quick wrist-shaking for drummers, and (3) an imaginary running the fingers up and down the keyboard for a pianist.

Fig. 20   Introducing a bass player

The Black Power handshake or greeting can be divided into five components executed in a given sequence. These components are illustrated in Figure 21; each is shown first from a distance and then at close range. They are:

1. Mutual encircling of the thumbs, interpreted as meaning *togetherness*.
2. Grasping each other's hands with bended fingers, interpreted as meaning *strength*.
3. Mutual grasping of wrists and hands, meaning *solidarity*.
4. Placing hands on shoulders with a slight amount of pressure, indicating *comradeship*.
5. Raising of the arm, flexing the biceps, and making a fist. This last gesture incorporates the meanings of the first four and symbolizes all of them: black pride, solidarity, and power. Sometimes Step 5 is elaborated by holding up both arms and fists simultaneously for emphasis.

These five steps are often abbreviated by just using Step 1 for close-distance contacts and just Step 5 for greater distances.

Fig. 21   Black Power handshake   STEP 1

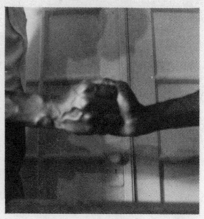

STEP 2

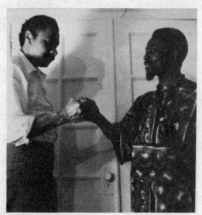

STEP 3

STEP 4

Fig. 21

STEP 5

Fig. 21

Hair and Clothing

Other aspects of nonverbal communication are hair and clothing. Originally what was known in Chicago as the Ranger Bush was worn by a Ranger leader and then adopted by other Rangers as a sign of their membership in that particular group. But the style became popular, and now there is no clear distinction. It consists of a thick bush of hair on top of the head tapered on a slant toward the back of the head and cut close on the sides of the head. This bush on top of the head was used before the "naturals" became popular; one informant suggested that the gang members found it helpful to have a "bush" on the top of the head to cushion the blows received in fights or from police.

As mentioned in the discussion of Figure 14, the natural hairstyle is a symbol of pride in self and heritage. This is a current trend of self-assertion of blackness among the males and females of the black community who, because of white racism, have been heretofore systematically separated from and kept unaware of their true identity. The "process" of hair straightening is now considered demeaning; most black brothers have abandoned it. Also symbolic of the emerging new Afro-American identity are the African-styled clothes and jewelry (dashikis, tikis, and dresses).

Just as clothes and hair consciously affirm black people's strength and unity of purpose for the achievement of control of their lives and destinies, so do the selected kinesic forms of nonverbal communication depicted here act on a deeper level of awareness. The greater awareness and appreciation of nonverbal communication created by this article should make intracultural communication even more meaningful and purposeful.

Photo Credits   Figures 1, 2, 3, 5c, 8a, 9a, 9b, 10, 11, 12, 13, 14a, 15, 16b, 17b, 17c, 18, 19a, 19c, 20, 21 by Benjamin Cooke; Figures 4, 5b, 5d, 6, 7, 8b, 9d, 14b, 14c, 16a, 17a, 17d, 19b by Collis Davis, Jr.; Figures 5a, 9c by Thomas Kochman.

NOTES

1. "The Black Athlete—A Shameful Story," *Sports Illustrated*, July 1, 1968, p. 18.

2. For a more complete explanation and discussion of the terms, see Ray L. Birdwhistell, "Some Relations between American Kinesics and Spoken American English," in *Communication and Culture*, ed. Alfred G. Smith (New York: Holt, Rinehart and Winston, 1966), pp. 182-183 and Alfred S. Hayes, "Paralinguistics and Kinesics," in *Approaches to Semiotics*, ed. T. Sebeok, A. Hayes, and M. Bateson (The Hague: Mouton & Co., 1964), p. 159.

3. More recently the palm-to-palm pattern of skinning illustrated in Figure 3 is being replaced by a fist-to-fist sequence. This variation has evolved out of the Black Power salute, which incorporates an upraised clenched fist as part of its message (see Figure 21).

4. Within the greeting phase, giving and getting skin has generally been replaced by the Black Power handshake. (See discussion and illustration below for the latter.) Skin is still operative within other phases of black interaction, however, as noted.

5. Any words which have been borrowed from the black idiom and which may need clarification will be footnoted and defined the first time they appear in the text. Thereafter any occurrences of the word or phrase will not be footnoted. "Cats" is a term for "men"; "digging" can mean listening to, observing, watching, or enjoying; "tellin' it like it is" means telling the truth.

6. "Keeping their cool" means staying calm, unexcited.

7. "Cappin' on" means engaging in one-upsmanship or winning a verbal contest.

8. "Rap" means to talk in a highly stylized manner.

9. "Cuts out" means to leave, depart.

10. "Groovy" means fine, excellent.

11. "Rapping" in this situation means the kind of personal talk a man engages in with a woman.

12. "Bad" means excellent.

13. "Running it down" is a manner of talking or rapping.

14. "Ready" means psychologically and emotionally prepared for a given confrontation.

15. Edward T. Hall, "Adumbration as a Feature of Intercultural Communication," *American Anthropologist* 66 (December 1964): 154-163.

16. "Uncle Tomism" from *Uncle Tom's Cabin*: a black person who is obsequious to the whites; currently called a "Negro."

17. "Down-home" referring to the South; since most blacks have roots there, this also refers to "soul."

18. "Hip" means aware of what's happening, of what's appropriate.

19. "Axes" is a term for musical instruments.

OBJECTIVE AND SUBJECTIVE PARAMETERS OF LANGUAGE ASSIMILATION AMONG SECOND-GENERATION PUERTO RICANS IN EAST HARLEM

Walt Wolfram

Spanish with its more than seven million speakers is by far the largest language community in the United States after English. See the Saville article in this volume for a description of some of its salient phonological and grammatical features. Like English speakers, Spanish speakers represent a number of speech communities and dialects. Among the Chicanos in the Southwest several varieties stemming from Mexican Spanish dominate; in Florida Cuban Spanish is spoken as well; in New York and other Northeastern cities Puerto Rican Spanish is the most widespread dialect. Spanish-speaking communities, most based on some dialect derived from those of the Southwestern states and Mexico, exist in almost every state. These Spanish communities differ from one another culturally as well as linguistically. Spanish speakers in the Southwest are descended from the first permanent European settlers. They have stable, often rural communities, and their ethnic heritage is both European and Native American. In contrast, the urban Spanish speakers of the Northeastern cities are often first- or second-generation immigrants from the Caribbean. Like all recent immigrants, they are undergoing the stress of linguistic and cultural change, as younger people reorient their identification and values from the old country to the new. And like other non-English-speaking groups in the United States, they find themselves trapped in economic and social marginality.

Walt Wolfram and his colleagues found that the processes of language contact are complicated in the case of New York Puerto Rican youth, for, besides the tension between Spanish, which represents ties to family and native culture, and English, which represents the society they would wish to find a place in, they are most frequently in contact not with an accepted variety of English but with the Black English Vernacular spoken by their equally marginal neighbors. In the present study Wolfram reports assimilation to English speaking by boys who are members of the street culture and by more standard-oriented "lames" (see Labov's "The Linguistic Consequences of Being a Lame" in this volume). Many informants have adapted pronunciation and grammatical features of Black English Vernacular to their own speech. Some have borrowed ritual exchanges unique to Black culture. This study is a complement to Kochman's review of the Black verbal repertoire and Labov's work on linguistic attitudes, also in this volume. Readers with a particular interest in Spanish-speaking peoples should also refer to the selection by Gumperz and Hernández-Chavez on Chicano bilingualism, relevant sections of Glazer's survey of language-maintenance efforts, and Saville's contrastive analyses of English with minority languages. A more detailed but technical discussion of the specific features of Puerto Rican English can be found in Walt Wolfram's "Overlapping Influence and Linguistic Assimilation in Second-

Generation Puerto Rican English" (David M. Smith and Roger W. Shuy, eds., *Sociolinguistics in Cross-Cultural Analysis*, Georgetown University Press, 1972, pp. 15-46).

The Negroes were in New York first and had a head start, but now the Puerto Ricans are copying them. They are borrowing the Negroes' gang structure. Also their jive talk and bop language (Rand 1958: 130).

Although there are a number of ways in which the sociolinguistic situation surrounding the second-generation Puerto Rican in East Harlem parallels that of other immigrant groups, there are also many ways in which this sociolinguistic situation is unique. As part of a major immigrant group in New York City, the Puerto Rican child is born into a relatively homogeneous adult Hispanic community. Typically, his parents have sought out social relations with other Puerto Rican immigrants with whom they can continue Puerto Rican cultural and linguistic traditions. As a young child, the second-generation Puerto Rican is usually raised within the context of this community. His first language is Spanish, and he initially adopts the traditional Puerto Rican culture of his parents. The child, of course, has very little to say in this matter.

As he reaches adolescence, however, he establishes his own peers, and at this point more alternatives open up. He can obviously choose to continue his association with Puerto Rican peers with backgrounds quite similar to his own. If this alternative is chosen, he may remain a fairly integral part of the community, revealing many of the linguistic and cultural traits which have been described for other homogeneous immigrant groups. But there are also other options which may arise because of certain physical and social conditions found in the context of East Harlem. It is a well-known fact that East Harlem is surrounded by the black community in the broader context of Harlem. Although there are obviously many differences between the lower-class black and Puerto Rican cultures, there is an affinity which may unite the groups because of the ethnic and social discrimination found in American society (this is particularly true of darker-skinned Puerto Ricans, who have fewer options in mainstream American culture than their lighter-skinned counterparts). Similar societal roles for Puerto Rican and black communities have been noted in a number of studies of Puerto Rican immigrants. For example, Mills et al. (1950: 133) note:

he [i.e., the Puerto Rican] must "become like" the Negro in the metropolitan community. The world in which he is to function inconspicuously is the Negro world. . . . He finds that he can hold only certain jobs, mix socially only with certain people. Almost always he must live in the Harlem ghetto, or in certain Negro sections of the Bronx.

The similarity in social position, the physical proximity of the groups, and the inevitable social contact that must take place in neighborhood facilities (e.g., schools, recreational centers, etc.) provide an ideal situation for the study of language contact.

Sample   In an attempt to describe the sociolinguistic situation that exists among second-generation Puerto Ricans we have recently completed a study of forty-four informants, twenty-nine Puerto Rican and fifteen black informants. Parents of the Puerto Rican informants were born in Puerto Rico and migrated to the United States. The children, however, were born and raised in New York City.

According to most of the current indices for objectively measuring socio-economic class, the informants would be classified as children of working- or lower-working-class parents. The occupational roles of the heads of households are mainly restricted to operatives, service workers, and laborers. Although we have not made evaluations of all the individual residences of the informants, a survey of the general neighborhoods and observation of a sample of the projects and tenements in which the informants live indicates that they are quite typical of working- or lower-working-class residences in Harlem. Many of the residences would clearly be classified as slum dwellings.

The school records of the informants further indicate that, for the most part, their educational achievement is far below the expected norms for their age level. This was true of their reading levels in particular, a fact which was well confirmed by a small reading passage which was given as a part of the interview. Several of the informants would have to be considered functionally illiterate and were unable to read even the word lists they were given. It is quite clear that the majority of our informants have been alienated from the schools and that their values do not coincide with the middle-class values placed on educational achievement. From background information available to us, it appears that many of the informants can be considered integral members of indigenous peer groups, participating fully in the street culture of New York City.

Our contacts with the informants were established through Youth Development, Inc., a clublike organization with recreational facilities such as table billiards, ping pong, and a basketball court open to the public daily. During the summer months, the organization has established camp facilities at Lake Champion, New York, where the same general activities available in the city are offered on an extended level. The fieldwork which serves as a basis for this analysis was conducted at the camp site. Follow-up interviews were also conducted with some of the informants in East Harlem.

The informants were not chosen randomly. Rather, a decision was made to start interviewing several informants who had considerable status among their peers. This decision was calculated in order to facilitate other interviews and to give us some sample of peer groups. It was anticipated that other individuals would recognize that the leaders had been chosen initially, and that to be asked for an interview would then be associated with status. It was further reasoned that positive reports from informants initially would enhance our chances of obtaining interviews with other informants.

Although somewhat of a risk (since negative reports by leaders would seriously hinder further interviewing), the procedure proved to be generally quite successful in obtaining informants. The association of the interviews with peer status apparently was understood by other members. In fact, several peer associates of our original contacts asked to talk to us before we had an opportunity to request an interview.

After establishing contacts with several of the peer leaders, we selected informants on the basis of either our acquaintance with them through informal contact, reference to other individuals from our initial interviews, recommendation from workers who knew the informants through more extensive interaction on a day-to-day basis, or a combination of these.

As a first step in looking at the linguistic assimilation of Black English among second-generation Puerto Rican teenagers in Harlem, it is necessary to separate Puerto Rican informants on the basis of their social interactions with blacks. There are a number of criteria which we might use for classifying Puerto Ricans into various groups with respect to their contacts with blacks, and in our more detailed study (Wolfram et al. 1971) we have examined several of them. It is clear that the most crucial of these is peer contacts. Who do they associate with in their friendship groups in the neighborhood? In order to elicit this information, each informant was asked to list his main friendship groups and to identify the race of each individual member of that group. The information elicited by this procedure was compared with observation by staff members who were familiar with the informants over an extended period and our participant observation of social interactions during the fieldwork. Although there is obviously a continuum with respect to the extent of black contacts revealed by our informants, we have chosen to separate informants into two groups on the basis of our sociological information: those with extensive black contacts and those with restricted black contacts. Those with extensive black contacts indicate a mixed or majority of blacks among their peers while those with restricted contacts have few or no blacks in their immediate peer groups. The types of group structures, initiation into peer groups, and the activities of the peer groups all give supportive information for our assessment (cf. Wolfram et al. 1971, for further detail on these assessments).

Parameters of Language Assimilation   There are a number of different vantage points from which we may view language or dialect assimilation. We may, for example, look at the assimilation of particular linguistic items by the speech communities in contact. This is the traditional way in which linguists have looked at the effects of linguistic systems in contact. We may also, however, look at communicative acts rather than linguistic items per se. On this level, verbal events such as narrative and conversational types are examined, as communities with different verbal "styles" come into contact. This type of assimilation usually is more apt to be examined by the ethnographer than the linguist, since it deals with the broader communicative functions of language.

Both the above aspects of languages in contact can be dealt with from a fairly objective point of view. But languages, or dialects, do not come into contact under neutral emotional conditions. There are always concomitant attitudinal reactions on the part of the groups in contact. This, of course, is a quite different vantage point from that taken by the traditional linguist. Yet it is an essential correlate of objective language data which must be considered when viewing language assimilation in the broader perspective of language and society.

In the illustrative account that follows, we shall examine the assimilation of black speech by Puerto Ricans in terms of the several different sociolinguistic levels cited above. First, we shall look at the assimilation of particular linguistic features of Black English by Puerto Ricans in New York City. This aspect of the description is based solely on objective data. (In this section, the concept of the "linguistic variable," as used in studies such as Labov 1966, 1968; Shuy, Wolfram, and Riley 1967; and Wolfram 1969 serves as our general model for description. Frequency tabulations of the variants of a variable are presented as quantitative evidence for assimilation.) In the second illustrative description, we shall examine the relative assimilation of certain black verbal activities. In this section, it is the cultural interpretation of verbal activity rather than specific linguistic items which is in focus. The cultural understanding of the form and function of such activities is our concern in this section. This account would probably be considered part of an ethnography of communication, since it deals with the function of communication. In the final section, we shall look at the perception of speech differences on the part of the different Puerto Rican groups. Our description in that section will be based primarily on indirect and open-ended comments by informants rather than on psychometrics. In part, this is due to the fact that the original interviews were not specifically focused on language attitudes. But it also appears that authentic subjective reactions to speech may be more likely when they appear as indirect and open-ended comments rather than forced choices with respect to predetermined categories of reaction.

The Assimilation of Linguistic Items   In order for us to attribute particular linguistic features used by Puerto Ricans in East Harlem to the influence of Black English, it is necessary for us to limit our examination to those items which are unique to Black English among the various dialects used in New York City. Specifically, this means that a number of the items generally described as an integral part of Black English must be eliminated from our consideration. As studies of Black English illustrate, many of the features characteristic of Black English also typify other nonstandard varieties of English. For example, the realization of morpheme-initial /ð/ as /d/ in items like *the, they,* and *that* or the frequent absence of postvocalic *r* in items like *four, sister,* and *board* are phenomena widespread among the various white and black nonstandard varieties of English.[1] To discover its widespread usage among Puerto Ricans does not necessarily indicate that its usage is acquired from blacks. We may interject here that it is not necessary that the features we choose be unique to Black English when compared with various dialects outside of New York City (e.g., Southern white speech), but only that they be unique among the various dialect options available in the local context.

In addition to our elimination of Black English features shared by other varieties of English spoken in New York City, it is also necessary to eliminate from consideration those features which might occur in Puerto Rican English because of interference from Spanish. We must be careful not to confuse interference and assimilation phenomena. For example, the reduction of certain word-final consonant clusters (e.g., [wɛs] "west" [mɛs] "messed") has sometimes been cited as one of the aspects characteristic of Black English phonology. But consonant-cluster reduction of this type may also be a phenomenon which is quite predictable on the basis of interference from Puerto Rican Spanish because of the morpheme structure rules of Spanish (Spanish morpheme structure rules do not allow word-final *st, nd, kt,* etc.). Consonant-cluster reduction is a well-known characteristic of Spanish interference and may be found independent of any of the English dialects with which Puerto Ricans come into contact. Because of the similarity in the realizations from these two sources, referred to elsewhere as "convergent processes," they must be eliminated as primary indicators of assimilation.[2]

One of the widespread features of Black English which qualifies in terms of the conditions stated above is morpheme-final /θ/. Quite typically, items like *tooth*, *mouth*, and *Ruth* are realized as [tuf], [mɑuf], and [ruf], respectively. We can look at the distribution of the *f* variant among the black informants used as a control group and the two groups of Puerto Ricans distinguished previously in Table 1. The tabulation is based on the extraction of variables from the spontaneous conversation of these informants during their initial tape-recorded interview.

The distribution of *f* realization in Table 1 is quite straightforward. The Puerto Ricans with extensive black contacts match (in fact, they exceed, but not to any significant degree) the extent of *f* realization found among the black informants, while the Puerto Ricans with limited black contacts reveal significantly less *f* realization than both groups.

The same pattern of distribution can be demonstrated by looking at another phonological variable, this time related to the vowel system of Black English. In Black English, there are a number of environments where the upgliding offset of diphthongs can be reduced or deleted, so that we have a centralized glide or a monophthong. Words like *time*, *try*, and *ride* may be realized as [ta⁽ə⁾m],

Table 1 Comparison of [f] Realization in Morpheme-Final Position for Blacks, Puerto Ricans with Extensive Black Contacts, and Puerto Ricans with Limited Black Contacts

	Occurrences of [f]	Occurrences of [θ]	% [f]
Black	36	8	81.8
PR with extensive Black contacts	20	3	87.0
PR with limited Black contacts	53	44	54.6

Table 2   Comparison of [a] Realization in Word-Final Position for Blacks, Puerto Ricans with Extensive Black Contacts, and Puerto Ricans with Limited Black Contacts[3]

	Occurrences of [a]	Occurrences of [ai]	% [a]
Black	190	57	76.9
PR with extensive Black contacts	104	44	70.3
PR with limited Black contacts	261	396	39.7

[tra$^{(ə)}$], or [ra$^{(ə)}$d]. Although this realization is quite common in some Southern varieties of white English, it is not typically used in white dialects spoken in Northern contexts such as New York City. The distribution of two main variants (i.e., the presence or absence of the upglide) is indicated in Table 2. Although there are a number of linguistic environments where this realization may occur, the table indicates only the incidence of the variants for word-final position. It is in this environment that the *a* variant is most likely to occur for all the groups.[4] Tabulation was made on the basis of the spontaneous conversation of the informants.

The same pattern observed in Table 1 is repeated in Table 2. There is no significant difference between the blacks and Puerto Ricans with extensive black contacts with respect to this feature. The Puerto Ricans with restricted black contacts and those with extensive black contacts differ quite significantly.

Although we have clearly demonstrated that there is a significant difference between the two groups of Puerto Ricans with respect to these phonological variables, it is essential to note that the differences are quantitative. That is, we observe a certain amount of black influence on both groups, but the one group simply shows a higher frequency of the assimilated variants. The black influence on both groups of Puerto Rican teenagers may be due to the fact that it is virtually impossible for a Puerto Rican teenager in Harlem to avoid some contact with blacks, despite the fact that he may not include them in his peer group. It may be that this restricted contact is sufficient for the assimilation of Black English features to a limited extent. But even if Puerto Ricans with restricted black contacts do not assimilate phonological features from the sporadic contact that they have with blacks, it is quite reasonable to suggest that some assimilation may be acquired indirectly. That is, Puerto Rican adolescents with restricted black contacts may be assimilating phonological features of Black English from Puerto Ricans with more extensive black contacts rather than the blacks themselves.

In the above discussion, we have made no mention of grammatical variables. In order to see if grammatical variables reveal the same type of distribution as the phonological ones, we may look at a grammatical feature unique to Black English in New York City.

One of the grammatical features which is considered unique to Black English in New York City is the use of "distributive *be*." This particular grammatical feature has been described by a number of linguists who vary slightly in their analysis but who generally agree that it refers to a repeated occurrence of some type (cf.

Fasold 1969: 764). The distributive function of *be* is illustrated in sentences such as:

1. He don't usually be home.
2. Sometimes he be at home; I know he do.

This particular function of *be* as a finite form should be distinguished from two other uses which are derived from underlying *will be* or *would be* by phonological processes. A sentence like 3 is derived from underlying *will be* since the negative form of this sentence is 4.

3. He be here in a few minutes.
4. He won't be here in a few minutes.

Similarly, sentence 5 is derived from *would be* since the negative counterpart to 5 requires the modal *would* in Black English, as in 6.

5. He be happy if he could come home.
6. He wouldn't be happy if he could come home.

The occurrences of distributive *be* as well as *be* derived from *will be* or *would be* are tabulated in Table 3 for representatives from the three groups.[5] In addition, however, another category includes the cases which are ambiguous. Despite considerable contextual clues which often clarify the derivation of *be*, there still remain some cases where it is impossible to determine the underlying source of *be*. This is due mainly to the fact that *will be* can often be used to refer to habitual activity of some type, a meaning which is quite close to the use of distributive *be* (e.g., *Whenever he's around his friends he'll be good*).

The figures in Table 3 clearly indicate the contrast between the groups. Although all three groups indicate several examples of *be* derived from underlying *will be* or *would be* (the forms derived through phonological processes), only the blacks and Puerto Ricans with extensive black contacts reveal distributive *be*. The categorical absence of distributive *be* for the three Puerto Rican informants with restricted black contacts indicates that it is a feature which may not be expected to be assimilated by Puerto Ricans unless they have extensive contacts with blacks.

Although we have only cited an illustrative example here, similar results have been obtained for a number of grammatical features unique to Black English among the nonstandard varieties of New York City (cf. Wolfram et al. 1971, particularly Chap. 4). This observation points to a basic difference in the assimilation of features when they are separated on the basis of phonology and grammar.[6] To some extent, the influence of Black English phonological features is common to both groups of Puerto Ricans, the differences between the groups being quantitative. Grammatical features, however, tend to reveal more qualitative differences between the groups. Whereas phonological features may be assimilated through indirect means or through limited contact with blacks, it is apparent that grammatical features unique to Black English are assimilated only through extensive peer contacts.

At this point, we can only hypothesize as to why phonological features are more subject to widespread assimilation by Puerto Ricans than grammatical ones.

Table 3 Occurrences of Invariant *be* for Blacks, Puerto Ricans with Extensive Black Contacts, and Puerto Ricans with Limited Black Contacts

	Distributive *be*/Potential	% *be*	Ambiguous	*will* or *would*/Potential
Black	20/53	37.7	6	2/4
PR with extensive Black contacts	7/46	15.2	2	2/9
PR with limited Black contacts	0/33	0.0	1	2/5

One possible reason may relate to the nature of the linguistic levels involved. For one, the units of phonology (i.e., systematic phonemes) are a relatively small, closed set of items which occur, for the most part, with quite high frequency. The restrictions of the inventory and the relatively high frequency with which the unit occurs may make phonological items more susceptible to assimilation through indirect means or restricted contact. Or, we may suggest that the more superficial the level of language involved, the more susceptible it is to borrowing. Since phonological rules operate on a much more superficial level of language than grammatical rules, they are the rules more susceptible to borrowing.

One might also hypothesize that the difference in the assimilation of phonological and grammatical phenomena is due to sociocultural reasons. Previous studies of socially diagnostic linguistic variables (cf. Wolfram 1969) indicate that grammatical variables more sharply differentiate social groups than do phonological ones. That is, various social groups are more definitely marked on the basis of grammatical features. Given the fact that Puerto Ricans with restricted black contacts often view linguistic assimilation from blacks negatively (a matter which we shall discuss in more detail later), it may be suggested that the relative obtrusiveness of grammatical features makes them less susceptible to borrowing than less obtrusive phonological ones.[7] Linguistic and sociocultural explanations for the difference in assimilation phenomena are, of course, not mutually exclusive. It is quite possible that they reinforce each other.

The Assimilation of Verbal Activities   In the preceding section, we have dealt with only those aspects of assimilation which are accounted for in a "conventional" linguistic description. That is, they are derived through the application of phonological and grammatical rules. But there is another aspect of language usage not generally accounted for when the description is limited to these types of phenomena, namely, the selection of those items from the speaker's linguistic repertoire which are appropriate for a given social situation. These sorts of phenomena are generally considered to be matters of "communicative competence" rather than "linguistic competence" per se. For example, understanding systems of address with respect to the appropriate titles for individuals in a given social relation involves this sort of competence. Competence of this type involves a common knowledge of the function or purpose of the linguistic message on the part of both speaker and hearer.

If the premises of the speaker and hearer are not the same, it is quite possible to misunderstand the function of a message despite the fact that all the phonological and grammatical structures are understood completely. Suppose, for example, a child, in one context, learned that adults with whom he was friendly could be addressed on a first-name basis. An adult, in another context, associates children's use of first names for adults as disrespectful of adult roles and considers it appropriate for children to address adults only by their last name. If the child assumes that he is indicating his friendship to the adult by addressing him on a first-name basis while the adult considers this an insult, we have an obvious gap in communicative content. This breakdown may occur despite the fact that both the addresser and addressee share a common competence in syntactic and phonological content. In some respects, variations in communicative competence across subcultures may lead to more serious communication breakdowns than variations in the linguistic items per se. In this section we shall look at one aspect of communicative competence as a potential indicator of assimilation among the Puerto Rican groups in East Harlem.

One of the characteristic aspects of lower socioeconomic black adolescent vernacular culture is the use of language in a prescribed and ceremonial fashion; that is, there are ritualistic patterns for certain types of verbal interactions. The ritualistic use of language has been described for black adolescent males in Harlem in detail by Labov et al. (1968, vol. II); it has also been described in other urban contexts by Abrahams (1963), Kochman (1969), and Mitchell-Kernan (1969). Probably the most well known of these rituals is what our black informants commonly call *sounding* (sometimes it is also referred to as "the dozens," but the use of this term is apparently decreasing). Other terms are also in use in other urban settings. To describe it briefly (for more detail see Labov et al. 1968: 2. 76-129), the activity is generally thought of in terms of insulting someone's mother, although other relatives might also be mentioned (e.g., grandmother, father, uncle). The presuppositions under which the activity is conducted are shared by the participants; namely, that the insult is not literally true. The proper cultural response to a ritualistic insult is another ritualistic insult. Typically, sounding takes place between two participants; but others are spectators and become judges of the quality of a sound (by laughter, jeering, or comments). The informal judging of such events should not be underestimated; it becomes clear who has the upper hand. The first participant initially insults someone's mother, and the respondent attempts to "outdo" him by responding with an insult that evokes a more effective response with the audience. Trading insults may stop at any stage, but effective sounders can trade verbal quips at some length. This verbal ritual may involve a number of topics, but probably the most prominent ones deal with the mother's sexual activity. Other topics include poverty, age, and physical attributes (skin color, weight, age, etc.).

During the course of our fieldwork, we had considerable opportunity to observe interactions involving ritualistic language usage, and each informant was interviewed about this topic. On the basis of this information we can discuss the verbal activity of sounding as it is an indicator of linguistic-cultural assimilation of black culture by Puerto Ricans. For the indigenous member of black culture, reference to this activity involves (1) an understanding of the procedural guidelines (i.e., the structure of the conversation exchange between interlocutors), (2) the function of the activity (i.e., its ritualistic rather than literal intention), and (3) the informal rules governing the content (i.e., topics and persons who can be the object of sounding). Obviously, a wide range of skill is represented by various members of the community. This is to be expected. For our purposes, we are more concerned with informants' cultural understanding of the activity than their actual verbal skill.

While sounding is widespread and a highly developed ritual among many indigenous black groups of adolescent males, there is no cultural analog for this activity in traditional Puerto Rican culture. This, of course, is not to say that there is no type of joking behavior or that ritualistic insults cannot occur. It is simply to say that the verbal activity that we described above does not have a specific analog in traditional Puerto Rican culture. In fact, ritualistic insults of mothers and relatives as they occur in sounding are generally considered taboo behavior. Mothers are not candidates for insults either ritualistically or literally. To insult a mother is to "curse" her, and this type of activity may readily lead to hostility between the insulter and the mother's son.

Because there is considerable cultural difference in how this activity may be interpreted by blacks and Puerto Ricans from traditional Puerto Rican culture, the observation of informants' reactions to this activity may be an important marker of Puerto Rican assimilation of black verbal styles. We may hypothesize that the Puerto Rican informants with many black peers will characteristically understand more of the rules for this activity and its cultural function as a ritualistic activity. First, of course, we expect that they should be familiar with how the activity proceeds. Our Puerto Rican informants with extensive black contacts quite typically indicate this knowledge. Consider, for example, the following exchange with one of these informants. The following excerpt should be prefaced by noting that the informant had previously been observed in extensive sounding sessions and had been reputed to have considerable verbal skill in the activity. (The fieldworker had also established quite good rapport with the informant through participation in a number of activities with him before the interview.)

FW: You're a pretty good sounder I hear. What if somebody said to you, "your mother drink pee"?

Inf: Your mother's a wino, tell you like that.

FW: Your mother's name Annie Oakley.

Inf: Your mother steal life preservers from Eastern Airlines.

FW: Your mother so old she fart dust.

Inf: Say your mother so old every time she snap her fingers she crack her knuckles.

FW: What if I said your mother's like a railroad track, she been laid all over the country?

Inf: Say your mother got more tracks than canal 47.

FW: What if I said your mother got legs coming out her nose?

Inf: Your mother got laid so many time she look like hopeless hoe (5: 8-9).[8]

In the above passage, the informant obviously demonstrates that he understands how the exchange of the discourse is structured. He further indicates that he is familiar with the topics which are suitable for ritualistic insult and the type of response which can "score" (i.e., bring about a positive effect as indicated by the evaluation of the peer participants). That is, he keeps the topic constant (i.e., if the participant insults his mother, his response is in terms of his mother) while elaborating on the theme of the comment (e.g., the insult "Your mother so old she fart dust" is responded to by the comment "Your mother so old every time she snap her fingers she crack her knuckles"). Although some of the other Puerto Rican informants with extensive black contact do not show the same degree of verbal skill in this activity, it is still quite obvious from their comments that they are quite familiar with how the activity proceeds. Consider, for example, the following excerpts.

Inf: Yeah, like yesterday we went over there and this guy name Rollie, me and him was sounding about mothers, you know, say "Hey man, your mother's a cab driver, no your mother this and that" . . . We joke with him like that and he came back with it, ah man, "Your mother this and how's your mother," and I say, "Oh yeah, your father too," we just keep it up, and then we stop and we shake hands, see that's the way I like people, don't take things serious.

FW: What would you say if Rollie said, "Your mother's a cab driver"?

Inf: I'll say your mother's a bus driver.

FW: What if he says your mother stink?

Inf: And your mother's a box, we gotta lot of ways to it.

FW: Your mother drink pee.

Inf: . . . I said that I got to your mother and then he say, "Your mother's a hole," and I tell him, "Your father's a faggot" and we kept on, but we never took it serious (18: 6-7).

Again there is obvious familiarity with the activity on the part of the informant. The procedure of the verbal exchange and the informal rules governing topics and comments is again illustrated, although this informant does not have the reputation for his skill that we indicated for the previously cited informant. Also indicated in the above passage is a cultural understanding of its ritualistic rather than its literal intent. Comments like "we never took it serious" and "that's the way I like people, don't take things serious" in the above passage are references to this cultural understanding. It is quite plain, then, that the informal rules and cultural function of this verbal activity have been assimilated by Puerto Rican adolescent males with extensive black contacts.

Now let us turn to the Puerto Rican group with restricted black contacts. With respect to the type of discourse involved in sounding, a majority of our informants indicated that they were quite familiar with the activity, although, in some cases, the term was not immediately related to the activity by the informants.

FW: What about sounding?
Inf: . . . Oh yeah, sounding, you mean like, you know, your mother eats . . .
FW: What did you think I meant?
Inf: I thought you meant cursing.
FW: What if I said your mother smelled like twenty pounds of yesterday?
Inf: Your father.
FW: What would be an example of one with a curse in it?
Inf: Well, your mother has hair on her chest, your father has a pussy, and, you know, all that silly stuff (7: 1).

Typically, informants are familiar with the procedural guidelines which govern this activity, but they do not spend nearly as much time engaged in the verbal activity as blacks or Puerto Rican informants with extensive black contacts. There are, however, several of the informants who indicate practically no familiarity with it, as illustrated by the following exchange with one informant.

FW: I hear a lot of sounding. Is sounding . . . ?
Inf: Like the way you talk?
FW: No, you know, sounding on each other.
Inf: Or like we're cursing at each other or something?
FW: Like if somebody said your mother has BO or something like that.
Inf: Oh yeah, body odor.
FW: What if they said your mother wears combat boots or your mother drinks pee?
Inf: No, that don't have nothing to do with it.
FW: Do you ever do any of it? Like, I hear a lot of it around here.
Inf: Like we do it, but they don't do it, you know . . . Like if you want to crack a little bit of jokes, you know, if you want to laugh, you know, my friend Izzie comes out with some good jokes (34: 11).

This type of response is more typical of Puerto Rican informants who are somewhat oriented toward the values of mainstream culture (as indicated by educational achievement, aspiration, peer-group activities, etc.) vis-à-vis the indigenous street culture. That is, they are cultural "lames."[9] This term, obviously borrowed from the contiguous black community, is used by informants themselves to describe either a social isolate who does not have extensive peer contacts or an individual who has peer contacts with a group that maintains values which conflict with the values of the indigenous culture. Although, as a part of this study, we interviewed several black informants who might qualify as lames, we may note that there was considerably more familiarity indicated by these informants than the Puerto Rican lames. The degree of unfamiliarity indicated above is not typical of the responses of the group as a whole. (Only three other informants in this group indicated this extent of unfamiliarity.) Generally speaking, we may conclude that Puerto Ricans with restricted black contacts are familiar with the form of the verbal exchange.

For the most part, the content is also familiar to the majority of Puerto Rican informants with restricted black contacts. That is, the topics we described previously as usually represented in sounding are verified by the informants. There is, however, one interesting restriction on the content indicated by several of the informants. These informants limit or redefine sounding so that mothers may be eliminated as topics for insult. This sort of restriction is indicated in the comments that follow.

> Inf: Everybody sounds sometime. Like if somebody has a pair of funny sneakers or something, then you, like start making jokes at it or like if once you were playing a game and you fell or something, they start, they bring it up and start laughing at it then everybody keeps on making more things.
> FW: Do they sound on mothers?
> Inf: No, 'cause some people's mothers are dead and like once this guy sound at his mother and the guy started crying and got mad and he was going to hit him with a bottle 'cause they don't like nobody cursing at they mothers (33: 7).

> FW: Do they sound on someone's mother?
> Inf: No, very seldom, no only on ourself. We don't talk about people's mothers . . . 'cause if somebody starts cussing on people's mother, you know, if they want to have a fight I got a pair of boxing gloves (43: 8).

It may be hypothesized that mothers are eliminated from the ritualistic insults because of the influence of the traditional Puerto Rican taboo on such insults. The general activity may be adopted, but it is modified in such a way as to make it more compatible with traditional Puerto Rican culture. Rather than take the risk of having the ritualistic insult misinterpreted with respect to traditional Puerto Rican culture, the topic of mothers simply may be eliminated.

Where there is not adaptation of the type mentioned above, we have a situation which may be subject to cross-cultural misunderstanding. The hostility that can be aroused if the functional intent is not precisely understood is a recurrent theme in the comments of the majority of Puerto Ricans with restricted black contacts. In several of the quotes mentioned above, sounding is associated with "cursing someone's mother," and we have already stressed the seriousness of this offense. We have many references to fights which have occurred as a result of the apparent misunderstanding of the function of sounding. Comments like the following are recurrent throughout our interviews with informants in this category.

> FW: Do the guys sound on one another?
> Inf: They usually do, man, ah like they be sounding on they mothers like that all they could think of mothers and your mother is this and that and that could really get a guy angry, you don't have no right of sounding on mines . . .

FW: What if somebody said your mother drinks pee?

Inf: I would punch them in the mouth for that or otherwise I would tell them to keep his cool (11: 7-8).

Our references to hostile activity resulting from sounding among some of the Puerto Ricans with restricted black contacts should not, of course, be taken to mean that hostilities never arise among blacks or Puerto Ricans with extensive black contacts. Hostilities can arise for a number of reasons (e.g., a sound is not sufficiently clear so that it can allow a literal rather than ritualistic interpretation or an opponent is sufficiently outdone so as to react hostilely out of embarrassment or frustration) among the other groups. But we are impressed by the recurrency of this theme in the comments of the Puerto Ricans with restricted black contacts as compared with the occasional and usually tangential mention of tensions surrounding the activity by the other groups. We may hypothesize that the obsession with the hostilities surrounding this activity are related to the potential for cross-cultural misinterpretation. Familiarity with the procedural guidelines of the verbal activity obviously does not necessarily ensure understanding of its cultural function.

The preceding illustrative description demonstrates that a thorough account of language assimilation must consider communicative as well as linguistic competence. These types of verbal activity may be diagnostic of assimilation in a manner which parallels the more traditional examination of linguistic variables. And, as we have stated earlier, the examination of verbal activities may be just as important, if not more so, than the examination of linguistic items in our description of language or dialects in contact.

The Subjective Level of Language Assimilation   In the previous descriptions of linguistic assimilation, we have focused primarily on objective aspects of language (although, of course, some of our description of language repertoire in the preceding section was based on informants' perceptions of specific verbal activities). In this section we shall look at some aspects of the more general perception of the language situation on the part of the Puerto Rican groups. The previous descriptive sections have given us an idea of what type of language assimilation is taking place. Now we want to know how Puerto Ricans view and react to the linguistic assimilation in a wider cultural framework. As with the other descriptive accounts, we are dependent on interviews with the informants, observation of various language contact situations, and reports by the informants.

To begin with, we must observe that there is a tendency for Puerto Ricans with extensive black contacts to minimize differences that exist between groups. We may thus get informants in this group who deny that the way blacks and Puerto Ricans speak English is different. For some of these informants, there is, of course, a great deal of objective similarity in the variety of English used by the two groups. But informants who would still perceptually be identified as being Puerto Rican may also tend to minimize these differences. The tendency to minimize speech differences that we observe on the part of Puerto Ricans is consistent with their perception of the social relations of these groups in a wider context. For example, we have observed that informants in this category may minimize physical differences between the groups, as one informant noted:

It's really hard to tell between a Puerto Rican and a Negro; it's really hard, you know (18: second interview).

Similarly, social tensions between the communities may be minimized.

You know, like before, it was a lot of race problem in East Harlem, like the community works together, you know, none of this bullshit about now, you black, get away from me, you're white, you better go to Hell or something like that. Ain't like that no more, you know (5: 7).

In reality, of course, there are considerably more differences than are admitted in the above comment. For example, a member of the Puerto Rican community generally would have little difficulty in distinguishing the blacks from the Puerto Ricans. And we know that there are still many tensions which exist between the black and Puerto Rican communities. For our purposes here, however, the actual situation is less important than the perception of social relations by Puerto Ricans in this category.

An interesting assessment of the unity of blacks and Puerto Ricans by the members of this group has been observed in relation to the use of Spanish in peer-group situations. In questioning about the use of Spanish with friends, several informants cited the fact that blacks learn to speak Spanish. One informant made the following observation when he was asked if any of the members of his peer group spoke Spanish.

Inf: Yeah, mostly the colored guys.

FW: The colored guys speak Spanish? Do you speak Spanish with one another?

Inf: You know, like sometime I say, "tu madre es puta," that means your mother's a whore, and the guy says, "tu abuela" you know, "your grandmother" and jive, and they say, "Vamos a comer," "let's go eat," stuff like that, yeah, and they know how to say like, somebody be talking, like two parents be talking, they say, "Estos ninos son tecatos," you know, like these kids are junkies, and they go around and they say, Hey man, your mother's over there saying we're junkies, I heard her, something like that (5: 11).

Another informant in this category confirms this impression when he says, "Colored dudes, you know, they know Spanish too" (18: second interview). In reality, we find that the extent of Spanish usage found among blacks in these peer groups is generally restricted to a few phrases or lexical items. One of the black informants in our corpus gives an illustration of this phenomenon when he is talking about a Puerto Rican who is a member of a predominantly black peer group.

We say like, "Eh mira," you know, we talk in Spanish and ask him for a cigarette, "Dame cigarillo" and he say I don't have none and he say, "look here," man, he make his speech, like if we have a party or something and that guy say, "Look at that Spanish guy over there" he walk over to him, he say, he make his little speech, he say, "Listen now, listen to me real good, I may be Spanyola on the outside, but inside I have a Negro heart, you know." Everybody look at him and say, you know, they start clapping, they say, "Reuben, say some more," and he be telling all that and then you know, most the time they say, "what's happening," you know, he consider hisself a Nigger, I wouldn't blame him (1: 17).

It is obvious from other comments by Puerto Ricans and our observation of social interactions that the claim concerning the acquisition of Spanish by blacks is quite exaggerated. The learning of a few fixed phrases is quite different from acquiring language competence in Puerto Rican Spanish. Statements by Puerto Rican informants also tend to contradict their observation that blacks speak Spanish. In other contexts, Puerto Ricans mention that Spanish is generally avoided around black peers. The reasons for this avoidance are stated succinctly by one Puerto Rican with extensive black peers who observes that the reason he does not use Spanish with his peers is "So the guy could know that I'm boss, I don't want to hide nothing." For Puerto Ricans to use Spanish with black peers is socially inappropriate since it may be associated with ineptness in cultural adaptation. As illustrated in the previously cited quote, Puerto Ricans with predominantly black peers have to prove that they belong. The use of Spanish with another Puerto Rican in the peer group would thus be counterproductive to this purpose. Furthermore, the use of Spanish may be disruptive to a social group. If a black peer does not understand it, he may view it suspiciously, in which case it could be disruptive to the social group. Informants mentioned that Puerto Ricans who talk Spanish around black peers may be suspected of criticizing or attempting to conceal information from their black peers.

If Spanish is not likely to be used around black peers, we may ask why some of the Puerto Ricans make special mention of the fact that blacks speak Spanish. Part of the reason may be related to the point that was mentioned earlier; that is, the tendency of Puerto Ricans with extensive black contacts to minimize differences that exist between the two groups. But we may also hypothesize that there is a desire on the part of these informants to interpret assimilation as reciprocal. That is, not only are Puerto Ricans assimilating aspects of the surrounding black culture, but blacks are also assimilating aspects of Puerto Rican culture. In reality, assimilation is largely one-way; it is the Puerto Ricans who are copying the blacks. Black teenagers do not pick up aspects of Puerto Rican English which might identify them as being Puerto Rican, such as occasional syllable-timing, the tendency not to reduce vowels in unstressed syllables, and so forth. Nor do they pick up any real conversational ability in Puerto Rican Spanish. When more integrative aspects of linguistic competence are considered, the few phrases or lexical items learned by some blacks in East Harlem must be considered tokens. These sorts of phrases indicate a relatively superficial level of borrowing. But these small tokens apparently are interpreted quite symbolically by some Puerto Ricans who desire to see the assimilation process working both ways.

Now let us turn to the Puerto Ricans with restricted black contacts. Unlike the Puerto Ricans with extensive black peer-group contacts, there is no tendency to minimize the speech differences between the groups. Therefore, we find informants in this category perceiving blacks and Puerto Ricans as talking quite differently. The following types of reactions are quite typical.

FW: Is there a difference between the way Puerto Ricans and blacks talk?

Inf: Say, like a white person, he will say, "you try to be cool," now a black person will say, "You all try to be cool." So there's an accent right there (39: second interview).

FW: Is there any difference between the way Puerto Ricans and blacks talk?

Inf: Yes, there is a big difference . . . Spanish, he'll say slap me five, but the Negro will come up and say, "Put some skin on my hand," you know, and he'll use "man" and he'll say, "Come on, man, let's go and do our little thing."

FW: Puerto Ricans don't say that, right?

Inf: They say it, but it's different, way different by the way Negroes say it (43: second interview).

FW: Do you think that black and Puerto Ricans sound any different when they talk?

Inf: Yeah, I think the Negro stretches the word.

FW: Give me an example of him stretching the word.

Inf: Like when they say man I would say, "Hey man, cut it out." Listening to a Negro, they don't speak like that, they say, "maaan," and it starts moving you know. They emphasize on the word more (11: second interview).

This perception of speech differences is consistent with the perception of differences between blacks and Puerto Ricans in East Harlem on a broader cultural level. Despite the fact that the social position of Puerto Ricans and blacks is quite similar in the wider context of American society, there is sometimes considerable intergroup tension. This tension tends to highlight the differences between the groups.

You see, we have half a building full of niggers, guys that really look for trouble. They all came down 'round about and a couple of guys from our building and we have room. 8 [sic] per cent of the guys round here are Spanish. They surrounded the niggers on the outside I went straight down and hit a couple of them on the head. Now I was at the bottom and when the Spanish finished with the niggers out there, they came in. They don't fool around with the Spanish cause, what you call it, Spanish take their ass and make it inside out (43: 13-14).

These types of tensions are not uncommon, despite superficial statements of solidarity about the relations between the groups.

Like some of these Negro guys, I don't hang around, most of the guys that stick around there, they always, you know, look for trouble (35: 9).

In such a context, then, it is quite predictable that differences in speech should be brought out to parallel the perception of other social differences.

At this point, we must remember that Puerto Ricans with restricted black contacts, despite their perception of speech differences, do show some influence in certain aspects of their speech. We have shown that there is some phonological influence regardless of the extent of contact. If we had included vocabulary in our study, we would also have seen that there are a number of indigenous black terms which have been borrowed into the lexicon of both groups of Puerto Ricans. But these similarities are perceived as insignificant when compared with the amount of assimilation revealed by Puerto Ricans with extensive black contacts. In fact, there is evidence that some Puerto Ricans are not conscious of the extent to which black speech may have influenced their own speech. This was vividly illustrated in one incident that occurred following an interview. The informant, never having heard his voice on a tape recorder, asked to play back part of the interview. After listening to his voice for a minute, he worriedly exclaimed to the interviewer, "Man, I sound just like a nigger." The assimilation of Black English may be viewed negatively by Puerto Ricans in this group, despite the fact that they have assimilated aspects of Black English in their own speech. Consider the following comments in this connection.

FW: Do a lotta Spanish kids sound like black kids?
Inf: Sometimes . . .
FW: How about you? Do you think you ever sound like a black when you talk?
Inf: I don't know, do I?
FW: I want your opinion. Do you think you'd like to?
Inf: No.
FW: Why not?
Inf: I want to talk like I always talk. I don't care if I can talk English, at least I can talk.
FW: Do you think that when a Spanish guy talks like a black guy that makes him sound cool?
Inf: Corny.
FW: Does it make him sound tough?
Inf: Not tough but corny.
FW: You know some guys who talk that way?
Inf: Yeah . . . I think they're trying to show off, like, if they got a colored friend, they want to show off in front of him.[10]

The extensive adoption of Black English by Puerto Ricans with extensive black contacts may be viewed as an attempt to be something that a Puerto Rican naturally is not, and therefore be considered pretentious. And even though Puerto Ricans with restricted black contacts may be further removed from traditional

Puerto Rican culture than their parents, they may define it as a symbol of the rejection of the Puerto Rican community of which they are still a part.

Any negative reactions toward the assimilation of Black English on the part of the teenagers with restricted black contacts are clearly reinforced in the homes. If parents perceive certain aspects of their children's English to be influenced by black speech, they may react quite negatively. In the first place, many parents speak to their children in Spanish and may require that the children answer them in Spanish. As it was put by one informant:

> Well, I have to [answer his parents in Spanish]. My father asks me a question in Spanish. He won't take it in English. I have to answer him in Spanish 'cause he says I'm not an Italian and I'm not a Negro, but I'm a Puerto Rican and have to speak to me in my language . . . [He says] I was born in Puerto Rico and . . . I'm gonna raise you like Puerto Ricans. So if we speak English, in front of him . . . it's like cursing right in front of him (10: 9).

In some instances, it is considered inappropriate for children to answer parents in English at all. To speak to parents in a dialect of English that is discernibly influenced by Black English is to elicit an even stronger reaction on the part of parents. One informant explained how a friend who talked like a black was smacked by his father who said "You *can* talk English, but normal English." There is considerable evidence that the parents view the acquisition of Black English features on the part of their children as quite insulting. The adoption of these features may be interpreted symbolically by a parent as a move away from traditional Puerto Rican culture.

The reactions of Puerto Ricans with restricted black contacts may be summarized as being basically ambivalent. On the one hand, they are quite aware of the differences that exist between the two groups in a number of areas of culture and they tend to perceive these differences in speech as in other areas. On the other hand, they are faced with the reality of the social situation in which it is very difficult to avoid some influence from the black community which surrounds them. By perceiving the amount of influence on their own speech as insignificant they do not have to deal with this limited assimilation while reacting negatively toward the amount of assimilation that takes place among the counterparts with extensive black contacts.

NOTES

1. See articles by Lourie, McDavid, and Labov's "General Attitudes towards the Speech of New York City" in this volume. [Eds.]

2. Although convergent processes cannot be considered primary indicators of linguistic assimilation from Black English, the frequency distribution of these types of phenomena differs for those Puerto Ricans with extensive black contacts and those with restricted black contacts (cf. Wolfram 1972).

3. Marie Shiels Djouadi is responsible for the extraction and tabulation of this variable.

4. There is a consistent ordering of environments which increase the probability of [a] for all the groups, but this shall not be considered here (cf. Wolfram et al. 1971: 156-164).

5. For this tabulation, only nine informants were used (three blacks, three Puerto Ricans with extensive black contacts, and three Puerto Ricans with limited black contacts).

6. Further investigation of the relation of grammatical and phonological assimilation reveals that Black English grammatical processes are assimilated as grammatical processes and phonological processes as phonological ones. At first glance, this may seem like a trivial observation, but a closer examination of some of the features which might be interpreted to result from either grammatical or phonological processes indicates that this is a significant observation (cf. Wolfram 1972: 37-40).

7. One of the arguments against this hypothesis comes from our observation of lexical borrowing. It is generally assumed that socially diagnostic lexical items are more obtrusive than both phonological and grammatical ones. Yet there is considerable lexical borrowing by both groups of Puerto Ricans.

8. The citation refers to the tape number assigned to the informant in our corpus and the page of the typescript on which the quote may be found. In cases where we have not transcribed the section quoted, we simply give the tape number and which interview we are quoting (i.e., our first or second interview with the informant).

9. See Labov's "The Linguistic Consequences of Being a Lame" in this volume. [Eds.]

10. This quote is excerpted from a supplemental series of interviews on Puerto Rican English by Paul Anisman. I am grateful to Mr. Anisman for bringing it to my attention.

References

Abrahams, Roger D. 1963 *Deep Down in the Jungle*. Chicago, Aldine.

Fasold, Ralph W. 1969 "Orthography in Reading Materials for Black English Speaking Children." In: *Teaching Black Children to Read*. Ed. by Joan C. Baratz and Roger W. Shuy. Washington, D.C., Center for Applied Linguistics.

——— 1969 "Tense and the Form *be* in Black English." *Language*. 45. 763-777.

——— 1971 "Minding your Z's and D's: Distinguishing Syntactic and Phonological Variable Rules." *Papers from the Seventh Regional Meeting of the Chicago Linguistic Society*.

Kochman, Thomas. 1969 "Rapping in the Black Ghetto." *Trans-action*.

Labov, William. 1966 *The Social Stratification of English in New York City*. Washington, D.C., Center for Applied Linguistics.

Labov, William, Paul Cohen, Clarence Robins, and John Lewis. 1968 *A Study of the Non-Standard English of Negro and Puerto Rican Speakers in New York City*. Final Report, Cooperative Research Project no. 3288, U.S. Office of Education.

Mills, C. Wright, Clarence Senior, and Rose Kahn Golsen. 1950 *The Puerto Rican Journey*. New York, Russell and Russell.

Mitchell-Kernan, Claudia. 1969 *Language Behavior in a Black Urban Community*. Unpublished Ph.D. dissertation, University of California, Berkeley.

Rand, Christopher. 1958 *The Puerto Ricans*. New York, Oxford University Press.

Shuy, Roger W., Walter A. Wolfram, and William K. Riley. 1967 *Linguistic Correlates of Social Stratification in Detroit Speech*. Final Report, Cooperative Research Project no. 6-1347, U.S. Office of Education.

Wolfram, Walt. 1969 *A Sociolinguistic Description of Detroit Negro Speech*. Washington, D.C., Center for Applied Linguistics.

Wolfram, Walt, in collaboration with Marie Shiels and Ralph Fasold. 1971 *Overlapping Influences in the English of Second-Generation Puerto Rican Teenagers in Harlem*. Final Report, U.S. Grant no. 3-70-003(508), Office of Education.

Wolfram, Walt. 1972 "Overlapping Influence and Linguistic Assimilation in Second-Generation Puerto Rican English." In: *Sociolinguistics in Cross-Cultural Analysis*. Ed. by David M. Smith and Roger W. Shuy. Washington, D.C., Georgetown University Press.

ENGLISH AS A SECOND LANGUAGE FOR NAVAJOS

Robert W. Young

According to 1970 census figures, the United States has 792,730 Native Americans, 268,205 (or about one-third) of whom claimed an American Indian language as their mother tongue. Although estimates of how many American Indian languages there are vary between fifty and several hundred, here are the major languages and language families, along with approximate numbers of speakers and their location in 1970:

Language family	Language and number of speakers	Location
Algonquin	Ojibwa: 30,000	Northern Midwest
	Blackfoot: 6000	Montana
	Cheyenne: 3500	Oklahoma, Montana
	Arapaho: 2500	Oklahoma, Wyoming
	Fox: 1500	Oklahoma, Iowa
	Delaware: 100+	Oklahoma
	Passamaquoddy: 100+	Maine
Salishan	Flathead: 1000	Montana
Athapaskan	Navajo: 100,000	Arizona, Utah, New Mexico
	Apache: 10,000	Arizona
Penutian	Yakima: 1000	Washington
	Shahaptian: 1000	Idaho
	Klamath: 100+	Oregon
Yuman	Yuma: 1000	Arizona
	Mojave: 1000	Arizona
Iroquoian	Cherokee: 10,000	Oklahoma, N. Carolina
	Seneca: 4000	New York
	Mohawk: 2000	New York
	Oneida: 1500	New York
Siouan	Sioux: 20,000	Northern Midwest
	Assiniboin: 1000	Montana
	Winnebago: 1500	Wisconsin, Nebraska
	Crow: 3500	Montana
	Omaha: 2000	Nebraska
	Osage: 100+	Oklahoma
Caddoan	Caddo: 100+	Oklahoma
	Pawnee: 100+	Oklahoma
Muskogean	Choctaw: 7000	Oklahoma, Mississippi
	Chickasaw: 2500	Oklahoma
	Creek: 7500	Oklahoma
	Seminole: 100+	Florida
Keresan	Keresan: 7000	New Mexico
Uto-Aztecan	Papago: 8000	Arizona
	Pima: 5000	Arizona
	Hopi: 4000	Arizona
	Ute: 3000	Utah, Colorado
	Shoshone: 5000	West
	Paiute: 2000	West

Language family	Language and number of speakers	Location
Uto-Aztecan	Comanche: 1500	Oklahoma
	Kiowa: 2000	Oklahoma
Tanoan	Tewa: 2000	New Mexico
	Tiwa: 2500	New Mexico
	Towa: 1000	New Mexico
Zuñi	Zuñi: 3500	New Mexico

Robert W. Young's article concentrates on Navajo, the largest of these speech communities, and illustrates the radical dissimilarity between the language and culture of the Navajos, on the one hand, and the language and culture of Euro-Americans, on the other. His distinction between material and nonmaterial culture and his description of cultural borrowing (actually enforced cultural lending by our schools) are apt definitions of the interaction between American education and any cultural minority. But Young's example of the Navajo world view—the absence of coercive tactics or language—makes it clear just how fundamentally the Navajos differ from the white Americans who surround them. (For more on semantics and world view, see "The Nature of Language" in the General Introduction.) Saville's section on Navajo phonology and syntax complements the present essay, pointing to potential linguistic conflict where Young emphasizes potential cultural conflict. We need similar linguistic and cultural information for many other groups of Native Americans if we hope to open more effective lines of communication between these communities and mainstream society. One such study is the Philips article, which analyzes how children in another group of Native Americans participate in learning structures at home and in school.

Cultural Borrowing

In everyday parlance we use the term *culture* in a wide variety of contexts and meanings ranging from "proper" social deportment to the acquisition of "refined" tastes in music, literature, and the arts. In addition, the term forms part of the specialized vocabulary of several disciplines, including agriculture, bacteriology, and anthropology. In the latter, and in this chapter, *culture* refers to the varied systems developed by human societies as media for adaptation to the environment in which their members live; in its totality, a cultural system constitutes the means through which the group to which it pertains achieves survival as an organized society. Such systems range from simple to the complex and sophisticated, and among themselves they exhibit a wide variety of differences in form and content.

When we speak of the culture of a society or community, we have reference to the entire gamut of tools, institutions, social values, customs, traditions, techniques, concepts, and other traits that characterize the way of life of the group. The specific items that make up a cultural system, or *elements* as they are called, fall into two broad categories: material and nonmaterial. In the first are included such features as tools (axes, hammers, jacks), vehicles (wagons, cars, airplanes), clothing (shirts, dresses, shoes) and shelter (houses, tents, hogans); and among the nonmaterial elements of culture are such institutions as social organization, kinship systems, marriage, government, religion, and language.

The content of a given cultural system is determined by a wide range of factors, including the physical environment, inventiveness of the people, influence of surrounding communities, trade, opportunities for borrowing, and many others. For obvious reasons the material content of traditional Eskimo culture contained elements of a type not found in the cultures of the peoples living in the tropical rain forests or of those living in the hot deserts. The physical environment, in each instance, imposed different requirements for survival, and a different framework for cultural development.

Borrowing and trade have had a tremendous influence on cultural content, in modern as well as in ancient times, and a cursory glance at the present-day Eskimo, the Navajo or, for that matter, virtually any community of people anywhere on earth, is sufficient to reflect the importance of these avenues for cultural change and growth. Guns, steel axes, knives, metal fishhooks, motorboats, rubber boots, stoves, tobacco, liquor, and a host of items have been borrowed and incorporated into Eskimo culture in the course of contact with outside cultural communities; horses, sheep, goats, iron tools, wagons, automobiles, radio, television, and many other elements have been borrowed by, and have become part of the cultural systems of such people as the Navajo since their first contact with Europeans. And in Japan, Western European and American influences have changed the way of life in less than a century.

In Alaska, in the American Southwest, and elsewhere, the pace of cultural change has quickened with each generation, as aboriginal peoples respond to changing conditions of life. To no small degree, the dominant Anglo-American system, with its emphasis on molding the environment itself to human need, has established new conditions for life and survival; new conditions so complex in nature that the institution of the school has come to occupy a position of primary importance providing, as it does, the training necessary for successful living.

Formal education, in modern American society, is designed to facilitate the successful adaptation and survival of its members within an environment and under conditions that the society itself, to a large extent, has created. The educational system is not only one that cultural minorities have *borrowed*, but one which the Anglo-American cultural community has imposed upon them. With reference to such culturally divergent minorities, formal education is the instrument used by the dominant society to generate and accelerate cultural change through the medium of induced "acculturation"—that is, the process through which such communities as the Navajo are induced and trained to participate in the dominant national cultural system. It is, in a broad sense, a form of cultural borrowing, differing, however, from the more usual process of voluntarily picking and choosing, on the part of the borrower, in that some of the stimuli for change are imposed and the initiative is taken by the "lending" system itself. Unfortunately, the process of induced or—as it often turns out, *compelled* —acculturation is not without its problems for the "lender" as well as for the "borrower." The need for change is not always as apparent to the latter as it is to the former, and in the absence of recognition of compelling necessity, the borrower is sometimes reluctant to accept what is held out to him. It may not appear, from his viewpoint, to fit his requirements, or its acceptance may threaten existing institutions and practices upon which he places value.

Consequently, compulsory education, when first imposed upon Indian communities by the federal government just before the turn of the century, met with strenuous resistance. From the hopeful point of view of the would-be "lender," schooling offered improved tools for survival in a changing environment; but from that of the "borrower" the educational process threatened cultural extinction. It removed the child from the home where he received his traditional training in the language, values, religion, and other institutions of his own culture and promised to leave him ill-prepared for life in the only world his parents knew. They resisted and the "lenders" applied force. A long tug-of-war followed.

A comparable situation developed when, in the 1930s, the compelling need to conserve natural resources in the Navajo country led to livestock reduction and the introduction of a wage economy as a new economic base for the Navajo people. From the point of view of the lending society, this was a new and superior device for survival; but from the Navajo viewpoint it threatened cultural extinction. Coupled with the process of formal education, the new economic system constituted a threat to the traditional social organization of the tribe, as well as to the religious life of the people, not to mention the economic pursuits, residence patterns, and associated values that were basic to the traditional Navajo way of life. Like compulsory education in the days of Black Horse,[1] the new economic urgings so necessary from the viewpoint of the "lender" met with violent resistance by the prospective "borrowers."

Time, among other factors, is usually an important ingredient in cultural change, whether the change takes place through a process of voluntary borrowing or through one of induced acculturation. *In the latter case, the degree of success and the quantity of time required hinge, to no small degree, on the depth of understanding attained by the "lender," and on the effectiveness of applied techniques.*

The fact is that a culture is more than a system of material and nonmaterial elements that can be listed, cataloged, and classified. A culture constitutes a complex set of habits of doing, thinking, and reacting to stimuli—habits that one acquires in early childhood and which, for the most part, he continues to share, throughout his life, with fellow members of his cultural community. In its totality, a cultural system is a frame of reference that shapes and governs one's picture of the world around him. Within this framework and, as Whorf[2] pointed out in 1956, within the frame of reference imposed by the structure of the language he speaks, one is conditioned to look upon the world about him in a manner that may differ substantially from that characterizing another and distinct cultural system.

As a consequence, from the point of view of his own system, one man, looking at a vast expanse of trees through his cultural window, may choose the expansiveness of the forest as the salient feature of the landscape, without reference to the species that compose it, and so describe the scene by applying appropriate terms in his language; another man, viewing the same scene from the vantage point of another cultural window might see and describe it quite differently as large numbers of specific types of trees—oaks, elms, maples. From the point of view of his own system one man, looking at the passage of time within the limits imposed by his cultural perspective, may conceive of it, measure, and describe it *only* in terms of the rising and setting of the sun, the recurring phases of the moon, or the sequence of seasons; another man may add mechanical and mathematical or astronomical measurements, including hours, minutes, seconds, days, months, years, decades, centuries, millennia, and light years—one system may place maximum importance on the element of time and its exact measurement, while another may attach little or no importance to the same phenomenon. Similarly, one may look at an object and describe its color as *green* in contradistinction to *blue*; but another may apply a term meaning both green and blue (Navajo *dootł'izh,* for example), and if the distinction is of paramount importance may make it by comparison with something possessing the proper shade (Navajo *tátł'id naxalingo dootł'izh*—blue like water-scum—green).[3]

The manner in which the members of one cultural community conceive of the world around them, and their relationship with it, may differ substantially from the manner in which the members of another such community look upon and react to it—this is true even where the cultural groups concerned occupy similar physical environments, and in situations where the concepts are not conditioned by geographical factors.

Likewise, what is "logical" and "reasonable" to one system may be quite the contrary to another. There are few, if any, cultural absolutes but many "relatives," in this regard. To a Navajo or Pueblo Indian, whose culture has developed an elaborate system through which man strives for the maintenance of harmony with nature, the Anglo-American concept of actively controlling natural forces in the interest of man's survival, and the media through which to accomplish this may not always appear reasonable. In the late fifties the Navajo Tribal Council, after long debate and against the better judgment of most of the Navajo community, authorized the use of a small amount (ten thousand dollars) of tribal funds to employ a technician to seed the clouds with silver iodide in an effort to break a period of severe drought. The experiment met with very limited success, especially in view of the paucity of appropriate clouds—and there were those who complained that the propellers of the airplane blew away such rainclouds as appeared over the horizon. In subsequent council action, which met with the enthusiastic support of most tribal leaders and members, the unused residue of the appropriation was diverted to defray the cost of reconstructing and carrying on a ceremony that had fallen into disuse, and which had formerly been relied upon to produce rain. The ceremonial procedure was "logical" to traditionally oriented members of the tribe because it was consonant with the position that man must maintain himself in harmony with nature; at the same time, the cloud-seeding process was "logical" to non-Navajos who were culturally conditioned to a scientific approach in attaining control over nature for man's benefit. The two processes reflect fundamentally different points of view regarding natural phenomena and man's relationship to them; they pertain to different cultural frames of reference—and, to the delight of the proponents of the ceremonial approach, it did, in fact, rain!

Borrowed elements of material culture generally find ready acceptance if they represent an obvious improvement or otherwise meet an immediate need in the estimation of the borrower. Replacement of a stone ax by one made of steel does not require radical complementary cultural changes; both instruments have the same function. Such patently practical improvements are capable of smooth incorporation into a system, with few if any repercussions. Even the horse, whose introduction revolutionized the way of life of peoples such as the Navajo and the Indians of the Great Plains, was readily accommodated within the Indian cultures, apparently without seriously shaking the foundations on which those systems rested. Wagons, automobiles, trucks, radios, television, Pendleton blankets, and a host of other objects have since entered the Navajo scene, and have become part of the system without creating insuperable problems or generating a high level of resistance. The cultural system merely flowed around such innovations, after the fashion of an ameba around its prey, and made them part of itself without seriously modifying its own basic structure. History seems to reflect the fact that people literally threw away their stone axes and knives when steel tools became available; and the production of pottery for utilitarian purposes has all but disappeared since the advent of more durable utensils for the Indian housewife.

Not so, however, with the nonmaterial elements of culture—the institutions pertaining to religion, social organization, kinship, language, marriage, or social values. The Navajo or the Pueblo did not junk his own religion for Christianity; discard his own language for Spanish or English; or drop his clan, kinship, or other social system in favor of a borrowed replacement. Such nonmaterial elements as these are among the mainstays in the cultural framework and, as such, they undergo change at a much slower rate than do those relating to the tangible material culture. The successful incorporation of such Anglo-American institutions as formal education, representative democratic government, the father-centered family, a system of justice based on coercive laws, and modern medicine into Navajo culture has been slow and painful because they are or were elements that did not fit the accustomed cultural framework; their incorporation necessitates a host of radical adjustments in the complex of fundamental cultural habits of the people before they can be accommodated—in fact, incorporation of the entire range of such alien institutions has profound implications for the very survival of the borrowing system itself.

The immediate value of these institutions as improved tools for survival, intangible and complex as they are, has not been as readily apparent to the potential borrower as it was in the case of the steel ax, the horse, or the gun. Material elements from non-Indian culture have continued to be accepted, and incorporated wholesale into that of the Navajo and other Indian tribes, but the values, customs, concepts, language, associated habits, and institutions of the outside community enter slowly and painfully, often only as the result of heavy pressure.

The concept of coercion, in the sense of imposing one's will on another person or animate being without physical contact or force, is part of the Anglo-American cultural heritage, and the English language is replete with terms expressing various aspects of the concept: *cause, force, oblige, make, compel, order, command, constrain, must, have to, ought to, shall* come quickly to mind. They are part of the heritage of a culture with a long history of kings, emperors, dictators, deities, governments, and family patriarchs, whose authority to impose their will on others has been long accepted as part of the world view of the communities participating in the system. So deeply ingrained is this area of habitual acceptance of the compelling, coercive need to do certain things that Anglos are astonished and annoyed by the lack of concern in the same area on the part of people like the Navajo, as reflected by the paucity of terms in the language of the latter corresponding to those listed above. How does one say *ought to, must, duty*, or *responsibility* in Navajo? Such circumlocutions, from the English point of view, as *ákǫ́ǫ́ deesháałgo t'éiyá yá' át'ééh—It is only good that I shall go there*, seem to lack the force of compelling necessity implicit in /*I must go there, I have to go there*. Likewise, when /*I make the horse run*, the action of the horse is implicitly the result of the imposition of my will over his. *Łį́į́' shá yilghoł—The horse is running for me*, implies an action, on the part of the horse, that is essentially voluntary. Again, to the English-speaking person the Navajo expression appears to be weak and lacking the important overtone of coercive authority—of forcing the beast to yield to the will of a master. And when Anglos find that not even the deities of the Navajo pantheon or the political leaders of the tribe are wont to issue mandates to be obeyed by men, they are likely to be as perplexed as the Navajo who finds the reverse to be true in Anglo-American society.

Navajo culture does not have a heritage of coercive religions or of political or patriarchal family figures, and in the Navajo scheme of things one does not usually impose his will on another animate being to the same extent, and in the same ways as one does from the English point of view. *I made my wife sing* becomes, in Navajo, simply *even though my wife did not want to do so, she sang when I told her to sing (she' esdzáán doo íinízin da ndi xótaał bidishníigo xóótááł)*. From the Navajo point of view, one can compel his children to go to school in the sense that he *drives* him (*bíníshchéén*) or them (*bíníshkad*) there; or he can *place* them in school (*nínínil*), but none of these terms reflect the imposition of one's will independently of physical force—the children do not comply with a mandate. They are animate "objects" with wills of their own.

On the other hand, with reference to inanimate objects, lacking a will of their own, appropriate causative verb forms exist. *Yibąs*, in Navajo means *it* [a wheel-like object] *is rolling along*, while a causative form, *yoołbąs*, conveys the meaning *he is making it roll along; he is rolling it along* [by physical contact]. *Naaghá* means *he is walking around*, and a causative form, *nabiishłá*, can be translated *I am making him walk around*—but only in the sense of *I am walking him around* (as a baby or a drunk person, for example, by holding him up and physically moving him about). The causative action expressed by *yoołbąs* and *nabiishłá* has in both instances the same connotation; both actions are produced as a result of physical contact, and not by the imposition of the agent's will with acquiescence by the actor. To express the concept of obliging a person to walk against his will, by mandate, one is likely to take the same approach as that described with reference to "making" one's wife sing, even though she does not wish to do so. One can, of course, *order* or *command* another person (*yił'aad*) but the term carries the connotation of *sending* him to perform an action; it does not follow that he complies. In the Navajo cultural-linguistic framework, animate objects are more frequently and commonly viewed as acting voluntarily than as acting as the result of imposition of another animate object's will.

The Navajo parent is likely to ask a child if it *wants* to go to school, rather than issuing a mandate to the effect that it *must* go. By the same token, coercive laws are distasteful from the Navajo point of view, and the tribal leadership has long preferred persuasion to force, even in applying "compulsory" education laws on the reservation. As a result, acceptance of the Anglo-American police and court system, based as it is on the principle of compulsive behavior—the enforcement of coercive laws—has still not been comfortably accommodated within the Navajo cultural framework, despite the fact that the tribal government supports a system of tribal courts and a well-equipped police force. Nor is the concept of impersonal punishment through the imposition of a fine or jail sentence, in lieu of payment to the victim of a crime or act of violence, "reasonable" from the traditional Navajo viewpoint. Many types of disputes, both civil and criminal, were customarily resolved in local community meetings in the very recent past, and the procedure probably continues to the present day. In some instances, such solutions involve payment of money or goods by one party to another.

The contrasting Anglo and Navajo viewpoints regarding coercion merely serve to exemplify the many other conflicting cultural values that serve to complicate interaction between these two societies.[4] In addition, we might elaborate a bit upon the cultural differences that exist regarding the nature of knowledge and the purposes and methods of education. Traditionally in Navajo society, the acquisition of knowledge involved rote learning of practical experience. The process of rote learning was predicated on the premise that the answers to all philosophical questions were already contained in the body of Navajo religious literature (mythology, as it is often termed), and one had only to seek it out; while adequate methods relating to such practices as animal husbandry and agriculture had already been developed in Navajo culture, and therefore one had only to learn them by experience. The learner was not expected to question the body of facts or the traditional methodology. To no small degree rote learning is a factor in the Anglo-American education system, but generally Anglos have accepted the fact that they do not possess all knowledge in an absolute sense, and they encourage their children to question and test theories and hypotheses and to strive to make their own contribution to the fund of human knowledge. This approach to the acquisition of knowledge reflects Anglo-American acceptance of change in the interest of "progress," and the requirement that opinions and practices be supported by a strong rationale. Rote learning is defensible on the premise that it provides the tools required to support initiative thinking, but it is not universally accepted in Anglo-American society as an ideal end in itself.

Such cultural conflicts cannot be readily resolved. They constitute divergent habits, habitual attitudes and systems, which are part of the main fabric of the societies to which they belong, and change in one area carries the need for change in others. Such situations sometimes resemble cards: the removal of one card in a key location threatens to tumble the entire structure.

Culture is a complex system of interrelated habits.

Linguistic Borrowing

The nature and function of language assume different perspectives as they are examined by different disciplines. The psychologist, the philosopher, the linguist, the physiologist, and the anthropologist are each concerned with different facets of the phenomenon of speech—but from the standpoint of the social scientist a language becomes an integral part of the culture of the people who speak it or, for that matter, who use it in any of its several secondary forms (writing, gestures, signals, signs, mathematical formulas, artistic and other representations). Whatever its form, language comprises a set of signals that serve the need, in human society, for the intercommunication of ideas and concepts. In addition, the structure and content of a given system of speech, as Whorf,[5] Sapir,[6] Hoijer,[7] and others have pointed out—in combination with associated cultural features—establishes a frame of reference within which the process of reasoning itself takes place; it is a framework that molds the world view of the speakers of a given language and one that tends to confine that view to the boundaries and perspective of the cultural system in which such speakers are participants. Like the rest of culture, a system of language, with its characteristic patterns of expression, elements of phonology, and structural features, comprises a complex set of distinctive habits. In short, the sum total of the values, attitudes, concepts, and modes of expression of a community constitute the frame of reference within which its members conceive of, look upon, describe, react to, and explain the world in which they live and their relationships with it—it is their window on the universe.

The lexicon, or elements of vocabulary, of a speech system can be compared to the material elements (tools, weapons, etc.) of culture—such elements of speech, like tools, may be borrowed from another language system, or existing terms, like existing tools, may be modified to meet new requirements. Words, as these units are commonly called, again like tools, may come and go. But unlike elements of vocabulary, the structural-grammatical features of a language and the characteristic pattern in which they are used to reflect the world of its speakers constitute a framework that changes much more slowly; structural, grammatical features (and the patterns governing the expression of ideas) are analogous, in this context, to the fundamental elements of a culture—its institutions of religion, social and political organization, and values.

As cultures change—and none are static—those changes reflect in language, because, as we have pointed out, language itself is a reflection of the total culture of its speakers—a catalog and transmitter of the elements and features of the entire social system. There are few, if any, "primitive" cultures in the sense that they are rudimentary in form and content; and by the same token there are few, if any, truly "rudimentary" speech forms. Cultural and linguistic systems may be, of course, relatively more or less complex, in a comparative sense; but their viability hinges on the extent to which they meet group requirements, and the demands of successful social living are rarely, if ever, simple. In fact, the languages of relatively simple cultural systems may be structurally highly complex, while those of comparatively complex societies may be quite simple, as exemplified by a comparison of Navajo and English.

Neither culture generally nor language in particular is static; both are in a constant state of change for a large variety of reasons, including cultural and linguistic borrowing. English *tobacco* is, in its origin, a Carib Indian word; and Navajo *béeso* (*money*) has its origin in Spanish *peso*. Sometimes vocabulary grows to meet new needs through a process of extending the meaning of a preexisting label: English *car* now describes any vehicle on wheels, but it was once a term applied to a Celtic war chariot; Navajo *K'aa'* is the name for *arrow* and, by extension, *bullet (bee'eldǫǫh bik'aa', gun's arrow=bullet), and łeetsoii—yellow ochre* is, by extension, applied to uranium ore. In other situations, new words are coined as labels for the identification of new objects: English *kodak, radar*; Navajo *chidí naa' na'í* (caterpillar tractor—literally *crawling automobile*). Verb labels, as well as names (nouns) are extended in meaning to meet new needs. Thus English *start* came to be applied to the process of causing a combustion engine to begin operation, and *run* came to be applied to the operation itself. Navajo *diits'a'* means *it is making a noise*, and the term was transferred to describe the operation of a gasoline motor, to meaning *it is running*. By analogy with other verbal constructions the term *diséłts' ą́ą́'—I caused it to make noise*, came into use to describe the act of starting a motor—that is, *causing* it to make noise.

These borrowings, with other developmental changes, are part of the process through which language grows to complement other types of cultural change. However, like the replacement of a stone ax with a steel implement, changes of this type do not seriously disturb the structural and conceptual framework underlying a given speech system: rather, they enrich it and maintain it abreast of changing communicational needs.

Sweeping .cultural change sometimes results in the discarding of an entire language, with adoption of the speech system of the new culture—or such change may result in the relegation of a language to a position of secondary importance. The introduction of English and other European speech forms as the languages of science and education in so-called "underdeveloped countries" (that is, countries inhabited by cultural minority peoples) seriously affects the status of the local language and may result in its sharp decline or extinction. Many American Indian languages, as well as many tribal languages of Africa and Asia, have followed, or may well follow, such a course to more or less quickly join the ranks of the myriads of dead languages (and associated cultures) of the world. At the same time, in other situations, the languages of minority cultures have survived (Welsh, for example) or have themselves become the vehicle of communication with reference to a radically changed cultural system (Japanese, for example). A system of language that does not keep pace with cultural change is not likely to survive.

Adapted from *English as a Second Language for Navajos: An Overview of Certain Cultural and Linguistic Factors*, revised edition, by Robert W. Young (Albuquerque: Bureau of Indian Affairs Area Office, 1968).

NOTES

1. Black Horse was a Navajo leader of the 1890s who was violently opposed to education. See The Bureau of Indian Affairs, "The Trouble at Round Rock," Navajo Historical Series no. 2 (Washington, D.C.: Government Printing Office, 1952).

2. Benjamin Lee Whorf, *Language, Thought and Reality*, ed. John B. Carroll (Cambridge, Mass.: M.I.T. Press, 1956).

3. Young employs the symbol /'/ for glottal stop, a full consonant phoneme in Navajo; /ł/ for a voiceless lateral; and /x/ for a voiceless palatovelar fricative as in German "na*ch*." Various symbols on vowels serve to modify them to accommodate the sounds of Navajo. [Eds.]

4. An excellent analysis of conflicting cultural values relating to Southwestern Indian and Mexican-American communities is provided in Miles V. Zintz, "Final Report, Indian Research Study" (Albuquerque: University of New Mexico College of Education, 1960).

5. Whorf, *Language, Thought and Reality*.

6. Edward Sapir, "Language and Environment," in *Selected Writings in Language, Culture, and Personality*, ed. David J. Mandelbaum (Berkeley: University of California Press, 1949).

7. Harry Hoijer, "Culture Implications of Some Navaho Linguistic Categories," *Language* 27 (1951): 111-120.

PART II

VARIATION WITHIN
SPEECH COMMUNITIES

*The normal person is never convinced by the mere content of speech
but is very sensitive to many of the implications of language behavior,
however feebly (if at all) these may have been consciously analyzed.
All in all, it is not too much to say that one of the really important
functions of language is to be constantly declaring to society the
psychological place held by all of its members.*

—Edward Sapir

The materials in Part I of this book demonstrate how our society is structured into socially, psychologically, and politically significant communities which can be identified by their linguistic behavior. Members of these various speech communities use special linguistic forms and practices to assert the strength of their personal group identifications. However, McDavid's pioneering 1948 study, reprinted here, suggests that experiential and attitudinal differences within a community may be likewise indicated through language behavior. Other readings in this section illustrate some of these individual differences within speech communities: the creative language use which individuates members within each American speech community and the function of language, even on the intragroup level, as a tool for maintaining social control.

One of the remarkable characteristics of human language learning is the multiplicity of linguistic varieties which each person comes to use. The term "monolingual" is somewhat misleading, for even speakers of only one language (e.g., English, Spanish, or Ojibway) command a *verbal repertoire* that extends from very formal styles for talking to school principals or census takers to various other styles for religious observance, public speaking, and talking with children, friends, family, and lovers. We can use language to keep interactions with strangers distant and brief or to turn a meeting into a personal conversation. One person's verbal repertoire may extend across several dialects or different languages or may be limited to variation within one. If more than one language is employed in a community, shifting from one style to another may be accomplished by switching from one language to another. In this section Gumperz and Hernández-Chavez discuss such *code switching* among Spanish-English bilinguals. Even within a monolingual community *style shifts* are indicated by verbal cues which a group member instantly, though perhaps unconsciously, recognizes and which sociolinguists can accurately describe. Styles are differentiated by a combination of conventions—phonological, lexical, and grammatical. In addition, speed and pitch of speech, as well as gestures and posture, may mark a shift in styles. For example, all American English speakers regularly use /-ɪn/ as the suffix on verbs (*riding, coming*) instead of /-ɪŋ/ in their casual speech. Studies have shown that even young children, like adults, style shift from primarily /-ɪn/ to primarily the more standard /-ɪŋ/ in interaction with adult strangers. Some lexical choices are also closely associated with particular styles. A customer returning spoiled fruit at the grocery might complain to a friend, *This is the worst damned crap I've ever bought in a store* and turn immediately to the approaching market manager to say, *I'm dissatisfied with this produce I purchased yesterday.*

Style shifts indicate an alteration in the individual's definition of and relation to the speech event. For example, a teacher might greet one student visiting his office hours with, *You are interested in discussing a term paper topic, I presume, Mr. Francisco?* thereby setting a limited agenda for the meeting and defining his role only as that of course instructor. A few minutes later the same teacher might greet his favorite graduate student with, *Hi, Matt. Oh, I see you've got the book for Judy Ross' nineteenth-century course. How d'you like her?* By indicating his willingness to discuss the student's general educational concerns and using a casual style, he defines himself not strictly as instructor but also as adviser and perhaps ultimately as friend.

The above example also points to the social function of language variation: maintenance of social roles and structures. It is the teacher, not the student, whose prerogative it is to set the topic and define the role he will play and thus that the student must play. In social interaction it is the person with power who makes the rules. Parents who come to the principal's office to discuss their unruly child feel they must do their best to shift to the style of speech which their schoolteachers used. The principal has an accustomed way of speaking at the office, but the parents may be forcing themselves into unfamiliar roles and speech patterns. In such situations speakers of nonstandard varieties, sensing a negative attitude toward their linguistic behavior, may exhibit *linguistic insecurity*, a feeling that their language is not "good enough" (through their own fault), often accompanied by exaggerated attempts to approximate the standard language (*hypercorrection*). Nonstandard speakers may find in an institutional setting that the very speech which expresses their personal identity and establishes rapport with most members of their community becomes the clearest indicator of their unfamiliarity with the institution and the greatest stumbling block to functioning effectively within it. Thus even within the normal range of activities for members of a community, their speech patterns and style may be turned against them.

The selections in Part II illustrate variation within speech communities and describe the pressure toward standardization and the internal dynamics of nonstandard and non-English-speaking communities. The two articles by Labov are central to an understanding of these issues. In his description of the speech of Harlem teenagers and Lower East Side ethnic groups he shows linguistic behavior ranging from strong identification with dominant groups and standard language to extreme rejection of mainstream language and culture.

The three articles on women's linguistic behavior by Conklin, Henley, and Zimmerman and West demonstrate that women share many language norms and patterns regardless of their class or ethnicity. However, since women are integrated into communities to which their families belong, it is more useful to regard their speech as variation within groups than as a separate speech community based on sex. It is perhaps these selections which reveal most clearly the use of language for maintenance of social roles within the speech community.

Further Readings

William Labov, "The Reflection of Social Processes in Linguistic Structures," Joshua A. Fishman, ed., *The Sociology of Language* (Mouton, 1968). Demonstrates and defines style shifting, linguistic insecurity, and hypercorrection, using New York City data; for a briefer description of these phenomena, see Labov's "The Social Stratification of Language" in *The Study of Nonstandard English* (National Council of Teachers of English, 1970).

Lewis Levine and H. J. Crockett, Jr., "Speech Variation in a Piedmont Community: Postvocalic r," *Sociological Inquiry* 36:2 (1966). Reprinted as *International Journal of American Linguistics* Publication 44. Demographic analysis of the encroachment of the Northern postvocalic r on a Southern community.

Joshua A. Fishman, Robert L. Cooper, and Roxana Ma, *Bilingualism in the Barrio* (Language Science Monographs 17, Indiana University Publications, 1971). Major study of code switching among Spanish-English bilinguals.

Wallace E. Lambert, "A Social Psychology of Bilingualism," *Journal of Social Issues* 23:2 (1967). Reprinted in Anwar S. Dil, ed., *Language, Psychology, and Culture* (Stanford University Press, 1972). Reports reactions of French-English bilinguals to speakers of their first and second language; similar subjective reaction techniques were employed by G. Richard Tucker and Lambert to elicit "White and Negro Listeners' Reactions to Various American-English Dialects," *Social Forces* 47 (1969).

Barrie Thorne and Nancy Henley, eds., *Language and Sex: Difference and Dominance* (Newbury House, 1975). The most valuable book on women's language to date, yet still contains articles of varying quality; two with sociolinguistic orientations reprinted below; contains excellent annotated bibliography.

Roger Brown and Albert Gilman, "The Pronouns of Power and Solidarity," Joshua A. Fishman, ed., *The Sociology of Language* (Mouton, 1968). Details use of German and French pronouns and terms of address for maintenance of social roles; pioneering study of the relation between language structure and social control.

Emanuel A. Schegloff, "Sequencing in Conversational Openings," *American Anthropologist* 70 (1968). Reprinted in John J. Gumperz and Dell Hymes, eds., *Directions in Sociolinguistics: The Ethnography of Communication* (Holt, Rinehart and Winston, 1972). A good introduction to discourse analysis.

Susan M. Ervin-Tripp, "An Analysis of the Interaction of Language, Topic, and Listener," John J. Gumperz and Dell Hymes, eds., *The Ethnography of Communication, American Anthropologist* 66:6, part 2 (1964). Reprinted in Joshua A. Fishman, ed., *The Sociology of Language* (Mouton, 1968). Among Japanese-English-speaking women, language used in the interaction influences perceptions of self.

POSTVOCALIC /r/ IN SOUTH CAROLINA:
A SOCIAL ANALYSIS[1]

Raven I. McDavid, Jr.

Raven I. McDavid's now classic 1948 study of the distribution of "r-less" dialects in South Carolina (the absence of /r/ after vowels, as in *car, card, father*) demonstrates the necessity of a sociological approach to language study as clearly as any later work, which has expanded and refined his methodology and analysis. By using a sociological approach, McDavid was able to account for otherwise conflicting data and establish the boundaries of social groups within a geographically defined dialect. This article sets out simply and clearly the reasoning upon which subsequent selections in this section have built in order to study variation within speech communities. In his concluding remarks McDavid points to the role sociolinguistic research is coming to play in measuring the group identification and social attitudes which influence the success of public programs and education.

The relationship between speech forms and the cultural configurations and prestige values within a civilization has been indicated by linguistic scientists, but so far most of the study of that relationship has been directed toward languages outside the Indo-European family.[2] It is, however, just as proper to utilize the data of linguistics, as derived from a study of dialects of our own language, in analyzing some of the problems within our own culture.[3]

As an example of a situation in which linguistic data and other cultural data must be correlated, one may examine the distribution in South Carolina and the adjacent parts of Georgia of postvocalic /r/ as constriction in such words as *thirty, Thursday, worm, barn, beard, father*.[4] (In popular terminology, speakers lacking constriction in words of these types are said not to pronounce their /r/.) A social analysis proved necessary for this particular linguistic feature, because the data proved too complicated to be explained by merely a geographical statement or a statement of settlement history. In this particular problem, moreover, the social analysis seems more significant than it might seem in others, because the presence or absence of postvocalic /r/ as constriction becomes an overt prestige symbol only on a very high level of sophistication. With little experience a speaker learns that the folk forms *lightwood* and *fireboard* do not have the prestige of the corresponding standard forms *kindling* and *mantelpiece*—that the folk forms are generally recognized as "countrified" or "common." Folk verb forms, like *I seen what he done when he run into your car*, are under a strong social taboo and as a rule may be used by highly cultured speakers only for deliberate, humorous effects. Even some pronunciations, such as [ˈaɪ ðə(r)], [ˈnaɪ ðə(r)], instead of [ˈiː ðə(r)], [ˈniː ðə(r)], *either, neither,* or the so-called "broad *a*" pronunciation [ˈhɑf,pɑst] instead of the more common [ˈhæf,pæst], *half past,* are fairly

MAP 1
REGIONS OF
SOUTH CAROLINA

generally known as symbols of real or fancied elegance. But there is little or no direct concern with a person's postvocalic /r/ except as part of the occupational training for such highly sophisticated crafts as elocution, pedagogy, concert singing, acting, radio announcing, and some branches of the ministry. Since the traditions of these professions generally require that their practitioners tinker with their speech in other ways, persons deliberately concerned about the presence or absence of constriction in their postvocalic /r/ would not be used as representatives of natural local usage on any cultural level. In short, constriction—or lack of it—in the speech of *Atlas* informants may be considered due to the normal operation of social forces and not to any conscious notions of elegance.

The first of the accompanying maps shows the geographical details essential to an understanding of the distribution of postvocalic /r/ in South Carolina. The tidewater area, extending inland about thirty miles through a network of islands and peninsulas and tidal creeks, except along the beach front of Horry County, was the area in which the first cultural centers were planted: Georgetown, Charleston, Beaufort, and Savannah. About thirty miles inland is a belt of pine barrens, which have never been suitable for large-scale plantation agriculture, and where small-scale farming is the prevailing pattern.[5] Above the pine barrens the rich coastal plain spreads inland for about seventy miles, to the infertile sand hills along and just below the fall line. Above the fall line—the old head of navigation on the rivers, and the shore line in an earlier geological period—the rolling Piedmont begins, gradually becoming more broken until in the northwestern corner of the state it merges into a fringe of the Blue Ridge Mountains. From the coast to the fall line is generally known as the low country; above the fall line, as the up-country.

The conventional statement about the Southern postvocalic /r/ is that it does not occur as constriction in words of the type here under examination. The fact that in every Southern state one may find locally rooted native speakers with constriction in at least some of these words has been either overlooked or deliberately ignored.[6] The usual statement is still that Southern and New England speech differs from so-called "general American" in that the two former types do not have constriction of postvocalic /r/.[7]

However, records made for the *Linguistic Atlas of the South Atlantic States* showed very early that postvocalic /r/ does occur with constriction in many Southern communities, including several of those first investigated in South Carolina by the late Dr. Guy S. Lowman. These data led Professor Hans Kurath, director of the *Atlas*, to set off tentatively two areas in South Carolina within which constriction occurred: the middle and upper Piedmont, and the area north of the Santee River.[8] A simple explanation of the evidence seemed possible at that time: The area north of the Santee was settled predominantly by Scotch-Irish planted from the coast, was adjacent to the Highlander settlements in the Cape Fear Valley of North Carolina, and could be looked upon generally as a cultural continuation of the Cape Fear settlements. The northwestern corner of the state was settled originally by the main Scotch-Irish migration southward from Pennsylvania, and would naturally represent a southward prong of the "Midland" area that Professor Kurath has set up as stemming from the Pennsylvania settlements.[9] The explanation was still on the basis of geography and the area of original settlement.

But if a geographical interpretation of the postvocalic /r/ was the proper one, it might have been expected that further field work would substantiate and simplify the picture. Instead, with further research the picture has become more complicated, as Map 2 indicates. Many speakers—even whole communities—are found with constriction of postvocalic /r/ in the area where the 1941 evidence did not indicate constriction to exist, and many speakers lack constriction in areas where constriction seemed indicated as normal. A purely geographical interpretation of the distribution is likely to be meaningless: it is difficult to see how, in a geographical sense, Barnwell and Orangeburg counties can be less "Midland" than Hampton and Berkeley, where constriction occurs. It is therefore necessary to make a statement of other social phenomena in order to explain the distribution of postvocalic /r/ in South Carolina.

In the communities where postvocalic /r/ occurs with constriction, it has been noticed that three variables operate toward decreasing the amount: normally, the more education an informant has, the less constriction; and within the same cultural level, younger informants generally have less constriction than older ones, and urban informants less than rural.

Moreover, the communities in which constriction occurs have in common a proportionately large white population—generally a majority, even in 1860, when the proportion of Negroes in South Carolina was largest.[10] These communities are

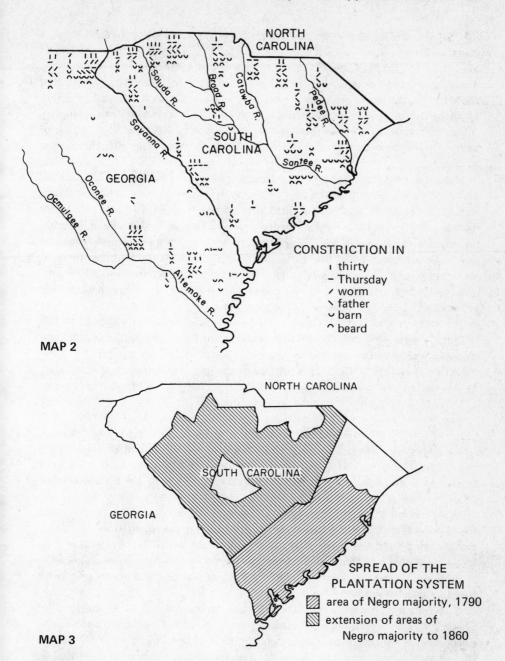

MAP 2

CONSTRICTION IN

ı thirty
‒ Thursday
⁄ worm
＼ father
ᴗ barn
⌒ beard

SPREAD OF THE
PLANTATION SYSTEM

▨ area of Negro majority, 1790
▧ extension of areas of
Negro majority to 1860

MAP 3

counties or parts of counties where farming, often scratch farming, was the rule, and where the cultural orientation was toward the county seat and the local religious congregation. They comprise the pine barrens, the hinterland of the Horry Beach, the sand hills, and the mountain margin—lands where the plantation system could not be even temporarily profitable—and the Dutch Fork between the Saluda and Broad rivers, where a cohesive, religious-centered Lutheran community with a tradition of self-sufficient farming was able to resist the lure of alleged money crops. Constriction in the speech of textile workers in Piedmont metropolitan centers is only superficially an exception to the observation that constriction is a mark of cultural isolation: the textile workers were originally recruited from the culturally peripheral areas, and the paternalistic company village that characterizes the Southern textile industry has created a pattern of cultural segregation as real and almost as strong as that setting off whites from Negroes.[11]

When one studies both the early settlement history and the current distribution of speech forms other than the postvocalic /r/, it is apparent that the original area without constriction was only a small part of the state.[12] The area settled by southern British speakers hardly reached above tidewater; farther inland, whether the settlers came in the great migration from Pennsylvania or first landed at Charleston or other ports, the early population was made up almost entirely of Scotch-Irish and Germans, who might be expected to retain their postvocalic constriction of /r/, just as they have retained much of their characteristic vocabulary.[13] Only in Beaufort, Charleston, and Georgetown districts—and only in the tidewater riceland sections of those districts—were the southern British settlers, in whose dialect constriction would have first been lost, the dominant group in 1790: and in those same sections plantation agriculture and large slave majorities prevailed.[14] Clearly, the spread of the loss of constriction accompanied the spread of the plantation system, both representing the imposition on the majority of the patterns, if not the will, of a minority.

The spread inland of the minority speech pattern, so far as constriction is concerned, naturally involved several types of social readjustment. The following social forces are known to have operated; given the established prestige of the original group that lacked constriction, the tidewater plantation caste,[15] each of these forces would have tended to reinforce the prestige of the constrictionless type of speech as a model:

1. Following the establishment of American independence, the reopening of the slave trade,[16] and the invention of the cotton gin, plantation agriculture spread inland from the coast, displacing many of the small farmers, who in their turn moved west into the frontier communities.[17]

2. Some successful up-country farmers became planters, and intermarried with the older plantation caste.[18]

3. As inland towns arose, they tended to become cultural outposts of Charleston. The original fall line trading posts—Augusta, Columbia, Camden, and Cheraw—were financed by Charleston capital for the Indian trade.[19] As the trading posts grew into towns, the local business and financial leaders had an increasing number of contacts with the group in Charleston that has always controlled the financial life of the state. Sometimes, Charlestonians even migrated to the up-country to establish offshoots of their family banks or business houses. The cotton of the up-country was marketed through Charleston factors until well into the twentieth century.[20]

Not only financial ties attached the up-country townspeople to Charleston. Both health and fashion contrived to make the low-country planters migrate inland during the malaria season to such health resorts as Aiken, Pendleton, Greenville, and Spartanburg.[21] Some of the low-country visitors settled permanently, to become the local elite. Even the Civil War did not disturb this trend; in fact, the siege of Charleston caused many Charlestonians to become refugees in the up-country, and some did not return with the cessation of hostilities. For the Charlestonian not completely above the salt in his home town, the up-country provided a greater sense of social prestige than he could have known between the Ashley and the Cooper. Even Irish Catholics transplanted to the up-country, though remaining exotic in the Protestant environment, found that a Charleston origin and a trace of Charleston accent helped them to become accepted as part of the socially preferred group.[22]

Charleston long continued to dominate the cultural and professional life of South Carolina. The state medical college is still located in Charleston, and apprenticeship in the office of a Charleston lawyer has long been considered the best type of legal training.[23] The moving of the state capital to Columbia, and the setting up of the state university there, did not change the picture materially; from the beginning, the dominant group in Columbia society was the plantation caste, the rulers of South Carolina.

The many Protestant colleges in the up-country did little to counteract the trend—partly because after 1830 (and almost all the up-country colleges were established after that date) there was but one approved social system and no room for competitors; partly because a rising educational institution tended to conform by way of showing its cultural legitimacy; partly because many of the founders and early faculty members of these inland institutions were themselves from tidewater areas, or at least educated in institutions located in these areas.[24]

None of these influences operated alone; they make up a complex, rooted in the desire of every ambitious South Carolinian to be accepted by, and, if possible, taken into, the ruling caste. Politically, this same desire was manifested in the ardor with which many up-country leaders adopted and championed the cause of Charleston and the interests of the large slaveholders.[25] In any event, the prestige of the old plantation caste has meant the spread inland of many of their speech ways, including the lack of constriction of postvocalic /r/, and the trend toward the loss of constriction continues. It even serves to reinforce Southern xenophobia, for among the phonetically sophisticated the lack of constriction has become a point of caste and local pride.[26]

It is true, of course, that prestige values can change. It should not be surprising, therefore, that indications already exist that constriction of postvocalic /r/ may some day become respectable in South Carolina. The presence in local military posts of many Northern and Western servicemen, with strong constriction of their /r/, as well as with a different and more sophisticated line of conversation, has led many Southern girls to the conclusion that a person with constriction can be acceptable as a date for the daughter of generations of plantation owners, or even possibly as a husband. Even in the heart of the low country, a number of girls in their late teens or early twenties are still speaking with a newly acquired constriction of postvocalic /r/, long after the training camps have closed.[27] Perhaps the trend is about to be reversed.

In the meantime, since practical applications of scientific information are always sought, there are some ways in which this analysis of the social distribution of postvocalic /r/ in South Carolina might be put to use by other social scientists. Just as in South Carolina, so probably in most of the other states of the Deep South, constriction is a linguistically peripheral feature found in culturally peripheral communities, generally on poor land among people who were driven onto that land—or, as with the textile workers, into their occupation—by the pressure of competition from the plantation system and Negro labor. It is among those people, whose cultural situation was originally brought about by Negro competition, that the fear of continuing Negro competition is keenest, and is most easily exploited by demagogues. It is from those people that the Ku Klux Klan, the Bleases and Talmadges and Bilbos, and the lynching mobs have tended to draw their strength.[28] Consequently, a Southern official whose job dealt with interracial problems might screen with a little extra care those native applicants for, say, police jobs whose speech showed strong constriction. And those interested in changing the racial attitudes of the whites might well concentrate their efforts on those areas where constriction has survived in greatest strength. Perhaps this suggestion is extreme, but it shows the possibilities.[29] For language is primarily a vehicle of social intercommunication, and linguistic phenomena must always be examined for their correlation with other cultural phenomena—as for the correlation between the spread of the unconstricted postvocalic /r/ in South Carolina and the rise of the plantation system.

NOTES

1. This paper was presented at the symposium on linguistics and culture sponsored by Section H (Anthropology) of the AAAS at Chicago, Dec. 27, 1947.

2. See, for example, the work of the late Benjamin L. Whorf, particularly "The Relation of Habitual Thought and Behavior to Language," in *Language, Culture and Personality*, Sapir Memorial volume (Menasha, Wis., 1941), pp. 75-93.

3. Raven I. McDavid, Jr., "Dialect Geography and Social Science Problems," *Social Forces*, XXV (1946), 168-172. The data for this study have been derived from the field records collected for the *Linguistic Atlas of the South Atlantic States* prior to 1941 by the late Dr. Guy S. Lowman, and since that time by McDavid. The latter's field work was made possible first by a fellowship in 1941 from the Julius Rosenwald Fund and later by an honorary fellowship from Duke University and grants from the American Council of Learned Societies.

4. The term "constriction" includes turning up of the tongue tip (retroflexion, perhaps the rarest type of constriction in English), retraction of the tongue, spreading of the tongue, and other tongue movements providing friction during the articulation of a vowel. Traditionally, "retroflexion" has been used where this paper uses "constriction."

5. The difference between a farm and a plantation is not merely one of size, but rather of the attitude of the owner toward participation in the work of farming. Even on the largest farms, in the up-country and north of the Santee, the farmer and his family normally did a great deal of the manual labor; on the plantations, the work of the planters was almost exclusively managerial.

6. It is a tradition among some schools of scientific investigation not to insist on facts and examples, and to ignore them when they conflict with previously formulated theories.

7. See, for example, George Philip Krapp, *The English Language in America* (New York, 1925), I, 38; Albert C. Baugh, *History of the English Language* (New York, 1935), pp. 444, 449; Eilert Ekwall, *British and American Pronunciation*, the American Institute in the University of Upsala, "Essays and Studies on American Language and Literature" (Upsala, 1946), II, 13.

8. Chart accompanying talk before the annual meeting of the Linguistic Society of America, New York, 1944.

9. The concept of the Midland group of dialects, spreading westward and southward from the Philadelphia area, is perhaps the most fruitful contribution Kurath has made to the study of American dialects. The division into Northern, Midland, and Southern types is generally a better explanation of the historical facts and the present distribution of vocabulary items than the older grouping of Eastern, Southern, and "General American," and is at least as good a framework for an analysis on the basis of phonetic types.

10. See Map 3. Since the available statistics are for counties, the large slaveholdings on the Sea Islands and the river ricelands obscure the presence of the many small farmers in the pinelands of Beaufort and Charleston districts.

11. The mill villages, regardless of size—some are over ten thousand in population—are usually unincorporated, with all municipal functions handled by the mill management. The company store, with bills deducted from millworkers' wages, has existed on a scale unparalleled in any other industry, except possibly coal mining. Separate schools are provided for mill children—at Greenville, even a separate high school—and each mill village has its separate Protestant churches. See Liston Pope, *Millhands and Preachers; a Study of Gastonia* (New Haven, 1941). In South Carolina, the paternalistic textile village dates from the founding of the Graniteville mill, in Aiken County, by William Gregg, in 1845. Gregg is also traditionally responsible for the pattern of employing only white labor in production operations in Southern textile mills. He advocated the building up of a textile industry as a philanthropic enterprise which would provide the poor whites with a means of livelihood secure from Negro (slave) competition.

12. The loss of initial /h-/ in *wheelbarrow, whetstone, whip*— a feature of southern British "received" pronunciation today—hardly occurs outside the immediate vicinity of the coastal centers, and is by no means universal even there. Such Midland vocabulary items as *a little piece* ("a short distance"), *jacket* ("vest"), *coal oil* or *lamp oil* ("kerosene"), and *quarter till* (the hour) may still be found in many low-country communities. Original settlement from southern Britain does not necessarily imply a tendency toward loss of constriction. Field records made in England by Dr. Lowman show constriction in many southern British folk dialects today. It does not, of course, weaken the argument for the influence of prestige factors to assert that the loss of constriction occurred principally in American communities which maintained close cultural contacts with the city of London; in fact, this assertion only reemphasized that influence.

13. Expansion inland from the coast in the eighteenth century was not the work of groups within the older communities as it was in New England. Instead, frontier townships were laid out, and groups of immigrants settled directly upon them. As a rule, the townships north of the Santee were settled originally by Scotch-Irish, those south of the Santee by Germans and German-Swiss. See Robert Lee Meriwether, *The Expansion of South Carolina 1729-1765* (Kingsport, Tenn., 1940).

14. See Map 3.

15. Although by the time of the American Revolution the bulk of the white population of South Carolina was to be found in the frontier townships and in the new settlements made by the immigrants from Pennsylvania, political power was held by the plantation group around Charleston. All the delegates to the Continental Congress and to the Constitutional Convention came from this group. The tidewater planters and merchants kept up their ties with England after the American Revolution, and a fair number of their sons were educated in England. Even today the socially elite in Charleston and Savannah tend toward uncritical admiration of things English, at least of the practices of the English upper classes.

16. Under the royal government several efforts were made to restrict the importation of slaves, generally by imposing high import duties, but profits from rice and indigo plantations kept these efforts from being very effective. See Julian J. Petty, *The Growth and Distribution of Population in South Carolina*, Bulletin 11, State Planning Board (Columbia, S.C., 1943), pp. 50-57.

17. Ibid., pp. 70-81.

18. A case history is cited by Wilbur Joseph Cash, *The Mind of the South* (New York, 1941), pp. 14-17.

19. See, for example, Meriwether, op. cit., pp. 69-71.

20. Interest rates were usually very high. For up-country resentment toward Charleston, especially toward the symbols of Charleston influence, the merchant and the banker, see Ben Robertson, *Red Hills and Cotton* (New York, 1942), pp. 81-84, 91-107. To my paternal grandfather, an up-country farmer, Charleston was a symbol of sharp business practices, if not of outright dishonesty.

21. See Lawrence Fay Brewster, *Summer Migrations and Resorts of South Carolina Low Country Planters*, Historical Papers of the Trinity College Historical Society (Durham, N.C., 1942).

22. Refugees from Charleston contributed particularly to the growth of Greenville. The Roman Catholic group in Greenville dates from the Civil War. Paradoxically, although the Roman Catholic Church has repeatedly served as a whipping boy for up-country Ku Klux Klan organizers, demagogues, and Protestant ministers, Roman Catholics as individuals have achieved far more complete cultural integration in Greenville than in the outwardly more tolerant culture of Charleston. Even today, Charlestonians not fully accepted in their native city have found their origin a password to social acceptance in the up-country. Typical of the colonial attitude of the older families in up-country towns is their reverence for the exclusive balls given by the St. Cecilia Society of Charleston. In Greenville, for instance, there is much more talk of the possibilities of being invited than one would hear in Charleston from people of the same social standing.

23. As for example, the apprenticeship served by the Hon. James F. Byrnes, in the firm of Mordecai and Gaston.

24. This was true even among the Baptists, the most loosely organized of the major Protestant sects. See William Joseph McGlothlin, *Baptist Beginnings in Education: a History of Furman University* (Nashville, 1926).

25. John C. Calhoun, the most eloquent orator for slavery and nullification and Southern separatism, was born on the South Carolina frontier, and in the early stages of his political career was a spokesman for the frontier philosophy represented nationally by Andrew Jackson. After marrying into a Charleston family, he became the spokesman for the plantation interests. Robertson, op. cit., pp. 101-102.

26. A former student of mine, the son of a Darlington County informant, explained, "The reason we Southerners resent the way the Yankees roll their /r/ is that it reminds us of the way the crackers talk." In South Carolina the term *crackers* is used (though less than formerly) by the townspeople, the plantation caste, and plantation-reared Negroes as a derogatory designation for the poor whites—nonslaveholders, or descendants of nonslaveholders—in areas where large slaveholdings once prevailed.

27. This phenomenon has been observed particularly in such constrictionless low-country towns as Walterboro and Sumter. The radio and the movies will probably reinforce this new trend. Similar effects may be expected from the recent and continuing migrations of Negroes northward and of up-country whites to coastal towns. An apparent tendency to replace the low-country ingliding diphthongs in *date, boat* [de·ᵊt, bo·ᵊt] with the up-country upgliding type [de·ɪt, bo·ʊt] also suggests a reversal of the trend in prestige values. One must remember, however, that in linguistic geography each phonological or lexical item must be judged on its own merits, and nothing could be more dangerous than to predict the fate of the postvocalic /r/ in South Carolina from the fate of the low-country diphthongs in *date* and *boat*.

28. South Carolina political observers have noticed that Horry County, the northeasternmost coastal county, has generally voted the same way as the upper Piedmont in state elections, and always gave a heavy Blease majority. Linguistic evidence—not only the preservation of constriction, but of many lexical items as well—indicates the cultural tie between the two sections.

29. It is not necessarily true, of course, that only those persons in the Deep South lacking postvocalic constriction of /r/ would be likely not to mistreat Negroes. Many of the plantation caste would resent the notion of equality, much as they would resist anti-Negro mob violence by poor whites. But since the revision of racial attitudes is largely a matter of education, it can hardly be without significance that in South Carolina the postvocalic /r/ loses constriction among the group with the greater amount of education. It is also worthy of note that almost every lynching in South Carolina in the last twenty-five years occurred in counties where the field work for the *South Atlantic Atlas* has disclosed strong constriction of postvocalic /r/.

GENERAL ATTITUDES TOWARDS
THE SPEECH OF NEW YORK CITY

William Labov

This selection is extracted from *The Social Stratification of English in New York City,* the first large-scale linguistic study to use social science survey methodology. In this landmark study, William Labov established that the natives of New York City exhibit the characteristics of a single speech community, both in their use of the English language and in their attitudes about "correct" speech. Labov discovered five phonological variables which both serve to differentiate New York City dialect from adjacent speech communities and function as markers of social class for speakers within the New York City speech community. Each of these phonological features—(r), (eh), (oh), (th), and (dh)—has two or more pronunciations in New York City. Labov indicates this inherently variable pronunciation by placing the item in parentheses.

1. The variable (r) refers to the presence or absence of postvocalic /r/ (as in McDavid's South Carolina study). Thus words like *car, card, beer,* and *beard* have both "r-less" and "r" pronunciations in New York City.

2. The variable (eh) represents the range of pronunciations of the low, front vowel of *bad, bag, ask, pass, cash, dance,* which has been written /æ/ in this book. In New York City speech the specific location of this vowel fluctuates widely within one person's speech and among speakers. In order to make fine discriminations, Labov divides the phonological space that (eh) ranges over into six sections: [eh-1] for the highest, frontest version through [eh-6] for the lowest, most central pronunciation. The /æ/ of most American dialects is in the [eh-3] or [eh-4] area of the New York City range; [eh-1] and [eh-2] are stigmatized varieties in New York City.

3. Similarly, Labov found a wider range of variation among pronunciations of the low back vowel /ɔ/ of *caught, talk, awed, dog, off, lost, all* in New York City than elsewhere in the United States. This vowel, too, is analyzed by setting up a six-point linear scale: [oh-1] for the highest, most rounded pronunciation through [oh-6] for the lowest, most central and unrounded. Many of these pronunciations are virtually unique to New York City speech, and the higher varieties, as in the (eh) variable, are stigmatized.

4, 5. The initial consonants (th) and (dh) of *thing, thigh; this, that* are phonological variables in New York City and throughout the United States. The prestige pronunciation with a fricative ([Θ], [ð]) varies to an affricate ([tΘ], [dð]) to the most stigmatized form, a stop ([t], [d]). (Complete phonetic descriptions of these variables and their scalings can be found on pages 50-56 in *The Social Stratification of English in New York City.*)

The American Language Survey (ALS), the source of the findings in this study, was carried out on the Lower East Side (LES) of Manhattan, an ethnically and socially mixed community. Residents were divided into "New Yorkers," on whom the description of the New York City dialect is based, and "out-of-towners," more recent in-migrants to the area. In this article, the attitudes of LES residents toward their own and their neighbors' speech contrasts with the reactions of "outsiders," who are non-New Yorkers. By going beyond analysis of the actual dialect of these speakers to considerations of their ideas about language, Labov discovers that the LES speech community is internally structured, with social class, sex, and ethnic group differences in both attitudes and behavior.

Appendixes C and D are tests of linguistic insecurity and language attitudes, adapted for more general use from those Labov developed for the American Language Survey. They are helpful in understanding the data reported here and could serve as the basis for similar research projects by individual readers.

At many points in the course of this study, it has been emphasized that the behavior which we are studying lies below the level of conscious awareness. Very few of the informants perceive or report their own variant usage of the phonological variables, and fewer still perceive it accurately. This does not mean that New Yorkers do not give a great deal of conscious attention to their language. Most of the informants in our survey have strong opinions about language, and they do not hesitate to express them. But their attention focuses only on those items which have risen to the surface of social consciousness, and have entered the general folklore of language. Just as the reporting of usage in the self-evaluation test is essentially inaccurate, so most perception of language is perception not of sense experience but of socially accepted statements about language.

It was common for our informants to condemn the language of a person, a group, or a whole city in very general terms: "sloppy," "careless," "hurried," "loud," or "harsh." When we asked for particular features in this style of speech which were offensive, most of the respondents could not think of any; the few examples which were given were morphological variants, such as *ain't* for *isn't*, *gonna* for *going to*, *whatcha* for *what are you*, or *aks* for *ask*. The only phonological form that was mentioned frequently and spontaneously was the stigmatized upgliding vowel [əy] in *bird, work, shirt*, etc.[1] Most voice qualities which the listener did not like were termed "nasal"; in New York City, this most frequently refers to a denasalized voice quality of lower-class speech.

In this chapter, we will be concerned with general attitudes toward New York City English, the kind of information which can be obtained from any informant directly: general approval or disapproval, comparisons with other regional dialects, feelings about correctness and the need to change one's language. The data will concern emotional attitudes rather than cognitive statements; most of these attitudes may be seen as expressions of the linguistic insecurity of the New York City speech community.

Methods and the Population Studied

The questions on linguistic attitudes which were used in the survey of the Lower East Side (LES) are given in Appendix C. This section of the interview was not applied with formal rigor: for some informants, the discussions were long and for others very brief. In many cases, the interview had already lasted an hour or more before this section was reached, and the strenuous effort of the Subjective Reaction (SR) test had left the subjects in no state of mind for extended formal questioning.[2] The linguistic attitudes section was therefore administered as if it were not a part of the formal interview, and the completion rate for various questions was somewhat irregular. If the informant had only a limited amount of time, other sections of the interview were given priority.

As a result of these limitations, only 68 of the 93 adult New York City informants gave responses to the section on linguistic attitudes, and there are usually only 40 to 50 responses for a given question. Twenty-eight of the 38 out-of-town respondents participated in this section of the survey, with comparable rates for particular questions.

There is a class bias in the losses, as Table 1 shows. A breakdown by classes will therefore be required to assess the effect of the bias on the overall results. Since the data consist of single answers and lack the quantitative reliability of the phonological indexes, only obvious and large-scale trends will be considered here.

The numerical data for the discussion are given in Table 2. In the following pages, the results will be discussed in general terms, with references to the figures in Table 2 only where necessary.

Table 1   New York City Respondents Participating in the Linguistic Attitudes Section by Class

Socioeconomic class	Lower class	Working class	Lower middle class	Upper middle class
Total ALS adult informants	27	32	22	12
Participating in linguistic attitudes section	15	24	18	11

Table 2   Responses to Questions on Linguistic Attitudes

	Adult New York respondents			
		Socioeconomic class		
	Total	Lower class	Working class	Middle class
Recognition by outsiders as New Yorker:				
Yes	24	8	9	7
No	8	2	3	3
As non-New Yorker	4	—	—	4
Opinion on outsiders' view of NYC speech:				
Not negative	15	4	6	5
Negative	30	5	10	15
Own attitude toward NYC speech:				
Positive	14	2	4	8
Negative	23	6	6	11
Neutral	9	2	6	1
Own attitude toward Southern speech:				
Positive	8	2	3	3
Negative	12	2	3	7
Neutral	4	1	2	1
Efforts to change own speech:				
Yes	32	4	9	19
No	14	3	6	5

Recognition of New Yorkers by Outsiders

The informants were asked if they had ever traveled outside New York City and if they had ever been recognized as New Yorkers by their speech. Some had never been outside the city limits, even on a vacation; but for those who had left the city at times, it seems to have been a common experience to be recognized as New Yorkers by the evidence of their speech alone.

"It's the first thing you open your mouth," reported one of the oldest ALS informants, a 73-year-old Irishman. A middle-class Jewish housewife admitted ruefully, "I know I sound like a New Yorker. I've been spotted instantly, innumerable times." A young Italian woman from a working-class family had the same experience: "Oh definitely, wherever I go."

Table 2 (continued)

| | Adult New York respondents | | | | | | | Out-of-town Respondents | |
| | Ethnic group | | | Sex | | Age | | | |
Italian	Jewish	Negro	M	F	20-39	40+	White	Negro
10	9	—	8	16	7	17		
—	6	1	—	8	2	6		
1	—	1	1	3	1	3		
6	6	2	7	8	6	9	6	4
5	15	2	11	19	11	19	4	—
3	5	4	7	7	7	7	5	5
6	13	1	5	18	4	19	6	2
1	6	1	6	3	2	7	2	7
2	4	—	2	6	1	7	—	—
3	3	4	5	7	4	8	3	7
—	3	—	2	2	1	3	—	—
5	19	3	10	22	14	18	4	5
3	6	—	8	6	4	10	3	—

Three-quarters of the lower-class and working-class informants reported that they had been recognized as New Yorkers, but only half of the middle-class informants did so. All but one of the Italian respondents had been identified by outsiders as New Yorkers, but only three-fifths of the Jewish group. But there were no Jewish respondents among the four middle-class speakers who could say that someone outside the city had thought that they were *not* New Yorkers. Those who made this report took considerable pride in doing so, for the overwhelming majority of respondents felt that recognition as a New Yorker was tantamount to stigmatization as a New Yorker.

Opinions on How Outsiders View New York City Speech

Immediately after the question on recognition, the subjects were asked if people who lived outside the city liked New York City speech, and why these outsiders felt as they did. (We will refer to such outside residents as *outsiders*, in contrast to the ALS informants who were raised outside the city and who are designated *out-of-towners* in this study.)

Two-thirds of the New York City respondents thought that outsiders did not like New York City speech. Only three thought that the speech of the city was looked on with interest or approval of outsiders; the balance thought that the outsiders were neutral, or didn't care much one way or the other. Among the working-class respondents, there was a higher proportion of respondents who felt that outsiders were neutral than for any other class. Yet even a majority of them voted for "dislike."

"They think we're all murderers," said the old Irish workingman. "To be recognized as a New Yorker—" thought a middle-class Jewish woman, "that would be a terrible slap in the face!" An older Jewish woman put it this way: "Somehow, the way they say, 'Are you a New Yorker?' they don't care so much for it."

Sometimes the New Yorker will pretend to be ignorant of the ridicule directed at his local speech pattern, but no one is deceived. An Italian girl in her early twenties, from a working-class family, gave the following view of her identification as a New Yorker by her husband's friends.

Bill's college alumni group—we have a party once a month in Philadelphia. Well, now I know them about two years and every time we're there—at a wedding, at a party, a shower—they say, if someone new is in the group: "Listen to Jo Ann talk!" I sit there and I babble on, and they say, "Doesn't she have a ridiculous accent!" and "It's so New Yorkerish and all!" [laughter]

I don't have the accent. I'm in a room with fifty people that have accents, and . . . I don't mind it, but I *never* take it as a compliment. And I can tell by the way people say it, they don't mean it complimentary.

Although the general consensus is that outsiders do condemn New York City speech, there is an opposing point of view held by some New Yorkers. Most of these are men, and the experience they draw upon was usually obtained in the armed services.

A thirty-year-old Jewish truck driver denied that other servicemen disliked New York City speech.

Some got quite a kick out of it. . . . I used to put on "thoity thoid 'n' thoid" [θɔɪti θɔɪdntθɔɪd] but I didn't really talk that way—I spoke that way because it was expected of me. Kidding, you know.

This minority point of view is stated even more strongly by Steve K., a 25-year-old Jewish ex-philosophy student.

The people in the army—respected New York. They liked New York. They were fascinated by it, all from Ohio, Chicago—they enjoyed the fact that I was from New York. It was never said as a put-down . . . it was a matter of curiosity.

Views of the Out-of-Town ALS Informants

What do the out-of-town informants in our survey actually think about New York City speech? Their view is almost exactly the contrary of the New York respondents. Only one in four reported that outsiders disliked New York City speech; most of the out-of-town informants believed that outsiders were neutral toward New York City speech, neither admiring it nor despising it. This was true for the white respondents as well as the Negroes, although Negroes lean even more heavily in favor of New York City.

When the out-of-town respondents reported their own feelings about New York City, the result was still more favorable. Ten liked the speech of the city, nine were neutral, and less than a third said that they disliked it. Again, this tendency was strongest among Negroes: 12 out of 14 Negro out-of-town respondents said that they liked the speech of the city or were neutral toward it. (For all Negro respondents, the figure is 17 out of 20.)

Sometimes the leaning toward New York was a part of a reaction against the respondents' own native region or town. "I don't like that midwestern drawl," said a post office clerk who was raised in Indiana. Some of the lower-class subjects from eastern Pennsylvania found little to admire in the declining fortunes of the coal-mining towns from which they came.

Pennsylvania? I wouldn't give five cents—too dead. I'm out of that graveyard. There's a lot of excitement in New York City.

But there is also the sincere desire to sound like a New Yorker. One woman who came to work in New York City as a young girl said: "When I came to New York City, I tried to talk like that, but I couldn't because my accent was too much Pennsylvania." When her aunt back home said that she spoke like a New Yorker, she took it as a compliment, which a true New Yorker would never have done.

There are some respondents who have spent most of their lives in New York City without showing any significant change in their native speech pattern. A teacher who had worked for thirty years in the New York City school system seemed to have preserved intact the phonological pattern of Beverly, Massachusetts, where she was raised. She said that when she was a little girl, a boy from New York City used to visit her:

He was always talking about his *aunt* [eh-3] Nelly—had to take a *bath* [eh-3]—we took the wrong *path* [eh-4] in the woods, and so forth. I just didn't like it, and when I came, I just made an effort not to change.

As a rule, upper-middle-class respondents from out of town showed the most resistance to the speech of the city, and lower-class and working-class subjects showed a more favorable response.

Attitudes of New York Respondents toward New York Speech

When most New Yorkers say that outsiders dislike New York City speech, they are describing an attitude which is actually their own. Whether or not their opinion about outsiders' views is a projection of their own feelings, New Yorkers show a general hostility toward New York City speech which emerges in countless ways. The term "linguistic self-hatred" is not too extreme to apply to the situation which emerges from the interviews. Only 14 New Yorkers expressed themselves favorably toward New York City; 9 were neutral, and 23 expressed dislike quite plainly. These overt reactions are the correlates of the phonological behavior and the unconscious subjective reactions which have been studied in the various chapters of the present work.

The terms which New Yorkers apply to the speech of the city give some indication of the violence of their reactions. "It's terrible." "Distorted." "Terribly careless." "Sloppy." "It's horrible." "Lou-zay!"

Again, we find that men express much less of this attitude than women. As Table 2 shows, a minority of the men expressed themselves negatively about New York City speech, but a large majority of the women respondents did so. Since our survey population is weighted somewhat in favor of women, it is possible that this aspect of the city's attitudes has been stressed too heavily. Yet it should be emphasized that men follow the same general pattern of stylistic variation and subjective reaction as women; their reactions are simply more moderate, and in this case, there is a third force which modifies their behavior even further in comparison to that of women. We will return to this discussion below.

The negative attitude toward New York City speech seems to have penetrated even to those who have never been outside the city. An old Italian woman who had been only to the fifth grade, cannot read even today, and had never been outside the city limits, remarked in answer to the interviewer's question, "Out of town they speak more refined."

A more neutral attitude characteristic of working-class men may be heard in a quotation from a working-class Italian man, raised in Williamsburg: "I was brought up in New York, and if I would talk any other way it would seem strange."

One may wonder how the ALS interview question could be asked in terms of "New York City speech" in general. It would seem natural for the respondents to distinguish between many kinds of New York City speech, since they did distinguish sharply the usage of various informants in the subjective reaction test. However, very few respondents felt the need for such equivocation. There seemed to be a general understanding that there was such a thing as "New York City speech," and whatever the respondent perceived as that entity was the object of the statements quoted above.

Informants' Dislike of Their Own Speech

Pressures from Above We find the negative attitude toward the city speech in general is directed by the respondent toward himself as well. More than half of the respondents thought poorly of their own speech, and two-thirds had attempted to change their speech in some way or another.

The pressures toward conformity with middle-class norms of speech are very strong. We have seen objective evidence of this tendency; in the course of the survey, respondents reported many incidents which showed the social contexts in which such pressures occur. A Negro man reported the following situation among his immediate friends:

I have some friends that speak very rough—when we are all together, with the careful group, we all try to be more careful.

Some fellas never come down—they stay up all the time—and you find that the ones that don't speak well—are more or less quiet.

Another form of correction comes from the respondents' children. A number of the oldest informants, especially among the lower-class subjects, had suffered for many years under the sharp corrections of their own children. A frequent comment is, "My son always laughs at me." One older Italian woman was particularly embarrassed at her own inability to distinguish *earl* and *oil*, which had apparently been a point of ridicule for many years in her own family. She cheered up considerably when she learned that this was once the prestige pronunciation of the highest levels of society.

As a rule, our informants show little tendency to respect the speech of their elders. "Lots of these words, they laugh at me," said one old Jewish woman. Another woman took a more hopeful view:

I'll tell you, you see, my son is always correcting me. He speaks very well—the one that went to [two years of] college. And I'm glad that he corrects me—because it shows me that there are many times when I don't pronounce my words correctly.

Under such pressures, a tendency toward linguistic insecurity on the part of older New Yorkers is not difficult to understand.

Pressures from Below   A great deal of the present study is devoted toward delineating the effect of pressures from above upon language. It has been pointed out that equally powerful pressures must be exerted from below, since the pattern of class stratification of language is becoming sharper rather than tending to disappear. Many New Yorkers are conscious of the need for the style shifts that we have observed by means of the phonological indexes. One respondent who is the owner of a small advertising agency shows the effects of pressures from above and below, and is himself aware of both influences on his own language. He was very conscious of the need for correct speech for his office staff: he said that he would have refused to hire any of the speakers on the SR test tape except the upper-middle-class speaker. "I think people have to have some respect for the way the language is written. Even if we all make mistakes, I think we can't say *'cause* [oh-1] 'n' *dat* 'n' *di udda ting.* It's no longer our language. I'm vehement about this." Yet he also said of himself:

As a performer—I change my style of speech. I will do a kind of gutsy talk, that's very different. It will not include four letter words, but I change the pattern almost entirely, 'cause I'm very good at that, and I enjoy it.

In the examples that he offered ("I'm gonna talk plain . . ."), he used r-lessness, [t] for [Θ], [d] for [ð], [oh-2]. He found this style essential for dealing with customers:

I said, "Thank you" for something, and he was annoyed, 'cause I thanked him—'cause he's a rough, tough kinda guy, y'know. So he says, "Aaah, ya fuckin' gentleman you!" 'Cause basically I am—he resents the fact that I'm courteous to him. So what I did was to put my head back in the door and say to him, "You know Jack, you're quite a character." He had a bunch of people—they're all close people, and he had made the remark in front of them. "What would you want me to do, take that thing from you, and call you a dirty name? Would that [dæt] be a sign of respect to you?" . . . . So he smiled and says, "Go on, kiddo, I'll see ya."

A lawyer explained to the interviewer why he made no effort to change his own speech, and why his speech had actually "deteriorated" in recent years.

. . . most of the people I associate with in this area are men with very little schooling . . . mostly Italian-American . . . so that these are the men I've gone out drinking with, the ones I go out to dinner with, and when I talk to them, my speech even deteriorates a little more, because I speak the way they speak . . .

This speaker had preserved the traditional r-less pattern, with raised (eh), more consistently than any other upper-middle-class speaker. He showed the mixture of feelings that are produced in any New Yorker who tries to go against the tide—yet the pressure from below was strong enough to allow him to resist the opposing pressure from his wife, his children, and their friends.

The people that I represent never criticize my speech—the only criticism I receive is primarily from my wife—I get it there—my children also ... self-criticism when I listen to myself. I find it important to be natural in my speech—I can express myself faster and clearer.

Pressure toward conformity with the native speech pattern is very strong among schoolchildren. Those who come to the city from out of town are quickly compelled to drop their own regional accents. One woman who had come from Atlanta as a ten-year-old, fifty years ago, could still remember how she had cried when the others made fun of her southern accent. The pressure is greatest against those who would attempt to use an acquired prestige pattern too early. A teacher who conducted a class of gifted children told me:

> I had a boy of Greek parentage, and oh! he spoke beautifully in class, and I happened to hear him on the street one day. He sounded just like everybody else in Chelsea, and when I mentioned it to him—the next day—he said that he knew which was correct, but he said: "I couldn't live here and talk like that."

One of the reasons for the resistance of children to the middle-class norms is that their teachers advocate a language, and an attitude toward language, which is quite remote from everyday life. The teacher quoted above told me of her difficulties in explaining to children the importance of pronouncing the word *length* as [lɛŋθ] and not [lɛnθ].

> Some children, you correct them—and they aren't anxious. They say, "What difference does it make?" And I try to tell them that it does make [a difference]. There might be two people applying for a position, and someone might talk about the length [lɛŋθ] of the room, and someone else about the length [lɛnθ] of a dress, and I said the one who spoke correctly, probably, in many instances *would* get the position.

The phonological variables we have been studying are seldom discussed by teachers. Instead, many of them concentrate on individual words that have become major issues in their own thinking. One young man, of Polish background, who now worked in a furniture warehouse, remembered two rules of pronunciation on which the speech teacher had drilled his high school class.

> I never paid attention to the rules of grammar until she started teaching to me, and I was so surprised at the way stuff is supposed to be pronounced. . . . She wrote the word *butter* on the board, and she asked me how to pronounce it, and I said [bədər]. She told me that was wrong, and that's when I learned to pronounce *t*'s like a *t*—I used to pronounce them as *d*'s all the time.

The pronunciation he used with me was exactly the same pronunciation of *butter* which almost all Americans use—with a semi-voiced intervocalic consonant.[3] When I asked him how the teacher had taught him to pronounce the word, he couldn't remember what it was supposed to sound like.

> I haven't been in school for a while, and I'm reverting back to the *d*'s again.

The only other rule of pronunciation which the teacher had stressed was the use of [ʍ] as the initial consonant of *when* and *where*, instead of the normal [w] which is used by New Yorkers of all classes and age levels. This young man used a high percentage of stops (e.g., [dɪs] for *this*) and affricates (e.g., [tɵɪŋ] for *thing*) in his careful conversation—but the teacher had never brought this feature to his attention.

Almost everyone in the sample agreed that the speech of their high school English teachers was a remote and special dialect which had no utility for everyday life. A few looked rather wistfully back at the lost possibility of "improving" their own speech in those days, but hardly a word was raised in defense of the English teacher.

A Negro man gave me this view of the pressure exerted against working-class children who adopt middle-class standards of speech:

> When I was small and going to school, if you talked that way, the kids would kid you, but we had a few kids that would do it, and we always kid them . . . There was a girl who was always very proper . . . so, she'd always walk up and say, "Pardon me." We'd all laugh, we knew it was correct, but we'd still laugh. Today, she end up successful.

One of the main factors which contribute support to the working-class speech pattern of the city is its association with cultural norms of masculinity. A middle-aged Italian man who was raised in Massachusetts explained why he lost his outside speech pattern very quickly when he came to the city:

> To me, I think [tɪŋk] I got the [də] New York speech. At one time, I had a good speech, and vocabulary too, when I first came from Massachusetts. But I lost it. When I first came here, to New York, they used to say, "You speak like a fairy—like they do in Massachusetts." When I kept going back to Massachusetts, they said, "Gee, you got the New York lingo."

The masculinity attributed to New York City working-class speech is described directly in Steve K.'s account of a primitive painter who had abandoned his earlier career as an archaeologist, and with it, his middle-class speech pattern.

> If E. has consciously gone back to Brooklyn for his language—his reasons are not social, they're sexual. Because his vulgarity was sexual: he's aware of himself sexually, as a sexual person. His idea of success isn't the American idea of success—it's not the money . . . If he's gone back to Brooklyn, it's for the same reason, he wants to be there grappling.

Differences in Linguistic Attitudes of Various Subgroups

Men vs. Women   As we compare the sexes' reports of linguistic attitudes, we find a series of significant differences. Only one man reported that he had not been recognized as a New Yorker when he left the city, but 11 out of 16 women made this statement. Both men and women share the view that outsiders dislike

New York speech, but women were more consistent in this respect. As we have seen, the sexes are opposed in their personal attitudes toward the speech of the city, with men favoring it slightly, and women heavily against. In the reports of efforts to change, women also show a more consistent tendency in this direction.[4] On every count, women show much greater linguistic insecurity than men. The masculine values associated with the working-class speech pattern used by men do not seem to be counterbalanced by any similar positive values with which women endow their native speech pattern.

Class Differences We have noted that only a few New Yorkers reported that they had been identified as *not* being from New York, and all of these were middle class. The linguistic goal of most of the middle-class speakers is to lose all resemblance to New Yorkers; almost all of them stated that they would be complimented if someone told them they did not sound like New Yorkers. There are also class differences in the perception of outsiders' views: three-quarters of the middle-class respondents thought that out-of-towners disliked New York speech, but smaller percentages of working-class respondents thought so, and even fewer from the lower class. In New Yorkers' attitudes toward their own speech, we find that the working class showed the smallest percentage of respondents who reacted negatively. This finding correlates with the results of the Index of Linguistic Insecurity, where working-class speakers showed the least linguistic insecurity.[5] In the tendency to change one's language, we find that the middle class led the others,[6] while the lower class showed the least effort in this direction.

We can summarize these findings by saying that the middle class shows the greatest linguistic insecurity, and the working class the least. But when we consider the recognition of norms imposed from above by the socioeconomic hierarchy, which we have called the social significance of the variables, the class groups are ranked in order: middle class highest, working class next, and lower class least. Despite their good knowledge of these unifying norms, the working-class speakers show the least tendency to reject their native speech pattern in favor of the prestige pattern. The lower class shows less ability to recognize middle-class norms, and less confidence in the native speech pattern. Thus the lower class forms an outside group in two senses: (1) many lower-class subjects fall outside the influence of the unifying norms which make New York City a single speech community, and (2) many seem to lack the cultural values which maintain the working-class pattern of speech in opposition to massive pressure from above.

Ethnic Differences We have already noted that Italians were almost unanimous in their report that they had been recognized as New Yorkers, while the Jews showed some exceptions to this rule. As far as our limited numbers of replies indicate, the Jews showed more tendency to think that outsiders disliked New York City speech, and to dislike it themselves. However, both groups showed equal dislike of their own speech, and equal effort to change their own speech.

The Negro informants, on the other hand, are separated from the rest of the sample population by more than a quantitative difference in trends. In almost all respects, the Negroes reverse the pattern of attitudes shown by the others. The numbers of New York City Negro respondents are too small to give us a very reliable report by themselves, but they seem to conform quite closely to the pattern shown by the out-of-town Negro respondents, and the two subgroups will be discussed together.

While most white New Yorkers thought that outsiders disliked New York City speech, almost all the Negroes who expressed an opinion thought that out-of-town residents did not dislike the speech of the city. While most white New Yorkers showed negative attitudes toward the New York speech pattern themselves, only three out of twenty Negro respondents expressed this opinion, and nine reported that they liked it.

The sharpest opposition between Negro and white occurred when the respondents were asked to compare their feelings about New York City speech with their feelings about Southern speech. Eight white informants said they liked Southern speech better, four were neutral, and only eight liked New York City speech better. As far as the Negroes were concerned, none liked Southern speech better than New York City speech.

A typical white attitude toward Southern speech was expressed by a woman white-collar worker:

[Southern speech?] I like the sound of it. A girl in the office comes from Kentucky, and people get me mixed up with her.

An old Jewish lady had grandchildren in Texas: "They sound adorable—I love to hear them talk."

A Negro woman, 50 years old, born and raised in the Bronx, said this about Southern speech:

When I was very young, and used to hear about some of the things that happened in the South, I had a physical reaction, as if my hair was standing on end . . . and if I would hear a white Southerner talk, I was immediately alerted to danger, and so I never could see anything pleasant in it . . .

Although Negro speakers share the white attitudes toward correctness, and are even more anxious to change their own speech, they reverse white attitudes toward the cultural values of New York City speech. For most Negro speakers, any feature of speech associated with Northern regional dialects (such as r-fullness), is considered good, cultivated, and educated usage, as opposed to Southern dialect features, which are considered uneducated and "rough." But in the same way that many younger New Yorkers prefer the rough outlines of the working-class dialect, so many young Negro speakers lean toward Southern characteristics in their casual speech. Many older Negro respondents told me that they were quite puzzled to find young Negro people, raised in the North, of Northern parents, talking "rough" just like Southerners. For the older Negro subjects, the sound of New York City English is a good sound, and the very qualities which make white New Yorkers shudder seem perfectly acceptable Northern speech to many Negroes. Thus in the SR test, about half of the New York City Negro respondents showed positive response to (oh), and two-thirds of the out-of-town Negro respondents did so. In the case of (eh), the majority showed negative response to [eh-2], but a much larger number of Negro respondents showed positive response to [eh-2] than white respondents.

Thus the Negroes of New York City react primarily against features of Southern English—the regional dialect speakers from the Lower South form a negative reference group for them.[7] The white New Yorkers react against their own speech, and their image of it: to many of them, Southern speech appears as attractively remote and not without glamor as compared to the everyday sound of New York City speech.

Age Differences   In the limited data which we have available, there were no differences by age in the respondents' reports of being recognized as New Yorkers, nor in their views of outsiders' evaluations of New York City speech. The younger respondents did not seem to have absorbed as much negative feeling about New York City speech as the older subjects. Finally, we may note that the younger people reported more efforts to change their language; this may reflect the greater number who have been required to take speech courses at one time or another.

The primary observation to be drawn from the data is that attitudes toward New York City speech have not changed radically in recent years, as attitudes toward (r) have. The strong feeling against the native speech pattern of the city seems to be shared by all age levels of the community.

The Negative Prestige of New York City Speech

Preceding chapters have dealt with patterns of behavior which revealed negative evaluations of New York City speech. In this chapter, we have brought forward a relatively small body of evidence from conscious reactions which illustrate the same orientation. As far as language is concerned, New York City may be characterized as a great sink of negative prestige. The reasons for this cultural bias fall outside the province of the linguist. However, we can present some evidence to indicate that the pattern is not a new one, but originated well before the arrival of the immigrants from southern and eastern Europe whose descendants occupy the Lower East Side today.

In the earlier history of New York City, New England influence and New England immigration preceded the influx of Europeans. The prestige dialect which is reflected in the speech of cultivated Atlas informants shows heavy borrowings from eastern New England.[8] There has been a long-standing tendency for New Yorkers to borrow prestige dialects from other regions, rather than develop a prestige dialect of their own. In the current situation, we see that the New England influence has retreated, and in its place, a new prestige dialect has been borrowed from Northern and Midwestern speech patterns. We have seen that for most of our informants, the effort to escape identification as a New Yorker by one's own speech provides a motivating force for phonological shifts and changes.

The failure of the New York City speech pattern to expand into its own hinterland is another aspect of the process of negative evaluation which we have been studying. Most of the important dialect boundaries of the Eastern United States fall along lines which are natural troughs in the network of communication.[9] The speech patterns of Boston, Philadelphia, Richmond, and Charleston expanded throughout the eighteenth and nineteenth centuries, to a radius of 75 to 150 miles around each of these influential cities; today we find that the limits of dialect regions which surround them are located in the more or less remote mountainous areas that impede the flow of communication. But the New York City dialect area is an exception to this pattern, and a radical exception. The influence of New York City speech is confined to a narrow radius, hardly beyond the suburbs that form the "inner ring" of the city; and even today the speech pattern fails to expand as New Yorkers move in large numbers into the outer ring.[10] The dialect boundary which surrounds New York City is crossed every day by at least a million people: it has no relation to any minimal lines in the pattern of communication.

Thus we see that most other dialect boundaries of the Eastern United States represent the limits of the expansion of prestige patterns, while the New York City boundary represents a circumscription of an area of negative prestige. This is not a recent pattern, but rather one which must date from at least the early part of the nineteenth century.

Summary

We have seen that the dominant theme in the subjective evaluation of speech by New Yorkers is a profound linguistic insecurity, which is connected with a long-standing pattern of negative prestige for New York City speech.

In this chapter, we have also touched on some of the less obvious sources of pressure from below, which maintain the structure of stylistic and social variation, and even seem to be leading toward increased stratification of speech performance within the city. The preponderance of some stigmatized speech forms among male speakers, despite their clear recognition of the social significance assigned by pressure from above, reinforces the suggestion that masculinity is unconsciously attributed to the unmodified native speech pattern of the city, as it is used by men. Thus the pressure exerted in conformity with the socioeconomic hierarchy is counterbalanced by a cultural tradition which we have described as pressure from below. The exact description of the covert values associated with the native speech pattern is one of the unfinished tasks which remain for future studies.

NOTES

1. Other phonological variables which were mentioned occasionally are: a strongly voiced [g] following [ŋ] in words such as *wrong, ringer, singer, Long Island,* called the *"ng click"* in college speech classes; "hard *t, d,* and *g"* in initial position (usually referring to velarized initial consonants); and the variables (eh) and (r), which we have been considering in this study.

2. For a description of subjective reaction behavior and testing, see Appendix E. [Eds.]

3. This is the fast speech pronunciation that makes *latter* and *ladder* homophonous. [Eds.]

4. There were three women who reported that their speech had "deteriorated" in their present surroundings, and who felt that they could do little about it. We may place these respondents among the ones who showed the most linguistic insecurity.

5. For an explanation of linguistic insecurity and a sample test, see Appendix D. [Eds.]

6. The upper-middle-class respondents showed as great a tendency in this direction as the lower middle class. The reason is probably that most of the upper middle class had been required to take speech courses for the city school system and other academic work. The difference between these two groups is that the upper-middle-class respondents had usually made the changes earlier, and with more consistent results.

7. This term is used in the technical sense developed by Robert K. Merton, *Social Theory and Social Structure* (Glencoe, Ill.: The Free Press, 1957), p. 300.

8. Evidence for both migration patterns and dialect influence is provided in Yakira A. Frank, *The Speech of New York City* (University of Michigan Dissertation, 1948, unpublished), chap. 1 and *passim.*

9. This statement is based upon the dialect boundaries shown in Hans Kurath, *A Word Geography of the Eastern United States* (University of Michigan Press, 1949), and Hans Kurath and Raven I. McDavid, Jr., *The Pronunciation of English in the Atlantic States* (University of Michigan Press, 1961), and calculations from traffic-flow maps provided by the highway departments of all Eastern states. An example of such a minimum line in the communication network is the line which divides Northern speech from Midland speech. It runs across Pennsylvania from east to west, separating the northern tier of counties from the rest. Even today, very few travelers go from Pittsburgh to Buffalo, or from Philadelphia to Schenectady, compared to the number that go from Albany to Buffalo, or from Philadelphia to Pittsburgh.

10. For the delineation of the terms *inner ring* and *outer ring,* see Edgar M. Hoover and Raymond Vernon, *Anatomy of a Metropolis* (Cambridge: Harvard University Press, 1959). The process in which the New York pattern is rejected, and children follow the pattern of an *r*-pronouncing dialect despite the presence of a very large number of *r*-less New York City adults, may be seen in the area of Bergen County where I live. In the elementary schools of Closter, New Jersey, one can hardly find a single instance of an *r*-less form spoken by the children; among their parents, *r*-less forms predominate.

THE LINGUISTIC CONSEQUENCES
OF BEING A LAME

William Labov

William Labov's study of Harlem adolescent peer culture was designed to find the most natural, casual speech style under the assumption that informal, un-self-monitored conversation is the most consistent and reliable data for linguistic analysis. His findings bear this out and further demonstrate that the vernacular language exists only as a process of group interaction and not as a characteristic of an individual speaker. In fact, "the consistency of certain grammatical rules is a fine grained index of membership in the street culture."

In the preceding selection, Labov describes factors which influence non-standard speakers to try to change their language for purposes of social acceptability. But teenage hang-out groups like the Aces and Thunderbirds no longer submit to the values, linguistic or otherwise, of the dominant society. While rejecting white, middle-class language norms, they have instead developed their own systematic, sophisticated linguistic system, which is a key to peer-group identity and prestige.

In this volume Kochman and Cooke provide introductions to the verbal and nonverbal skills so highly developed among Blacks in the street culture, while Lourie summarizes many of the linguistic variables that Labov uses in this excerpt. Wolfram shows how the Black street culture has become a model for Puerto Rican ghetto youths as well.

Because portions of this study are highly technical linguistic descriptions of the sociolinguistic variables, we have abridged the original and summarized the findings. Readers interested in the fuller version should consult Chapter 7 of Labov's *Language in the Inner City*.

Who's the lame who says he knows the game,
And where did he learn to play?

—"The Fall"

Locating the Vernacular

The largest part of our recent research of the speech community has focused upon the language used by primary peer groups in natural, face-to-face interaction. We focus upon natural groups as the best possible solutions to the *observer's paradox*: the problem of observing how people speak when they are not being observed. The natural interaction of peers can overshadow the effects of observations and helps us approach the goal of capturing the vernacular of everyday life in which the minimum amount of attention is paid to speech: this is the most systematic level of linguistic behavior and of greatest interest to the linguist who wants to explain the structure and evolution of language.

But there is a second even more compelling reason for us to select natural groups of speakers rather than isolated individuals. The vernacular is the property of the group, not the individual. Its consistency and well-formed, systematic character is the result of a vast number of interactions: the group exerts its control over the vernacular in a supervision so close that a single slip may be condemned and remembered for years.[1] The overt norms of the dominant social class can operate to produce a consistent superordinate dialect, if class is reasonably cohesive and protected from large-scale invasions from below. Thus the Received Pronunciation described by H. C. Wyld was a class dialect rigorously controlled in the British public (private) schools (1936: 3). At the other end of the social spectrum, the covert norms of the street culture operate to produce the consistent vernacular of the urban working class. The lower-class culture differs from upper-class culture in that its base in the population becomes progressively narrower with age. In the early adolescent years, the focal concerns of lower-class culture (Miller 1958) involve all but the upper-middle and upper class in America. But individuals are gradually split away from involvement in these concerns, so that only a small percentage of "lower-lower-class" adults retain this orientation wholeheartedly as they grow older.[2]

We usually find that the most consistent vernacular is spoken by those between the ages of 9 and 18. It is well known that in most cities peer-group membership reaches a peak at the ages of 15 to 16 (Wilmott 1966); as the young adult is detached from the teenage hang-out group he inevitably acquires a greater ability to shift toward the standard language and more occasions to do so. In some sharply differentiated subsystems, a consistent vernacular can be obtained only from children and adolescents: the grammars of adults seem to be permanently changed by their use of standard rules. This is the case with both Hawaiian Creole English ("Hawaiian Pidgin") and black vernacular. In general, working adults will use a sharper degree of style shifting than adolescents in their careful speech with outside observers, and only under the most favorable circumstances will their vernacular system emerge. In old age, much of this superposed variation disappears. But it is still an open question how much the basic vernacular system changes in the course of a lifetime.[3]

Members and Lames

In our work on sound change, we are concerned with the working-class vernacular rather than an upper-class dialect because it forms the main stream in the history of the language. The vernacular affects a much larger number of speakers in a more intimate way than the standard, and the transmission of linguistic tradition through successive peer groups takes place in the subculture dominated by the vernacular (which we refer to as the *vernacular culture*). But even in the most solid working-class areas, many isolated children grow up without being members of any vernacular peer group and a steadily increasing number of individuals split away from the vernacular culture in their adolescent years.

The Black English Vernacular (BEV) currently refers to such isolated individuals as *lames*. They are not *hip*, since they do not hang out. It is only by virtue of being available and on the street every day that anyone can acquire the deep familiarity with local doings and the sure command of local slang that are needed to participate in vernacular culture. To be *lame* means to be outside the central group and its culture; it is a negative characterization and does not imply any single set of social characteristics. Some lames can't or won't fight—they are cowards or weaklings; some are "good" in that they do not steal, smoke, shoot up dope, or make out, but others may be just as tough or just as "bad" as peer-group members; they may merely be distant, going their own way with their own concerns. What all lames have in common is that they lack the knowledge which is necessary to run any kind of a game in the vernacular culture. The term *lame* can carry a great deal of contempt especially where someone pretends to knowledge he doesn't have. One of the epic statements of vernacular culture, "The Fall," begins on this note as shown in the epigraph to this chapter. Again we find that in "Mexicali Rose" the protagonist puts down his main man, Smitty, because he hit on a girl and failed.

> Smitty dipped easy and from behind
> "Lame, you think your game is stronger than mine?"
> Sam said, "Not only is my game stronger, but my spiel is tougher,
> So move over, Jake, and watch me work."[4]

There are many reasons for someone to be lame. Separation from the peer group may take place under the influence of parents, or of school, or of the individual's own perception of the advantages of the dominant culture for him; on the other hand, he may be too sick or too weak to participate in the peer-group vernacular activities, or he may be rejected by the peer groups as mentally or morally defective (a *punk*). In our work in south-central Harlem, we encountered many examples of all these factors; one of the most important is the active intervention of parents. For example, a swimming team at Milbank recreation center is said to have been broken up when the mother of Ricky S. objected to his "hanging around with Stanley an' 'em."

A high concentration of lames will be found in any selective social institution or activity which requires the active participation of parents, such as Vacation Day Camps.[5] Since parents had to enroll boys in the program, and it was run in schools by adults, this "VDC" series contrasts as a whole with data provided by the Thunderbird, Jet, and Cobra peer groups, formed apart from and in spite of the influence of parents and schools.

Social institutions like the early grades of the public schools will of course include both lames and members of the vernacular culture (hereafter referred to as *members*). Teachers, testers, educational psychologists, and linguists who work or hang out only in schools have no way of distinguishing these categories. Only by

Table 1 Relation of Central Peer Groups to All Boys 6 to 19 in 1390 Fifth Avenue Apartment Building

Boy's age	Floor												Total
	2	3	4	5	6	7	8	9	10	11	12	13	
6	n	n								n			4
7	n				nn						n		4
8						n		n	nn	n			5
9		n				n	T		ñ	TT	n	nn	9
10		n	ñ		ñ			TT		T	nñ		8
11				n	TT		T			T	ñ	T	7
12							T	T			ñ		3
13	nññ	T			n	n	Th	T̃			n	T	11
14	n	n	n	n	n		n		n	n	nn	nn	12
15	nn	n			n	n	n		nn			nn	10
16	n	nn				0		n	nñ	0		n0	10
17						0		n0	0	ñ		n	6
18				n		0			n	nñ			5
19													0
													94

T = Thunderbird   ñ = Puerto Rican nonmember
0 = Oscar Brother   T̃ = Puerto Rican Thunderbird
n = nonmember   ñ = West Indian nonmember
h = kept at home

working outside these institutions can we obtain an overall view of students' status and estimate the relative size of the vernacular component. The importance of this knowledge for an analysis of educational problems cannot be overstated. Lames in Harlem schools read only one or two grades behind the national norms and generally follow an upward curve of reading achievement; but the large body of peer-group members shows a very much lower pattern with a ceiling at the fourth grade reading level. The ability to distinguish lames from members is even more important for linguists trying to study the vernacular, for as we shall see, lames and members differ systematically in their grammars as well as in their school performance.

What are the percentages of members and lames in any inner-city population? One answer to this question appears in our study of the peer groups located in a 13-story apartment building in a low-income project, 1390 Fifth Avenue. With help from the boys themselves, we carried out an enumeration of all youth living in this building. Table 1 shows the population of boys from 6 to 19 years old. The 17 Thunderbirds range from 9 to 13 years, and make up 45 percent of the 38 boys in this range. The 7 Oscar Brothers, a related older group, make up 33 percent of the boys in the 16 to 18 age range.[6] Table 1 also indicates some of the reasons that boys are not members. Some have different family backgrounds— West Indian or Puerto Rican. At least one is kept at home by his parents. Some go to Catholic schools. In any case, it is evident that the Thunderbirds are the only

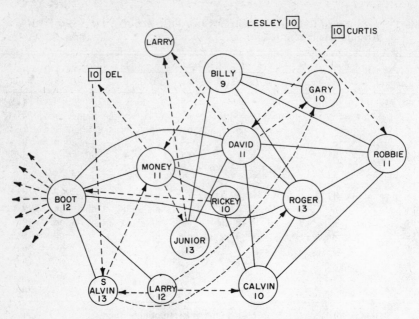

Figure 1   Hang-out Pattern of the Thunderbirds

self-organized peer group in their age range, and the rest are isolated individuals, who are lames by definition. We interviewed four of these boys individually; we will refer to them as the "1390 Lames."

Membership is demonstrated by actual participation in group activities, but it appears quite clearly in answers to the hang-out question in individual interviews. We can plot answers to "Who are all the cats you hang out with?" on sociometric diagrams such as Figure 1, which shows members of the Thunderbirds from 10 to 13.[7] The double lines show symmetrical naming; the lighter lines with arrowheads indicate a naming by someone who is not named in return. The leaders Boot and Roger and central members Money, David, Rickey, Junior, Calvin are bound by a network of mutual namings. A younger subgroup is formed by Billy, Gary, and Robbie. The isolated position of lames Del, Lesley, and Curtis is apparent.

Linguistic Differentiation of Preadolescent Members and Lames

We can make the most precise comparison of lames and peer-group members by pairing the 1390 Lames with the Thunderbirds. The Aces, who were located in the neighboring project building, are a peer group which we can expect to match the Thunderbirds. On the other hand, the Vacation Day Camp series should be intermediate, since it includes some local boys we know as members as well as a good many lames. The VDC series also covers a much wider area than the Jet, Cobra, and Thunderbird territory, and some boys reported membership in named groups that we were not familiar with.

In the following analysis we will then present four groups of preadolescent speakers: The Thunderbirds, the Aces, 10 boys from the VDC series, and the 1390 Lames. It must be remembered that all these boys appear to speak the black vernacular at first hearing. None of them are middle-class or standard speakers who would stand out from the others as obviously speaking a different dialect; the linguistic differences we will show here emerge only on close analysis. All groups use the same linguistic variables, and the differences in the system are internal variations in the organization of similar rules: differential weightings of variable constraints.

To illustrate this general point, consider the following fight story from Lesley C., one of the 1390 Lames:

> See, Book pushed the door and Calvin pushed it back on him an' then they start pushing each other an' then they started to fight . . . Book was holding Calvin by the neck and Calvin had his han' up at his face . . . Book was almost crying and then Book got a cut right down his nose. (Who won that fight?) I say it was Calvin 'cause he ain't cry or bleed.

There are no grammatical items here which distinguish Lesley's speech from BEV; it has the characteristic syntax of a BEV fight narrative and ends with one of the most marked BEV forms, *ain't* for *didn't*. But Lesley is a lame,[8] and his language reflects this fact. To see how it does so, we will have to look more closely at the Lame use of BEV variable rules.

[In this section Labov provides a thorough, technical analysis of several linguistic variables which are diagnostic for social class among blacks in New York City. His findings can be summarized as follows:

On the variable (r); that is, presence or absence of /r/ after vowels as in *car, card, four o'clock*; Lames of 1390 5th Avenue demonstrate more frequent use of the standard /r/ pronunciation than peer-group members and intermediate VDC informants in all styles tested, increasing in word lists to 50 percent.

On the variable (dh), the use of nonstandard /d/ for /ð/ in *this, then*, etc., Lames are lower than peer-group members, with the VDC group resembling the Lames in reading style only.

On the variable (ing), in *running, coming*, etc., a particularly sensitive variable in this community, all the informants perform in typical BEV fashion by using near 100 percent /ɪŋ/ in more formal styles (reading, word lists); however, members of the Thunderbirds and Aces exhibit less than 5 percent /ɪŋ/ in casual speech, while the VDC group and the Lames maintain the standard /ɪŋ/ about 25 percent of the time in conversation.

On the variables (Consonant+d) and (Consonant+t); that is, loss of final consonant in clusters with /d/ and /t/ as in *past* and *passed*; Labov discovers actual differences in phonological rules between Lames, on the one hand, and Aces, Thunderbirds, and VDC informants on the other. There are four different environments which determine whether (Consonant+d, t) deletion will occur: as the past-tense marker before a vowel, which hinders deletion; as the past-tense marker before a consonant, which enhances deletion; as simply the last consonant of a word before a vowel; as the last consonant of a word before a consonant. Some deletion of /d/ and /t/ occurs in all these environments, but the likelihood of deletion varies widely. A first, primarily phonological rule predicts the /t/, /d/ deletion of Thunderbirds, Aces, and VDC informants as:

a. Most deletion where /t/, /d/ is part of the root and followed by a consonant (*past me*)

b. Second most deletion where /t/, /d/ is the past-tense marker and followed by a consonant (*passed me*)

c. Third most deletion where /t/, /d/ is part of the root and followed by a vowel (*past us*)

d. Least deletion where /t/, /d/ is the past-tense marker and followed by a vowel (*passed us*)

The Lames, however, follow a second, primarily grammatical rule common to BEV-speaking adults and the white New York City population. This rule reverses the likelihood of deletion so that deletion in *past us*, with a /t/, /d/ in the root followed by a vowel, is more frequent than deletion in *passed me*, the past-tense marker followed by a consonant (i.e., the ordering is altered from the above to acbd). Eds.]

This qualitative difference in the organization of the deletion rule emerges from a quantitative study of natural speech. It represents a regular development with age as well as a difference among social groups, since even the peer-group members shift to the primarily grammatical rule when they become adults. The predominant standard English (SE) pattern is heavily against deletion in past-tense forms, and its influence is thus felt in the internal reorganization of the vernacular rule; since the 1390 Lames are isolated from the black vernacular and are most sensitive to SE influence, they are aligned in the SE direction from the outset.[9]

In the overall pattern, the VDC series is closer to the BEV peer groups than to the 1390 Lames. There are, however, several measures where the VDC subjects are shifted in the direction of the Lames and away from the peer groups. For all these variables, the T-Birds and the Aces are remarkably similar.

We next consider a more complex phenomenon: the operation of rules for contraction and deletion of *is* as a realization of the copula and auxiliary *be*. Here the comparison will be confined to two groups—the Thunderbirds and the 1390 Lames, who are directly opposed in their relation to the BEV subculture.

[Again, Labov finds that the relative importance of factors causing the contraction and deletion of the copula *be* (as in "He fast in everything he do," "But everybody not Black") differs for peer-group members and for Lames. In a complex of phonological and grammatical environments, the Thunderbirds' behavior is predictable from rules governing BEV; the Lames delete *be*, but not systematically or as often as peer-group members. See Labov's "Contraction, Deletion, and Inherent Variability of the English Copula," 1972a. Eds.]

The Lames' use of the rule is minimal: they delete the copula often enough so that it is evident that the rule is present in their system, but it is plainly being suppressed. In this respect, as in the case of /t/, /d/ deletion, the 1390 Lames have brought their rule system into alignment with that of the dominant white society.

There are also a number of grammatical features of BEV which demonstrate the linguistic differentiation of the Lames. For these grammatical variables we can contrast 12 of the Thunderbirds with four 1390 Lames.

1. BEV uses the dummy subject *it* where standard English uses *there*, as in *It's a difference* or *It's a policeman at the door.* This is not a categorical rule, but it rises to a very high frequency in the vernacular. The T-Birds use 79 percent *it* and only 21 percent *there*; the 1390 Lames use 91 percent *there* and only 9 percent *it.*

2. In BEV, the rule of negative concord applies regularly to indefinites *any* and *ever* within the clause, so that *Nobody knows nothing about it* is expected in place of *Nobody knows anything.* In all white nonstandard dialects, this is an optional rule. The T-Birds apply the negative concord rule in 98 percent of these cases, the 1390 Lames only 76 percent of the time. We have here a qualitative contrast between a semicategorical use of the rule and a variable one.

3. One of the characteristic features of informal southern syntax is the use of inverted word order in embedded questions: *I asked him could he do it* instead of the northern form *I asked him if he could do it.* This is the normal use in BEV but is heard only rarely in northern white dialects. The Thunderbirds use the inverted order without *if* 80 percent of the time, the 1390 Lames only 20 percent. This feature was quite compelling for many members, but it is not so for Lames.

There are many more such indicators which we might select from our grammatical studies of BEV, but by now the overall pattern should be apparent. Rules that are in strong use in BEV are reduced to a low level by the Lames. Whenever there is a contrast between SE and BEV, the language of the Lames is shifted dramatically toward SE. In many cases, this leads to a close alignment between the Lames and white nonstandard vernaculars. This does not necessarily imply that the Lames are modeling their behavior directly on the white nonstandard speakers, but rather that their interaction with SE patterns brings them from a point farther away from SE to roughly the same distance as members of the white vernacular culture.

If we now return to the speech of Lesley C. on page 209, his distance from the vernacular becomes more apparent. Lesley uses the [ɪŋ] version three times in a row in connected speech, which is simply not done by members. He preserves consonant clusters in the second *pushed* (the first is neutralized), and in *almost crying,* though he deletes the /d/ in *and* and *hand.* The use of the preterit *ain't* shows that Lesley is within the BEV system, but his use of that system is lame.

Verbal Agreement and Disagreement for Members and Lames

For a broader view of the contrast between the language of members and lames, we can turn to a series of measures which are very sensitive to distance from the vernacular culture. In general, we can say that the black vernacular has no

Table 2 Person-Number Agreement of *Have, Do, Want, Say* for BEV Peer-Group Members and Other Groups

Group		Have +3s	Have −3s	Do +3s	Do −3s	Don't +3s	Don't −3s	Want +3s	Say +3s
Club members (31)	-s:	5	0	0	0	2	0	2	1
	∅:	21	44	20	44	61	163	16	26
Oscar Brothers (3)	-s:	6	0	2	1	7	0	3	3
	∅:	10	41	4	20	11	83	0	9
Lames (10)	-s:	6	0	1	0	10	0	7	0
	∅:	4	29	8	8	18	107	4	12
Inwood (8)	-s:	26	0	13	0	8	0	6	19
	∅:	0	23	0	40	17	74	2	0

+3s = third singular subjects
−3s = other subjects

Table 3 Person-Number Agreement for *Was* and *Were* for BEV Peer-Group Members and Other Groups

Group	1st singular be *as* auxiliary	1st singular be *as* main verb	3rd singular be *as* auxiliary	3rd singular be *as* main verb	Elsewhere be *as* auxiliary	Elsewhere be *as* main verb
Club members (31):						
was	40	54	54	117	54	51
were	2	2	13	5	9	8
Oscar Brothers (3):						
was	11	13	8	32	2	3
were	0	0	0	0	7	6
Lames (10):						
was	13	19	28	20	3	5
were	1	0	0	0	15	4
Inwood (8):						
was	11	24	25	76	0	4
were	0	0	0	0	21	8

agreement between subject and verb. There is one exception: some agreement is clearly registered in the finite forms of *be*. Here the first person singular regularly has contracted *'m*, third person singular has *is* or *'s* when realized, and other persons when realized mostly have *are*, sometimes *is*. Aside from this, we have invariant verb forms with no relation to the person and number of the subject. Forms in *-s* are rarely found for *have, do, don't, want,* or *say*. The invariant form for *be* in the past is *was*, not *were*. These facts are illustrated by Tables 2 and 3, which show the actual forms used by 31 club members, including T-Birds, Aces, Jets, and Cobras. A total of 10 *-s* forms are found for all 31 club members for the five verbs, as against 395 zero forms—hardly enough to indicate any basis for

Table 4 Use of Standard Verb Forms by Club Members, Lames, and Whites

	Percent		
Present tense forms of verb	Club members	Lames	Inwood
has (3d sg.)	19	60	100
doesn't (3d sg.)	03	36	32
were (2d sg., pl.)	14	83	100
does (3d sg.)	00	13	100
says (3d sg.)	04	00	100
No. of subjects	31	10	8

subject-verb agreement. The ratios of zero to -*s* forms for the five successive verbs are 21/5, 20/0, 61/2, 16/2, and 26/1. In Table 3, *was* predominates and *were* is used occasionally in all environments.

The second line of Tables 2 and 3 shows the figures for three Oscar Brothers. As an older, informal peer group they are already beginning to modify their speech in the direction characteristic of adults. They show 22 -*s* forms altogether in Table 2, though the predominant use is still the zero form in all cases except *want.* In Table 3, they show a clear tendency toward the use of *were* with the plural and second person singular.

The third line of Tables 2 and 3 shows the figures for 10 Lames, drawn from the T-Bird, Cobra, and Jet areas. There is a clear reversal of the BEV pattern for *have* and *want*, where *has* and *wants* are preferred in third person singular contexts. There is also a pronounced shift toward *doesn't.* In Table 2, only *do* and *say* keep their vernacular forms. In Table 3, the Lames have clearly adopted subject-verb agreement. They show almost no *were* with first and third person singular and use mainly *were* forms elsewhere.

The last line of Tables 2 and 3 gives us a comparison with the white Inwood groups, speakers of the nonstandard New York City vernacular. There is no deviation from the standard pattern of agreement for *have, do,* or *say.* A few anomalies appear for *want* and *was/were.* The only place where there is any sizable lack of agreement is with the predominant use of *don't* for *doesn't* with third person singular subjects. Note that the Lames match the Inwood group closely on this verb and differ from the Inwood group only on *do* and *say.*

The pattern of agreement and disagreement is summed up in Table 4, which shows the use of the standard marker of agreement for the five auxiliaries studied in Tables 2 and 3. The club members use these forms with very low frequency. The Lames use *has* and *were* and show some use of *doesn't.* The white Inwood group uses all of them except *doesn't*, where its use is about that of the Lames.

We can therefore conclude that the use of *has, were,* and *doesn't* is a clear sign of shifting away from the black vernacular which distinguishes lames from members.

The Prevalence of Lames

The term *lame* carries the negative connotation that was originally intended by the members of the BEV culture who applied it to the isolated individuals around them. But it is evident that the lames are *better* off than members in many ways. They are more open to the influence of the standard culture, and they can take advantage of the path of upward mobility through education, if they are so inclined or so driven. They are less open to social pressures to fight, steal, or take drugs. Of course, some lames steal, shoot up, and drop out; but as a group, they have a better record. In a study of 37 addict and nonaddict sibling pairs, Glaser et al. (1971) found that 22 of the addicts said that they had hung out in gangs as kids, and only seven of the nonaddicts. In 16 of the cases, it was agreed that the nonaddict had stayed home most as a teenager, and in only seven was this said of the addict. There are any number of positive terms that I might have applied to lames which would reflect this side of the matter, contrasting them with the members of the lower-class peer groups: *nondelinquents* as against *delinquents*, *culture-free* as against *culture-bound*, *upwardly mobile* as against *downwardly mobile*. Even a neutral term such as *isolates* would have avoided the pejorative sense of *lame* which must inevitably irritate readers who realize that lames are better individuals from the standpoint of middle-class society—and even more importantly, that it is to the personal advantage of any individual to be a lame. Even if he does not go to college, he has a better chance of making money, staying out of jail and off of drugs, and raising children in an intact family. Given hindsight or a little foresight, who would not rather be a lame?

The term *lame* serves to remind us that it is the normal, intelligent, well-coordinated youth who is a member of the BEV culture and who is suffering from the social and educational depression of the ghetto. The lames are exceptional in one way or another. Some unusually intelligent and some unusually stupid boys are lames; some lames are courageous and self-reliant individuals who go their own way with no need of group support, and some are weak or fearful types who are protected from the street culture by their mothers, their teachers, and their television set. Some lames gain safety or success through isolation, but in exchange they give up the satisfaction of a full social life and any firsthand knowledge of the vernacular culture. Other lames have gained nothing through their isolation: they are the victims of a disorganized and demoralized subsection of the community. Many descriptions of the poor and disadvantaged are explicitly about lame areas and lame children. The study by Pavenstedt et al. of deprived children in the North Point Project of Boston was concerned with disorganized families exhibiting "social and/or psychological pathology":

> They do not belong to a "culture," having neither traditions nor institutions. No ethnic ties nor active religious affiliations hold them together. In fact we speak of them as a group only because of certain common patterns of family life and a form of peripheral social existence (Pavenstedt 1967: 10).

The descriptions of the language of these children match the picture of "verbal deprivation" which we find in educational psychologists who have developed the "deficit hypothesis" (Labov 1972b, chap. 8; Ginsburg 1971). We have not studied children of this type, but many of the apparently unrealistic descriptions of the language behavior of lower-class black children may be based on such specially selected populations.[10] It should also be noted that "verbal deprivation" may occur in isolated upper-working-class families where both parents work, and preschool children are kept at home, forbidden to play with others on the street.

In other discussions of the vernacular we have indicated that the lames have suffered a loss of some magnitude in their isolation from its rich verbal culture.[11] The members themselves, who have responded to the definition of man as a social animal, see most clearly the overwhelming disadvantages of being a lame. For those who are trying to understand the structure and evolution of social behavior, the disadvantages of dealing with lames will eventually appear just as clearly. At first glance, lames appear to be members of the community; they are much more accessible to the outsider than members are; and the limitations of their knowledge are not immediately evident. But the result as we have seen may be an inaccurate or misleading account of the vernacular culture. Many of the informants used by linguists and anthropologists are lames—marginal men who are detached from their own society far enough to be interested and accessible to the language, the problems, and preoccupations of the investigator.[12] It is even more common for the linguist to work with captive populations—classes of students who are tested as a whole without regard to their group membership or participation in the culture being studied. Subjects selected with the assistance of teachers, psychologists, or parents are even more heavily biased toward the lame population, and unfortunately studies of Black English Vernacular made in schools far outnumber studies done by direct contact with members in a vernacular context.[13] If the vernacular culture is the main stream of linguistic and social evolution, as we have argued elsewhere, then this is a serious matter. Let us consider for a moment some of the ways in which lames fall short as informants.

We have already seen that Lesley and the other 1390 Lames used a kind of black vernacular that was much closer to some of the other nonstandard vernaculars than to BEV. They show subject-verb agreement, variable negative concord, contraction of *is* but very little deletion, and so on. If we begin to explore broader aspects of the vernacular culture, the data are even more skewed. One of the most important regulations in peer-group society is the rules for fair fighting and the violations of those rules that make up street fighting. The information we can get from Curtis is only hearsay. He has been in no major fights of his own, and his accounts of T-Bird fights are those of a bystander who never understands how they started. One of our basic questions in the "Fight" section of our interview schedule is, "What was the best fight you ever saw?" To get the same message across to lames, we have to translate this into "What was the worst fight you ever saw?" A great many lames actually deny the fights they were in—partly because they lost, and partly because they have been trained to think of fighting as a bad thing to do. As a result, lame narratives of personal experience are lame, too.

If we are interested in toasts, jokes, sounds, the dozens, riffing, or capping, we cannot turn to the lames. They have heard sounding from a distance, but proficiency at these verbal skills is achieved only by daily practice and constant immersion in the flow of speech. Lames do not know "Signifying Monkey," "Shine," "The Fall," or any of the other great toasts of the oral literature. But away from home, some lames look back on the vernacular culture and try to claim it as their own; the result can be a very confused report for the outsider who relies on such data.

At recent scholarly meetings on black studies, there have been violent objections from black students and professionals to the use of the term *black English,* with repeated demands for a definition which could not be satisfied. Some educated black speakers argue that *black English* should be used for the language that they themselves use, since they are black, and deny that they use many of the words or grammatical forms quoted by the linguist as "black English." This objection seems to be valid. It seems much more appropriate to use the term *Black English Vernacular, BE vernacular,* or *BEV* to identify the consistent grammar of the peer-group members that has been analyzed by linguists. We will then avoid the improper opposition of "standard English" to "black English," implying that this is the major axis dividing the English language. Instead, we should oppose the standard language to all nonstandard dialects or vernaculars. One of these is the Black English Vernacular.

Most of the black professors and students that I have met in the universities are intent on absorbing whatever the "high culture" of Western literature, European literature, art, and scholarship has to offer, but without losing what they feel are the essential values of their own background. But at the same time, many condemn "ghetto English" as an inferior means of communication and claim that black people can improve their social and economic position only if they acquire the formal means of expression used by this high culture. There is a division of opinion on the place for the vernacular, usually referred to as "our own language," "home language," or "soul language." Most college students will claim to have a deep and intimate knowledge of it and insert into their basically standard grammar quotations from the "language of the street." But very few are willing to examine the grammar of this dialect.

But the findings presented here indicate that unless these speakers were raised within the majority peer-group culture and broke away from their group only in late adolescence, their grammar will be peripheral to the Black English Vernacular. They may be at a greater disadvantage than they realize in dealing with complex rules such as those involved in negative concord, since their own grammars may be influenced by other dialects in a number of subtle and indirect ways. In any case, black students are not yet making the major contribution to linguistics and the investigation of the Black English Vernacular that we hope for.[14] This is a serious problem, for it is hard to imagine the study of the BE vernacular making good progress without black linguists carrying the major share of the field work and analysis. Given our present social situations, most black graduate students will be lames; but even with the limitations shown here, it should be clear that they are much closer to the black vernacular than any white student will be. More importantly, they have the background and credentials to become as close as they want to. To do this it is only necessary that they achieve a firm understanding of what the vernacular is, who speaks it, and how they stand in relation to it.

The position of the black graduate student in linguistics is no different from that of any linguist in his removal from the vernacular. If a black student should take seriously Chomsky's claim that the primary data of linguistics are the intuition of the theorist and begin to write an introspective BEV grammar, the results would be bad—but no worse than other grammars now being written on the same basis. The problem we are dealing with here is one of the greatest generality, for it must be realized that most linguists are lames.

The Linguist as Lame

There are communities where the basic vernacular is a prestige dialect which is preserved without radical changes as the adolescent becomes an adult. The class dialect used in British public schools had that well-formed character, and presumably a British linguist raised as a speaker of Received Pronunciation can serve as an accurate informant on it.[15] There are middle-class French and Spanish children who may be in the same favorable position in relation to their prestige dialect. To a lesser extent, this may be said about a few Americans who grow up in upper-middle-class communities where 90 percent of the high school graduates go on to college. On the surface, they seem to continue using the dialect that was the main vehicle of communication by peer groups in their preadolescent years and are able to represent that group in speech as well as intuition.

The great majority of linguists are probably not in that position. They were already detached from the main peer-group activity in early adolescence as they pursued their own interests, and by the time they enter graduate studies in linguistics are at some distance from the majority of vernacular speakers in their community. I was a lame myself in my adolescent years; my knowledge of the nonstandard vernacular of the working-class majority in Fort Lee, New Jersey, is as indirect as the James' knowledge of black vernacular described above. The knowledge I now have of how to deal with the vernacular culture of adolescent and adult groups was gained in contacts since then—in factories, in the service, and in many field trips to urban and rural areas—always with a full recognition of this initial distance. Fortunately for linguists interested in the study of language in its social context, the problem of gaining access to peer groups and of observing natural interaction does not require that the full distance be crossed in each encounter. The linguist can learn principles of social organization which are very much the same in regions as distant as Hawaii, Chicago, Kingston, Glasgow, and Paris.

Even if the linguist is raised in a community of peers, fully immersed in the main stream of social life in his high school years, he inevitably broadens his horizon when he pursues college and graduate training and weakens his command of the vernacular. Our studies of sound change in progress in cities throughout England and America show that college students are in general a very poor source of data. The sharp, clear patterns shown in the working-class speakers are blurred, limited, and mixed in the speech of the college student. The principle seems to hold that learning closely related dialect rules affects the form of the original ones. The linguist who is alert to the widest range of dialect differences, who may construct the broadest pan-dialectal grammar, is often the worst informant on his own local dialect. There are of course exceptions—some speakers show an extraordinarily tenacious hold on their original dialect. But we do not know who the exceptions are until we have studied the vernacular in the intact speech community itself.

I do not believe that it is natural or inevitable that the linguist be a lame, or that only lames go to college. I am not convinced that linguistic analysis—or a future linguistic science—must be carried out in the grammar of the high culture. Nor is it inevitable that black students who go to college and graduate school be lames. In our present social system, the best way for a lower-class youth to achieve upward social mobility, money, and security is by breaking away from his group. The social and psychological price for this move is well known. But there is some reason to think that the group can move as a whole, and a few signs that this might indeed happen in our society. If this should happen, the gains would be very great for everyone concerned, including the linguist who has more to learn from members than lames.

When we now hear linguists speaking at every hand about "my dialect" and "dialect variation" we are bound to wonder what basis they have for their claims. The only data usually provided are that some other linguist has disagreed with their intuitive judgments on certain sentences, and it is therefore decided that the critic is speaking a different dialect. "My dialect" turns out to be characterized by all the sentence types that have been objected to by others. Although it has been claimed that some speakers differ from each other repeatedly and reliably, no correlation is claimed with geography, peer group, family, or fraternity. Such idiolectal variations are said to be correlated with the systematic development of syntactic rules in particular directions, a product of the language-learning faculty in its most subtle and efficient form. If so, it will undoubtedly appear that no two linguists have the same dialect, unless they are colleagues jointly responsible for the same theory. These are lame dialects, and it is appropriate that they be conceived, developed, and analyzed in isolation.

It is difficult for us, caught up in current linguistic practice, to evaluate the overwhelming reliance of our field on the theorist's own intuitions as data. Scholars of the future who must eventually review and explain our behavior may find it hard to understand our casual acceptance of confused and questionable data, the proliferation of ad hoc dialects, and the abandonment of the search for intersubjective agreement. They may point out that most scholars will do whatever they have been told is right and proper by other scholars. But their analysis may also indicate that our current trend is supported by more than local ideology; a theoretical stance can become a congenial way of life. To refine the intricate structure of one's own thoughts, to ask oneself what one would say in an imaginary world where one's own dialect is the only reality, to dispute only with those few colleagues who share the greatest part of this private world—these academic pleasures will not easily be abandoned by those who were early detached from the secular life. The student of his own intuitions, producing both data and theory in a language abstracted from every social context, is the ultimate lame.

NOTES

1. A classic case, reported in Whyte 1955, is that of the Cornerville group known as the Cream Puffs for many years, because someone had heard one member say "Aw shucks!" when a store was out of something he wanted to buy.

2. In any survey, we run across a few lower-class subjects who openly and defiantly endorse lower-class values. A woman of 55 answered all the questions in the Lower East Side survey (Labov 1966) in this style. She told me that when asked by a previous interviewer about her job aspirations, she had answered, "To be a prostitute!" and claimed that she would curse and swear to anyone, it didn't matter who. But one of her married daughters disagreed, "Not when you answer the phone, Ma!"

3. This is a crucial question for the interpretation of standard dialectological materials and even more important for our current work in tracing sound changes in progress through distribution through age levels ("apparent time"). Earlier reports in real time are of course essential supports for any argument about change in progress, no matter how fragmentary they may be. But it is also possible to show from internal distribution what changes have been occurring later in life, since these superposed rules do not have the regular character of the earlier vernacular. Responses to formal questions, like minimal pair tests, will often show a newly acquired norm, quite distinct from the pattern of speech. An 80-year-old man from central Pennsylvania, for example, made a clear distinction between *hock* and *hawk*, *Don* and *dawn* in his connected speech, but reported them as the same and merged them in his production of minimal pairs—at a completely different point in phonological space.

4. From the version of Big Brown, recorded in New York City in 1965.

5. Although the selection of Vacation Day Camps was done on a geographically random basis, the individual subjects in the camps were not chosen randomly. They were boys who were not engaged in sports or any other social activity at the time, and the bias of the VDC selection was therefore increased in the direction of isolates or lames.

6. The Oscar Brothers are not in fact a named group like the Thunderbirds. They are an informal hang-out group of older boys, including several older brothers of the Thunderbirds, who have helped them out once or twice in fights with other groups in the neighborhood. No one is sure how the name "Oscar Brothers" originated: it probably refers to the Big O (Oscar Robertson). The Oscar Brothers themselves say the name is used only by the younger boys. In accounts of great fights in the history of the Thunderbirds, the leader Boot is quoted as saying, "Go get the Oscar Brothers!"

7. There are several nine-year-olds involved who were not interviewed. The verbal leader Boot has a great many connections with outsiders, while the nonverbal leader, Roger, is located entirely within the Thunderbirds.

8. Lesley is far enough outside of the group that he has gotten Boot's name wrong. It is usually pronounced without any final consonant [bu], and for a long time we ourselves thought his name was Boo, but one day he visited us with sneakers labeled across the toes BOOT. Lesley has reconstructed a [k] for the final consonant, a common form of hypercorrection in a dialect where *den* has become *dent*.

9. The influence on the 1390 Lames may come from several directions: parents, the mass media, teachers, or other adolescents outside the BEV influence. The fact that their pattern matches that of the white nonstandard speakers in many details does not necessarily show any direct influence, since they are moving toward SE along the same axes from a greater distance.

10. Note that some such projects explicitly concentrate on subjects with histories of psychological pathology or work in areas with high concentrations of mental retardation. This was the case with the study of Heber, Dever, and Conry 1968.

11. See Abrahams 1964, chaps. 7 and 8 in Labov 1972a, and section 4.2 in Labov et al. 1968 for evidence that BEV culture is the most verbal subculture within the United States. As a whole, the lames have lost out on this, although many have managed to transfer their verbal skills into a superbly elaborated version of the Bernsteinian elaborated code.

12. The classic case is the work of Loflin 1967 whose descriptions of the grammar of Black English Vernacular are explicitly based on data obtained over a period of approximately a year from one 14-year-old boy. Data supplied by an isolated individual in response to direct questions may be skewed from the vernacular in the direction of the standard, as in the data given above. But if the informant understands that the linguist is interested primarily in those features which are most different from the standard, he will produce a stereotyped version in the opposite direction. A comparison of Loflin's descriptions with the spontaneous group data from the same community collected in Loman 1967 shows that this kind of distortion is most common: as for example, reporting that there is no preterit *-ed* or *have + en* in the dialect.

13. For school-based studies see Loban 1966, Henrie 1969, Entwisle and Greenberger 1969, Baratz 1969, Cazden 1968, Garvey and McFarlane 1968, and many others. For secular studies, see Wolfram 1969, Mitchell-Kernan 1969, those cited in this study, and not many others.

14. A number of graduate students from black communities in the United States are now working on problems of black English in various research groups throughout the country; there is a good possibility that the statement made here will be obsolete by the time this book appears.

15. The social controls exerted on that dialect have been discussed at some length and are well known, and deviations from the standard are penalized by members looking for linguistic evidence of an inadequate background. If it is true that Received Pronunciation cannot be mastered by someone who has been to the wrong school, this would stand as additional confirmation of the fact that the regular rules of the vernacular must be formed in the preadolescent years. [Received Pronunciation is the standard for British speech, established by interviewing graduates of established boarding schools, members of Parliament, etc. Eds.]

References

Abrahams, Roger, 1964   *Deep Down in the Jungle.* Aldine.

Baratz, Joan C. 1969   "Teaching Reading in an Urban Negro School System," Joan Baratz and Roger Shuy, eds., 1969. *Teaching Black Children to Read.* Center for Applied Linguistics.

Bernstein, Basil, 1966   "Elaborated and Restricted Codes: Their Social Origins and Some Consequences," *American Anthropologist* 66, no. 6, part 2.

Cazden, Courtney, 1968 "The Acquisition of Noun and Verb Inflections," *Child Development* 39: 433-438.

Chomsky, Noam, 1957 *Syntactic Structures.* Mouton.

Entwisle, Dorris R., and Ellen Greenberger, 1969 "Racial Differences in the Language of Grade School Children," *Sociology of Education* 42, no. 3.

Garvey, Catherine, and Paul T. McFarlane, 1968 *A Preliminary Study of Standard English Speech Patterns in the Baltimore City Public Schools.* John Hopkins University, no. 16.

Ginsburg, Herbert, 1971 *The Myth of the Deprived Child.* Prentice-Hall.

Glaser, Daniel, Bernard Lander, and William Abbott, 1971 "Opiate-Addicted and Non-Addicted Siblings in a Slum Area," *Social Problems* 18: 510-521.

Heber, R., R. Dever, and J. Conry, 1968 "The Influence of Environmental and Genetic Variables on Intellectual Development," J.H. Prehm, L.A. Hamerlynck, and J.E. Crossom, eds., 1968. *Behavioral Research in Mental Retardation.* University of Oregon Press.

Henrie, Samuel N., Jr., 1969 *A Study of Verb Phrases Used by Five-Year-Old Non-Standard Negro English Speaking Children.* Dissertation, University of California (Berkeley), unpublished.

Labov, William, 1966 *The Social Stratification of English in New York City.* Center for Applied Linguistics.

———, 1972a *Language in the Inner City: Studies in the Black English Vernacular.* University of Pennsylvania Press.

———, 1972b *Sociolinguistic Patterns.* University of Pennsylvania Press.

Labov, William, Paul Cohen, Clarence Robins, and John Lewis, 1968 *A Study of the Non-Standard English of Negro and Puerto Rican Speakers in New York City.* Report on the Co-operative Research Project 3288. Columbia University.

Loban, Walter, 1966 *Language Ability: Grades Seven, Eight and Nine.* Government Printing Office.

Loflin, Marvin, 1967a "A Note on the Deep Structure of English in Washington, D.C.," *Glossa* 1: 1.

———, 1967b "On the Structure of the Verb in a Dialect of American Negro English." Center for Applied Linguistics, mimeo.

Loman, Bengt, 1967 *Conversations in a Negro American Dialect.* Center for Applied Linguistics.

Miller, Walter B., 1958 "Lower Class Culture as a Generating Milieu of Juvenile Delinquency," *The Journal of Social Issues* 14: 5-19.

Mitchell-Kernan, Claudia, 1969 *Language Behavior in a Black Urban Community.* Working Paper no. 23, Language Behavior Research Laboratory, Berkeley.

Pavenstedt, Eleanor, ed., 1967 *The Drifters: Children of Disorganized Lower-Class Families.* Little, Brown.

Whyte, William F., 1955 *Street Corner Society: The Social Structure of an Italian Slum,* enlarged ed. University of Chicago Press.

Wilmott, Peter, 1966 *Adolescent Boys of East London.* Routledge & Kegan Paul.

Wolfram, Walt, 1969 *A Sociolinguistic Description of Detroit Negro Speech.* Urban Language Series no. 5, Center for Applied Linguistics.

Wyld, H.C., 1936 *A History of Modern Colloquial English,* 3d ed. Basil Blackwell.

THE LANGUAGE OF THE MAJORITY:
WOMEN AND AMERICAN ENGLISH

Nancy Faires Conklin

In any community there are separate norms for the behavior of men and women, and language behavior is no exception. Until recently, the traditional view of speech communities as uniform groups of speakers has masked the role of gender in language variation. In some cultures, men and women have fairly distinct languages with different names for things, different pronunciations, and sometimes even systematically distinct grammatical structures (e.g., word orders, verb endings). By contrast, English appears relatively undifferentiated by sex, but, as Nancy Faires Conklin points out in this survey of recent research into "women's language," the differences may be more subtle but just as systematic. Conklin relates men's and women's varieties of English to the roles assigned to the sexes in American society. In a period of rapid change in gender roles, women's language behavior should prove an interesting area for observation. Concomitant rapid linguistic change might be evidenced in a wide range of language variation among women, in heightened linguistic sensitivity, and possibly in increased linguistic insecurity, as women grope for roles which they find both socially and personally acceptable.

The two articles which follow this selection focus on specific aspects of gender-related language variation: Henley on nonverbal communication and Zimmerman and West on discourse strategies. Appendix F offers a test of attitudes toward features of women's language discussed in these articles.

As in so many fields, in linguistics the study of women has only recently begun. Up until five years ago, it was tacitly assumed that sex was not a significant variable for describing language behavior. Just as in the 1960s linguists "discovered" the importance of socioeconomic and ethnic background in accounting for speakers' behavior and attitudes, in the 1970s we are "discovering" the importance of gender to accurate linguistic description.

Because the study of "women's language" is so new, linguistic data must be drawn from studies which focus not on sex differences but on other factors such as social class or ethnicity. In some of the major sociolinguistic surveys, however, sex is reported, though largely unanalyzed. Other information on women's linguistic behavior and attitudes can be extracted from psychological and sociological studies of gender and sex roles. Because sex-variant linguistic behavior is deeply embedded in the context of interaction and the role play of participants, research into women's language is pushing forward the shift in focus of language study from isolated words, sentences, and texts toward a true ethnography of communication. It is in aspects such as intonation, order of speaking, discourse style, gesture and body language, politeness, and role taking that sex-linked language differences are beginning to emerge most systematically. This description of sex-linked language differences in American English follows linguistic research from the traditional categories of vocabulary, pronunciation, and grammar, through the newer, exciting research in style, discourse structure, and nonverbal communication.

Vocabulary

Vocabulary differences between men and women are a direct result of, and an excellent indicator of, the roles to which each sex has been assigned in our society. For example, men would be more likely to know the terminology of sports or auto mechanics, women to be familiar with terms necessary for working with fabrics, cookery, or children. Since our categorizations for men are based above all on occupation, men who do command the lexicon of "women's world" are most often taken for "experts" of some sort—an interior decorator, a gourmet chef, a child psychologist, or a pediatrician. Since women are not viewed as having any profession, their knowledge of traditional women's fields is not awarded any special notice, unless it is lacking, and command of "men's" terms is viewed somewhat suspiciously rather than respected.

In addition to subject areas which are sex-stratified, a number of adjectives and adverbials are, surprisingly, attributed almost exclusively to women: *adorable, charming, sweet, lovely, divine.* They just seem to go best with nouns from "women's world" like *baby, dress,* or *party.* Likewise terms such as *delighted* and *thrilled* and intensifiers *so, quite, such (a)* belong in woman's traditional domain. For instance, it seems fine, though very "feminine" to say:
    "That was such a lovely party you gave last night!"
but outside the traditional sphere these same terms might seem odd in a woman's mouth:
    "That was such a lovely report you turned in last week!"
Indeed, one of the ramifications of this "women's language" is that women must divest themselves of extremely "feminine" manners of speaking if they are to be taken seriously in their professional lives. Adjectives such as *lovely* and *sweet* are already passing out of favor as sex roles and life styles change.[1]

Women's intensifiers contrast radically with men's—men use "four-letter words" as emphasizers. There has been a virtual taboo against use of "obscenities" by women, at least in middle-class society; however this, too, is beginning to fall away. An intensity marker is used to underline how emphatically the speaker holds the expressed opinion. The taboo on "strong language" is indicative of the seriousness with which women are expected to hold opinions and have their opinions taken by others. The relationship obscenities hold to politeness and deference will be explored below.

Pronunciation

The common stereotype of women's language behavior includes the "school-marm" forcing innocent young children to learn antiquated pronunciations and incessantly correcting their grammar. And in part this stereotype is true. Women are sometimes linguistic conservatives, but they are radicals as well. Studies to date have shown that women's rate of linguistic change, in grammar as well as pronunciation, is different from men's, although both sexes usually are moving in the same direction.

The Detroit Dialect Study, carried out in the late 1960s, reports data on sex differences quite consistently. One of the most significant innovations reflected in Detroit speech is fronting of vowels, particularly low vowels. That is, *caught* (/kɔt/) is coming to be pronounced more like *cot* (/kat/), which itself is moving forward toward *cat* (/kæt/). The vowel of *cat* is coming to sound closer to /kɛt/ (see Figure 1). These vowel changes are similar to shifts in the location of pronunciation of vowels which have characterized the entire history of English. In Detroit, the rate of this change is not uniform across the entire population. Some ethnic groups are ahead of others. But for all groups, female members are, as a whole, well in advance of their male counterparts. Table 1 indicates vowel fronting by sex for the entire (black and white) Detroit sample population. In all cases except /a/ among working-class speakers, women are fronting their vowels more than men.[2] Sociolinguistic studies have revealed over and over that the lower middle and/or upper working class is the most sensitive to "dialect" or nonstandard features in their own and others' speech and is the most anxious to avoid them. This is the class on the margin of respectability, most eager for upward mobility. The most extreme differences in fronting of vowels occur between men and women of the lower middle class, an indication that the women in that group are particularly attuned to the "new" vowels. Indeed lower-middle-class women are the most frequent vowel fronters overall.

This example from Detroit is only illustrative of a great many similar discrepancies between men's and women's rates of phonological change. William Labov estimates that women may be about thirty years, or one generation, ahead of men in such shifts.[3]

Figure 1 Schematic Representation of Vowel Fronting

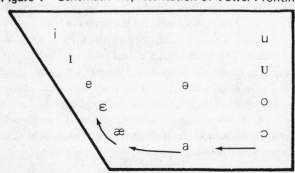

Table 1 Percentage of Low Vowels with Fronted Articulation in Detroit Blacks and Whites, by Sex and Social Class

	/ɔ/		/a/		/æ/	
	Male	Female	Male	Female	Male	Female
Upper middle class	23	35	66	69	37	48
Lower middle class	26	59	64	88	35	67
Working class	19	28	84	61	38	40

Adapted from Fasold, as cited in Shuy, p. 12.

It came as a surprise to dialect researchers that women were in the vanguard of significant linguistic changes. It clashes with the conservative schoolmarm stereotype. And that stereotype is upheld by other data. In 1954-1955, John Fischer studied children in a small New England town to determine how their speech changed as they went from formal, intimidating situations to more relaxed and familiar ones. He focused on the "dropping of g" (/Iŋ/ becomes /In/) in gerundives like *runnin', comin'*. Fischer found that significantly more instances of the full form (*running, coming*) occurred in the children's speech when the atmosphere was formal and the interviewer a stranger, when the child ranked low on aggressiveness, and when the child was female. Thus girls in general, but especially in formal situations, were more likely to use the "approved" pronunciation. In the Detroit study, on a larger, much more diverse population, the average frequency of the nonstandard /In/ form was 62.2 percent of all occurrences among men but only 28.9 percent among women.

What causes these radically different behaviors in women? In the first instance, vowel fronting, the linguistic change does not have social value. The restructuring of the vowel system which is happening in Detroit and elsewhere in the United States is an extremely significant change in the linguistic system, but speakers are largely unaware of it. With *ing/in'*, however, a linguistically minor shift has taken on tremendous social importance. Those who overuse the *in'* form (we all use it sometimes) risk stigmatization as stupid, lazy, unintelligent, or uneducated. Women of all social and ethnic groups surveyed exhibit conservative behavior when a change has become socially significant and innovative behavior toward socially insignificant changes.

A further comparison will illustrate how this dynamic of women's sociolinguistic sensitivity operates in a single population. Among the linguistic variables which differentiate the speech of Detroit blacks from that of whites some have taken on the role of social indicators. Others, linguistically equally significant, pass practically unnoticed by the general community as well as black speakers themselves. The difference in women's behavior on these two sorts of variables is striking. Figure 2 illustrates one of the most highly stigmatized features of Black English Vernacular, pronunciation of the "th" sound of *tooth, bath*, etc., as [f] (*toof, baf*) or [t] (*toot, bat*) or its deletion (*too, ba*). In all classes black women produce fewer of the nonstandard variants. In the upper working class, the social

Figure 2   Frequency of Alternate Pronunciation for /Ө/ in Detroit Blacks, by Sex and Class (/Ө/ becomes [t] or [f] or is deleted)

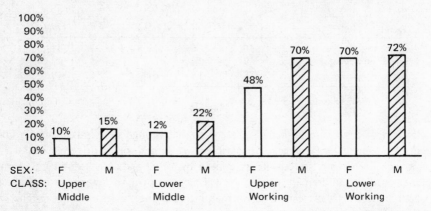

(Adapted from Wolfram, p. 92)

class which exhibited the greatest style shifting and linguistic insecurity in the study, the sex differences are particularly marked. The data from Table 2, on the other hand, show insignificant differences between the sexes. Deletion or reduction of final /d/, while it might seem a more likely feature to avoid, since it creates a large number of homophones (*bead=beet=be* before consonants), has not become a vehicle for social stigmatization. This is no doubt partly due to the fact that some white nonstandard dialects also exhibit it. Because reduction or deletion of /d/ goes unnoticed in conversation, women do it as frequently as men.

Women's leading role in linguistic change is perhaps most dramatic in situations in which a "new" form that is coming into local speech is moving it toward the prestige language, rather than away from it. One of the most salient characteristics demarcating Southern from Northern white speech is the absence of postvocalic /r/ in words like *car, barn, farmer*. "/r/-lessness" has been the traditional prestige pronunciation, but in areas of the South which have become industrialized and attracted large populations of Northern skilled and professional workers, Northern speech appears to young people as the speech of the economic and social elite.

Table 2   Percentage of Alternate Pronunciations for Final /d/ before Consonants in Detroit Blacks, by Sex (/d/ Becomes [t] or Is Deleted)

	Male	*Female*
/d/	52	57
/t/	32	31
Deletion	16	12

Adapted from Wolfram, p. 105.

Table 3   Percentage of /r/-full Pronunciations among Piedmont
Speakers, Contrasting Sentence Style with Single
Word-List Style, by Age, Occupation, Education,
and Sex

	Sentences	Word lists	/r/ increase
Age, years:			
21-39	57	65	8
40-59	54	60	6
Over 60	44	49	5
Occupation:			
Nonmanual	53	62	9
Manual	54	60	6
Education:			
Some college	53	59	6
H.S. diploma	55	66	11
Some H.S.	50	57	7
0-6 years	52	57	5
Sex:			
Female	53	61	8
Male	52	57	5

Adapted from Levine and Crockett, p. 223.

This perception is reinforced by the broadcast media. The data in Table 3, from the Raleigh-Durham area of North Carolina, represent the difference between the percent of postvocalic /r/ in sentences (i.e., when speech cannot be monitored so closely) and in word-list pronunciation (i.e., when extreme care can be exercised over speech). While women are only slightly ahead of men in adoption of the new "/r/-full" standard overall, they demonstrate significantly more sensitivity to the Northern prestige pronunciation, increasing their rate of /r/-full pronunciations by 8 percent, to men's 5 percent, when they move from reading texts to single words, the most careful style. In the other demographic categories, higher sensitivity toward /r/ is shown by young people, nonmanual (i.e., more socially mobile) workers, and people with a high school degree only (who in other studies as well have demonstrated high sensitivity to sociolinguistic variables combined with low linguistic security).

In each of these examples men and women have been reacting to linguistic change in similar ways, although women are acting more extremely, positively or negatively, depending on the social value attached to the change. Women are apparently more attuned to the norms of middle-class culture or simply are more willing to change their own behavior to fit those norms. All the speakers in the examples cited above have modified their speech in the direction of a perceived external language norm, but women have moved more quickly over time and more extremely across styles. In a recent survey of the working-class dialect of Norwich, England, Peter Trudgill discovered a community in which women and men do not move in the same direction and have apparently adopted separate norms for "desirable" speech. Norwich is a stable, industrial community with a dialect which is radically divergent from British standard speech, which is known as Received Pronunciation (RP). Norwich dialect (N) has become the butt of jokes and serves as the stereotype for dumb, uneducated people in the British media, much as an exaggerated version of Brooklyn dialect is used to represent the working class in the United States (e.g., Archie Bunker). In such a situation the members of the stigmatized speech community ordinarily react with extreme embarrassment about their own speech, adopting the low opinion of themselves which is projected onto their speech by outsiders. The high level of linguistic insecurity manifests itself in a conscious negative attitude toward their own speech, in extreme style shifting toward the external norm in more formal styles, and often in hypercorrection, avoiding dialect features even where they are actually used in the standard language. Women in the Norwich working-class speech community do act in just this fashion. Men, however, do not. Table 4 illustrates women's and men's divergent reaction to one of the highly stigmatized features of Norwich pronunciation. Norwich speakers were asked whether they primarily used the standard RP form /ɪə/ for *ear* or the local stigmatized pronunciation /ɛ:/. Comparing their response to tapes of their actual speech, an index of their accuracy in describing their speech was established. Both men and women had difficulty judging themselves. Women erred primarily in declaring themselves more likely to be standard speaking than they actually were. However, the men overidentified themselves, not as RP speakers but as nonstandard speakers. This difference in attitude toward dialect usage was borne out in analysis of the actual speech samples. Women overall did employ the RP forms with greater frequency than the men. Even more remarkable was the behavior of the men as they shifted from conversation to reading to word-list styles during the course of the interviews. Whereas the women shifted more and more toward RP norms as they moved to the more careful reading and citation styles, the men shifted not toward, but away from the standard, hypercorrecting their Norwich features to contexts where they do not occur in the actual dialect.

Table 4   Percent of Over- and Under-Reporting of
Their Use of RP Pronunciation for *ear*
(/ɪə/) by Women and Men in Norwich

	Male	*Female*	*Total*
Report RP/use N	22	68	43
Report N/use RP	50	14	33
Accurate	28	18	23

Adapted from Trudgill, p. 98.

The linguistic behavior of Norwich men and women reflects their values and self-identification. Women recognize the middle-class speech norm and acquiesce to it. Men, though they recognize what "correct" speech should be (as their hypercorrections indicate), purposefully deviate from it in order to assert their positive identification with working-class culture. An explanation for these language and attitude differences may lie in the roles assigned to men and women. While men are expected to provide economically for their families, it is women who bear the primary responsibility for maintaining and passing on social and cultural norms, as part of their child-care and family role. It is women, for example, who keep up old world ties in immigrant families, through activities in religious organizations, native foods, holiday customs, etc. It is women, as well, who are expected not only to instill the traditional values but also to prepare the children with the social skills and cultural knowledge necessary to take advantage of upward economic mobility. Thus women are especially concerned with their children's religious training, educational success, and social contacts. In lower- and working-class families it is also the women who have most contact with middle-class people—social workers, religious and educational professionals, employers in shops, offices, and private homes. For men, primary contact is with other working-class colleagues, in the factory and in the neighborhood. Thus women may have more opportunity to learn what is "correct" speech behavior, as well as a stronger sense of responsibility for bringing this knowledge into the family. Women's role in child care may also influence their rate of linguistic change in cases (such as the Detroit vowel-fronting example) where social variables do not intrude: girls are in ongoing contact with younger children, while boys are more often free to associate only with their peers.

Grammar

Women's sociolinguistic sensitivity can also be seen in their grammatical preferences. Turning again to the Detroit Dialect Study, two highly stigmatized nonstandard features will illustrate that sex transcends both social class and race as a linguistic variable. Negative concord, the use of a negative in all possible grammatical slots ("*Nobody* did*n't* do *no*thing"), rather than a single one, is a regular rule of Black English Vernacular (BEV) and also occurs in some white nonstandard speakers. Figure 3 represents the frequency of negative concord in Detroit speech. In all classes, women are significantly lower than their male counterparts in use of the stigmatized negative structure. It is no surprise that the greatest percentage differential between men and women is among the lower working class, that group just on the margin of social acceptability and eager for upward mobility.

Similar evidence appears in the behavior of blacks toward "zero copula," a regular feature of BEV. In contexts such as existential statements ("She my older sister"), the copula *be* does not appear (see Figure 4). Frequency of the BEV zero copula construction decreases as one moves up the social ladder with a corresponding decrease from men to women within each social class. This

Figure 3 Distribution of Negative Concord among Detroit Blacks and Whites, by Sex and Socioeconomic Class

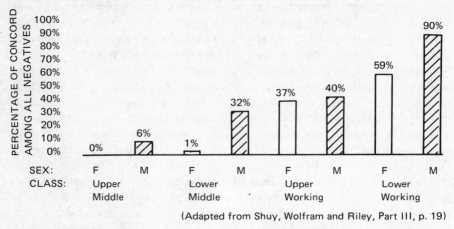

(Adapted from Shuy, Wolfram and Riley, Part III, p. 19)

Figure 4 Frequency of Zero Copula among Detroit Blacks, by Sex and Socioeconomic Class

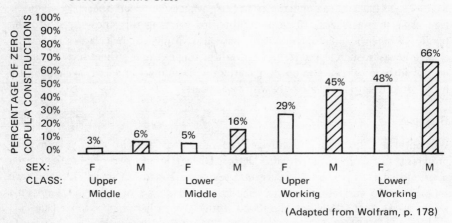

(Adapted from Wolfram, p. 178)

tendency to move toward more "standard" or "acceptable" speech forms is reflected in other areas of women's grammatical behavior. Robin Lakoff has described several structures that are used more frequently by women than by men; tag questions, "hedges," and subjunctives all tend to add a deferential, polite, or formal color to speech. Tag questions are statements with an interrogative "tag" on the end, which requests assent or confirmation from the listener. For instance,

"You'd rather go by train, wouldn't you?"
"It looks like it's going to rain, doesn't it?"

are typical cases of speculative statements in which a response is logically solicited. Women, however, says Lakoff, extend these tag questions even to statements which do not require external confirmation, for example, the expression of a personal opinion:

"It's really hot today, isn't it?"

"The inflation rate is awfully high, isn't it?"

or a statement of fact about oneself, which cannot be easily evaluated by an outsider:

"I've gained two or three pounds, haven't I?"

Such "hedges" as *I think, it seems (to me), I guess, it sort of looks like* are also added to sentences to create the same kind of verbal "out" for the listener who in fact does not agree with the speaker's observation. Women, Lakoff reports, have a greater tendency to avoid direct commands and requests. Rather than telling her husband directly to fulfill his part of their housekeeping agreement, a wife might say:

"Wouldn't you like to dry the dishes?"

Of course, he "wouldn't like" to, but this is not really the question being asked. Even pleasant occupations can be presented as choices. For instance, a woman who has spent two hours preparing dinner may say to her family:

"Would you like to eat now?"

or even the ultra-deferential ("please don't do it if you don't want to"):

"Wouldn't you like to eat now?"

rather than:

"Dinner's ready. Let's eat."

The stereotype of nurses or child-care workers using *we* forms for requests may also stem from the same desire to make others feel that the decision is their own, rather than imposed by the woman speaker:

"We're going to take our nap now and go right to sleep."

"We're going to have our temperature taken, aren't we?"

Choice of subjunctive forms over indicatives also has this same effect:

"I would like to go."

rather than:

"I want to go." or "I will go."

Each of these syntactic devices functions to mitigate a confrontation between the speaker and the listener. Tags on statements specifically set up an opportunity for the listener to respond with a dissent. The circumlocutions of the *it appears to me* type mark the speaker as somewhat ambivalent or unsure, so that dissent is not awkward. By avoiding direct commands and letting others "decide" if they want to do the dishes, eat dinner, or go to bed, a speaker can suggest an action without presuming the authority to order it. Given women's relative position of powerlessness in society, this sort of linguistic behavior is not surprising and is perhaps quite functional.

Intonation and Pitch

Yet another form of mitigation is the use of question intonation when the content of the sentence is actually declarative. In extreme cases question intonation is used when the person answering the question is the only one with the information. An example from a Virginia woman's speech is:[4]

  Male: "What color is your new car?"

  Female: "White?"

The young woman had just purchased a new car and her friend had not seen it yet. The question intonation offers that same doubtfulness, not this time in her opinion as to which color she did indeed choose, but about the friend's possible disapproval of her choice.

There are major, systematic differences between the intonation patterns of men and women in American English. Ruth Brend posits four meaningful pitch levels in women's intonation, contrasting with a male three-pitch system. Women have a wider range of variation in their pitch, with an extra, highest pitch which is lacking in men's speech.[5] This results in a voice characteristic which is often thought of as "sing-songy." Mimic of women's intonation contours is a most frequent element in attempts to stigmatize male homosexuals. Words with the high pitch are perceived as particularly emphasized. Expressions with high pitch might be:[6]

  "How ARE you?"

  "What a deLIGHTful party!"

  "Good-BYE-e."

Like female-associated words and grammar, these intonation contours can stand in the way of women's acceptance in professional settings. Women university lecturers have been labeled "impossible to understand" or "hard to listen to," perhaps solely on the basis of their intonation.

Although control of pitch and intonation may seem to be highly sophisticated linguistic skills, even young children learn to mimic their gender role models' speech. The "voice change" in boys is a secondary sex characteristic which occurs with puberty as the larynx (voice box) enlarges and the vocal cords within it become correspondingly longer. Longer cords produce lower pitch, so that in adults fundamental frequency of voice pitch differs markedly between men and women. For young boys and girls the entire vocal tract is anatomically identical. Yet it is often possible to tell a girl from a boy by voice alone. Intrigued by this observation, Jacqueline Sachs, Philip Lieberman, and Donna Erickson tape-recorded a group of four- through twelve-year-old American boys and girls, matched in height and weight. Contrary to the expectation based on anatomy, the group of boys did have a lower fundamental frequency than the girls. Even at preschool ages, children are learning to distort their vocal tracts in order to attempt the norms they perceive as appropriate for their sex. The differences in the children's tape-recorded speech, minute though they were, were adequate for a group of listeners to make extremely accurate judgments as to their sex.[7]

Discourse Styles

The study of different styles of speaking and the structure of texts which are longer than a single sentence has barely begun. It is clear already that, just as variation in language at the level of sounds, words, phrases, and sentences is a regular and meaningful part of communication, different structures and different choices among available structures characterize utterances, exchanges, and entire conversations. Choices are colored by the topic and the setting and by the number, sex, age, race, ethnicity, and social and geographical background of the speakers. Just as with other speech behavior, there are norms for intragroup talk and norms for talk with outsiders. Women's talk has been popularly characterized by such pejoratives as "gossip," "chatter," "kaffeeklatching." Stereotypically, women talk incessantly and only about trivial and personal matters. Actual research on men's and women's discourse styles does show strong distinctions between men's and women's talk, sometimes but not always along the lines of popular notions.

In a study of the narrative structure of white working-class adolescents (14 to 18 years old), Janet Eisner discovered significant differences in content and style between girls and boys. Boys' stories are "action-oriented," most frequently about fights. They consist almost exclusively of a simple recounting of a sequence of events. Girls' stories are frequently about movies or television soap operas, and often about personal experiences, including a few fights as well. Structurally they are considerably embellished with personal evaluations of the action, with reactions of other people to the event (including moral and social judgments) and self-analysis of their personal motivations for participating in actual events. Physical details of fights, which the boys relish, for instance, are less likely to be mentioned and then only reluctantly.

Donald Graves' analysis of compositions by seven-year-olds revealed similar differences in thematic choices. "Basic themes of aggression, territorial expansion were visible in the boys' writing. Themes of dependency and limited territory were noted in the girls." (p. 1103) The choice of narrative structure with expression of personal feelings and development of characteristics again appeared in the girls' work. In fact, the boys' and girls' stories contrasted very clearly in the use of pronouns: girls used the first person *I* or *me* very commonly, whereas boys "projected themselves into a vicarious use of the third person." (p. 1103)

It is just a short step from this sort of written and oral language behavior to the "consciousness raising" (CR) groups which have become a major vehicle of the feminist movement. The much maligned *Kaffeeklatch* really stems from a tradition in which women, usually isolated in their homes with small children, turn to each other for advice, consolation, and stimulation. Adolescent girls grow up with a "best friend" with whom to share their innermost feelings. It should come as no surprise, then, that women are more adept at personal essay writing, at embellishing and evoking an oral story.

The very discourse styles which are deprecated as "subjective," "personalistic," "gossipy" in girls and women are those which teachers of writing encourage in prospective novelists. For creative writing, "pure plot" is bad style. In a board room, however, evaluative or personal remarks on a report would be "irrelevant," "trivial," and "inappropriate." Women's discourse styles are well suited for highly interactive situations: establishing people's needs, getting them to express their opinions, reporting events so that others can actually sense the situation themselves. There is no question of men's or women's style being "better." But men and women both should learn to control as many speech styles as possible and to apply them to appropriate situations.

What sort of success do women have when they apply their unique verbal style to impersonal or professional situations? Many of the features of women's speech discussed above (avoidance of obscenities, tag questions, hedges, intensifiers, question intonation in declarative sentences, etc.) add up to an impression of politeness, even deference. O'Barr and Conley used some of these features to study what language is most convincing to trial-jury members. They first established, from tapes of trials, that it is predominantly women who use these forms, both in giving testimony and in questioning witnesses in their capacity as lawyers. Since these forms were also frequent in the speech of some men, O'Barr and Conley termed this mode of speaking "powerless" language, contrasted with "power" language which did not exhibit these forms. They created a series of taped "testimony" in which the "witnesses" differed from one another in these specific features and had them rated on characteristics such as believability, intelligence, competence, likeability, and assertiveness. Both female and male "witnesses" were rated lower, and less likely to be credible to the jury, when they used the "powerless" style. The ramifications of these findings extend far beyond the courtroom. Women in any professional situation, or in any situation in which they must speak convincingly of factual matters, will be less effective if they employ the speech styles which they have developed as part of the female role. Women, as well as men, are apparently less convinced of the reliability and competence of a speaker who uses "women's style."

Nonverbal Language

Differences between men's and women's gestures, walk, seated and standing postures, and other nonverbal behaviors are clear to all of us. After raising or lowering the voice, gesture and facial expression are probably the most ready ways for mimicking the opposite sex. Novelist Marge Piercy provides a lovely description of Wanda, a feminist theater director, teaching her students how to relearn walking, standing, and sitting:

> Wanda made them aware of how they moved, how they rested, how they occupied space. She demonstrated how men sat and how women sat on the subway, on benches. Men expanded into available space. They sprawled, or they sat with spread legs. They put their arms on the arms of chairs. They crossed their legs by putting a foot on the other knee. They dominated space expansively.
>
> Women condensed. Women crossed their legs by putting one leg over the other and alongside. Women kept their elbows to their sides, taking up as little space as possible. They behaved as if it were their duty not to rub against, not to touch, not to bump a man. If contact occurred, the woman shrank back.

If a woman bumped a man, he might choose to interpret it as a come-on. Women sat protectively, using elbows not to dominate space, not to mark territory, but to protect their soft tissues.

Further, men commented on how women looked and walked on the streets. Women did not stand in groups observing men critically and aloud informing them of their approval or disapproval, commenting that they found a man attractive or ugly, that they wanted to use him sexually or that they thought he could be bought for a price. A woman walked with a sense of being looked at: either she behaved as if being evaluated by men were a test and she tried to pass it; or she walked with chin lowered, eyes lowered. She pretended that, if she did not look at the men, the men could not see her. She walked very fast, pretending to be invisible, deaf, dumb, blind.[8]

Studies of white middle-class groups have shown that women smile more, that women seek eye contact more frequently but do not maintain it, and that women do not initiate touching. The implications of the nonverbal behavior, like the verbal deference behavior, are profoundly undermining for women who are in or are seeking positions of authority and responsibility.

Women are better interpreters of nonverbal behavior. Since emotional messages and reactions are predominantly coded into the nonverbal channel of language, it is not surprising that women, with their role-focus on family and personal issues (rather than the external, more impersonal affairs of men's roles), pick up silent cues more readily. Robert Rosenthal and his colleagues tested subjects' ability to guess the topic in video-taped sequences in which the verbal message was diminished to intonation contours or totally obliterated. In some tapes only part of the body was shown. They found that women could detect the situation with greater speed and accuracy. The few men who were as skilled as women at decoding nonverbal language were all in occupations of a "nurturant, artistic or expressive nature" (e.g., teachers, clinical psychologists, designers). Children as young as third graders were tested with significantly better scores for girls than boys, although the accuracy level declined for all subjects younger than their early twenties. Research into this fascinating area has just begun. Uncovering sex differences in nonverbal communication and in discourse style in particular may serve as a very significant first step toward identifying and altering gender-role-determined language behavior and the consequent stereotyping by sex.

Attitudes toward Language

The heightened sensitivity to nonverbal communication which was reported above is paralleled in the verbal aspect of language by women's keen awareness of language varieties, and of the social implications of language usages. The sections on phonology and grammar above illustrated that women exhibit higher frequencies of standard forms when a dialect feature is stigmatized. At this time it is impossible to say whether this stems from a greater sensitivity to phonological and grammatical minutiae or, as the Trudgill study may imply, a greater willingness to adopt features dictated by the dominant language group. A middle-ground interpretation is that men may have a passive knowledge of sociolinguistic significance but fail to make active use of such knowledge to enhance their own speech socially as women do.

The stronger hypothesis, that women are actually more acute sociolinguistically, is supported by women's behavior on subjective reaction tests. Some studies have shown that women tend to be more skillful in detecting dialect features on taped speech samples than men—both in identifying the speaker as "nonstandard" and in isolating the linguistic feature which triggered their identification. In all events women have a markedly stronger tendency to judge people negatively because of nonstandard speech features than do men. Women are much harsher evaluators on subjective reaction ratings, on both sociological and personality variables.

Similarly, women have tended to show greater linguistic insecurity both by their more extreme style shifting toward standard features and by hypercorrection. In specific tests for linguistic insecurity, they show a larger discrepancy between what they think is their own speech form and what they perceive as the "correct" usage.

These attitudes and the linguistic behavior they evoke correlate closely with the accepted roles for women in American society. Women are expected to be socializers, cultural bastions, standard setters for the younger generation given into their care. These are heavy responsibilities, and women have reacted to them by monitoring and modifying their language to best suit the family's ambitions. However important, the family is not the locus of power in this society, perhaps because it is the domain of women. The standards for behavior, like the goals of the family, are actually set by men. Women are left with the task of fitting the young people for a world which they themselves do not control. In such a situation it is little wonder that women are linguistically insecure and use language which reveals an overattention to authority and a lack of self-confidence and self-assertion. As options for women and men widen, perhaps women and men can learn from each other the specialized linguistic skills which make men better at describing factual situations and asserting their opinions and women more adept in noting and responding to the personal aspects of interaction.

NOTES

1. Some of these phenomena were first remarked upon by Lakoff (1973).

2. This apparent exception may be accounted for by the fact that fronting of /a/ is stigmatized *within* the Detroit speech community. It "sounds awful" to local speakers. Women's lower rate of fronted /a/ would thus be an indication of their sensitivity to sociolinguistically negatively valued features. [Eds.]

3. Labov points specifically to British vowel shifts and to the merger of /a/ and /ɔ/ which is taking place across the United States, beginning in the Middle Atlantic states and the Far West.

4. Linda Coleman, who brought this example to my attention, feels that this question intonation in women's declaratives is particularly common in the South, especially in male-female interactions.

5. The obvious anatomically determined differences between the fundamental frequencies of men and women are a separate issue from this socially determined language behavior. Fundamental frequencies are discussed below.

6. Brend, following Kenneth L. Pike, glosses the following:

Women only: 'oh,   'that's   'awful!

Women contrasted with men:

Women: 'yes,   'yes,   I   'know.

Men: 'yes,   'yes,   I   'know.

7. Of the entire group of children only two, both girls, were consistently misidentified. Both were described by friends as "tomboys." Clearly other linguistic clues such as intonation or articulation were revealing some sex-inappropriate "aggressiveness" factor in these girls' speech.

8. Marge Piercy, *Small Changes.* Doubleday, 1973, pp. 438-439.

References

Brend, Ruth M., 1971   "Male-Female Intonation Patterns in American English," Barrie Thorne and Nancy Henley, eds., *Language and Sex: Difference and Dominance.* Newbury House, 1975, 84-87.

Conklin, Nancy Faires, 1974   "Toward a Feminist Analysis of Linguistic Behavior," *The University of Michigan Papers in Women's Studies* 1:1, 51-73.

Eisner, Janet Margaret, 1975   *A Grammar of Oral Narrative.* Ph.D. Dissertation, The University of Michigan, unpublished.

Fischer, John L., 1958   "Social Influence in the Choice of a Linguistic Variant," *Word* 14, 47-56. Reprinted in Dell Hymes, ed., *Language in Culture and Society: A Reader in Linguistics and Anthropology.* Harper & Row, 1964, 483-488.

Graves, Donald H., 1973   "Sex Differences in Children's Writing," *Elementary English* 50: 7, 1101-1106 (Special Issue: *Women and Girls*).

Lakoff, Robin, 1973   "Language and Woman's Place," *Language and Society* 2, 45-79.

Levine, Lewis, and Harry J. Crockett, Jr., 1966   "Speech Variation in a Piedmont Community: Postvocalic r," *Sociological Inquiry* 36:2, 204-226 (Special Issue: *Explorations in Sociolinguistics,* Stanley Lieberson, ed.).

O'Barr, William M., and John M. Conley, 1976   "When a Juror Watches a Lawyer," *Barrister* 3: 3, 8-11, 33.

Rosenthal, Robert, Dane Archer, M. Robin DiMatteo, Judith Hall Koivumaki, and Peter L. Rogers, 1974   "Body Talk and Tone of Voice: The Language without Words," *Psychology Today* 8: 4, 64-68.

Sachs, Jacqueline, Philip Lieberman, and Donna Erickson, 1973   "Anatomical and Cultural Determinants of Male and Female Speech," Roger W. Shuy and Ralph W. Fasold, eds., *Language Attitudes: Current Trends and Prospects.* Georgetown University Press, 74-84.

Shuy, Roger W., 1969   "Sex as a Factor in Sociolinguistic Research," ERIC-PEGS pamphlet. U.S. Office of Education, publication ED 001720.

Shuy, Roger W., Walter A. Wolfram, and William K. Riley, 1967   *Linguistic Correlates of Social Stratification in Detroit Speech* (Final Report of the *Detroit Dialect Study*). U.S. Office of Education, publication ED 022187.

Trudgill, Peter, 1974   *Sociolinguistics: An Introduction.* Penguin Books.

Wolfram, Walter A., 1969   *A Sociolinguistic Description of Detroit Negro Speech.* Center for Applied Linguistics.

POWER, SEX, AND NONVERBAL COMMUNICATION

Nancy M. Henley

Just as there are separate language norms among the various speech communities in the United States, standards for nonverbal behavior also vary from group to group. Sometimes this variation among groups causes confusion in the meaning of an identical gesture or posture. For instance, Chicano and Black children are taught that direct eye contact with adults is rude and presumptuous. An Anglo teacher interprets watchfulness on the part of pupils as a sign of attention and deference. Thus in the same situation in which a white child is told, "Look at me when I'm talking to you," a Black child is warned, "Don't you cut eye with me!" A familiar clash of nonverbal communication norms is our discomfort among a group of people who are notably more or less physically affectionate than our own family. The Headnote to Cooke's article on gestures and postures in the Black community outlines the general role of nonverbal behavior in communication.

Within a single speech community, nonverbal language, like linguistic structures, is used to establish relationships and social standing. Nancy M. Henley selects just a few affective channel cues in order to demonstrate the use of nonverbal behavior to reinforce gender roles and status. Readers may wish to analyze other nonverbal cues listed in Appendix G in terms of Henley's analysis for cross-ethnic group or social class interactions as well as for those between males and females in the same speech community.

In front of, and defending, the larger political-economic structure that determines our lives and defines the context of human relationships, there is a micropolitical structure that helps maintain it. The "trivia" of everyday life—using "sir" or first name, touching others, dropping the eyes, smiling, interrupting, and so on—that characterize these micropolitics are commonly understood as facilitators of social intercourse but are not recognized as defenders of the status quo—of the state, of the wealthy, of authority, of all those whose power may be challenged. Nevertheless, these minutiae find their place on a continuum of social control which extends from internalized socialization (the colonization of the mind) at the one end to sheer physical force (guns, clubs, incarceration) at the other.

Micropolitical cues are, moreover, of particular importance in the study of woman's place in our society, for several reasons. First, like any other oppressed group, women should know all the chains binding them. Second, women are likely targets for this subtle form of social control for two reasons: they are particularly socialized to docility and passivity, and their physical integration around centers of power (as wives, secretaries, etc.) ensures their frequent interaction (verbal and nonverbal) with those in power.[1] Finally, women are more sensitive than men to social cues in general, as many studies have shown, and to nonverbal cues in particular (Argyle et al., 1970).

This paper will seek to examine certain nonverbal behaviors, and some subtle verbal ones, in their social context as a step toward understanding the myriad faces of power.

Sexual Dimorphism or Unimorphism?

From the beginning we should guard against the mistake of assuming that the observed nonverbal (or even verbal) differences between the human sexes result from biology. In 1943, Galt pointed out humanity's long journey from an apparently little-acknowledged distinction between the sexes (and early bisexuality and natural "polymorphous perversity") to the present "Western" cultural assumption of extreme sexual distinction (and narrowly channeled sexuality). He writes,

> it should be clear that the *either-or* type of sexual behavior demanded of man and woman by the mores of Western culture under threat of severe penalty is not in line with the trend of sexual adjustment as it has developed throughout biological evolution. (p. 9)

Birdwhistell (1970) writes that when different animal species are rated on a spectrum by the extent of their sexual dimorphism, on the basis of secondary sexual characteristics "man seems far closer to the unimorphic end of the spectrum than he might like to believe" (p. 41). He states that his work in kinesics leads him to postulate "that man and probably a number of other weakly dimorphic species necessarily organize much of gender display and recognition at the level of position, movement, and expression" (p. 42). Thus we must realize that much of our nonverbal behavior, far from being "natural," has been developed and modified to emphasize and display sex differences, much like our manner of dress. (Class differences are signaled and emphasized in these ways too.)

Communication—Verbal and Nonverbal

Our culture emphasizes verbal over nonverbal communication. English is taught in our schools through all grades, with the aims of both better understanding (diagramming sentences, learning Latin roots) and better expression (writing compositions). Nonverbal communication isn't taught: we never learn to analyze what certain postures, gestures, and looks mean, or how to express ourselves better nonverbally. (Of course, nonverbal communication is learned informally, just as language is learned before we enter schools to study it.) This doesn't mean everybody doesn't *know* that looks and postures mean something, perhaps everything, especially in emotion-charged interaction. But mentioning looks and postures is illegitimate in reporting communication; legal transcripts and newspaper accounts don't record them. And they are seldom allowed in personal argument ("What look? What tone of voice? Look, did I say OK, or didn't I?").

Yet, with all our ignorance about nonverbal communication, the evidence is that the nonverbal message greatly overpowers the verbal one; one estimate (Argyle et al., 1970) is that it carries 4.3 times the weight. In the face of the facts that nonverbal communication is more important than verbal, that it helps maintain the power structure, that women are particularly influenced by it, and that it is glaringly ignored in our education and disallowed in argument, it becomes important for all those deprived of power, and particularly women, to learn all they can about how it affects their lives, and to apply that knowledge to their struggle for liberation.

Most of the literature on nonverbal communication emphasizes solidarity relations (friendship, liking, attraction) rather than power relations. The popular literature on "body language" (e.g., Fast, 1970; Montagu, 1971; Morris, 1971), where it's not charlatanry, concentrates primarily on intimacy and communication between supposed equals. The empirical literature (e.g., Duncan, 1969; Mehrabian, 1972; Scheflen, 1972) likewise tends to focus on the emotional and solidarity aspects of nonverbal communication.

For insights into the *status* aspects of nonverbal communication, a more fruitful source is the anecdotal descriptions of writers like Goffman and Haley. Haley in a well-known essay (1962) discusses "The Art of Psychoanalysis" from the point of view of gamesmanship. He notes the importance of the physical aspects of this status-laden interaction:

> By placing the patient on a couch, the analyst gives the patient the feeling of having his feet up in the air and the knowledge that the analyst has both feet on the ground. Not only is the patient disconcerted by having to lie down while talking, but he finds himself literally below the analyst and so his one-down position is geographically emphasized. In addition, the analyst seats himself behind the couch where he can watch the patient but the patient cannot watch him. This gives the patient the sort of disconcerted feeling a person has when sparring with an opponent while blindfolded. Unable to see what response his ploys provoke, he is unsure when he is one-up and one-down.... Another purpose is served by the position behind the couch. Inevitably what the analyst says becomes exaggerated in importance since the patient lacks any other means of determining his effect on the analyst. (pp. 209-210)

Goffman (1956), in his intriguing essay "The Nature of Deference and Demeanor," points to many characteristics associated with status. "Between superordinate and subordinate," he writes, "we may expect to find asymmetrical relations, the superordinate having the right to exercise certain familiarities which the subordinate is not allowed to reciprocate." Goffman cites such familiarities as using familiar address, asking for personal information, touching, teasing, and informal demeanor.

Some Conceptual Problems   As Mehrabian (1972) has pointed out, "nonverbal behavior," in its traditionally broad usage, has included subtle aspects of verbal behavior as well. This article will not dwell on problems of terminology in a rather confused field where distinctions are made or not made between such terms as paralinguistic, extralinguistic, linguistic, subtle, implicit, nonverbal, kinesic, and proxemic. I will discuss first some of those aspects of language which are not part of familiar linguistic analysis, and then a group of nonlanguage behaviors. It should be kept in mind at all times, however, that the artificial divisions created by traditions of study and by this particular account are not real: communication is integral, carried on at many levels and in many channels simultaneously.

I will not investigate the relationships of these behaviors to *power* and *status* separately. Status and power are usually confounded; when writing of specific findings, I will be specific about which variable the researchers investigated. When writing of my own theories regarding nonverbal communication, however, I may refer either to power or to status or to both.

Since males are likely to have more status and power than females, it may be difficult to determine whether sex or status is the appropriate variable to be associated with a particular behavior. For example, are female secretaries touched because they are subordinates, or because they are females, or both? The answer is probably both. Many studies demonstrate separately the effects of status and sex, but for some questions we will have to await further research.

The relation of nonverbal cues to the exercise of power is complex. On a simple behavioral level, we may observe first that they are *associated* with power or the lack of it. Further they may *affect* the power relationship, for example, when in an established relationship a dominance gesture is not met with submission. On an analytical level, we may decide that the gestures act as cues *symbolic* of power, both to display for observers and to *express* for both sender and receiver the power relation. On a theoretical level, we may suggest that nonverbal behaviors are used overall to *maintain* the power relations of a society, but in individual situations may help *establish* such relations, as when people in a competitive situation begin to seek dominance over each other. For the most part this article will deal with the association between behavior and status in the maintenance of social structure.

The observations and descriptions cited in the following studies are based at times on somewhat unrefined methods of observation, but that only indicates the developing state of this field of investigation and ought not stop us from reviewing them and seeing the relations between them. The questions thus raised, and conclusions drawn, will point toward future directions for research, in the continual interplay that the relation between theory and research requires.

Subtle Aspects of Language

Although we are focusing on nonverbal communication, we know that language also carries messages of status in its structure and usage. Sociolinguists have for some years pursued political, class, and status aspects of language, but until recently only feminists looked into ("complained about") sexism in our language.

Male/Female Distinctions Two comprehensive reviews of male/female distinctions in languages have now been made. Lakoff (1973) discusses both the concept of "woman's language" in English (which, when used, works against her) and the deprecation of women implicit in general usage. Examples of woman's language are given in the lexicon, syntax, intonation, and other suprasegmental patterns. There is also provocative discussion of sex-differentiated language learning in children and of the interaction of sex and class with language. Lakoff illustrates the weakness introduced into woman's English by its use of tag questions (e.g., "The Vietnam war is terrible, isn't it?") and tag orders (e.g., "Won't you please close the door?"). Other examples can be added to this list: hesitating, apologizing, and disparaging one's own statement (e.g., "I don't know anything about it, but. . . .").

Key (1972) examines the linguistic behavior of males and females in phonological, grammatical, and semantic components, emphasizing analysis in situational context. She looks both at differences in women's and men's usages and at the implicit sexism in structure and usage in the phonological realm (pronunciation and intonation patterns, including pitch and stress), in the grammatical component (syntactic patterns and grammatical gender), and in the semantic component (grammatical categories, gender vs. sex, and pronominal and nominal referents). Recent papers by other authors have analyzed such topics as gender in English (Nichols, 1971), male-female differences in intonation (Brend, 1972) and anatomical and cultural determinants of male and female speech (Sachs et al., 1973).

Austin (1965) has commented on sex and status differences in speech:

In our culture little boys tend to be nasal . . . and little girls, oral. Nasality is considered 'tough' and 'vulgar' and is somewhat discouraged by elders. 'Gentlemanly' little boys tend to be oral also. (p. 34)

A 'little girl's voice' (innocence, helplessness, regression) is composed of high pitch and orality. (p. 37)

The dominant middle-class white culture in the United States has certain set views on lower-class Negro speech. It is 'loud,' 'unclear,' 'slurred,' 'lazy.' The myth of loudness should be exorcised at once. Any minority or 'out-group' is characterized as 'loud'—Americans in Europe, Englishmen in America, and so on. (p. 38)

When considering women as the out-group, at first it may seem that the characterization "loud" does not apply: their speech is renowned as soft, quiet (the "lady's" speech is golden). However, only the acceptable members of the out-group (i.e., those allowed into some legitimate relationship with the in-group) are identified as having the in-group characteristics and are not stereotyped as loud. Nonladies are often characterized by their loudness, and female advocates of women's liberation are used to being described as "shrill." Of course, the word *shrill* simply adds the connotation of loudness to that of high pitch (commonly associated with the female voice, though not determined by biology—see Sachs et al., 1973).

Terms of Address   The use of different terms of address is one very familiar distinction made with language. Inferiors must address superiors by title and last name (Mr., Dr., Professor Jones) or by other polite address, such as "sir," or polite second-person forms (*vous, Sie, usted*) in languages which have them. Superiors may address inferiors by first name or by the familiar form (*tu, du, tú*). Brown and his colleagues (Brown, 1965; Brown and Ford, 1961; Brown and Gilman, 1960) have demonstrated how terms of address are used to indicate both status and solidarity relations: status is characterized by asymmetry of address as described above, and solidarity by symmetric use of familiar (close) or polite (distant) address. Historically the polite form has been used symmetrically within the upper classes, and the familiar form symmetrically within the lower classes.

In a detailed analysis of the status and solidarity dimensions of interpersonal relationships, Brown has gone beyond the terms of address to a generalization of the rules that govern their use; this generalization applies to other forms of communicative behavior we will examine later. He has pointed out a universal norm in terms of address that has the generalized formula: "If form X is used to inferiors it is used between intimates, and if form Y is used to superiors it is used between strangers" (Brown, 1965, p. 92). Furthermore, when there is a clear difference of status between two persons, the right to initiate a change to more intimate forms of relationship (e.g., mutual first name or familiar address) belongs to the superior.

Self-Disclosure   Goffman (1956) writes:

in American business organizations the boss may thoughtfully ask the elevator man how his children are, but this entrance into another's life may be blocked to the elevator man, who can appreciate the concern but not return it. Perhaps the clearest form of this is found in the psychiatrist-patient relation, where the psychiatrist has the right to touch on aspects of the patient's life that the patient might not even allow himself to touch upon, while of course this privilege is not reciprocated. (p. 64)

A study of address and social relations in a business organization by Slobin, Miller, and Porter (1968) confirms both the basic analysis of address made by Brown and the observations about self-disclosure made by Goffman. Individuals in the company studied were "more self-disclosing to their immediate superior than to their immediate subordinates" (p. 292); that is, personal information flows opposite to the flow of authority. This finding may be juxtaposed with that of Jourard and Lasakow (1958), who found that females disclose themselves more to others than do males. Although this effect has been frequently replicated, a number of studies have failed to find sex differences in self-disclosure; however, no study has reported greater male disclosure (Cozby, 1973).

The whole question of the relation of self-disclosure to status, and its special importance for women, is further illuminated in comparing the controlled aura of the professional or VIP (doctor, corporation head, judge) with the more variable demeanor of ordinary people, particularly children, working-class people, women, and persons of "ethnic" background.[2]

"Cool" is nothing more than the withholding of information, that is, refusing to disclose one's thoughts and emotions, and the value it gives to street people, poker players, and psychiatrists is of the same sort. But while it is practically a class characteristic for the upper classes, for lower-class people it can only be an individual or situational variable. Disadvantaged people find it difficult to withhold personal information; poor people and national minorities are forced to reveal any information about themselves that is wanted by the authorities. They are the focus of endless questioning by social workers and government officials, and of endless investigation by anthropologists and sociologists. The cultures of most poor and "ethnic" peoples in our societies, and those of women and children, allow for a broader and deeper range of emotional display than that of adult white males, and members of those cultures are commonly depicted as "uncontrolled" emotionally. Male children are socialized away from this, but the socialization of female children to be more expressive emotionally sets them up for their vulnerability as "emotional" women, with little control over the visibility of their affect.[3] This involuntary self-disclosure, giving knowledge that gives power over oneself ("Whoever said 'Knowledge is power'/had power first"—Gitlin, 1971), is related to the self-disclosure that comes with visibility, which will be discussed in a subsequent section.

Nonverbal Communication

Demeanor   In the area of demeanor, Goffman (1956) observes that in hospital staff meetings, "medical doctors had the privilege of swearing, changing the topic of conversation, and sitting in undignified positions" (p. 78), while attendants were required to show greater circumspection. Furthermore, doctors' freedom to lounge on the nursing station counter and to joke with the nurses could be extended to other ranks only after it had been initiated by doctors.

The rules of demeanor recognized by Goffman may also be examined with special reference to women: women, too, are denied such privileges as swearing and sitting in undignified positions, which are allowed to men, and are explicitly required to be more circumspect than men by all standards, including the well-known double one.

Space   There are silent messages in the nonhuman environment as well as the human one, and the distribution of space is one carrier of such messages. The imposing height and space of courtrooms and governmental buildings intimidate, as they are meant to, the people whose lives are affected there. A storefront structure is designed to draw people in; a courthouse or library, with distant stone facade and discouraging high steps, is designed to turn people away.

Brown (1965, pp. 78-82) discusses spatial relations (as one of five types of interpersonal relationship) in terms of solidarity and status dimensions, noting that status differences are marked by being above or below, in front or behind. Sommer (1969) observes that dominant animals and human beings have a larger envelope of inviolability surrounding them than do subordinate ones (dominants may not be approached as closely).[4] Sex status in the unequal distribution of personal space is demonstrated in a study reported by Willis (1966). He found, in studying the initial speaking distance set by an approaching person, that women were approached more closely than were men, by both men and women.

Silveira (1972) reports that in public observations of who gets out of the other's way when passing on the sidewalk, the woman moved out of the man's way in 12 of 19 observed mixed-sex encounters (in four cases both moved, and in three cases the man did). When women approached women or men approached men, about 50 percent of the time both moved out of each other's way; the rest of the time only one moved.

Touch Popular writers (e.g., Montagu, 1971; Morris, 1971) who have written on touching have generally advanced sexual explanations for it or see it only in a context of intimacy. Jourard and Rubin (1968) take the view that "touching is equated with sexual intent, either consciously, or at a less-conscious level" (p. 47). Lewis (1972) writes: "In general, for men in our culture, proximity (touching) is restricted to the opposite sex and its function is primarily sexual in nature" (p. 237).

But there are clearly status connotations in touching, and it will be valuable to consider the touching between the sexes in this light. Goffman (1956) writes of the "touch system" in a hospital: "The doctors touched other ranks as a means of conveying friendly support and comfort, but other ranks tended to feel that it would be presumptuous for them to reciprocate a doctor's touch, let alone initiate such a contact with a doctor" (p. 74).

Touching is also one of the closer invasions of one's personal space and may be related to the deference shown the space surrounding the body. It is even more a physical threat than space violation, pointing, or staring, perhaps a vestige of the days when dominance was determined by physical prowess. The status dimension of touching is illustrated in the following interactions between pairs of persons of differing status (which would be more likely to put an arm around the shoulder, a hand on the back, tap the chest, or hold the wrists?): teacher and student; master and servant; policeman and accused; doctor and patient; minister and parishioner; counselor and client; foreman and worker; businessman and secretary.

Even those who put forward a sexual explanation for males' touching of females have to admit that there is at least a status overlay: female factory workers, secretaries, students, servants, and waitresses are often unwillingly felt or pinched, but women of higher status (e.g., "boss ladies," "first ladies," and "ladies" in general) aren't.

In fact, women are expected to accept as normal behavior the daily violations of their persons. However, when they reciprocate or, especially, initiate touch with men they are likely to be interpreted as conveying specific sexual intent. The question of sexuality as explanation for touching will be taken up later.

What investigation of touching there has been by psychologists provides evidence in support of the thesis that females are touched by others more than males are (Jourard, 1966; Jourard and Rubin, 1968). Studies of child-mother interaction have reported greater touching of female than of male children, at least from age six months on (Clay, 1968; Goldberg and Lewis, 1969; Lewis, 1972).

It is interesting to examine some of the consequences of being handled more as a child. Lewis (1972) puts forward the thesis "that the major socialization process, in terms of attachment or social behavior, is to move the infant from a proximal mode of social interaction (e.g., touching, rocking, holding) to a distal mode (e.g., smiling and vocalizing)" (p. 234). His data suggest that boys are moved faster from the proximal to distal form of interaction than girls are, and indeed, that girls are never socialized as thoroughly as boys in this regard, i.e., to distal relations, associated with more independence. Thus greater touching of females is part of the larger picture in which they are socialized to dependence, to be not the manipulators of their environment, but the objects in it.[5]

An observational study by this author (1970, 1973) investigated touching with regard to several status dimensions (socioeconomic status, sex, and age) and found that in all these cases those of higher status (higher SES, male, older) touched those of lower status significantly more. With regard to sex, observed frequencies were: for males (M) touching (T) females (F), 42; FTM, 25; MTM, 17; and FTF, 17. The pattern of touching between and within the sexes was particularly striking when other factors were held constant, i.e., when women did not have other status advantages in the absence of the sex one. A breakdown of observations into indoor and outdoor[6] settings showed a clear sex status touching pattern only outdoors. This finding was interpreted as suggesting either that subtler cues (e.g., eye contact, voice shifts) sufficed to maintain the status relation indoors, while grosser physical acts were necessary outdoors; or that more public outdoor settings necessitated stricter attention to the status structure than the more intimate indoor ones.

Sexual Explanations of Touching The greater frequency of touching between the sexes, when compared to within sexes, may suggest components of both heterosexual attraction and homosexual inhibition. However, sexual attraction is not sufficient to explain men's greater touching of women, since it would predict that women would touch men as frequently. It can hardly be claimed any longer that men have greater "sex drives";[7] therefore, a lesser expression of sex must be attributed to an inhibition on the part of women to display sexual interest in this manner. At this point we are back where we started: the question becomes one of why one sex feels free to express its motivation tactually and the other does not. The status difference, which is a common variable underlying the differential utilization of touch in other status dimensions, best explains the difference in touching between the sexes.[8]

Duality of Touch Symbolism   The hypothesis that touch communicates power is not necessarily in conflict with an alternative interpretation that it communicates intimacy. There is no question that persons who are close exchange touch more. Touch may be regarded as a nonverbal equivalent of calling another by first name; used reciprocally, it indicates solidarity; when nonreciprocal, it indicates status. Even when there is mutuality, however, we may note that there is some indication of status difference. Consider for example, who, over the course of dating by a couple, initiates touching: usually the male is the first to place his arm around the female, rather than vice versa.

Furthermore, as with Brown's (1965) status norm discussed previously, there is evidence that the behavioral form used toward subordinates or members of a lower class is found in reciprocal use among the members of that class: Clay (1968), Hore (1970), and Lewis and Wilson (1971) all report greater physical contact among mother-child pairs in lower classes than in higher ones.

Eye Contact   Perhaps the most extensively researched area in nonverbal communication is that of eye contact. And according to one researcher: "Perhaps the most powerful single variable [in eye contact] is sex" (Duncan, 1969, p. 129). There is, first of all, a common finding that in interactions, women look more at the other person than do men (Exline, 1963; Exline, Gray, Schuette, 1965; Rubin, 1970). Women also have a higher percentage of mutual looking; Exline, Gray, and Schuette (1965) suggest that this "willingness to engage in mutual visual interaction is more characteristic of those who are oriented towards inclusive and affectionate interpersonal relations" (p. 207).

It is important to put eye contact into its political context, taking into account the importance of social approval to women's survival. The hypothesis that "[Subjects] maintain more eye contact with individuals toward whom they have developed higher expectancies for social approval" was supported in Efran and Broughton's (1966) study of visual interaction in males. And Exline (1963) writes: "Women . . . may look at other persons more than do men because they value more highly the kinds of information they can obtain through such activity" (p. 18).[9] More pointedly, Rubin (1970) suggests that "gazing may serve as a vehicle of emotional expression for women and, in addition, may allow women to obtain cues from their male partners concerning the appropriateness of their behavior" (p. 272).

There is another reason for women's greater eye contact: the listener in a conversation tends to look at the speaker rather than vice versa (Exline, 1963; Duncan, 1969), and men tend to talk more than women (Argyle, Lalljee, and Cook, 1968).

Exline notes that Simmel (1921) specifically distinguishes the mutual, communion-signifying glance from the nonmutual one, and that Sartre implies that "when two glances meet, a wordless struggle ensues until one or the other succeeds in establishing dominance" (p. 3). Exline asks: "A dominance which is, perhaps, signaled by the lowered glance of the loser?" Here we have reverberations of the parlor game in which one person stares another down, but this "game" is enacted at subtler levels thousands of times daily when a subordinate averts or lowers the eyes from the gaze of a superior.

Dominance communicated through eye contact (with other nonverbal cues) is illustrated by O'Connor (1970) in this account:

> A husband and wife are at a party. The wife says something that the husband does not want her to say. . . . He quickly tightens the muscles around his jaw and gives her a rapid but intense direct stare. . . . The wife, who is actually sensitive to the gestures of the man on whom she is dependent, immediately stops the conversation, lowers or turns her head slightly, averts her eyes or gives off some other gesture of submission which communicates acquiescence to her husband and reduces his aggression. (p. 9)

Research reported by Ellsworth, Carlsmith, and Henson (1972) supports the notion that the stare can be perceived as an aggressive gesture. These authors write: "The studies reported here demonstrate that staring at humans can elicit the same sort of responses that are common in primates; that is, staring can act like a primate threat display" (p. 310). The suggestion that the averted glance may be a gesture of submission is supported by the research of Hutt and Ounsted (1966). These authors, in writing about the characteristic gaze aversion of autistic children, remark that

> these children were never attacked despite the fact that to a naive observer they appeared to be easy targets; this indicated that their gaze aversion had some signalling function similar to 'facing away' in the kittiwake or 'head-flagging' in the herring gull—behavior patterns which Tinbergen (1959) has termed 'appeasement postures.' In other words, gaze aversion inhibited any aggressive or threat behavior on the part of other conspecifics. (p. 354)

There seems to be some discrepancy between the notions that dominance is established or maintained by the nonmutual glance, and that women do more looking. But there are several factors that resolve this conflict. First, of course, we must remember that a greater portion of women's looking consists of *mutual* eye contact. Also, women may look at the other more and still not use nonmutual looking to dominate, by looking when another is speaking (an act outside the realm of competition). They may furthermore be the first to look away (the submissive gesture) when mutual glance is maintained for some while. More detailed research on sex differences in the initiation and termination of eye contact, in coordination with speaking patterns, would further our understanding here.

Visibility   Visibility is related to both eye contact and self-disclosure: it is the availability of (visual) information about oneself to others, with all the power that information conveys. Further insight into the politics of visibility is given by Argyle et al. (1968), in whose experiments the visibility of one of the two communicators was varied. These authors hypothesize that "if A can see B better than B can see A, A becomes the 'perceiver' and comes to dominate the encounter" (p. 13). In their experiments, females found communication more difficult when they could not see the other person and wanted to see even when invisible themselves. While women when invisible *decreased* their speech by 40 percent, males when invisible *increased* their amount of speech by 40 percent in addition to talking more than females in general. A significant interaction between visibility and sex was found in which "males talk more when invisible *and* talking to females" (p. 12). These results suggest sex differences in the effects of invisibility; though invisibility conveys a certain advantage, perhaps women are not as able (because of past experience outside the laboratory) to take advantage of it as are men.

Argyle and Williams (1969) report that in interview situations an asymmetry is established, that subjects felt themselves to be subordinate, to be "observed" rather than "observer," when they were being interviewed (as opposed to interviewing), were female, were younger, or if female, were with a male. The authors' comments about females' reactions to visibility are interesting:

It is expected that there would be sex differences. Women, in most societies, dress up more colorfully and decoratively than men, and can be regarded as taking the role of performer rather than audience. It is suggested that women are more concerned about their appearance, not because they are personally insecure, but because they are going to be performers and going to be 'observed.' We predict then that in a dyadic encounter between a male and a female the female will feel herself more observed than a male; and that this difference will not be due to differences of security or dominance. (pp. 398-399)

Later, however, they state:

It is possible that people who feel observed have in the past been stared down by others, and adopted a low level of looking themselves—i.e., their feelings of being observed are based on real experiences of being looked at in the past. (p. 410)

In a society in which women's clothing is designed explicitly to reveal the body and its contours; in which women are ogled, whistled at, and pinched while simply going about their business; in which they see advertisements in magazines, on billboards, on TV in their own homes, showing revealingly clad women; in which tactual information about them is freely available, their bodies accessible to touch like community property; in which even their marital status is the first information by which a stranger identifies them—in such a society it is little wonder that women feel "observed." They are.

Gestures of Dominance and Submission   Dominant and submissive gestures have long been described by students of animal behavior, often with some reference to their similarity to the gestures of human beings. We noted earlier that the direct stare has been characterized as a threat, and the averted glance as a sign of submission, among humans. Anthony (1970) compares the "presenting" submissive gesture of chimpanzees to that of chorus girls, and O'Connor (1970) makes similar comparisons. O'Connor describes some subtle distinctions that make a gesture submissive rather than dominant:

> Women use [the direct stare] as well as men, but often in modified form. While looking directly at a man, a woman usually has her head slightly tilted, implying the beginning of a presenting gesture or enough submission to render the stare ambivalent if not actually submissive. (p. 9)

Staring, pointing, and touching may be considered as dominance gestures with the corresponding submissive gestures being, respectively, lowering or averting the eyes, stopping action or speech, and cuddling to the touch. Veiled physical threats may be seen in the playful and casual lifting and tossing around that is often done by men with women—swinging them (hard) at square dances, picking them up and spanking them (in "play"), threatening to drop them or throw them in water (and doing it), or just lifting them to demonstrate their lightness and the male's strength. Smiling is another recognized submissive gesture, the badge of women and of the shuffling Tom.

Interruption may also be considered a dominance gesture, and allowing interruption, the corresponding submissive gesture. Argyle et al. (1968) allude to a finding that men dominate an interaction by interruption, though the supporting data are not directly presented. Our own conversational experiences will confirm that superiors can more readily interrupt others, and more readily resist interruption by others, than subordinates.

When Power Becomes Sex: Violation of Sex-Status Norms   We noted earlier that women's touch was more likely to be interpreted as having sexual intent than men's. Similarly, women's stare, physical closeness, and loosening of demeanor may all be taken by men as sexual invitations. Other characteristics that are associated with men, such as a husky voice or the withholding of information (the "woman of mystery"), are considered sexy in women. We have seen that these behaviors and characteristics are not just "natural" or pointless properties in men but carry status and power connotations, helping maintain their place in the social order. Why should these concomitants of status lose those connotations, and in addition, take on sexual connotations, when used by the wrong sex? It is because the implication of power is unacceptable when the actor is a woman, and therefore must be denied.

Sex is a convenient alternative interpretation because (1) many of these behaviors—touching, gazing, proximity, and relaxed demeanor—are also expressive of solidarity and intimacy, and appropriate to a sexual relationship; and (2) attribution of sexual aggressiveness to a woman both compliments the man and disarms the woman, and places her back in her familiar unthreatening role as sex object (as in "You're so cute when you're mad, baby."). There are other ways in which women are put down for exhibiting "male" characteristics: they are labeled deviant and abhorrent (castrating, domineering), or, when all else fails, lesbian.

Conclusion

We have noted the importance of nonverbal and subtle verbal cues in the maintenance of the social structure and of power relationships, and their particular importance in restricting women to "their" place. In grammar, vocabulary, voice quality, and intonation patterns, women's language keeps them at a disadvantage, while men's (the dominant) language tends to ignore women completely or deprecate them. Terms of address, conversational patterns, self-disclosure, demeanor, distribution of space, touch, eye contact, and visibility all contribute to the maintenance of the status quo. The accessibility of information about subordinate persons and groups, including women, is used to subordinate and subdue them.

When subordinate groups defy the norms governing micropolitical acts, authority's first attempt at control is the denial of the norm violation, and substitution of an interpretation (for women, sexual aggression) which reestablishes the former relationship. The dual nature of many of the signals, used differently as indicators of either status or solidarity, makes them particularly available for this ploy.

The findings presented here have certain implications for women and others in inferior positions who wish to counteract the power expressed over them. They may begin to become conscious of the nonverbal symbolism of power, in order to resist it when it is used by others to exert control, and to exercise it themselves to help reverse the power relationships in their environment (see Henley, 1971). Similarly, those reluctantly in positions of power, like men who wish to divest themselves of "foreskin privilege," can begin to monitor their own acts toward others and their reactions to others' acts, in an attempt to exorcise the subtle power indicators from their daily interactions.

Manipulating these status cues will not, of course, change the fundamental power relationships in our society. Knowledge of them will, however, raise consciousness and enable people to detect the subtle ways in which they are inhibited, coerced, and controlled.

This paper was written with the partial support of Special Research Fellowship 1F03MH35977 from the National Institute of Mental Health. It has benefited from criticism and discussion with numerous friends and associates, including Roger Brown, Ann Calderwood, editors of the *Berkeley Journal of Sociology*, and many women, particularly women of the Center for Cognitive Studies, Harvard University.

NOTES

1. Personal servants, of course, are also physically integrated around power. However, other oppressed groups in our society are often physically separated (e.g., in ghettos and reservations) from power centers.

2. The unemotional demeanor associated with Anglo-Saxon culture is, of course, an asset in a society dominated by persons of Anglo-Saxon descent.

3. Many factors in female socialization have this effect, such as the fostering of passivity, nonaggressiveness, physical weakness, unconcern with achievement, etc. One especially

important, and usually overlooked, factor is the socialization of women to *care* more than men about personal relationships. Ross articulated in 1921 the "Law of Personal Exploitation" which states: "In any sentimental relation the one who cares less can exploit the one who cares more" (p. 136). It is put more broadly (without restriction to sentiment) by Waller and Hill (1951) as the "Principle of Least Interest": "That person is able to dictate the conditions of association whose interest in the continuation of the affair is least" (p. 191).

4. Space, of course, is the prerogative of the rich and the powerful; only the poor must live in crowded rooms, without yards, in crowded cities.

5. In fact, I relate this socialization to receive touch to the sexual abuse of girls and women. Rush (1971) argues that "sexual abuse of [female] children is permitted because it is an unspoken but prominent factor in socializing and preparing the female to accept a subordinate role; to feel guilty, ashamed, and to tolerate, through fear, the power exercised over her by men. ... In short, the sexual abuse of female children is a process of education which prepares them to become the sweethearts and wives of America" (p. 10).

6. Indoors: bank, stores, restaurant, doctor's office, college buildings. Outdoors: shopping plaza, beach, college campus, concert, party.

7. Sherfey (1966), in fact, has written of (primitive) woman's sexual drive as "too strong" for society's good: "the *forceful* suppression of women's inordinate sexual demands was a prerequisite to the dawn of every modern civilization and almost every living culture" (1970, p. 224; emphasis hers. See also Sherfey, 1973).

8. Of course, Millett's (1970) analysis has shown us that the realm of sexuality certainly does not exclude the political.

9. Exline relates women's "visual dependence" in the social field, however, to a supposed personality variable, that women are more field-dependent in studies in the physical field (i.e., in making judgments of horizonticality and verticality they tend to rely on reference points in the environment rather than on their own internal body cues). This explanation overlooks the social context in which the visual information is both more important to women and generally less available to them (because of their exclusion from informative interaction, and men's greater concealment of affect). Both the physical and social examples, nevertheless, do illustrate women's reliance on visual perception rather than gut feelings (both literally and figuratively), perhaps because of learned distrust for their own judgments.

References

Anthony, N., 1970   "Open Letter to Psychiatrists." *Radical Therapist* 1, 3, 8.

Argyle, M., M. Lalljee, and M. Cook, 1968   "The Effects of Visibility on Interaction in a Dyad." *Human Relations* 21, 3-17.

Argyle, M., V. Salter, H. Nicholson, M. Williams, and P. Burgess, 1970   "The Communication of Inferior and Superior Attitudes by Verbal and Nonverbal Signals." *British Journal of Social and Clinical Psychology* 9, 222-231.

Argyle, M., and M. Williams, 1969   "Observer or Observed? A Reversible Perspective in Person Perception." *Sociometry* 32, 396-412.

Austin, W.M., 1965   "Some Social Aspects of Paralanguage." *Canadian Journal of Linguistics* 11, 31-39.

Birdwhistell, R.L., 1970   *Kinesics and Context: Essays on Body Motion Communication.* Philadelphia: University of Pennsylvania Press.

Brend, R.M., 1972   "Male-Female Differences in American English Intonation." *Proceedings of the Seventh International Congress of Phonetic Sciences, 1971.* The Hague: Mouton. Reprinted in Barrie Thorne and Nancy Henley, eds., 1975, *Language and Sex: Difference and Dominance.* Rowley, Mass.: Newbury House.

Brown, R., 1965   *Social Psychology*. Glencoe, Ill.: Free Press.

Brown, R., and M. Ford, 1961   "Address in American English." *Journal of Abnormal and Social Psychology* 62, 375-385.

Brown, R., and A. Gilman, 1960   "The Pronouns of Power and Solidarity." In T.A. Sebeok, ed., *Style in Language*. Cambridge, Mass.: M.I.T. Press.

Clay, V.S., 1968   "The Effect of Culture on Mother-Child Tactile Communication." *Family Coordinator* 17, 204-210.

Cozby, P.C., 1973   "Self-Disclosure: A Literature Review." *Psychological Bulletin* 79, 73-91.

Duncan, S., 1969   "Nonverbal Communication." *Psychological Bulletin* 72, 118-137.

Efran, J.S., and A. Broughton, 1966   "Effect of Expectancies for Social Approval on Visual Behavior." *Journal of Personality and Social Psychology* 4, 103-107.

Ellsworth, P.C., J.M. Carlsmith, and A. Henson, 1972   "The Stare as a Stimulus to Flight in Human Subjects: A Series of Field Experiments." *Journal of Personality and Social Psychology* 21, 302-311.

Exline, R., 1963   "Explorations in the Process of Person Perception: Visual Interaction in Relation to Competition, Sex, and Need for Affiliation." *Journal of Personality* 31, 1-20.

Exline, R., D. Gray, and D. Schuette, 1965   "Visual Behavior in a Dyad as Affected by Interview Content and Sex of Respondent." *Journal of Personality and Social Psychology* 1, 201-209.

Fast, J., 1970   *Body Language*. New York: Evans.

Galt, W.E., 1943   "The Male-Female Dichotomy in Human Behavior." *Psychiatry* 6, 1-14.

Gitlin, T., 1971   "On Power Structure Research." *100 Flowers* 1, 35.

Goffman, E., 1956   "The Nature of Deference and Demeanor." *American Anthropologist* 58, 473-502. In E. Goffman, 1967, *Interaction Ritual*. New York: Anchor, 47-95.

Goldberg, S., and M. Lewis, 1969   "Play Behavior in the Year-Old Infant: Early Sex Differences." *Child Development* 40, 21-31.

Haley, J., 1962   "The Art of Psychoanalysis." In S.I. Hayakawa, ed., *The Use and Misuse of Language*. Greenwich, Conn.: Fawcett, 207-218.

Henley, N., 1970   "The Politics of Touch." Paper read at American Psychological Association. In P. Brown, ed., 1973, *Radical Psychology*. New York: Harper & Row, 421-433.

———, 1971   "Facing Down the Man." *Radical Therapist* 2, 2, 22. In Rough Times Staff, eds., 1973, *Rough Times*. New York: Ballantine.

———, 1973   "Status and Sex: Some Touching Considerations." *Bulletin of the Psychonomic Society* 2, 91-93.

Hore, T., 1970   "Social Class Differences in Some Aspects of the Nonverbal Communication between Mother and Preschool Child." *Australian Journal of Psychology* 22, 21-27.

Hutt, C., and C. Ounsted, 1966   "The Biological Significance of Gaze Aversion with Particular Reference to the Syndrome of Infantile Autism." *Behavioral Science* 11, 346-356.

Jourard, S.M., 1966   "An Exploratory Study of Body Accessibility." *British Journal of Social and Clinical Psychology* 5, 221-231.

Jourard, S.M., and P. Lasakow, 1958   "Some Factors in Self-Disclosure." *Journal of Abnormal and Social Psychology* 56, 91-98.

Jourard, S.M., and J.E. Rubin, 1968   "Self-Disclosure and Touching: A Study of Two Modes of Interpersonal Encounter and Their Inter-relation." *Journal of Humanistic Psychology* 8, 39-48.

Key, M.R., 1972   "Linguistic Behavior of Male and Female." *Linguistics* 88 (Aug. 15), 15-31.

Lakoff, R., 1973   "Language and Woman's Place." *Language in Society* 2, 45-79.

Lewis, M., 1972   "Parents and Children: Sex-Role Development." *School Review* 80, 229-240.

Lewis, M., and C.D. Wilson, 1971 "Infant Development in Lower-Class American Families." Paper read at Society for Research in Child Development.

Mehrabian, A., 1972 *Nonverbal Communication.* Chicago: Aldine-Atherton.

Millett, K., 1970 *Sexual Politics.* Garden City, N.Y.: Doubleday.

Montagu, A., 1971 *Touching: The Human Significance of the Skin.* New York: Columbia University Press.

Morris, D., 1971 *Intimate Behavior.* New York: Random House.

Nichols, P.C., 1971 "Gender in English: Syntactic and Semantic Functions." Paper read at Modern Language Association.

O'Connor, L., 1970 "Male Dominance: The Nitty Gritty of Oppression." *It Ain't Me Babe* 1, 9-11.

Ross, E.A., 1921 *Principles of Sociology.* New York: Century.

Rubin, Z., 1970 "Measurement of Romantic Love." *Journal of Personality and Social Psychology* 16, 265-273.

Rush, F., 1971 "The Sexual Abuse of Children." *Radical Therapist* 2, 4, 9-11.

Sachs, J., P. Lieberman, and D. Erickson, 1973 "Anatomical and Cultural Determinants of Male and Female Speech." In R. Shuy, and R. Fasold, eds., *Language Attitudes: Current Trends and Prospects.* Washington, D.C.: Georgetown University Press.

Scheflen, A.E., 1972 *Body Language and the Social Order.* Englewood Cliffs, N.J.: Prentice-Hall.

Sherfey, M.J., 1966 "The Evolution and Nature of Female Sexuality in Relation to Psychoanalytic Theory." *Journal of the American Psychoanalytic Association* 14, 28-128. Abridged in R. Morgan, ed., 1970, *Sisterhood Is Powerful.* New York: Random House, 220-230.

———, 1973 *The Nature and Evolution of Female Sexuality.* New York: Random House.

Silveira, J., 1972 "Thoughts on the Politics of Touch." *Women's Press* (Eugene, Ore.) 1, 13, 13.

Simmel, G., 1921 "Sociology of the Senses: Visual Interaction." In R.E. Park and E.W. Burgess, eds., *Introduction to the Science of Sociology.* Chicago: University of Chicago Press.

Slobin, D.I., S.H. Miller, and L.W. Porter, 1968 "Forms of Address and Social Relations in a Business Organization." *Journal of Personality and Social Psychology* 8, 289-293.

Sommer, R., 1969 *Personal Space.* Englewood Cliffs, N.J.: Prentice-Hall.

Tinbergen, N., 1969 "Comparative Study of the Behavior of Gulls: A Progress Report." *Behavior* 15, 1-70.

Waller, W.W., and R. Hill, 1951 *The Family, a Dynamic Interpretation.* New York: Dryden.

Willis, F.N., Jr., 1966 "Initial Speaking Distance as a Function of the Speakers' Relationship." *Psychonomic Science* 5, 221-222.

SEX ROLES, INTERRUPTIONS, AND SILENCES IN CONVERSATION

Don H. Zimmerman and Candace West

Recent research in the analysis of discourse, such as the study by Don H. Zimmerman and Candace West of cross-sex conversation, has shown that everyday interaction is rarely a simple sequence of utterances alternating among speakers but rather a highly complex system of turn-taking, in which split-second overlaps and pauses must be employed and interpreted. Zimmerman and West present a model for the description of turn-taking which captures the social and psychological messages inherent in speakers' use of conversational "space." The radical differences in discourse behavior which show up between middle-class white men and women point to probable greater differences in discourse style across speech communities. It is clear from these data that what would be "pushy" in a woman is acceptable behavior in a man. The potential for cross-cultural misunderstanding, where a set of shared speech norms of role-appropriate behavior does not exist, is correspondingly greater.

Zimmerman and West touch on just a few of the important considerations in the comparison of discourse styles. Labov's "Modes of Mitigation and Politeness" in this volume contrasts Black and White communities' discourse norms. Gumperz and Hernández-Chavez discuss language switching among Chicano Spanish-English bilinguals as a discourse strategy.

Zimmerman and West employ a small set of conventions for transcribing conversations. Using this notation, other parameters, such as those suggested in Appendix G, could be easily observed and contrasted across language, ethnic group, social class, and sex boundaries. Here is the way Zimmerman and West describe their conventions:

Transcribing Conventions

The transcript techniques and symbols were devised by Gail Jefferson in the course of research undertaken with Harvey Sacks. Techniques are revised, symbols added or dropped as they seem useful to the work. There is no guarantee or suggestion that the symbols or transcripts alone would permit the doing of any unspecified research tasks; they are properly used as an adjunct to the tape-recorded materials.

(x) I've (x) I've met him once	Parentheses encasing an "x" indicate a hitch or stutter on the part of the speaker.
// J: Well really//I	Double obliques indicate the point at which one speaker is overlapped or interrupted by another.

C: I don't care	When nothing appears to the right of this symbol, the speaker has been overlapped in the middle of the last syllable preceding the slashes.
[ ] J: If I//could D: [But] you can't	Brackets around the first part of a speaker's utterance mean that the portion bracketed overlapped or interrupted a previous speaker's utterance.
::: A: Well::: now	Colons indicate that the immediately prior syllable is prolonged.
= A: 'Swat I said= B: But you didn't	An equal sign is used to indicate that no time elapses between the objects "latched" by the marks. Often used as a transcribing convenience, it can also mean that a next speaker starts at precisely the end of a current speaker's utterance.
————————	Underscoring is utilized to represent heavier emphasis (in speaker's pitch) on words so marked.
(?), (!), (,), (.) Are you sure (?)	Punctuation marks are used for intonation, not grammar.
(word) If you (will) please	Single parentheses with words in them indicate that something was heard, but the transcriber is not sure what it was. These can serve as a warning that the transcript may be unreliable.
( ) Why do you ( ) it	Single parentheses without words in them indicate that something was said but not caught by the transcriber.
((softly)) Ha ((chuckles))	Double parentheses enclose "descriptions," not transcribed utterances.
(#) But (#) you said	Score sign indicates a pause of one second or less that wasn't possible to discriminate precisely.
(1.2)	Numbers encased in parentheses indicate the seconds and tenths of seconds ensuing between speaker's turns. They may also be used to indicate the duration of pauses internal to a speaker's turn.

Power and dominance constitute significant aspects of many recurring interactions such as those between whites and blacks, adults and children, and—of specific interest here—men and women. It should not be surprising, then, that the distribution of power in the occupational structure, the family division of labor, and other institutional contexts where life chances are determined, has its parallel in the dynamics of everyday interaction. The preliminary findings of the research reported here indicate that there are definite and patterned ways in which the power and dominance enjoyed by men in other contexts are exercised in their conversational interaction with women.

Interruptions, lapses in the flow of conversation, and inattentiveness are commonplace occurrences, seemingly far removed from sociological concerns with such things as institutionalized power. Employing recent developments in the study of conversational interaction (Sacks et al., 1974; Sacks, n.d.; Schegloff, 1972a, b; Schegloff and Sacks, 1973) as a resource, this paper shows how these events may be related to the enduring problems of power and dominance in social life.

Specifically, we report striking asymmetries between men and women with respect to patterns of interruption, silence, and support for partner in the development of topics. We discuss these observations in this paper and draw implications from them concerning the larger issue of sexism in American society. Prior to presenting our results, we must briefly consider the relationship of our research to the study of language and social interaction.

Sex Roles, Language, and Social Interaction

The recognition that sex-role differences are reflected in language patterns has stimulated a good deal of recent research in this area (cf. Henley and Thorne, 1975). To consider just one example, Robin Lakoff (1973) suggests that a separate "woman's speech" exists, characterized by a greater preponderance of such forms as tag questions, compound requests, and questioning intonational patterns offered in the context of otherwise declarative answers. She also examines the semantics of sexism by focusing on the discrepancies in supposed referential equivalents (e.g., "master" and "mistress"), and typically female euphemisms (e.g., "lady") for which there is no colloquial male equivalent.

Even a cursory review of studies of sex roles and language patterns suggests that various features of language and speech furnish the resources for male dominance (and, for that matter, female submissiveness) in pervasive and often subtle ways (cf. also Bernard, 1968; Brend, 1972; Key, 1972; and Kramer, 1973). There can be little doubt that speech patterns and particular syntactic, semantic, phonological, and intonational structures function to communicate the cultural and social meanings that cluster around sex roles. We, however, wish to stress the role of language and its constituent structures in the *organization* of social interaction in general and from that perspective view the characteristics of interaction between men and women. Conversation is clearly one very basic form of social interaction, and it is the analysis of conversational structure in relation to sex roles that concerns us here.

While studies dealing with the exchange of talk between men and women can be found (e.g., Strodtbeck and Mann, 1956; Strodtbeck, James, and Hawkins, 1957; and Soskin and John, 1963), they typically lack any explicit model of conversational interaction per se in terms of which their findings could be interpreted. An appropriate model can be found, however, in recent work by Sacks, Schegloff, and Jefferson (1974), and Sacks (n.d.), which provides a systematic approach to turn-taking or speaker alternation in naturally occurring (i.e., uncontrived) conversation. This model, taken in conjunction with other work on the structure of conversation by Sacks and Schegloff (Sacks, 1972a, 1972b; Sacks, Schegloff, and Jefferson, 1974; Schegloff, 1972a, 1972b), furnishes a general approach to the study of conversational interaction strongly rooted in meticulous empirical examination of audiotaped natural conversations.[1]

In this paper, we attempt to adapt relevant portions of this turn-taking model and other work in conversational analysis to the concerns already announced. We wish to make it clear that we do not view our efforts as a contribution to conversational analysis per se but rather as an attempt to apply it to a particular problem. In order to carry through this application, it is necessary to spell out the relevant aspects of the model in a brief and simplified form. The first part of this paper is, therefore, an exposition of Sacks, Schegloff, and Jefferson (1974).

The Model

Sacks et al. (1974) suggest that speech exchange systems in general are organized to ensure that (1) one party speaks at a time and (2) speaker change recurs. These features are said to hold for casual conversation as well as for formal debate and even high ceremony. Thus it appears that the range of speech exchange systems found in our society (and possibly all societies) is constrained by some form of turn-taking mechanism.

What distinguishes conversation from debate and ceremony is the variability of the distribution of turns, turn size, and turn content. In debate, there is preallocation of turns, and standardization of turn size; in ceremony, the content of speech is predetermined as well.

The model Sacks et al. (1974) offer describes the properties of the turn-taking mechanism for conversation. A turn consists of not merely the temporal duration of an utterance but of the right (and obligation) to speak which is allocated to a particular speaker. The turn is spoken of as something valued and sought (or sometimes avoided) and allusion is made to the distribution of turns as a kind of economy. This analogy will prove useful to the purposes of this paper in subsequent discussion.

A turn is constructed by the speaker out of what Sacks et al. (1974) call "unit-types" which can consist of single words, phrases, clauses, or sentences. Each speaker, upon being allocated a turn, has an initial right to produce one such unit. In general, the terminal boundary of a unit-type, e.g., the end of a sentence, is a possible transition place, and the transfer of a turn from one speaker to another properly occurs at that place.

Unit-types are generally projective; that is, the beginning portion of the unit frequently furnishes a basis for anticipating when it will be concluded and hence signals the upcoming transition place for purposes of speaker change. This property of unit-types assumes that the listener performs a syntactic (and/or intonational) analysis of the unit in the course of its production—the internal structure of the sentence, for example, indicating its possible completion point. Elsewhere, Sacks (n.d.) suggests that the phenomenon of sentence completion furnishes evidence for this "on line" analysis. For example, in the following segment,[2] a young man attempting to arrange a date with a young woman he has just met appears to anticipate her objection by completing her sentence for her (lines 4 and 5):

	1	A:	How would'ja like to go to a movie later on tonight?
(3.2)	2	B:	Huh?=
	3	A:	A movie y'know like a like (x) a flick?
(3.4)	4	B:	Yeah I uh know what a movie is (.8) It's just that=
	5	A:	You don't know me well enough?

With appropriate transformation of the pronouns, the sentence reads: "It's just that I don't know you well enough," a syntactically and semantically coherent utterance jointly produced by two speakers. It should also be pointed out that the completion is done with precise timing, i.e., no gap or overlap between the two speakers.

With regard to the timing of transitions between utterances, Sacks et al. (1974) observe that much of the time the alternation of speakers is achieved with little or no gap, suggesting a considerable degree of next-speaker readiness to commence a turn upon the occurrence of a possible transition place. These considerations establish the ground for what is undoubtedly presupposed by parties to conversations, namely, that a conversation involves both active speakership and active listenership, with these roles alternating between persons.

Minimal Responses: A Brief Digression Active hearership is a fundamental prerequisite for the production of instances of a particular class of utterances which may not be considered as unit-types, and hence may not count as filling turns. Such items as "um hmm," "uh huh," and "yeah," when interspersed through a current speaker's ongoing utterance, are not seen as interrupting the current speaker (cf. Schegloff, 1972b), but instead serve to display continuing interest and coparticipation in topic development. Fishman (1973) continues along these lines to point out the agility with which speakers are able to insert such comments—rarely do they overlap a current speaker's utterance, being interjected virtually between breaths. Characteristically, the current speaker will continue her turn after insertion of a "yeah" or "um hmm" with little if any discernible pause. Fishman (1973) suggests that these phenomena serve to do "support work," functioning as indicators that the listener is carefully attending to the stream of talk.

These "minimal responses" which monitor a speaker's utterance may of course be coupled with energetic nonverbal cues such as nodding of the head, and such gestures often replace the verbal comments when conversationalists are face-to-face. Although the purposes at hand prohibit examination of this matter in detail, it is interesting to note that parties to talk are likely to time these nonverbal signals to coincide with pauses in a current speaker's utterance. Thus items like "um hmm," "uh huh," and "yeah" may be viewed as a kind of positive reinforcement for continued talk where the provider of such cues must do active listening work to determine proper placement.

The Operation of the Rule-Set   The specific mechanism for speaker alternation is furnished by an ordered set of rules which are applied recursively to generate the distribution of turns and turn sizes for any actual conversation. In order to simplify this presentation the operation of the rule-set is represented in Figure 1 as a flow diagram of the sequence of "decisions" involved.[3] The rule-set is represented by a vertical array of decision points, with the highest-priority decision point at the top.

Inspecting Figure 1 we see that for a given transition place within a turn, the highest-priority decision is whether or not current speaker has selected next speaker. Current speaker selects next speaker by such techniques as addressing her by name (or title) or by directing a question to her, or both, where the term of address or question is constructed as part of the unit-type the terminal boundary of which marks the next transition place. If next speaker has been selected by current speaker at this point, the rule-set recycles to the beginning (I) in preparation for the occurrence of the next transition place, the speaker just selected having the exclusive right (and obligation) to speak next.

In the event that next speaker has not been selected by current speaker, the next decision point (II) presents the *option* to potential speakers other than current speaker to self-select. (Self-selection is an option available to each potential next speaker; thus more than one speaker could start to speak, the right to the turn belonging to the first starter.) The rule-set recycles to (I) if self-selection occurs; if it does not, the third decision point (III) is reached.

In the absence of self-selection by other parties, the current speaker may (but is not obligated to) continue speaking. The exercise of this option recycles the rule set to (I), the process repeating itself until speaker change occurs. If current speaker does not speak, the rule-set recycles to (II), the first decision point (current speaker selects next speaker) being obviously inapplicable.

This model of turn-taking, Sacks et al. propose, accounts for a number of regularly occurring features of observed conversations—including the alternation of speakers in a variable order with brief (if any) gaps or overlaps between turns, as well as variable length of turns. That is, the model provides for the systematic initiation, continuation, and alternation of turns in everyday conversation.

Sacks et al. (1974) characterize their model as a "locally managed" system, by which they mean that over a series of turns the rule-set operates to effect transitions between successive pairs of adjacent turns, one turn at a time, the

Figure 1   Flow diagram of the "decision" process in Sacks' et al. (1974) model of turn-taking in naturally occurring conversation

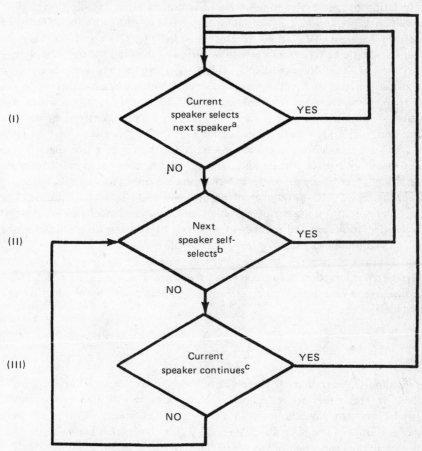

Notes:

[a]The person selected by current speaker has the exclusive right (and obligation) to speak next.

[b]Next speaker other than current speaker.

[c]Current speaker is not obligated to continue speaking.

focus of the system being the next turn and the next transition. Turn size is also locally managed since the concatenation of unit-types to construct longer turns is also provided for by the system's organization.

Moreover, the system is said to be "party administered," i.e., turn order and turn size are under the control of parties to the conversation who exercise the options provided. The system is also characterized as "interactionally managed," turn order and turn size being determined turn by turn by conversationalists, each of whom exercises options which are contingent upon, and undertaken with the awareness of, options available to the other. The point of immediate concern here is that the turn-taking system described by Sacks et al. (1974) can be viewed as a representation of speakers' methods for achieving a preferred organization of their conversational interaction, i.e., the intended conversational order from the point of view of speakers. (Violations of this intended order can and do occur, of course, and should be observable as such by virtue of the rules for turn-taking.)

Sacks et al. (1974) suggest that this model approaches the status of a context-free mechanism which is, moreover, finely context-sensitive in its application. Here, "context-free" means analytically independent of a wide range of features exhibited by actual conversations, e.g., topics, settings, number of parties, and social identities (which could be subject to analysis in their own right). This independence establishes the basis for the context-sensitivity of the system since, by virtue of its indifference to the particulars of any given conversation, it can accommodate the changing circumstances of talk posed by variation in topic, setting, number of parties, and identity of participants. The model generates an infinite set of possible turn-taking sequences varying in terms of turn order, turn size, and number of speakers, by recourse to a limited set of organizational principles usable on any occasion of conversation.[4]

Our task in this paper is to bring relevant aspects of this model to bear on conversational interaction between men and women. The next section deals with the collection, transcription, and analysis of our data and is followed by the presentation of our findings.

Methods

Recording Conversations   Three-quarters of the 31 conversational segments analyzed in this paper were two-party interactions recorded in coffee shops, drugstores, and other public places in a university community. Such places were viewed as routine settings in which everyday "chit chat" takes place—the kind of talking we all do, even when others are likely to overhear us.

The tape recorder was carried by one or the other author, and what they could hear by virtue of their routine and unquestioned access to public areas was deemed eligible for taping. Whenever possible, conversationalists were subsequently informed of our recording and their consent obtained. In some of these cases, however, the abrupt departure of parties to the talk precluded such debriefing. In the process of transcription, identifying references were disguised and the tape erased after the transcript was completed and checked, thus protecting the anonymity of the persons involved. Some recording was done in private residences to which the authors normally had casual access. In these cases (which comprise the remaining fourth of the data), consent was uniformly obtained after recording, and no refusals to permit the use of the tape or complaints about the covert procedure were encountered. Data collection, moreover, was designed to collect equal numbers of male-male, female-female and male-female conversations for comparative purposes.[5]

Of the conversations among same-sex pairs (equally divided between 10 male-male and 10 female-female pairs), all parties were white, apparently middle-class persons from approximately twenty to thirty-five years of age with relationships varying from close friendship to that between nurse and patient. The eleven cross-sex pairs were also apparently middle class, under thirty, and white. All but one were university students. Relationships varied from intimacy to first-time acquaintanceship, with one instance of a formal status relationship (see footnote 5). The topics of these exchanges varied widely, touching on everyday concerns. Close friends and lovers quarreled and confessed insecurities to one another, and people meeting for the first time exchanged social amenities.

Classifying Overlaps and Interruptions   Each author inspected the transcripts for instances of simultaneous speech and employed the definitions of overlap and interruption specified below to produce an initial classification of these events. The results of this independent classification were then compared. Of 86 instances of simultaneous speech classified, there was agreement between the authors on 80 (93 percent). The disagreements were resolved by discussion of the particular utterance.

Two-Party Conversations   The selection of two-party conversations was not accidental. The model outlined above applies, in principle, to any number of participants in a given conversation, although Sacks et al. (1974) suggest that for larger groups (e.g., four or more) there is a tendency for talk to divide into two or more distinct conversations. Our reason for choosing two-party talk was that it is a simpler case to analyze.

In conversations with three or more participants, *who* speaks next is problematic; this is not the case in two-party talk where the alternation of speakers follows an ABAB . . . pattern. Moreover, certain phenomena will be observed only infrequently in two-party talk, e.g., simultaneous starts by two speakers. Simultaneous starts in two-party conversation can be observed after what appear to be lapses, i.e., where current speaker stops for an interval and then elects to continue, and next speaker self-selects.

These considerations notwithstanding, *when* a next speaker commences her utterance remains an interesting problem. A next speaker needn't concern herself that some other next speaker will commence speaking if she doesn't start first, thus eliminating the systemic pressure toward early starts characteristic of multiparty conversations. Thus two-party conversations are perhaps the best case to inspect for the purposes at hand.

Transcription   Transcription was done by the authors according to a set of conventions modeled after those suggested by Gail Jefferson (see Headnote). Silences between utterances were timed by stop watch twice and averaged. Those portions of our tapes actually transcribed were selected by the criteria that a segment exhibit a pattern (more than two instances) of (1) noticeable silence between speaker turns and/or (2) instances of simultaneous speech, without regard to other features present, e.g., who overlapped whom. Portions of our tapes which were not transcribed included many stretches of talk containing neither noticeable silences nor instances of simultaneous speech (for both same-sex and cross-sex pairs). However, no segment of two-party conversation excluded from transcription by our selection criteria contained any instance of simultaneous speech initiated by a female in a cross-sex pair. Insofar as was possible, the topical coherence of each segment was preserved.

Generality   This collection of conversations does not, of course, constitute a probability sample of conversationalists or conversations. Hence simple projections from findings based on this collection to conversationalists or conversations at large cannot be justified by the usual logic of statistical inference. The stability of any empirical finding cannot, in any event, be established by a single study. The present research serves to illustrate the utility of the Sacks et al. (1974) model as a means of locating significant problems in the area of language and interaction and as a point of departure for further study. Further, more systematic research should settle the question of the stability and generality of our findings concerning sex-role differences in conversation. With this note of caution entered, we proceed to the examination of our data.

Using the Model: Simultaneous Speech

The turn-taking mechanism described by Sacks et al. (1974) is so constructed that under ideal conditions conversations generated via its use would exhibit, among other features, a minimum of perceptible gaps between speaker turns and no instances of simultaneous talk (e.g., "overlaps"). Parties to such conversations would be observed to alternate their turns at speaking precisely on cue.

As noted earlier, clean and prompt transitions between speaker turns are conditional in part on the competent listenership of the potential next speaker; i.e., the current speaker's utterance must be analyzed in the course of its development in order for the listener to be prepared to commence a turn at a transition place, either by virtue of being selected to speak next or on the basis of self-selection. Indeed, the provision that the self-selector who speaks first gains the turn encourages the intended next speaker in a multiparty conversation to begin at the earliest point of a transition place. This leads to the systematic possibility of briefly overlapping the current speaker. The likelihood of an overlap is also increased if the current speaker varies the articulation of the last syllable or syllables of a unit-type:

> A1: I know what you thought I know you://
> A2: [Ya] still see her anymore (?)

or adds a tag question:

> A2: Oh I did too::: it just doesn't sit well with them not being specialized
> enough//right (?)
> A1: [Or] empirically grounded enough ha (!).

A speaker who has been allocated a turn has the initial right to one unit-type, e.g., a sentence. A sentence, in the course of its development, may project a possible completion point (i.e., the end of a sentence):

> B: Well::: my appointment was for two o'clock.

However, this sentence (and hence, the unit-type) can be extended by the speaker:

> B: Well::: my appointment was for two o'clock 'n (x) I have a class at three.

A listener, presumably performing an ongoing analysis of this sentence, may exercise a legitimate option to self-select as next speaker:

> B1: ... 'n I have a class at three//so
> B2: [I'm] sure you'll be in by then dear. ...

In our view, overlaps are instances of simultaneous speech where a speaker other than the current speaker begins to speak at or very close to a possible transition place in a current speaker's utterance (i.e., within the boundaries of the last word). It is this proximity to a legitimate point of speaker alternation that leads us to distinguish overlaps from interruptions.[6]

An interruption in this context, then, is seen as penetrating the boundaries of a unit-type *prior* to the last lexical constituent that could define a possible terminal boundary of a unit-type:

> B2: Know what 'cha mean (#) we went camping in Mojave last//
> B1: [Oh] didja go with Mark in August (?)[7]

or

> B: That sounds fantastic (#) not everybody can jus' spend a day in some//place
> A: [Well] we've already established the fact that um he's not y'know just anyone (.)

The category of overlaps, as we have defined them, explicitly allows some margin of error in the transition between speaker turns. However, interruptions can be viewed as *violations* of the turn-taking system rules (which provide that the proper place for transition between speakers is at the terminal boundary of a unit-type or possible unit-type). How are these "errors" and "violations" distributed in our transcripts?[8]

Patterns of Overlap and Interruption   Because of the small number of observations involved, we have collapsed the results of our tabulations for same-sex conversations (male-male and female-female) into one table (see Table 1). There were 7 instances of simultaneous speech classified as interruptions and 22 classified as overlaps.[9] What is striking about Table 1 is that both overlaps and

Table 1 Interruptions and Overlaps in 20 Same-Sex Two-Party Conversational Segments

	First speaker*	Second speaker	Total
Interruptions	43% (3)	57% (4)	100% (7)
Overlaps	55% (12)	45% (10)	100% (22)

*For a given segment, the person speaking first is designated first speaker; the person speaking second is thus a second speaker. There is no necessary implication that "first speaker" is the one who initiated the conversation, e.g., the first to utter a greeting, etc.

Table 2 Interruptions and Overlaps in 11 Cross-Sex Two-Party Conversational Segments

	Males	Females	Total
Interruptions	96% (46)	4% (2)	100% (48)
Overlaps	100% (9)		100% (9)

interruptions appear to be symmetrically distributed between speakers. That is, speaker transition errors (overlaps) and violations (interrupts) seem to be fairly equally divided between the first and second speakers in these conversations; or, put another way, the distribution approaches maximum variance.

Turning to Table 2, in cross-sex conversations there were 48 instances of simultaneous speech classified as interruptions and 9 classified as overlaps. The pattern displayed by Table 2 is dramatic: virtually all the interruptions and overlaps are by the male speakers (98 and 100 percent, respectively). The cross-sex conversational segments we examined are thus clearly asymmetrical with regard to the occurrence of violations and speaker errors.

Since our observations of simultaneous speech are based on a collection of conversational segments, it is possible that one or two conversational pairs could have contributed a disproportionate number of these instances to the overall pattern. If this were the case, it is conceivable that some unusual circumstances or some quirk of personality could have produced these remarkable distributions.

Reviewing the transcripts, we found that 5 out of the 11 male-female segments contained a total of 9 overlaps; 18 percent of the segments contained 66 percent of the overlaps. All were, of course, done by males. For the 20 same-sex pairs, half yielded a total of 22 overlaps, with 64 percent of the overlaps located in 15 percent of the segments. Thus if the distribution of overlaps across the segments is construed as evidence of clustering, we would have to conclude that the pattern is essentially identical for both cross-sex and same-sex pairs.

Ten of the 11 male-female segments exhibited interruptions, ranging from a low of 2 to a high of 13 and averaging 4.2 per transcript. The segment containing

13 interruptions (27 percent of the total) occurred between the female teaching assistant (see footnote 6) and a male undergraduate who repeatedly interrupted her attempts to explain a concept. The 7 interruptions that occurred in the same-sex conversations, in contrast, were concentrated in only 3 of the 20 or 15 percent of the segments. Thus it might be argued that the occurrence of interruptions is clustered in a few conversations for the same-sex pairs, while almost uniformly distributed across cross-sex pairs. This contrast in the distribution of interruptions vis-à-vis overlaps cannot be fully analyzed here, although it suggests, if anything, that interruptions are idiosyncratic in same-sex conversations and systematic in cross-sex conversations. For example, one possibility is that males conversing with females orient themselves to the role of listener differently than they do with one another. For, if interruptions are viewed as violations of a speaker's rights, continual or frequent interruption might be viewed as disregard for a speaker, or for what a speaker has to say. Here, we are dealing with a class of speakers, females, whose rights to speak appear to be casually infringed upon by males.

Hence, on the basis of these observations, we note that at least for the transcripts we have inspected, there is a marked asymmetry between males and females with respect to interruption, and, perhaps to a lesser extent, with respect to overlap. The incidence of interruptions, which are violations of a speaker's right to complete a turn, and of overlaps, which we have viewed as errors indigenous to the speaker transition process, are much higher and more uniformly distributed across the male-female segments than proves to be the case for the same-sex transcripts.

Using the Model: Silences

Silences in the conversational interchange are also possible outcomes provided by the model. The operation of the rule-set does not *command* participants to speak; even a next speaker selected by the current speaker (and thus obliged to take the turn thereby transferred) may pause before speaking. Moreover, since, at some points, potential next speakers may elect not to speak in the absence of selection by current speaker and current speaker may not elect to continue, a discontinuity in conversational flow—which Sacks et al. (1974) term a "lapse"—may occur. Many conversations proceed with few if any lapses; yet others are characterized by frequent and sometimes lengthy gaps between speaker turns. (Recall that our segments were selected partly on the basis of silence.)

There is nothing inherent in the turn-taking model which would suggest that, over a range of turns and of different conversations, one party to a conversation would fall silent more frequently than another. Indeed, all the model furnishes by way of a characterization of speakers are the categories "current speaker" and "next speaker." Accordingly, we would expect that on the average silences *between* speaker turns would tend to be symmetrically distributed (we cannot consider the silence within speaker turns here).

For two-party conversations, this assumption can be expressed as a ratio of silences (measured in seconds and tenths of seconds) with 1.0 indicating equality (either exactly equal silences or the absence of any gaps whatsoever). This is admittedly a crude measurement which does not distinguish between types of silences (e.g., those that represent a thoughtful pause before answering a question, or those following upon a brusque interruption), but it should inform us as to the existence of gross asymmetries.

The ratio of silence was computed as follows. The total silence in seconds (and tenths of seconds) for the least silent speaker was divided by the total for the most silent speaker for each of the same-sex pairs, thus avoiding any ratio greater than 1.0 (and hence, an arbitrary maximization of any differences that might exist).

A speaker's total silence was determined by counting the elapsed time prior to speaking after the previous speaker had concluded a turn. If a previous speaker spoke again after a period of time—without a next speaker beginning an utterance—the intervening silence was treated as *internal* to that speaker's turn and thus not counted.

Patterns of Silence   Table 3 charts the silence ratios for the three sets of conversational segments. It is immediately evident that each female in the cross-sex segments exhibits the most silence, where for same-sex conversations, the distribution of silence is more nearly equal. It is also worth noting that the female-female and male-female distributions do not overlap, and that the other same-sex distribution does so only slightly. For our transcripts, there is an obvious asymmetry in the allocation of silences between men and women conversationalists relative to their same-sex counterparts.

What accounts for these differences? We can begin to address this question by observing that 62 percent of the females' aggregate silence in the cross-sex segments followed upon three types of events in the preceding turns: (1) a delayed "minimal response" by the male, (2) an overlap by the male, and (3) an interruption by the male. In the two instances where a female interrupted a male, there was no ensuing silence prior to the male speaking again. A few silences do follow delayed minimal responses, overlaps, and interrupts in the same-sex conversations. However there are fewer (45 percent vs. 67 percent) of such ensuing silences spread across the three types of events and the average aggregate silence is 1.35 seconds (with a range from 1.0 to 2.2) as compared with 3.21 seconds (with a range from 1.0 to 12.0) for females in the cross-sex segments.

If we subtract all the silences following the delayed minimal responses, overlaps, and interruptions for the cross-sex segments, we may gain some information about the effect of these male-initiated events on their female co-conversationalists. (Since the delayed minimal response is, by our definition, preceded by at least one second of silence, these silences must also be excluded if the silence following them is to be disregarded.)

Although some slight equalization in the silence ratio does occur by discounting silences following delayed minimal responses, overlaps, and interrup-

Table 3 Distribution of Silence between Partners

Lengths of silences of one partner compared to the other	Least equal						Most equal
Same-sex dialogues:							
Female-female (number of conversations=10)							x xxx x xxx xx
Male-male (number of conversations=10)					x		xxx x xx xxx x
Cross-sex dialogues* (number of conversations=11)	xx x	xx	x x x	x x	x		

*In all cases of cross-sex conversation, women were the more silent partners.

tions, it appears to us that the overall asymmetry between males and females still remains. One reason for this may be that the occurrence of one or more of these three silence-inducing events in the course of conversation may affect the subsequent conversational participation of the female, a possibility that we cannot elaborate here. It is quite evident, however, that there is a relationship between the occurrence of delayed minimal responses, overlaps, and interruptions, on the one hand, and noticeable silence prior to a next speaker's turn on the other. This relationship is most pronounced for females in cross-sex conversations. We now turn to a more detailed consideration of this relationship.

Delayed Minimal Responses   Consider the following excerpt from a male-female transcript:

(A is the male, and B the female)

```
 1   B:   This thing with uh Sandy 'n Karen
 2        'n Paul is really bugging me
(5.0)

 3   A:   Um
(3.0)

 4   B:   Well it's really complicating things
 5        y'know between Sandy 'n Karen 'n I
 6        because I know what's (   ) going on
 7        'n I can see uh there's no contradiction
 8        to me at all//

 9   A:   [Um] hmm
(#)

10   B:   In between Sandy finding (#) I mean in
11        between Paul finding Sandy attractive (#)
```

```
12          'n Paul finding um uh Karen
13          attractive
(4.0)

14    A:    Mm hmm
(6.0)

15    B:    Y'know an' sleeping with either
16          of 'em or whatever (2.0) the
17          problem (x) problem is that when
18          he started finding Karen attractive
19          um (#) it was at the same
20          time uh as he was finding Sandy
21          unattractive
(10.0)
```

It seems evident that B (the female) introduces a topic in lines 1 and 2 (her feelings about the relationship among the three persons mentioned) and attempts to elaborate it in her subsequent remarks. It is also obvious that A (the male), in response to B's attempts, employs several minimal responses ("Um," "Um hmm") which were discussed earlier as types of supportive responses one party gives to another in conversation (Fishman, 1973; Schegloff, 1972b). The difference here is that these minimal responses are (with the exception of the "um hmm" of line 9) preceded by pauses up to 10 seconds in length. Instead of finely timed placement within the structure of the current speaker's utterance, as suggested by Fishman (1973), these are retarded beyond the end of the utterance.

In our male-female segments, the mean silence for all females following a delayed minimal response was 3.85 seconds (vs. 1.4 seconds for the three instances found in the same-sex conversations). Eleven of the 13 delayed minimal responses observed in our data were followed by perceptible silences, and ten of these were timed as longer than one second.

The difference between a monologue and a dialogue is not the number of persons present but the articulation of the roles of speaker and listener. We are inclined to the view that the "promptly" issued minimal response serves to display active listenership (in effect, "I understand what you are saying") with, moreover, the least intervention in the development of a topic by the other speaker (in effect, "Go on, say more"). That speakers currently holding the floor are oriented to the display of active listenership is sometimes indicated by the use of question-like forms ("you know") to elicit response from the putative listener.

Such displays of active listenership can, of course, be simulated. We have in mind here the "yes dear" response that husbands are said to utter while their wives talk and they read the newspaper, a kind of minimum hearership sustained by an artfully located standardized response. Poor timing (among other things) can quickly betray feigned involvement or at least call attention to some difficulty in the course of talk.

The delayed minimal response and the ensuing silence may thus *locate* a point in conversation found to be problematic by its participants. If we assume that the demonstration of active attention and the invitation to continue a turn support the speaker's developing a topic, then retarding the response may function to signal a lack of understanding or even disinterest in and inattention to the current talk. The silence that follows a delayed minimal response reflects, we believe, the other speaker's uncertainty as to her partner's orientation to the current state of the conversation, an uncertainty generated by these several possibilities. The implications of the foregoing in the context of the pattern of male-initiated retarded responses will be discussed in connection with the examination below of the silences following interruptions.

Interruptions and Ensuing Silences　We have already noted the tendency for speakers in our transcripts to fall silent for noticeable (if brief) periods of time subsequent to being interrupted. This observation relies almost entirely on the response of women in the cross-sex segments who, in the aggregate, paused for an average of 3.14 seconds after 32, or 70 percent, of the interruptions recorded. Two women in the same-sex conversations each paused for 1 second in response to 2 of the seven, or 29 percent, of the interruptions recorded there. Silence also followed overlaps, but less frequently and for shorter average durations than it did interruptions.

Our position, which follows that of Sacks et al. (1974), is that interruptions are a violation of a current speaker's right to complete a turn, or more precisely, to reach a possible transition place in a unit-type's progression. In an earlier, unpublished manuscript, Sacks (n.d.) discusses the social control devices available to conversationalists in dealing with violations such as interruptions. One type of negative sanction is the complaint, i.e., a formulation of a speaker's previous utterance as a certain kind of act. Such a complaint could be: "You just interrupted me" or, in the case of a series of such acts, "You keep interrupting me."

We have observed a variant of this type of sanction which includes a counterinterruption reclaiming the turn just lost:

```
(A1 and A2 are both males)
  1    A1:   Well (,) I moved again ya know (x)
  2          you know Del Playa (?) Well I//
  3    A2:   [Shee] :::et (!) You don't mean//
  4    A1:   [Let] me finish::: no I didn't move
  5          back in with Cathy (.)
```

The above example is the only instance in our data where an explicit negative sanction follows on an interruption and it occurs in a male-male segment. Indeed, even after repeated interruptions, women in our transcripts enter no such complaint, and as the preceding remarks suggest, when the interrupting male completes his utterance, the female typically pauses before speaking again. A possible explanation for the relative absence of sanctioning in our data lies in the locally managed character of conversation. Elsewhere (Sacks, n.d.) it is suggested that complaints must be entered in the turns immediately subsequent to violations if they are to be effective. However, voicing a complaint also constitutes changing the topic of the talk at that point. A speaker interrupted in the course of topic development may choose to disregard the violation in order to continue her trend of thought. In this respect, the females' pauses before speaking again might indicate points at which the foci of topic development must be recollected after interruptions.

While we cannot demonstrate it here, we believe that both retarded minimal responses and interruptions function as topic control mechanisms. For example, if retarded minimal responses are indeed signals of nonsupport for the continued development of a topic by one speaker over a series of turns (or by continuation of the same turn) a series of retarded responses should serve, at a minimum, to bring the topic to a close. We have observed this pattern in 3 of the 10 male-female transcripts.

Similarly, repeated interruptions of the same speaker by her partner also seem to be followed by topic change. If the interrupter is the one who is developing a topic, the interruptions appear to restrict the rights of the person being interrupted to contribute to the developing topic. We view the production of both retarded minimal responses and interruptions by male speakers interacting with females as an assertion of the right to control the topic of conversation reminiscent of adult-child conversations where in most instances the child has restricted rights to speak and to be listened to (cf. Sacks, 1972b). Indeed, our preliminary work on a set of adult-child transcripts indicates that the patterns of interruption found there (adults interrupt children overwhelmingly) most closely resemble the male-female patterns and contrast with those of the same-sex adult conversants we have discussed in this paper.

Concluding Remarks

It will be useful at this point to recall that Sacks et al. (1974) view the turn-taking system as an economy in which the turn is distributed in much the same fashion as a commodity. Differences between males and females in the distribution of turns may, for example, be parallel to the differences between them in the society's economic system, i.e., a matter of advantage. It can be noted that, in effecting the distribution of turns, the operation of the turn-taking system determines the distribution of resources for accomplishing interactional events *through* conversation, e.g., introducing and developing topics. Just above, we suggested that males assert an asymmetrical right to control topics and do so without evident repercussions. We are led to the conclusion that, at least in our transcripts, men deny equal status to women as conversational partners with respect to rights to the full utilization of their turns and support for the development of topics. Thus we speculate that just as male dominance is exhibited through male control of macro-institutions in society, it is also exhibited through control of at least a part of one micro-institution.

Before closing, we wish to reiterate one point. We are not claiming that male-female conversations invariably exhibit the asymmetric patterns reported in this paper. A challenging task for further research is the specification of conditions under which they occur, i.e., the conditions under which sex-roles become relevant to the conduct of conversationalists and sex-linked differences in conversational interaction emerge.

NOTES

1. This paper does not concern itself specifically with the nonverbal component of conversational interaction. Gestures, posture, patterns of eye contact, and intonation are clearly involved in the total communicative exchange between speakers. Moreover, research by Duncan (1972) suggests that nonverbal cues (e.g., hand gesticulation) are relevant to turn-taking in the interview situation. However, since our data consist of transcripts of audiotapes, we obviously cannot address such matters. Thus we ignore them in our discussion even though they are potentially important variables to consider.

2. The transcribing conventions used for our data are presented in the Headnote to this paper. Here, the = sign following a speaker's last word indicates a transition to the first word of the next speaker's utterance which is free of any perceivable gap.

3. The use of the term "decision" here does not necessarily imply any *conscious* choice or deliberation of the sort that could be retrieved by introspection or elicited by interview, but instead is used descriptively as a shorthand reference to the process of selection from sets of alternative acts that constitute different states of talk.

4. The analogy to the notion of a generative grammar is obvious.

5. The research plan called for ten segments each for the male-male, female-female, and male-female conversations. In the course of recording these conversations, we were given a tape of a discussion section conducted by a female teaching assistant. One segment of this tape contained a two-party interaction with the teaching assistant and a male undergraduate. Inclusion of this segment increased the number of male-female segments to 11, but since it contained the only instances of a female interrupting a male we could not exclude it. It is worth noting that in this case of female-initiated interruption, the female is the status superior (teaching assistant vis-à-vis undergraduate). Nevertheless, the male undergraduate interrupted this woman eleven times to her two. Our future research will, in part, deal with the relationship between sex-role status differentials and other types of status inequalities, e.g., employer-employee.

6. In coding instances of simultaneous speech in terms of our distribution between overlap and interruption, we relied on our intuitive knowledge of the English language to decide where possible completion points occurred. In cases where an utterance was ambiguous (e.g., could receive more than one syntactic analysis) we relied on the topical context for disambiguation. We hope to employ more formal linguistic analysis in subsequent research.

7. The careful reader will note that the excerpt to the left of the double slashes could be interpreted as a possibly complete sentence. However, the context of B2's utterance led the authors to decide that "last" was used as an adjective rather than an adverb; thus B1's intrusion constituted an interruption of B2's unit-type completion.

8. In the analysis, we do not take certain steps that some would assume to be routine. We do not apply a chi-square test to our percentage tables because more than one of the units of analysis (interruptions and overlaps) can be contributed by each individual, thus violating the assumption of independent observations. Since our collection of segments is not a probability sample, we do not present tests of significance which depend for their interpretation on just such a sample. We feel that the regularities in our data are sufficiently strong to warrant reporting them here if caution is exercised in their interpretation.

9. The segments from which these instances were drawn were not standardized, and the figures presented are thus not rates of interruption or overlap per some unit measure. Among the many possible units are number of words uttered, temporal duration of speech, number of turns, number of unit-types in a turn, number of unit-types, etc. There are a number of problems connected with each of these choices, not the least of which is determining the theoretical rationale for selecting among them. For present purposes, we have elected not to introduce any arbitrary standardization since whatever unit we selected would not alter the basic fact that in our transcripts an overwhelming proportion of interruptions are done by men to women. These considerations also pertain to the discussion of silences.

References

Bernard, Jesse, 1968   *The Sex Game.* Englewood Cliffs, N.J.: Prentice-Hall.

Brend, Ruth M., 1972   "Male-Female Intonation Patterns in American English." *Proceedings of the Seventh International Congress of Phonetic Sciences, 1971.* The Hague: Mouton. Reprinted in Barrie Thorne and Nancy Henley, eds., 1975, *Language and Sex: Difference and Dominance.* Rowley, Mass.: Newbury House.

Duncan, Starkey, Jr., 1972   "Some Signals and Rules for Taking Speaking Turns in Conversations." *Journal of Personality and Social Psychology* 23, 283-292.

Fishman, Pamela, 1973   "Interaction: The Work Women Do." Unpublished master's paper, University of California, Department of Sociology, Santa Barbara.

Henley, Nancy, and Barrie Thorne, 1975   "Sex Differences in Language, Speech and Nonverbal Communication: An Annotated Bibliography." In Barrie Thorne and Nancy Henley, eds., *Language and Sex: Difference and Dominance.* Rowley, Mass.: Newbury House.

Key, Mary Ritchie, 1972   "Linguistic Behavior of Male and Female." *Linguistics* 88 (Aug. 15), 15-31.

Kramer, Cheris, 1973   "Women's Speech: Separate but Unequal?" *Quarterly Journal of Speech* 60, 14-24. Reprinted in Barrie Thorne and Nancy Henley, eds., 1975, *Language and Sex: Difference and Dominance.* Rowley, Mass.: Newbury House.

Lakoff, Robin, 1973   "Language and Woman's Place." *Language and Society* 2, 45-79.

Sacks, Harvey, 1972a   "An Initial Investigation of the Usability of Conversational Data for Doing Sociology." In David Sudnow, ed., *Studies in Social Interaction.* Glencoe, Ill.: The Free Press.

———, 1972b   "On the Analyzability of Stories by Children." In John Gumperz and Dell Hymes, eds., *Directions in Sociolinguistics.* New York: Holt, Rinehart and Winston.

———, n.d.   "Aspects of the Sequential Organization of Conversation." Unpublished manuscript.

Sacks, Harvey, Emanuel A. Schegloff, and Gail Jefferson, 1974   "A Simplest Systematics for the Organization of Turn-Taking for Conversation." *Language* 50, 696-735.

Schegloff, Emanuel A., 1972a   "Notes on a Conversational Practice: Formulating Place." In David Sudnow, ed., *Studies in Social Interaction.* Glencoe, Ill.: The Free Press.

———, 1972b   "Sequencing in Conversational Openings." In John Gumperz and Dell Hymes, eds., *Directions in Sociolinguistics.* New York: Holt, Rinehart and Winston.

Schegloff, Emanuel A., and Harvey Sacks, 1973   "Opening Up Closings." *Semantica* 8, 289-327.

Soskin, William F., and Vera P. John, 1963   "The Study of Spontaneous Talk." In Roger Barker, ed., *The Stream of Behavior.* New York: Appleton-Century-Crofts.

Strodtbeck, Fred L., and Richard D. Mann, 1956   "Sex Role Differentiation in Jury Deliberations." *Sociometry* 19, 3-11.

Strodtbeck, Fred L., Rita M. James, and Charles Hawkins, 1957   "Social Status in Jury Deliberations." *American Sociological Review* 22, 713-719.

BILINGUALISM, BIDIALECTALISM, AND CLASSROOM INTERACTION

John J. Gumperz and Eduardo Hernández-Chavez

Because they constitute a significant proportion of the population in the American Southwest, are not cut off from their mother culture, and form a cohesive, ethnically distinct group, Chicanos have been able to maintain their Spanish-speaking communities for generations. Although many Chicanos are monolingual Spanish speakers, a great number have developed functional bilingualism in order to achieve social and economic mobility in our linguistically stratified nation. Bilinguals are often perceived as suffering from some sort of "confusion" of languages—as possessing incomplete portions of two language systems. John J. Gumperz and Eduardo Hernández-Chavez, in this study of the second author's professional colleagues, demonstrate that *code switching* (altering their speech not just gradually from style to style but radically from language to language within a single conversation) among Spanish-English bilinguals is an extremely sophisticated and well-controlled linguistic technique which defines social distance and the speaker's relation to the topic under discussion.

In the second section of their article, Gumperz and Hernández-Chavez move to a discussion of attitudes and practices in the education of linguistically and culturally different children. The extent to which public education has failed to meet the needs of Spanish-speaking students was pointed out in a study published by the National Assessment of Educational Progress in 1977. This survey of 350,000 students revealed that only 54 percent of Hispanic seventeen-year-olds have reached the eleventh grade, as compared to 61 percent of Blacks and 76 percent of Whites.

The pedagogical observations in this article relate directly to the materials in Part III of this book, particularly the work of Philips on learning styles in a group of Native Americans and Fishman's typology of bilingual education in the United States. Readers may also wish to refer to other selections on Spanish-speaking Americans, especially Wolfram's study of Puerto Ricans' English and its Headnote, which sets out information about the various Spanish-speaking communities in the United States, and Saville's contrastive analysis of Spanish and English phonological and grammatical features. Appendix G offers guidelines for analyzing discourse style, including code switching.

I

Recent systematic research in the inner city has successfully disproved the notions of those who characterize the language of low-income populations as degenerate and structurally underdeveloped. There is overwhelming evidence to show that when both middle-class and non-middle-class children, no matter what their native language, dialect, or ethnic background, come to school at the age of five or six, they have control of a fully formed grammatical system. The mere fact that their system is distinct from that of their teacher does not mean that their speech is not rule-governed. Speech features that strike the teacher as different do not indicate failure to adjust to some universally accepted English norm; rather, they are the output of dialect or language-specific syntactic rules every bit as complex as those of Standard English (Labov, 1969).

It is clear furthermore that the above linguistic differences also reflect far-reaching and systematic cultural differences. Like the plural societies of Asia and Africa, American urban society is characterized by the coexistence of a variety of distinct cultures. Each major ethnic group has its own heritage, its own body of traditions, values, and views about what is right and proper. These traditions are passed on from generation to generation as part of the informal family or peer-group socialization process and are encoded in folk art and literature, oral or written.

To understand this complex system, it is first of all necessary to identify and describe its constituent elements. Grammatical analysis must be, and has to some extent been, supplemented by ethnographic description, ethnohistory, and the study of folk art (Hannerz, 1969; Stewart, 1968; Abrahams, 1964; Kochman, 1969). But mere description of component subsystems is not enough if we are to learn how the plurality of cultures operates in everyday interaction and how it affects the quality of individual lives. Minority groups in urbanized societies are never completely isolated from the dominant majority. To study their life ways without reference to surrounding populations is to distort the realities of their everyday lives. All residents of modern industrial cities are subject to the same laws and are exposed to the same system of public education and mass communication. Minority-group members, in fact, spend much of their day in settings where dominant norms prevail. Although there are significant individual differences in the degree of assimilation, almost all minority-group members, even those whose behavior on the surface may seem quite deviant, have at least a passive knowledge of the dominant culture. What sets them off from others is not simply the fact that they are distinct, but the juxtaposition of their own private language and life styles with those of the public at large.

This juxtaposition, which is symbolized by constant alternation between in-group and out-group modes of acting and expression, has a pervasive effect on everyday behavior. Successful political leaders, such as Bobby Seale and the late Martin Luther King, rely on it for much of their rhetorical effect. C. Mitchell-Kernan, in her recent ethnographic study of verbal communication in an Afro-American community (1969), reports that her informants' everyday conversation reveals an overriding concern—be it positive or negative—with majority culture.

Majority-group members who have not experienced a similar disjuncture between private and public behavior frequently fail to appreciate its effect. They tend merely to perceive minority-group members as different, without realizing the effect that this difference may have on everyday communication. This ignorance of minority styles of behavior seems to have contributed to the often-discussed notion of "linguistic deprivation." No one familiar with the writings of Afro-American novelists of the last decade and with the recent writings on black folklore can maintain that low-income blacks are nonverbal. An exceptionally rich and varied terminological system, including such folk concepts as *sounding, signifying, rapping, running it down, shucking, jiving, marking,* etc., all referring to verbal strategies (i.e., different modes of achieving particular communicative ends), testifies to the importance Afro-American culture assigns to verbal art (Kochman, 1969; Mitchell-Kernan, 1969). Yet inner-city black children are often described as nonverbal, simply because they fail to respond to the school situation. It is true that lower-class children frequently show difficulty in performing adequately in formal interviews and psychological tests. But these tests are frequently administered under conditions that seem unfamiliar and, at times, threatening to minority-group children. When elicitation conditions are changed, there is often a radical improvement in response (Labov, 1969; Mehan, 1970).

The fact that bilingualism and biculturalism have come to be accepted as major goals in inner-city schools is an important advance. But if we are to achieve these goals we require at least some understanding of the nature of code alternation and its meaning in everyday interaction. Bilingualism is, after all, primarily a linguistic term, referring to the fact that linguists have discovered significant alternations in phonology, morphology, and syntax in studying the verbal behavior of a particular population. Although bilingual phenomena have certain linguistic features in common, these features may have quite different social significance.

Furthermore, to the extent that social conditions affect verbal behavior, findings based on research in one type of bilingual situation may not necessarily be applicable to another socially different one.

Sociolinguistic studies of bilingualism for the most part focus on the linguistic aspects of the problem. Having discovered that speakers alternate between what, from a linguistic point of view, constitute grammatically distinct systems, investigators then proceed to study where and under what conditions alternates are employed, either through surveys in which speakers are asked to report their own language usage (Fishman, 1965) or by counting the occurrence of relevant forms in samples of elicited speech. The assumption is that the presence or absence of particular linguistic alternates directly reflects significant information about such matters as group membership, values, relative prestige, and power relationships.

There is no doubt that such one-to-one relationships between language and social phenomena do exist in most societies. Where speakers control and regularly employ two or more speech varieties and continue to do so over long periods of time, it is most likely that each of the two varieties will be associated with certain activities or social characteristics of speakers. This is especially the case in formal or ceremonial situations, such as religious or magical rites, court proceedings, stereotyped introductions, greetings, or leavetakings. Here language, as well as gestures and other aspects of demeanor, may be so rigidly specified as to form part of the defining characteristics of the setting—so much so that a change in language may change the setting.

There are, however, many other cases where such correlations break down. Consider the following sentences cited in a recent study of bilingualism in Texas:

(1) Te digo que este dedo (*I tell you that this finger*) has been bothering me so much.

Se me hace que (*it seems that*) I have to respect her porque 'ta ... (*because she is*).

But this arthritis deal, boy you get to hurting so bad you can't hardly even ... "cer masa pa" tortillas (*make dough for tortillas*). (Lance, 1969, pp. 75-76)

Similar examples come from a recently recorded discussion between two educated Mexican-Americans.

(2a) Woman: Well, I'm glad that I met you. Okay?

M———: Andale, pues (*okay, swell*) and do come again, mmm?

(b) M———: Con ellos dos (*with the two of them*). With each other. La señora trabaja en la canería orita, you know? (*The mother works in the cannery right now*). She was ... con Francine jugaba ... (*she used to play with Francine ...*) with my little girl.

(c) M———: There's no children in the neighborhood. Well ... sí hay criaturas (*there are children*).

(d) M———: ... those friends are friends from Mexico que tienen chamaquitos (*who have little children*).

(e) M———: ... that has nothing to do con que le hagan esto ... (*with their doing this*).

(f) M———: But the person ... de ... de grande (*as an adult*) is gotta have something in his mouth.

(g) M———: An' my uncle Sam es el más agabachado (*is the most Americanized*).

It would be futile to predict the occurrence of either English or Spanish in the above utterances by attempting to isolate social variables that correlate with linguistic form. Topic, speaker, setting are common in each. Yet the code changes sometimes in the middle of a sentence.

Language mixing of this type is by no means a rarity. Linguists specializing in bilingualism cite it to provide examples of extreme instances of interference (Mackey, 1965). Some native speakers in ethnically diverse communities are reluctant to admit its existence. It forms the subject of many humorous treatises, and in Texas it tends to be referred to by pejorative terms, such as Tex-Mex. Yet in spite of the fact that such extreme code switching is held in disrepute, it is very persistent wherever minority language groups come in close contact with majority language groups under conditions of rapid social change.

One might, by way of an explanation, simply state that both codes are equally admissible in some contexts and that code switching is merely a matter of the individual's momentary inclination. Yet the alternation does carry meaning. Let us compare the following passage from a recent analysis of Russian pronominal usage with an excerpt from a conversation.

(3) An arrogant aristocratic lieutenant and a grizzled, older captain find themselves thrust together as the only officers on an isolated outpost in the Caucasus. Reciprocal formality at first seems appropriate to both. But while the latter is sitting on the young lieutenant's bed and discussing a confidential matter he switches to *ty* (familiar). When the lieutenant appears to suggest insubordination, however, the captain reverts to *vy* (polite) as he issues a peremptory demand. . . . [Friedrich, 1966, p. 240]

(4) M———: I don't think I ever have any conversations in my dreams. I just dream. Ha. I don't hear people talking: I jus' see pictures.
E———: Oh. They're old-fashioned, then. They're not talkies yet, huh?
M———: They're old-fashioned. No. They're not talkies, yet. No. I'm trying to think. Yeah, there too have been talkies. Different. In Spanish and English both. An' I wouldn't be too surprised if I even had some in Chinese. (*Laughter*). Yeah, E———. De veras (*really*). (M——— *offers* E——— *a cigarette, which is refused.*) Tú no fumas, ¿verdad? Yo tampoco. Dejé de fumar. (*You don't smoke, right? Neither do I. I quit smoking.*)

The two societies, the social context, and the topics discussed differ, yet the shift from English to Spanish has connotations similar to the alternation between the formal (second person pronoun) *vy* and the informal *ty*. Both signal a change in interpersonal relationship in the direction of greater informality or personal warmth. Although the linguistic signs differ, they reflect similar social strategies. What the linguist identifies as code switching may convey important social information. The present paper is an attempt (1) to elucidate the relationship among linguistic form, interactional strategies, and social meaning on the basis of a detailed study of a natural conversation, and (2) to suggest implications for understanding language use in the culturally diverse classroom.

The conversation cited in items 2 and 4 was recorded in an institution specializing in English instruction for small Mexican immigrant children. The staff, ranging in age from recent high school graduates to persons in their middle fifties, includes a large number of people of Mexican or Mexican-American descent as well as some English-speaking Americans. Of the latter group, several speak Spanish well. The recording was made by a linguist (E———), a native American of Mexican ancestry who is employed as an adviser for the program. His interlocutor (M———) is a community counselor employed in the program. She is a woman without higher education who has been trained to assist the staff in dealing with the local community. She has had some experience in public affairs. In spite of the difference in education and salary, both participants regard each other as colleagues within the context of the program. When speaking Spanish they address each other by the reciprocal *tú*. The program director or a Spanish-speaking outsider visitor would receive the respectful *usted*. Conversations within the office are normally carried on in English, although, as will be seen later, there are marked stylistic differences that distinguish interaction among Mexican-Americans from interaction across ethnic boundaries.

For analysis the taped manuscript was roughly divided into episodes, each centering around a single main topic. Episodes were then subdivided into "turns of speaking" (i.e., one or more sentences reflecting a speaker's response to another's comment). The author and the interviewer cooperated in the analysis of social meaning.

Two types of information were utilized. Turns containing a code switch were first examined as to their place within the structure of the total conversation in terms of such questions as, What were the relevant antecedents of the turn and what followed? or, What was the turn in response to, either in the same or preceding episodes? The purpose here was to get as detailed as possible an estimation of the speaker's intent. In the second stage a phrase from the other language would be substituted for the switched phrase in somewhat the same way that a linguistic interviewer uses the method of variation within a frame in order to estimate the structural significance of a particular item. By this method it was possible to get an idea of what the code switch contributed to the meaning of the whole passage.

Before discussing the social aspects of code switching, some discussion of what it is that is being switched is necessary. Not all instances of Spanish words in the text are necessarily instances of code switching. Expressions like *ándale pues* (item 2a) or *dice* (he says) are normally part of the bilingual's style of English. Speakers use such expressions when speaking to others of the same ethnic background in somewhat the same way that Yiddish expressions like *nebbish, oi gewalt*, or interjections like *du hoerst* characterize the in-group English style of some American Jews. They serve as stylistic ethnic identity markers and are frequently used by speakers who no longer have effective control of both languages. The function of such forms as an ethnic identity marker becomes particularly clear in the following sequence, already cited in item 2b, between M——— and a woman visitor in her office.

(5) Woman: Well, I'm glad that I met you. Okay?
M———: Andale, pues (*okay, swell*) and do come again, mmm?

The speakers, both Mexican-Americans, are strangers who have met for the first time. The *ándale pues* is given in response to the woman's *okay*, as if to say, "Although we are strangers we have the same background and should get to know each other better."

Aside from loan word nouns such as *Chicano, gabacho*, or *pocho*, the ethnic identity markers consist largely of exclamations and sentence connectors. For example:

(6) M———: I say, Lupe no hombre (*why no*), don't believe that.

(7) M———: Sí (*yes*) but it doesn't.

(8) M———: That baby is . . . pues (*then*).

Mexican-Spanish is similarly marked by English interjections. Note, for example, the *you know* in the sentence:

(9) M———: Pero, como, you know . . . la Estela . . .

The English form here seems a regular part of the Spanish text, and this is signaled phonetically by the fact that the pronunciation of the vowel *o* is relatively undiphthongized and thus differs from other instances of *o* in English passages. Similarly, words like ice cream have Spanish-like pronunciations when they occur within Spanish texts, and English-like pronunciations in the English text.

The greater part of the instances of true code switching consist of entire sentences inserted into the other language text. There are, however, also some examples of change within single sentences, which require special comment. In the items below, the syntactic connection is such that both parts can be interpreted as independent sentences.

(10) M———: We've got all these kids here right now, los que están ya criados aquí (*those that have been raised here*).

This is not the case with the noun qualifier phrase in item 2d and the verb complement in item 2e. Other examples of this latter type are:

(11) M———: But the person . . . de . . . de grande (*as an adult*) is gotta have something in his mouth.

(12) M———: ¿Será que quiero la tetera? para pacify myself? (*It must be that I want the baby bottle to . . .*)

(13) M———: The type of work he did cuando trabajaba (*when he worked*) he . . . what . . . that I remember, era regador (*he was an irrigator*) at one time.

(14) M———: An' my uncle Sam es el más agabachado (*is the most Americanized*).

Noun qualifiers (2d), verb complements (2e), parts of a noun phrase (13), the predicate portion of an equational sentence (14), all can be switched. This does not mean, however, that there are no linguistic constraints on the co-occurrence of Spanish and English forms. The exact specification of these constraints will, however, require further detailed investigation. Clearly, aside from single loan words, entire sentences are most easily borrowed. Sentence modifiers or phrases are borrowed less frequently. And this borrowing does seem to be subject to some selection constraints (Blom and Gumperz, 1970). But some tentative statements can be made. Constructions like *que have chamaquitos* (*who have boys*) or *he era regador* (*he was an irrigator*) seem impossible.

When asked why they use Spanish in an English sentence or vice versa, speakers frequently come up with explanations like the following taken from our conversation:

(15) If there's a word that I can't find, it keeps comin' out in Spanish.

(16) I know what word I want and finally when I . . . well, bring it out in Spanish, I know the person understands me.

Difficulty in finding the right word clearly seems to account for examples like *para pacify myself* (item 12). In other instances, some items of experience, some referents or topics are more readily recalled in one language than in another, as in:

(17) M———: I got to thinking vacilando el punto este (*mulling over this point*).

(18) M———: They only use English when they have to . . . like for cuando van de compras (*when they go shopping*).

Linguistically motivated switches into English occur when the discussion calls for psychological terminology or expressions, e.g., *pacify, relax, I am a biter.* Such expressions or modes of talking seem rarely used in typically Mexican-American settings. On the other hand, ideas and experiences associated with the speaker's Spanish-speaking past such as items 20 and 21 below trigger off a switch into Spanish.

In many other instances, however, there seems to be no linguistic reason for the switch. *Sí hay criaturas* (item 2c) is directly translated without hesitation pause in the following sentence. Many other Spanish expressions have English equivalents elsewhere in the text. Furthermore, there are several pages of more general, abstract discussion that contain no Spanish at all.

One might hypothesize that codes are shifted in response to E———'s suggestion and that M——— answers him in whatever language he speaks. This is clearly not the case. Several questions asked in English elicit Spanish responses and vice versa.

In discussing the social aspects of switching, it is important to note that while the overt topic discussed is the use of English and Spanish, much of the conversation is dominated by a concern with Mexican versus non-Mexican, i.e., common middle-class values or group membership. Spanish occurs most in episodes dealing with typically Mexican-American experiences. In several places fears are expressed that Mexican-American children are losing their language and thus, by implication, denying their proper cultural heritage. To some extent the juxtaposition of English and Spanish symbolizes the duality of value systems evidenced in the discussion.

At the start of the conversation several exchanges dealing with the mechanics of tape-recorder operation are entirely in English. Code shifts begin with a sequence where M——— asks E——— why he is recording their talk and E——— responds:

(19) E———: I want to use it as a . . . as an example of how Chicanos can shift back and forth from one language to another.

(20) M———: Ooo. Como andábamos platicando (*Oh. Like we were saying*).

M———'s switch to Spanish here is a direct response to his, E———'s, use of the word *Chicanos.* Her statement refers to previous conversations they have had on related subjects and suggests that she is willing to treat the present talk as a friendly chat among fellow Chicanos rather than as a formal interview.

Codes alternate only as long as all participants are Chicanos and while their conversation revolves around personal experiences. Toward the end of the recording session, when a new participant enters, talk goes on. The newcomer is an American of English-speaking background who, having lived in Latin America, speaks Spanish fluently. Yet in this context she was addressed only in English and did not use her Spanish. Furthermore, in the earlier part of the session, when E——— and M——— were alone, there was one long episode where M——— spoke only English even when responding to E———'s Spanish questions. This passage deals with M———'s visit to San Quentin prison, to see an inmate, and with prison conditions. The inmate was referred to only in English and the conversation contained no overt reference to his ethnic background. Further inquiries made while analysis was in progress revealed that he was a non-Chicano. It is evident from the first example that it is social identity and not language per se that is determinant in code selection. The second example indicates that, when conversations have no reference to speakers or their subjects' status as Chicanos, and when as in the present case a subject is treated in a generally detached manner without signs of personal involvement, code switching seems to be inappropriate.

On the whole, one has the impression that, except for a few episodes dealing with recollections of family affairs, the entire conversation is basically in English. English serves to introduce most new information, while Spanish provides stylistic embroidering to amplify the speaker's intent. Spanish sentences frequently take the form of precoded, stereotyped, or idiomatic phrases.

While ethnic identity is important as the underlying theme, the actual contextual meanings of code alternation are more complex.

Turning to a more detailed analysis, many of the Spanish passages reflect direct quotes or reports of what M——— has said in Spanish or of what other Mexican-Americans have told her, for example:

(21) Because I was speakin' to my baby ... my ex-baby-sitter, and we were talkin' about the kids you know, an' I was tellin' her ... uh, "Pero, como, you know ... uh ... la Estela y la Sandi ... relistas en el telefón. Ya hablan mucho inglés." Dice, "Pos ... sí. Mira tú," dice, "Pos ... el ... las palabras del televisión. Ya que me dice ... ya me pide dinero pa'l ayscrín y ..." You know? "Ya lue ... y eso no es nada, espérate los chicharrones, you know, when they start school ..." (But, how, you know ... uh ... "Estela and Sandi are very precocious on the telephone. They already speak a lot of English." She says, "Well, yes, just imagine," she says, "well, the words on television, and she already asks me for money for ice cream and" ... You know? "And then ... and that isn't anything, wait for the kids, you know, when they start school ...")

Throughout the conversation Spanish is used in quoting statements by individuals whose Chicano identity is emphasized. However, the following passage in which Lola, who is of Mexican origin, is quoted in English seemed at first to contradict this generalization.

(22) An' Lola says, "Dixie has some, Dixie" . . . So Dixie gave me a cigarette.

Lola, however, is in her late teens; and members of her age group, although they know Spanish, tend to prefer English even in informal interaction. Later on, however, if they marry within the Chicano community, they are quite likely to revert to the predominant usage pattern. The use of English in her case reflects the fact that for the present, at least, Lola identifies with the majority group of English monolinguals with respect to language-usage norms.

The pattern of quoting Chicanos in Spanish and talking about them in English is reversed in the following passage, in which M——— reports on the way she talks to her children:

(23) Yeah. Uh-huh. She'll get . . . "Linda, you don' do that, mija . . . (*daughter*). La vas . . . (*you are going to . . .*) you're going to get her . . . give her . . . a bad habit." Le pone el dedo pa' que se lo muerda (*she gives her her finger to bite*), you know, "Iiya, she'll bite the heck out of you." "Ow!" La otra grita (*the other one yells*). So, una es sadist y la otra es masochist (*so, one is a sadist and the other is a masochist*). (*Laughter.*)

Further enquiry again reveals that in M———'s family children are ordinarily addressed in English.

Aside from direct quotes, Spanish occurs in several modifying phrases or sentences, such as *friends from Mexico que tienen chamaquitos* (item 2d). The effect here is to emphasize the ethnic identity of the referent. The use of *sí hay criaturas* (item 2c) is particularly interesting in this respect. It is preceded by the following exchange:

(24) M———: There's no children. The Black Panthers next door. You know what I mean.
E———: Do they have kids?
M———: Just the two little girls.
E———: No, no. I mean, do some of the other people in the neighborhood have kids?
M———: They don't associate with no children . . . There's no children in the neighborhood. Well . . . sí hay criaturas (*there are children*).

M——— goes on to talk about the one other Mexican family in the building. The *sí hay criaturas* here serves to single out Mexican children from others and in a sense modifies the *there's no children* several sentences above. The implication is that only the other Chicano children are suitable playmates.

In the next group of examples the switch to Spanish signals the relative confidentiality or privateness of the message. The first example, cited in item 2b above, is a case in point:

(25) With each other. La señora trabaja en la canería orita, you know? (*The mother works in the cannery right now*).

Here M———'s voice is lowered, the loudness decreasing in somewhat the same way that confidentiality is signaled in English monolingual speech. Next, consider the following:

(26) E———: An' how ... about how about now?
M———: Estos ... me los hallé ... estos Pall Malls me los hallaron (*These ... I found ... these Pall Malls ... they were found for me ...*) No, I mean ...

M——— has been talking about the fact that she smokes very little, and E——— discovers some cigarettes on her desk. Her Spanish, punctuated by an unusually large number of hesitation pauses, lends to the statement an air of private confession. She is obviously slightly embarrassed.

Note the almost regular alternation between Spanish and English in the next passage:

(27) Mm-huh. Yeah. An' ... an' they tell me, "How did you quit, Mary?" I di'n' quit. I ... I just stopped. I mean it wasn' an effort I made que voy a dejar de fumar porque me hace daño o (*that I'm going to stop smoking because it's harmful to me, or ...*) this or that, uh-uh. It just ... that ... eh ... I used to pull butts out of the ... the ... the wastepaper basket. Yeah. (*Laughter.*) I used to go look in the (*unclear*) se me acababan los cigarros en la noche (*my cigarettes would run out at night*). I'd get desperate, y ahi voy al basurero a buscar, a sacar, you know? (*and there I go to the wastebasket to look for some, to get some*). (*Laughter.*)

The juxtaposition of the two codes here is used to great stylistic effect in depicting the speaker's attitudes. The Spanish phrases, partly by being associated with content like "it is harmful to me" or with references to events like "cigarettes running out at night" and through intonational and other suprasegmental clues, convey a sense of personal feeling. The English phrases are more neutral by contrast. The resulting effect of alternate personal involvement and clinical detachment vividly reflects M———'s ambiguity about her smoking.

A further example derives from a discussion session recorded in Richmond, California, by a black community worker. Participants include his wife and several teen-age boys. Here we find alternation between speech features that are quite close to Standard English and such typically Black English features as lack of postvocalic "r," double negation, and copula deletion.

(28) You can tell me how your mother worked twenty hours a day and I can sit here and cry. I mean I can cry and I can feel for you. But as long as I don't get up and make certain that I and my children don't go through the same, *I ain't did nothin' for you,* brother. That's what I'm talking about.
(29) Now Michael is making a point, where that everything that happens in that house affects all the kids. It does. And Michael and *you makin' a point, too. Kids suppose' to learn how to avoid these things.* But let me tell you. We're all in here. *We talkin' but you see ...*

Note the italicized phrase in item 28, with the typically Black English phrase *ain't did nothin'* embedded in what is otherwise a normal Standard English sequence. On our tape the shift is not preceded by a pause or marked off by special stress or intonation contours. The speaker is therefore not quoting from another code; his choice of form here lends emphasis to what he is saying. Item 29 begins with a general statement addressed to the group as a whole. The speaker then turns to one person, Michael, and signals this change in focus by dropping the copula "is" and shifting to black phonology.

It seems clear that, in all these cases, what the linguist sees merely as alternation between two systems serves definite and clearly understandable communicative ends. The speakers do not merely switch from one variety to another, but they build on the coexistence of alternate forms to convey information.

It can be argued that language choice reflects the speaker's minority status within the English-speaking majority, and that selection of forms in particular cases is related to such factors as ethnic identity, age, sex, and degree of solidarity or confidentiality. But the relationship of such social factors to speech form is quite different from what the sociologist means by correlation among variables. One could not take a rating of, for instance, ethnicity or degree of solidarity, as measured by the usual questionnaire techniques or other scaling devices, and expect this rating to predict the occurrence of Spanish or black dialect and Standard English in a text. Such ratings may determine the likelihood of a switch, but they do not tell *when a switch will occur, nor do they predict its meaning*. What seems to be involved here, rather, is a symbolic process akin to that by which words convey semantic information. Code switching, in other words, is meaningful in much the same way that lexical choice is meaningful.

To be sure, not all instances of code alternation convey meaning. Our tapes contain several instances where the shift into Black English or the use of a Spanish word in an English sentence can only be interpreted as a slip of the tongue, frequently corrected in the next sentence, or where its use must be regarded merely as a sign of the speaker's lack of familiarity with the style he is employing. But, even though such errors do occur, it is nevertheless true that code switching is also a communicative skill, which speakers use as a verbal strategy in much the same way that skillfull writers switch styles in a short story.

How and by what devices does the speaker's selection of alternate forms communicate information? The process is a metaphoric process somewhat similar to what linguists interested in literary style have called *foregrounding* (Garvin, 1969). Foregrounding, in the most general sense of the term, relies on the fact that words are more than just names for things. Words also carry a host of culturally specific associations, attitudes, and values. These cultural values derive from the context in which words are usually used and from the activities with which they are associated. When a word is used in other than normal context, these associations become highlighted or foregrounded. Thus to take an example made famous by Leonard Bloomfield (1933), the word *fox* when it refers to a man, as in "He is a fox," communicates the notions of slyness and craftiness that our culture associates with the activities of foxes.

We assume that what holds true for individual lexical items also holds true for phonological or syntactic alternates. Whenever a speech variety is associated with a particular social category of speakers or with certain activities, this variety comes to symbolize the cultural values associated with these features of the nonlinguistic environment. In other words, speech varieties, like words, are potentially meaningful, and in both cases this is brought out by reinterpreting meanings in relation to context. As long as the variety in question is used in its normal environment, only its basic referential sense is communicated. But when it is used in a new context, it becomes socially marked, and the values associated with the original context are mapped onto the new message.

In any particular instance of code switching, speakers deduce what is meant by an information-processing procedure that takes account of the speaker, the addressee, the social categories to which they can be assigned in the context, the topic, etc. (Blom and Gumperz, 1970). Depending on the nature of the above factors, a wide variety of contextual meanings derives from the basic meaning inclusion (we) versus exclusion (they). This underlying meaning is then reinterpreted in the light of the co-occurring contextual factors to indicate such things as degree of involvement (5), anger, emphasis (7), change in focus (8), etc., the numbers in parentheses referring to the items on pages 280-281.

We have chosen our examples from a number of languages to highlight the fact that the meanings conveyed by code switching are independent of the phonological shape or historical origin of the alternates in question. The association between forms and meaning is quite arbitrary. Any two alternates having the same referential meaning can become carriers of social meaning.

The ability to interpret a message is a direct function of the listener's home background, his peer-group experiences, and his education. Differences in background can lead to misinterpretation of messages. The sentence "He is a Sikh" has little or no meaning for an American audience, but to anyone familiar with speech behavior in northern India it conveys a whole host of meanings, since Sikhs are stereotypically known as bumblers. Similarly, the statement "He is a fox," cited above, which conveys slyness to middle-class whites, may be interpreted as a synonym for "He is handsome" by blacks. Communication thus requires both shared grammar and shared rules of language usage. Two speakers may speak closely related and, on the surface, mutually intelligible varieties of the same language, but they may nevertheless misunderstand each other because of differences in usage rules resulting from differences in background. We must know the speakers' normal usage pattern, i.e., which styles are associated as unmarked forms with which activities and relationships, as well as what alternates are possible in what context, and what cultural associations these carry.

Note that the view of culture that emerges from this type of analysis is quite different from the conventional one. Linguists attempting to incorporate cultural information into their descriptions tend to regard culture as a set of beliefs and attitudes that can be measured apart from communication. Even the recent work that utilizes actual speech samples by eliciting "subjective reactions" to these forms or evaluations, going considerably beyond earlier work, does not completely depart from this tradition, since it continues to rely on overt or conscious judgment. Our own material suggests that culture plays a role in communication that is somewhat similar to the role of syntactic knowledge in the decoding of referential meanings. Cultural differences, in other words, affect judgment both above and below the level of consciousness. A person may have every intention of avoiding cultural bias, yet, by subconsciously superimposing his own interpretation on the verbal performance of others, he may nevertheless bias his judgment of their general ability, efficiency, etc.

Communication problems are compounded by the fact that we know very little about the distribution of usage rules in particular populations. For example, there seems to be no simple correlation with ethnic identity, nor is it always possible to predict usage rules on the basis of socioeconomic indexes. While the majority of the speakers in a Puerto Rican block in Jersey City used Spanish in normal in-group communication and switched to English to indicate special affect, there are others residing among them, however, whose patterns differ significantly. A Puerto Rican college student took a tape recorder home and recorded informal family conversation over a period of several days. It is evident from his recording, and he himself confirms this in interviews, that in his family English is the normal medium of informal conversation while Spanish is socially marked and serves to convey special connotations of intimacy and anger.

II

It follows that, while the usual sociological measures of ethnic background, social class, educational achievements, etc., have some correlation with usage rules, they cannot be regarded as accurate predictors of performance in particular instances. On the contrary, social findings based on incomplete data, or on populations different from those for which they were intended, may themselves contribute to cultural misunderstanding. The use of responses to formal tests and interviews to judge the verbal ability of lower-class bilinguals is a case in point. Rosenthal (1968) has shown that teachers' expectations have a significant effect on learning, and psychological experiments by Williams (1969) and Henrie (1969) point to the role that dialect plays in generating these expectations. *When expectations created by dialect stereotypes are further reinforced by misapplied or inaccurate social science findings, education suffers.*

Imagine a child in a classroom situation who in a moment of special excitement shifts to black speech. The teacher may have learned that black speech is systematic and normal for communication in Afro-American homes. Nevertheless, intent as she is upon helping the child to become fully bilingual, she may comment on the child's speech by saying, "We don't speak this way in the classroom," or she may ask the child to rephrase the sentence in Standard English. No matter how the teacher expresses herself, the fact that she focuses on the form means that the teacher is not responding to the real meaning of the child's message. The child is most likely to interpret her remark as a rebuff and may feel frustrated in his attempt at establishing a more personal relationship with the teacher. In other words, by imposing her own monostylistic communicative norms, the teacher may thwart her students' ability to express themselves fully. An incident from a tape-recorded classroom session in Black Language Arts will illustrate the point.

Student (*reading from an autobiographical essay*): This lady didn't have no sense.
Teacher: What would be a Standard English alternate for this sentence?
Student: She didn't have any sense. But not this lady: *she didn't have no sense.*

Note the difference in focus between teacher and student. The former, in her concern with Standard English, focuses on the deviant double negatives, while the student is concerned with creating the proper narrative effect. If the teacher were able to interpret the social meaning conveyed by the child's use of particular linguistic forms, her teaching would be enhanced. All too often, however, his use of forms other than Standard English has a negative effect—not because linguistic differences per se would prevent the child from learning to read but because they affect how the teacher behaves toward him.

Classroom observation of first-grade reading sessions in a racially integrated California school district illustrates some of the problems involved. Classes in the district include about 60 percent White and 40 percent Chicano, Black, and Oriental children. College student observers find that most reading classes have a tracking system such that children are assigned to fast or slow reading groups, and that these groups are taught by different methods and otherwise receive different treatment.

Even in first-grade reading periods, where presumably all children are beginners, the slow reading groups tend to consist of 90 percent Blacks and Chicanos. Does this situation reflect real learning difficulties, or is it simply a function of our inability to diagnose reading aptitude in culturally different children? Furthermore, given the need for some kind of ability grouping, how effective and how well adapted to cultural needs are the classroom devices that are actually used to bridge the reading gap?

One reading class was divided into a slow reading group of three children, and a second group of seven fast readers. The teacher worked with one group at a time, keeping the others busy with individual assignments. With the slow readers she concentrated on the alphabet, on the spelling of individual words, and on supposedly basic grammatical concepts such as the distinctions between questions and statements. She addressed the children in what white listeners would identify as pedagogical style. Her enunciation was deliberate and slow. Each word was clearly articulated, with even stress and pitch, as if to avoid any verbal sign of emotion, approval, or disapproval. Children were expected to speak only when called upon, and the teacher would insist that each question be answered before responding to further ideas. Unsolicited remarks were ignored even if they referred to the problem at hand. Pronunciation errors were corrected whenever they occurred, even if the reading task had to be interrupted. The children seemed distracted and inattentive. They were guessing at answers, "psyching out" the teacher in the manner described by Holt (1964) rather than following her reasoning process. The following sequence symbolizes the artificiality of the situation:

Teacher: Do you know what a question is? James, ask William a question.
James: William, do you have a coat on?
William: No, I do not have a coat on.

James asks his question and William answers in a style that approaches in artificiality that of the teacher, characterized by citation form pronunciation of [e] rather than [ə] of the indefinite article, lack of contraction of *do not*, stress on the *have*, staccato enunciation as if to symbolize what they perceive to be the artificiality and incomprehensibility of the teacher's behavior.

With the advanced group, on the other hand, reading became much more of a group activity and the atmosphere was more relaxed. Words were treated in context, as part of a story. Children were allowed to volunteer answers. There was no correction of pronunciation, although some deviant forms were also heard. The children actually enjoyed competing with each other in reading, and the teacher responded by dropping her pedagogical monotone in favor of more animated natural speech. The activities around the reading table were not lost on the slow readers, who were sitting at their desks with instructions to practice reading on their own. They kept looking at the group, neglecting their own books, obviously wishing they could participate. After a while one boy picked up a spelling game from a nearby table. He started to work at it with the other boy, and they began to argue in a style normal for black children. When their voices became raised, the teacher turned and asked them to go back to reading.

In private conversation, the teacher (who is very conscientious and seemingly concerned with all her children's progress) justified her ability grouping on the grounds that children in the slow group lacked books in their homes and "did not speak proper English." She stated they needed practice in grammar, abstract thinking, and pronunciation and suggested that, given this type of training, they would eventually be able to catch up with the advanced group. We wonder how well she will succeed. Although clearly she has the best motives and would probably be appalled if one were to suggest that her ability grouping and her emphasis on the technical aspects of reading and spelling with culturally different children is culturally biased, her efforts are not so understood by the children themselves. Our data indicate that the pedagogical style used with slow readers carries different associations for low-middle-class and low-income groups. While whites identify it as normal teaching behavior, blacks associate it with the questioning style of welfare investigators and automatically react by not cooperating. In any case, attuned as they are to see meaning in stylistic choice, the black children in the slow reading group cannot fail to notice that they are being treated quite differently from and with less understanding than the advanced readers.

What are the implications of this type of situation for our understanding of the role of dialect differences in classroom learning? There is no question that the grammatical features of black dialects discovered by urban dialectologists in recent years are of considerable importance for the historical study of the origin of these dialects and for linguistic theory in general, but this does not necessarily mean that they constitute an impediment to learning. Information on black dialect is often made known to educators in the form of simple lists of deviant features with the suggestion that these features might interfere with reading. There is little if any experimental evidence, for example, that the pronunciations characteristic of urban Black English actually interfere with the reading process.

Yet the teacher in our classroom spent considerable time attempting to teach her slow readers the distinction between *pin* and *pen.* Lack of vowel distinction in these two words is widespread among blacks, but also quite common among whites in northern California. In any case, there is no reason why homophony in this case should present more difficulty than homophony in such words as *sea* and *see* or *know* and *no* or that created by the midwestern dialect speaker's inability to distinguish *Mary, marry,* and *merry.*

The problem of contextual relevance is not confined to contact with speakers of Black English. It also applies, for example, to the teaching of both English and Spanish in bilingual schools. When interviewed about their school experiences, Puerto Rican high school students in New York as well as Texas and California Chicano students uniformly complain about their lack of success in Spanish instruction. They resent the fact that their Spanish teachers single out their own native usages as substandard and inadmissible, in both classroom speech and writing.

On the contrary, a recent study, using testing procedures specifically adapted to black school children, shows that children who fail to distinguish orally between such word pairs as *jar* and *jaw, toe* and *tore, six* and *sick* are nevertheless able to distinguish among them when presented with the written forms.

It is not enough simply to present the educator with the descriptive linguistic evidence on language or dialect differences. What we need is properly controlled work on reading as such, work that does not deal with grammar alone. Our data suggest that urban language differences, while they may or may not interfere with reading, *do have a significant influence on a teacher's expectation, and hence on the learning environment.* In other words, regardless of overtly expressed attitudes, the teachers are quite likely to be influenced by what they perceive as deviant speech and failure to respond to questions and will act accordingly, thus potentially inhibiting the students' desire to learn. Since bilinguals and bidialectals rely heavily on code switching as a verbal strategy, they are especially sensitive to the relationship between language and context. It would seem that they learn best under conditions of maximal contextual reinforcement. Sole concentration on the technical aspects of reading, grammar, and spelling may so adversely affect the learning environment as to outweigh any advantages to be gained.

Experience with a summer program in language arts for minority-group members—mostly of Chicano origin—suggests a method of dealing with this problem (Waterhouse, 1969). Course attendance in this program was voluntary, and it soon became evident through group discussion that if the course were to be continued it could not start with the usual grammar and instruction. Several weeks of discussion were therefore devoted to achieving some agreement on the kind of communicative goals that would be relevant to students and that would require Standard English. Once this agreement had been achieved, students set out to enact such interaction sequences in the classroom, using a role-play technique. Texts then produced in this way were discussed in relation to their communicative effectiveness, and in the course of this discussion students soon began to correct their own and fellow students' grammar. The teacher's role was reduced to that of a discussion moderator, an arbiter of effectiveness, with the result that student motivation increased tremendously and learning improved dramatically.

It seems clear that progress in urban language instruction is not simply a matter of better teaching aids and improved textbooks. Middle-class adults have to learn to appreciate differences in communicative strategies of the type discussed here. Teachers themselves must be given instruction in both the linguistic and ethnographic aspects of speech behavior. They must become acquainted with code-selection rules in formal and informal settings as well as with those themes of folk literature and folk art that form the input to these rules, so that they can diagnose their own communication problems and adapt methods to their children's background.

Research reported on in this paper has been supported by grants from the Urban Crisis Program and the Institute of International Studies, University of California, Berkeley. We are grateful to Louisa Lewis for assistance in field work and analysis.

The point of view expressed in this paper leans heavily on the work of Claudia Mitchell-Kernan (1969).

References

Abrahams, Roger D., 1964   *Deep Down in the Jungle*. Hatboro, Pa.: Folklore Associates.

Blom, Jan Petter, and John J. Gumperz, 1970   "Social Meaning in Linguistic Structures." In John J. Gumperz and Dell Hymes, eds., *Directions in Sociolinguistics*. New York: Holt, Rinehart and Winston, 407-434.

Bloomfield, Leonard, 1933   *Language*. New York: Holt, Rinehart and Winston.

Fishman, Joshua, 1965   "Who Speaks What Language to Whom and When." *La Linguistique* 2, 67-88.

Friedrich, Paul, 1966   "Structural Implications of Russian Pronominal Usage." In William Bright, ed., *Sociolinguistics*. The Hague: Mouton and Co., 214-253.

Garvin, Paul, ed., 1969   *A Prague School Reader*. Washington, D.C.: Georgetown University Press.

Gumperz, John J., and Eduardo Hernández, 1969   "Cognitive Aspects of Bilingual Communication." Working Paper no. 28, Language Behavior Research Laboratory, University of California at Berkeley, December.

Hannerz, Ulf, 1969   *Soulside.* New York: Columbia University Press.

Henrie, Samuel N., Jr., 1969   *A Study of Verb Phrases Used by Five Year Old Non-Standard Negro English Speaking Children.* Doctoral dissertation, University of California at Berkeley.

Holt, John Caldwell, 1964   *How Children Fail.* New York: Pitman.

Kochman, Thomas, 1969   " 'Rapping' in the Black Ghetto." *Trans-action,* February, 26-34.

Labov, William, 1969   "The Logic of Non-Standard English." In James E. Alatis, ed., *Linguistics and the Teaching of Standard English.* Monograph Series on Languages and Linguistics, no. 22. Washington, D.C.: Georgetown University Press, 1-43.

Lance, Donald M., 1969   "A Brief Study of Spanish-English Bilingualism." Research report, Texas A. and M. University.

Mackey, William F., 1965   "Bilingual Interference: Its Analysis and Measurement." *Journal of Communication* 15, 239-249.

Mehan, B., 1970   Unpublished lecture on testing and bilingualism in the Chicano community, delivered to the Kroeber Anthropological Society Meetings, Apr. 25.

Melmed, Paul J., 1970   *Black English Phonology: The Question of Reading Interference.* Doctoral dissertation (Language Behavior Research Laboratory, Monograph I), University of California at Berkeley.

Mitchell-Kernan, Claudia, 1969   *Language Behavior in a Black Urban Community.* Doctoral dissertation (Working Paper no. 23, Language Behavior Research Laboratory), University of California at Berkeley.

Rosenthal, Robert, and Lenore Jacobson, 1968   *Pygmalion in the Classroom.* New York: Holt, Rinehart and Winston.

Sacks, Harvey, 1970   "On the Analyzability of Stories by Children." In John J. Gumperz and Dell Hymes, eds., *Directions in Sociolinguistics.* New York: Holt, Rinehart and Winston, 325-345.

Schegloff, Emanuel A., 1970   "Sequencing in Conversational Openings." In John J. Gumperz and Dell Hymes, eds., *Directions in Sociolinguistics.* New York: Holt, Rinehart and Winston, 346-380.

Shuy, Roger W., 1964   *Social Dialects and Language Learning.* Proceedings of the Bloomington, Indiana, Conference. N.C.T.E. Cooperative Research Project no. OE5-10-148.

Stewart, William A., 1968   "Continuity and Change in American Negro Dialects." *The Florida FL Reporter,* spring, 3-4, 14-16, 18.

Troike, Rudolph C., 1969   "Receptive Competence, Productive Competence and Performance." In James E. Alatis, ed., *Linguistics and the Teaching of Standard English.* Monograph Series on Languages and Linguistics, no. 22. Washington, D.C.: Georgetown University Press, 63-73.

Waterhouse, John, 1969   Final report, Comparative Literature 1A (Section 4) and Comparative Literature 1B (Section 5), English for Foreign Students Program, University of California at Berkeley. Typescript.

Williams, Frederick, 1969   "Psychological Correlates of Speech Characteristics: On Sounding 'Disadvantaged.' " Institute for Research on Poverty, University of Wisconsin, March.

PART III

EDUCATIONAL IMPLICATIONS

As a result of cultural reasons of one kind or another a local dialect becomes accepted as the favored or desirable form of speech within a linguistic community . . . The speakers of [other] local dialects begin to be ashamed of their peculiar forms of speech because these have not the prestige value of the standardized language; and finally the illusion is created of a primary language . . . and of the many local forms of speech as uncultured or degenerated variants of the primary norm.

—Edward Sapir

In American schools all the complex language diversity described in Parts I and II of this collection comes squarely up against the expectation of linguistic as well as cultural uniformity. Just as they have served as our chief means of acculturation and purveyors of the melting-pot myth, so our schools have traditionally been among the primary perpetuators of Standard American English. Though existing in the midst of remarkable ethnic, racial, and economic diversity, American schools have consistently operated as if all Americans shared a single history, similar economic opportunities, identical cultural attributes, and a common language background. And it has been naïvely assumed that children will either come to school speaking Standard English or will be able to pick it up by memorizing a few prescriptive rules of grammar. Yet, as this anthology indicates, the language situation in the United States is more complicated and Standard English more nebulous than educators had supposed. Consequently, the difficulties and dangers of teaching Standard English are now becoming apparent for the first time. Among the dangers of enforcing a standard language on a various U.S. population are widespread insecurity about language use, the attempted eradication of non-English mother tongues even in the home, and the alienation of minority children from our educational process. The articles by Philips, Wolfram and Christian, and Labov in this section describe some of the language-related difficulties such children confront in school.

The tendency toward language standardization in the schools cannot, however, simply be dismissed as wrongheaded or repressive. There are solid arguments to be made in favor of preserving a national standard: it minimizes cultural slippage in communication situations and provides a reassuring norm for use in public or formal exchanges. There are also solid reasons for training all Americans to control the standard. Our government affairs, major business transactions, and media reports are all presently conducted in Standard English. Short of abolishing the standard, the only way to assure all Americans access to this power structure is to educate them in the language of the powerful. Clearly, the issue of how or whether to teach Standard English in the schools is not as simple as it once seemed.

The Standard English issue once seemed simple for reasons that have to do with the history of grammar instruction in the schools. During the eighteenth century several intellectual and social currents left their stamp on the teaching of grammar in England and America. It was the age of Neoclassicism, so that Latin and Greek were exalted at the expense of living languages like English, which were viewed as the deteriorating descendants of a noble classical lineage. Hence English was considered elegant or proper only to the extent that it conformed to the static rules of Latin grammar. Latin-based grammars legislated—against popular usage—that what would not work in Latin should not work in English: sentences should not end with prepositions nor should infinitives be split.

The eighteenth century was also the age of Reason, which influenced grammarians to think that language, like all other natural phenomena, should follow divine and immutable laws of logic. Thus in spite of its frequent use in popular speech and writing, grammarians outlawed multiple negation (e.g., *Henry wouldn't hit no child*) on the logical, though certainly not linguistic, grounds that two negatives equal a positive and therefore logically reverse the intended meaning (supposedly, *Henry would hit any child*).

And finally, the eighteenth century was the age of the Industrial Revolution, which introduced the possibility of upward mobility and with it the desire of the middle classes to assert their newly acquired social status through the readiest of social indicators—language. To this end, grammarians were commissioned to produce school grammars of English, and the Anglo-American obsession with linguistic "correctness" began in earnest. By the nineteenth century the popular schoolbook grammarian Lindley Murray would epitomize this obsession by defining English grammar as "the art of speaking and writing the English language with propriety."

These eighteenth-century attitudes toward English grammar have survived virtually unrevised until the present day and are largely responsible for the continued American faith in and insistence upon Standard English. Grammarians and educators alike have assumed that English, like the dead language Latin, could be handily codified and conveyed to students as a single entity. They have further assumed that any nonstandard variety of English represents a threat to the purity of a divinely ordained standard, an affront to natural logic, and a signal of linguistic—and perhaps even moral—corruption. Moreover, no student, it was supposed, could succeed either academically or societally without knowing

Standard English. It seemed the clear duty of every self-respecting English teacher to stamp out any deviation from such a virtuous norm.

As descriptive linguistics began to find its way into post-World War II school curricula, some Latin-based grammars were replaced with more systematic and accurate accounts of English. But even descriptive grammars were used mainly in the service of inculcating the national standard rather than exploring the intricacies of language system. The concept of the inevitable and valid variation in all natural languages was slow to get a foothold in American education.

In the last decade, however, sociolinguistics has finally penetrated the schoolroom. Unfortunately, the result has been more chaos than clarity. While many teachers now acknowledge that their former notion of a hallowed and unalterable standard was erroneous, there is little agreement about how to handle the new information that all language varieties are equally logical, expressive, and coherent. Burling's article summarizes the various and conflicting approaches to nonstandard varieties proposed in recent years—approaches which vary from eradicating all nonstandard varieties (the traditional solution) to fostering all nonstandard varieties regardless of the context.

Since 1974, the distress and disagreement over Standard English in the schools have accelerated. On the one hand, developments in sociolinguistics have led the Conference on College Composition and Communication of the National Council of Teachers of English to issue a pamphlet (excerpted in this section, along with replies by Baxter and Stewart) which urges the maintenance of whatever language variety a student brings to school. On the other hand, parents and educators are clamoring for a return to the three R's after the liberalization of curricula in the 1960s. Their demands, which include the teaching of Standard English, were spurred by a decline in College Entrance Examination scores which began in 1963 but became precipitous between 1974 and 1975 when the average score on the verbal section dropped ten points. This drop and other pressures from the educationally conservative persuaded the College Entrance Examination Board to add a Written Test of Standard English to the verbal section of the Scholastic Aptitude Test in 1974. The lines of disagreement in the Standard English controversy are sharply drawn, and solutions will not come easily.

The confusion over how to treat nonstandard varieties of English is compounded by the need to offer equal education to Americans with native languages other than English. Federal guidelines published in 1975 require all school systems with twenty or more students from a single language background to provide bilingual education, not just instruction in English as a second language, at the elementary and intermediate levels. Fishman's article describes the possible types and goals of such bilingual programs. Obviously, these guidelines call for drastic changes in many American school systems, and they, too, are bound to engender debate.

Part III, then, examines some of the linguistic problems that inevitably arise when a pluralistic society, especially one that suffered too long under a monocultural illusion, tries to provide the best possible education for all its youth.

Readers are encouraged to weigh all the considerations that bear on this vital question. Only from informed and careful evaluation of linguistic evidence by teachers, language professionals, and educational policy makers can viable solutions be reached.

Further Readings

Alfred C. Aarons, ed., *Issues in the Teaching of Standard English*, Special Issue of *Florida Foreign Language Reporter* (Spring/Fall, 1974). Published in late 1975, this collection represents the most recent thinking about the role of Standard English in the schools; diverse viewpoints presented.

Alfred C. Aarons, Barbara Y. Gordon, and William A. Stewart, eds., *Linguistic-Cultural Differences and American Education*, Special Anthology Issue of *Florida Foreign Language Reporter* (Spring/Summer, 1969). Although somewhat outdated, an inclusive and useful anthology which uses sociolinguistic and ethnographic approaches to communities with more than one language or language variety; separate section on pedagogical implications.

Frederick Williams, ed., *Language and Poverty: Perspectives on a Theme* (Markham Publishing Company, 1970). Readings on the relationship between language and the cognitive development of minority children; some of the articles define nonstandard speakers as "disadvantaged"; helpful annotated bibliography on language, poverty, and child development.

Ralph W. Fasold and Roger W. Shuy, eds., *Teaching Standard English in the Inner City* (Center for Applied Linguistics, 1970). An accessible reader on language variation in the cities; suggests specific pedagogical approaches for teaching Standard English.

Joan C. Baratz and Roger W. Shuy, eds., *Teaching Black Children to Read* (Center for Applied Linguistics, 1969). Discusses reading problems created by dialect interference and a range of possible solutions, including the use of readers written in nonstandard dialect; useful background for the current controversy on reading and writing skills.

WHAT SHOULD WE DO ABOUT IT?

Robbins Burling

Robbins Burling's book *English in Black and White* is a reliable and readable account of the structure, use, and origins of Black English Vernacular. Its two concluding chapters, the first of which is reprinted below, offer sound suggestions for instructing speakers of this or other nonstandard varieties in the language arts. In this selection, Burling summarizes the four alternative methods for initiating nonstandard speakers into a society which links success with Standard English. Burling himself opts for a compromise between accepting the student's original dialect and encouraging *bidialectalism*—a crucial linguistic concept for educators to grasp and one that Burling defines carefully in this chapter. Readers should scrutinize each alternative and try to articulate their positions on this complicated issue.

In his consideration of what aspects of Standard English to teach nonstandard speakers and when to teach them, Burling assumes that nonstandard speakers can learn to read Standard English before they learn to speak it and refers readers to his concluding chapter for supporting arguments. In essence, what he argues there is that nonstandard speakers should be able to learn to read Standard English because (1) all English speakers use the same basic vocabulary, (2) English spelling so little resembles the phonology of any spoken variety that it can be interpreted equally well by all English speakers, and (3) spoken grammar differs from written grammar for Standard as well as nonstandard speakers, and so Standard written grammar should pose no insurmountable obstacles in teaching minority students to read. Rather, Burling maintains, it is the disparaging attitude that teachers display toward nonstandard varieties that bars minority students from reading success and should therefore be changed. See the Wolfram and Christian article and the CCCC Language Statement in this collection for further discussion of techniques for teaching nonstandard speakers to read.

The Dilemma and Our Alternatives

We cannot avoid this dismal fact: The children of our inner city ghettoes fall far behind the national average on every measure of reading skill and on all standard measures of verbal ability. Many subtle, interwoven factors combine to handicap these children, and no one should be so rash as to suggest that a single cause lies at the heart of all their problems. No single program will bring a rapid solution. Children who are hungry have difficulties not shared by children with full stomachs. Children from homes where reading is encouraged and where books are treasured learn to read more eagerly than children whose parents are effectively illiterate. Black children who confront white teachers may rebel against everything their teachers represent. When the schools are but tiny middle-class islands barely afloat in a great lower-class sea, it may be difficult for the schools and the children to learn much from each other. Nevertheless, whatever other factors contribute to reading failure, the language that black ghetto children bring to school is surely one part of the problem. Language differences, poverty, and poor educational attainment seem to be indissolubly linked.

Every teacher in every classroom in the inner city must grapple with the problem of language. She will be surrounded by children who speak strongly stigmatized forms of English, and, in one way or another, she will have to come to terms with the way her children talk. She may accept their language, or she may reject it. She may accept it intellectually but reject it emotionally. She may accept it part of the time but reject it at others. The one thing she can never do is ignore it. The language of her children is too much a part of their personality ever to be forgotten.

The thoughtful teacher will ask herself what she should do or what the schools should do, and she may find herself puzzled. How much, she may ask, should she interfere with the natural speech of the children? How much should she insist upon change? Few questions concerning inner-city education need more urgent answers, but no answers have been harder to find. The pages remaining in this book will certainly not be sufficient to give final answers to such a knotty set of questions, but perhaps, given the facts of dialectal variability that we have surveyed in the earlier chapters, we can at least begin to find the directions in which plausible answers lie.

From the broadest perspective, we can conceive of four alternative policies that our schools and their teachers might implement with respect to dialect variability: (1) try to achieve dialect uniformity by wiping out nonstandard English; (2) achieve dialect uniformity by teaching nonstandard English to standard speakers; (3) accept dialect diversity, and when children speak nonstandard English in school, make no effort to change it; (4) encourage bidialectalism and hope that children can learn Standard English in school while they continue to use their home language with their friends and family. Each of these four policies has serious drawbacks, but each needs to be considered.

1. Wipe Out Nonstandard English The oldest and most familiar American policy toward nonstandard dialects has simply been to treat them as wrong. Children who speak "badly" are clearly instructed to give up their errors and to learn to speak "correctly." This policy has the great virtue of simplicity and clarity. Anyone who wants to advance, anyone who wants to continue his education or to get a better job than his father, must conform. Anyone who fails to conform can be assumed to have feeble aptitudes and can safely be cast aside. It is a tribute to our educational system that the overwhelming majority of Americans have been instilled with a rocklike conviction that certain linguistic forms are correct, while others are wrong. Even those Americans who are uncertain about precisely which forms are correct are usually confident that to find the answer they need only look the matter up in the right book or consult the proper authority. This is our conventional wisdom about language, but our conventional wisdom is wrong. As we have seen, there are usually many ways of saying the same thing, and there is no possible way of determining in every case that just one of the alternatives is correct. Variability is a permanent fact of language.

Our conventional wisdom about correctness in language is worse than simply mistaken, however, for it places an impossible burden upon the child whose native dialect happens to diverge widely from the standard. If by school policy or even by the unconscious attitudes of his teachers his dialect is dismissed as wrong, he is offered a grim choice. If he accepts the school's authority, he will come to see the language of his parents, his family, and his friends as evidence of their stupidity or laziness. On the other hand, if he refuses to reject his family, it will be difficult for him not to reject his school. Our educational system has persuaded many children to reject their own heritage and to adapt their language to the demands of society, but it is difficult to exaggerate the personal and psychological cost of this adaptation. Far more children have fallen by the wayside, rejecting and rejected by a rigid social system to which they could not conform.

The worst to be said against the policy of trying to wipe out nonstandard English, however, is simply that it has never worked. Generations of school teachers have struggled valiantly to persuade their children to conform to school standards. Generations of children have successfully defied their teachers and continued to speak with nonstandard forms. We ought to forget a policy that has failed so badly and for so long.

2. Teach Nonstandard English to Standard Speakers   If dialect uniformity cannot be achieved by wiping out nonstandard English, what about attempting the opposite? If we feel that a common dialect is needed in our country (and this is often offered as a reason for teaching a new dialect), a plausible argument could be made for achieving unity by choosing nonstandard English as the common tongue and teaching that dialect to standard speakers. In many ways this would seem much fairer than to force Standard English upon nonstandard speakers, most of whom have more than their share of problems already. To add to the problems of poverty and discrimination the burden of having to learn a new dialect seems a gross injustice. If, in the interest of uniformity, some of our people are going to have to change their language, it ought to be the more privileged members of the community. They have so many compensating advantages that they should be willing to make this sacrifice.

This suggestion, alas, is little short of ludicrous. Suggest to a standard speaker that he learn nonstandard English, and he is likely to snort with derision. Why, indeed, should he? He has no conceivable motivation for changing his speech. He already speaks the language that opens the doors of opportunity. It hardly seems profitable to urge the school boards of our white middle-class suburbs to introduce courses on how to speak nonstandard English, however much such a policy might serve the ends of equality and social justice.

3. Leave the Dialect Alone   Trying to teach nonstandard English to standard speakers is even more hopeless than trying to wipe out nonstandard English, but can we accept all dialects as equally legitimate in the classroom? A few educators have argued that spoken language, even the spoken language of nonstandard speakers, should be left entirely alone. They suggest that our diverse home dialects should all be welcome in the classroom and accepted as equally valid ways to speak, just as we accept British and American dialects as equally valid in their differing areas. If the schools worried less about correct usage, more time would be available for reading and for all the other subjects that children should study. It is certainly possible to discuss geography, mathematics, physics, or philosophy in any dialect. If Frenchmen, Japanese, and Englishmen can talk about these subjects in their own language, why can lower-class black students not talk about them in their natural language too? The schools might have a better prospect of turning out educated people if they squandered less energy in trying to change their dialect.

The policy of full acceptance of the dialect should appeal to our sense of democracy. We may feel that each man should be allowed to speak in his own way and that no child should be handicapped by having to divert his attention from other subjects while coping with a new spoken style. But the dangers of this policy are obvious. It is doubtful that even the most splendidly educated young man or woman will find employment if he continues to speak the language of the black ghetto, and many educators argue that the practical if unjust world demands the standard dialect. If a man or woman fails to learn this dialect as a child, his speech may become so firmly set that he may never be able to learn it at all.

Beyond these practical problems, there is also a more purely linguistic problem: Black spoken language can differ enough from the written language of our books and magazines to pose special obstacles when learning to read. It is often argued that a child has to speak and understand the standard language before we can hope to teach him to read. It is hardly fair to abandon a child with nothing but his nonstandard dialect if that will result in his permanent exclusion from full participation in our national life.

4. Encourage Bidialectalism Few educators argue with much conviction today for the absolute rejection of the children's home language, for they have recognized the widespread failure of the schools to replace one dialect with another, and they have become uncomfortable with the arrogance of so casually condemning the language of a child's parents. At the same time, they hardly dare leave a child with nothing but his nonstandard dialect. They seek some sort of compromise, and today thoughtful educators often support the policy of bidialectalism in which nonstandard English is regarded as an alternative and well-formed dialect that presents its speakers with problems somewhat analogous to those of a speaker of a foreign language.

When a child has foreign parents, it seems natural to accept his home language as an honorable and worthy medium of communication and to encourage the child to continue to use that language with pride. We can try to help him learn the English he will need for life in the United States without rejecting the language of his parents. We can encourage him to become bilingual. Analogously, it is argued that when we teach a child Standard English in school, we ought to avoid disparaging the nonstandard English of his home. If one child can become bilingual, another should be able to become bidialectal. He can be encouraged to speak his home dialect with his parents and even with his friends on the street, but in the practical adult world he will be impossibly handicapped if he cannot also control the forms of Standard English. One always thinks of the job interview, the terrible moment when a young man or woman has to impress someone with his intelligence and responsibility. Most interviewers expect Standard English, and in the United States today anyone who does not speak Standard English will probably be judged as hopelessly ignorant. Is the situation of the non-standard-speaking child any different from that of the child of foreign parents? If the one can learn a new language, cannot the other learn a new dialect?

Sadly, the black child is likely to have an even harder time than the child of immigrants. Several factors contribute to his difficulty. One should not, of course, minimize the difficulties that immigrants faced, or the loss of self-esteem they had to suffer, for they were also often made to feel ashamed of their native language; but the immigrants, at least, often came to America with an attitude that expected and even welcomed change. They planned to build a new life in a new country, and learning a new language could be seen as one requirement of the move. Those not wishing to change could decline to migrate. Blacks are given no choice. They have not made the personal commitment of a European immigrant, but they are still told to change. They are simply told that the language they have grown up with in their own country is inadequate. At the same time, they are subject to even more severe segregation than European immigrants ever were, and so they are given fewer natural opportunities to merge their speech with that of the surrounding community.

Differences in attitude and in the degree of segregation partly explain the relative success of European immigrants when compared with that of blacks, but the most important reason for the special difficulties faced by nonstandard speakers is certainly that nonstandard and Standard English are simply too much alike. When a child speaks a foreign language, his teacher understands his problem, and so does he. She realizes that he has to start at the beginning and understands why he cannot easily make himself understood. The teacher may have little respect for his home language, but she knows what it is. A non-standard-speaking child also comes to school with a language that differs in some respects from his teacher's, but neither he nor the teacher is as likely to grasp the nature of the difference. It is too much like Standard English. The child who speaks a foreign language can simply set aside all his old linguistic habits and start fresh. The non-standard-speaking child has a whole battery of English habits, and he cannot simply put these all aside. It is difficult for him to know which of his many English habits are acceptable in his new environment and which he must discard.

In spite of these difficulties, the goal of bidialectalism is certainly more humane than the older policy of trying to wipe out all alternative forms of English. In an attempt to encourage bidialectalism, sophisticated programs have been developed for drilling ghetto children in the forms of the new dialect. Teaching guides are available that contrast standard and nonstandard constructions. These are designed to help teachers guide their pupils into a new dialect suitable for new occasions, and they carry the stern command to the teacher not to disparage the older dialect simply because a new one is being taught. Every American child is said to "have the right" to learn Standard English so that he will be able to compete on an equal basis and share fully in all aspects of American life. (See, for instance, *Nonstandard Dialect*, published by the New York Board of Education and the National Council of Teachers of English, 1968.)

Unfortunately, a child whose parents and friends all speak one way does not have an easy time with a new dialect that he practices only with his teachers. The non-standard-speaking child hears ample Standard English on radio and television, and he may learn to understand it with ease, but if he suddenly started to talk like a radio announcer, he would sound silly to his friends on the street and impertinent to his family. Furthermore, the differences between his own and the standard dialect are far more subtle than either he or his teacher is likely to realize. If the drills for imparting Standard English were carried out consistently, they would consume a significant portion of the school day. This would inevitably cut into the time available for other subjects. Moreover, if the lessons are to be learned well, they can hardly be confined to special periods of drill. Children certainly cannot be expected to practice standard forms very faithfully at home or on the streets; so they must be encouraged to use them during all the hours they spend in school. Only if the arithmetic teacher demands Standard English, only if the geography teacher does the same, are the drills of the English teacher likely to be sufficiently reinforced to bring much change.

If all these teachers conspire to insist upon Standard English, the goals of bidialectalism are likely to be forgotten, and as the policy of bidialectalism becomes translated into daily practice in the classroom, it is likely to come across to the children as something like this: "It is all right to speak in that crude way at home and to your friends if you really want to, but while you are in this classroom, you had better speak correctly." The child may be no better off than he would be under the older policy that simply assumes one dialect to be correct. Indeed, he may be worse off, for the simplicity and clarity of the old policy is lost. Books and teachers now make pious statements about the value of the street dialect, but the faith that only one dialect is really correct runs so deep that these pious statements are often contradicted by everyday attitudes. The child fails to gain the respect that should be implied by the new policy. All that has changed is that attitudes and policies have become ambiguous.

There are other problems. Many teachers in inner-city schools, including many black teachers, have themselves struggled to escape the nonstandard dialect of their own parents. For many, the struggle has been a difficult one, but they have paid the price in order to move up the social ladder and into the teaching profession. They may have lost a bit of their heritage as they left their parents' dialect behind, but having won their struggle, they may feel justified in their contempt for others who have not made it. They may be particularly authoritarian with their pupils, particularly insistent that their pupils follow their own enlightened example.

At the same time these teachers may still be insecure about their own speech. Having learned all too well the lesson that there is but one "correct" way to speak, they may sometimes remain uncertain about exactly which form is the "correct" one. Afraid of reverting to the familiar but nonstandard patterns of her own childhood, a teacher may overcompensate and assume an excessively formal style, which can only deepen the gulf that separates her from her children. If she is sensitive, and if, like most teachers, she yearns to help her children, she may be torn by conflicting urges: to set an example of "correct" usage or to speak in the natural dialect that she herself learned as a child and that her pupils still use—the only language that either she or they can use easily to convey real human warmth and understanding. A good many teachers caught in this dilemma slide back and forth between relatively formal and relatively informal styles. This may offer a realistic example for children who may thereby be helped to learn to shift among various styles themselves. With good luck, the example set by the teacher may help them to adapt to the varied and complex situations that the world will hold for them. But few teachers have the background or the training needed to recognize just what they do when they shift styles, and the result is that they may tell their children to do one thing while demonstrating something quite different in their own speech.

I once watched a lively, intelligent teacher helping her slowest first grade reading group to sound out words. The teacher and her students were all black, and it was obvious that they enjoyed each other's company. They smiled and joked and took pleasure in the challenge of the lesson, but the children were not learning very quickly. The teacher was having them sound out words such as *pin*, *fin*, and *tin*, and to help them grasp the relationship between sound and symbol she had them say the words slowly and with exaggerated articulation: *pi-i-nnn*, *fi-i-nnn*, *ti-i-nnn*. Then, to clinch the lesson the teacher had them read more rapidly. Speaking more naturally, they now left off the final *n* of these words, but, in a manner common among black speakers and by no means unknown among whites, they nasalized the vowel in a sort of echo of the missing *n*. (We can symbolize their pronunciation as *pĩ, fĩ, tĩ*, in which the "~" indicates the nasalization of the vowel.) To pronounce the words this way struck me as skillful interpretation of the written word into their natural spoken language. The teacher smiled and said, "That's good, but I want to hear the *n*'s. I want to hear what they *soũ* like." Unaware of the patterns of her own dialect, she had used a natural pronunciation that allowed easy, rapid communication with her children. At the same time she had demonstrated by her own behavior the very thing she was telling them not to do, for she had omitted the *n* of *sound* (and the *d* as well) while nasalizing the vowel. She was a fine teacher. She was working with warmth and enthusiasm to help her children over the earliest hurdles in reading. But she had been taught that the *n*'s are supposed to be pronounced when appearing at the ends of words, and like almost all Americans, whether black or white, she was unaware that she sometimes omitted them herself.

For these many reasons it is difficult to build a serious and successful program of bidialectalism. Children spend only a few hours each day in school, and because of de facto school segregation, much of their time even in school is spent speaking to and listening to other children who share their dialect. As we have just seen, even the teachers in inner-city schools may have inconsistent or uncertain control over the standard language. Faced with this situation, practical teachers may decide that if they are ever going to get any arithmetic or history across to their children, they will have to compromise on the language. A bit guiltily, perhaps, they let the children speak in whatever way they can, so long as they seem to learn their other lessons. Immersed from morning to night in the nonstandard language of his community, the child has little chance to learn standard. All he is likely to learn is shame and uncertainty about his own speech. The bidialectal program has collapsed.

We seem to be left with four bad policies. Americans like to imagine that every problem is matched with an ideal solution, but here we seem to have a problem with nothing but poor solutions. Yet the problem will not go away. Teachers have to face it, and if there is no single ideal solution, we will have to search for a compromise that avoids the worst pitfalls of each of the existing alternatives. Perhaps we can dismiss the first one, that of trying to wipe out nonstandard English, for it is a solution that is not only arrogant in principle but futile in practice. Perhaps we can also dismiss the second, that of teaching nonstandard English to standard speakers, since it is surely hopeless in practice. We might at least try to teach standard speakers something *about* nonstandard English, however. We will never convert them to the use of nonstandard, but we might give them an understanding of what nonstandard English is like and why some people speak it. We might encourage a greater tolerance among the privileged segment of our nation for dialect diversity. Putting these two policies aside, however, we are left with the third and fourth, that of permitting and even encouraging the use of nonstandard English and that of encouraging bidialectalism. What seems to be called for is some kind of compromise between these two. The following sections offer a few suggestions about the kind of compromise toward which we might reasonably work.

Priorities

We can begin to cut through our difficulties by recognizing that we are not really faced with so simple a question as whether or not to teach Standard English. Instead, we have the far more complex question of what aspects of Standard English to teach and of when in a child's education to present them. Perhaps we can agree without too much argument that we have a number of priorities. We might like a child to have all of the following language skills, but those high on the list seem to have priority over those that follow:

1. Ability to understand the spoken language of the teacher.
2. Ability to make oneself understood to the teacher.
3. Ability to read and understand conventional written English.
4. Ability to speak with standard grammar.
5. Ability to write with the conventions of standard written English.
6. Ability to speak with standard pronunciation.

Teaching and learning each of these six skills present somewhat special problems. We will complicate every issue if we confuse them.

Understanding and Being Understood   We can start by recognizing that a child who can understand the language of his teacher shows that he has already taken the first, and most important step in learning Standard English. American children, even the impoverished children of the ghettoes, spend long hours before the television set, and most of the dialogue they hear approximates Standard

English. A child who has listened to thousands of hours of television will probably understand the English of his teachers without much difficulty. When a child does have trouble, it is usually overcome in his early school years by the natural willingness of those who talk to small children to speak simply enough and repetitiously enough to get them to understand. Getting even the poorest, most segregated child to understand the spoken English of his teachers, then, is rarely a serious problem. The first, most fundamental step in language education is usually accomplished with little or no help from the schools.

Second only to understanding is the reciprocal ability to make oneself understood, and on this point the testimony of teachers is somewhat varied. Many teachers who work in ghetto schools, including many middle-class white teachers from quite different backgrounds, claim to have had no serious difficulty understanding their children. In extreme situations, where dialect differences are at a maximum, problems occasionally arise.

Part of the difficulty surely lies in the attitude of some teachers. A teacher who is rigid, one who is contemptuous of the way her children talk, may, consciously or unconsciously, be unwilling to adapt to her children's style, and she may report that she cannot understand them. Another teacher, less rigid in her outlook and emotionally more willing to meet them halfway, may find that she can understand them with no great difficulty. With small children, certainly, but probably with older children as well, much of the burden of adaptation should surely lie with the teacher. We might remember the old Army rule: Never order a man to do what you would be unwilling to do yourself. If we apply the same rule to a classroom, we can suggest that any teacher who asks her children to learn *her* kind of English ought, at least, to be willing to understand their kind of English.

Whatever difficulties in understanding exist would be eased if teachers could concentrate upon the goal of communicating ideas and information and worry less about the superficial details of style. In Europe, where those who speak entirely different languages must often cooperate, people manage to get their ideas across. Even the casual traveler who really wants to say something experiments to find the words that seem to work and supplements them with gestures and smiles. When people are eager enough to communicate, they can make themselves understood across far wider, deeper language barriers than any that divide standard and nonstandard English.

A teacher who really wants to speak with her children quite naturally experiments until she finds the words and expressions that are most successful. This does not mean that she has to learn to speak the nonstandard English of her children. Any deliberate attempt to imitate their dialect would be awkward and stilted, and any teacher who mimics her children's speech is likely to have her best efforts interpreted as mocking. The children will soon detect the artificiality of her language. But a teacher who finds herself naturally using words and expressions that she has learned from her children need hardly feel guilty about it. As long as they come naturally, these expressions are a sign of interest and of respect. Whether or not a teacher ever uses a single word that she learns from her children, however, she owes them at least the courtesy of working to understand their natural language. This is only courteous reciprocity for her expectation that they will work to understand hers. If the teacher can demonstrate her genuine interest to her children, they will naturally be encouraged to meet her halfway. They, too, will search for ways to make themselves understood. At this stage it is far more important to encourage the natural eagerness of children to talk and to give them confidence in their ability to express themselves freely in their own dialect than it is to worry about details of their spoken style. A teacher must at least learn to understand their home dialect easily enough to make them feel comfortable with her. They must be encouraged to speak freely and easily.

Usually it is the teacher who really prefers not to speak with her children who has the most difficulties. The children quickly grasp the fact that she is uninterested in them, and unconsciously they react by refusing to make adjustments in their own language. The teacher may rationalize her difficulties by blaming them upon the language barrier. She may then focus even more attention on the form of the language, drilling the children on new grammar and pronunciation. Sadly, this may have an effect exactly the opposite of that desired, for whether or not the drills accomplish anything in teaching new grammatical patterns, they clearly demonstrate the teacher's stubbornness about her form of the language. The children are all too likely to respond with the same kind of stubbornness about *their* form of the language and, actively or passively, to reject the suggestion that they change. Children probably absorb more of their teacher's language when they work together with enthusiasm on a project in history or science or art, paying no outward attention to language at all, than when they struggle with language drills that tend to put the dialects in competition with each other and to put the children on the defensive.

It must be stressed again, however, that mutual understanding between teacher and child is not the major problem. All but a small minority of teachers have enough natural goodwill and adaptability to bridge whatever dialect differences divide them from their children. Perhaps what teachers need most is simply to be reassured that they are by no means neglecting their duties when they refrain from criticizing dialect patterns so that they can encourage free, natural self-expression.

Speaking Standard English The priority that follows understanding and making oneself understood is reading. This is such a complex and important topic that it deserves a chapter of its own, and, accordingly, the final chapter of this book considers reading in some detail. One of the conclusions must be anticipated here, however. I argue that the ability to speak Standard English is *not* a prerequisite for learning to read Standard English. You may want to reserve final judgment about this conclusion until you consider the arguments as they are presented in full later: I realize that only if it seems possible to teach reading without first teaching a new dialect can it make sense to postpone deliberate effort to teach standard spoken English until late in a child's education. Since I believe that this is possible, I maintain that the major effort of the primary school should be in reading and that instruction in speaking Standard English can safely wait until later.[1]

For many years to come, however, the realities of our discriminatory society will persuade many older children that they must learn to speak Standard English, and when a young person decides for himself that he wants to gain proficiency in the prestige dialect, our schools owe him all the help they can give. By clearly separating the task of learning to read from the task of learning to produce a new oral style, and by postponing all explicit attention to the second task until the child is old enough to be well motivated, both tasks might be greatly simplified.

Motivation is all-important. It is hopeless to teach a new dialect to a child or youth who has no desire to learn it. It is arrogant even to try. If every American should have the "right" to speak Standard English if he so desires, it ought to be equally insisted that it is the right of every American *not* to speak Standard English if he does not want to. Schools would simplify their task if they could separate those students who want to learn to speak the new dialect from those who do not; and since high schools in the United States offer a good deal of choice among courses, it should not be too difficult to provide alternate English classes, some announced as spending time on Standard English, others not. This would not be a matter of "tracking," for there need be no real or implied prestige attached to either choice, any more than there is prestige attached to the choice between music and art. But by offering students a choice, those with the least motivation to learn Standard English might be removed from the class, and this would leave the rest with a better chance of success. Given the choice, many lower-class students would certainly select the course that offered them help with Standard English, and simply by forcing them to make a choice, some of the burden of stimulating motivation would be shifted to the students.

One way of encouraging students and one way of making the goal of bidialectalism seem attainable might be to have them instructed by bidialectal teachers. It seems a bit unreasonable to expect our young people to become bidialectal if we cannot demonstrate to them that such a thing is possible. Can they retain their respect for their older dialect while learning a new one if their teacher is unwilling to make a similar switch herself? One might suppose that only a genuinely bidialectal teacher could effectively communicate the idea that two ways of talking can both have an honorable place in a man's life.

The situation would also be simplified if we could concentrate our efforts upon the most severely stigmatized aspects of nonstandard speech. Nonstandard grammar, for instance, is far more stigmatized than nonstandard pronunciation. Americans are relatively tolerant of diverse pronunciation as long as the grammar conforms to the standard, and this should allow us to concentrate our efforts on grammar. It is for this reason that standard pronunciation was shown with the lowest priority in the list given earlier in this chapter, but there is probably little the schools can do about pronunciation anyway. The only people who are likely to acquire a new, more prestigious pronunciation are those who decide for themselves that they want to do so, and perhaps the best advice we can give them is to suggest that they imitate those whose pronunciation they admire. With pronunciation, even more than with grammar, motivation is crucial. The schools can do little to motivate unwilling students, but the relative American tolerance for diverse pronunciation makes it unnecessary for them to try.

In view of this, then, if the teacher wants to help her students adjust to the prejudices of the dominant society (and there is no other reason for teaching Standard English), she ought to concentrate on those aspects of the language that are most likely to evoke negative responses. Since she cannot possibly change everything, she would be well advised to concentrate all her attention on helping her pupils to substitute prestige grammatical forms for the most stigmatized of their earlier patterns. How can she help them?

Sadly, neither of the two most obvious techniques holds much hope for success. These are (1) to correct random "errors" as teachers have always done, and (2) to proceed as we do in second-language instruction—that is, to start at the very beginning and build the new dialect step by step, just as one must build an entirely new language. Why are these two techniques so unpromising?

To try to correct random "errors" is too unsystematic. No teacher can ever correct all the stigmatized forms in her pupils' speech. She may not even notice many of them, particularly if she is interested enough in her students to listen to what they say, so that she does not spend all her energies in merely listening to how they say it. The best she can do is to make corrections part of the time, while at other times she may let the same "errors" slip by. She may be able to say that a construction is stigmatized but be unable to explain what should be substituted for it. Moreover, the random correction of "errors" is a dismally negative process. It is destined to strip students of all motivation.

To imagine that we must start from scratch and build up what amounts to an entirely new language may seem to be a more positive approach. Certainly it could be more systematic than the correction of random errors. It fails, however, to capitalize upon the enormous amount of English that the pupils have already mastered. To treat Standard English like a foreign language condemns a child to "learning" a great deal in this new "language" that he has thoroughly mastered in his old. This is an utter waste of everybody's time and energy.

What seems to be called for, then, is neither random correction of errors nor a completely fresh beginning but rather a systematic comparison between the two dialects and systematic instruction in how to convert forms of one dialect to those of the other. If a student can understand how negatives and interrogatives are formed in the two dialects, he might learn to switch from one pattern to the other. In effect, he must learn to translate, and anyone hoping to teach Standard English must be prepared to teach skillful translation.

To do this, of course, the teacher should herself be a good translator, or she must at least have a clear understanding of the differences between the dialects. She must understand which forms are equivalent and be able to help her students learn to select the Standard English forms when the situation calls for them. What is needed is an educational program that builds upon what the students already know and that helps them to expand and develop the linguistic system they have already mastered. The teacher needs a thorough understanding of the grammatical patterns of her students and of the ways in which standard and nonstandard English differ. It should not be necessary either to wipe out the old system or to make people ashamed of their older language, and it is misleading to imagine that the new style represents something entirely new.

One promising technique for helping students to learn new dialect patterns is to have them act out small dramatic situations. The students can assume varying roles—reporter, doctor, employer, policeman, salesman, and so on—but their lines should be spontaneously produced rather than memorized. Skits could involve either dramatic, realistic situations or humorous ones, but in any case the students should act out roles that are not their usual ones. Challenged to act as realistically as possible, they must assume the speech styles used by people of different backgrounds or different social classes; and if the various members of the class take turns acting out similar skits, they can profit by the example of others, so that each student can seek to improve his own performance. Such role playing provides a situation where varying verbal styles can be deliberately assumed and then deliberately set aside, and it clarifies, as no other type of instruction is likely to do, exactly what is required when one must switch styles in real life. The youth who hopes to approximate Standard English in a job interview must respond to a dramatic challenge that is not entirely different from that of a classroom skit. In the job interview, as in the skit, rewards go to the skillful actor and the skillful role player. As a technique for teaching a student to assume Standard English, this type of deliberate role playing should have the profound advantage over most other techniques of instruction of posing no threat to the student's own role in life. With a technique that is fun rather than threatening, students can gradually help themselves and each other gain confidence and skill in acting out new roles and the new speech styles appropriate to these roles (June R. McKay, John Waterhouse, Sylvia Taba, and Shirley Silver, Report on Neighborhood Youth Corps Summer Language Program, University of California, Berkeley, Mimeo, 1968).

Other than a modest amount of explicit instruction in Standard English patterns and some practice with role playing, the most effective way to lay a foundation for speaking Standard English is probably to give it as little explicit attention as possible. People always tend naturally to imitate the language of those whom they most admire, and children are most likely to admire those who respect them as they are, not those who are intent on changing them. The teacher who works constructively with her children on projects having nothing to do with language may be the most effective model of language use, a model that the children will naturally want to imitate. The language arts teacher who carefully corrects her children's speech but who is not much concerned with the content of what they say will evoke little but antagonism. Nobody will want to imitate her. Without even trying, a gym teacher or science teacher may convey more of the standard language than the English teacher who is armed with the most sophisticated, up-to-date linguistic techniques. The emotional reactions of children and of teachers toward one another are all-important in promoting or inhibiting the imitation of language. No technique will work if the emotional climate is unsuitable. This is one good reason for postponing any explicit instruction in Standard English at least until high school, when the students can understand and agree upon the objectives.

Conclusions

When we teach standard grammar, we are doing no more and no less than teaching verbal etiquette, teaching people to mimic the style of the more privileged classes. While we can hardly refuse the requests of nonstandard speakers when they ask for help in achieving the prestige forms, many teachers will always be uncomfortable with the job.

We do not want to teach people to be ashamed of their own background or to make them pretend to be something they are not, but when we teach a new form of speech, we must try, quite deliberately, to help our students hoodwink those in authority, to fool those who guard the gates to higher education and the doors to employment. There is simply no other reason to teach standard grammar. And even as we help students with standard grammar, we must admit to serious doubts about our chances for success. Those in power do not really discriminate against the language itself so much as they discriminate against people. Language is only a convenient symbol, an excuse to exclude those who are disliked. Even if the language of lower-class black Americans more and more approaches the standard, it is unlikely ever to become identical with the language of privileged whites until there is a complete end to segregation and complete social equality. As long as any difference in language remains, no matter how trivial that difference may be, it can serve as a pretext for discrimination.

If the present linguistic differences seem to be great, it is easy to imagine that by reducing them we will ease the problem of discrimination. We may instead merely produce discrimination on the grounds of ever more subtle linguistic differences. In the end we must acknowledge that it is not language that determines social relationships, but rather it is the social relations that are reflected in the way people speak. When society ceases to discriminate, linguistic differences will either disappear or will cease to matter. Until society stops discriminating, any tiny linguistic trait can be seized upon in justification. It seems unlikely that even the most sophisticated program imaginable for teaching a new dialect will ever be a match for the ability of men to discriminate against their brothers.

NOTE

1. We have abundant and persuasive evidence that the ability to speak is in no way a prerequisite either for the ability to understand or for the ability to read. As they are learning their language, all children are able to understand far more than they can actually say, and adults can always read certain passages that they would have difficulty reproducing. An obvious example: Standard-speaking adults have very little difficulty reading and understand-

ing a nonstandard passage. More dramatic evidence can be obtained from the occasional child who has severely crippled vocal organs but who is otherwise normal. Such a child can learn to understand spoken language perfectly without ever saying a word. Deaf-mutes can become fluent readers even when they can neither hear nor speak. There may be sound reasons why a child might want to learn Standard English. Its need as a foundation for reading is certainly not one of them. [See Headnote for a brief summary of what Burling argues in his final chapter. Eds.]

STUDENTS' RIGHT TO THEIR OWN LANGUAGE

Committee on the CCCC Language Statement

In April 1974, the membership of the Conference on College Composition and Communication (CCCC), a subdivision of the influential National Council of Teachers of English, adopted the bold resolution and accompanying background statement reprinted below. Basically, this resolution adduces current linguistic research in an attempt to reverse the stand on language diversity prevalent for two hundred years in American schools. Whereas English teachers at all levels have traditionally tried to enforce Burling's first alternative ("Wipe out nonstandard English"), the CCCC now proposes that they support his third alternative ("Leave the dialect alone") instead—a more radical approach than Burling's. The profound effect that such a change would have on teaching methods, materials, and attitudes can scarcely be overestimated. Educators therefore need to scrutinize the implications of this statement, comparing the sections on reading and standardized testing with the more detailed ones in the Wolfram and Christian selection.

The present extract omits several sections between the "Introduction" and "Does Dialect Affect the Ability to Read?" because they repeat basic sociolinguistic concepts outlined in the "Variation in Language" section of the General Introduction. Also omitted are a concluding list of areas in language study that English teachers should know something about and a lengthy bibliography of readings in sociolinguistics.

Introduction

American schools and colleges have, in the last decade, been forced to take a stand on a basic educational question: what should the schools do about the language habits of students who come from a wide variety of social, economic, and cultural backgrounds? The question is not new. Differences in language have always existed, and the schools have always wrestled with them, but the social upheavals of the 1960s, and the insistence of submerged minorities on a greater share in American society, have posed the question more insistently and have suggested the need for a shift in emphasis in providing answers. Should the schools try to uphold language variety, or to modify it, or to eradicate it?

The emotional nature of the controversy has obscured the complexities of the problem and hidden some of the assumptions that must be examined before any kind of rational policy can be adopted. The human use of language is not a simple phenomenon: sophisticated research in linguistics and sociology has demonstrated incontrovertibly that many long held and passionately cherished notions about language are misleading at best, and often completely erroneous. On the other hand, linguistic research, advanced as much of it is, has not yet produced any absolute, easily understood explanation of how people acquire language or how habits acquired so early in life that they defy conscious analysis can be consciously changed. Nor is the linguistic information that is available very widely disseminated. The training of most English teachers has concentrated on the appreciation and analysis of literature, rather than on an understanding of the nature of language, and many teachers are, in consequence, forced to take a position on an aspect of their discipline about which they have little real information.

And if teachers are often uninformed, or misinformed, on the subject of language, the general public is even more ignorant. Lack of reliable information, however, seldom prevents people from discussing language questions with an air of absolute authority. Historians, mathematicians, and nurses all hold decided views on just what English teachers should be requiring. And through their representatives on Boards of Education and Boards of Regents, businessmen, politicians, parents, and the students themselves insist that the values taught by the schools must reflect the prejudices held by the public. The English profession, then, faces a dilemma: until public attitudes can be changed—and it is worth remembering that the past teaching in English classes has been largely responsible for those attitudes—shall we place our emphasis on what the vocal elements of the public think it wants or on what the actual available linguistic evidence indicates we should emphasize? Shall we blame the business world by saying, "Well, we realize that human beings use language in a wide variety of ways, but employers demand a single variety"?

Before these questions can be responsibly answered, English teachers at all levels, from kindergarten through college, must uncover and examine some of the assumptions on which our teaching has rested. Many of us have taught as though there existed somewhere a single American "Standard English" which could be isolated, identified, and accurately defined. We need to know whether "Standard English" is or is not in some sense a myth. We have ignored, many of us, the distinction between speech and writing and have taught the language as though the *talk* in any region, even the talk of speakers with prestige and power, were identical to edited *written* English.

We have also taught, many of us, as though the "English of educated speakers," the language used by those in power in the community, had an inherent advantage over other dialects as a means of expressing thought or emotion, conveying information, or analyzing concepts. We need to discover whether our attitudes toward "educated English" are based on some inherent superiority of the dialect itself or on the social prestige of those who use it. We need to ask ourselves whether our rejection of students who do not adopt the dialect most familiar to us is based on any real merit in our dialect or whether we are actually rejecting the students themselves, rejecting them because of their racial, social, and cultural origins.

And many of us have taught as though the function of schools and colleges were to erase differences. Should we, on the one hand, urge creativity and individuality in the arts and the sciences, take pride in the diversity of our historical development, and, on the other hand, try to obliterate all the differences in the way Americans speak and write? Our major emphasis has been on uniformity, in both speech and writing; would we accomplish more, both educationally and ethically, if we shifted that emphasis to precise, effective, and appropriate communication in diverse ways, whatever the dialect?

Students are required by law to attend schools for most of their adolescent years, and are usually required by curriculum makers to take English every one of those years, often including "developmental" or "compensatory" English well into college if their native dialect varies from that of the middle class. The result is that students who come from backgrounds where the prestigious variety of English is the normal medium of communication have built-in advantages that enable them to succeed, often in spite of and not because of, their schoolroom training in "grammar." They sit at the head of the class, are accepted at "exclusive" schools, and are later rewarded with positions in the business and social world. Students whose nurture and experience give them a different dialect are usually denied these rewards. As English teachers, we are responsible for what our teaching does to the self-image and the self-esteem of our students. We must decide what elements of our discipline are really important to us, whether we want to share with our students the richness of all varieties of language, encourage linguistic virtuosity, and say with Langston Hughes:

I play it cool and dig all jive
That's the reason I stay alive
My motto as I live and learn
Is to dig and be dug in return.

It was with these concerns in mind that the Executive Committee of the Conference on College Composition and Communication, in 1972, passed the following resolution:

We affirm the students' right to their own patterns and varieties of language—the dialects of their nurture or whatever dialects in which they find their own identity and style. Language scholars long ago denied that the myth of a standard American dialect has any validity. The claim that any one dialect is unacceptable amounts to an attempt of one social group to exert its dominance over another. Such a claim leads to false advice for speakers and writers, and immoral advice for humans. A nation proud of its diverse heritage and its cultural and racial variety will preserve its heritage of dialects. We affirm strongly that teachers must have the experiences and training that will enable them to respect diversity and uphold the right of students to their own language.

The members of the Committee realized that the resolution would create controversy and that without a clear explanation of the linguistic and social knowledge on which it rests, many people would find it incomprehensible. The members of the Executive Committee, therefore, requested a background statement which would examine some common misconceptions about language and dialect, define some key terms, and provide some suggestions for sounder, alternate approaches. What follows is not, then, an introductory course in linguistics, nor is it a teaching guide. It is, we hope, an answer to some of the questions the resolution will raise.

Does Dialect Affect the Ability to Read?

The linguistic concepts can bring a new understanding of the English teacher's function in dealing with reading and writing skills. Schools and colleges emphasize one form of language, the one we called Edited American English (EAE). It is the written language of the weekly newsmagazines, of almost all newspapers, and of most books. This variety of written English can be loosely termed a dialect, and it has preempted a great deal of attention in English classes.

If a speaker of any dialect of a language has competence (but not necessarily the ability to perform) in any other dialect of that language, then dialect itself cannot be posited as a reason for a student's failure to be able to read EAE. That is, dialect itself is not in impediment to reading, for the process of reading involves decoding to meaning (deep structure),[1] not decoding to an utterance. Thus the child who reads

Phillip's mother is in Chicago.

out loud as

Phillip mother in Chicago.

has read correctly, that is, has translated the surface of an EAE sentence into a meaning and has used his own dialect to give a surface form to that meaning. Reading, in short, involves the acquisition of meanings, not the ability to reproduce meanings in any given surface forms.

Reading difficulties may be a result of inadequate vocabulary, problems in perception, ignorance of contextual cues that aid in the reading process, lack of familiarity with stylistic ordering, interference from the emotional bias of the material, or combinations of these. In short, reading is so complicated a process that it provides temptations to people who want to offer easy explanations and solutions.

This larger view should make us cautious about the assumption that the students' dialect interferes with learning to read. Proceeding from such a premise, current "dialect" readers employ one of two methods. Some reading materials are written completely in the students' dialect with the understanding that later the students will be switched to materials written in the "standard" dialect. Other materials are written in companion sets of "home" version and "school" version. Students first read through the "dialect" version, then through the *same* booklet written in "school" English. Both methods focus primarily on a limited set of surface linguistic features, as for example, the deletion of *ed* in past tense verbs or the deletion of *r* in final position.

To cope with our students' reading problem, then, we cannot confine ourselves to the constricting and ultimately ineffectual dialect readers designed for the "culturally deprived." We should structure and select materials geared to complex reading problems and oriented to the experience and sophistication of our students. An urban eight-year-old who has seen guns and knives in a street fight may not be much interested in reading how Jane's dog Spot dug in the neighbor's flower bed. Simply because "Johnny can't read" doesn't mean "Johnny is immature" or "Johnny can't think." He may be bored. Carefully chosen materials will certainly expose students to new horizons and should increase their awareness and heighten their perceptions of the social reality. Classroom reading materials can be employed to further our students' reading ability and, at the same time, can familiarize them with other varieties of English.

Admittedly, the kinds of materials we're advocating are, at present, difficult to find, but some publishers are beginning to move in this direction. In the meantime, we can use short, journalistic pieces, such as those found on the editorial pages of newspapers, we might rely on materials composed by our students, and we can certainly write our own materials. The important fact to remember is that speakers in any dialect encounter essentially the same difficulties in reading, and thus we should not be so much interested in changing our students' dialect as in improving their command of the reading process.

Does Dialect Affect the Ability to Write?

The ability to write EAE is quite another matter, for learning to write a given dialect, like learning to speak a dialect, involves the activation of areas of competence. Further, learning to write in any dialect entails the mastery of such conventions as spelling and punctuation, surface features of the written language. Again, native speakers of *any* dialect of a language have virtually total competence in all dialects of that language, but they may not have learned (and may never learn) to punctuate or spell, and, indeed, may not even learn the mechanical skill of forming letters and sequences of letters with a writing instrument. And even if they do, they may have other problems in transferring ease and fluency in speech to skill in writing.

Even casual observation indicates that dialect as such plays little if any part in determining whether a child will ultimately acquire the ability to write EAE. In fact, if speakers of a great variety of American dialects do master EAE—from Senator Sam Ervin to Senator Edward Kennedy, from Ernest Hemingway to William Faulkner—there is no reason to assume that dialects such as urban black and Chicano impede the child's ability to learn to write EAE while countless others do not. Since the issue is not the capacity of the dialect itself, the teacher can concentrate on building up the students' confidence in their ability to write.

If we name the essential functions of writing as expressing oneself, communicating information and attitudes, and discovering meaning through both logic and metaphor, then we view variety of dialects as an advantage. In self-expression, not only one's dialect but one's idiolect is basic. In communication one may choose roles which imply certain dialects, but the decision is a social one, for the dialect itself does not limit the information which can be carried, and the attitudes may be most clearly conveyed in the dialect the writer finds most congenial. Dialects are all equally serviceable in logic and metaphor.

Perhaps the most serious difficulty facing "nonstandard" dialect speakers in developing writing ability derives from their exaggerated concern for the *least* serious aspects of writing. If we can convince our students that spelling, punctuation, and usage are less important than content, we have removed a major obstacle in their developing the ability to write. Examples of student writing are useful for illustrating this point. In every composition class there are examples of writing which is clear and vigorous despite the use of nonstandard forms (at least as described by the handbook)—and there are certainly many examples of limp, vapid writing in "standard dialect." Comparing the writing allows the students to see for themselves that dialect seldom obscures clear, forceful writing. EAE is important for certain kinds of students, its features are easily identified and taught, and school patrons are often satisfied when it is mastered, but that should not tempt teachers to evade the still more important features of language.

When students want to play roles in dialects other than their own, they should be encouraged to experiment, but they can acquire the fundamental skills of writing in their own dialect. Their experiments are ways of becoming more versatile. We do not condone ill-organized, imprecise, undefined, inappropriate writing in any dialect; but we are especially distressed to find sloppy writing approved so long as it appears with finicky correctness in "school standard" while vigorous and thoughtful statements in less prestigious dialects are condemned.

Does Dialect Limit the Ability to Think?

All languages are the product of the same instrument, namely, the human brain. It follows, then, that all languages and all dialects are essentially the same in their deep structure, regardless of how varied the surface structures might be. (This is equal to saying that the human brain is the human brain.) And if these hypotheses are true, all controversies over dialect will take on a new dimension. The question will no longer turn on language per se, but will concern the nature of a society which places great value on given surface features of language and proscribes others, for any language or any dialect will serve any purpose that its users want it to serve.

There is no evidence, in fact, that enables us to describe any language or any dialect as incomplete or deficient apart from the conditions of its use. The limits of a particular speaker should not be interpreted as a limit of the dialect.

Just as people suppose that speakers who omit the plural inflection as in "six cow" instead of "six cows" cannot manipulate the concept of plurality, so also some believe that absence of tense markers as in "yesterday they *look* at the flood damage" indicates that the speaker has no concept of time. Yet these same people have no difficulty in understanding the difference between "now I *cut* the meat/yesterday I *cut* the meat," also without a tense marker. The alternative forms are adequate to express meaning.

And experience tells us that when speakers of any dialect need a new word for a new thing, they will invent or learn the needed word. Just as most Americans added "sputnik" to their vocabularies a decade or more ago, so speakers of other dialects can add such words as "periostitis" or "interosculate" whenever their interests demand it.

What Is the Background for Teaching One "Grammar"?

Since the eighteenth century, English grammar has come to mean for most people the rules telling one how to speak and write in the best society. When social groups were clearly stratified into "haves" and "have-nots," there was no need for defensiveness about variations in language—the landlord could understand the speech of the stable boy, and neither of them worried about language differences. But when social and economic changes increased social mobility, the members of the "rising middle class," recently liberated from and therefore immediately threatened by the lower class, demanded books of rules telling them how to act in ways that would not betray their background and would solidly establish them in their newly acquired social group. Rules regulating social behavior were compiled in books of etiquette; rules regulating linguistic behavior were compiled in dictionaries and grammar books. Traditional grammar books were unapologetically designed to instill linguistic habits which, though often inconsistent with actual language practice and sometimes in violation of common sense, were intended to separate those who had "made it" from those who had not, the powerful from the poor.

Practices developed in England in the eighteenth century were transported wholesale to the New World. Linguistic snobbery was tacitly encouraged by a slavish reliance on rules "more honored in the breach than the observance," and these attitudes had consequences far beyond the realm of language. People from different language and ethnic backgrounds were denied social privileges, legal rights, and economic opportunity, and their inability to manipulate the dialect used by the privileged group was used as an excuse for this denial. Many teachers, moved by the image of the "melting pot," conscientiously tried to eliminate every vestige of behavior not sanctioned in the grammar books, and the schools rejected as failures all those children who did not conform to the linguistic prejudices of the ruling middle class. With only slight modifications, many of our "rules," much of the "grammar" we still teach, reflect that history of social climbing and homogenizing.

What Do We Do about Handbooks?

Many handbooks still appeal to social-class etiquette and cultural stasis rather than to the dynamic and creative mechanisms which are a part of our language. They attempt to show one public dialect (EAE) which generates its own writing situations and its own restraints. By concentrating almost exclusively on EAE, such handbooks encourage a restrictive language bias. They thus ignore many situations which require other precise uses of language. We know that American English is pluralistic. We know that our students can and do function in a growing multiplicity of language situations which require different dialects, changing interconnections of dialects, and dynamic uses of language. But many handbooks often present only the usage of EAE for both written and spoken communication. Usage choices are presented as single-standard etiquette rules rather than as options for effective expression. This restrictive attitude toward usage is intensified by the way school grammar is presented as a series of directives in which word choice, syntax, surface features of grammar, and manuscript conventions are lumped together in guides of "correctness." These restrictive handbooks, by their very nature, encourage their users toward imitation, not toward generation of original written statements. By appealing to what is labeled "proper," they encourage an elitist attitude. The main values they transmit are stasis, restriction, manners, status, and imitation.

Teachers who are required to use such handbooks must help their students understand the implied restrictions of these texts. At best they are brief descriptions of the main features of EAE, and they clearly point out the limits of their own structures. Students should be encouraged to think of the handbook simply as a very limited language resource, and to recognize that its advice usually ignores the constraints of the situation. We alter our choices to create appropriate degrees of social intimacy. You don't talk to your kids as if they were a senate committee. A personal letter is not a technical report. Students use different forms of language in talking to their friends than they use in addressing their teachers; they use yet another style of language in communications with their parents or younger children; boys speak differently to boys when they are in the presence of girls than when the boys are alone, and so on—the list can be expanded indefinitely by altering the circumstances of time, place, and situation.

The man who says, "He had a pain in his neck, the kind you get when you've suffered a bore too long," is creating an emotional bond with his hearers. Using the handbook rule, "avoid unnecessary shifts in person," to criticize the speaker's choice denies a very important language skill, a sense of how to adjust the tone to the situation.

Furthermore, students need to recognize the difference between handbook rules and actual performance. When, after a half hour's work on pronoun reference practice, carefully changing "everyone/their" to "everyone/his," the teacher says, "Everyone can hand in their papers now," students can recognize the limits of the rule. They can compare the handbook's insistence on "the reason that" with the practice of the national newscaster who says, "the reason for the price increase is because. . . ." They can go on to consider what assumption underlies the claim that "he does" is always clearer than "he do."

By discussions of actual student writing both students and teachers can learn to appreciate the value of variant dialects and recognize that a deviation from the handbook rules seldom interferes with communication. The student who writes, "The Black Brother just don't believe he's going to be treated like a man anyway," is making himself completely clear. Students and teachers can go on to discuss situations in which adherence to handbook rules might actually damage the effectiveness of the writing. Through such discussions of tone, style, and situation, students and teachers can work together to develop a better understanding of the nature of language and a greater flexibility and versatility in the choices they make. The handbook in its clearly limited role can then be serviceable within the framework of a flexible rhetoric.

How Can Students Be Offered Dialect Options?

Teachers need to sensitize their students to the options they already exercise, particularly in speaking, so as to help them gain confidence in communicating in a variety of situations. Classroom assignments should be structured to help students make shifts in tone, style, sentence structure and length, vocabulary, diction, and order; in short, to do what they are already doing, better. Since dialects are patterns of choice among linguistic options, assignments which require variety will also open issues of dialect.

Role playing in imaginary situations is one effective way of illustrating such options, especially if the situations are chosen to correspond with a reality familiar to the students. Materials that demonstrate the effective use of variant dialects are also useful. A novel like John O. Killens' *Cotillion*, for instance, combines an exciting, coherent narrative structure with a rich, versatile range of black speech patterns used in various social situations, and thus can be used to show both literary and linguistic artistry.

Discussions must always emphasize the effectiveness of the various options, and must avoid the simplistic and the patronizing. Tapes, drills, and other instructional materials which do nothing more than contrast surface features (the lack of *s* in third person singular present tense verbs, or *ed* in past tense verbs, for instance) do not offer real options. Instead, because they are based on a "difference-equals-deficit" model, they imply that the students' own dialects are inferior and somehow "wrong" and that therefore the students' homes, the culture in which they learned their language, are also "wrong." Such simplistic approaches are not only destructive of the students' self-confidence, they fail to deal with larger and more significant options.

Linguistic versatility includes more than handbook conformity. Becoming aware of a variety of pitch patterns and rhythms in speech can reduce failures in understanding caused by unfamiliarity with the cadence another speaker uses. Listening for whole contexts can increase the ability to recognize the effect of such ponderous words as "notwithstanding" or "nevertheless" as well as pick up the meaning of unfamiliar names of things. Recognizing contradictions and failures in logic can help students concentrate on the "sense" of their communication rather than on its form. Identifying the ways language is used in politics and advertising can help students see when they are being manipulated and reduce their vulnerability to propaganda. Practice in exercising options can make students realize that vividness, precision, and accuracy can be achieved in any dialect, and can help them see that sloppiness and imprecision are irresponsible choices in any dialect—that good speech and good writing ultimately have little to do with traditional notions of surface "correctness."

By building on what students are already doing well as part of their successes in daily living, we can offer them dialect options which will increase rather than diminish their self-esteem, and by focusing on the multiple aspects of the communication process, we can be sure we are dealing with the totality of language, not merely with the superficial features of "polite usage."

What Do We Do about Standardized Tests?

Standardized tests depend on verbal fluency, both in reading the directions and in giving the answers; so even slight variations in dialect may penalize students by slowing them down. Not only are almost all standardized tests written in test jargon and focused on EAE, they also incorporate social, cultural, and racial biases which cannot hold for all students. Rural Americans may not know much about street life, and urban students will know little about the habits of cows. Words like "punk," "boody," or "joog," if they appeared in tests, would favor one dialect group over others. Tests which emphasize capitalization, punctuation, and "polite usage" favor one restrictive dialect. Even literature tests which emphasize the reading lists of the traditional anthologies favor one kind of school literature. Consequently, those students fluent in test jargon and familiar with the test subject matter are excessively rewarded.

Another problem of standardized tests is that they may further restrict the students' worlds and ultimately penalize both those who do well and those who "fail." Those who succeed may become so locked into the rewarding language patterns that they restrict their modes of expression and become less tolerant of others' modes. Those who do not succeed may be fluent in their own dialects but, because they are unable to show their fluency, get a mistaken sense of inferiority from the scores they receive.

Some test makers have recognized these biases and are trying to correct them, but theories governing test construction and interpretation remain contradictory. At least four major theories begin with different images and assumptions about genetic and environmental forces or verbal fluency and differences. To some extent the theory of test construction controls test results. In a sense, what goes in also comes out and thus tests tend to be self-validating. Furthermore, test results are reported in terms of comparisons with the groups used for standardizing, and thus unless the purpose in giving the test is properly related to the comparison group, the results will be meaningless. For instance, a test intended to measure verbal ability for purposes of predicting probable success in reading difficult textual material is improperly used if it is part of the hiring policy for electrical technicians or telephone repairmen, as is being done in one major American city.

Ideally, until standardized tests fair to all students from all backgrounds can be developed, they should not be used for admitting, placing, or labeling students. Since they are built into the system, however, those who use and interpret the test results must recognize the biases built into the tests and be aware of the theory and purpose behind the tests. Used carelessly, standardized tests lead to erroneous inferences as to students' linguistic abilities and create prejudgments in the minds of teachers, counselors, future employers, and the students themselves.

Resolutions of the Annual Meetings of NCTE in 1970 and 1971 challenged the present forms and uses of standardized tests. Because our schools and colleges continue to administer them, we must continue to deal with the effects of such testing on students and curricula. In response to the problem, we can employ caution in using and trusting test results, and seek positive ways to neutralize the negative effects. We should develop and employ alternative methods for the measurement of our students' performance. Various types of written and oral performance-in-situation testing can be done in the classroom. Various forms of in-class study of dialect can lead students to understand what is common to all dialects and what is particular to individual dialects, and can determine, through discussion, which alternatives most effectively represent the intentions of the speaker or writer.

Tests should not be focused on whether students can think, speak, or write in the institutional dialect, but on whether they can think, speak, and write in their own dialects. If it is also necessary to know whether students have mastered the forms of EAE, that should be tested separately.

What Are the Implications of This Resolution for Students' Work in Courses Other than English?

Teachers from other fields who view English as a service course, one which will save them the labor of teaching writing, often implicitly define writing as the communication of information within a limited social context. Perhaps when they (and some English teachers) fuss about spelling and usage, they are merely avoiding difficult problems of writing or, at least, avoiding talking about them. Sometimes, what they see as incompetence in writing is merely a reflection that the student doesn't understand the materials of the history or sociology course. But often they see the student's skill only in terms of limited needs. Whatever the reason for the complaint, courses which limit themselves to a narrow view of language in hopes of pleasing other departments will not offer a view of dialect adequate to encourage students to grow more competent to handle a fuller range of the language, and thus will defeat their own purpose.

What is needed in the English classroom and in all departments is a better understanding of the nature of dialect and a shift in attitudes toward it. The English teacher can involve the entire teaching staff in examining sample essays and tests from the various departments to determine whether a student's dialect in an essay examination from Mr. Jones in Geography *really* obscures clarity, whether Mary Smith's theme for Mr. Rogers is *really* worthless because of the "she don'ts" and because "receive" is spelled with an "ie." Such activities would help everyone in defining the areas which are vitally important to us.

We can also provide help for students who find themselves in courses whose teachers remain unreasonably restrictive in matters of dialect. In business and industry secretaries and technical writers rescue the executive and engineer. Science professors have been known to hire English teachers to rewrite their articles for publication. Even a popular technical magazine, such as *QST*, the journal for ham radio operators, offers services which will "standardize" a variant dialect:

> Have you a project which would make a good *QST* story? We have a technical editing staff who can *pretty* up the words, should they need it—*ideas are more important for QST articles than a finished writing job.* (Italics added) (*QST*, April 1971, p. 78)

We must encourage students to concentrate on crucial exactness of content, and we must persuade our colleagues to forget their own biases about dialect long enough to recognize and respect this better kind of exactness. Students—all of us—need to respect our writing enough to take care with it. Self-expression and discovery as much as communication demand care in finding the exact word and phrase, but that exactness can be found in any dialect, and the cosmetic features of polite discourse can be supplied, when needed for social reasons.

How Does Dialect Affect Employability?

English teachers should be concerned with the employability as well as the linguistic performance of their students. Students rightly want marketable skills that will facilitate their entry into the world of work. Unfortunately, many employers have narrowly conceived notions of the relationship between linguistic performance and job competence. Many employers expect a person whom they consider for employment to speak whatever variety of American English the employers speak, or believe they speak. Consequently, many speakers of divergent dialects are denied opportunities that are readily available to other applicants whose dialects more nearly approximate the speech of the employer. But a plumber who can sweat a joint can be forgiven confusion between "set" and "sat." In the same way, it is more important that a computer programmer be fluent in Fortran than in EAE. Many jobs that are normally desirable—that are viewed as ways of entering the American middle class—are undoubtedly closed to some speakers of some nonstandard dialects, while some of the same jobs are seldom closed to white speakers of nonstandard dialects.

Spoken dialect makes little difference in the performance of many jobs, and the failure of employers to hire blacks, Chicanos, or other ethnic minorities is often simply racial or cultural prejudice. One of the exceptions is the broadcast industry, where most stations at least used to require that almost all newscasters and announcers speak "network standard," but ethnic stations that broadcast "soul" (black) or country or western or Chicano programs tend to require the appropriate dialect. A related social bias is implied by certain large companies which advertise for receptionists who speak BBC (British Broadcasting Company) dialect, even though British English is a minority dialect when it is spoken in this country. For them prestige requires the assumption that Americans are still colonials.

The situation concerning spoken dialect and employability is in a state of change; many speakers of minority dialects are now finding opportunities that five or ten years ago would have been closed to them. Specific data are understandably difficult to find, yet it would seem that certain dialects have a considerable effect on employability. Since English teachers have been in large part responsible for the narrow attitudes of today's employers, changing attitudes toward dialect variations does not seem an unreasonable goal, for today's students will be tomorrow's employers. The attitudes that they develop in the English class will often be the criteria they use for choosing their own employees. English teachers who feel they are bound to accommodate the linguistic prejudices of current employers perpetuate a system that is unfair to both students who have job skills and to the employers who need them.

Teachers should stress the difference between the spoken forms of American English and EAE because a clear understanding will enable both teachers and students to focus their attention on essential items. EAE allows much less variety than the spoken forms, and departure from what are considered established norms is less tolerated. The speaker of a minority dialect still will write EAE in formal situations. An employer may have a southern drawl and pronounce "think" like "thank," but he will write *think*. He may say "y'all" and be considered charming for his quaint southernisms, but he will write *you*. He may even in a "down home" moment ask, "Now how come th' mail orda d'partment d'nt orda fo' cases steada five?" But he'll write the question in EAE. Therefore it is necessary that we inform those students who are preparing themselves for occupations that demand formal writing that they will be expected to write EAE. But it is one thing to help a student achieve proficiency in a written dialect and another thing to punish him for using variant expressions of that dialect.

Students who want to write EAE will have to learn the forms identified with that dialect as additional options to the forms they already control. We should begin our work in composition with them by making them feel confident that their writing, in whatever dialect, makes sense and is important to us, that we read it and are interested in the ideas and person that the writing reveals. Then students will be in a much stronger position to consider the rhetorical choices that lead to statements written in EAE.

NOTE

1. Framers of this statement earlier argue that "differences among dialects in a given language are always confined to a limited range of *surface* features that have no effect on what linguists call *deep structure*, a term that might be roughly translated as 'meaning' " (p. 6). See Stewart's article in this collection for an important counterargument. [Eds.]

EDUCATING TEACHERS
ABOUT EDUCATING THE OPPRESSED

Milton Baxter

While generally sympathetic to the goals of the CCCC Language Statement, Milton Baxter issues three important caveats to educators who may be implementing it: (1) He wishes to soften the thrust of the statement somewhat by applying the "students' right to their own language" only to spoken, not written, varieties. (2) He reminds readers of the deep-seated social prejudices that stand in the way of widespread tolerance for language diversity. (3) He, along with Kochman and Cooke and other authors in this collection, maintains that dialects have nonverbal as well as verbal components. If we are to encourage cultural pluralism in our classrooms, we cannot artificially set apart certain linguistic features as objects of toleration while we let other aspects of the communication process in minority cultures continue to alienate us.

Introduction

The role of dialects which students bring with them into the classroom has been at the center of much controversy among the linguists and English instructors. Recently it has flourished in the form of a radical resolution adopted by members of the Conference on College Composition and Communication.[1]

Clearly the statement of the CCCC has important implications today for the education of many black children who are desperately floundering in an educational system that unfortunately has been for them alienating, constricting, irrelevant, and uncompromising.

There is a grave danger, however, that the CCCC resolution will be propagated without concern for its implications as to actual classroom policy. This danger stems from the failure to spell out explicitly what is meant by the students' right to their own language. The purpose of this paper is to discuss these implications so that educators can gain a much needed perspective for the implementation of this resolution in the English curriculum. There are three crucial areas in which the CCCC statement can be considered undeveloped:

1. It ignores the distinction between spoken expression and written expression.

2. It ignores the social aspect of social dialects.

3. It ignores the network of speech-related behavior that is an integral part of the communication process; that is, it ignores the fact that dialects are enmeshed in a cultural context.

Spoken versus Written Expression in the Dialect

Many educators today will agree that language patterns or dialects are intricately a part of the students' identity, and will also acknowledge that much of the students' resistance to adopting classroom Standard American English (hereafter SAE) at the expense of discarding the native dialect stems from the unwillingness of students to acquire any speech patterns which might set them apart from peers and, more importantly, for which they can perceive no immediate relevance at home or in their community.

These same educators will quickly point out, however, that dialect-speaking students want to attain proficiency in written SAE grammar and compositional skills to enable them to pursue their careers successfully. In other words, although many students resist adopting the SAE speech patterns used by teachers, they do not necessarily resist the learning of SAE written usage and conventions (generally referred to as "Edited American English," and hereafter as EAE). Some teachers who would like to change the students' spoken language to more closely approximate SAE have therefore had to adjust their priorities, giving highest priority to the students' attainment of EAE. The statement of the CCCC ignores this important distinction that many educators and students have made between speaking and writing in dialect.

Since it is generally agreed that dialect users must learn to write EAE, the CCCC statement could head off some opposition if it limited itself clearly to spoken language. Even here, it will meet resistance enough, for many teachers who stubbornly resist the intrusion of dialects in their classroom and who painstakingly attempt to erase the various dialect patterns in their students' speech do so in keeping with the belief that SAE is the superior form of English—a belief which was cultivated during *their own* education when they learned to reject *their own* local dialects.

Social Parameters of a Dialect

Another pitfall of the CCCC statement is that it ignores the differences in attitudes that people have about social dialects and regional dialects. Regional dialects are generally regarded with less disdain than social dialects, particularly when a social dialect is associated with a lower socioeconomic group of people, as is the case with that variety of English spoken by many blacks in America. That social dialect, which we will refer to as Black English Vernacular (or BEV), is spoken by lower-class, uneducated (or undereducated), poor, largely ghettoized blacks. These social factors are important considerations upon which linguists come to label BEV as a *social* dialect, rather than as a *regional* dialect. While linguists and enlightened educators can acknowledge the theoretical validity of a social dialect such as BEV, they know full well that the acceptance of BEV by the intellectual community will not ameliorate the disdain with which BEV is generally regarded, for our society's intolerance of social dialectal differences can be clearly understood only within the broader pattern of racial and social discrimination. The rejection of BEV is just one manifestation of the racial and class prejudice that permeates our society.

To date, our understanding and treatment of BEV as a social dialect has been myopic in that a great deal of attention has been focused on the *dialect* aspect (i.e., on the nature of the systematic differences between SAE and BEV phonological and syntactic rules, as well as on vocabulary differences) while the *social* aspect has been neglected or willfully ignored, particularly when pedagogical implications are considered. When dialect-enlightened linguists and educators address meetings and conferences, they too often focus most of their attention on grammatical aspects of the dialect, ignoring the association of BEV with stigmatized social status. After the conference fanfare, those teachers influenced by the conference speakers are left with the arduous task of implementing in their curriculum and classroom practices these newfound notions of dialect relativity and, more importantly, of combating the social attitudes held toward nonstandard varieties of speech by colleagues, students, and the general community, many of whom are irreconcilably opposed to the very notion of BEV.

One cannot introduce BEV into the English curriculum as just another variety of English with pronunciation and grammatical differences (accountable for by perhaps some later ordered, overgeneralized rules or perhaps decreolization rules). An educator may be backed by a body of research to support his judgment that the difficulties students are having acquiring EAE are a result of cross-dialectal interference patterns (i.e., BEV influences on the learning of SAE); but this is usually not enough to withstand opposition by persons unable to transcend the social stigma of the dialect and accept BEV as a valid language system. It is, then, the failure to address the *social* aspect of a social dialect such as BEV that threatens to undermine any serious attempts educators might make to implement—in the form of innovative curriculum and pedagogic approaches—their newfound awareness of the need to uphold the students' right to their own language in the classroom.

It is, no doubt, the social stigmatization of BEV that has prompted many middle-class blacks to oppose the recognition of BEV as a bona fide dialect. But can we blame the educated middle-class blacks for the school system's blatant opposition to dialect-oriented curricula? Not unless they are also to blame for the more pervasive discrimination that exists in this society against lower-class, poor, and undereducated people, whatever their speech patterns. We are involved in a form of prejudice that is larger in scope than language; it resides in the social system itself. Although BEV is a full-fledged dialect with systematic phonological and grammatical rules, it is perhaps doomed to be shunned by many educators, parents, and even students themselves as an inferior variety of English because of its association with lower-class, poor, undereducated black people.

Those black parents who in their lifetime have experienced the degradation of having lower socioeconomic status want their children not only to learn SAE but also to be rid of any remnants of a social dialect that will possibly hamper their success. Many students under pressure from parents, teachers, and their own individual needs to succeed will pursue the acquisition of SAE. But at the same time, they remain cognizant of the need to retain those BEV speech patterns that will foster their acceptance and participation in peer-group situations. From such parents and students little argument, if any, will be found about the ultimate purpose of education: to provide upward social mobility. In this perspective we must examine more closely the social implications of any systematic attempt by educators to permit students, in the province of the classroom, a right to their own language. Such an attempt is always susceptible to being interpreted as institutionally promoting a veneer of cultural diversity, while actually condoning the stigma of lower socioeconomic citizenry in the midst of a society in which socially upward-aspiring Americans are the norm.

Perhaps implicit in the CCCC's statement is the belief that the classroom acceptance of language diversity among the students will be a catalyst for ultimately bringing about general acceptance of social class and cultural differences. If, however, the introduction of BEV into the classroom is really to be used as a means of exposing and eliminating the various forms of societal prejudice against lower-social-class behavioral differences, then it is inappropriate and deceitful to disguise these goals.

BEV as a Communication System

If the English class is to be the battleground for the struggle to uphold cultural diversity and pluralism in America, then English teachers will need to do more than involve themselves in in-service teacher training programs dealing with dialect variation. They will need to become sensitized to other communicative behavior of BEV speakers, including gestures, intonation patterns, and various sorts of body language. For example, the common use of falsetto voice among blacks has stirred much informal discussion among linguists about BEV intonational patterns and pitch ranges, some of which have been linked with African sources. Unfortunately, when educators envision the classroom use of a dialect such as

BEV, they have in mind BEV-speaking students who will utter their dialect patterns with SAE mannerisms, gestures, pitch ranges, intonational patterns, etc.—no doubt to facilitate the teachers' understanding of BEV. Surely the CCCC statement does not call for such a restricted conception of the students' language. Yet, no specific mention is made of these paralinguistic elements. We cannot afford to ignore them. Teachers whose cultural backgrounds are different from the students' will find it hard to interpret these communicative elements used by their students in the classroom.

Along with phonological suprasegmental differences such as pitch ranges and intonational patterns, there are differences in gesticulation (e.g., hand movements, body stances). No doubt many of the gestures used by BEV speakers can be found also among speakers of other varieties of English—in the same way that many of the grammatical features of BEV appear in other dialects. What is important here is that such gestures are important for the speech act itself, because they facilitate communication. Examples are "slapping five" to express acceptance, support, or approval, or perhaps "eyeballing" to indicate derision.

Should teachers allow such speech-related behaviorisms in the classroom? If not, are we promoting what may be an artificial situation in which dialect speakers are granted the right to talk in dialect, but only with SAE speech-related mannerisms (which are in keeping with established "classroom decorum")? If, on the other hand, we permit these dialect-related mannerisms, will we not be asking teachers to go beyond a narrow conception of the linguistic retraining required of them?

Educating Teachers about Educating the Oppressed

Granting students a right to their own language in the classroom places a great deal of responsibility on teachers' shoulders, if indeed the CCCC statement is not to become a meaningless catch phrase. Teachers can give life and substance to the CCCC statement not only by acknowledging dialect differences in the classroom, but also by developing and using curricula that are based on linguistically sound analyses of the English language varieties, and more specifically, that utilize cross-dialectal contrastive methodology for teaching SAE or EAE.

Unless teachers are provided retraining which focuses not only on grammatical characteristics of BEV, but also on culturally defined speech-related behavior, many unwittingly will be exposing their ignorance of important subtleties in their students' communication patterns.

Most important, however, it will be necessary to provide training which will increase the teachers' sensitivity to the apprehensions of students who are speakers of social dialects which carry no prestige in the society, and the use of which in the classroom may be regarded by the students and their parents as a constant reminder of their "inferiority" and lower-class status. Each student must be considered individually to determine his or her particular sensitivities. No presumptions can be made about the homogeneity of the student population in its attitudes toward classroom use of dialect-oriented materials, just as it should not be assumed that all BEV speakers use the dialect to the same degree. If we are to seriously advocate the students' right to their own language in the classroom, we as educators must ensure a constant dialogue with our students. We will run the risk of learning their language, just as they will run the risk of learning ours.

NOTE

1. The resolution, adopted by the Executive Committee of the Conference on College Composition and Communication in 1972, was supported by a position statement published in a Special Fall Issue of *College Composition and Communication* in 1974. [This resolution and position statement are reprinted as the preceding selection in this volume. Eds.]

THE LAISSEZ-FAIRE MOVEMENT IN ENGLISH TEACHING: ADVANCE TO THE REAR?

William A. Stewart

William A. Stewart is a cultural pluralist and a creolist who believes strongly that Black English Vernacular (BEV) is a descendant of West African creoles and that it therefore differs in quite basic ways from Standard English. (For evidence of the creole origins of BEV, see the articles by Dreyfuss and Lourie in this volume.) That is why in his review article, reprinted below, Stewart severely criticizes the CCCC Language Statement both for its major premise that differences between BEV and Standard English are only superficial and for its consequent plea that such minimal differences need not and should not concern the schools. Rather, Stewart would contend, teachers should admit the considerable differences between BEV and Standard English, should understand the deep-seated American prejudice against BEV, and should teach their black students to control the standard variety in addition to their own. In terms of the four options proposed by Burling, Stewart would wish teachers to "encourage bidialectalism."

The bulk of Stewart's article comprises a history of the ideological considerations that have led scholars in recent decades to minimize the linguistic and cultural differences between black and white Americans. For Stewart, *Students' Right to Their Own Language* is simply the latest document in this long and complicated history of assimilationism, a history which flies in the face of every American's common-sense knowledge that blacks have a different language and culture than whites. This article should, of course, be read in conjunction with the CCCC Language Statement and Baxter's comment on it, also reprinted in this collection.

"The road to hell," as the saying goes, "is paved with good intentions." Unfortunately, the same bids fair to be true for the well-meant document under consideration except that it leads, not straight downward to an obvious hell which all would seek to avoid, but rather back through a circuitous route to—ultimately—an educational purgatory of bygone days: vocational tracking. And by "vocational tracking" I mean just that; not a generalized trend within the entire student population toward more practical and service-oriented preparation (though that may also occur, and will undoubtedly be used to explain away vocational tracking), but rather the concentration of lower-class Negroes, Indians, and the like into low-level vocational training schools (perhaps by then euphemized as "community universities")—ostensibly on a voluntary basis, but actually as a survival response to the failure of higher (and indeed primary and secondary) education to furnish them with a viable academic preparation for the pursuit of advanced degrees or professional work beyond the university.

This view of *Students' Right to Their Own Language* (hereafter SROL) is likely to startle those who have read the document with approval, since they will in all probability have approved of it precisely because it seems to open the way to a more equitable (and hence, it may appear, a more successful) pedagogical approach to minority-group students through equal instructional treatment regardless of "the dialects of their nurture" (read: regardless of their ability to use Standard English). And indeed such an approach ought to make classwork easier for those students who lack proficiency in Standard English, and teaching (or at least grading) correspondingly easier for their instructors. But it would be well to ask whether this happy state would come about because those students' lifetime linguistic needs had already been met by their preschool socialization, with the school finally acknowledging that fact, or because a very real linguistic need and an important but difficult pedagogical obligation had simply been defined away. Though the question seems obvious enough when so put, it is nevertheless one which teachers who are overwhelmed by the language-usage problems of their minority students and who are desperately looking for a socially sanctioned easy way out (such as is offered in SROL) might not care to ask themselves. But then what kind of linguistic need might reasonably entail a pedagogical obligation?—which is really to ask, What is the function of formal education? For this is the fundamental question underlying any issue of pedagogical policy, and most certainly that raised by SROL. Yet the question is hardly touched on there, although much of the rhetoric of the document clearly reflects an assumed answer to it. In the very first paragraph of the Introduction, for example, the authors ask, "Should the schools try to uphold language variety, or to modify it, or to eradicate it?" (p. 1). Now, unless they intend for "try" to be an exercise in futility, they must be assuming here that it is quite possible for school policy to alter language attitudes in the larger society. Indeed, they go on to assert that "past teaching in English classes has been largely responsible for [public linguistic prejudices]" (p. 1), and then to chide their colleagues with the statement that "many of us have taught as though the function of schools and colleges were to erase differences" (p. 2), showing that they believe the potential of formal education for determining public language attitudes to be considerable. And it is this tacit belief which evidently constitutes the justification for their announced policy goal of making the school an agent of generalized linguistic relativism, and for their assumption that the school will be able to instill linguistic tolerance in the marketplace before the products of its policy of instructional linguistic laissez-faire begin to arrive there.

Unfortunately for all these plans, there is simply too much evidence against scholastic sociolinguistic power for a belief in it to be made the basis of policy recommendations. And some of this counter-evidence, it should be pointed out, is well within the realm of common knowledge. Who in the English-teaching profession can be unaware that Latin was the scholastic language *par excellence* of medieval and even Renaissance Europe, and that in spite of this fact it eventually had to give way to the common tongues (French, etc.)? Less known, perhaps, are such later but more peripheral cases as the extinction of scholastically preferred Persian in Islamic India and Manchu in Imperial China. Nor may it be much better known in the English-teaching profession that, in spite of government-inspired and school-based attempts to foster Hindi in modern India and Mandarin in modern China, the local vernaculars are not being abandoned. But any perceptive American English teacher who has vacationed in the formerly British Caribbean will certainly have noticed what little effect an educational policy of condemning Creole English has had. And for American teachers who know French, a visit to Haiti will have provided an even more dramatic example. In West and Central Africa, on the other hand, national schools which have tried to encourage vernacular education have met with as much popular resistance as earlier colonial schools had; while in the Republic of Ireland, school encouragement of Irish has done little to reverse the steady replacement of that language by English in even the rural counties. With respect to popular attitudes toward details within specific languages, too, scholastic sociolinguistic power has proved weak. French and German orthoepic preference for apical /r/ has had as little effect in discouraging the spread of uvular /r/[1] as, in the United States, classroom insistence on object *whom* has had in eradicating the general use of object *who*. But just the same, what about the general decline of nonstandard dialects—in America and Europe, at least—in the sense of their perceptible structural shift (seen at any given moment as variability) toward commonly shared features? Is not this process, which can be called *dialect leveling*, a direct result of educational pressures? So it might appear, except that there are enough examples of dialect leveling and decreolization[2] occurring in illiterate populations to suggest that, even here, one may be dealing more with general sociolinguistic dynamics than with the impact of the school.

Altering language attitudes in the general society (which educators in fact seldom if ever claim to be able to do) is of course a very different thing from teaching specific language skills to individuals and small groups, so that evidence of the school's ineffectiveness at the first should not be taken as proof of its incapacity for the second. Rather, educationalist claims of routine success in teaching language skills should be taken as more exaggerated than false. Sometimes there is dazzling success, and sometimes abysmal failure, with the accomplishment mean falling somewhere in between these extremes. And the determinant variables relate to individuals, groups, curriculum content, and methodology, plus the interaction of all of these. What obviously follows from all this is that, while educators are unlikely to be able to obliterate the linguistic "prejudices" and expectations of their larger society, they could at least teach their students specialized linguistic skills which would bypass the prejudices and meet the expectations. Yet the authors of SROL would advise English teachers to give up attempting the latter, in order to accomplish the former!

Inside the back cover of the Special Issue of *College Composition and Communication* (hereafter CCC) which constitutes the version of SROL being reviewed, the Committee on CCCC Language Statement is described as having consisted of Melvin A. Butler (Chairman), Adam Casmier, Ninfa Flores, Jenefer Giannasi, Myrna Harrison, Robert F. Hogan, Richard Lloyd-Jones, Richard A. Long, Elizabeth Martin, Elisabeth McPherson, Nancy S. Prichard, Geneva Smitherman, and W. Ross Winterowd. With two exceptions, these were academics who were recruited to draft the Statement (that is, over and above the original Resolution, on which more in a moment). The two exceptions were Hogan and Prichard, NCTE officials serving *ex officio* on the CCCC Committee. The four C's are of course the initials of the Conference on College Composition and Communication, a subdivision of the publisher of CCC, the National Council of Teachers of English (NCTE).

On the inside front cover of SROL, Richard L. Larson (Assistant Chairman and then Chairman of CCCC during the 1972-1974 period when the Statement was drafted) gives a short history of the document. The essential parts of his summary are:

> This special issue of CCC includes the resolution on language adopted by members of CCCC in April 1974; the background statement explaining and supporting that resolution; and the bibliography that gives sources of some of the ideas presented in the background statement. . . . This publication climaxes two years of work, by dedicated members of CCCC, toward a position statement on a major problem confronting teachers of composition and communication: how to respond to the variety in their students' dialects.
>
> A first draft of the resolution on language was presented to the Executive Committee at its meeting in March 1972, by a committee specially appointed by the officers in the fall of 1971 to prepare a position statement on students' dialects. After some amendments [it was] adopted by the Executive Committee at its meeting in November 1972. . . .
>
> Realizing that the Resolution would be controversial, and that it contained many assertions that could best be explained by reference to current research on dialects and usage, the Executive Committee appointed a special committee

to draft a statement that would offer this explanatory background. The special committee reported at its New Orleans meeting in 1973, where its initial draft statement was thoroughly discussed. A revised draft was presented to and accepted by the Executive Committee at the Philadelphia NCTE meeting in November 1973. The resolution and background statement were then distributed to members of CCCC, and the resolution was considered at the regular business meeting in Anaheim in April 1974 [where] it was adopted as the policy of CCCC. . . .

I cite this much of Larson's history of SROL to show that, from its inception, the resolution which constitutes the heart of the Statement was intended by the CCCC leadership to become the official policy of that organization. Even more of the interesting history of this document can be obtained from the secretary's reports in CCC 22 (1971) through CCC 25 (1974) where one can learn, for example, that an unsuccessful attempt to develop a CCCC language statement was made in 1969-1970 (CCC 22:293, 300; 23:323) or that Larson himself was the initiator of the successful second attempt (CCC 23:322).

In spite of the fact that both Larson's historical summary and the secretary's reports give much information on the development of SROL, they leave two important matters unclarified—both relating to committee membership in the drafting of the resolution and background statement. Larson and the reports indicate that the resolution was drawn up well before it was decided to add the background statement, and that different committees were formed for each. Yet the authorship of the resolution is never made known, since the only committee whose members are listed is the later one which produced the background statement. Thus the impression given on the inside back cover that the CCCC Committee on Language Statement authored everything in SROL may be misleading. In fact, during one of the later Executive Committee meetings (November 1973) when the Language Committee was asked about changing the wording of the original resolution, the response was that it had no mandate to do so (CCC 25:331). The second matter left unclarified is that of the criteria which were involved in the selection of the members of the later Language Committee. Larson says that they were "dedicated members of CCCC," though one hopes—and suspects—that there was more to it than this. Yet, following a tentative discussion at the March 1972 Executive Committee meeting of how such a committee should be formed (CCC 23:323-4), the very next report lists a relatively full and operating committee at the November 1972 meeting (CCC 24:333). It would be nice if someone who was privy to all these unrecorded goings-on would give an account of them, just for posterity.

The original resolution, now embedded in SROL, reads:

We affirm the students' right to their own patterns and varieties of language—the dialects of their nurture or whatever dialects in which they find their own identity and style. Language scholars long ago denied that the myth of a standard American dialect has any validity. The claim that any one dialect is unacceptable amounts to an attempt of one social group to exert its dominance over another. Such a claim leads to false advice for speakers and writers, and immoral advice for humans. A nation proud of its diverse heritage and its cultural and racial variety will preserve its heritage of dialects. We affirm strongly that teachers must have the experiences and training that will enable them to respect diversity and uphold the right of students to their own language. (SROL, pp. 2-3)

At least the structure of this declaration (it can hardly be called a proposition) is reasonably clear. The first sentence asserts the right of students to their own dialects, the second supplies a linguistic justification for the assertion, the third a political justification, the fourth a moralistic and the fifth a cultural one, while the sixth constitutes a call for more linguistic training on dialects for English teachers. But the line of argumentation is nevertheless elusive. Even the justifications which follow the opening assertion turn out to be mere assertions themselves, so that the entire resolution consists of nothing but a series of assertions. Thus there is really no argumentation to follow, and the reader is left with nothing to do but wonder about those assertions. Since the resolution is a declaration by teachers to teachers about students, one can assume that the "right" being affirmed is that of students to use their own dialects in the classroom. And since the organization sponsoring the resolution is primarily concerned with the teaching of composition, one can further assume that this would cover written use in formal composition as well as use in formal speaking. But does this "right" also cover a student's rejection of a teacher's evaluation of a particular form or turn of phrase as awkward or ungrammatical in terms of the known structure of the student's own dialect? In spite of the last sentence of the resolution, which I take as implying that teachers should learn about their students' dialects, there seems to be no corresponding affirmation of "teachers' right to their own knowledge." How, under such circumstances, can the proposed students' right to their own dialects be kept from becoming in effect a prohibition against the teaching of style? Yet these questions about the scope of the students' right to their own dialects as a pedagogical policy must take their place beside still others which arise in connection with the linguistic, political, moral, and cultural justifications offered in support of it. Who are the "language scholars" who "long ago denied that the myth of a standard American dialect has any validity," if not the same dialect geographers who have just as long and with equal certainty denied the existence of Black English? And is it really true that claims to the effect that particular dialects are unacceptable for certain purposes necessarily amount to attempts at social dominance rather than, say, constituting observations of sociolinguistic fact? And how is it more immoral to warn students of such sociolinguistic conventions in their society than not to warn them? And why, finally, should it be assumed that a pedagogical policy of linguistic laissez-faire will prevent dialect leveling from occurring by itself?

It would be nice to think that the then-members of the Executive Committee of CCCC were perceptive enough to ask such questions themselves, and that a healthy skepticism was therefore behind their appointment of another committee to clarify the original resolution. Yet against this there is Larson's recollection that, "Realizing that the resolution would be controversial, and that it contained many assertions that could best be explained by reference to current research on dialects and usage, the Executive Committee appointed a special committee to draft a statement that would offer this explanatory background," which clearly indicates that the Executive Committee saw potential controversy over the resolution as residing less in doubtful claims than in insufficient explanations. Under such circumstances, it was probably inevitable that the newly formed Committee on CCCC Language Statement would contrive to produce, and the Executive Committee to accept, an "explanatory" statement which in fact misrepresented "current research on dialects and usage" as much as the original resolution had ignored it. Indeed, so obvious must this misrepresentation be to any knowledgeable reader of SROL that I find it hard to believe a claim of Larson's that the document "has won the praise of many linguists and rhetoricians." If true, then the fact reflects even more unfavorably on the judgment of those unnamed linguists and rhetoricians than do the shortcomings of SROL on the ability of its authors, since the former ought to have known better, while the latter may well have been recruited more in deference to organizational or ethnic politics than on the basis of any demonstrated technical competence in dialectology, stylistics, or sociolinguistics.

There has already been some discussion in this review of the opening sociolinguistic misstatement in SROL, i.e., the assertion that English teaching has in large part created popular language prejudices. But it is now relevant to note that the claim first appears in the paragraph immediately following an authoritative warning that "sophisticated research in linguistics and sociology has demonstrated incontrovertibly that many long held and passionately cherished notions about language are misleading at best, and often completely erroneous" (p. 1). Thus an impression is created in the reader's mind that all assertions made in SROL, and particularly those which go against "passionately cherished notions" (read: common knowledge), are based on linguistic and sociological research. Yet the discussion earlier in this review of the claim advanced in SROL as to the sociolinguistic power of formal education should show that this is not necessarily the case. Furthermore, three important qualifications need to be borne in mind with respect to the SROL warning on linguistic and sociological research vs. common knowledge. The first is that research may end up supporting common knowledge just as often as not; the second is that researchers may disagree, since differing ideologies or methodologies may cause them to preselect different data; and the third is that, where research and common knowledge are at variance, the researchers are not necessarily always right.

Although the authors of SROL seem not to have noticed, the fact is that all these eventualities are illustrated in the counterpoint of scientific vs. popular assessments of black-white speech relationships in the United States. To state the popular position first, it had always been a matter of common knowledge among both black and white Americans that at least their folk speech was perceptibly different, and that black folk speech was similar enough throughout the country to warrant being considered in some sense a single entity—hence such designations as *Black English* (18th century term, recently revived) and *Negro English* or *Negro dialect* (19th and 20th century terms). This view remained unchallenged until the second quarter of the present century, when it began to be called into question by certain language historians and dialect geographers who were socially assimilationist, culturally regionalist, and methodologically lexicographic in orientation. By the 1950s, this movement had been so successful (for reasons which will be touched upon shortly) that it was routine for American scholars of English to denounce the popular belief in black-white speech differences as essentially fallacious. But in the 1960s, research conducted by creolists and sociolinguists—both having theoretical and methodological orientations at variance with those of traditional historical linguistics and dialect geography—began to offer evidence in support of the popular view that black and white speech were, and are, different. Thus the history of this issue (which is reviewed in Stewart 1969a and 1969b, and more fully in Dillard 1972 and Stewart 1974) furnishes examples of research at variance with common knowledge, research in support of it, and of course substantive disagreement between different camps of researchers.

One related issue on which there might at first seem to be a clear dichotomy between research findings and common knowledge is that of the structural and functional normalcy of Black English, especially as spoken by lower-class preschoolers and schoolchildren. It is true that virtually all linguists (by no means all of them researchers) have argued that it is normal language, while many nonlinguists have assumed that it is not. Yet even on this issue, the polarization is not really between researchers and laymen as such, since the main proponents of the view that Black English is underdeveloped or unstructured have in fact been educational psychologists with a heavy research commitment. Among laymen, moreover, the deficiency view of Black English is far from universally held; it is more commonly found among those in the North than in the South, and more among blacks than whites—a startling set of facts if one fails to realize that the deprecation of Black English is, at least among laymen, more a part of the rhetoric of black upward mobility than of white racism.

There is a widespread notion that common experience yields such faulty information about social phenomena that one must look to sophisticated research for an accurate accounting of them, and indeed expect scientific refutation of common knowledge as the rule rather than the exception. This notion may well be an extrapolation from what holds in the physical realm, where forms and events are not often discernible to the unaided senses nor relationships easily understood in common-sense terms. But to extrapolate thus is to miss the important point that human beings are eminently social creatures—ones more qualified by nature than by scholarship to gather, analyze, and store social information. In fact, it is likely that a very different quality of natural competence is involved in an intuitive judgment such as whether blacks and whites speak alike than in, say, one as to whether they possess the same vocal physiology.

For if past judgments on these and similar sets of analogous social and nonsocial matters are any indication, popular intuition is every bit as capable as formal scientific procedure of being correct on questions of the first type, but much less so on questions of the second type.

It would be a great service to intergroup understanding if, along with this natural ability to assess social-behavioral variables, there were an equally natural awareness of its limitations. But such an awareness does not come naturally, and the common tendency has long been to regard social behavior as of a single phenomenological class with human biology. Because of this, it has been commonplace to see behavioral differences of whatever type as necessarily caused by biological differences (the latter being taken as, in some sense, more fundamental), and therefore to attempt to associate instances of each where both have been observable, or to infer a causal existence of the latter where only the former might be seen. By this process, an accurate observation that blacks and whites speak differently becomes an indication that they have differing vocal physiologies, and a series of observations that they react differently to certain heuristic challenges is interpreted as evidence that they possess unequal cerebral equipment. Thus an observational ability which could have aided intergroup understanding has turned out to work largely at cross purposes with that end—an unhappy situation which it is left to the social and behavioral sciences to attempt to remedy.

To the extent that the problem is one of invalid inferences being drawn from valid data, it would seem only reasonable to counter by making clear why it is that the inferences are invalid. And it is difficult to imagine a better way to do so than by educating people as to the actual nature of those very real social-behavioral differences which they have observed. Yet this is not the approach which the social and behavioral sciences have adopted—at least not in their efforts to educate the general public. Instead, most scientists have given in to the expedient of simply denying the existence of the kinds of group differences in social behavior from which biological inferences had been or might be drawn. In other words, while the common-knowledge problem largely involved the drawing of invalid inferences from valid data, the scientific counterposition was to treat it as the exact opposite, i.e., as if it involved the drawing of (otherwise) valid inferences from invalid data. Thus the popular conclusion that blacks and whites had differing vocal physiologies was scientifically countered by denying that they spoke differently, while the conclusion that they had different mental capacities was dismissed on the grounds that they did not really behave differently on intellectual tasks. But of course blacks and whites, as groups, did speak differently, did perform differently on certain kinds of intellectual tasks, and too obviously so for these differences and others like them to escape notice. Rather, if they were to count for nothing, such differences had to be officially denied and deliberately ignored. The irony of it all was that, because of the rhetorical strategy chosen, the social-scientific stand against racism became a stand against reality as well, with its educational mission accordingly requiring a measure of cooperative self-deception on the part of those with whom it would succeed. Moreover, once it became an acceptable scientific posture to deny true behavioral differences when their popular recognition gave rise to untrue conclusions about the innate capabilities of racial or ethnic groups, it was an easy matter for the professional apologists and image makers in such groups to manage the extension of the strategy to include the denial of all group characteristics which could in any sense be regarded as unfavorable, regardless of whether false conclusions were derived from them or not. And since, given any two unfavorable observations, the truer one is likely to seem least favorable (it somehow being more insulting to call a pauper poor than prodigal, and so on), the inevitable result—which certainly must have struck some social scientists as ironic indeed—was that ethnic behavioral descriptions became politically controversial in direct proportion to their adherence to fact. Thus cultural differences in American society, and above all culture conflict as a prime factor in American racism, ceased to be an approved subject of scientific inquiry and became instead the problem child of what in effect were human-relations programs carried out by the various social-science disciplines.

The moral justification advanced for thus converting American social science into a social-policy instrument was a historical assumption that 18th and 19th century American social thought had been dominated by racism (here in the technical sense of a biological theory of group differences in behavior and capabilities, rather than in the much looser sense of a synonym for *prejudice*), coupled with another—the so-called "melting-pot" theory—that all the major American ethnic groups had successfully acculturated to the dominant Anglo-Saxon mainstream by the early part of the present century. (Clear exceptions, such as Indians and Mexican-Americans, were either ignored by the melting-pot theory or considered of too little significance to affect the generalization.) Taken together these historical assumptions reinforced the increasingly modish view that current intergroup conflicts and inequities were necessarily the result of racism, pure and simple, rather than of real cultural differences, and to that extent clearly set the task of the social sciences as one of lessening intergroup conflicts and inequities by repudiating racist beliefs.

Not surprisingly, this educational mission was taken up with the greatest enthusiasm by the sociologists, theirs being the social-science discipline with the strongest professional commitment to improving intergroup relations. (Perhaps coincidentally, but perhaps not, theirs was also the discipline with the least adequate theoretical framework for dealing with cultural differences as such, and therefore with culture conflict as a cause of intergroup tensions.) But in their enthusiasm, the extremes to which sociologists sometimes went in attempting to repudiate supposedly racistic modes of thinking could be ludicrous to anyone not sharing their acceptance of fact distortion for a good cause. At one point, for example, it seems to have been an accepted sociological tactic to teach that American racial categories were essentially arbitrary, on the grounds that borderline distinctions proved difficult if not impossible to make. As it had to in order to be taken seriously, this line of reasoning carefully ignored the fact that to demonstrate the fuzziness—or even the absence—of boundaries between any given categories is not sufficient to invalidate them, since seemingly adjacent categories may in fact be predicated upon noncontiguous points (such as poles or concentrations of differences) along an uneven continuum of differentiation, with any apparent interface between categories being simply an effect of generalizing outward from each such point to some abstract line of demarcation. This aspect of the psychology of categorization is nicely illustrated by the color spectrum, which is in reality a continuum of wavelength change, but which is normally subcategorized by naïve viewers (e.g., in popular descriptions and artistic representations of rainbows) as consisting of discrete bands of color. Given the psychological reality of such judgments, it would be as absurd to deny in general the type of categorization which they represent as it would be to specifically avoid using such distinctions as *hill:mountain, child:youth:adult, Old:Middle: Modern English, British:American accent,* or (please note for further reference!) *standard:nonstandard dialect,* simply because no clear-cut or nonarbitrary borderlines exist between them.

One could conclude from all this that the onetime sociological attempt to dismiss popular racial categorizations as nebulous was itself without substance, even if the categories involved were indeed abstractions from a physical continuum, as had been assumed. In fact, one may go further and question whether these categories are anywhere near as boundaryless as they would appear to be when simply defined. If they were—that is, if judgments on racial identity were made strictly in terms of single-attribute categories which matched reality only at the poles of a physical continuum—then one would expect mistaken judgments to be made in direct proportion to the proximity of individuals to the center of such a continuum, which would mean a goodly number. Yet, while Americans collectively make thousands of daily judgments as to the racial identity of their fellows, the number of mistakes appears to be so far below this expectation that one is forced to conclude that very few individuals are truly borderline cases. Why it might be that so few individuals pose a racial-classificatory dilemma for their compatriots becomes rather clear when one considers, first, that "race" in the American sense is as much a matter of social identity as of physical type and, second, that American racial categories are not really single-attribute categories but rather composites each of a number of subcategories, some of which involve physical attributes (e.g., skin color, hair texture, features, and body type), while others involve cultural ones (speech, posture, gait, dress, etc.). And since all these subcategories are only loosely interdependent, the chance of any individual's being truly borderline on a majority of them (assuming them also to be without discrete boundaries) would be too small to affect a correct judgment in most instances. Thus the attempted sociological refutation of popular racial categories was doomed to failure before it was ever begun, while its transparent absurdity curtailed it to a period of vogue much shorter than was enjoyed by the simultaneous sociological attempt (not necessarily by the same authorities) to deny distinctive American-Negro cultural patterns (Myrdal 1944, Frazier 1949) and linguistic attempt, already discussed, to deny Black English. After all, while Black English could be explained away as Southern dialect gone North and black culture characterized as environmental pathology, it was no easy thing to dismiss Negroes as Southern-whites-as-viewed-in-the-North or their physical characteristics as due to dusty cottonfields and sooty cities.

Again, the social-scientific motivation for this comprehensive denial of popular perceptions of racial and race-related differences—particularly when relating to Negroes—was the historical assumption that perceptions of this type were essentially a legacy of 18th and 19th century racism, and accordingly that the alleged differences themselves had little real substance. And it of course followed that if such differences were largely the fabrications of a popular state of mind, it should be possible to eradicate them by changing that state of mind through education. It was hoped that the social-relations problems popularly ascribed to them would then diminish considerably. But social policy intended as a corrective to history will at best be only as successful as the historical interpretation is accurate, and 18th and 19th century American attitudes toward race were never to be so easily categorized or refuted. If there were advocates of polygenism (the theory that human races sprang from different original sources), they were offset by a tendency toward environmentalism so strong that William Stanhope Smith could, at the end of the 18th century, gain a following for the theory that Negroes had dark skins because their mothers left them in the sun while working in the fields—with albino Negroes being the exception which proved the rule! If there was a general tendency to attribute a great deal to heredity, it was one which applied as much to family as to national as to racial attributes. Perhaps the closest thing to modern racism in its practical implications was not a form of hereditarianism at all, but rather an early version of social Darwinism which held different races and nationalities to be at different stages of development toward civilization and enlightenment. What is important to note about this view is that it was based largely upon comparisons (albeit ethnocentric ones) of actual behavior. In other words, people (the "savage" no less than the "civilized") in the 18th and 19th centuries were noticing real behavioral differences between human groups and drawing inferences—of inconsistent accuracy, to be sure—from these, just as people have continued to do in the course of the present century. Of course it is quite true that while a large portion of the North American population consisted of foreign-born in the 18th and 19th centuries, this was no longer the case by the time the middle of the 20th century was being approached. Yet if acculturation in the descendants of these original "foreigners" has in fact proceeded more slowly than melting-pot rhetoricians have generally maintained, then the legacy to be reckoned with from past centuries may be, not imaginary differences in capacity between races, but rather quite real differences in behavior between subcultures.

But this possibility was given scant consideration, and it remained common-place in "enlightened" circles to regard the denial of ethnic behavioral differences as a stand against racism, and by extension, to interpret even the most guarded hint of their existence as a manifestation of racist tendencies. Had this not been so, perhaps social scientists would have been a little more cautious about advocating social-change policies based blindly on the assumption that Americans were, if not without social-class stratification, at least culturally homogeneous within each class stratum. Or at least they might have been better prepared to deal with the problems which might arise were such policies to collide with a culturally pluralistic reality. As it was, few seemed to have had any inkling at midcentury that just such a collision was imminent, much less that the impact site would be that institutional symbol of acculturation, the school, or that the group destined to be hit the hardest would be both the intended beneficiary and the ethnicity long pointed to by social scientists as the prime example of total acculturation to Anglo-Saxon norms, the American Negro.

Since the view of American society held by the majority of social scientists at midcentury discounted appreciably different subcultures, it also discounted culture conflict as a cause of intergroup tensions. Ethnic groups were recognized in this view, but as little more than interest groups, competing with each other for their place in the sun when power was equally distributed between them, but sometimes becoming oppressor and oppressed when one gained the upper hand. Race relations in the Deep South were seen as an extreme example of the latter, so that white resistance to racial integration of the schools was anticipated there more than in the North. And since class differences were admitted by social scientists, albeit reluctantly, there was also an expectation that poor black children might fare somewhat more poorly in terms of academic achievement than the majority of white children with whom they were being integrated, though not necessarily much more poorly than rural Southern poor-white children. Any significant difference between the two latter types would be the result of less self-confidence in the black children, since psychologists had found evidence of what they interpreted as a "poor black self-image"; but this would be temporary, since it was held to be the result of segregation, and would accordingly disappear soon enough when integration had been achieved. What was not anticipated, however, was the vast difference in academic achievement between the majority of black children and even poor-white ones which turned up when the two populations were brought together in the same school settings and tested by the same instruments, and which gave every appearance of being far from temporary. Nor was the established social-science framework really able to explain this endemic black-white performance gap, which came to be known as the "postintegration educational crisis" of the late 1950s and early 1960s (though one could now add the late 1960s and early 1970s). Traditional dialectology, for example, which had maintained that black speech was merely general Southern folk speech, simply could not account linguistically for the fact that, even in the South, black children did significantly more poorly on school-language tasks than white children, and this even when differences in social class (here in the strict sense, rather than as a euphemism for race or ethnicity) were allowed for. Worst of all, black-white differences in academic achievement could not easily be dismissed offhand as illusory, since they were showing up as significantly different scores on well-defined curriculum and assessment tasks. Inevitably, there were vague conjectures from some quarters that these curriculum and assessment tasks were culturally biased against black children, but then such conjectures could have little weight when embedded in a general social-scientific insistence that there were no black-white cultural differences.

At this rather embarrassing juncture, a small group of educational psychologists came to the rescue with a theory of "cultural deprivation" (*cum* psychological and linguistic corollaries, "cognitive deprivation" and "verbal deprivation") which, for all its empirical limitations, was but a logical consequence of the melting-pot theory. For if it could be assumed that American Negroes had long since lost all vestiges of African culture, and yet failed to perform adequately in terms of Anglo-American cultural norms, then it could be concluded that they must be without a culture, or at least without an adequate one. The scientific problem would then be to explain why this condition turned out to be so prevalent among Negroes, since they had been among the first non-British arrivals on American shores, and therefore a group upon which the melting-pot mechanism had had an unusually long time to work its acculturative magic. The problem was solved by asserting that Negroes generally lived in a debilitating social and physical environment (a claim which the growing national concern with racism and its effects lent a great deal of credence to), and that this led to abnormally restricted psychological and linguistic development in black children. The implication was that, while the melting-pot mechanism might well have brought about full acculturation for American Negroes as a group, environmental deprivation prevented the adequate socialization of large numbers of individual Negroes to the cultural norms which their group as a whole embodied—which were those of the nation at large. Deprivation theory was thus able to explain low Negro academic achievement without having to recognize either cultural differences between blacks and whites or genetic ones—a fact which no doubt accounts for the general popularity which deprivation theory enjoyed when it was first proposed. Moreover, the policy implications were quite clear; what the black population needed was cognitive and linguistic "enrichment" at the weak point of the natural socialization process, early childhood. In consequence, a rash of early-childhood "intervention" programs were initiated in the early 1960s to achieve this end. Considering how scrupulously the deprivation theorists had avoided genetic considerations, it is more than a little ironic that the disappointing results of these programs stimulated, more than anything else, a resurgence of speculation on hereditary causes for endemically low black achievement on academic tasks and standardized IQ tests. So it was that the denial of black-white cultural differences, originally adopted as an antiracism strategy, ended up promoting racism by discounting the only viable nongenetic explanation of differences between black and white intellectual performance.

It almost seems natural, in a chain of events as replete with ironies as the one under examination, that the strongest challenge to the trend toward scientific racism would first come from the remnant of a minor anthropological-linguistic movement which, when it originated around 1940, had been regarded by many sincere egalitarians as itself constituting a trend toward racism. The movement was that begun by the anthropologist Melville J. Herskovits, whose *Myth of the Negro Past* (1941) argued for the widespread existence of African cultural survivals among New World Negroes, including those of the United States. As pointed out earlier, the view of American Negroes as incompletely acculturated Africans was the prevailing one in the previous century, and therefore could hardly be called original with Herskovits. What he did, however, was to propose this view as the correct one to a body of American social scientists who were strongly committed to melting-pot theory. Under the circumstances, it was inevitable that he would be challenged, as he was by the Negro sociologist E. Franklin Frazier (1949), and equally so that Frazier's early version of assimilation-*cum*-pathology would carry the day. Thereafter, followers in the Herskovitsian tradition concentrated on New World Negro populations outside the United States, with the Caribbean quite naturally attracting a great deal of attention. Linguists with a Herskovitsian bent pursued there the study of creole languages, i.e., special varieties of such languages of maritime expansion as English and French which showed the structural effects of having originally been informally learned by Africans and substantially reshaped in the process. This of course made creole forms of English, etc., structurally rather deviant from their closest noncreole counterparts, particularly in syntax, and (at least as far as the Herskovitsians were concerned) suggested something of a general acculturative model for the New World Negro. It also suggested (though at the time there seemed to be no direct evidence) that, in the United States, black and white folk speech might well be different because of creole vestiges in the former, and therefore that the popular American belief in black-white speech differences might be correct in spite of academic assertions that it was not. Linguists who studied creole languages in the Caribbean also became quite familiar with the endemic school-language problems of creole-speaking students in such countries as Haiti and Jamaica, where, because the creole and official languages used essentially the same words and because the grammar of the creole was not formally recognized, the official or standard language was considered the only "real" language, with the creole dismissed as merely a "broken" form of it. Consequently, schoolchildren in these countries were taught the official language as if it were their native speech—with predictably disastrous results.

With this background, creole-language scholars living in the United States at the beginning of the postintegration educational crisis were understandably intrigued when news of it began to spread beyond educationalist and governmental circles. To these creolists, the chronically poor school-language performance of lower-class black children, compared even to Southern poor whites, did not mean what it did to the deprivationists or hereditarians. Rather, it strongly suggested school performance in terms of formally unrecognized black-white speech differences, hence the unexpected racial differences in curriculum performance among lower-class children, in addition to the more general standard-nonstandard speech differences which accounted for social-class-related performance differences cutting across race. Needless to say, this kind of speculation brought the creolists into direct conflict with established dialectological theory (the evolution of which has already been traced in the discussion of research findings vs. common knowledge), and a heated controversy ensued between the two linguistic camps over the existence of distinctively black varieties of English in colonial and present-day North America. Thus while the controversy was in part historical in nature, it also involved the question of whether contemporary speech did or did not show evidence of structural differences correlating with ethnicity—in this case, with being black or white. The latter issue, in particular, attracted to the controversy a number of sociolinguists who formed a third linguistic camp, siding at first with the dialectologists but gradually moving closer to the creolist position as their data base expanded. And since the controversy had in fact been touched off by an educational crisis—the endemically low school-language performance of black children—it was natural that much of the associated field research would be directed toward the resolution of this much larger problem. Thus while one outcome of the sociolinguistic research was the identification of distinctively black speech patterns, and hence the recognition (or, rather, the re-recognition) of Black English, another was a set of recommendations for improving the teaching of Standard English to speakers of Black English through the use of a contrastive approach reminiscent of foreign-language teaching. Applied to the Black English speaker, the goal of such an approach was to produce conscious "split-level" control of equivalent rules in Black English and Standard English, i.e., *bidialectalism* in the usual sense of the word.

While the linguistic recognition of Black English and the consequent recommendation for its pedagogical recognition implicitly threatened the melting-pot ideal to which American education was still heavily committed, as these did even more the mechanics of the "equal treatment" policy which the schools were attempting to achieve through integration, educators flocked nevertheless to the early linguistic workshops on the "disadvantaged" which were so much a part of the mid-1960s. Perhaps they came in innocence, since many arrived clearly expecting to be reinforced with deprivation theory. But few, if any, expected to hear nonstandard speech treated as real language, much less hear black speech linguistically labeled as such in public. Yet even when this occurred, none of the white educators seemed at all prepared for the histrionic reactions of their black colleagues. It was usual during those early workshops, once nonstandard black speech had been characterized by the linguist as having its own unique structure, for black teachers of English to get up and deny the existence of the linguistic forms cited (often using these very forms in the process, as Standard English broke down under the emotional involvement of denying Black English). At this point, seeing the distress of their black colleagues, the white teachers would typically come to a quick decision to subordinate the educational problems of their black school children to the psychological needs of their black copartici-pants, and they would join in the denial. A denial of the linguistic forms of Black

English would then quickly lead to a denial of black students' "mistakes" in Standard English (since these often amounted to the same thing), and soon the entire body of participants was busy assuring the linguist that the problem which they had all come together to learn how to deal with did not really exist! Needless to say, very few teachers went away from such workshops with a better understanding of the educational problems of their black pupils.

The situation was even more turbulent when attempts were made to experiment with the use of pedagogical materials incorporating Black English for the purpose of teaching Standard English and beginning-reading skills to speakers of Black English. Self-appointed black image makers and "community representatives" protested and, where possible, marshaled the support of black parents. These people obviously felt that, given its content, the pedagogical solution being proposed was more embarrassing to their racial public image than the original educational problem—and this at the height of the Black Awareness Movement. (Joan Baratz and I once had a black educator tell us that, if lower-class black children could indeed only be taught to read via Black English primers, then she would prefer that they remain illiterate! Only recently have there been any signs that this set of image priorities might be reversing). Nor was black resistance the only disquieting feature of the pedagogical recognition of Black English from the educator's point of view. For one thing, its greater specificity placed an unaccustomed knowledge load on the teacher (who now found roles suddenly reversed in being expected to learn the students' dialect), while at the same time it made the teacher more directly accountable for student failure. Still another disquieting feature of the pedagogical recognition of Black English was of course the fact that, if extended to curriculum development, it would violate the "equal treatment" principle, since it would call for different materials for monolectal Black English speakers than for those who already knew Standard English. Indeed, the trouble here was that, quite apart from what kind of materials might be used, the mere recognition of the language-learning problem raised the issue of unequal treatment in the form of an unequal workload, since monolectal Black English speakers had another dialect to learn, while Standard English speakers did not. What too few educators stopped to consider was that equal treatment (especially in the commonly understood sense of identical treatment) in the classroom could, under a number of circumstances, lead to unequal education as a school product. Apparently, given the increasingly sociosymbolic and political function of the schools, what really mattered was that they were democratic, not that they were effective. And while it was to be expected that any formulation of educational process-and-goal which made explicit a greater learning load for the "underprivileged" would be regarded as grossly unfair by egalitarian-minded educators, it was by the same token all too rare for these same educators to then ask themselves how, especially in a complex and pluralistic society, any useful teaching could go on in the face of a requirement that the curriculum provide the same work load for all students *ab initio*—or, indeed, how this work-load balance would be determined for purposes of curriculum development and assessment.

Again, it seemed only to matter that the schools were democratic. (Significantly, both these misgivings concerning the pedagogical recognition of Black English recur in SROL, the latter stated outright on p. 2, and the former implicit both in the view expressed on p. 7 that beginning-reading texts in Black English are "constricting" and intended for the "culturally deprived" and in the claim on p. 11 that the contrastive approach to second-dialect teaching equates "different" with "deficit.")

All this should give some idea of why it was that, by the close of the 1960s, the English-teaching profession was ready to beat a hasty retreat back to the comfortable (and far less controversial) pedagogical ethnocentrism of melting-pot and deprivation-theory days. Yet that route had been effectively closed by the linguistic research on Black English and by the subsequent linguistic attack on deprivation theory. Moreover, if the Black Awareness Movement accomplished nothing else, it succeeded in rendering melting-pot ideology decidedly out of style in the black rhetorical scheme of things. Indeed, even if it were possible to undo the rediscovery of Black English and eliminate the effects of Black Awareness rhetoric, there would still be the problem of low black school-language performance to be faced. Clearly, the retreat from the pedagogical recognition of Black English had to be carried out in such a way as to avoid any appearance of denying or condemning the dialect, while at the same time refraining from admitting its pedagogical implications. But then, neither could traditional English-teaching methodology really be reverted to with confidence, since it was after all the gross ineffectiveness of the traditional approach with speakers of Black English which had motivated a search for methodological alternatives in the first place. With the pedagogical options thus closed off by controversy on one side and embarrassment on the other, it was as inevitable that the English-teaching profession would begin to question its avowed goal of teaching Standard English (at least to black students) as it had been for Aesop's fox to finally doubt the edibility of those unreachable grapes. With the motivation for a laissez-faire movement in English teaching present, all that was needed was someone to provide the kind of rationale which would make pedagogical laissez-faireism appear morally responsible and socially progressive.

A first step in the development of just such a rationale had actually been taken at mid-decade by James Sledd (1965) in a paper which, while it contained fleeting references to "the children of the poor and ignorant," was primarily an argument against teaching General American Standard English norms (equated by Sledd and many other Southerners with "Yankee" speech) to speakers of other—especially Southern—varieties of English. Moreover, partly for personal reasons, one suspects, but also perhaps to make his case against the need for teaching dialectal alternatives appear as strong as possible, Sledd argued as if the range of standard-nonstandard dialect differences in the United States were typified by the minor structural differences (largely phonological in nature) between General American Standard English and (White) Southern Standard English. In other words, the structural and functional differences between two varieties of Standard

English were supposed to be representative in scope of the differences between a standard and a nonstandard variety—even, one was left to conclude, between General American Standard English and the "deepest" variety of Black English. Judging from the general lack of reaction at the time, however, Sledd's early plea for a laissez-faire policy toward dialect differences fell on deaf ears. The English-teaching profession had not yet become desperate enough to consider moving toward the very antithesis of its traditional normativism, of course, but there is also the consequence to be considered of Sledd's having presented the issue largely in terms of Southern white linguistic integrity. Who, after all, cared in the mid-60s what was happening to whites, much less Southern ones? By the end of the decade, however, the profession was willing to look at laissez-faireism (at least for black students) in a much more favorable light, and Sledd's next paper on the subject (1969) made full use of the prevailing political winds by giving his linguistic cause the rhetorical momentum of the Civil Rights Movement, with just enough Black Revolution thrown in to add a note of avant-garde radicalism to what might otherwise (already in 1969) have sounded too liberally platitudinous. Rhetoric aside, the assumptions and assertions in this paper and its 1972 sequel are quite similar to those already discussed as appearing in SROL (and quite probably derived from Sledd). If there is any difference it is that Sledd, speaking as an individual rather than as a committee, and for himself rather than for a national organization, is able to make much stronger claims that the teaching of Standard English to speakers of Black English amounts to the imposition of the former on the latter—"enforced . . . , mandatory . . . , compulsory . . . , coercive bi-dialectalism" are his terms (Sledd 1969, *passim*)—with the alleged oppressors being "white supremacists" (as if General American Standard English were really "white," those who taught it to black students always white, and real white supremacists at all eager for Negroes to talk "educated"). If Standard English is "imposed" in the classroom, it, like mathematics or any other subject, is imposed as necessary knowledge by the older on the younger, not by whites as whites on blacks as blacks. That is why black parents are every bit as hostile as white educators to the pedagogical use of Black English in language-arts materials and, above all, in beginning-reading texts. Indeed, they are likely to be more hostile, since linguistic insecurity and the desire to change one's speech, no less than other social-mobility attitudes, are likely to originate within the lower classes themselves, rather than being imposed from above. Yet this obvious possibility passes undigested through the rhetoric of White Liberalism, the Civil Rights Movement, and the Black Revolution, since there is no place in their ideologies for the hypothesis that the "oppressed" might often be their own greatest oppressors.

But Sledd was still white, and the English-teaching profession had already sidled into a policy position, earlier adopted by governmental agencies and philanthropic foundations, that nothing pertaining to blacks could be said or done without black approval or, if at all possible, direct black participation. (This policy did not require that the black contribution be original; it was enough to have a black simply restate what had already been said by whites.) Fortunately for

Sledd, a certain amount of black support for his laissez-faire ideal was guaranteed from the start by the fact that, if adopted as pedagogical policy, it would remove one continuing source of racial public embarrassment: low black performance on the Standard English component of the curriculum. (All the better for racial public-image purposes was the fact that laissez-faire teaching would not actually throw out the Standard English component; it would be retained at the symbolic level in that students would be taught in it alone, and textbooks would be tolerated only in it. In other words, speakers of Black English would be treated by their educators *as if* they were speakers of Standard English, just as many public-school students are now being made symbolic literates by being distributed textbooks without having been taught to read.) Less expectedly, Sledd's strategic trivialization of the structural and functional differences between Standard English and Black English—a *sine qua non* for any laissez-faire rationale—received a welcome boost from a black rhetorician responding to the ideological needs of Black Nationhood (Smitherman 1971, 1973).

A shared but unique and historically associated language can be a powerful symbol of identity and solidarity in a nationalistic movement—a fact which did not escape proponents of Black Nationhood in the United States, some of whom at various times considered the adoption of such languages as Arabic, Swahili, or Yoruba for that purpose. The trouble was that these languages had long since become truly foreign to the entire American Negro population, while the contemporary sociolinguistic situation was not such as to make their learning an easy matter in the foreseeable future. It was therefore quite natural that Black English would come in for consideration, especially once linguistic studies had brought about some formal acknowledgment of its existence as real language. But there were two problems even here: the first was that by no means all American Negroes actually spoke Black English, at least as defined by linguists, since some were monolectal speakers of Standard English; and the second problem was that the nonstandard grammatical features of Black English were still, in spite of linguistic explanations to the contrary, commonly regarded as "mistakes"—even by the majority of its own speakers. In her 1971 article, Geneva Smitherman succeeded at least partially in overcoming these problems by tacitly rejecting the grammatical criteria which linguists had used to define Black English, substituting instead "idiom" (unfortunately, never clearly defined) and prosodic features which she called "rhythm" and "cadence" (terms which reappear in SROL). Since this in effect collapsed Black English (as previously defined by linguists) and Standard English (at least as spoken by many blacks) into a single entity, Smitherman quite appropriately referred to her concept by a different name, *Black Idiom*. But for those who did not follow the definitional subtleties of this terminological shift, or understand its real purpose, and especially for those who failed to perceive that Smitherman's "Black English" in 1973 was synonymous with her "Black Idiom" of 1971 rather than with the linguists' use of the term, Smitherman was furnishing the needed black support for Sledd's trivialization of the structural and functional differences between Black English and Standard

English, and hence for the English-teaching profession's abandonment of the teaching of Standard English.

To judge from SROL, the strategy finally adopted has been as follows: first, to diffuse the sociolinguistic focus on Black English by extending the pedagogical problem to cover "the language habits of students who come from a wide variety of social, economic, and cultural backgrounds" (p. 1); second, to weaken the argument for the contrastive (bidialectal) approach by trivializing the structural and functional differences between Black English and Standard English; third, to define away what remains of the school-language problem by disavowing the original pedagogical goal of imparting productive competence in Standard English, thus eliminating the chance of classroom failure by excluding the possibility of classroom success.

Of these essentially definitional strategems, the second is by far the most revealing on the relationship of SROL to the earlier public-relations tradition of attempting to improve intergroup relations by de-emphasizing conflict-producing intergroup differences. For the fact is that argumentation in the SROL attempt to trivialize the structural differences between Black English (whether so called, or euphemized) and Standard English is virtually identical to that used in the earlier sociological attempt to define away black-white physical differences, while the SROL arguments against functional conflicts between Black English and Standard English amount to simple denial, and thereby parallel the earlier social-science stand on black-white cultural differences.

Early in SROL, the common-knowledge distinction between Black English (or any other nonstandard dialect) and Standard English is put under attack by the argument that "most linguists agree that there is no single homogeneous American 'standard' " (p. 5). And since Black English has already been diffused amid "the language habits of students who come from a wide variety of social, economic, and cultural backgrounds"—i.e., amid a hodgepodge of dialects of varying degrees of nonstandardness—this has the effect of implying a continuum of difference, and hence no boundary between standard and nonstandard usage. ("Edited English," rather than Standard English, is seen as an acceptable pedagogical goal by the authors of SROL; but what "Edited English" might be if not written Standard English per definition 3 of the term in Webster's Third is never made clear.) Then, just to make sure that the nonstandard-standard boundary is sufficiently obscured, the reader is swamped by repeated claims to the effect that most Americans are at least passively multidialectal and that all American dialects of English are (for that reason and for structural ones as well) mutually intelligible. In other words, the nonstandard-standard boundary is trivialized, if not denied completely, by the implication that it is bridged by the linguistic competence of most Americans. Yet when one examines the actual statements made in SROL concerning multidialectalism, they turn out really to be referring more to different styles within a single dialect than to different dialects in the usual linguistic sense, e.g., ". . . most speakers, consciously or unconsciously, use more than one dialect" (p. 3). In part, inherent variability involving features which originally come from different dialects (a stage in the dialect-leveling process mentioned earlier) seems to be taken here for multidialectalism. The confusion is neither unique nor original to the authors of SROL, it must be said, since some fairly prominent sociolinguists have actually concluded from looking at sociolinguistic continuum situations (and ignoring cases of clear-cut bidialectalism in the process) that "code switching" does not normally occur within a single language. From this, educators have concluded (again ignoring cases of clear-cut bidialectalism) that speakers of Black English simply cannot be taught to be bidialectal in Standard English. If Standard English is taught in such a way that its features merely increase the inherent-variability range of the Black English speaker, as has resulted from piecemeal correction techniques in the past, then such a pessimistic conclusion will of course turn out to be true. On the other hand, all that this may actually amount to is a strong argument for the pedagogical recognition of Black English, particularly in the teaching of Standard English through contrastive-structure techniques, since one obvious result of such an approach would be to turn unconscious inherent variability into conscious selective bidialectalism—even if (as would be unlikely) no new forms or constructions were involved.

As the argument shifts to structural matters, the authors of SROL distort what they claim to be an "insight from linguistic study" in asserting that "differences among dialects in a given language are always confined to a limited range of *surface* features that have no effect on what linguists call *deep structure*, a term that might be roughly translated as 'meaning' " (p. 6). The distortion is in the use of the word "always," which would be appropriate only if one were to use it as the defining term for distinguishing dialects from closely related languages—a usage which even then few linguists would subscribe to. Furthermore, the question still remains as to how deep-structural (i.e., meaning) differences can be perceived by a listener (or reader) if they do not appear in the surface structure. The authors of SROL are themselves victims of this problem, since they overlook the fact that the Black English construction *Mary daddy home*, for which they give only one Standard English meaning (p. 6), actually has two Black English deep structures, and hence two Standard English equivalents, i.e., "Mary's daddy is at home" (the one they give) and "Mary's daddy's home" (i.e., "The home of the father of Mary"). Within Black English, the sequence *Mary daddy home* is merely ambiguous, and unperplexingly so at that. But what is simple structural ambiguity in one dialect can become a barrier to comprehension to the listener who speaks another when the ambiguity is not paralleled across the two dialects, since the listener is not warned by his own dialect to expect ambiguity. Thus the fact that Standard English *you* is ambiguous with respect to number causes few if any problems for listeners within the same dialect, since they know intuitively that *you* supplies no information as to number. But to the speaker of Black English who uses *y'all* for the plural and who therefore expects *you* to always indicate the singular, the Standard English use of *you* for plural is likely to create misunderstanding. In the same vein, a similar problem is created in the other direction by the fact that Gullah (an unquestionably creole form of Black English) does not, in contrast to Standard English, formally mark the plural of nouns. This means, of course, that unmarked Gullah nouns are ambiguous with respect to number, just as is Standard English *you*. In discussing plans for a picnic, for example, one Gullah might say to another *I go bring my sister*. The listening Gullah, intuitively knowing that no information as to the number of sisters has been supplied, but needing to know (since, let us say, the speaker is known to have several sisters), may elicit it by asking *How many you go bring?* or some such question. A Standard English-speaking listener, on the other hand, would not be trained by his dialect to expect number ambiguity in unmarked nouns and would therefore be likely to interpret Gullah *I go bring my sister* as necessarily indicating only one sister, and might well be wrong. Moreover, the same speaker of Standard English might get a quite mistaken idea of Gullah intelligence, if, on stating, *I'm going to bring my sister*, he were asked by the Gullah listener *How many you go bring?*

Nor does one need structural ambiguity to create faulty or inadequate comprehension across dialects. It would be utterly unrealistic to claim, as SROL implies, that Standard English speakers are at all likely to take Black English *be VERB-in'* and *been VERB-ed* in the true sense in which they are used by Black English speakers, or that Black English speakers will generally understand the distinction between Standard English *I insist that he go* and *I insist that he goes*. Speakers of the other dialect may get the general idea, of course, particularly if there are plenty of contextual clues to assist in the effort at comprehension. But then so can beginning learners of a foreign language often guess at the general meaning of a sentence in that foreign language when they do not really know all its grammatical rules. To call this sort of guesswork "receptive competence," however, is to largely abandon the technical meaning of the term. Even worse, to summarily charge comprehension failures across dialects to negative social attitudes, as the authors of SROL do, is to engage in pseudo-moralistic bombast at the expense of an important, if unpalatable, truth.

The SROL position on intelligibility across dialects can be little more than adherence to a discourse convention which "liberal" thought now seems to impose on any acknowledgment of ethnic behavioral differences among Americans, i.e., that such differences never be depicted as creating problems. It is the kind of polite self-deception which admits to the existence of cultural differences, but considers the uncomfortable fact of ethnic preferences and performance differences in various types of work and play as imposed by some all-powerful ruling elite; and it is the kind of self-imposed blindness which admits to the existence of dialect differences, but considers the markedly different school-language and reading performance of students from different dialect backgrounds as evidence only of unfavorable attitudes on the part of their teachers.

At this point, one should wonder about the probable effect of a professional "position statement" which attempts to define away a very real problem. Over the short run, a laissez-faire policy in English teaching will undoubtedly take much of the stress and strain off both teacher and minority student. But in the long run, it is doubtful that it will have accomplished any major attitudinal changes toward language usage, nor will the functional problems which it has defined away really have disappeared.

NOTES

1. Stewart means that grammarians have preferred the apical [r], pronounced by tapping the tongue tip against the hard palate (as in Spanish) but that the uvular [r], pronounced by trilling the uvular flap at the back of the throat, continues to be more popular anyway. [Eds.]

2. Decreolization is the process whereby a creole gradually assimilates to the dominant language from which it is partially descended. See the Dreyfuss article in this collection for an extended discussion. [Eds.]

References

Committee on CCCC Language Statement, 1974   *Students' Right to Their Own Language.* Special Issue of *College Composition and Communication*, separately paginated.

Dillard, J.L., 1972   *Black English: Its History and Usage in the United States.* New York: Random House.

Frazier, E. Franklin, 1949   *The Negro in the United States.* New York: Macmillan.

Herskovits, Melville J., 1941   *The Myth of the Negro Past.* New York: Harper & Brothers.

Myrdal, Gunnar, 1944   *An American Dilemma: The Negro Problem and Modern Democracy.* New York: Harper & Brothers.

Sledd, James, 1965   "On Not Teaching English Usage." *English Journal* 54: 698-703.

———, 1969   "Bi-Dialectalism: The Linguistics of White Supremacy." *English Journal* 58: 1307-1315, 1329.

———, 1972   "Doublespeak: Dialectology in the Service of Big Brother." *College English* 33: 439-456.

Smitherman, Geneva, 1971   "Black Idiom." *Negro American Literature Forum* 5: 88-116.

———, 1973   " 'God Don't Never Change': Black English from a Black Perspective." *College English* 34 :828-833.

Stewart, William A., 1969a   "Sociopolitical Issues in the Linguistic Treatment of Negro Dialect." In James E. Alatis, ed., *Monograph Series on Language and Linguistics*, no. 22. Washington, D.C.: Georgetown University.

———, 1969b   "Historical and Structural Bases for the Recognition of Negro Dialect." In James E. Alatis, ed., *Monograph Series on Language and Linguistics*, no. 22. Washington, D.C.: Georgetown University.

———, 1974   "Acculturative Processes and the Language of the American Negro." In William W. Gage, ed., *Language in Its Social Setting.* Washington, D.C.: The Anthropological Society of Washington.

EDUCATIONAL IMPLICATIONS OF
DIALECT DIVERSITY

Walt Wolfram and Donna Christian

Much of this anthology emphasizes ethnicity as a chief causal factor in the diversity of American language. But it is important to recall that variables such as social class and geographical region can also mark off distinct speech communities, even among white Anglo-Saxon Protestants, who are usually considered the ethnic norm. Because of its relative poverty and isolation, the Appalachian Mountain region—comprising parts of Kentucky, Virginia, North Carolina, Tennessee, and all of West Virginia—provides an excellent example of a white Anglo-Saxon speech community, largely of Scottish extraction, whose language differs significantly from Standard English.

In their book *Appalachian Speech*, Walt Wolfram and Donna Christian describe the phonological and grammatical features of the Appalachian English (AE) spoken by the working-class rural population in Monroe and Mercer Counties of West Virginia. They noticed that this variety shares a number of features with other nonstandard varieties and with Southern regional speech generally. And, like other linguists, they found variation among their informants by age, sex, and social class and also observed the expected fluctuation between Standard English and AE forms in each informant. Nevertheless, they were able to distinguish as characteristic of AE the phonological and vocabulary features cited in Appendix H and the grammatical features listed in the table below. Several of these features (1, 4, 7, possessive + n in 10a), Wolfram and Christian note, are retained in AE from older forms of British English and testify to the isolation and consequent slow change of some language features in this mountain region. Notice also the similarity of many of these features to Black English Vernacular.

Nonstandard Grammatical Features of Appalachian English

AE feature	Examples
1. *A* prefix on *-ing* verbs	he was *a-tellin'*, a bear come *a-runnin'*
2. Subject-verb nonconcord	we was, he don't
3. Irregular verbs	
a. regularized simple past	we *throwed* them a party
b. variant simple past	we *set* there one day
c. uninflected simple past	finally the state *come* by
d. simple past same as past participle	that's all I *seen* of it
4. Perfective *done*	I *done* forgot when it opened
5. Comparatives and superlatives	
a. *-er*, *-est* generalized	awfulest, beautifulest
b. redundant markers	more older, most stupidest
c. regularized	baddest, worser
6. Frequent absence of *-ly* on adverbs	I come from Virginia *original*

Nonstandard Grammatical Features of Appalachian English (continued)

7. Negative concord	
a. negative indefinite after negative verb	I did*n't* have *nothing* to do
b. negative indefinite before negative verb	*Nobody* did*n't* see him
c. negative auxiliary and negative indefinite sometimes inverted	Did*n't nobody* get hurt
d. negative sometimes carried to dependent clause	I was*n't* sure that *nothin'* was*n't* (i.e., anything was) gonna come up
8. *Ain't (hain't)*	I *ain't* been there; *hain't* that awful?
9. Plurals	
a. uninflected in nouns of measure	two *gallon* of moonshine
b. regularized	deers, wifes
c. *-s* added to irregular plurals	mens, oxens, childrens
10. Pronouns	
a. nonstandard variants	hisself, theirself, *them* boys, *this here* one, his'n, y'all
b. object case in compound subject	*me* and my baby sleep the day
c. relative pronoun deleted	I got some kin people lived there
d. conjunctive *which*	I went to Cleveland *which* my cousin lives there
e. personal dative	We had *us* a cabin
11. Existential *it* and *they*	*it's* too much murder; *they's* copperheads around here
12. Nonstandard use of prepositions	*at/of* wintertime; *at/of* the morning; I lived Coal City; I just go *at* my uncle's; *upside* the head, etc.
13. Indirect questions marked by direct question word order rather than *if* or *whether*	I asked him *could I* come downstairs

Item numbers keyed to Tables 1 and 2 in the Wolfram and Christian excerpt.

In a final chapter, Wolfram and Christian discuss the educational implications of the gap between Standard English and AE, concentrating particularly on standardized tests and reading skills. Their discussion can be readily generalized to any nonstandard variety and should be compared with the Burling selection and the CCCC Language Statement. It would also be instructive to use the tables in this article as models for contrasting another nonstandard variety like Black English Vernacular with "correct" answers to any standardized grammar test.

Dialect Diversity and Testing

The importance that mainstream society places on standardized tests is fairly obvious to most educators. Crucial decisions in the diagnosis of educational abilities are often based on standardized test scores of one type or another—

decisions that affect children's current and future lives in our society. Admittedly, test scores are difficult to resist, given their widespread use by all types of agencies. Standardized tests are used as instruments that produce objectified, quantitative information of one type or another. Quantifiable scores do show significant distinctions between various groups of individuals, so that their use as an objectifiable parameter of measurement can become a highly valued basis for evaluating a group or an individual's performance. Obviously, when a test reveals significant differences between various groups in the population, we have demonstrated something. But the uneasy question which arises is whether the instrument actually measures what it is designed to measure. Do the scores faithfully represent the domain set forth by the tests? And, we may take this one step further and ask what can be inferred about other behavior on the basis of a test. This would involve assessing the usefulness of the measurement as an indicator of some other variable or as a predictor of behavior. These questions deal with the test *validity* (the former case being a matter of *content validity* and the latter *criterion-related validity*).

Although there are various aspects of validity that have at times become controversial issues with respect to standardized testing, one of the recurrent themes relates to the appropriateness of such measurements for different cultural groups. Included in the concern for cross-cultural applicability is consideration for some of the rural, relatively isolated groups found in regions of Appalachia. In many instances, we find that the distribution of scores among these groups is disproportionate when compared with mainstream populations. These findings have raised several different questions concerning the tests. One of the questions posed has been whether higher test scores from high socioeconomic groups reflect genuine superiority of one type or another. Or, do high scores result from an environmental setting which provides certain advantages? Or, do the differential scores reflect a bias in the test materials and not important differences in capabilities at all? Recent research in testing (Roberts, 1970; Meier, 1973; Cicourel et al., 1974) indicates the last question is becoming increasingly important in the consideration of test application across different social and cultural groups in American society. It is also the area in which linguistics can play a significant role in suggesting ways of examining specific tests and the testing process in general.

Although we might look at the general question of test bias from several different approaches, our central concern here is that of a sociolinguistic perspective. From this perspective, we are interested in how language diversity in the context of society may be used to the advantage of certain groups as opposed to others. Our research into language diversity in American English has shown that there are considerable differences in language systems. Our knowledge of those differences may serve as a basis for understanding certain types of potential sociolinguistic interference in testing. Although we shall examine in some detail the effects of these types of dialect differences on testing language skills, the crucial nature of the testing question will carry us somewhat further than the differences in linguistic form.[1]

Differences in Linguistic Form   One aspect of test interference involves the differences in linguistic items which speakers may have as a part of their linguistic system. The background of this sort of investigation is found in the descriptive accounts of various linguistic systems as they contrast with responses to linguistic items considered correct by tests. In a sense, this is what is done in *contrastive linguistics* where the descriptive accounts of linguistic systems are placed side by side in order to observe where the patterns of a language are similar and where they are different. In contrastive studies as they are applied to different languages or dialects, these comparisons often serve as a basis for predicting where a speaker of Language Variety A will encounter difficulty when confronted with Language Variety B. Although all predicted interference will not, of course, be realized for one reason or another, the comparison can anticipate many of the patterns or items which will, in fact, interfere. On the basis of a contrastive analysis of Standard English and a nonmainstream variety such as AE, we may therefore predict what types of interference we would expect a test to hold potentially for the speaker of AE.[2]

Language tests may be used for a wide range of purposes, including the assessment of language development, auditory discrimination, the diagnosis of learning disabilities, reading assessment, and achievement in language arts. In all these cases, the norms called for in the test may systematically conflict with the language system of a nonmainstream speaker. Although each of these language tests might be dealt with in detail, we may most efficiently discuss our perspective by illustration. For this purpose, we shall focus on the Illinois Test of Psycholinguistic Abilities (henceforth ITPA), a widely used test in several different disciplines, particularly in speech pathology and learning disabilities assessment.

The ITPA consists of a battery of tests to measure various facets of cognitive abilities. It is essentially a diagnostic tool in which specific abilities and disabilities in children may be delineated in order for remediation to be undertaken when needed (ITPA Examiner's Manual, 1968: 5). Among the various subtests is one entitled "grammatical closure," which was designed to "assess the child's ability to make use of the redundancies of oral language in acquiring automatic habits for handling syntax and grammatic inflections" (ITPA Examiner's Manual, 1968: 11). While the manual mentions that the test elicits the ability to respond in terms of Standard American English, no warning is given about the use of this test with children who may speak nonmainstream varieties of English. The test is, in fact, routinely administered to quite different dialect and social groups. In the grammatical closure subtest, the child is asked to produce a missing word as the tester points to a picture. For example, the examiner shows a plate with two pictures on it, one with one bed and the other with two beds. The examiner points to the first picture as he says, "Here is a *bed.*" He then points to the second picture and says, "Here are two _____ ," with the child supplying the missing word. The focus is on a particular grammatical form, such as the plural *-s* in this case. All the responses must be in Standard English in order to be considered correct.

With this background information in mind, let us consider the specific items of the grammatical closure test in terms of the grammatical description of AE. Based on our contrastive analysis of the items considered to be correct responses according to the test manual and the different grammatical rules of AE, we may predict those cases of possible divergence accounted for by the grammatical rules of AE. According to the manual for scoring, all these items would have to be considered "incorrect," even though they are governed by legitimate linguistic rules which simply differ from dialect to dialect. Table 1 gives each of the stimulus items in the test, the responses considered to be "correct" according to the test manual and, where applicable, the corresponding dialect form which would be an appropriate response for AE speakers. In all the cases cited in the table, the legitimate AE form would have to be considered incorrect according to the scoring procedures in test manuals. In each case where the dialect form of AE would be different from the expected correct response, we have cited the number of the item in the Headnote.

Table 1   ITPA Grammatical Closure Subtest with Comparison of "Correct" Responses and Appalachian English Alternant Forms

Stimulus with "correct" item according to Test Manual	AE alternant	Number of feature in Headnote
1. Here is a dog. Here are two *dogs/doggies.*		
2. This cat is under the chair. Where is the cat? She is on/(any preposition—other than *under*—indicating location).		
3. Each child has a ball. This is hers; and this is *his.*	*his'n*	10a
4. This dog likes to bark. Here he is *barking.*		
5. Here is a dress. Here are two *dresses.*		
6. The boy is opening the gate. Here the gate has been *opened.*		
7. There is milk in this glass. It is a glass *of/ with/for/o'/lots of* milk.	No preposition	12
8. This bicycle belongs to John. Whose bicycle is it? It is *John's.*		
9. This boy is writing something. This is what he *wrote/has written/did write.*	*writed/writ, has wrote*	3abd
10. This is the man's home, and this is where he works. Here he is going to work, and here he is going *home/back home/to his home.*	*at home*	12
11. Here it is night, and here it is morning. He goes to work first thing in the morning, and he goes home first thing *at night.*	*of the night*	12
12. This man is painting. He is a *painter/ fence painter.*	*a-paintin'*	1
13. The boy is going to eat all the cookies. Now all the cookies have been *eaten.*	*eat, ate, eated*	3acd

Table 1 (continued)

14. He wanted another cookie; but there weren't *any/any more.*	*none/no more*	7a
15. This horse is not big. This horse is big. This horse is even *bigger.*	*more bigger*	5b
16. And this horse is the very *biggest.*	*most biggest*	5b
17. Here is a man. Here are two *men/gentlemen.*	*mans/mens*	9bc
18. This man is planting a tree. Here the tree has been *planted.*		
19. This is soap and these are *soap/bars of soap/more soap.*	*soaps*	9
20. This child has lots of blocks. This child has even *more.*		
21. And this child has the *most.*	*mostest*	5c
22. Here is a foot. Here are two *feet.*	*foots/feets*	9bc
23. Here is a sheep. Here are lots of *sheep.*	*sheeps*	9b
24. This cookie is not very good. This cookie is good. This cookie is even *better.*	*gooder*	5c
25. And this cookie is the very *best.*	*bestest*	5c
26. This man is hanging the picture. Here the picture has been *hung.*	*hanged*	3a
27. The thief is stealing the jewels. These are the jewels that he *stole.*	*stoled/stealed*	3a
28. Here is a woman. Here are two *women.*	*womans/womens*	9bc
29. The boy had two bananas. He gave one away; and he kept one for *himself.*	*hisself*	10a
30. Here is a leaf. Here are two *leaves.*	*leafs*	9b
31. Here is a child. Here are three *children.*	*childrens*	9c
32. Here is a mouse. Here are two *mice.*	*mouses*	9b
33. These children all fell down. He hurt himself; she hurt herself. They all hurt *themselves.*	*theirselves/ theirself*	10a

We see, in Table 1, that 25 of the 33 items in the test have alternant forms in AE. These are forms which are a legitimate part of the AE grammatical system, but according to the instructions for scoring the test, they would have to be considered incorrect responses. To understand what the implication of such divergence may be for diagnosis of language abilities, consider the hypothetical case of a ten-year-old AE speaker. Suppose that such a speaker obtains correct responses for all the other items in the test, but his appropriate AE responses are considered to be incorrect according to the guidelines given for scoring this section. When the raw score of eight correct responses is checked with the psycholinguistic age norms for this test, we find his abilities to be equivalent to those of a child of four years and five months. This, of course, may be somewhat exaggerated, given the fact that most of the features of AE are variable and a particular speaker may not use all these features as a part of his system. Instead we may arbitrarily say that the AE speaker realizes only approximately half of the potential AE alternants in his actual performance on such a test. This would give him a raw score of 20 correct responses, and his psycholinguistic age level according to this measurement would be that of a child six years and eight months of age. This is still over three years below his actual age, and would, in many cases, be sufficient to recommend such a child for remedial language training. The implications for using such a test to assess the language capabilities of the AE-speaking child appear quite obvious given the norms of the test and the legitimate differences found in the AE system. On the basis of a test such as this, it would be quite possible to misdiagnose a child's language abilities and penalize him for having learned the language of his community.

Testing as a Social Occasion   Although a primary focus in this study has been the linguistic form of AE, the extent of sociolinguistic considerations in tests is not restricted to different linguistic items. There are other matters which take us beyond the limitations of systematic differences between linguistic items per se as discussed above. One of the important considerations in any test is the context of the testing situation. Testing, like other types of behavior, necessarily involves the existence of a social occasion. The testing process is not devoid of cultural context regardless of how standardized the testing procedure may actually be. Testing is "social" in several ways. First of all, it is social in the sense that it involves interaction between the test administrator and the test taker. Second, it involves a particular division of labor that distinguishes the testing situation from other aspects of behavior. And finally, it is social in the sense that it operates on the output of socialization that has taken place prior to the actual situation.

Test construction involves elaborate plans for the manipulation of the subject's behavior. These plans are first based on the assumption that the test designer has a viable (though perhaps implicit) model which can serve as a guide for his own actions in constructing the test. It is further assumed that the researcher knows the ways in which the properties of situations might influence the behavior of the subjects, and how to place these properties under control in the standardization of procedures.

In order to promote the orderly interpretation of data that are derived from the test situation, the researcher has no other alternative but to presume that the subject can enter and remain in the experimental frame constructed for the test. In other words, he must assume that the subject can play the researcher's game. And, if he cannot bring the subject into the experimental frame, there is no objectifiable way in which the abilities of the subject which the tester wants to measure can be tapped.

The basic issue here, then, concerns the assumption of the "sameness" of the environment and the irrelevance of potentially different socialization processes which may lead to this test situation. From a sociolinguistic viewpoint, the question at this point is determining the extent to which potentially different historical backgrounds may be individualistic or cultural. We cannot completely dismiss the individual aspects which may result in different perceptions of the social occasion, since there seems to be some evidence that certain individuals from all socioeconomic groups may be adversely affected by the judgmental and competitive conditions that characterize the testing situation. But we must go one step further and look at the systematic cross-cultural aspects of the testing situation. For a number of reasons, we are led to believe that the testing situation is culturally biased in favor of particular classes. The regulation of the testing situation, the social style of the test administration, the expectations of the experimental frame, and the expected behavior of the test takers while engaged in the testing activity all point to a particular class orientation. Those individuals who are not members of this class, then, are likely to be at some disadvantage when in this situation.

The importance of the social occasion in testing can be illustrated best by citing the instructions from a fairly typical test guide. The "hints" for successful test taking given below are taken from a brochure on taking aptitude tests, published by the U.S. Department of Labor (1968), but they could have come from any number of test instructions.

1. Get ready for the test by taking other tests on your own.

2. Don't let the thought of taking a test throw you, but being a little nervous won't hurt you.

3. Arrive early, rested, and prepared to take the test.

4. Ask questions until you understand what you are supposed to do.

5. Some parts of the test may be easier than others. Don't let the hard parts keep you from doing well on the easier parts.

6. Keep time limits in mind when you take a test.

7. Don't be afraid to answer when you aren't sure you are right, but don't guess wildly.

8. Work as fast as you can, but try not to make mistakes. Some tests have short time limits.

All the above "hints" are really concerned with the socialization process involved in test taking. For example, hint 1 deals with the development of test taking as a type of social activity into which one should become enculturated by exposure to the process of test taking itself. Chances of success on any given test are enhanced by having been exposed to previous test-type activities, whether they be other tests, preparatory test activities, or other socialization processes that simulate the types of activities called for in tests. Or, for example, hints 5, 7, and 8 deal with particular types of orientation procedures which tell how we are to assess different variables in the test. Hint 5 deals with a "coping" task in which the test taker should know he can compensate for the difficult parts by concentrating on the easier sections. Hint 7 deals with an assessment of the role of guessing as opposed to only answering questions of which the test taker is certain. And hint 8 deals with an understanding of how the relation of time should be dealt with in respect to accuracy. Now the interesting paradox found in the hints for test taking is that a number of them are theoretically part of the assumptions about the neutrality of the testing situation at the same time that they are admitted as contributing factors to success or failure in a test. If it is admitted that these hints may change how a person scores in a test, then the assumption about neutrality or control of the social occasion cannot be entirely valid.

The importance that the social occasion may have in testing has, in fact, led some educators to endorse the teaching of test taking as a distinct, important, and learnable skill in itself. While this may not be a completely satisfactory answer to the problem for other reasons, efforts to equalize the orientation to the testing occasion do deserve consideration.

Task Bias In addition to the aspects of the social occasion discussed above, testing makes certain types of assumptions concerning the specific tasks involved in test taking. The standardization process of testing requires not only that the test be uniformly administered, but that the test materials be understood and interpreted uniformly by the subjects taking the test. The assumption that there is one correct answer is based on the constructor's faith that he and the test taker share a common symbolic background in which objects have only one meaning which is apparent to all. From this perspective, meaning is not negotiated and built up over the course of the interaction, but it is assumed to share a commonness by the way in which the task is arranged.

All tests, no matter what the focus of the particular subject matter, must start with the assumption that the test taker comprehends the instructions (whether written or oral). These instructions are dependent upon linguistic comprehension of some type, so that even tests which do not seek to measure language skills at all still involve language and certain assumptions about it. From a linguistic standpoint, this involves the comprehension of sentence meanings, including the presuppositions and implications of questioning.

The obviousness of the instructions and questions becomes a point at which we must investigate the possible discrepancy between the interpretations of the test designer and testee. The first observation is that not all presumed obvious information is in fact necessarily obvious. In some cases, the appeal to obviousness comes from an inability to design the task clearly enough so that only the intended interpretation is possible. However straightforward the task may appear to the test designer, we can never exclude the possibility of ambiguity in the task. Although psychometric means of "validating" procedures may exist, there is no assurance that this is sufficient. We know, of course, that there are a number of reasons why an individual may not obtain the "correct" response. From our vantage point, it becomes crucial to know exactly why a subject or group of subjects did not come up with the correct response. A subject may give an incorrect response because he is unfamiliar with the vocabulary; or he may obtain the incorrect answer because he interpreted the question in terms of his own common sense; or because his presuppositions did not match those of the test designer. In terms of potential task interference, it becomes important to identify exactly why the answer is considered inappropriate by the test designer but not by certain test takers. One type of investigation of this is an analysis of errors using patterns that correlate with membership in socially and linguistically defined groups. However, another investigative approach is available that makes use of the test material itself as data (see Cicourel et al., 1974, for important studies of test material as data). From a sociolinguistic perspective, it becomes essential to identify some of the potential ways in which the task as presented may interfere with the identification of correct responses. We are here concerned not so much with the stated protocol in test administration, but with the subtleties of the task which may interfere with the assumption of "obviousness."

Different groups may share a desire to succeed in their performance on a test, but simply interpret the protocol of "obvious" instructions differently. Take, for example, the simple instruction to repeat something. The first problem we must recognize is that the instructions to repeat allow for more than one interpretation. One interpretation calls for verbatim repetition, whereas another allows for similarity in communicative content through paraphrase. The second problem lies in the assumption that the test taker can extract from his real life uses of repetition (which are drastically different) and remain in the experimental frame where repetition is an end in itself. Interestingly enough, an informal survey of lower-class children's performance on a sentence-repetition task showed two types of departures in the performance of the task (King, 1972). One was a tendency to respond in terms of language use outside the context of the specified experimental frame which called for verbatim repetition. Thus asked to repeat a sentence like "Is the car in the garage?" while being shown a picture of a car in the garage, many children chose to answer by giving the information relevant to the question rather than simply repeating the question. This, of course, is a reasonable way to respond to a question—outside the specialized testing situation. The other problem involved a tendency to give more detail than the verbatim repetition called for in the response. In essence, many of the stimuli were paraphrased rather than repeated verbatim. From the children's perspective, the paraphrase had to be interpreted as an attempt to succeed at the task, but from the test designer's perspective, the task was not followed as prescribed. Strict verbatim was the avenue for success in this task, not detailed recapitulation. But suppose the child's experience suggests that positive value should be placed on those types of language use which might involve a paraphrase or caricature of what a first party has said rather than verbatim recall. One can see how interpretations of this sort would lead to serious misunderstandings of the "simple" instructions to repeat.

Quite obviously, task interference may be reflected in the choice of a general method for obtaining the desired information. The information which the test taker has to give back is relatively constant, but one method may tap this information to a much greater extent than another. Consider, for example, the notion of "word knowledge" as an illustration. Word knowledge may be obtained in a number of different ways, one of which is synonymy. The notion of synonymy as such involves a task which is fairly well restricted to the testing situation and fairly educated writing styles. This, however, is not to say that the notion of "word knowledge" is not found outside of these situations. There is ample evidence that all individuals can give approximate definitions or uses of words, but it does not necessarily involve the notion of "word replaceability" which is a part of synonymy. As Meier (1973: 10) puts it:

A synonym is only one approach to "word definition" and involves a quite abstract notion about the replaceability of one word for another. If pressed for a "meaning," children (and adults) generally give a story example that describes the word or context which uses it appropriately.

Similarly, antonymy is another method commonly used to get at the notion of word meaning or relationship. However, the notion of opposition may in fact imply different relationships than those which the test designer intends when he illustrates the notion with an "obvious" example of antonymy. Meier points out that the notion of opposite may in fact quite legitimately be interpreted as something which is "very different." By this interpretation items like "tall" and "far" might be considered opposites, just as surely as "tall" and "short." Failure to obtain the "correct" notion of antonymy might then be interpreted not as a result of an inability to get the right answer, but as a result of focus on a different relationship. The assumed neutrality of tasks must indeed be questioned as it relates to different individuals and different social groups. Middle-class children, because of their familiarity with specific tasks as they are employed to get certain types of information, would appear to hold a serious advantage over their working-class counterparts in playing the test game. Given the fact that testing tasks involve a particular type of extraction from real-life language tasks, the only way an equal chance for success can be assured for all social groups is to ensure similar familiarities with the tasks.

Principles to Guide the Test User   In the previous sections we have presented a sociolinguistic perspective on testing. We have also provided examples of the types of potential sociolinguistic interference that may be found in tests. At this point, we may summarize our discussion by setting forth some principles to guide the test user in the consideration of tests.[3] Although some of the principles relate specifically to a sociolinguistic perspective on testing, others are more general in nature. In terms of general standards and guidelines for tests, we strongly recommend that all test users become familiar with the principles set forth in *Standards for Educational and Psychological Tests*, which gives a much more extended set of guidelines.

Principle 1: *The test user must compare what the test claims to be testing with what it actually tests.* It cannot always be assumed that a test actually assesses what it claims to. With respect to language, we must ask what aspects of a language are actually being tested as compared to what the test claims to tap. All tests which consistently differentiate groups of individuals measure something, but not necessarily what they set out to measure. For example, the Peabody Picture Vocabulary Test, which is widely used in a number of different disciplines, may be an effective measure of a person's receptive ability to recognize the pictorial referents of dialectally specific lexical items. This, however, is quite different from the general claims about assessing vocabulary acquisition it makes, let alone any indications of intelligence which may be a derivative of the test. The initial question of content validity is the touchstone for evaluating any testing instrument.

Principle 2: *The test user must consider the types of assumptions which underlie the testing task.* Tests which involve participation of some type involve certain assumptions about the nature of this participation. The range of assumed abilities may, of course, vary greatly from test to test. For example, one test of language may require only that a child show recognition of a pictorial reference through the activity of pointing. Others may involve the assumption of reading ability and an orientation of a particular multiple-choice format. If the assumptions necessary for performance on the test cannot be met satisfactorily by all the test takers, then the test will prohibit the collection of adequate data on the actual test items.

Principle 3: *The test user must ask what specific problems may be encountered by the speaker of a nonmainstream variety of English.* Given the current faddishness of ridiculing tests, it is imperative for the test user to give an account of the specific ways in which a test may hold potential for bias. For example, we have given specific cases where the speaker of AE may be expected to give alternant forms according to the grammatical rules for AE. The demand for specific information naturally requires a knowledge of the dialect in question and available reference works. In cases where descriptive reference works may not be available, the observant test user may pay attention to the linguistic form of an individual and check his usage against that of the speaker's peers to see if test performance can be attributed to a legitimate dialect difference or not.

Principle 4: *The test user should consider the accessibility of scoring information on individual items in the test.* In some cases, recurrent patterns in the answers of test takers may give important clues as to the nature of sociolinguistic interference. In order to perform the type of item analysis necessary to discover such patterns, however, it is necessary to be able to retrieve not only information on specific test items, including the categories of "wrong" answers. Unfortunately, there are a number of standardized tests where the results are available only in terms of total scores. This means that there is no potential for looking at the distribution of specific responses. On one level, test scores must be considered as important sociolinguistic data, and there are a number of ways in which the data can be analyzed if the test user has access to information on specific items. Without such specific information, however, the sociolinguistic usefulness of test results is minimal.

Principle 5: *The test user should know how to interpret the results of a test for nonmainstream speakers.* Given the possible ways in which a test may systematically favor certain groups, it becomes essential to know how the results from a given test must be interpreted. For example, it is important to know what a raw score of 8 out of 33 correct responses on the ITPA grammatical closure subtest may mean for the AE speaker who systematically uses legitimate AE alternants for many of the items which would have to be scored incorrect according to the directions for scoring in the test manual. The language capabilities of such a speaker may be very different from those of the speaker of the mainstream variety who obtains a score of 8 or the AE speaker who obtains a low score not because of the AE alternants but because he has a genuine language disability.

Principle 6: *The test user must know what justifiable classifications and assessments can be made in light of the test's potential for sociolinguistic bias.* Ultimately, the use of test results in the decision-making process is the most crucial aspect for the test user to consider. Given the potential for bias that many tests hold, the test user must proceed with extreme caution in accepting diagnoses and classifications based on test scores. In fact, it is reasonable to suggest that no diagnosis or classification of language capabilities should be made solely on the basis of a standardized test score. Evidence from tests must be coupled with other types of data, including observations outside the testing situation. Ultimately, attention must be given to the individual's use of language in a number of different social settings before any decision can be made regarding a child's language capabilities.

An Illustrative Case   The principles set forth above may be illustrated by turning again to an actual test. For illustrative purposes, we have chosen the language skills subtest of the California Achievement Test (1963) which has fairly wide distribution in various sections of the United States. We observe that the California Achievement Test (CAT) is designed "for the measurement, evaluation, and diagnosis of school achievement" (CAT Manual, 1963: 2). While this is what the test claims to be measuring with reference to language, the language subtest turns out, for the most part, to be a test in the recognition of written Standard English sentences.[4] This recognition may or may not be related to skills achieved in school. For the speaker of a nonmainstream variety who is being taught Standard English in school, it might relate to school achievement; however, for the speaker of a mainstream variety who comes to school speaking a mainstream variety, it has no direct relation to what is being learned in the schools. There is, then, a discrepancy between what the test claims to be testing and what it actually assesses for different groups of speakers (Principle 1).

The test makes two important assumptions about the test taker's participation in the task (Principle 2). For one, it assumes reading ability. Although the recognition of Standard English may exist independent of reading, it cannot be tapped here unless the child can read. Furthermore, the test presumes familiarity with a mutually exclusive response format such as

$$He \begin{Bmatrix} are \\ is \end{Bmatrix} my\ cousin.$$

One additional point in terms of the task involves the instructions to "make an *x* on the one you think is correct in each sentence." This direction requires that a child extract from the typical real-life situation, where the *x* is used to cross out wrong answers.

The specific items which may vary in this test for the AE speaker as opposed to the speaker of a mainstream variety are seen in Table 2 (Principle 3). In this case, the answers considered correct according to the test manual are italicized. In those cases where an alternant form would be acceptable according to the rules of AE, we have listed the number of the item in the Headnote where the particular rule is discussed.

Table 2   California Achievement Test with AE Alternant Forms

Stimulus with "correct" item according to Test Manual	Number of feature in Headnote
1. He $\left\{ \begin{array}{l} \text{are} \\ \textit{is} \end{array} \right\}$ my cousin.	
2. Can you $\left\{ \begin{array}{l} \textit{go} \\ \text{went} \end{array} \right\}$ out now?	
3. Beth $\left\{ \begin{array}{l} \text{come} \\ \textit{came} \end{array} \right\}$ home and cried.	3c
4. We $\left\{ \begin{array}{l} \textit{were} \\ \text{was} \end{array} \right\}$ told to sit down.	2
5. Mark read the poem $\left\{ \begin{array}{l} \text{too} \\ \textit{to} \end{array} \right\}$ the class.	
6. My sister $\left\{ \begin{array}{l} \text{am} \\ \textit{is} \end{array} \right\}$ six years old.	
7. I have read $\left\{ \begin{array}{l} \textit{those} \\ \text{them} \end{array} \right\}$ books before.	10a
8. She $\left\{ \begin{array}{l} \text{were} \\ \textit{was} \end{array} \right\}$ a nice girl.	
9. He $\left\{ \begin{array}{l} \text{run} \\ \textit{ran} \end{array} \right\}$ all the way to school.	3c
10. She $\left\{ \begin{array}{l} \text{see} \\ \textit{saw} \end{array} \right\}$ the cow in the barn.	
11. I $\left\{ \begin{array}{l} \textit{am} \\ \text{are} \end{array} \right\}$ a good pupil.	
12. A man $\left\{ \begin{array}{l} \textit{came} \\ \text{comed} \end{array} \right\}$ to the door.	3a
13. I didn't hear $\left\{ \begin{array}{l} \text{no} \\ \textit{any} \end{array} \right\}$ noise.	7a
14. There $\left\{ \begin{array}{l} \textit{were} \\ \text{was} \end{array} \right\}$ no ducks on the lake.	2

Table 2 (continued)

15. I try not to talk $\left\{ \begin{array}{c} too \\ to \end{array} \right\}$ much.	
16. Is $\left\{ \begin{array}{c} this\ here \\ this \end{array} \right\}$ your pencil?	10a
17. He $\left\{ \begin{array}{c} can \\ may \end{array} \right\}$ read very well.	
18. She will give me $\left\{ \begin{array}{c} them \\ those \end{array} \right\}$ dolls.	10a
19. We have $\left\{ \begin{array}{c} run \\ runned \end{array} \right\}$ many blocks.	3a
20. When $\left\{ \begin{array}{c} can \\ may \end{array} \right\}$ I come again?	
21. She $\left\{ \begin{array}{c} doesn't \\ don't \end{array} \right\}$ read very well.	2
22. She and $\left\{ \begin{array}{c} I \\ me \end{array} \right\}$ are good friends.	10b
23. I just $\left\{ \begin{array}{c} began \\ begun \end{array} \right\}$ my lessons.	3d
24. I have just $\left\{ \begin{array}{c} wrote \\ written \end{array} \right\}$ a poem.	3d
25. $\left. \begin{array}{c} Isn't \\ Aren't \end{array} \right\}$ most houses painted white?	2

Of the 25 items in the test, there are 15 in which the alternant form in the list of choices is a legitimate AE linguistic item. In these 15 cases, the AE speaker who intuitively follows the rules of his dialect will obtain answers which would be marked incorrect. The speaker of a mainstream variety, however, should obtain correct responses here simply by following intuitively the rules of his dialect.

The scoring of the test may provide a breakdown in terms of the individual items if hand-scored (Principle 4). It is unclear if the alternate procedure involving machine scoring allows for the retrieval of answers to individual items, but such information would appear necessary to see how much influence the speaker's intuitive rules of AE may actually have on his answers.

The interpretation of results for the speaker of a nonmainstream variety can best be done by comparison with what the results may mean for the speaker of a mainstream variety (Principle 5). For the majority of items, the mainstream dialect speakers are tested on the recognition of their mainstream dialect rules in writing. Following their intuitions in terms of the rules they have acquired from their community, they should obtain correct responses without assistance from the school. For speakers of a nonmainstream variety, however, it measures the ability to recognize written Standard English, a dialect different from the one they have acquired in their community. Dependence on intuitions from the dialect they have acquired would lead them to responses quite different from that of mainstream dialect speakers. If Standard English is being taught in the school, the test might tap some facet of school achievement in language for the speaker of a nonmainstream variety. It is, however, inappropriate to compare results from the mainstream and nonmainstream speakers as aspects of school achievement, since the test may be measuring quite different things in each case.

In connection with the observations made above, the test user should know what legitimate assessments can be made on the basis of this test (Principle 6). As an indicator of the recognition of written Standard English in a particular testing format, it may hold some validity. However, as an assessment instrument of basic school achievement in language skills, it must be viewed quite cautiously, for the results may lead to unfounded conclusions.

Integrating Dialect Diversity into Language Arts We should note the potential that the study of AE has for the investigation of dialect diversity and general linguistic inquiry as a part of language arts. In a number of the more recent language arts materials developed for both primary and secondary levels, the nature of dialect diversity has been given some attention. Within this context, the study of AE can provide a rich data source for the firsthand observation of such diversity. For the most part, individuals within the Appalachian range are aware of language differences between this area and other regions of the United States. Unfortunately, in many cases, such diversity is often seen in terms of unwarranted stereotypes rather than as a valid object of study in order to determine the nature of these differences. Data from the AE system can provide a base from which an accurate understanding of the systematic nature of linguistic diversity could be developed. Both individual introspection and the collection of samples from other residents in the area may serve as a data base.

The knowledge of a language is a somewhat unique kind of knowledge in that a speaker has it simply by virtue of the fact that he speaks a language. While much of this knowledge is, to be sure, on a tacit rather than a conscious level, it allows the potential for systematic tapping that few disciplines can match. Examining how a speaker of AE uses his language provides a natural laboratory for making generalizations based on an array of data. In this context, our knowledge of the language can be used as the basis for hypothesizing rules which govern the use of particular linguistic items. These hypotheses, formulated on the basis of initial observation, can then be checked against additional data that we provide as speakers of a language. In a sense, then, hypothesis construction and testing as an approach to the nature of scientific inquiry can be examined through the unique laboratory of language. While the formalization of particular aspects of the system may call for specific training, it is quite clear that accurate generalizations are not the unique domain of the professional linguist; they are open to any speaker of a language. From this perspective, the speaker of AE should be encouraged to use his knowledge of the system as an introduction to the systematic nature of dialect diversity.

Although the above suggestion may, at first glance, seem somewhat abstract and removed from the actual situation in the language arts classroom, it can readily be translated into practical language arts exercises. For example, take an item such as perfective or completive *done*. In an attempt to introduce students to the systematic way in which this form operates, a teacher might ask them to construct sentences where the time or aspect perspective makes the use of *done* permissible. This would then be compared with instances where it would not be permissible. On the basis of the acceptable and unacceptable contexts, students may then come up with a hypothesis which in turn could be checked against the data. The rules must, of course, ultimately account for all but only the cases where the form is permissible. The significance of such an exercise lies as much in the process as in the result. That is, the fact that the students provide the data, make the hypothesis, and then check this against the data is an important aspect of learning. In this way, students may learn about the nature of scientific inquiry in language and the systematic nature of linguistic diversity. Many of the descriptive features in the Headnote and Appendix H would lend themselves conveniently to such types of exercises. In fact, hypotheses that students arrive at may be checked with the analyses provided here, and revisions made on this basis. While this type of exercise may appear to be more appropriate to students on a secondary level, such an approach has been experimented with quite successfully on a primary level as well.

In addition to the use of introspective techniques such as those described above, it is possible to use the linguistic diversity within Appalachia itself to considerable advantage in the language arts curriculum. For example, language change can be examined through the comparison of speakers from different age levels. An important dimension of the diversity within AE relates to age differences. Students could interview older and middle-aged residents and then look for ways in which their own usage differed from that observed in the interviews. Here again, we must point out that the expertise of the professional linguist is not necessary to make valid observations.

The use of the community as a base for looking at diversity within Appalachia may have advantages other than the examination of age differences. For one, it may serve as an impetus to look at the roots of the English language as it has developed through the years. In this way, the study of the history of the English language can be a meaningful and vibrant subject matter for classroom discussion. Another advantage of sending students into the community itself relates to the preservation of the cultural and oral traditions of the region. There is, for example, a rich oral tradition and verbal art which has developed around story telling in Appalachia. An indication of the recognition of this art is found in the fact that most people in the community can readily recall individuals who are recognized as "good story tellers." Using such residents as sources for preserving the traditions of the region could be a rewarding activity as well as provide an opportunity to look at the art of story telling. The qualities that make a person a good story teller could be investigated by comparing different individuals recognized as story tellers as well as by eliciting comments from the community concerning the characteristics of a good story. While we shall not detail them here, there are many ways in which community themes can be tapped in meaningful educational and cultural ways. The success of Eliot Wigginton's *Foxfire* (1972) collections attests to the cultural and educational advantages of using the community itself as a primary source in language arts. In the context of the linguistic tradition of Appalachia, there is great opportunity for the language arts specialist to use firsthand data in a meaningful way in the education of children from the region. In many cases, however, such resources are not going to be tapped if activities are limited to the conventional approaches to the curriculum in language arts. The creative language arts specialist will have to go beyond such sources in utilizing the potential of the community itself. Although this admittedly requires a different type of preparation and some creativity, language arts specialists who invest their energy in such an effort should reap rich rewards for their work.

Dialect Diversity and Reading

The distance from written Standard English to nonmainstream varieties of English is greater than that to varieties of spoken Standard English. This fact naturally has implications for children acquiring the skill of reading, since they bring with them the variety of English from the community around them and are faced with a form of written Standard English as reading material. The question that has been raised by sociolinguists and educators is how great an effect this mismatch has on the acquisition of reading skills.

The role language plays in the acquisition and process of reading is an important one. In speech, language rules mediate between sound and meaning. While the purposes for which written language is used may differ from those of speech, the reading process must also involve these rules, mediating instead between visual symbols and meaning. This interrelationship between language and reading is thus a crucial one and may have even further implications for the learning processes involved. Frank Smith (1971: 45) observes:

> Whatever the relation of speech to writing, the fact that almost all children have acquired a good deal of verbal fluency before they face the task of learning to read has a dual significance for understanding the reading process. In the first place children have a basis of language that is obviously relevant to the process of learning to read—the written language is basically the same language as that of speech, even if it has special lexical, syntactic, and communicational aspects. But equally important, study of the manner in which children learn to speak and understand spoken language can provide considerable insight into the manner in which they might approach the task of learning to read.

Given the influence of language in reading, we must ask how great a problem the mismatch between spoken language and the language of reading materials poses for the child in developing reading skills. This mismatch is present to some extent for all children, owing to the characteristic differences between speech and writing. Our focus here, however, is on those cases where dialect diversity makes the distance even greater. While it is not yet known what degree of difference leads to difficulty in learning to read, there is evidence that children who speak nonmainstream varieties of English show a higher rate of failure in reading than others. While this higher rate is undoubtedly a product of other social factors as well, it seems likely that language patterns are involved. (See Baratz, 1973; Venezky and Chapman, 1973.)

There are obviously a large number of areas of potential conflict due to differing language patterns when someone is developing reading skills. For instance, when reading aloud, a very common activity in the earlier grades, an AE speaker might say *acrosst* when the printed word is *across*. If this and other comparable features are counted as reading errors rather than being recognized as features of spoken language, the student's reading ability may be underestimated. Frequent correction in these cases might also lead to confusion on the student's part, since the task of acquiring reading skills may become enmeshed with learning standard forms of English.

Sociolinguists and educators who have considered the problem of differing language patterns and reading have suggested various ways of dealing with it. The options basically involve changing the methods or the materials for teaching reading in order to accommodate dialect diversity. These four alternatives are discussed in detail by Wolfram (1970). It is not our intention to advocate any one of the options but rather to state briefly the advantages and disadvantages each has. An important consideration in all cases is the need for an understanding of the features of the dialect before any special measures can be undertaken. With an inventory of features modifications in programs can be suited to the specific groups involved. That is, materials or methods designed with Vernacular Black English speakers in mind, for example, would not be appropriate for use with AE speakers because of the significant differences between the two varieties. In most cases, it would be preferable to retain programs geared to mainstream varieties of English rather than assuming that nonmainstream varieties were enough alike to allow the same approach for all of them.

Two of the alternative ways of handling dialect diversity with respect to reading have the advantage that no change in materials would be required. The first of these involves changing the child instead. In this approach, Standard English would be taught before any reading instruction began, in order to reduce the gap between the spoken language and the reading materials. Then the teaching of reading could proceed, ideally with no problems caused by dialect interference. The rationale for this method takes two very different forms. Those who believe that nonmainstream varieties are deficient in some way advocate it, not only as a way to facilitate the acquisition of reading skills but also to remedy the cognitive handicap such children are assumed to have because of their language system. This interpretation cannot be justified, and so any program dependent on it could not be seen as desirable. Other advocates of this position, however, recognize nonmainstream dialects as legitimate linguistic systems. They feel that Standard English must be taught prior to reading to ease some of the difficulties there. In this way, the student would control both varieties and could call on the standard one during the development of reading skills.

The proposal stemming from the second type of rationale seems very attractive until the practical implementation is considered, when certain disadvantages become apparent. First of all, teaching Standard English first would mean that all reading instruction would have to be postponed for some period of time. This delay might have some effect on learning to read itself and would certainly cause the students involved to lag behind the other members of their grade for a while at least. Second, and probably most important, it is not at all clear that widespread success can be expected in teaching Standard English. If success in teaching the language forms is uncertain, delaying reading instruction until it is accomplished would not appear to be a desirable course of action.

The second alternative provides for allowing nonmainstream speakers to read in their own dialect (noticeable mainly during reading "aloud"). This has the advantage that it can be implemented immediately with no change in the student or the materials. In this case, the teacher would accept alternant forms from the standard materials as accurate renditions if they represent features of the student's spoken language variety. This approach particularly demands a familiarity with the variety on the part of the teachers so that a clear distinction can be maintained between true reading errors and dialect features. The teachers in this case must also be observers of the students' spoken language to be confident that the features are in fact part of their systems. According to this approach, an AE speaker who reads *There were four yellow flowers* as *They was four yeller flowers* would not be corrected if the teacher has noticed this type of concord, final unstressed *-ow*, and existential *they* as features of the student's speech. It would, in fact, seem likely that such students are exhibiting good comprehension by interpreting the sentence according to their own language patterns.

There are potential disadvantages to this approach as well, although they appear less severe than those for teaching Standard English first. Although most of the differences between mainstream and nonmainstream varieties are apparently surface-level phenomena, there is a possibility that some meaning will be missed or misinterpreted by nonmainstream speakers when reading Standard English materials. Little evidence is available on this point, and hence it is impossible to determine how greatly comprehension would be affected if this method is adopted. Also, those who advocate teaching Standard English would object to this approach on the grounds that it would not necessarily contribute to the learning of standard forms. However, it is important to remember that learning spoken Standard English and learning to read are different activities and, as goals of teaching, should be clearly distinguished.

The remaining two alternatives involve changing the materials to lessen the gap between a student's language patterns and those of the reading materials. Where modification of materials is required, there is naturally the practical disadvantage of cost. Again, it is extremely important to have available an accurate description of the variety in question, as well as some idea as to the generality and importance of the features to justify designing materials around them. The restructuring of materials would also mean that different sets would need to be developed for the various nonmainstream varieties where dialect diversity was found to cause difficulty for students in learning to read since the nature and extent of features different from Standard English vary.

The development of "dialect-fair" or "dialect-free" materials, the third option on our list, is probably the less controversial of the remaining two. This proposal basically aims at reducing the problems caused by dialect differences by eliminating, as far as possible, those features in the Standard English texts which have alternant forms in the nonmainstream variety. In this approach, a text intended for AE speakers would, for example, have no instances of existential *there* due to the nonstandard concord patterns it can follow and would avoid using past tense irregular verbs for the same reason. The rationale for this approach is based on the belief that learning to read is facilitated by eliminating those features which would be unfamiliar to the nonmainstream speaker. None of the alternant nonstandard forms are used; only standard forms that are also part of the variety are included.

The major disadvantage to this approach lies in its assumption that it is feasible to construct reading materials in this way, that mainstream and nonmainstream varieties have enough in common to provide for such neutral texts. The number of features which have alternant forms in a nonmainstream variety can be quite large. To avoid them in composing a text might cause the language of the materials to be very unnatural. For instance, in materials designed with AE in mind, no relative clauses like *I know the people who lived up there* could be used owing to potential relative pronoun deletion, adverbs that had standard forms ending in *ly* such as *originally* and *certainly* would have to be avoided because of the possibility of *ly* absence, and so on. Some evaluation measure might be used, however, to determine a ranking for the features so that only the more important ones would need to be involved. In this way, the gap might be reduced without making the materials too unnatural. Constructing entirely new texts, although time-consuming, might allow for the use of this method. Attempts to alter existing materials might prove more difficult, as Wolfram and Fasold (1974: 197) point out:

> Even if the overall differences between the standard and nonstandard dialect are significantly less than the similarities, the clustering of differences may make this strategy virtually unusable for particular types of passages.

Neutralization of reading materials with respect to nonmainstream varieties could have certain advantages, however. Eliminating the features that might be unfamiliar to nonmainstream speakers could simplify the task of learning to read for them. Neutralization of texts without incorporation of nonstandard forms also avoids the controversy over whether or not it is desirable to include socially stigmatized language patterns. It would be possible for teachers to use this strategy to some extent without costly revisions of materials by designing certain texts on their own, provided, of course, they are aware of which features should be neutralized.

The fourth alternative that has been suggested by certain sociolinguists and educators is the use of dialect readers for beginning materials. This proposal involves developing texts written in the nonmainstream variety spoken by the students, with a gradual conversion to Standard English materials once reading skills have been established. Those who advocate this strategy (see Baratz, 1973, and the discussion of these readers in Leaverton, 1973) argue that learning to read is facilitated if the language patterns of the student's speech are more closely matched by those appearing in beginning readers. An additional advantage comes from the confidence this may give the student with respect to his speech; that is, feelings that it is somehow "inferior," which are fairly common, may be lessened if the variety is represented in printed materials and not stigmatized in the classroom.

This alternative would require not only development of early reading materials written using the nonmainstream variety but also a set of transitional readers which would gradually introduce the various alternant standard forms. An example sentence in a test intended for AE speakers might be developed in the following way: A first representation might be *They come here about three year ago.* Then, a later stage might add the plural ending, giving *They come here about three years ago* and finally, the standard form of the irregular past tense would be introduced, giving *They came here about three years ago.* Naturally, because of the development of reading skills that would be going on, as well as the fact that sets of materials would be different, the sentences would not be replicated exactly as in this example. A schema for introducing standard features would need to be devised, though, based on an accurate descriptive account of the variety and some decision procedure for establishing an order for the entry of particular forms or patterns at various levels.

We mentioned above that this strategy is the most controversial of the alternatives. Looking at it in a purely practical light, the difficulties of implementation, in terms of developing the materials alone, present quite an obstacle. The strongest criticisms, however, have come from those who believe that Standard English should be taught and feel that the use of dialect readers will only reinforce the nonmainstream language patterns, and thus delay the acquisition of Standard English. This objection often is voiced by members of the community from which the students come who are sensitive to the social stigmatization of the various dialect features. There is also a feeling that the use of different materials for a particular group signifies some inferiority on the part of that group, in that it is assumed they are unable to learn to read in the same way as everyone else. This type of criticism is made as well by others who feel it is the job of the schools to teach Standard English and this approach can only impede progress toward that goal. Leaverton (1973) discusses the difficulty of convincing school personnel to allow dialect readers to be used even on an experimental basis to determine their effectiveness. Thus the controversy that surrounds this approach is a disadvantage that may be impossible to overcome at this time.

Another problem with dialect readers is the identification of the population for whom they are appropriate. Care must be taken to ensure that these materials are truly reflective of the language patterns of the students, since a reverse mismatch would occur if they are not. In some cases, the texts have inappropriately been used as general remedial materials, for students having difficulty with the acquisition of reading skills when not all the students were speakers of the nonmainstream variety in question. This would undoubtedly only lead to greater confusion on the part of such students. Dialect readers are not remedial materials, and precautions should be taken to prevent this type of misuse.

It should be apparent from the above discussion that none of the alternatives provides a foolproof way of dealing with dialect diversity and the teaching of reading. There is as yet no clear way to resolve the sociopolitical issues and at the same time treat the problems that occur in learning to read because of linguistic differences. Much more evidence of the effectiveness of the various approaches needs to be gathered.

There are, however, certain suggestions that can be made for those who cannot wait for this evidence because they must face the situation immediately. An important distinction that needs to be kept clear is that between the goals of teaching Standard English and teaching reading. Although a policy decision on the spoken-language question may limit the alternatives in terms of reading, the two activities should be separated so that the acquisition of reading skills is a well-defined goal in itself. A first step that can be taken follows the second option discussed above, that of allowing students to read in their own dialect. This can be immediately implemented, provided that the teacher has the information needed to discriminate between reading errors and valid patterns of the students' spoken language. In this way, the task of learning to read will not be confused with language instruction and the mismatch we have spoken of will be somewhat less intense.

Other activities can also be planned to supplement the school reading curriculum. In our discussion of language arts, the community was viewed as a valuable source of a number of possible activities. There are also a variety of applications of these suggestions for teaching reading, following an approach similar to the "language experience" type of program. In addition to having the students recount stories which can then be read back (the most common form "language experience" activities take), tapping the oral traditions of the community can also provide a source of reading materials. The stories that could be gathered by the students would be told in the language of the community and so would be linguistically appropriate as texts for reading in terms of the match between spoken and written language. There would, of course, be additional benefits in terms of preserving the traditions of the area, providing meaningful experiences for the students, and generally adding some excitement to the task of developing reading skills. A model for this type of activity can be found in the *Foxfire* collections, compiled by Eliot Wigginton, which have met with great success, both in terms of the learning experiences for the students involved and in its value for the community as a whole. It would appear that the model could be adapted to any grade level and would be extremely useful if implemented in beginning reading. The materials would, in a sense, be designed by the students and the community and so would be linguistically and culturally appropriate. This could be very effective in facilitating the development of reading skills, for both the beginning student and the older student needing some remedial work. It would also, of course, be a useful and interesting activity for more advanced readers.

There are certain other considerations that relate to dialect diversity and reading beyond the specific approaches to teaching reading. One aspect involves the evaluation of reading skills in the form of standardized and individual classroom testing. We saw in the previous general discussion of testing that dialect diversity has potentially a great effect on performance on standardized tests, and the implications of this are far-reaching. These comments hold as well for tests of reading, since often the knowledge of standard forms of English is implicitly or overtly part of the evaluation. As Principle 3 stated, the test user must consider carefully what problems the nonmainstream speaker of English might face in an attempt to identify what parts of the test truly evaluate reading ability and what parts do not.

Another dimension of dialect diversity that should be mentioned here is the cultural and social diversity that generally accompanies it. These factors enter into the consideration of comprehension (and tests of comprehension) as well as in the concern which is often voiced for making materials "relevant." For instance, an urban student might have difficulty with a story that dealt with life on a small farm, even though the reading of the story could be successfully accomplished. In the same way, a student who had always been in a rural environment might find the reading task unduly complicated by subject matter involving street life in a big city. These types of gaps show up often as poor comprehension skills in testing situations. For example, a common type of question in comprehension tests is something like "Why do you think the author wrote this story?" This might well be answered in a way considered incorrect if the values in the cultures of the test designer and the student do not match. These sorts of problems are ones teachers and other test users should be aware of when they choose to use a test, or use its results for some evaluation of a student. Reading tests are particularly susceptible to this difficulty, owing to the comprehension component.

There are, of course, many other considerations and suggestions that could be made with respect to dialect diversity and the teaching/learning of reading. This outline of some of the advantages and disadvantages of alternatives to dealing with the situations is intended to be suggestive of ways in which different strategies may be used and what sorts of problems might occur. Since none of the options emerges as the clear solution, no recommendations can be made at this time. However, programs designed with an awareness of the relationship of dialect diversity to reading are needed to minimize the effect of linguistic differences on the task of learning to read for the speaker of a nonmainstream variety.

NOTES

1. The framework discussed here is essentially that presented in Wolfram (1976), with special adaptation for AE.

2. The prediction of linguistic interference in tests should, of course, be followed up with studies of test responses to observe the actual patterning of interference.

3. A *test user* is defined here to mean anyone who is involved in choosing a test to be used or who makes decisions based on test scores.

4. In addition to the majority of sentences in this subsection which are related to the recognition of written Standard English sentences, there are several sentences related to the spelling of one item (*to/too*) and several sentences which relate to the recognition of sentences which would violate the grammatical rules of both mainstream and nonmainstream varieties.

References

Baratz, Joan C., 1973   "The Relationship of Black English to Reading: A Review of Research." In James L. Laffey and Roger W. Shuy, eds., *Language Differences: Do They Interfere?* International Reading Association.

Cicourel, Aaron V., et al., 1974   *Language Use and School Performance.* Academic Press.

Illinois Test of Psycholinguistic Abilities, 1968   University of Illinois Press.

King, Pamela, 1972   *An Analysis of the Northwestern Syntax Screening Test for Lower Class Black Children in Prince George's County.* Unpublished MA thesis, Howard University.

Leaverton, Lloyd, 1973   "Dialectal Readers: Rationale, Use and Value." In James L. Laffey and Roger W. Shuy, eds., *Language Differences: Do They Interfere?* International Reading Association.

Meier, Deborah, 1973   *Reading Failure and the Tests.* Workshop Center for Open Education.

Roberts, Elsa, 1970   "An Evaluation of Standardized Tests as Tools for the Measurement of Language Development," *Language Research Reports*, no. 1. Language Research Foundation.

Smith, Frank, 1971   *Understanding Reading: A Psycholinguistic Analysis of Reading and Learning to Read.* Holt, Rinehart and Winston.

Tiegs, Ernest, and Willis Clark, 1963   California Achievement Test. McGraw-Hill.

U.S. Department of Labor, 1968   "Doing Your Best on Aptitude Tests." Government Printing Office.

Venezky, Richard L., and Robin S. Chapman, 1973   "Is Learning to Read Dialect Bound?" In James L. Laffey and Roger W. Shuy, eds., *Language Differences: Do They Interfere?* International Reading Association.

Wigginton, Eliot, 1972   *The Foxfire Book.* Doubleday.

Wolfram, Walt, 1970   "Sociolinguistic Alternatives in Teaching Reading to Nonstandard Speakers," *Reading Research Quarterly* 6, 9-33.

———, 1976   "Levels of Sociolinguistic Bias in Testing." In Deborah Harrison and Thomas Trabasso, eds., *Black English: A Seminar.* Lawrence Erlbaum Associates.

Wolfram, Walt, and Ralph W. Fasold, 1974   *The Study of Social Dialects in American English.* Prentice-Hall.

MODES OF MITIGATION AND POLITENESS

William Labov

Beginning in 1965 with funding from the Office of Education, William Labov and several colleagues conducted a comprehensive study of the vernacular language spoken by Black and Puerto Rican youths in south-central Harlem. This research convinced him that educators need to understand not only the phonological and grammatical structure but the entire cultural context of minority speakers if they are to work effectively with them. Thus Labov examines the peer culture in "The Linguistic Consequences of Being a Lame," included in this volume. And elsewhere he concludes that many Black students fail at reading and other academic tasks only partly because the structure of their language differs from the structure of Standard English; but they fail mainly because their cultural and political values, which their language symbolizes, conflict with those of the dominant society, represented by classroom language.

Another result of Labov's emphasis on cultural context is his experimentation with the new field of discourse analysis in the present excerpt from *The Study of Nonstandard English,* a pamphlet for secondary school teachers on the structure and educational implications of nonstandard English. Essentially, discourse analysts (like Zimmerman and West in this volume) maintain that there are rules for putting sentences together in a text or conversation just as there are rules for assembling words into sentences (see "The Structure of Language" of the General Introduction). Furthermore, these discourse rules may vary from one subculture to another within one language community. And, as Labov implies in his analysis of commands and questions, these variations in discourse rules may present even more formidable barriers to communication than phonological and grammatical differences because, while largely unconscious, they affect our entire interpretation of a speech event. Appendix G provides guidelines for readers who wish to pursue discourse analysis on their own.

We are only beginning to describe the rules for the use of language, but in this area we can observe many differences between nonstandard and standard speakers. The nonstandard speaker is undoubtedly handicapped in many ways by his lack of control over mitigating forms which are more highly developed in middle-class and school language. These forms are used to avoid conflict between individuals who meet in some kind of face-to-face encounter. The child may not know the mitigating ways of disagreeing with the teacher which make such disagreement acceptable in the school situation. It is not uncommon for Negro children to simply accuse the teacher of lying where middle-class white children might say, "There's another way of looking at it." Faced with the statement "You a lie!" most teachers find it necessary to react forcefully. After one or two such confrontations, most students learn to say nothing. But some students continue to object without learning the means of doing so without conflict. In the school records of boys we have studied, we find many cases where they have been reprimanded, even demoted, for their failure to use mitigating forms of politeness. For one fourteen-year-old named Junior, who can be described as a verbal leader of his subgroup, we find such entries as the following:

Nov. 63   Frequently comes to school without a tie. . . . He frequently calls out answer. When told not to call out he made an expression of disgust. He then refused to accept the rexographed sheet the teacher gave to the class.

Nov. 63   When asked to re-write a composition he adamantly refused. He said, "I will not." He doesn't practice any self control.

Dec. 63   Was fighting with another boy in class today . . .

Sept. 66   *F* in citizenship.

May 67   Mother has been in touch with school regarding son's truancy.

This record can be interpreted in several ways. Junior may be unable to compete with the smart kids and finds a way out in being "bad." Or it may be that he does not care at all about school and is simply expressing his defiance for the system. It is just as hard for us to interpret the school record by itself as it is for the teacher to deal with the student in this formal situation without any knowledge of the vernacular culture.

When we listen to Junior speaking outside of school, we can see that he has a natural command of language and has no difficulty in expressing his ideas. The following quotations are taken from a session with Junior, a black fieldworker, and Ronald, one of Junior's best friends. First of all, it is apparent that Junior does have strong feelings of resentment against the school and white society.

Junior: Like I'ma tell you the truth. They jus' want everythin' taken away from us. . . . Who do we work for? Whities! Who do we go to school for? Whities! Who's our teachers? Whities!
. . .
Interviewer: If the whitey's not different from you, how come he has everything?
Ronald: They don't have everything.
Junior: Yes they do!

It is important to note here that Junior and Ronald are members of the Jets, a group which is quite indifferent and even hostile to black nationalism and the Muslim religion. Junior has not been taught to be militant; the resentment expressed here is a product of Junior's own thinking—the result of his own experience. Despite his antagonism toward the dominant white society, he has retained a strong sense of realism in his evaluation of it. An argument with Ronald as to whether high school diplomas are necessary:

Ronald: And I'm 'onna tell you; I'm 'onna say *why* what they say you have to have a high school diploma. Some whitey's probably ain't got a high school diploma, and he still go out to work. My father ain't got a high school diploma.

Junior: Your father ain't no whitey, is he?

Ronald: No, but he has no high school diploma, but he go out there and work, right?

Junior: O.K.! . . . But . . . I'ma tell you, you're wrong in a *way*—cause ev'ry whitey—ev'ry whitey, if they out o' school, they went through *high* school. If they didn't go to college they went through *high* school. If the whities didn't go through high school, how come they got everything? . . . 'Cause they had the *knowledge.*

It seems clear that Junior is a much better speaker than Ronald. In complex arguments of this sort, Ronald's syntax gets him into problems like the double *but* clauses or the unsolved labyrinth of his first sentence quoted above. Junior has no such difficulty expressing his ideas. Furthermore, he has the ability to put one argument on top of another which is characteristic of those who win verbal contests.

Junior: If you—if you was in a high school—right? Why do people graduate?

Ronald: 'Cause they try hard to grad—'cause they *want* to graduate.

Junior: 'Cause they *learn* . . . 'cause they *learn.* If they didn't learn, and they just stood around, they wouldn't have everything. 'Cause you got to *work* to get to high school, you got to *work* to get from elementary to junior high . . .

In this dialogue, Junior seems to express very well the values of middle-class society. He shows a full cognitive awareness of the importance of education. It comes as something of a shock then to learn that at the time of this interview he was in the eighth grade and his reading score was 4.6—more than three years behind grade. And the disciplinary record cited above indicates that he is very unlikely to be graduating from high school himself. Note that the *they* of *they learn* seems at first reading to refer to a very general *people* who graduate; it seems to be an inclusive rather than an exclusive *they.* But when Junior says "*they* wouldn't have everything . . .'' it is clear that he is not including himself among the people who graduate.

Is there any internal evidence within this record as to why Junior is not learning to read—why he is not taking advantage of the school system to get what he so plainly wants? It is obviously not a question of his verbal intelligence. A reading of disciplinary events shows serious sources of conflict between him and his teachers which are preventing him from using his intelligence for the acquisition of knowledge. Each of these reported incidents was the occasion for an interruption in his school work, a violent confrontation with authority. The teachers report that he "calls out answers" and "doesn't practice any self control." The kinds of skills which Junior is lacking appear to be those verbal routines of mitigation which would make it possible for him to object and refuse without a major confrontation. Of course the record reflects the teachers' subjective impressions rather than what actually happened, but we can see enough to reconstruct the kinds of events involved and to isolate the problems for further study. Note that Junior's disciplinary record begins in the fifth grade, when he was eleven. The exchange between him and the teacher must have been something like this:

Teacher: Junior, this is very sloppy work.
Junior: No it isn't!
Teacher: Now you take that composition and write it over again!
Junior: I will not!

The sentence "I will not" was striking enough to be quoted in the teacher's report. It is an elliptical response, short for "I will not write that composition over again," but it is certainly not illogical. We hear a good deal about the faults of nonstandard language, but its strong points certainly include brevity and clarity. The problem with "I will not" is that it is altogether too clear: it lacks the verbal indirection which could have been used to make the objection and perhaps win the argument. Instead, the direct refusal without mitigation led to the end of the verbal exchange ("You go right down to the office . . .").

To show what Junior did not do, it is necessary to analyze the rules for commands, and for refusing commands, which prevail for Standard English and the middle-class society in which that language is embedded. Commands and refusals are actions; declarations, interrogatives, imperatives are linguistic categories—things that are said, rather than things that are done. The rules we need will show how things are done with words and how one interprets these utterances as actions: in other words, relating what is done to what is said and what is said to what is done. This area of linguistics can be called "discourse analysis"; but it is not well known or developed. Linguistic theory is not yet rich enough to write such rules, for one must take into account such sociological, nonlinguistic categories as roles, rights, and obligations. What small progress has been made in this area is the work of sociologists and philosophers who are investigating informally the rules which lie behind everyday "common sense" behavior.

We have, however, begun work in this field relative to requests and commands, so that it is possible to indicate what Junior might have done besides answering "I will not." Commands or requests for action are essentially instructions from a person A to a person B to carry out some action X at a time T.

$$A \rightarrow B: X!/T$$

This is the explicit form of such a command. But there are a number of unstated preconditions which must hold if the receiver B is to hear the command as valid (or a "serious" command). It is necessary that he believe that the originator A believes four things: that, at time T,

a. X should be done.
b. B has the obligation to do X.
c. B has the ability to do X.
d. A has the right to request that B do X.

These four preconditions are not only part of the process of judging and reacting to a command. They are also used for indirect ways of making the command or request. Either a statement or a question about any of these four preconditions can stand for and be heard as the command itself. Thus the teacher could have said:

a. This has to be done over. *or*
   Shouldn't this be done over?
b. You'll have to do this over. *or*
   Don't you have to do neater work than this?
c. You can do better than this. *or*
   Don't you think you can do neater work than this?
d. It's my job to get you to do better than this. *or*
   Can I ask you to do this over?

Some of these forms are heard as forceful requests, but many are heard as mitigated and very polite forms, even more than "Would you please . . . ?" Furthermore, not only are these preconditions used in making requests, but they are also utilized for mitigated forms of refusal. Denials of any of these preconditions, or questions about them, will serve the same purpose as "I will not" as far as the activity of refusing is concerned. Thus Junior could have said:

a. I don't think it's sloppy enough to do over. *or*
   It's not that sloppy, is it?
b. I'm not supposed to be doing penmanship today. *or*
   If it's right it doesn't have to be pretty, does it?
c. I sprained my wrist and I can't write good. *or*
   That's the best I've done so far, isn't it?
d. You have no right to tell me that. *or*
   Are you telling me to do everything twice?

Except for the last two forms, which concern the teacher's rights and are therefore extremely challenging, these kinds of refusals leave the door open for further negotiation. They are heard as partial refusals, in the sense that it is clear Junior will not rewrite the composition unless the teacher repeats the command. But most importantly, they are *deniable* refusals. If someone is accused of refusing a command by such forms, he is entitled to say, "I didn't refuse, I was only . . ." Furthermore, if the teacher wants to retreat, he too can say that Junior did not refuse, avoiding the loss of face involved in accepting a refusal. There are thus many adult ways of doing business in this situation. But the form "I will not" stands in contrast to all of these and signals an unwillingness to use the mitigated forms; it thus represents a direct challenge to the authority of the teacher. Perhaps Junior was angry and wanted to precipitate a crisis: the question is, did this eleven-year-old have the skills to avoid that crisis if he wanted to?

It is not suggested that all of these indirect, mitigating forms be taught in school. Much of this unnecessary elaboration may be expendable, just as much of the elaboration of formal syntax may be a matter of ritual style. But differences in the knowledge of such rules must be studied to isolate the areas of conflict which proceed from ignorance on both sides. It is not entirely clear that all of the adjustment must be on the part of the nonstandard language and the vernacular culture.

Asking Questions

One of the most common speech events which occurs in school is the asking of questions. Teachers ask students questions with astonishing frequency—sometimes five or six a minute or in some schools as high as fifteen or twenty a minute. Students occasionally ask teachers questions, though not as often. Sometimes the teacher asks questions to get students to ask questions, or at least to get them to talk as much as possible. In one way or another, teacher questions are often conceived of as ways of getting students to talk.

In sociolinguistic research, we also use questions to obtain speech—as much as possible—and we have therefore given a great deal of attention to the form of questions, their underlying presuppositions, and the kind of question that gets the most results. We observe very different patterns in speakers of different ages and social backgrounds, and different styles of questioning on the part of middle-class and working-class interviewers. But, on the whole, it appears that questions may not be very good means of getting people to talk. In order to understand why, it may be helpful to compare questions to the requests and commands discussed in the previous section.

A *question* may be used to execute many different kinds of speech acts, including commands, insults, jokes, and challenges. Here we are properly considering *requests for information*. This is a subtype of requests for action, discussed above, but with several different properties. Abstractly, these have the general form that A asks B to perform one particular act—to give him, by speaking or writing, certain information. The time is normally unstated and is understood as "right now."

$$A \rightarrow B: \text{tell me X!}$$

It has been noted, particularly by Skinner, that questions have a mandatory force. In answer to a question, one can lie or equivocate, but there is a strong social compulsion to respond; it is indeed very difficult to say nothing when someone asks you the time. Requests for information are harder to refuse than requests for action. In many social situations, including the schoolroom, two of the four conditions are presumed to hold at all times: B believes that A believes that

    d. A has the right to ask B the question.
    b. B has the obligation to answer.

Students may object to questions asked by the teacher on the ground that they are unfair, unclear, or not included in the assignment, but they cannot object that he has no right to ask. Thus (unless the teacher is a substitute, where anything goes), we do not have reports of

> Teacher: How much is 7 and 9?
> Student: You have no right to ask me that!

Correspondingly, the student knows that he is under an obligation to answer, if only to say that he does not know. Given these two constants in the situation, the student then must consider whether the other two conditions hold in order to see what is being done—whether the teacher believes that

a. X needs to be told to A.
c. B has the ability to answer.

Under normal conditions, this is not a simple problem to resolve. In the schoolroom, the situation is particularly difficult, since there are different options exercised in rapid succession. Sometimes condition (a) holds: the student believes that the teacher really does not know X and wants to know it. If condition (c) also holds—the teacher believes that the student has this information—we are dealing with a genuine request for information.

> Teacher: Did you find this homework too hard?

But this is not the usual case; in the classroom, condition (a) normally does *not* hold. There are then several possibilities which the student must consider. He may be dealing with

1. A known-answer question. A believes that he knows the answer and that B may not know it.
2. A no-answer question. A believes that there is no correct answer to the question.
3. A rhetorical question. A believes that he knows the answer and that B knows it too.

The first of these is the most typical—the test question. It is not a request for information about X but about B's ability to give X. More generally, it is *a request for proof.* Students generally understand that they are to say the minimum necessary to establish this proof. On various occasions, they have discovered that this is a situation where anything they say may indeed be held against them. One wrong remark added to an acceptable answer may act as a disproof, whereas a short but correct answer may be accepted as evidence of a larger body of correct information. Answers to test questions are therefore usually quite short.

The second type of no-answer question is essentially a *request for display.* "Tell me everything you can about *this*!" says the educational tester and places a free-form blank in front of a child. The response desired is for the child to begin talking and continue as long as he can. Discussion questions in high school classes are frequently of this type—leading questions designed to "draw out" the student.

The third type is equally common, but the work done by these rhetorical questions is often difficult to analyze. If the teacher asks "Now how many eyes do I have?" this may be a prelude to a discussion of bilateral symmetry among animals, a preface to a disciplinary rebuke, or an introduction to a discussion of odd and even numbers. The "correct" response is to give the obvious answer so that the teacher can continue with whatever he has in mind. Yet many rhetorical questions of this sort turn out to be forms of entrapment. After a certain number of bad experiences, many students learn not to volunteer answers to riddles, "come-ons," or invitations.

If we now consider the task of deciding which of these various possibilities holds at any given moment and what the consequences of a wrong decision may be, it appears that students are required to develop a very high level of expertise. Our intuitive responses to such situations run far ahead of our ability to analyze them. Even so, the situation may be quite unclear for many students. Consider the intelligence test in which the examiner holds up an orange and says, "What is this?" The child must ask himself: Is this a known-answer question, or a rhetorical question? If the latter, what is it a prelude to? Such "controlled testing" of educational psychologists provides a constant stimulus, but there is no control on the interpretations which intervene between the stimulus and the response. What is the question getting at? What type of question is it? What are the consequences of answering or not answering? The safest port in these storms may appear to be a simple "I don't know." The problem for the examiner is then to interpret the meaning of this "D.K." If he takes it as evidence of B's ability to give the information, it may be seriously misleading. Given the various pressures and uncertainties of the test situation and the fact that it is impossible for the child not to answer, it follows very often that he will utilize "don't know" as his only available means of refusing the request for information. This is the only assertion he can make which cannot be contradicted.

If we are to understand verbal behavior in the schoolroom situation we must begin to solve the general question posed here. How do students know, in a given situation, what kind of question is being posed, and what is requested of them? When we have the answers to this, we may simultaneously begin to understand some of the reasons for failure, confusion, and rejection in the classroom.

We will also be in a better position to carry out research on the verbal skills and linguistic habits of schoolchildren. It is a simple matter to ask a question, but to obtain a meaningful answer is much harder.

PARTICIPANT STRUCTURES AND COMMUNICATIVE COMPETENCE: WARM SPRINGS CHILDREN IN COMMUNITY AND CLASSROOM

Susan U. Philips

Like Labov in "Modes of Mitigation and Politeness," Susan U. Philips assumes that communication breakdowns between minority students and their teachers are traceable not just to differences in language structure but to divergent cultural assumptions about how verbal exchanges should be structured. Thus she analyzes how Warm Springs Indian children learn in their homes and community in order to illuminate their nonparticipation in the typical pattern of classroom interaction. In the terms of "The Nature of Communication" from the General Introduction, Philips is exploring the *ethnography of communication* in this Native American community and discovers considerable *cultural slippage* when Warm Springs children encounter their white teachers.

Using Philips as a model, readers are encouraged to observe rules for appropriate speech behavior in a cultural group other than their own (Appendix G can serve as one aid to such observation) and to consider whether these rules might result in communication failure between members of that culture and members of another. Also readers should be sure to take a position on how teachers should resolve cultural slippage once it is discovered. Should they (and can they) accommodate their teaching style to the cultural expectations of their students (a position analogous to affirming nonstandard dialects); is it their responsibility to enculturate students in the speech norms of the dominant society (analogous to insisting that they speak Standard English); or is there a useful and feasible middle ground?

Introduction

Recent studies of North American Indian education problems have indicated that in many ways Indian children are not culturally oriented to the ways in which classroom learning is conducted. The Wax-Dumont study (Wax et al., 1964) of the Pine Ridge Sioux discusses the lack of interest children show in what goes on in school, and Wolcott's (1967) description of a Kwakiutl school tells of the Indian children's organized resistance to his ways of structuring classroom learning. Cazden and John (1968) suggest that the "styles of learning" through which Indian children are enculturated at home differ markedly from those to which they are introduced in the classroom. And Hymes (1967) has pointed out that this may lead to sociolinguistic interference when teacher and student do not recognize these differences in their efforts to communicate with one another.

On the Warm Springs Indian Reservation in central Oregon, where I have been carrying out research in patterns of speech usage, teachers have pointed to similar phenomena, particularly in their repeated statements that Indian children show a great deal of reluctance to talk in class, and that they participate less and less in verbal interaction as they go through school. To help account for the reluctance of the Indian children of Warm Springs (and elsewhere as well) to participate in classroom verbal interactions, I am going to demonstrate how some of the social conditions governing or determining when it is appropriate for a student to speak in the classroom differ from those that govern verbal participation and other types of communicative performances in the Warm Springs Indian community's social interactions.

The data on which discussion of these differences will be based are drawn, first of all, from comparative observations in all-Indian classes in the reservation grammar school and non-Indian or white classes in another grammar school at the first- and sixth-grade levels. The purpose here is to define the communicative contexts in which Indian and non-Indian behavior and participation differ, and to describe the ways in which they differ.

After defining the situations or social contexts in which Indian students' verbal participation is minimal, discussion will shift to consideration of the social conditions in Indian cultural contexts that define when speaking is appropriate, attending to children's learning experiences both at home and in the community-wide social activities in which they participate.

The end goal of this discussion will be to demonstrate that the social conditions that define when a person uses speech in Indian social situations are present in classroom situations in which Indian students use speech a great deal, and absent in the more prevalent classroom situations in which they fail to participate verbally.

There are several aspects of verbal participation in classroom contexts that should be kept in mind during the discussion of why Indians are reluctant to talk. First of all, a student's use of speech in the classroom during structured lesson sessions is a communicative performance in more than one sense of "performance." It involves demonstration of sociolinguistic competency, itself a complex combination of linguistic competency and social competency involving knowledge of when and in what style one must present one's utterances, among other things. This type of competency, however, is involved in every speech act. But in the classroom there is a second sense in which speaking is a performance that is more special although not unique to classroom interactions. In class, speaking is the first and primary mode for communicating competency in all the areas of skill and knowledge that schools purport to teach. Children communicate what they have learned to the teacher and their fellow students through speaking; only rarely do they demonstrate what they know through physical activity or creation of material objects. While writing eventually becomes a second important channel or mode for communicating knowledge or demonstrating skills, writing, as a skill, is to a great extent developed through verbal interaction between student and teacher, as is reading.

Consequently, if talk fails to occur, the channel through which learning sessions are conducted is cut off, and the structure of classroom interaction that depends on dialogue between teacher and student breaks down and no longer functions as it is supposed to. Thus while the question "Why don't Indian kids talk more in class?" is in a sense a very simple one, it is also a very basic one, and the lack of talk a problem that needs to be dealt with if Indian children are to learn what is taught in American schools.

Cultural and Educational Background of the Warm Springs Indians

Before embarking on the main task of the discussion outlined above, some background information on the setting of the research, the Warm Springs Indian Reservation, is necessary to provide some sense of the extent to which the cultural, linguistic, and educational situation there may be similar to or different from that of North American Indians in other parts of the country.

Today the reservation of 564,209 acres is populated by some 1500 descendants of the "bands" of Warm Springs Sahaptin, Wasco Chinook, and Paiute Indians who gradually settled there after the reservation was established in 1855. The Warm Springs Indians have always been the largest group numerically, followed by the Wasco, with the Paiutes so small in number that their influence in the culture of the reservation has been of relatively small significance. Although they spoke different languages, the Warm Springs and Wasco groups were geographically quite close to one another before the reservation was established and were culturally similar in many respects. Thus after over a hundred years together on the reservation, they presently share approximately the same cultural background.

The "tribe," as the Indians of Warm Springs now refer to themselves collectively, today comprises a single closely integrated community with strong tribal leadership, which receives the full backing of the people. Until after World War II the Indians here experienced considerable poverty and hardship. Since that time, however, tribal income from the sale of reservation timber has considerably improved the economic situation, as has tribal purchase of a sawmill and a small resort, which provide jobs for tribal members.

With the income from these enterprises, and drawing as well on various forms of federal aid available to them, the tribe has developed social programs to help members of the tribe in a number of ways. Chief among their concerns is the improvement of the education of their children, whom they recognize to be less successful in school than their fellow non-Indian students. Tribal leaders have taken numerous important steps to increase the educational opportunities of their young people, including the establishment of a scholarship program for college students and a tribal education office with half a dozen full-time employees supervising the tribally sponsored kindergarten, study halls, and community center courses as well as the federally sponsored programs such as VISTA, Head Start, and Neighborhood Youth Corps. The education office employees also act as liaisons between parents of children with problems in school and the administrators and teachers of the public schools the children attend. In sum, the tribe is doing a great deal to provide the Warm Springs children with the best education possible.

Despite their efforts, and those of the public school officials, who are under considerable pressure from tribal leaders to bring about changes in the schools that will result in the improvement of the academic performance of Indian students, the Indians continue to do poorly in school when compared to the non-Indian students in the same school system.

One of the most important things to know about the schools the Indian children attend is the "ethnic" composition of their classes. For the first six grades, Warm Springs children attend a public school that is located on the reservation. Here their classmates are almost all Indians and their teachers are all non-Indians or whites. After the first six grades, they are bused into the town of Madras, a distance of fifteen to thirty miles, depending on where they live on the reservation. Here, encountering their fellow white students for the first time, the Indian students are outnumbered by a ratio of five to one. From the point of view of tribal leaders, it is only when they reach the high school, or ninth grade, that the Indian students' "problems" really become serious, for it is at this point that hostility between Indian and non-Indian is expressed openly, and the Indian students' failure to participate in classroom discussions and school activities is recognized by everyone.

There is, however, abundant evidence that Indian students' learning difficulties begin long before they reach the high school. The statistics that are available on their educational achievements and problems are very similar to those which have been reported for Indians in other parts of the country (Berry, 1969). On national achievement tests the Warm Springs Indian children consistently score lower than the national average in skills tested. Their lowest scores are in areas involving verbal competencies, and the gap between their level of performance on such tests and the national averages widens as they continue into the higher grade levels (Zentner, 1960).

Although many people on the reservation still speak an Indian language, today all the Warm Springs children in school are monolingual speakers of English. The dialect of English they speak, however, is not the Standard English of their teachers, but one that is distinctive to the local Indian community, and that in some aspects of grammar and phonology shows influence from the Indian languages spoken on the reservation.

In addition, there is some evidence that many children are exposed to talk in the Indian languages that may affect their acquisition of English. Because older people on the reservation are very concerned about the Indian languages' dying out, many of them make a concerted effort to teach young children an Indian language, particularly the Warm Springs Sahaptin. Thus some infants and young children are spoken to consistently in both Warm Springs and English. Every child still knows some Indian words, and many informants report that while their children refuse to speak the Warm Springs Sahaptin—particularly after they start school—they understand much of what is said to them in it.

The effects of the acquisition of a very local dialect of English and the exposure to the Warm Springs language on classroom learning are difficult for local educators to assess because children say so little in the presence of the teachers. Observations of Indian children's verbal interactions outside the classroom indicate a control and productive use of linguistic rules that is manifested infrequently in classroom utterances, indicating that the appropriate social conditions for speech use, from the Indians' point of view, are lacking. It is this problem with appropriate social contexts for speaking that will now be considered in greater detail.

Conditions for Speech Use in School Classrooms

When the children first enter school, the most immediate concern of the teachers is to teach them the basic rules for classroom behavior upon which the maintenance of continuous and ordered activity depends. One of the most important of these is the distinction between the roles of teacher and student. In this there is the explicit and implicit assumption that the teacher controls all the activity taking place in the classroom and the students accept and are obedient to her authority. She determines the sociospatial arrangements of all interactions; she decrees when and where movement takes place within the classroom. And most important for our present concern with communication, she determines who will talk and when they will talk.

While some class activities are designed to create the sense of a class of students as an organized group with class officers, or student monitors carrying out various responsibilities contributing to the group, actual spontaneous organization within the student group that has not been officially designated by the teacher is not encouraged. It interferes with the scheduling of activities as the teacher has organized them. The classroom situation is one in which the teacher relates to the students as an undifferentiated mass, much as a performer in front of an audience. Or she relates to each student on a one-to-one basis, often with the rest of the class as the still undifferentiated audience for the performance of the individual child.

In comparing the Indian and non-Indian learning of these basic classroom distinctions which define the conditions in which communication will take place, differences are immediately apparent. Indian first-graders are consistently slower to begin acting in accordance with these basic arrangements. They do not remember to raise their hands and wait to be called on before speaking, they wander to parts of the room other than the one in which the teacher is conducting a session, and they talk to other students while the teacher is talking, much further into the school year than do students in non-Indian classes. And the Indian children continue to fail to conform to classroom procedure much more frequently *through* the school year.

In contrast to the non-Indian students, the Indian students consistently show a great deal more interest in what their fellow students are doing than in what the teacher is doing. While non-Indian students constantly make bids for the attention of their teachers, through initiating dialogue with them as well as through other acts, Indian students do very little of this. Instead they make bids for the attention of their fellow students through talk. At the first-grade level, and more noticeably (with new teachers only) at the sixth-grade level, Indian students often act in deliberate organized opposition to the teacher's directions. Thus at the first-grade level, if one student is told not to put his feet on his chair, another will immediately put his feet on his chair, and he will be imitated by other students who see him do this. In non-Indian classrooms, such behavior was observed only at the sixth-grade level in interaction with a substitute teacher.

In other words, there is, on the part of Indian students, relatively less interest, desire, and/or ability to internalize and act in accordance with some of the basic rules underlying classroom maintenance of orderly interaction. Most notably, Indian students are less willing than non-Indian students to accept the teacher as director and controller of all classroom activities. They are less interested in developing the one-to-one communicative relationship between teacher and student, and more interested in maintaining and developing relationships with their peers, regardless of what is going on in the classroom.

Within the basic framework of teacher-controlled interaction, there are several possible variations in structural arrangements of interaction, which will be referred to from here on as "participant structures." Teachers use different participant structures, or ways of arranging verbal interaction with students, for communicating different types of educational material, and for providing variation in the presentation of the same material to hold children's interest. Often the notion that different kinds of materials are taught better and more efficiently through one sort of participant structuring rather than another is also involved.

In the first type of participant structure the teacher interacts with all the students. She may address all of them, or a single student in the presence of the rest of the students. The students may respond as a group or chorus in unison, or individually in the presence of their peers. And finally, student verbal participation may be either voluntary, as when the teacher asks who knows the answer to her question, or compulsory, as when the teacher asks a particular student to answer, whether his hand is raised or not. And always it is the teacher who determines whether she talks to one or to all, receives responses individually or in chorus, and voluntarily or without choice.

In a second type of participant structure, the teacher interacts with only some of the students in the class at once, as in reading groups. In such contexts participation is usually mandatory rather than voluntary, individual rather than chorus, and each student is expected to participate or perform verbally, for the main purpose of such smaller groups is to provide the teacher with the opportunity to assess the knowledge acquired by each individual student. During such sessions, the remaining students who are not interacting with the teacher are usually working alone or independently at their desks on reading or writing assignments.

A third participant structure consists of all students working independently at their desks, but with the teacher explicitly available for student-initiated verbal interaction, in which the child indicates he wants to communicate with the teacher by raising his hand, or by approaching the teacher at her desk. In either case, the interaction between student and teacher is not witnessed by the other students in that they do not hear what is said.

A fourth participant structure, and one that occurs infrequently in the upper primary grades, and rarely, if ever, in the lower grades, consists of the students' being divided into small groups that they run themselves, though always with the more distant supervision of the teacher, and usually for the purpose of so-called "group projects." As a rule such groups have official "chairmen," who assume what is in other contexts the teacher's authority in regulating who will talk when.

In observing and comparing Indian and non-Indian participation or communicative performances in these four different structural variations of contexts in which communication takes place, differences between the two groups again emerge very clearly.

In the first two participant structures where students must speak out individually in front of the other students, Indian children show considerable reluctance to participate, particularly when compared to non-Indian students. When the teacher is in front of the whole class, they volunteer to speak relatively rarely, and teachers at the Warm Springs grammar school generally hold that this reluctance to volunteer to speak out in front of other students increases as the children get older.

When the teacher is with a small group, and each individual must give some kind of communicative verbal performance in turn, Indian children much more frequently refuse, or fail to utter a word when called upon, and much less frequently, if ever, urge the teacher to call on them than the non-Indians do. When the Indian children do speak, they speak very softly, often in tones inaudible to a person more than a few feet away, and in utterances typically briefer than those of their non-Indian counterparts.

In situations where the teacher makes herself available for student-initiated communication during sessions in which students are working independently on assignments that do not involve verbal communication, students at the first-grade level in the Indian classes at first rarely initiate contact with the teachers. After a few weeks in a classroom they do so as frequently as the non-Indian students. And at the sixth-grade level Indian students initiate such relatively private encounters with teachers much more frequently than non-Indian students do.

When students control and direct the interaction in small group projects, as described for the fourth type of participant structure, there is again a marked contrast between the behavior of Indian and non-Indian students. It is in such contexts that Indian students become most fully involved in what they are doing, concentrating completely on their work until it is completed, talking a great deal to one another within the group, and competing, with explicit remarks to that effect, with the other groups. Non-Indian students take more time in "getting organized," disagree and argue more regarding how to go about a task, rely more heavily on appointed chairmen for arbitration and decision making, and show less interest, at least explicitly, in competing with other groups from their class.

Observations of the behavior of both Indian and non-Indian children outside the classroom during recess periods and teacher-organized physical education periods provide further evidence that the differences in readiness to participate in interaction are related to the way in which the interaction is organized and controlled.

When such outside-class activity is organized by the teachers, it is for the purpose of teaching children games through which they develop certain physical and social skills. If the games involve a role distinction between leader and followers in which the leader must tell the others what to do—as in Simon Says, Follow the Leader, Green Light Red Light, and even Farmer in the Dell—Indian children show a great deal of reluctance to assume the leadership role. This is particularly true when the child is appointed leader by the teacher and must be repeatedly urged to act in telling the others what to do before doing so. Non-Indian children, in contrast, vie eagerly for such positions, calling upon the teacher and/or other students to select them.

If such playground activity is unsupervised, and the children are left to their own devices, Indian children become involved in games of team competition much more frequently than non-Indian children. And they sustain such game activities for longer periods of time and at younger ages than non-Indian children. While non-Indian children tend more to play in groups of two and three, and in the upper primary grades to form "friendships" with one or two persons from their own class in school, Indian children interact with a greater number of children consistently, and maintain friendships and teams with children from classes in school other than their own.

In reviewing the comparison of Indian and non-Indian students' verbal participation under different social conditions, two features of the Warm Springs children's behavior stand out. First of all, they show relatively less willingness to perform or participate verbally when they must speak alone in front of other students. Second, they are relatively less eager to speak when the point at which speech occurs is dictated by the teacher, as it is during sessions when the teacher is working with the whole class or a small group. They also show considerable reluctance to be placed in the "leadership" play roles that require them to assume the same type of dictation of the acts of their peers.

Parallel to these negative responses are the positive ones of a relatively greater willingness to participate in group activities that do not create a distinction between individual performer and audience, and a relatively greater use of opportunities in which the point at which the student speaks or acts is determined by himself, rather than by the teacher or a "leader."

It is apparent that there are situations arising in the classroom that do allow for the Indian students to verbalize or communicate under or within the participant structures their behavior indicates they prefer; otherwise it would not have been possible to make the distinctions between their behavior and that of non-Indians in the areas just discussed. However, the frequency of occurrence of such situations in the classroom is very low when compared to the frequency of occurrence of the type of participant structuring in which Indian students fail to participate verbally, particularly in the lower grades.

In other words, most verbal communication that is considered part of students' learning experience does take the structure of individual students' speaking in front of other students. About half of this speaking is voluntary insofar as students are invited to volunteer to answer, and half is compulsory in that a specific student is called on and expected to answer. In either case, it is the teacher who establishes when talk will occur and within what kind of participant structure.

There are many reasons why most of the verbal communication takes place under such conditions. Within our particular education system, a teacher needs to know how much her students have learned or absorbed from the material she has presented. Students' verbal responses provide one means—and the primary means, particularly before students learn to write—of measuring their progress, and are thus the teacher's feedback. And, again within our particular educational system, it is not group but individual progress with which our teachers are expected to be concerned.

In addition, it is assumed that students will learn from each others' performances both what is false or wrong, and what is true or correct. Another aspect of this type of public performance that may increase educators' belief in its efficacy is the students' awareness that these communicative acts *are* performances, in the sense of being demonstrations of competency. The concomitant awareness that success or failure in such acts is a measure of their worth in the eyes of those present increases their motivation to do well. Thus they will remember when they made a mistake and try harder to do well to avoid public failure, in a way they would not were their performances in front of a smaller number of people. As I will try to demonstrate further on, however, the educators' assumption of the validity or success of this type of enculturation process, which can briefly be referred to as "learning through public mistakes," is not one the Indians share, and this has important implications for our understanding of Indian behavior in the classroom.

The consequences of the Indians' reluctance to participate in these speech situations are several. First of all, the teacher loses the primary means she has of receiving feedback on the children's acquisition of knowledge, and is thus less able to establish at what point she must begin again to instruct them, particularly in skills requiring a developmental sequencing, as in reading.

A second consequence of this reluctance to participate in speech situations requiring mandatory individual performances is that the teachers in the Warm Springs grammar school modify their teaching approach whenever possible to accommodate, in a somewhat ad hoc fashion, what they refer to as the Indian students' "shyness." In the first grade it is not easy to make many modifications because of what teachers perceive as a close relationship between the material being taught and the methods used to teach it. There is some feeling, also, that the teaching methods that can be effective with children at age six are somewhat limited in range. However, as students go up through the grades, there is an increasing tendency for teachers to work with the notion, not always a correct one, that given the same body of material there are a number of different ways of "presenting" it, or in the terms being used here, a range of different participant structures and modes of communication (e.g., talking versus reading and writing) that can be used.

Even so, at the first-grade level there are already some changes made to accommodate the Indian children that are notable. When comparing the Indian first-grade classes with the non-Indian first-grade classes, one finds very few word games being used that involve students' giving directions to one another. And even more conspicuous in Indian classes is the absence of the ubiquitous "show and tell" or "sharing," through which students learn to get up in front of the class, standing where the teacher stands, and presenting, as the teacher might, a monologue relating an experience or describing a treasured object that is supposed to be of interest to the rest of the class. When asked whether this activity was used in the classroom, one teacher explained that she had previously used it, but so few children ever volunteered to "share" that she finally discontinued it.

By the time the students reach the sixth grade, the range of modes and settings for communication has increased a great deal, and the opportunity for elimination of some participant structures in preference to others is used by the teachers. As one sixth-grade teacher put it, "I spend as little time in front of the class as possible." In comparison with non-Indian classes, Indian classes have a relatively greater number of group "projects." Thus while non-Indian students are learning about South American history through reading texts and answering the teacher's questions, Indian students are doing group-planned and -executed murals depicting a particular stage in Latin American history; while non-Indian students are reading science texts and answering questions about how electricity is generated, Indian students are doing group-run experiments with batteries and motors.

Similarly, in the Indian classes "reports" given by individual students are almost nonexistent, but they are a typical means in non-Indian classes for demonstrating knowledge through verbal performance. And finally, while in non-Indian classes students are given opportunities to ask the teacher questions in front of the class, and do so, Indian students are given fewer opportunities for this because when they do have the opportunity, they don't use it. Rather, the teacher of Indians allows more periods in which she is available for individual students to approach her alone and ask their questions where no one else can hear them.

The teachers who make these adjustments, and not all do, are sensitive to the inclinations of their students and want to teach them through means to which they most readily adapt. However, by doing so they are avoiding teaching the Indian children how to communicate in precisely the contexts in which they are least able but most need to learn if they are to "do well in school." The teachers handicap themselves by setting up performance situations for the students in which they are least able to arrive at the evaluations of individual competence upon which they rely for feedback to establish at what level they must begin to teach. And it is not at all clear that students do acquire the same information through one form of communication as they do through another. Thus these manipulations of communication settings and participant structures, which are intended to transmit knowledge to the students creatively through the means to which they are most adjusted, may actually be causing the students to miss completely types of information their later high school teachers will assume they picked up in grammar school.

The consequences of this partial adaptation to Indian modes of communication become apparent when the Indian students join the non-Indian students at the junior and senior high school levels. Here, where the Indian students are outnumbered five to one, there is no manipulation and selection of communication settings to suit the inclinations of the Indians. Here the teachers complain that the Indian students never talk in class, and never ask questions, and everyone wonders why.

It does not necessarily follow from this that these most creative teachers at the grade school level should stop what they are doing. Perhaps it should be the teachers at the junior and senior high school levels who make similar adaptations. Which of these occurs (or possibly there are *other* alternatives) depends on the goals the Indian community has for its youngsters, an issue that will be briefly considered in the conclusion of the paper.

Conditions for Speech Use in the Warm Springs Indian Community

To understand why the Warm Springs Indian children speak out readily under some social conditions but fail to do so under others, it is necessary to examine the sociolinguistic assumptions determining the conditions for communicative performances, particularly those involving explicit demonstrations of knowledge or skill, in the Indian community. It will be possible here to deal with only some of the many aspects of communication involved. Attention will focus first on the social structuring of learning situations or contexts in which knowledge and skills are communicated to children in Indian homes. Then some consideration will be given to the underlying rules or conditions for participation in the community-wide social events that preschool children, as well as older children, learn through attending such events with their families.

The Indian child's preschool and outside-school enculturation at home differs from that of many non-Indian or white middle-class children's in that a good deal of the responsibility for the care and training of children is assumed by persons other than the parents of the children. In many homes the oldest children, particularly if they are girls, assume these responsibilities when the parents are at home, as well as when they are not. Frequently, also, grandparents, uncles, and aunts assume the full-time responsibility for care and instruction of children. Children thus become accustomed to interacting with and following the instructions and orders of a greater number of people than is the case with non-Indian children.

Equally important is the fact that all the people with whom Indian children form such reciprocal nurturing and learning relationships are kinsmen. Indian children are rarely, if ever, taken care of by "babysitters" from outside the family. Most of their playmates before beginning school are their siblings and cousins, and these peer relationships typically continue to be the strongest bonds of friendship through school and adult life, later providing a basis for reciprocal aid in times of need, and companionship in many social activities.

Indian children are deliberately taught skills around the home (for girls) and in the outdoors (for boys) at an earlier age than many middle-class non-Indian children. Girls, for example, learn to cook some foods before they are eight, and by this age may be fully competent in cleaning a house without any aid or supervision from adults.

There are other areas of competence in which Indian children are expected to be proficient at earlier ages than non-Indian children, for which the means of enculturation or socialization are less visible and clear-cut. While still in grammar school, at the age of ten or eleven, some children are considered capable of spending afternoons and evenings in the company of only other children, without the necessity of accounting for their whereabouts or asking permission to do whatever specific activity is involved. At this same age many are also considered capable of deciding where they want to live, and for what reasons one residence is preferable to another. They may spend weeks or months at a time living with one relative or another, until it is no longer possible to say that they live in any particular household.

In general, then, Warm Springs Indian children become accustomed to self-determination of action, accompanied by very little disciplinary control from older relatives, at much younger ages than middle-class white children do.

In the context of the household, learning takes place through several sorts of somewhat different processes. First of all, children are present at many adult interactions as silent but attentive observers. While it is not yet clear how adult activities in which children are not full participants are distinguished from those in which children may participate fully, and from those for which they are not allowed to be present at all, there are clearly marked differences. What is most remarkable, however, is that there are many adult conversations to which children pay a great deal of silent, patient attention. This contrasts sharply with the behavior of non-Indian children, who show little patience in similar circumstances, desiring either to become a full participant through verbal interaction, or to become completely involved in some other activity.

There is some evidence that this silent listening and watching was, in the Warm Springs culture, traditionally the first step in learning skills of a fairly complex nature. For example, older women reminisce about being required to watch their elder relatives tan hides when they were very young, rather than being allowed to play. And certainly the winter evening events of myth telling, which provided Indian children with their first explicitly taught moral lessons, involved them as listening participants rather than as speakers.

A second type of learning involves the segmentation of a task by an older relative, and the partial carrying out of the task or one of its segments by the child. In household tasks, for example, a child is given a very simple portion of a job (e.g., in cleaning a room the child may begin by helping move the furniture) and works in cooperation with and under the supervision of an older relative. Such activities involve a small amount of verbal instruction or direction from the older relative, and allow for questions on the part of the child. Gradually the child comes to learn all the skills involved in a particular process, consistently under the supervision of an older relative who works along with him.

This mode of instruction is not unique to the Warm Springs Indians, of course; many non-Indian parents use similar methods. However, there are aspects of this type of instruction that differ from its use among non-Indians. First of all, when it occurs among the Indians it is likely to be preceded by the long periods of observation just described. The absence of such observation among non-Indian children is perhaps replaced by elaborate verbal instructions outlining the full scope of a task before the child attempts any part of it.

A second way in which this type of instruction among the Warm Springs Indians differs from that of non-Indians is the absence of "testing" of the child's skill by the instructing kinsman before the child exercises the skill unsupervised. Although it is not yet clear how this works in a diversity of situations, it appears that in many areas of skill, the child takes it upon himself to test the skill unsupervised and alone, without other people around. In this way, if he is unsuccessful his failure is not seen by others. If he is successful, he can show the results of his success to those by whom he has been taught, whether it be in the form of a deer that has been shot, a hide tanned, a piece of beadwork completed, or a dinner on the table when the adults come home from work.

Again there is some evidence that this type of private individual's testing of competency, followed by public demonstration only when competency is fully developed and certain, has been traditional in the Warm Springs Indian culture. The most dramatic examples of this come from the processes of acquisition of religious and ritual knowledge. In the vision quests through which adolescents, or children of even younger ages, acquired spirit power, individuals spent long periods in isolated mountain areas from which they were expected to emerge with skills they had not previously demonstrated. While some of these abilities were not fully revealed until later in life, the child was expected to be able to relate some experience of a supernatural nature that would prove that he had, in fact, been visited by a spirit. Along the same lines, individuals until very recently received and learned, through dreams and visions, ritual songs that they would sing for the first time in full and completed form in the presence of others.

The contexts described here in which learning takes place can be perceived as an idealized sequence of three steps: (1) observation, which of course includes listening; (2) supervised participation; and (3) private, self-initiated self-testing. It is not the case that all acquisition of skills proceeds through such phases, however, but rather only some of these skills that Indian adults consciously and deliberately teach their children, and which the children consciously try to learn. Those which are learned through less deliberate means must to some extent invoke similar structuring, but it is difficult to determine to what extent.

The use of speech in the process is notably minimal. Verbal directions or instructions are few, being confined to corrections and question answering. Nor does the final demonstration of skill particularly involve verbal performance, since the validation of skill so often involves display of some material evidence or nonverbal physical expression.

This process of Indian acquisition of competence may help to explain, in part, Indian children's reluctance to speak in front of their classmates. In the classroom, the processes of *acquisition* of knowledge and *demonstration* of knowledge are collapsed into the single act of answering questions or reciting when called upon to do so by the teacher, particularly in the lower grades. Here the assumption is that one will learn, and learn more effectively, through making mistakes in front of others. The Indian children have no opportunity to observe others performing successfully before they attempt it, except for their fellow classmates who precede them and are themselves uninitiated. They have no opportunity to "practice," and to decide for themselves when they know enough to demonstrate their knowledge; rather, their performances are determined by the teacher. And finally, their only channel for communicating competency is verbal rather than nonverbal.

Turning now from learning processes in the home to learning experiences outside the home, in social and ritual activities involving community members other than kinsmen, there is again considerable evidence that Indian children's understanding of when and how one participates and performs individually, and thus demonstrates or communicates competence, differs considerably from what is expected of them in the classroom.

Children of all ages are brought to every sort of community-wide social event sponsored by Indians (as distinct from those sponsored by non-Indians). There is rarely, if ever, such a thing as an Indian community event that is attended by adults only. At many events children participate in only certain roles, but this is true of everyone. Sociospatially and behaviorally, children must always participate minimally, as do all others, in sitting quietly and attentively alongside their elders.

One of the social features that characterizes social events that are not explicitly kin-group affairs, including activities like political general councils, social dinners, and worship dances, is that they are open to participation by all members of the Warm Springs Indian community. While different types of activities are more heavily attended by certain Indians rather than others, and fairly consistently sponsored and arranged by certain individuals, it is always clear that everyone is invited, both by community knowledge of this fact and by explicit announcements on posters placed in areas where most people pass through at one time or another in their day-to-day activities.

A second feature of such activities is that there is usually no one person directing the activity verbally, or signaling changes from one phase to another. Instead the structure is determined either by a set procedure or ritual, or there is a group of people who in various complementary ways provide such cuing and direction. Nor are there any participant roles that can be filled or are filled by only one person. In dancing, singing, and drumming there are no soloists, and where there are performers who begin a sequence, and are then joined by others, more than one performer takes a turn at such initiations. The speaking roles are handled similarly. In contexts where speeches are appropriate, it is made clear that anyone who wants to may "say a few words." The same holds true for political meetings, where the answerer to a question is not necessarily one who is on a panel or council, but rather the person who feels he is qualified, by his knowledge of a subject, to answer. In all situations thus allowing for anyone who wants to to speak, no time limit is set, so that the talking continues until everyone who wants to has had the opportunity to do so.

This does not mean that there are never any "leaders" in Indian social activities, but rather that leadership takes quite a different form from that in many non-Indian cultural contexts. Among the people of Warm Springs, a person is not a leader by virtue of holding a particular position, even in the case of members of the tribal council and administration. Rather, he is a leader because he has demonstrated ability in some sphere and activity, and many individuals choose to follow his suggestions because they have independently each decided they are good ones. If, for example, an individual plans and announces an activity, but few people offer to help him carry it out or attend it, then that is an indication that the organizer is not a respected leader in the community at the present time. And the likelihood that he will repeat his efforts in the near future is reduced considerably.

This type of "leadership," present today among the people of Warm Springs, is reminiscent of that which was described by Hoebel for the Comanche chiefs:

> In matters of daily routine, such as camp moving, he merely made the decisions himself, announcing them through a camp crier. Anyone who did not like his decision simply ignored it. If in time a good many people ignored his announcements and preferred to stay behind with some other man of influence, or perhaps to move in another direction with that man, the chief had then lost his following. He was no longer chief, and another had quietly superseded him (Hoebel, 1954, p. 132).

A final feature of Indian social activities, which should be recognized from what has already been said, is that all who do attend an activity may participate in at least some of the various forms participation takes for the given activity, rather than there being a distinction made between participants or performers and audience. At many Indian gatherings, particularly those attended by older people, this aspect of the situation is reflected in its sociospatial arrangement: People are seated in such a way that all present are facing one another, usually in an approximation of a square, and the focus of activity is either along one side of the square, or in its center, or a combination of the two.

And each individual chooses the degree of his participation. No one, other than, perhaps, those who set up the event, is committed to being present beforehand, and all participating roles beyond those of sitting and observing are determined by the individual at the point at which he decides to participate, rather than being prescheduled.

In summary, the Indian social activities to which children are early exposed outside the home generally have the following properties: (1) they are community-wide, in the sense that they are open to all Warm Springs Indians; (2) there is no single individual directing and controlling all activity, and, to the extent that there are "leaders," their leadership is based on the choice to follow made by each person; (3) participation in some form is accessible to everyone who attends. No one need be exclusively an observer or audience, and there is consequently no sharp distinction between audience and performer. And each individual chooses for himself the degree of his participation during the activity.

If one now compares the social conditions for verbal participation in the classroom with the conditions underlying many Indian events in which children participate, a number of differences emerge.

First of all, classroom activities are not community-wide, and, more importantly, the participants in the activity are not drawn just from the Indian community. The teacher, as a non-Indian, is an outsider and a stranger to these events. In addition, by virtue of her role as teacher, she structurally separates herself from the rest of the participants, her students. She places herself outside the interaction and activity of the students. This encourages their cultural perceptions of themselves as the relevant community, in opposition to the teacher, perhaps much as they see themselves in opposition to other communities, and on a smaller scale, as one team is in opposition to another. In other words, on the basis of the Indians' social experiences, one is either a part of a group or outside it. The notion of a single individual being structurally set apart from all others, in anything other than an observer role, and yet still a part of the group organization, is one that children probably encounter for the first time in school, and continue to experience only in non-Indian-derived activities (e.g., in bureaucratic, hierarchically structured occupations). This helps to explain why Indian students show so little interest in initiating interaction with the teacher in activities involving other students.

Second, in contrast to Indian activities where many people are involved in determining the development and structure of an event, there is only one single authority directing everything in the classroom, namely, the teacher. And the teacher is not the controller or leader by virtue of the individual students' choices to follow her, as is the case in Indian social activities, but rather by virtue of her occupation of the role of teacher. This difference helps to account for the Indian children's frequent indifference to the directions, orders, and requests for compliance with classroom social rules that the teacher issues.

Third, it is not the case in the classroom that all students may participate in any given activity, as in Indian community activities. Nor are they given the opportunity to choose the degree of their participation, which, on the basis of evidence discussed earlier, would in Indian contexts be based on the individual's having already ascertained in private that he was capable of successful verbal communication of competence. Again these choices belong to the teacher.

Conclusion

In summary, Indian children fail to participate verbally in classroom interaction because the social conditions for participation to which they have become accustomed in the Indian community are lacking. The absence of these appropriate social conditions for communicative performances affects the most common and everyday speech acts that occur in the classroom. If the Indian child fails to follow an order or answer a question, it may not be because he doesn't understand the linguistic structure of the imperative and the interrogative, but rather because he does not share the non-Indian's assumption in such contexts that use of these syntactic forms by definition implies an automatic and immediate response from the person to whom they were addressed. For these assumptions are sociolinguistic assumptions that are not shared by the Indians.

Educators cannot assume that because Indian children (or any children from cultural backgrounds other than those that are implicit in American classrooms) speak English, or are taught it in the schools, that they have also assimilated all the sociolinguistic rules underlying interaction in classrooms and other non-Indian social situations where English is spoken. To the extent that existing cultural variation in sociolinguistic patterning that is not recognized by the schools results in learning difficulties and feelings of inferiority for some children, changes in the structuring of classroom learning situations are needed. Ultimately the nature of the changes to be made should be determined by the educational goals of the particular communities where this type of problem exists.

If, as may be the case on the Warm Springs Indian Reservation, the people's main concern is to enable Indian children to compete successfully with non-Indians, and to have the *choice* of access to the modes of interaction and life styles of non-Indians, then a conscious effort should be made in the schools to teach the children the modes for appropriate verbal participation that prevail in non-Indian classrooms. Thus rather than shifting away from situations in which children perform individually in front of their peers only with great reluctance, conscious emphasis on and encouragement of participation in such situations should be carried out in the early grades.

If, on the other hand, as also may be the case in Warm Springs (there are strong differences of opinion here on this issue that complicate the teachers' actions), there is strong feeling in the community that its culturally distinctive modes of communication should be maintained and encouraged to flourish rather than be eliminated through our educational system's apparent pursuit of cultural uniformity throughout the country, then quite a different shift in the orientation of classroom modes of instruction would be called for. Here an effort to adapt the community's conditions for appropriate speech usage to the classroom should be made, not in an ad hoc and partial fashion as at Warm Springs, but consistently and systematically. And where the classroom situation is one in which children of more than one cultural background come together, efforts should be made to allow for a complementary diversity in the modes of communication through which learning and measurement of "success" take place.

References

Berry, Brewton, 1969   *The Education of American Indians: a Survey of the Literature.* Prepared for the Special Subcommittee on Indian Education of the Committee on Labor and Public Welfare, United States Senate. Washington, D.C.: Government Printing Office.

Cazden, Courtney B., and Vera P. John, 1968   "Learning in American Indian Children." In *Styles of Learning among American Indians: An Outline for Research.* Washington, D.C.: Center for Applied Linguistics.

Hoebel, E. Adamson, 1954   *The Law of Primitive Man.* Cambridge, Mass.: Harvard University Press.

Hymes, Dell, 1971   "Competence and Performance in Linguistic Theory." In Renira Huxley and Elisabeth Ingram, eds., *Language Acquisition: Models and Methods.* New York: Academic Press.

Wax, Murray, Rosalie Wax, and Robert V. Dumont, Jr., 1964   *Formal Education in an American Indian Community.* Social Problems Monograph no. 1. Kalamazoo, Mich.: Society for the Study of Social Problems.

Wolcott, Harry, 1967   *A Kwakiutl Village and School.* New York: Holt, Rinehart and Winston.

Zentner, Henry, 1960   *Oregon State College Warm Springs Research Project.* vol. II: Education. Corvallis: Oregon State College.

BILINGUAL EDUCATION: WHAT AND WHY?

Joshua A. Fishman

It has only been in the last decade that the U.S. government has begun to recognize the educational problems posed by its large numbers of non-English-speaking children who must make their way in monolingual English schools. The Bilingual Education Act of 1968, which Joshua A. Fishman mentions below, was amended by the Bilingual Education Act of 1974, which required evaluation of bilingual education programs, enlarged the non-English-speaking constituency to which the Act applied, and defined a bilingual education program as "instruction given in, and study of English, and to the extent necessary to allow a child to progress effectively through the educational system, the native language of the children of limited English-speaking ability." This definition roughly corresponds to the "transitional bilingualism" that Fishman describes in the present selection. Then, in its 1974 *Lau v. Nichols* decision, the Supreme Court, citing the general antidiscrimination statute of the 1964 Civil Rights Act, held that school districts must devise programs to ensure equal education to students of non-English-speaking backgrounds. To implement this decision, the Office of Civil Rights in

1975 issued a set of guidelines which specify that, whenever a school district has twenty or more students from a single language group, a bilingual program—not just instruction in English as a second language—is required at both the elementary and intermediate levels. That is, subject matter courses like math and science must be taught in the students' first language.

Since 1975, school districts in areas with large non-English-speaking populations—California and Chicago, for instance—have begun efforts to comply with these stringent guidelines. As other areas develop programs to meet the federal regulations, it will be increasingly important that all educators familiarize themselves with the typology of bilingual education which Fishman offers below.

With the Bilingual Education Act (signed into law by Lyndon B. Johnson on January 2, 1968), America found itself with a new panacea for "whatever it is" that ails a segment of our economically disadvantaged. The segment that this act (ultimately Title VII of the Elementary and Secondary Education Act of 1965, as amended in 1967, or Public Law 90-247) recognized for special assistance consisted of those "who came from environments where the dominant language is other than English." Although the act does not restrict itself either to the poor or to the Hispanic and Indian populations of the United States, President Johnson did make this restriction when signing the bill into law, and the "Draft Guidelines to the Bilingual Education Act" prepared by USOE for implementing the act did so quite explicitly. Thus while any hopes (or fears) that the United States would support bilingual education more generally (see the *Proceedings* of the Spring 1967 *Hearings on S428*) were quickly dissipated, the act as such has slowly but surely supported (or, together with state and local authorities co-supported) a steadily growing number of programs.

At this writing, some 220 bilingual education programs are receiving at least partial support under this act, and a like number of others—some that received support in former years and others that have been stimulated by the act indirectly—function entirely on nonfederal funds. Indeed, while five years *before* passage of the act few envisaged any such possibility, now only five years after its passage, half of our states and many local education authorities have instituted bilingual education codes or programs of their own (among them California, Illinois, New York, Texas, Maryland, Massachusetts), and bilingual education has become an established part of the programs of all major language teachers' associations. In the spring of 1973 new bilingual education bills were introduced in conjunction with congressional plans to revise the Elementary and Secondary Education Act of 1965. These resulted in a substantial budgetary increase for Title VII at a time when many other educational budgets were cut. Bilingual education has also enjoyed a modicum of publicity in struggles for control of local school boards or as state and local education budget reviews have come to realize that it "costs money" to prepare and obtain the personnel, curricula, and materials that bilingual education requires. It is at such junctures that the questions have begun to be raised—as they must inevitably be raised, for all promising educational solutions to social problems—"does it work and is it worth it?"

What Is Bilingual Education?

In very general terms, bilingual education implies some use of two (or more) languages of instruction in connection with teaching courses other than language per se. Thus neither the smattering of foreign-language instruction that FLES (Foreign Language in Elementary Schools) programs have long been providing to many grade schoolers in the United States nor the smatterings more normally offered subsequently in most American secondary schools, in the course of foreign-language instruction, qualify as bilingual education. However, wherever courses such as mathematics or history or science (or Bible or Talmud) are taught via a language other than English, while other courses (such as mathematics or history or . . .) are taught via English, then bilingual education may be said to obtain. However, within this broad definition, it is obvious that vastly different types of programs and program goals can be and are being pursued.

Four Broad Categories of Bilingual Education Programs

It may be instructive to propose (as I have in the past; Fishman and Lovas, 1970) a tentative sociolinguistic typology of bilingual education programs based on four differing kinds of community and school objectives. Each of these types will be briefly illustrated by an existing or proposed bilingual education program for some Spanish-speaking community.[1] In presenting this typology of bilingual education programs, I would like to distinguish clearly between them and English-as-a-second-language programs. The latter are programs which include no instruction in the student's mother tongue as part of the program.

Another point about this typology is that it is not based on student and schedule characteristics such as proportion of students speaking a certain language and proportion of time devoted to each language. Rather it looks to the kinds of sociolinguistic development implied in the program objectives and suggests that various kinds of programs assume and lead to particular societal rules for the language taught.

Type I: Transitional Bilingualism   In such a program Spanish is used in the early grades to the extent necessary to allow pupils to "adjust to school" and/or to "master subject matter" until their skill in English is developed to the point that it alone can be used as the medium of instruction. Such programs do not strive toward goals of fluency and literacy in both languages with opportunity throughout the curriculum for the continuing improvement toward mastery of each. Rather, they state goals such as "increasing overall achievement of Spanish-speaking students by using both Spanish and English as media of instruction in the primary grades." Such programs (consciously or unconsciously) correspond to the societal objective of language shift and give no consideration to long-range institutional development and support of the mother tongue. An example of such a program can be found in the grant proposal of the Las Cruces (N.M.) School District No. 2 for support of their Sustained Primary Program for Bilingual Students. Perhaps the best way to characterize this program would be to cite the three primary objectives against which the program is to be evaluated:

1. To increase the achievement level of Spanish-speaking youngsters through the use of a sustained K-3 program.

2. To determine whether Spanish-speaking youngsters achieve more in a program that utilizes instruction in both Spanish and English or in a program that is taught in Spanish only.

3. To involve the parents of Spanish-speaking students in the educational program as advisers and learners, thus enriching the home environment of the child.

The entire proposal makes no mention of measuring performance in Spanish or continuing Spanish in the curriculum past grade 3—or of making any survey of the language situation in the community. Such programs (and there are many of this kind) are basically interested only in transitional bilingualism, i.e., in arriving at the state of English monolingual educational normality just as soon as is feasible without injuring the pupil or arousing the community.

Type II: Monoliterate Bilingualism   Programs of this type indicate goals of development in both languages for aural-oral skills but do not concern themselves with literacy skills in the non-English mother tongue. Thus such programs emphasize developing fluency in Spanish as a link between home and school, with the school providing recognition and support for the language in the domains of home and neighborhood; but they are not concerned with the development of literacy skills in the non-English mother tongue which would facilitate the child's use of the language in conjunction with work, government, religion, or book culture more generally. This type of program is intermediate in orientation between language shift and language maintenance. The likely societal effect of such a program might be one of language maintenance in the short run, but, given the exposure of students to American urban society which stresses and rewards literacy, it might well lead to shift. One example of such a program can be found in Christine McDonald's proposal for the El Rancho United School District in Pico Rivera, California. The program is designed for preschool children, and the parents' and children's home language is used throughout its entire course. However, the focus of the program would be on ultimately developing literacy in English with no reference to similar development in Spanish. Bilingual programs for American Indians frequently fall into this category because, in many instances, there is no body of written literature for the child to learn in his mother tongue. Obviously the intellectual imbalance between English literacy and mother-tongue illiteracy poses a difficult situation for any language-maintenance-oriented community, particularly if it is exposed to occupational mobility through English.

Type III: Biliterate Bilingualism, Partial   This kind of program seeks fluency and literacy in both languages, but literacy in the mother tongue is restricted to certain subject matter, most generally that related to the ethnic group and its cultural heritage. In such a program, reading and writing skills in the mother tongue are commonly developed in relation to the social sciences, literature, and the arts, but not in science and mathematics. This kind of program is clearly one of language maintenance coupled with a certain effort at culture maintenance (perhaps even cultural development should the program result in the production of journalism, poetry, and other literary art forms). In general, the program in the Dade County (Florida) Public Schools (as described in the administrative guideline) exemplifies this type of bilingual education. (See also Rojas, 1966.) The program provides special instruction in English in all skills for all Spanish-speaking students who need it. Additionally, the program provides formal instruction in reading and writing Spanish with emphasis on Spanish literature and civilization as subject matter. Other areas of the curriculum do not utilize Spanish as a medium of instruction. Other programs of this type are conducted by numerous American ethnic groups in their own supplementary or parochial schools.[2] Such programs imply that while non-English mother tongues are serious vehicles of modern literate thought, they are not related to control of the technological and economic spheres. The latter are considered to be the preserve of the majority whose language must be mastered if these spheres are to be entered. Nationalist protest movements since the mid-nineteenth century have consistently rejected any such limiting implication.

Type IV: Biliterate Bilingualism, Full   In this kind of program, students are to develop all skills in both languages in all domains. Typically, both languages are used as media of instruction for all subjects (except in teaching the languages themselves). Clearly this program is directed at language maintenance and development of the minority language. From the viewpoint of much of the linguistically and psychologically oriented literature this is the ideal type of program, since, in the words of one specialist, it results in "balanced, coordinate bilinguals—children capable of thinking and feeling in either of two languages independently."

Programs such as these enable us to ponder the difference between developing balanced competency in individuals and producing a balanced bilingual society. Though highly bilingual societies might find individuals with highly developed competency in all skills and domains very useful in a variety of roles (teachers, translators, business representatives), a fully balanced bilingual speech community seems to be a theoretical impossibility. Balanced competence implies languages that are functionally equivalent, and no society can be motivated to maintain two languages if they are really functionally redundant. Thus this type of program does not seem to have a clearly articulated goal with respect to societal reality.

Several examples of this type of program exist, but all of them are small pilot or experimental programs. The Coral Way Elementary School (Dade County,

Florida) and the Laredo Unified Consolidated Independent School District (Texas) are two frequently cited instances which exemplify this kind of program (Gaarder, 1967; Michel, 1967; Andersson, 1968), not to mention much more recent experiments by Lambert. In the Coral Way School, students take all subjects in both languages, English in the morning from one teacher, Spanish in the afternoon from another teacher. At Laredo Unified, students receive all instruction from the same teacher, who uses English half the day and Spanish the other half. The evidence so far suggests that these programs are quite successful, but looking at them from the view of the functional needs of the community, there is serious reservation in my mind whether they should serve as ideal models for large-scale American programs.

Clearly, few American educators or laymen have pondered the four alternatives presented above, let alone their societal implications and requirements. In part this is due to the fact that most American bilingual education programs are of Types I and II above and, therefore, are minimalist insofar as their non-English-language/culture components are concerned. In part this is because Americans tend to view bilingual education as if it were a strictly American sin or virtue; i.e., without any historical or cultural perspective whatsoever.

Why Bilingual Education?

It may be possible to examine at least some of the worldwide and timewide span of bilingual education while reviewing the rationales advanced for it and the evidence pertaining thereto. Clearly, most American bilingual education programs are viewed as academically *compensatory* to begin with, and therefore, it is hoped, also as socioeconomically compensatory for the disadvantaged *minority-group child* from non-English-speaking environments (Gaarder, 1970).

Compensatory Programs   This constriction of bilingual education to overcoming "diseases of the poor," distasteful though it may be, has its well-established precedents in other climes and in other centuries, but most particularly in Europe since the Reformation, wherever the expansion of educational opportunity (or obligation) was stymied by the fact that the official language of education was not always the mother tongue of students new to the educational system. In such circumstances, whether in early-modern France or Germany, in turn-of-the-century or in recent-day Yucatan, Manila, or Moncton, the same claim has been advanced: start the learner off in the language he knows best. The more rapid progress made as a result, insofar as developing learning confidence and satisfaction are concerned, will then pay off in terms of much more rapid progress when the majority language is turned to (and, as some would have it, when more serious educational work is begun). Thus this approach, when transferred to the American context, typically claims that "learning English" and "getting educated" are not one and the same and that it is worth pursuing the latter via the mother tongue until the former can be tackled and, indeed, that the one will facilitate the other.

A serious evaluation of the above claim is still to come, if by "serious" we mean an opportunity to disentangle the mother-tongue effect per se from the social, cultural, economic, linguistic, and educational contexts in which it is necessarily embedded. What little research there has been in connection with this claim indicates that there are certainly circumstances under which it is supported[3] but that, on the whole, bilingual education is too frail a device, in and of itself, to alter significantly the learning experiences of the minority-mother-tongue-poor in general or their majority-language-learning-success in particular. It is of course true that foisting a language other than their own upon such children is equivalent to imposing an extra burden upon those least capable of carrying it. However, precisely because there are so many other pervasive reasons why such children achieve poorly the goals of majority-oriented and -dominated schools (and societies), removing this extra burden above—and leaving all else as it was—does not usually do the trick, particularly when the teachers, curricula, and materials for bilingual education are as nonoptimal as they currently usually are. My own feeling is that just as there is no simple school-based solution to the learning problems of the alienated-in-general, we cannot and should not expect bilingual education to provide such a solution for the non-English-mother-tongue-alienated-poor in particular. If there is a sufficient rationale for bilingual education, and I believe there is, it must be found on other than compensatory grounds, particularly inasmuch as most compensatory programs are merely transitional or monoliterate and, therefore, hardly constitute bilingual education in a context in which it is most likely to succeed. Who among us would care to defend the contribution of (or the prospects for) science education or social studies education on the basis of its effectiveness with alienated and dislocated populations such as those receiving compensatory bilingual education?

Enrichment Programs   When we turn our gaze from the poor to the middle class and above, we find bilingual education typically far more intensive and justified not on the grounds of compensation but of enrichment: "To them that hath shall be given." Those who are relatively secure in their social, economic, and political power can afford and, indeed, often seek an additional educational and cultural exposure to that afforded them by their own mother tongue and immediate milieu. Thus rather than merely being a palliative for the poor, bilingual education has been long and widely viewed by advantaged groups as "an elitist thing." Whether we are interested in the classical world or in the modern, in the West or in the East, bilingual education has been savored by the fortunate few and, apparently, found to be very good indeed.[4]

There have been several attempts to expand such efforts in recent decades so that the enrichment formerly reserved for the patrician might be made more widely available. Most of these have not been exposed to research evaluations, but the impressions of serious and sophisticated observers are positive regarding the bilingual schools of Singapore (largely in Chinese and English), or of LWC schools in the Soviet Union (Lewis, 1972), of areas in Wales, and of the Yeshiva movement in the United States.[5] It is felt that the intellective and nonintellective results obtained are generally as good as or better than those in monolingual schools for students of comparable backgrounds. However, the one serious study of truly widespread compulsory bilingual education, the one conducted in Ireland (Macnamara, 1966), disclosed negative findings as well. Because of the time and effort invested in teaching Irish per se, as well as in teaching via Irish, to children who neither knew it nor used it out of school, elementary school graduates were on the average a year behind students of comparable backgrounds in England with regard to tested achievement in English and in mathematical problem solving—at the same time that their active grasp of Irish remained rather marginal at best. Once again, it is not possible to say, on the basis of one such study, whether it is the overextension of bilingual education per se that exacted this toll or whether it was exacted by the particular context of widespread disinterest in and perceived uselessness of Irish in present-day Ireland. On the whole, I would tend to favor the latter interpretation of the Irish findings (primarily because it agrees with my own preliminary findings based on international data) and to believe that well-disposed and supported schools, serving well-disposed and reasonably comfortable clienteles, can carry on bilingual education as successfully as most others carry on monolingual education and that the resulting educational product may be deemed well worth the additional cost and effort that may be entailed.

Group-Maintenance Programs   No matter how successful enrichment-oriented bilingual education for the relatively comfortable and secure may be, it still does not come to grips with the problems of self-perceived minorities, poor or otherwise. What spokesmen for some of the latter have been emphasizing (and, once more, throughout the world and across time) is neither "compensation" nor "enrichment" but rather the preservation and enhancement of the group as such. However, bilingual education rationalized in group-maintenance and culture-maintenance terms is also considered to help the individual learner. A minority student who is confident of and recognized in his more intimate primary-group membership relates more positively both to school and to society (both of which are majority-dominated) and, as a result, profits more from schooling. There is hardly any research evidence pertaining to such claims in conjunction with bilingual education, although the view itself is a long- and well-established one, particularly in the context of cultural pluralism and minority rights. In this context, however, it is primarily an article of faith, a moral and ethical position, a basic social right, and as such, not likely to benefit seriously from, or to be much subjected to, objective and empirical research.

The common argument *against* group-maintenance-oriented bilingual education is that it is conducive to sociopolitical tensions, at the very least, and to sociopolitical ruptures, at worst. This may well be so, in certain minority-majority contexts at particular times and in particular places and, therefore, would seem to merit more or less consideration as local circumstances dictate. Certainly the demand for group-maintenance-oriented bilingual education has been advanced by both groups and individuals who have had only sociocultural goals rather than sociopolitical ones. As a result of such demands the growth of mother-tongue instruction for minority-group children, at least during the early elementary school years, has been truly phenomenal during the past quarter century and may become worldwide before this century is out. The result of this movement has been a corresponding increase in partial bilingual education, if the entire period of school attendance is considered. Very few, if any, secessionist movements have been spawned thereby or related thereto, and it would seem to me to be more wicked than wise to raise any such bugaboo in conjunction with discussions of bilingual education in the United States today. The right of large concentrations of parents to have their children educated in their own mother tongue at public expense; the right of individuals to defend and protect the primary groups to which they belong most intimately, at the same time that they hold and cultivate multiple loyalties to more inclusive groups; the right of much smaller groups to coexist within the larger groups with which they have symbiotic ties—all these must not be philosophically beclouded by possibly baseless innuendos. When coterritorial groups move toward separatism, it is almost never because of conflicts over bilingual education.

Like much else that has transpired in American education during the past decade, bilingual education has come about as a result of the confluence of organized pressures and innovative initiatives. Like much else that is promising in American education today, bilingual education suffers from four serious lacks: a lack of funds (Title VII has been pitifully starved), a lack of trained personnel, a lack of evaluated experience (with respect to curricula, materials, and methods), and a lack of sociohistorical perspective. It is not and cannot be a cure-all for the myriad disadvantages faced by the millions of poor non-English-mother-tongue children in our society. It could possibly be a powerful enrichment for the many other millions of more affluent American children, but such is our current blindness with respect to it that we largely insist on seeing it merely as "something for the poor." Nevertheless, it is in this latter *general* enrichment manifestation, as well as in the context of the self-maintenance efforts of our various non-Anglo cultural groups, that its true contribution to American education and society will ultimately be made.

NOTES

1. Many examples of other than Spanish-related bilingual education at the elementary level are provided in John and Horner, 1971; and in Andersson and Boyer, 1970. An appreciably different (and much more detailed) typography of bilingual education is available in Mackey, 1970.

2. Over a thousand such programs under other than Jewish auspices are reviewed in Fishman, 1966, chap. 5: "The Ethnic Group School and Mother Tongue Maintenance" (pp. 92-126).

3. Among the supportive evidence cited by John and Horner is that contained in reports by Modiano, 1968; Osterberg, 1961; Pryor, 1967; Richardson, 1968; pertaining to Mexican Indians, Swedes, Mexican-Americans, and Cuban-Americans, respectively. In Osterberg's project young speakers of Pitean (a nonstandard Swedish dialect) learning to read in their dialect fared better than Pitean-speaking children learning to read the literary dialect.

Indirect support is also available from other programs that employ a nonstandard dialect for transitional or monoliterate purposes.

4. Two recent and well-done evaluative case studies of such programs, both with general positive findings, are to be found in Mackey, 1972 and in Lambert and Tucker, 1972.

5. The bilingual nature of traditional Jewish education does not properly fit into our discussion here because, on the one hand, it was not rationalized on the grounds of enrichment, and on the other, it was a reflection of *within-group* bilingualism (Yiddish and Loshen Koydesh) rather than of between-group bilingualism such as that best characterizing all the other examples cited in this paper.

References

Andersson, Theodore, 1968   "Bilingual Elementary Schooling: A Report to Texas Educators," *Florida FL Reporter* 34, 6, 25.

Andersson, Theodore, and Mildred Boyer, eds., 1970   *Bilingual Schooling in the United States.* 2 vols. Government Printing Office.

Fishman, Joshua A., 1966   *Language Loyalty in the United States.* Mouton.

Fishman, Joshua A., and John Lovas, 1970   "Bilingual Education in Sociolinguistic Perspective," *TESOL Quarterly* 4, 215-222.

Gaarder, A. Bruce, 1967   "Organization of the Bilingual School," *Journal of Social Issues* 23, 110-120.

———, 1970   "The First Seventy-six Bilingual Education Projects," *Georgetown University Monograph Series in Language and Linguistics,* 23, 69-76.

John, Vera P., and Vivian M. Horner, 1971   *Early Childhood Bilingual Education.* Modern Language Association of America.

Lambert, Wallace E., and G.R. Tucker, 1972   *Bilingual Education of Children.* Newbury House.

Lewis, E. Glyn, 1972   *Multilingualism in the Soviet Union.* Mouton.

Mackey, William F., 1970   "A Typology of Bilingual Education," *Foreign Language Annals* 3, 596-608.

———, 1972   *Bilingual Education in a Binational School.* Newbury House.

Macnamara, John, 1966   *Bilingualism and Primary Education.* Edinburgh University Press.

Michel, John, 1967   "Tentative Guidelines for a Bilingual Curriculum," *Florida FL Reporter* 5, 3, 13-16.

Modiano, Nancy, 1968   "National or Mother Language in Beginning Reading: A Comparative Study," *Research in the Teaching of English* 1, 32-43.

Osterberg, T., 1961   *Bilingualism and the First School Language.* Vasterbottens Tryckeri.

Pryor, G.C., 1967   *Evaluation of the Bilingual Project of Harlandale Independent School District in the First Grades of Four Elementary Schools during the 1966-67 School Year.* Harlandale School District, San Antonio, Tex.

Richardson, M., 1968   *An Evaluation of Certain Aspects of the Academic Achievement of Elementary Pupils in a Bilingual Program, Coral Gables, Florida,* Ph.D. dissertation. University of Miami.

Rojas, Pauline, 1966   "The Miami Experience in Bilingual Education." In Carol J. Freidler, ed., *Teaching English to Speakers of Other Languages.* National Council of Teachers of English.

APPENDIX A: WORD LISTS FOR REGIONAL PRONUNCIATION

Regional pronunciation differences range from specific qualities of a single sound to the presence or absence of several phonemes. Within a single geographic or metropolitan area, the particular words which exhibit a feature vary from speaker to speaker. To fully account for the data of language variation, it is necessary to take into account such sociological data as age, sex, occupation, education, ethnic background, trips, and residences outside the region, as well as more subtle factors such as the sensitivity of informants to speech differences and their attitudes toward their own speech. However, regional differences are basic to any further analysis and provide a good introduction to the study of language variation.

The materials in this appendix are designed briefly to introduce the best-known regional pronunciation differences while providing readers who wish to expand the data with a basis for further exploring regional variation. Unlike similar exercises, these tests require no knowledge of the phonetic alphabet. But readers should refer to the phonological charts in the "Structure of Language" section of the General Introduction for clarification of the relationships among sound variants.

Demographic Data

For the tests below, as well as for most of the other exercises in these appendixes, it is important to gather a short personal history for each informant. This information will allow you to speculate about which factors in an informant's life influence test results. Here is a sample demographic questionnaire:

Please supply the following information about yourself:

Name _____ sex _____ race or ethnicity _____

year of birth _____ highest grade level of formal education _____

Residence: state _____ county _____ town _____

                length of residence _____

Birthplace _____

Other places you have lived for appreciable lengths of time (places and years):

Places you have traveled outside your native region:

Parents' birthplace (town and state or country):

                                                his father _____

   father _____

                                                his mother _____

mother _____

her father _____

her mother _____

Your occupation _____

father's occupation _____

mother's occupation _____

Do you speak any language other than English? _____

If so, which _____

How did you learn it (them)? _____

Testing for Variation in Consonants and Vowels

In administering these tests, it is important to remind informants not to rely on spelling; it is *pronunciation* which is being tested. Also, remember that informants who use marked regional varieties may have a tendency to employ what they think are "Standard English" forms when under pressure. A relaxed atmosphere will therefore produce the most reliable test results.

Consonant Test

This test demonstrates variation in the pronunciation of American English consonants. In some cases dialect differences lie in the choice of one consonant over another; in other cases a consonant is present or absent. Ask informants to read these lists of words aloud, drawing a line that surrounds all the words in which the underlined consonant sounds the same. If one form is used consistently for one entire list, take note of which one this is.

Your data should show some of these major regional consonant pronunciation differences (numbers correspond to the numbered lists of test words):

1. /s/ *or* /z/: Southern speakers will have /z/ sounds in more of these words than speakers from other areas will. For example, *greasy* will be pronounced with a /z/.

2. *presence of* /h/: New York City area speakers will not have /h/ sounds before /yu/ as in *human, humorous,* or *Hugh.* Inland Southern speakers may omit /h/ in *humble.* Highly educated speakers will omit /h/ in *herb* and *homage.*

3. /n/ *or* /ng/: New York City area speakers tend to pronounce the "g" of "ng" wherever it occurs in spelling.

4. /h/ *or* /ǰ/: Contact with Spanish speakers will increase likelihood of /h/ pronunciation.

5. /θ/ *or* /ð/: Northern speakers will have more /ð/ sounds, as in *with.*

6. /n/ *or* /ŋ/: New York City speakers often have /n/ for "ng" before "th." All speakers commonly use /n/ for final "ng" in casual conversation.

7. /hw/ *or* /w/: Northern speakers have /hw/ where "wh" is written.

8. *presence of* /l/: Southern speakers omit /l/ before /p/, /b/, or /f/, as in *help.* Presence of /l/ before /m/ is highly variable and seems to depend on such factors as the quality of the preceding vowel and how early the word was learned.

9. *presence of* /r/: /r/ is not pronounced after vowels in the coastal and deep South, in Eastern New England, in New York City, and generally among blacks. Final /r/ is the most likely and /r/ between vowels the least likely to be lost. Eastern New England speakers have intrusive /r/ after final vowels, as in *idea*. Midland speakers have intrusive /r/ before "sh" and in other isolated words; hence, /warš/. Presence or absence of /r/ in *February* and *library* does not seem to depend on geographic location.

Consonant Word Lists

1. */s/ or /z/*

me<u>ss</u>	Mr<u>s</u>.	grea<u>s</u>y
lou<u>s</u>e	Mi<u>ss</u>es	lou<u>s</u>y
grea<u>s</u>e	hou<u>s</u>es	dai<u>s</u>y
Mi<u>ss</u>		

2. *presence of* /h/

<u>h</u>onest	fore<u>h</u>ead	<u>h</u>umorous
<u>h</u>erb	<u>H</u>ugh	<u>h</u>umble
<u>h</u>omage	<u>h</u>uman	<u>h</u>at

3. */ŋ/ or /ŋg/*

a<u>ng</u>er	lo<u>ng</u>er	si<u>ng</u>ing
li<u>ng</u>er	Lo<u>ng</u> Island	si<u>ng</u>er
fi<u>ng</u>er	ha<u>ng</u>er	duri<u>ng</u>

4. */h/ or /ǰ/*

<u>J</u>une	Mo<u>j</u>ave	<u>J</u>uan
<u>j</u>unta	Nava<u>j</u>o	<u>J</u>uanita

5. */θ/ or /ð/*

ba<u>th</u>	wid<u>th</u>	pa<u>th</u>s
leng<u>th</u>	wi<u>th</u>	ba<u>the</u>
leng<u>th</u>s	wi<u>th</u>in	

6. */n/ or /ŋ/*

si<u>ng</u>	comi<u>ng</u>	le<u>n</u>gth
doi<u>ng</u>	stre<u>ng</u>th	si<u>n</u>
jumpi<u>ng</u>		

7. */hw/ or /w/*

<u>wh</u>ether	<u>wh</u>ale	<u>w</u>eather
<u>wh</u>ich	<u>wh</u>eel	<u>w</u>itch
<u>wh</u>en	<u>w</u>eep	<u>w</u>atch
<u>wh</u>ip	<u>w</u>ell	

8. *presence of* /l/

Dallas	balm	calmed
polka	psalm	help
folk	palm	walk
calm	alm	talk

9. *presence of* /r/

Asia	sauce	library
idea	February	source
wash	car	cork
Washington	card	compare
gosh	park	comparative
lozenges	sister	carried
familiar	gunner	run

Vowel Test

Because they are defined by the location of the tongue in the open space of the mouth and not by a specific point of contact, it is not surprising that pronunciation of vowels varies widely from one part of the United States to another. Vowels are far more difficult to analyze than consonants, which are "there" or "not there." Some vocalic sound is always "there" between groups of consonants, even if it is little more than a transition as the tongue passes from one consonantal point to another. The question becomes, then: Just where is the tongue at the moment of strongest vowel articulation?

This test is devised to show contrasts among vowels of different dialects so that they can be detected without knowledge of the phonetic alphabet. Informants should be asked to say these lists of words out loud, drawing a line around all the words whose vowel sounds are the same. Words from more than one list may go together; a single list may be divided into two or even three parts. Large groups of identical words can be connected with each other by arrows. Be sure to go over each large group of encircled words at the end of the test, asking the informant if adjacent lists are the same.

The actual vowel sound which is present in each cluster of words can be determined by checking with the key words on the vowel chart in the "Structure of Language" section of the General Introduction. Your informants may have more or fewer vowels than are represented there. Because /r/ has a strong influence over vowels preceding it, a whole series of "vowel + /r/" lists is included. Even in /r/less dialects, the vowel may exhibit effects from the deleted /r/.

Your data should show some of these major regional vowel pronunciation differences:

1. /I/=/ɛ/ so that *pin* and *pen* become homophones in the South, the Midwest, the Far West, and in Black English Vernacular.

2. /ɛ/ becoming /e/ in more and more words like *egg*, especially in the Midwest.

3. /æ/ becoming /ɛ/ in more and more words like *catch*, especially in the South.

4. /a/ in words like *aunt, path, can't* for New Englanders where others have /æ/.

5. /a/=/ɔ/ so that *cot* and *caught* are homophones in the Middle Atlantic states and on the Pacific coast. This vowel collapse is spreading and may be found in other parts of the country as well. In the East the /ɔ/ of *caught* serves for both vowels, while in the West the /a/ of *cot* remains.

6. /ʊ/ in words like *roof, room* for New Englanders and Inland Northerners where others have /u/.

7. /yu/ in words like *Tuesday, due, news* for South Midland and Southern speakers where others have /u/.

8. /ai/=/au/=/a/, especially before voiced consonants, so that *find=found= fond* for Southern and some South Midland speakers.

9. /ɔi/=/ɔ/ or /o/, especially before /l/, so that *boil=bawl* or *bowl* for Southern and some South Midland speakers.

10. before /r/, /æ/=/ɛ/ so that *marry* and *merry* are homophones in the South; /e/=/ɛ/ so that *Mary* and *merry* are homophones in New England; /æ/=/e/=/ɛ/ so that *marry, Mary,* and *merry* are homophones in the Midlands and much of the rest of the country. The three vowels remain distinct in New York City.

11. before /r/, /a/ occurs in more words like *foreign* for New Yorkers while /o/ occurs in more words like *tomorrow* for Midland speakers.

12. before /r/, /ʊ/ in words like *assured* and *pure* for Northern speakers where others have /u/.

13. before /r/, /i/=/e/ so that *beer* and *bear* are homophones for Southerners.

14. before /r/, /u/=/o/ so that *poor* and *pour* are homophones for Southerners.

Vowel Word Lists

								just	hut
								bus	hung
		milk	bail		lag				bud
		sister	cape		can				done
		dinner	bay		catch				
peel	been		bait		pal				fond
be	bin		vague		rat		father		rot
beat	pin	any	plague	said	map	laugh	spa		rock
keep	since	penny	egg	pet	have	path	ah		prod
bead	Jim	Ben	leg	mess	thank	cast	mirage		bomb
	bill	pen	peg	bell	bag	aunt	palm		hot
	bit	sense	bread			chance	calm		lot
	bid	gem	fed			can't	psalm		God
		get							

aisle	fowl
find	towel
pride	found
right	mouse
try	out
dive	proud
buy	now
time	down
ice	

spirit	merry	care	carrot	fire	our
syrup	ferry	aware	narrow	hired	flower
mirror	berry	scarce	comparative	mired	power
nearer	bury	hair	marry	choir	sour
weary	Mary	cared	Harry	tire	
weird	dairy	bear	Harold		
fierce	vary				
spear	hairy				
beer	compare				
hero					
zero					

Vowel Word Lists (continued)

much							
dull	Don	want	talk	dope	full	fool	
bulge	wander	on	cross	soul	bull	do	
	cot	cog	hawk	rogue	put	spook	
	cod	log	dawn	loathe	foot	food	
	watch	hog	caught	home	look	boot	
	waffle	dog	saw	shone	bosom	spoon	
	awful	long	paw	go	hoof	lute	few
	law	off	all		roof	dew	feud
		moth	ball		room	due	beauty
		loss	sauce		buoy	news	cute
						Tuesday	view

buoy
boy
oil
boil
coin
noise
Boyd

aren't	forest	source	tour	hurry	bird
arms	foreign	pour	poor	curry	girl
bar	horrid	for	boor	flurry	fir
heart	borrow	horse	moor	courage	fern
large	tomorrow	cord	sure	furry	merge
are	sorry	fork	assured	worry	fur
guard		oar	endure	syrup	urn
star		more	pure		earn
starry		door	fury		burr
		court			word
		sore			Earl
		four			
		hoarse			

APPENDIX B: A CHECKLIST OF REGIONAL EXPRESSIONS

Linguistic atlas surveys have determined that checklists like the one below can be used to trace the distribution of vocabulary items by speakers' geographical and cultural origins, age, education, occupation, and sex. The best expressions to include in such a vocabulary survey are names of common objects, landscape and natural features, and other items of home and family life.

To administer this checklist, read the descriptions aloud to your informants. Try to avoid using the expression you are trying to solicit. If informants respond with more than one expression, ask them whether there are differences in meaning between them and when they would use each term. A group of informants who vary in age, length of residence, and education will produce the most interesting results. Be sure to solicit the demographic data suggested in Appendix A.

For some of the checklist items below, distribution among major regional dialect areas is given in parentheses (N=Northern, M=Midland, S=Southern); others are left for individual field workers to discover. Since the linguistic atlas surveys began in the 1930s, there have been marked increases in nationwide marketing and advertising and greater population mobility. These factors tend to suppress unusual usages. Thus your results may not indicate as great a variety of regional expressions as earlier surveys have reported.

Checklist Items

1. Container used for milk or water: pail (N, Northern M), bucket (S, M)
2. Devices at edges of roof to carry off rain: eave spout (N), gutter (M), guttering (M), eaves trough (N), rain gutter, water trough (N, S), spouts (M), spouting (M), eave troft (N)
3. Playground item that consists of a board balanced across a sawhorse: teeter board (N), teeter totter (N, M), seesaw (S, M), ridy-horse (S), hickey horse (S)
4. Worm used for fish bait: night crawler (N), fishing worm (M), fish worm (M), redworm (Southern M), bait worm (S, M), rainworm, angleworm (N), earthworm
5. A carbonated drink: cold drink (S), soda (New York and New England), tonic (Boston area), pop (M), soda pop, soft drink, coke, soda water
6. A stream of water not big enough to be a river: creek (M), crick (N, Northern M), brook (N), branch (S, Southern M), run (Northern M), draw, resaca
7. To put a single room of the house in order: clean up, do up, redd up (M), ridd up (M), straighten up, tidy up, put to rights, slick up
8. Paper container for groceries, etc.: bag (N), sack (M, S), poke (M), toot (Pennsylvania German)
9. Device found on outside of house or in yard or garden: faucet (N), spicket (S, M), spigot (S, M), hydrant (S, M), tap
10. Window covering on rollers: blinds (M), curtains, roller shades, shades, window blinds, window shades

11. Metal utensil for frying: creeper, fryer, frying pan, fry pan, skillet (M), spider (N, S)

12. Device over a sink: faucet (N), spigot (S, M), spicket (S, M), hydrant, tap

13. Large porch with roof: gallery, piazza, porch, portico, stoop, veranda

14. Furry stuff that collects under beds and on closet floors: dust, bunnies, dust kittens, lint balls, pussies

15. Family word for father: dad, daddy, father, pa, papa, pappy, paw, pop

16. Family word for mother: ma, mama, mammy, maw, mom, mommer, mommy, mother

17. People related by blood: my family, my folks, my parents, my people, my relatives, my relations, my kin, my kinfolks, my kind

18. Of children: brought up, fetched up, raised, reared

19. Large truck with trailer attached: truck, truck and trailer, semi, rig, trailer-truck

20. New limited-access road: turnpike, toll road, freeway, parkway, pay road, tollway, thruway, expressway, interstate

21. Grass strip in the center of a divided road: median, center strip, separator, divider, barrier, grass strip, boulevard

22. Place where firemen attach hose: fire hydrant, fire plug, plug, hydrant, water tap

23. Animal with strong odor: skunk (N, M), polecat (S), woodspussy (M), woodpussy (M)

24. Small, squirrel-like animal that runs along ground: chipmunk (N), grinnie, ground squirrel (S, M)

25. Dog of no special kind or breed: common dog, cur, cur dog, fice, feist, mongrel, no-count, scrub, heinz, sooner, mixed dog, mutt

26. Insect that glows at night: fire bug (M), firefly (urban N), glow worm, june bug, lightning bug (S, M, rural N), candle bug

27. Large winged insect seen around water: darning needle (N), devil's darning needle (N), dragon fly, ear-sewer, mosquito hawk (S), sewing needle, snake doctor (S, M), snake feeder (S, M), sewing bug (N)

28. Center of a cherry: pit (N), seed (S, M), stone, kernel, heart

29. Center of a peach: pit (N), seed (S, M), stone, kernel, heart

30. Bunch of trees growing in open country (particularly on a hill): motte, clump, grove, bluff

31. A spreadable luncheon meat made of liver: liver sausage, liverwurst, braunschweiger

32. A glass containing ice cream and root beer: float, root beer float, black cow, Boston cooler

33. Corn served on cob: corn-on-the-cob (N, M), garden corn, green corn (N), mutton corn, roasting ears (S, M), sugar corn, sweet corn

34. Bread made of corn meal: corn bread, corn dodger, corn pone (S), hoe cake, johnnycake (N), pone bread

35. Cooked meat juices poured over meat, potatoes, or bread: gravy, sop, sauce, drippings, jus, au jus

36. Large sandwich designed to be a meal: hero (New York), submarine, hoagy (Philadelphia), grinder (Boston), poor-boy (S)

37. Children's cry at Halloween time: trick or treat! tricks or treats! beggar's night! help the poor! Halloween! give or receive!

38. Call to players to return because a new player wants to join: allie-allie-in-free, allie-allie-oxen-free, allie-allie-ocean-free, bee-bee bumble bee, everybody in free, newcomer-newcomer

39. To coast on sled lying down flat: belly-booster, belly-bump, belly-bumper, belly-bunker, belly-bunt, belly-bust, belly-buster, belly-down, belly-flop, belly-flopper, belly-grinder, belly-gut, belly-gutter, belly-kachug, belly-kachuck, belly-whack, belly-whop, belly-whopper, belly-slam, belly-smacker

40. To hit the water when diving: belly-flop, belly-flopper, belly-bust, belly-buster, belly-smacker

41. To be absent from school: bag school, bolt, cook jack, lay out, lie out, play hookey, play truant, run out of school, skip class, skip school, skip off from school, ditch, flick, flake school, blow school

42. Holds small objects together: rubber band, rubber binder, elastic binder, gum band, elastic band

43. Outer garment of a heavy material worn for working: levis, overalls, overhauls, dungarees, jeans, blue jeans, pants

44. A time of day: quarter before seven, quarter of seven (N), quarter till seven (S, M), quarter to seven (N, S), 6:45

45. Become ill: be taken sick, get sick (N), take sick (S, M), be taken ill, come down

46. Become ill with a cold: catch a cold (N), catch cold, get a cold, take cold, take a cold (S, M), come down with a cold

47. Sick_____ : at one's stomach, in one's stomach (M), on one's stomach (M), to one's stomach (N), of one's stomach, with one's stomach

48. I_____ you're right: reckon, guess, figger, figure, suspect, imagine, expect

49. Grass strip between sidewalk and street: berm, boulevard, boulevard strip, parking strip, parkway, parking, sidewalk plot, tree lawn, neutral ground, devil strip, tree bank, city strip, yard extension

50. Of peas: to hull (M), to pod, to shell, to shuck (S)

APPENDIX C: LINGUISTIC ATTITUDES QUESTIONNAIRE

(Adapted from William Labov, The Social Stratification of English in New York City, *Center for Applied Linguistics, 1966, p. 600)*

This questionnaire is easy to administer and provides straightforward information on people's conscious attitudes toward their own speech and the speech of others. It can be used alone as an indicator of speakers' linguistic self-esteem or in conjunction with other appendixes which provide information on actual rather than perceived speech behavior. Appendixes C and D can be used together to establish levels of linguistic insecurity, which, in turn, point to attitudes toward standardization and the prestige dialect.

Ideally, these questions should be asked in a conversational setting. Fill in the materials in square brackets to reflect ethnic group, sex, and geographic location of the informant. Demographic data included in Appendix A would be useful here as well.

Introduction

"I would like to find out some information about the speech in this area and specifically how people feel about it. I'll just ask your opinion on a number of things and you tell me what you think."

Questions

1. What do you think of your own speech?

2. Have you ever tried to change your speech? What particular things have you tried to change?

3. Have you ever taken any courses in speech? What did the teacher mention in connection with pronunciation?

4. What do you think of [this locality's] speech?

5. When you traveled outside [this locality], were you picked up as being from here?

6. Do you think people from other places like the local speech? Why?

7. What do you think of
  [for Southerners] : Northern speech?
  [for non-Southerners] : Southern speech?
  [for blacks] : white speech?
  etc.

8. Have you heard [a well-known local-dialect speaker, e.g., a Senator, or a dialect speaker personally known to the informant] speak? As far as his speech is concerned (not his politics, but his way of talking), how do you like it? Have you heard [a well-known "standard" speaker, e.g., Walter Cronkite] speak? How do you like it? Which do you think is better? [Probe for opinions on other speakers the informant thinks good and bad.] Which of these do you think you sound more like?

9. Going back to the time you were growing up, I'd like to get some ideas of the kind of speech that your friends used. Were most of your friends [same race, religion, geographical origin as informant]? Did you have any friends who were [other races, religions, geographical origins]?

10. Can you remember a time when people actually argued about what was the right way to say things?

APPENDIX D: A TEST OF LINGUISTIC INSECURITY

(Adapted from William Labov, The Social Stratification of English in New York City, *Center for Applied Linguistics, 1966, p. 601)*

This test is designed to measure the discrepancy between what people perceive as "correct" pronunciations and their own. For these purposes it is irrelevant whether the informant selects the *a* or *b* form of the word. What counts is whether the form designated as "correct" is the same as that designated as "what I use." The greater the difference between the pronunciation speakers recognize as "standard" and their own usage, the greater their linguistic insecurity. Linguistic insecurity is a group as well as an individual phenomenon and is most prominent among speakers of stigmatized varieties. Its impact on attitudes toward standardization and on school performance is all too frequently overlooked.

This test is administered to an informant by reading alternate pronunciations aloud. Pick out fifteen or twenty words which have competing pronunciations in your area. Study the words aloud in advance so that your pronunciation is natural. You may need to adapt the phonetic form here to your own speech. Be sure, though, that the two forms you offer your informant differ from each other only in one sound. Speak slowly, pausing between the words. Disregard answers in which the informant indicates one of the forms is unknown. You may also wish to solicit the demographic data in Appendix A.

Introduction

"If someone should come to you, say a high school student, and ask you which of these pronunciations is correct, which would you say, the first or the second?" After the informant has responded, ask, "Is this the way you would usually say it? Let me know if there's a difference between the correct way and the way you might say it, for each of these words."

Test Words

1. Joseph   a. /jŏsɪf/   b. /jŏzɪf/
2. catch   a. /kæč/   b. /kɛč/
3. tomato   a. /təmeto/   b. /təmato/
4. diapers   a. /daipərz/   b. /daiəpərz/
5. aunt   a. /ant/   b. /ænt/
6. often   a. /ɔftən/   b. /ɔfən/
7. garage   a. /gəraǰ/   b. /gəraž/
8. humorous   a. /hyumərəs/   b. /yumərəs/
9. vase   a. /vez/   b. /vaz/   c. /ves/
10. length   a. /lɛnθ/   b. /lɛŋθ/
11. February   a. /fɛbrueri/   b. /fɛbyueri/
12. catsup   a. /kæčəp/   b. /kɛčəp/   c. /kætsəp/
13. avenue   a. /ævənu/   b. /ævənyu/
14. half   a. /hæf/   b. /haf/
15. escalator   a. /ɛskəletər/   b. /ɛskyuletər/
16. singing   a. /sɪŋɪŋ/   b. /sɪŋɪn/
17. Missouri   a. /mɪzuri/   b. /mɪzurə/
18. this   a. /ðɪs/   b. /dɪs/
19. sure   a. /šər/   b. /šur/
20. car   a. /kar/   b. /ka/
21. greasy   a. /grisi/   b. /grizi/
22. roof   a. /ruf/   b. /ruf/
23. calm   a. /kalm/   b. /kam/
24. wash   a. /waš/   b. /warš/
25. poor   a. /pur/   b. /por/
26. houses   a. /hausəz/   b. /hauzəz/
27. egg   a. /ɛg/   b. /eg/
28. across   a. /əkrɔst/   b. /əkrɔs/
29. sock   a. /sak/   b. /sɔk/
30. rouge   a. /ruž/   b. /ruǰ/
31. ask   a. /æks/   b. /æsk/
32. hanger   a. /hæŋgər/   b. /hæŋər/
33. marry   a. /mæri/   b. /mɛri/
34. get   a. /gɛt/   b. /gɪt/
35. iron   a. /arn/   b. /aiərn/
36. Mary   a. /meri/   b. /mɛri/
37. overalls   a. /ovərɔlz/   b. /ovərhɔlz/
38. police   a. políce   b. pólice
39. comparable a. cómparable   b. compárable
40. pecan   a. pecán   b. pécan

APPENDIX E: SUBJECTIVE REACTION TESTING

Subjective reaction tests reveal how people judge the character traits of others based solely on their speech. Short taped passages of various language varieties are played to people who rate the taped voices on such traits as these: high intelligence/low intelligence; good upbringing/bad upbringing; good education/poor education; ambition/laziness; self-confidence/lack of self-confidence; manual laborer/professional; trustworthiness/untrustworthiness; sincerity/insincerity; friendliness/unfriendliness; good sense of humor/no sense of humor; kindness/lack of kindness. The subjects mark an "x" on a scale for each trait to indicate where they feel the speaker falls on the continuum:

Character scales can be divided into any odd number of segments, depending on how fine a distinction is desired. The tester then assigns a number to each segment of the continuum and averages the scores assigned by all the subjects to each trait.

People who do not ordinarily express their attitudes about other groups may reveal their biases in their reaction to the speech of group members. Specifically, subjects are likely to discriminate against speakers of low-status language varieties by assigning them negative personality traits. The same is true for speakers of the lower-status language in a bilingual situation. Our faith in our ability to judge others by their speech is so great that we infer from speech samples not only indicators of social standing, such as amount of education and profession, but also individual personality characteristics like friendliness. It is this entrenched and unconscious stereotyping by speech that non-standard-speaking children face in school and public life.

Tapes for subjective reaction testing can be made from snatches of conversation or oral reading by speakers of various dialects, or commercial dialect recordings can be used. Speaking style and subject matter should be as similar as possible for every sample. Age and sex of the speakers may also influence the results.

The *matched guise technique* is a further refinement of subjective reaction testing. By this method, bilingual or bidialectal speakers are recorded in each of their languages or dialects and rated twice by the subjects. This eliminates every variable except choice of language or dialect.

Major studies which illustrate subjective reaction and matched guise testing are G. Richard Tucker and Wallace E. Lambert's "White and Negro Listeners' Reactions to Various American-English Dialects," reprinted in *Varieties of Present-Day English*, edited by Richard W. Bailey and Jay L. Robinson (Macmillan, 1973) and Wallace E. Lambert's "A Social Psychology of Bilingualism," *Journal of Social Issues* 23: 2 (1967), 91-109; reprinted in *Language, Psychology, and Culture*, edited by Anwar S. Dil (Stanford University Press, 1972).

APPENDIX F: RATING SCALES FOR ATTITUDES TOWARD SEX-MARKED LANGUAGE

The subjective reaction test format (see Appendix E) can be adapted to measure sex marking in language and attitudes toward it. Select several of the rating scales mentioned in Appendix E, adding this scale for probable sex of speaker:

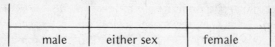

A separate set of scales should follow each of the test sentences below. Subjects who often guess the sex of the speaker can be considered sensitive to sex-marked language. In addition, the personality trait scales can be correlated with both the perceived sex of the speaker and the sex of the speaker indicated in parentheses below. This test should be given in written form in order to avoid bias due to the sex of the tester.

Test Sentences

(f)   1. I had such a delicious lunch today.
(f)   2. It's hot out today, isn't it?
(m)   3. You have some pulmonary congestion, but tetracycline should clear it right up.
(f)   4. Would you like to help me in the garden?
(m)   5. Get that dog out of my yard.
(f)   6. The walls in our bathroom are cerise.
(f)   7. You have a lovely apartment.
(f)   8. How *do* you do?
(m)   9. That's the worst shit I ever ate.
(m)   10. I ain't goin' with 'em.
(f)   11. To whom am I speaking?
(m)   12. They were real laid back.
(f)   13. Could you please give me the time?
(f)   14. Should it rain today, we would cancel the picnic.
(f)   15. We're feeling better today, aren't we?
(m)   16. Productionwise, we're doing real well.
(f)   17. I think I hear you saying that you feel depressed.
(m)   18. I'll need a Phillipshead to fix that.
(f)   19. There's an eensy-weensy problem here.
(f)   20. I think you may be sitting on my magazine.
(m)   21. I don't give a damn what you think.

APPENDIX G: WORKSHEETS FOR ANALYZING INTERACTION

Participants in an interaction use discourse style and structure and nonverbal behavior to encode their perceptions of their relationships to each other and to establish status and degree of intimacy. The nonverbal channel is also used to convey their feelings about the topic and the other members of the conversational group. Like other linguistic indicators, norms for discourse and nonverbal communication vary widely among speech communities, especially by race and ethnicity. Other factors which influence the definition of communication norms include sex, age, social class, occupation, and geographic region. Within these parameters, individual behavior varies according to the conditions of the interaction, that is, the setting, topic, kind, and number of participants. The worksheets below are designed to determine the communication norms in any given interaction and how individuals operate within them.

Using the suggestions below, it is easy to observe interaction, either as an outside observer or as a participant. For teachers, it is particularly important to analyze the structure of classroom interaction. Interesting contrasts can be found by observing conversations between strangers, friends, adults and children, teachers and students, employers and employees, customers and clerks. It is a profitable way to pass time standing in line, waiting for movies to begin, sitting in a restaurant, waiting your turn in the beauty parlor, barber shop, or doctor's office, or at meetings, parties, family gatherings. If you have the opportunity to tape-record a conversation, it can be analyzed with the notation in the Headnote to the Zimmerman and West article.

Discourse Style and Structure

I.   Initiating the interaction
   A. Who is allowed to initiate the interaction? Do they get this authority from their position (e.g., teacher, employer, older child, parent) or from their personal traits (peer-group leaders, talented talkers)?
   B. How is the conversation group established? Does it consist of everyone within hearing? If not, how is it determined who is included (e.g., in a small conversation group at a large party)?
   C. Are there ritual formulations for opening a conversation and ritual responses to them (e.g., "How are you?" "Fine, thanks, how are you"; "Hello, is Susie there?" "Speaking"; "Can I buy you a drink"; "Hey, man, what's happening?")?
   D. What rules are established for the interaction?
      1. What is the register, and how is it communicated (e.g., *casual or intimate conversation*: slang, simple syntax, fast speech, informal greeting; *formal discussion*: latinate vocabulary, complex syntax, explanatory preface, parliamentary procedure; *baby talk*: high pitch intonation, repetition, elliptical sentence structure, "y" and "ie" word endings)? Who establishes the register?

2. What is the topic and/or purpose (giving or getting information or opinions, giving or getting assurance of interest in other person, entertaining, sharing feelings and experiences, a ritual exchange like "sounding")? Who sets it and how?

3. How are status and role relationships defined (e.g., order in which people are greeted; terms of address like first names, titles, "sir," "ma'am," "honey," "ladies," "hey you," "teacher," "you guys," "junior")?

II. Maintaining the interaction
A. What do speakers do?
1. What are speakers' attitudes toward what they are saying (e.g., serious, joking, emotionally involved, detached, comfortable, insecure)? What are the verbal cues which indicate this (e.g., speed of speech, choice of words, intonation, voice quality, hesitation)?

2. What are speakers' attitudes toward the audience and the verbal cues that indicate them (e.g., *deferential*: question intonation, tag questions, pausing for assent; *condescending*: demands for assent, loudness, imperatives; *friendly*: terms of endearment, permitting interruptions; *detached*: monologue, ignoring interruptions, inappropriate register)?

B. What do nonspeakers do?
1. How do people indicate they are part of the interaction (if yes, nodding, murmuring agreement; if no, starting another interaction or a competing activity)?

2. How do they indicate their attitude toward the speaker (e.g., laughing, booing, answering politely, disagreeing, swearing)?

C. How do speakers rotate?
1. How do participants know when a speaker's turn is over?
   a. How long can one speaker speak?
   b. How long can a speaker pause without losing the floor?
   c. What cues do speakers give that they have finished ("in conclusion," "what I've been trying to say is," "you know?" "Do you see what I mean?" final falling intonation, end of a plot, punch line)?

2. How does a group member get a turn?
   a. Can one speaker overlap or interrupt another? Who can do this?
   b. What interrupting phrases and tactics do people use ("I think," "uh . . . uh," clearing throat, raising hand)? Which are successful and which not? Is success connected with the tactic or the status of the person using it?

3. How many speakers share the talking time? What is their status in the group?

D. How do ritual exchanges affect the interaction?
1. What cues are there that this type of interaction is going to begin ("Dearly Beloved"; "Knock, knock"; "You mama drink pee")?

      2. Does a ritual exchange have its own rules which are different from the rules for the larger conversation?

      3. How is the regular conversation resumed?

III.   What causes shifts in register, language or dialect, turn taking, or the general rules for the interaction (change of group composition, topic, setting)?

IV.   Terminating the interaction

    A. Does the conversation end naturally (e.g., end of story), because one or more people refuse to participate, because of external interruption? Who can terminate it and how? Is it a group or individual decision?

    B. Are there ritual formulations for closing an interaction ("See you later," "We'll pick up here tomorrow," "bye-bye")?

V.   What happens when individuals do not conform to group-interaction norms (e.g., interrupting too soon or too often, using the wrong register, taking too long a turn)?

    A. Are they punished (sent to the principal's office, jeered, cut off, ridiculed, cursed)?

    B. Are they rewarded (applauded, encouraged to speak fully, affirmed with phrases like "right on," "that's more like it," "hear, hear")?

Nonverbal Communication

Below are a number of nonverbal signals given with various parts of the body. When analyzing interaction, consider who uses these signals to whom and when, what they communicate and what response they evoke. Nonverbal cues can substitute for verbal cues (e.g., waving a hand for "good-bye"), but more often they convey emotion, self-concept, attitude toward other participants, or power relationships. Remember that the meaning of nonverbal cues can be different for men and women and also varies from culture to culture and sometimes from situation to situation.

I.   Expressive elements

    A. Head: nodding, shaking

    B. Face: smiling, frowning, wrinkling nose, wrinkling forehead, blushing

    C. Eyes: winking, rolling, staring, sidelong glances, maintaining/avoiding/breaking eye contact

    D. Hands: raising a hand, waving a hand or arm toward front with palm out, motioning hand or fingers toward front of body, extending arm toward side with thumb pointing back, palms out in front of body, arms outstretched toward other person, hand to chin or forehead, hands covering face, clenched fist, various finger and hand motions accompanying speech for emphasis or explanation

    E. Touching: arm around another's shoulder, hand on another's shoulder or upper arm, handshake, holding hands, hand under another's elbow, hand on another's knee, patting another's head, kissing (lips, cheek, hand, forehead), patting another's buttocks, hugging, elbow dig, touching another's torso

    F. Posture: slouching, erect, concealing or emphasizing various body parts with hands or other objects

      1. Sitting: hands in lap, arms crossed in front of body, sitting on hands, hands or elbows extended to adjacent seats; feet and legs close together, ankles crossed, knees crossed, one leg crossed over other at right angles, knees spread, legs or feet up (e.g., on desk)

      2. Standing: shoulders thrust back and pelvis forward, leaning with torso/foot/outstretched arm against wall; hands in front pockets, arms crossed in front of body, hands on hips, thumbs in belt loops or suspenders, arms hanging at sides; feet apart, legs crossed, one leg and hip forward, feet together

    G. Gait: long or short stride, fast or slow pace, toes in or out, knees together or apart, controlled or exaggerated hip movement

II.   Interactive elements

    A. Sitting and rising: Who sits and rises for whom in different situations (e.g., in meetings, introductions, crowded busses or waiting rooms, social gatherings, theaters)? How do people choose among empty seats (e.g., in a classroom, restaurant, bus, at a social gathering)?

    B. Interpersonal distance: How far apart do people remain in various kinds of conversations, waiting in lines, at counters, in crowds, dancing? How do they react when their space is violated?

    C. Orientation of body with respect to others: What direction do head, shoulders, torso face? What direction does crossed leg point? What direction are arms extended?

APPENDIX H: SAMPLE TEXTS

Black English Vernacular

Larry, a fifteen-year-old core member of the Jets, a Harlem teenage hangout group, speaks with field worker John Lewis:

JL: What happens to you after you die? Do you know?

Larry: Yeah, I know. (What?) After they put you in the ground, your body turns into—ah—bones, an' shit.

JL: What happens to your spirit?

Larry: Your spirit—soon as you die, your spirit leaves you. (And where does the spirit go?) Well, it all depends . . . (On what?) You know, like some people say if you're good an' shit, your spirit goin' t'heaven . . . 'n' if you bad, your spirit goin' to hell. Well, bullshit! Your spirit goin' to hell anyway, good or bad.

JL: Why?

Larry: Why? I'll tell you why. 'Cause, you see, doesn' nobody really know that it's a God, y'know, 'cause I mean I have seen black gods, pink gods, white gods, all color gods, and don't nobody know it's really a God. An' when they be sayin' if you good, you goin' t'heaven, tha's bullshit, 'cause you ain't goin' to no heaven, 'cause it ain't no heaven for you to go to.

JL: Well, if there's no heaven, how could there be a hell?

Larry: I mean—ye-eah. Well, let me tell you, it ain't no hell, 'cause this is hell right here, y'know! (This is hell?) Yeah, this is hell right here!

JL: ... but, just say that there is a God, what color is he? White or black?

Larry: Well, if it is a God ... I wouldn' know what color, I couldn' say,—couldn' nobody say what color he is or really *would* be.

JL: But now, jus' suppose there was a God—

Larry: Unless'n they say . . .

JL: No, I was jus' sayin' jus' suppose there is a God, would he be white or black?

Larry: . . . He'd be white, man.

JL: Why?

Larry: Why? I'll tell you why. 'Cause the average whitey out here got everything, you dig? And the nigger ain't got shit, y'know? Y'unnerstan'? So—um—for—in order for *that* to happen, you know it ain't no black God that's doin' that bullshit.

Appalachian English

The following text shows a number of phonological, grammatical, and vocabulary features described by Wolfram and Christian in *Appalachian Speech*. In addition to the grammatical features outlined in the Headnote to "Educational Implications of Dialect Diversity," Wolfram and Christian observed the following:

Phonological features of AE	Examples
/əz/ plural following -st, -sk, -sp	testes, deskes, waspes
intrusive /t/, especially after /s/	oncet, acrosst
/l/lessness before /p/, /b/, /f/	he'p, wo'f
deletion of unstressed initial syllable, initial /ð/, initial /w/ more generalized than in Standard English	'llowed, 'ccording, 'fore, 'em, 'uz, 'un
archaic /h/ retention in stressed positions	hit, hain't
a before nouns beginning with vowel	a apple
high rate of /ɪn/ for /ɪŋ/	tellin', huntin'
final unstressed "ow" becomes "er"	holler, tobaccer, yeller
final /ə/ becomes /i/	sody, Virginny, extry

Vocabulary Items in AE   but it still didn't *learn* (teach) him anything; I *took* (caught) a virus; come and *take up* (live) with us; I been *aiming* (planning) to go down and see him; I got *blessed out* (scolded); it was just *fixing* (preparing) to bite me; I'll get *fussed at* (scolded); she *got* (became) sixteen; you couldn't *go* (travel) the road; they sometimes *happen in* (arrive) at the same time; I've *heared tell* (heard) of some; I *reckon* (guess) she's done sold it; I hollered *right* (quite) loud; the house burnt *plumb* (completely) down; would you *druther* (rather) I did something; he *ain't but* (is only) thirteen; I *yet* (still) eat a lot; it's *subject* (likely) to kill 'em; it'll get better *some of these days* (one of these days); we tromped through the woods 'til *long about* (about) six o'clock; an old horse way back up *yonder* (at a considerable distance); trees that're *pert' near* (almost) square; I'm not *for sure* (certain)

Appalachian English Text   An Appalachian informant (Inf), a 67-year-old retired miner, speaks with a field worker (FW) who tape records the conversation:

FW: Did you read in the paper, a Huntington paper, where this couple had a young girl come in and babysit with their six-weeks-old daughter and while they were away, the parents were away, this girl had some friends in and they started taking pills, and she apparently went crazy or something and she put the baby in the oven, she thought that she was cooking a turkey.

Inf: No, I didn't read that.

FW: That was in the news.

Inf: But my aunt one time, she left the oven door down to put out a little more heat in the kitchen, it was in the wintertime, the old cat got up in 'ere to cool down to where he liked it and got in 'ere and set down and somebody come along, closed the oven door, so the next morning she gets up and builds a fire in the old coal range and baked the cat. She opened the door to put her bread in to bake it and there set the cat. Hide done busted off his skull and fell down and his meat just come off'n his bones.

FW: Oh, you're kidding!

Inf: It's a fact.

FW: Oh, isn't that awful?

Inf: Oh, I want to tell you one, maybe I shouldn't on this thing, but I'm a-gonna tell it anyway. My aunt was sick, and my uncle cooked breakfast. So, he washed his dishes up and everything and went out and harnessed up his horses to go plowing and run his hands in his pockets. Well, he hunted for the dishrag first, he couldn't find it. So he got him a new one, went out and harnessed his horses after while and went on to work and him, he chewed tobacco, you know, and reached his hand in his pocket to get him a chew of tobacco and found his dishrag. He'd stuck it in his pocket!

Inf: Do you remember any more interesting stories, Ike? Like, cooking the cat?

Inf: No, not right off hand, now, if it come to a bunch of jokes I could tell you enough to run that thing crazy.

FW: Well, have you heard any good jokes lately?

Inf: Well, they wouldn't be fit for that. Uh, I laughed at John Parker. Do you know John Parker over at Ashmeade?

FW: No.

Inf: Him and me and Jack Stern, we went to Bath County, Virginia, coon hunting. Went up to Leroy Buzzie's. And before I forgets I wanna tell you there's a Leroy Buzzie lived up there, and Al Crawley and Chuck McCoy, all of 'em lived in the same hollow 'ere.

FW: Buzzie. Where did you go, up in Bath County?

Inf: Bath County, Virginia. Up on Little Bath Creek.

FW: I think that's where Charley goes every year.

Inf: Yeah, I expect it is. Well, now they've got a cabin back down this side of that. Way down this side.

FW: They're mountain people, aren't they, Ike?

Inf: No, not really. No . . . They . . . he used to be an Army man, the old man Leroy Buzzie, see, he's dead now. He was a retired Army man, and, we went up 'ere and John supposedly had a sack to put the coon in if we caught one. We's gonna try to bring it back alive, so we tromped through the woods 'til along about six o'clock in the morning. The dogs treed up a big hollow chestnut oak, and we proceeded to cut the thing down. It's about three or four inches all the way around. About four foot through the stump. We tied the dogs and cut the thing down. Well, we cut it down and turned one dog loose, and he went down in that thing, way down in the old hollow of the tree and it forked, and we couldn't get up in there so he backed out and he tied 'im. And we's a-gonna chop the coon out if it was in there, I's a kinda halfway thought maybe it just treed a possum or something. Well, I chopped in and lo and behold, right on top of the dang coon. Eighteen pounder, Jack Stern says, kitten coon. I run in with the axe handle down in behind him to keep him from getting out or backing down in the tree. He reached, fooled around and got him by the hind legs and pulled that thing out it looked big as a sheep to me. Turned 'im loose, he said "kitten, Hell." We had an old carbide light and he turned that over and the lights were . . . that's all the light we had. And, we had to hunt it then and the dogs took right after the coon right down the holler and the dogs caught it and Jack beat us all down there. Went down there and he's a-holding three dogs in one hand and the coon in the other hand. And they's all a-trying to bite the coon and the coon a-trying to bite Jack and the dogs, and Jack pulled out a sack and it wasn't a dang thing but an old pillow case that Maggie had used, his wife, it was about wore out. So we fumbled around 'ere and finally got that coon in that sack and he aimed to close the top of it and the coon just tore the thing in half, in two, and down the holler he went again. With that sack on him, half of it and we caught that thing, and you know, E.F. Wurst finally pulled off his coveralls and we put that thing down in one of the legs of his coveralls and tied that coon up. He's tearing up everything we could get, we couldn't hold him he's so stout. And I brought that thing home and kept 'im about a month, fed 'im apples and stuff to eat so we could eat 'im. Well, I did I killed him and tried eat that thing, I'd just soon eat a tomcat or a polecat, I wouldn't make much difference. And, that's about the best coon hunt I believe I was on.

Gullah

This text, recorded by Lorenzo Turner in his *Africanisms in the Gullah Dialect* (University of Michigan Press, 1949, pp. 264-265), represents the speech of an elderly woman. She is describing a severe food shortage which the population was experiencing at the time. In addition to the phonetic symbols represented on the charts in the General Introduction, this selection utilizes:

/ɟ/ to represent a voiced palatal stop (somewhere between English /g/ and /j/)

/˜/ over vowels, to indicate nasalization of the vowel; over "n," to represent a nasal with palatal articulation (as in Spanish *señor*).

/ɔi sɛ: "dɛm bəkrə sɛn fid yɛ fə fid wi,
I say, "Them white people [the Red Cross] send feed here to feed we,
an dɛm ča əm ɟi dɪ
and them [the white people on Edisto Island] carry it [and] give [it to] the
ñɔŋ pipl wɔt də wək dɛ ɔn dɛm ples. de en də ɟi əm no
young people what were working there on them place. They ain't give it [to] no
wɪdo. dɛm də ča əm də ɟi əm dɪ pipl wɔt haw
widow. Them were carrying it [and] were giving it [to] the people what have
man n waɪf n čɪlən də wək fə dɛm."
man and wife and children working for them."
de ẽ ɟi wi nən. de lɔ sɛ wi tu ɔɪ. wi kã wək fə
They ain't give we none. They say [that] we too old. We can't work for
dɛm. yɛs mam! nɔu də fɔɪw ə wi ol pipl dɛ ẽ
them. Yes, Mam! Now there [are] five of we old people there [who] ain't
ɟit "taŋkɪ." si? fɔɪw! ẽ ɟit "taŋkɪ." si? dɛm dɛ
get [a] "thank you." See? Five! Ain't get [a] "thank you." See? Them there
kəmplen. ɔɪ tɛl əm ɔɪ dõ kəmplen. ɔɪ lɛf ɔl
[the old people] complain. I tell them I don't complain. I leave all
tɪŋ in gɔd han. ɔɪ sɛ: "sɪstə ɟeni" ɔɪ sɛ, "gɔdz gɔɪn mɛk diz
thing in God hand. I say: "Sister Janie," I say, "God's going [to] make these
bəkrə ɟəmp əp ɔn ɛdɪsto." ɔɪ sɛ: "gɔdz gɔɪn in dɛm bɛd n
white people jump up on Edisto." I say, "God's going in them bed and
tək dɛm aut." ɔɪ tɛl əm so. de ẽ—nən əw əm—bɪn dɛ tɔk
take them out." I tell them so. They ain't—none of them—been there talk
lɔŋ tɔɪm. wɛn de si mi, de aks ples fə sɪt dɔu ŋ aftə unə g̣ɔn.
[in a] long time. When they see me, they ask place to sit down after you gone.
... yu no wɔt dɛm pe fə bin? yu no wɔt dɛm pe fə
... You know what them pay for bean? You know what them pay for
bin? fɔɪw n wən sɛnt fə—wɛn yu pɪk əp dɛm bin—dat lɔɪmə
bean? Five and one cent for—when you pick up them beaŋ—that lima
bin—yu ẽ nɛwə gɔt bət fɔɪw n wən sɛnt in tred. tu kret kəm
bean—you ain't never got but five and one cent in trade. Two crate come

tu–ẽ nəf fə bɔɪ mɔɪ bakə. dat dɪ dɛwəl we de də
to—ain't enough to buy my tobacco. That [is] the devil way they are
ji yu nɔu. dɛn yu nɔk ɔf wɛn sən hɔt. dɛn yu go bak in
giving you now. Then you knock off when sun hot. Then you go back in
fil. dɛn wɛn yu ho kɔn, de ji yu twɛlw sɛnt fə ho kɔn—
field. Then when you hoe corn, they give you twelve cent to hoe corn—
twɛlw sɛnt—twɛlw sɛnt—ɔl de. wɛn de kɔl bak fə go bak
twelve cent—twelve cent—all day. When they call [you] back to go back
yu go raɪt bak in dɪ sem sən. mi ẽ kəmɪn bak in dat bəkrə
you go right back in the same sun. Me ain't coming back in that white man
fil an du dat tɪŋ. nɔt mi! no! nɔt diše dɔɪanə. dɔɪanə dən
field and do that thing. Not me! No! Not this here Diana. Diana done
bɪn tru so məč tɪŋ in rɛbəl tɔɪm: tɛk wɔtə, pɪjɪn, n ɔl dɛm tɪŋ./
been through so much thing in slavery: take water, piggin, and all that thing.

Pennsylvania German

Since the first religious refugees arrived in the latter seventeenth century, German has been spoken widely in the southeastern part of Pennsylvania. Various groups of dissenters—Amish, or "Plain People"; Mennonites; Moravians; and others—settled into rural communities, isolating themselves as much as possible from the outside world. During the nineteenth century they moved to farmlands all over Pennsylvania, and in regions farther west as well. Their well-known tenacity in holding to traditional ways of farming, dressing, and traveling extends to their language as well. Pennsylvania German, descended from the mix of German dialects spoken by the immigrants, can still occasionally be heard today. It is frequently called "Pennsylvania Dutch," a corruption of the Germans' word for themselves, *Deutsch*.

Pennsylvania German has been heavily influenced by its English-speaking environment. English vocabulary has been adopted extensively, with the pronunciation often altered to conform to the standard German phonological system. The text and word lists below illustrate what sorts of vocabulary tend to be borrowed and reflect the history of Pennsylvania German speakers' contact with their neighbors. Some effects on the syntax can also be detected, particularly on word order. Although the primary direction of influence has been from English to Pennsylvania German, a few vocabulary items which have become common among English speakers in the region indicate that the linguistic and cultural borrowing has not been entirely one-sided.

Pennsylvania German Text

Diefe Gedonke

Ess wohr goot wedder fer fische. Der parre wohr am fische uf ee seidt fun die grick un eens fun seine eldischter wohr am fische uf die onner seidt. Iwwereweil hutt der parre en beis grickt, un er hutt en wunderbohrer scheener fisch g'heecheldt; eens fun denne oss mer nett lieye braych defun. Er hutt g'schpielt mitt den fisch, fer'n longi tzeit. Der eldischter hutt tzugeguckt.

Endlich iss der fisch miedt warre un hutt gerhucht owwe uf'm wasser. Der parre hutt der fisch geech sich getzoge un wie er der fisch schier gohr haldt hatte, hutt macht sich der fisch ee letschter tzuckt; er hutt die ongel ferbruche un hutt sich ferschlupt unnich's wasser.

Der parre hutt datte g'huckt und hutt geguckt oss wonn der ferschondt hutt schtill schtee deet. Der eldischter hutt die gons g'schickt g'seehne. Er hutt so schpettlich iwwer's wasser niwwer gegrische, "Parre wass bischt am denke?" "Well," sawgt der parre, "ich binn am denke wass du sawge deetscht."

Deep Thoughts

It was good weather for fishing. The preacher was fishing on one side of the creek and one of his elders was fishing on the other side. After a while the preacher got a bite, and he hooked a very beautiful fish; one that we need not lie about. He played with the fish, for a long time. The elder watched.

Finally the fish became tired and rested on the water. The preacher pulled the fish toward himself and as he had almost got hold of the fish, the fish made one last pull; he broke the hook and disappeared underneath the water.

The preacher sat there and looked out where it had disappeared and stood still. The elder had seen the whole story. He finally called across the water, "Preacher what are you thinking about?" "Well," said the preacher, "I am thinking about what you would say."

English influences on Pennsylvania German vocabulary

Pennsylvania German	English	Standard German
daadi	daddy	Vater
bu	boy	Junge, Knabe, Bube
faektri	factory	Fabrik
schtori, g'schickt	story	Geschichte
humbuk	humbug	
kaesch	cash, money	Geld, Bargeld
weri	very	sehr
lof-letter	love letter	Liebesbrief
schtaert	start	anfangen
boggi	buggy	Wagen
duh; geduh	do; done	tun; getan
blaum	plum	Pflaume
juscht	just	jetzt
figgeren	figure (do arithmetic)	rechnen
waschkessel, waschboiler	wash kettle, wash boiler	Waschkessel
weck; aweck	wake; awake	wecken; wach
gemixte pickles	mixed pickles	gemischte Gurken
eul, aul	owl	Eule
eicharnch, schwgerl	squirrel	Eichhörnchen

Some examples of extreme language mixing

Mein *stallion* hat ueber den *fenz* ge*schumpt* und dem nachbar sein *whiet* ge*daemaetscht*. My stallion jumped over the fence and damaged my neighbor's wheat.

Es gibt gar kein *use*. It is no use.

Ich muss den gaul ab*harnessen* und den *boggi greasen* befor wir ein *ride* nehmen. I must harness up the horse and grease the buggy before we take a ride.

Midlands dialect terms influenced by Pennsylvania German

fat cakes (doughnuts)	from	*fettkuche*
thick milk (curdled milk)		*dickmilch*
saw buck (saw horse)		*saegebock*
liverwurst (liver sausage)		*leberwurst*
toot (paper bag)		*tuette*
rain worm (earthworm)		*regenworm*
a little piece (a short distance)		*ein kurzes stueck*